A SECOND TREASURY OF THE FAMILIAR

A SECOND TREASURY OF THE FAMILIAR

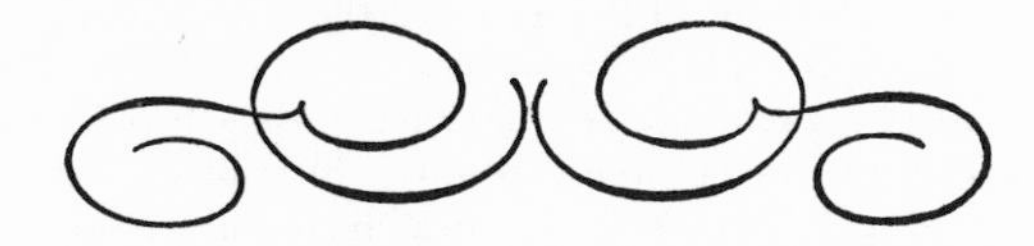

EDITED BY

Ralph L. Woods

THE MACMILLAN COMPANY

NEW YORK

Ninth Printing 1967

THE MACMILLAN COMPANY, NEW YORK

ACKNOWLEDGMENTS

Grateful acknowledgment is made to the following, who have granted permission to reprint herein the copyrighted material listed below:

MRS. YOUNG E. ALLISON for "Derelict" by Young E. Allison.

BOBBS-MERRILL COMPANY, for James Whitcomb Riley's "The Raggedy Man," "An Old Sweetheart of Mine," and "A Life Lesson," from *Rhymes of Childhood, Pipes o' Pan at Zekesbury,* and *Afterwhiles,* respectively; Frank L. Stanton's "Sweetes' Li'l Feller" from *Songs from Dixieland,* copyright 1900, 1928, used by special permission of the publishers, The Bobbs-Merrill Company.

MR. GELETT BURGESS for his "The Purple Cow" and the quatrain sequel to it.

BURNS OATES AND WASHBOURNE, LTD., for Francis Thompson's

"A Child's Prayer" and Alice Meynell's "The Shepherdess" and a passage from Francis Thompson's *Essay on Shelley.*

CASSELL & COMPANY, LTD., for passages from Winston Churchill's *The End of the Beginning,* copyright 1943, and from his *Blood, Sweat and Tears* (English title, *Into Battle*), copyright 1941 by Winston Churchill.

CHRISTY & MOORE, LTD., for "The Gate of the Year" from M. Louise Haskins's *The Gate of the Year.*

W. B. CONKEY COMPANY for Ella Wheeler Wilcox's "You Never Can Tell" and "Whatever Is—Is Best."

DAVID CORY for his poem "Miss You."

MRS. ROBERT H. DAVIS for Robert H. Davis's "The Printing Press."

J. M. DENT & SONS, LTD., for passages from the W. F. Trotter translation of Blaise Pascal's *Pensées;* "St. Francis and Poverty" from T. W. Arnold's translation of the anonymous *Little Flowers of St. Francis;* the Lucas translation of Hans Christian Andersen's "The Emperor's New Clothes."

DODD, MEAD & COMPANY for "Poetical Economy" from Harry Graham's *Deportmental Ditties;* "Barney Magee" and "The Sea Gypsy" from *More Songs from Vagabondia* by Bliss Carman and Richard Hovey, copyright 1896 by Dodd, Mead & Company; "The Law of the Yukon" from *The Complete Poems of Robert W. Service,* copyright by Dodd, Mead & Company; "Lepanto" from *The Collected Poems of G. K. Chesterton,* copyright 1911, 1932 by Dodd, Mead & Company; "Differences" from *Complete Poems of Paul Laurence Dunbar,* copyright by Dodd, Mead & Company; "My Financial Career" by Stephen Leacock; passages from Anatole France's *The Opinions of Jerome Coignard* and *The Seven Wives of Bluebeard,* translated by Mrs. Wilfrid Jackson and D. B. Stewart, respectively; all reprinted by permission of Dodd, Mead & Company.

DOUBLEDAY & COMPANY, INC., for "Rouge Bouquet" from *Poems, Essays and Letters* by Joyce Kilmer, copyright 1914, 1917, 1918 by Doubleday & Company, Inc.; for a prose passage from the Preface to *Leaves of Grass,* "Out of the Cradle Endlessly Rocking" and "I Hear America Singing" also from *Leaves of Grass* by Walt Whitman, copyright 1924 by Doubleday & Company, Inc.; "Baseball's Sad Lexicon" from *The Column Book of F.P.A.* by Franklin P. Adams, copyright 1928 by Doubleday & Company, Inc.; "the song of mehitabel" from Don Marquis' *Archy and Mehitabel,* copyright 1927 and 1930 by Doubleday & Company, Inc.; "When Earth's Last Picture Is Painted" from Rudyard Kipling's *The Seven Seas,* "Tommy" and "Danny Deever" from Rudyard Kipling's *Departmental Ditties and Barrack Room Ballads,* and "The Female of the Species" from Rudyard Kipling's *The Years Between,* copyright 1911 by Rudyard Kipling, and all reprinted by permission of Mrs. George Bambridge and Doubleday & Company, Inc.

GERALD DUCKWORTH & COMPANY, LTD., for "The Yak" by Hilaire Belloc.

THE EXECUTORS OF THE ESTATE OF CARRIE JACOBS-BOND for the words of "I Love You Truly."

FORBES & COMPANY for Ben King's "If I Should Die Tonight."

FOUNTAIN INN (S.C.) TRIBUNE for Robert E. Quillen's "Popular Young Couple Married This Week."

THE GROLIER SOCIETY, INC., for "Change the Name of Arkansas" from Vol. 2 of *Folklore of Romantic Arkansas,* by Fred W. Allsopp, copyright 1931 by The Grolier Society, Inc.

ROBERT BROWNING HAMILTON for his poem "Along the Road."

JUDGE LEARNED HAND for his address "The Spirit of Liberty."

HARCOURT, BRACE & COMPANY for "Mia Carlotta" from *Selected Poems of T. A. Daly,* copyright 1926 by Harcourt, Brace & Company; "Caliban in the Coal Mines" from *Selected Poems and Parodies of Louis Untermeyer,* copyright 1935 by Harcourt, Brace & Company.

HARPER & BROTHERS for R. H. Conwell's "Acres of Diamonds"; "The Mendicant's Will" by Williston Fish, from *Harper's Weekly;* the use of the trade-marked name "Mark Twain" in connection with several passages by him; "A Soldier: His Prayer" by Gerald Kersh, from *Poems from the Desert,* verses by members of the Eighth Army, published 1944; "A Little Work: A Little Play" from Du Maurier's *Trilby.*

HARVARD UNIVERSITY PRESS and THE LOEB CLASSICAL LIBRARY for a passage from N. H. Watts's translation of Cicero's *Pro Archia Poeta,* from The Loeb Classical Library.

HENRY HOLT & COMPANY for "Fire and Ice" and "Stopping by Woods on a Snowy Evening" from *Complete Poems of Robert Frost, 1949,* by Robert Frost, copyright 1949 by Henry Holt & Company; "Old Susan" and "Martha" from *Collected Poems, 1901–1918,* by Walter de la Mare, copyright 1920 by Henry Holt & Company, copyright 1948 by Walter de la Mare; "The Death of Captain Waskow" from *Brave Men* by Ernie Pyle, copyright 1944 by Henry Holt & Company; for a passage from *Cyrano de Bergerac* by Edmond Rostand, translated by Brian Hooker, copyright 1923 by Henry Holt & Company.

HOUGHTON MIFFLIN COMPANY for a passage from Winston Churchill's *Sinews of Peace;* "The Face Against the Pane" and "Memory" from *The Poems of Thomas Bailey Aldrich;* Charles E. Carryl's "The Walloping Window-Blind" from *Davy and the Goblin;* Bret Harte's "The Aged Stranger"; Amy Lowell's "Patterns" from *Men, Women and Ghosts;* Frank Dempster Sherman's "A Prayer" from *Lyrics of Joy;* and for various passages from the Works of Henry Wadsworth Longfellow, James Russell Lowell, Dr. Oliver Wendell Holmes, James T. Fields, John Hay, Edward Rowland Sill, John Greenleaf Whittier, Ralph Waldo Emerson.

BRUCE HUMPHRIES, INC., for "Money" from Richard Armour's *Yours for the Asking,* copyright 1942, by permission of Bruce Humphries, Inc.

ALFRED A. KNOPF for "Velvet Shoes" from *Collected Poems of Elinor Wylie,* copyright 1921, 1932 by Elinor Wylie; the words of "It's the Syme the Whole World Over" as given in Downes and Siegmeister's *A Treasury of American Songs;* "The Yak" from Hilaire Belloc's *Cautionary Verses,* copyright 1931 by Hilaire Belloc.

BEN HUR LAMPMAN for his essay "Where to Bury a Dog."

JOHN LANE THE BODLEY HEAD, LTD., for passages from Anatole France's *The Opinions of Jerome Coignard* and *The Seven Wives of Bluebeard,* translated by Mrs. Wilfrid Jackson and D. B. Stewart, respectively.

WILLIAM LIVINGSTON LARNED for his essay "Father Forgets."

LITTLE, BROWN AND COMPANY for "Song of the Open Road" from Ogden Nash's *The Face Is Familiar,* copyright 1940 by Ogden Nash, "Autres Btes, Autres Mœurs" from Ogden Nash's *Hard Lines,* copyright 1931 by Ogden Nash; five poems from *Poems by Emily Dickinson,* copyright 1944 by Martha Dickinson Bianchi; Justice Oliver Wendell Holmes's Broadcast on His Ninetieth Birthday.

LONGMANS, GREEN AND COMPANY, INC., for a passage from George F. R. Henderson's *Stonewall Jackson,* published 1936.

R. J. MACBEAN, Independent executor of estate of John A. Lomax, deceased, for the words of "Jesse James," "Home on the Range," and "The Cowboy's Lament" from *Cowboy Songs and Other Frontier Ballads,* copyright 1910, 1916, 1938, by John A. and Alan Lomax.

McCLELLAND AND STEWART, LTD., for Stephen Leacock's "My Financial Career," and for passages from Winston Churchill's *The End of the Beginning* and *Blood, Sweat and Tears.*

THE MACMILLAN COMPANY for a passage from Alfred Austin's "Is Life Worth Living?" from *Songs of England;* passages from *The Public Papers and Addresses of Franklin D. Roosevelt;* "When You Are Old" from *Poems* by W. B. Yeats, copyright 1906 by The Macmillan Company and used with their permission; "In Tenebris" from *Collected Poems* by Thomas Hardy, copyright 1925 by The Macmillan Company, used with their permission; a passage from John Masefield's *The Everlasting Mercy,* copyright 1911 by John Masefield; "On Growing Old" from *Enslaved* by John Masefield, copyright 1920 by John Masefield; "Stupidity Street" from *Poems* by Ralph Hodgson, copyright 1917 by The Macmillan Company; "Let Me Live Out My Years" from *The Quest* by John G. Neihardt, copyright 1916 by The Macmillan Company; "Barter" from *Love Songs* by Sara Teasdale, copyright 1917 by The Macmillan Company; "An Old Woman of the Roads" from *Wild Earth and Other Poems* by Padraic Colum, copyright 1916 by The Macmillan Company; "General William Booth Enters Into Heaven" by Vachel Lindsay, from *General William Booth Enters Into Heaven* by Vachel Lindsay, copyright 1913 by The Macmillan Company; "To Our Lady" from Mary Dixon Thayer's *The Child on His Knees,* copyright 1926 by The Macmillan Company; passages from the Smith and Miller translation of Homer's *Iliad,* copyright 1944 by The Macmillan Company; passages from Israel Zangwill's *The Melting Pot,* copyright 1909, 1914, by The Macmillan Company.

MACMILLAN & COMPANY, LTD., for a passage from Alfred Austin's "Is Life Worth Living?" from *Songs of England;* to Macmillan & Company, Ltd., and Miss Nancy McIntosh for Sir W. S. Gilbert's "Little Buttercup," "The First Lord's Song," and "A Wand'ring Minstrel," all from *The Savoy Operas,* and "The Yarn of the Nancy Bell" from *Bab Ballads* by Sir W. S. Gilbert; to Macmillan & Company, Ltd., and the trustees of the Thomas Hardy Estate for "In Tenebris" from *Collected Poems* by Thomas Hardy.

THE MACMILLAN COMPANY OF CANADA, LIMITED for Rudyard Kipling's "Tommy," "Danny Deever," "The Female of the Species," and "When Earth's Last Picture Is Painted"; and William Butler Yeats's "When You Are Old."

REVEREND AND MRS. JOHN G. MAGEE for the sonnet "High Flight" by John Gillespie Magee, Jr.

MESSRS. MANN, MATHEWSON, LAFLEUR, AND BROWN, AND MRS.

DAVID CRAIG, for William Henry Drummond's "The Wreck of the Julie Plante."

VIRGIL MARKHAM for Edwin Markham's "Lincoln, the Man of the People," "A Creed," and "Earth Is Enough."

JUANITA JOAQUINA MILLER for Joaquin Miller's "Kit Carson's Ride."

HENRY BEDINGER MITCHELL for Ernest Temple Hargrove's "Letter from Fra Giovanni," copyright by The Quarterly Book Department, published by The Yale University Press.

MRS. WILBUR D. NESBIT for Wilbur D. Nesbit's "Who Hath a Book."

NEW DIRECTIONS for Thomas Merton's "For My Brother" from his *A Man in the Divided Sea and Thirty Poems,* copyright 1946 by New Directions.

THE NEW YORK HERALD TRIBUNE for "High Flight" by John Gillespie Magee, Jr.

THE NEW YORK, NEW HAVEN AND HARTFORD RAILROAD CO. for "The Kid in Upper Four" by Nelson C. Metcalf.

THE NEW YORK SUN for the editorial "Lindbergh Flies Alone" by Harold MacDonald Anderson and "Is There a Santa Claus?" by Francis P. Church.

THE NEW YORK TIMES for the editorial "Flag Day—1940."

OUR SUNDAY VISITOR for Frances Angermayer's "Conversion."

OXFORD UNIVERSITY PRESS for Alfred Austin's "In After Days" and "Before Sedan," and for Gerard Manley Hopkins's "Pied Beauty" from *The Poems of Gerard Manley Hopkins,* copyright 1948 by Oxford University Press. Permission also granted by the families of Alfred Austin and Gerard Manley Hopkins for these poems.

L. C. PAGE & COMPANY, INC., for Miss Will Allen Dromgoole's "The Bridge-Builder" from *Rare Old Chums* by Will Allen Dromgoole, by permission of the publisher, L. C. Page & Company, Boston, Mass.

G. P. PUTNAM'S SONS for passages from Winston Churchill's *Blood, Sweat and Tears,* copyright 1941 by Winston Churchill; for a stanza from "Alumnus Football" from Grantland Rice's *The Sportlights of 1923,* copyright 1924 by Grantland Rice; "So Long, Son" from Howard Vincent O'Brien's *So Long, Son,* copyright 1944 by Howard Vincent O'Brien.

RANDOM HOUSE, INC., for Franklin D. Roosevelt's First Inaugural Address, from *The Public Papers and Addresses of Franklin D. Roosevelt.*

VIRGINIA RICE for a passage from the play *You Can't Take It with You* by Moss Hart and George S. Kaufman, published by Farrar and Rinehart, copyright 1937.

RINEHART & COMPANY, INC., for Lizette Woodworth Reese's "Tears" from her *Selected Poems,* copyright 1926 by Lizette Woodworth Reese, reprinted by permission of Rinehart and Company, Inc.

KENNETH ALLAN ROBINSON for his poem "American Laughter."

SAMUEL I. ROSENMAN for passages from *The Public Papers and Addresses of Franklin D. Roosevelt.*

THE RYERSON PRESS for "The Law of the Yukon" from *Complete Poems of Robert W. Service,* published by The Ryerson Press.

MARGARET E. SANGSTER for her grandmother's poem "The Sin of Omission."

CHARLES SCRIBNER'S SONS for four quotations from the *Works* of President Theodore Roosevelt; Edwin Arlington Robinson's "Calvary," "An Old Story," and "Cliff Klingenhaven," all from *Children of the Night;* Francis Thompson's "A Child's Prayer"; Alice Meynell's "The Shepherdess"; a passage from Francis Thompson's *Essay on Shelley;* "Mr. Dooley on New Year's Resolutions" by Finley Peter Dunne; Robert Louis Stevenson's "The Two Matches," "Eulogy of the Doctor," "Document Giving a Child His Birthday," "The Land of Storybooks," "The Whole Duty of Children," "Escape at Bedtime," "The Gardener," "My Bed Is a Boat," "The Celestial Surgeon," and "Happy Thought"; Henry van Dyke's "America for Me," reprinted from *The Poems of Henry van Dyke,* copyright 1911 by Charles Scribner's Sons, 1939 by Tertius van Dyke, used by permission of the publishers; "The Dinkey Bird" by Eugene Field, reprinted from *Love Songs of Childhood,* by Eugene Field, copyright 1894 by Eugene Field, 1922 by Julia Sutherland Field, used by permission of the publishers, Charles Scribner's Sons; "O World" reprinted from *Poems* by George Santayana, copyright 1923 by Charles Scribner's Sons, used by permission of the publishers.

VIOLET ALLEYN STOREY for her "Prayer for a Very New Angel," copyright 1927 by Violet Alleyn Storey.

GILBERT THOMAS, and GEORGE ALLEN & UNWIN, LTD., for "Red Sky at Morning."

TIME, The Weekly Newspaper, for the "Letter from a Yugoslavian Guerrilla Fighter to His Unborn Child," copyright Time, Inc., 1943.

THE UNIVERSITY OF NORTH CAROLINA PRESS for "What the Governor of N.C. said to the Governor of S.C.," from *North Carolina: A Guide to the Old North State,* Compiled and Written by the Federal Writers' Project, copyright 1939.

THE VIKING PRESS for Dorothy Parker's "Coda" from *The Portable Dorothy Parker,* copyright 1928, 1944, by Dorothy Parker, reprinted by permission of The Viking Press, New York.

A. P. WATT & SON and the executors of the late George Macdonald for "Sweet Peril" and "The Wind and the Moon" from *George Macdonald's Poetical Works;* A. P. Watt & Son and Mrs. George Bambridge for "When Earth's Last Picture Is Painted" from Rudyard Kipling's *The Seven Seas;* for "Tommy" and "Danny Deever" from *Barrack Room Ballads* by Rudyard Kipling; and for "The Female of the Species" from *The Years Between* by Rudyard Kipling; A. P. Watt & Son and Mrs. W. B. Yeats for "When You Are Old" from *The Collected Poems of W. B. Yeats;* A. P. Watt & Son and the executrix of the late Mr. G. K. Chesterton for "Lepanto" from *Collected Poems of G. K. Chesterton.*

COLONEL CLAYTON E. WHEAT, U.S.A., Retired, for his "Cadet Prayer."

ARTHUR E. YOUNG, Acting Chief, Manuscript Division, The Library of Congress, for John Vance Cheney's "The Happiest Heart."

I am also personally grateful to the following: Lillias W. Woods, Patricia J. Woods, Henry F. Woods, Robert L. Barret, Gloria Ruggerio for valuable suggestions. Frank Lenney gave me generous practical assistance. Mrs. Francis Byers and Patricia J. Woods did much excellent typing of manuscript. Miss Hazel Felleman of The *New York Times Book Review* and Miss Carol Bridgman of The American Society of Composers, Authors, and Publishers supplied me with useful copyright guidance. Lillias W. Woods checked typescript, prepared the indexes, and otherwise gave a helping hand. Finally, R. L. De Wilton, Assistant Editor-in-Chief of The Macmillan Company, whose contributions to this book were varied, important, and often above and beyond the call of duty.

R. L. W.

PORT WASHINGTON, N.Y.
January 1950

EDITOR'S NOTE

I am deeply grateful to the many readers of the First TREASURY OF THE FAMILIAR who have suggested and urged including in this volume those of their favorites not in the initial collection.

R. L. W.

Again to

PATRICIA JOAN WOODS

When Time, who steals our years away,
Shall steal our pleasures, too,
The mem'ry of the past will stay,
And half our joys renew.

—THOMAS MOORE, Song

WHICHEVER WAY THE WIND DOTH BLOW

Caroline A. Mason

Whichever way the wind doth blow
Some heart is glad to have it so;
Then blow it east or blow it west,
The wind that blows, that wind is best.

My little craft sails not alone;
A thousand fleets from every zone
Are out upon a thousand seas;
And what for me were favoring breeze
Might dash another, with the shock
Of doom, upon some hidden rock.
And so I do not dare to pray
For winds to waft me on my way,
But leave it to a Higher Will
To stay or speed me; trusting still
That all is well, and sure that He
Who launched my bark, will sail with me
Through storm and calm, and will not fail
Whatever breezes may prevail
To land me, every peril past,
Within His sheltering Heaven at last.

Then whatsoever wind doth blow,
My heart is glad to have it so;
And blow it east or blow it west,
The wind that blows, that wind is best.

* * *

If you measure your shadow, you will find it no greater than before the victory.

Archidamus to Philip of Macedon

THE BIRTH OF A NATION

John Adams

Yesterday, the greatest question was decided, which ever was debated in America, and a greater, perhaps, never was nor will be decided among men. A resolution was passed without one dissenting colony, "that these United Colonies are, and of right ought to be, free and independent States, and as such they have, and of right ought to have, full power to make war, conclude peace, establish commerce, and to do all other acts and things which other States may rightfully do." You will see in a few days a Declaration setting forth the causes which have impelled us to this mighty revolution, and the reasons which will justify it in the sight of God and man. A plan of confederation will be taken up in a few days.

You will think me transported with enthusiasm, but I am not. I am well aware of the toil, and blood, and treasure, that it will cost us to maintain this declaration, and support and defend these States. Yet, through all the gloom, I can see the rays of ravishing light and glory. I can see that the end is more than worth all the means, and that posterity will triumph in that day's transaction, even although we should rue it, which I trust in God we shall not.

(From a letter to his wife, July 3, 1776)

LITTLE BUTTERCUP

W. S. Gilbert

For I'm called Little Buttercup—dear Little Buttercup,
Though I could never tell why,
But still I'm called Buttercup—poor Little Buttercup,
Sweet Little Buttercup I!

I've snuff and tobaccy, and excellent jacky,
I've scissors, and watches, and knives;
I've ribbons and laces to set off the faces
Of pretty young sweethearts and wives.

I've treacle and toffee, I've tea and I've coffee,
Soft tommy and succulent chops;
I've chickens and conies, and pretty polonies.
And excellent peppermint drops.

Then buy of your Buttercup—dear Little Buttercup;
  Sailors should never be shy;
So, buy of your Buttercup—poor Little Buttercup;
  Come, of your Buttercup buy!

ADDRESS TO THE OCEAN

Lord Byron

Roll on, thou deep and dark blue Ocean—roll!
Ten thousand fleets sweep over thee in vain:
Man marks the earth with ruin—his control
Stops with the shore;—upon the watery plain
The wrecks are all thy deed, nor doth remain
A shadow of man's ravage, save his own,
When for a moment, like a drop of rain,
He sinks into thy depths with bubbling groan,
Without a grave, unknell'd, uncoffin'd and unknown.

His steps are not upon thy paths—thy fields
Are not a spoil for him—thou dost arise
And shake him from thee; the vile strength he wields
For earth's destruction thou dost all despise,
Spurning him from thy bosom to the skies,
And send'st him, shivering in thy playful spray,
And howling, to his Gods, where haply lies
His petty hope in some near port or bay,
And dashest him again to earth—there let him lay.

The armaments which thunderstrike the walls
Of rock-built cities, bidding nations quake,
And monarchs tremble in their capitals,
The oak leviathans, whose huge ribs make
Their clay creator the vain title take
Of lord of thee, and arbiter of war—
These are thy toys, and, as the snowy flake,
They melt into thy yeast of waves, which mar
Alike the Armada's pride, or spoils of Trafalgar.

Thy shores are empires, changed in all save thee—
Assyria, Greece, Rome, Carthage, what are they?
Thy waters washed them power while they were free,

And many a tyrant since: their shores obey
The stranger, slave or savage; their decay
Has dried up realms to deserts:—not so thou,
Unchangeable save to thy wild waves' play—
Time writes no wrinkle on thine azure brow—
Such as creation's dawn beheld, thou rollest now.

Thou glorious mirror, where the Almighty's form
Glasses itself in tempests: in all time,
Calm or convulsed—in breeze, or gale, or storm,
Icing the pole, or in the torrid clime
Dark-heaving;—boundless, endless, and sublime—
The image of Eternity—the throne
Of the Invisible; even from out thy slime
The monsters of the deep are made; each zone
Obeys thee; thou goest forth, dread, fathomless, alone.

And I have loved thee, Ocean! and my joy
Of youthful sports was on thy breast to be
Borne, like thy bubbles, onward: from a boy
I wanton'd with thy breakers—they to me
Were a delight; and if the freshening sea
Made them a terror—'twas a pleasing fear,
For I was as it were a child of thee,
And trusted to thy billows far and near,
And laid my hand upon thy mane—as I do here.

(From Childe Harold's Pilgrimage)

"I'M NOBODY! WHO ARE YOU?"

Emily Dickinson

I'm nobody! Who are you?
Are you nobody, too?
Then there's a pair of us—don't tell!
They'd banish us, you know.

How dreary to be somebody!
How public, like a frog
To tell your name the livelong day
To an admiring bog!

THE WHISTLE

Benjamin Franklin

When I was a child of seven years old, my friends on a holiday filled my little pocket with hapence. I went directly to a shop where they sold toys for children; and being charmed with the sound of a whistle that I met by the way, in the hands of another boy, I voluntarily offered and gave all my money for it. When I came home, whistling all over the house, much pleased with my whistle, but disturbing all the family; my brothers, sisters, and cousins, understanding the bargain I had made, told me I had given four times as much for it as it was worth; put me in mind what good things I might have bought with the rest of the money; and laughed at me so much for my folly, that I cried with vexation; and the reflection gave me more chagrin than the whistle gave me pleasure.

This however was afterwards of use to me, the impression continuing on my mind; so that often, when I was tempted to buy some unnecessary thing, I said to myself, "Do not give too much for the whistle"; and I saved my money.

As I grew up, came into the world, and observed the actions of men, I thought I met many, "who gave too much for the whistle." —When I saw one ambitious of court favor, sacrificing his time in attendance at levees, his repose, his liberty, his virtue, and perhaps his friend, to obtain it, I have said to myself, "This man gives too much for his whistle."—When I saw another fond of popularity, constantly employing himself in political bustles, neglecting his own affairs, and ruining them by that neglect, "He pays," says I, "too much for his whistle."—If I knew a miser, who gave up every kind of comfortable living, all the pleasure of doing good to others, all the esteem of his fellow-citizens, and the joys of benevolent friendship for the sake of accumulating wealth, "Poor man," says I, "you pay too much for your whistle."—When I met a man of pleasure, sacrificing every laudable improvement of his mind or of his fortune, to mere corporeal satisfactions, and ruining his health in their pursuit, "Mistaken man," says I, "you are providing pain for yourself instead of pleasure; you pay too much for your whistle."—If I see one fond of appearance, or fine clothes, fine houses, fine furniture, fine equipage, all above his fortune, for which he contracts debts, and ends his career in prison, "Alas!" says I, "he has paid dear, very dear, for his whistle."—When I saw a beautiful, sweet-tempered girl, married to an ill-natured brute of a husband, "What a pity," says I, "that she should pay so much for a whistle!"—In short, I conceived that great part of the miseries of mankind were brought upon them by the false estimates they have made of the value of things, and by their "giving too much for their whistles."

Yet I ought to have charity for these unhappy people, when I consider that with all this wisdom of which I am boasting there are certain things in the world so tempting; for example, the apples of King John, which happily are not to be bought, for if they were put to sale by auction, I might very easily be led to ruin myself in the purchase, and find that I had once more "given too much for the whistle."

THE SIN OF OMISSION

Margaret E. Sangster

It isn't the thing you do, dear,
It's the thing you leave undone
That gives you a bit of a heartache
At setting of the sun.
The tender word forgotten,
The letter you did not write,
The flowers you did not send, dear,
Are your haunting ghosts at night.

The stone you might have lifted
Out of a brother's way;
The bit of heartsome counsel
You were hurried too much to say;
The loving touch of the hand, dear,
The gentle, winning tone
Which you had no time nor thought for
With troubles enough of your own.

Those little acts of kindness
So easily out of mind,
Those chances to be angels
Which we poor mortals find—
They come in night and silence,
Each sad, reproachful wraith,

When hope is faint and flagging,
And a chill has fallen on faith.

For life is all too short, dear,
And sorrow is all too great,
To suffer our slow compassion
That tarries until too late;
And it isn't the thing you do, dear,
It's the thing you leave undone
Which gives you a bit of a heartache
At the setting of the sun.

THE BEGINNING OF THE NEW DEAL

Franklin D. Roosevelt

I am certain that my fellow Americans expect that on my induction into the Presidency I will address them with a candor and a decision which the present situation of our nation impels.

This is pre-eminently the time to speak the truth, the whole truth, frankly and boldly. Nor need we shrink from honestly facing conditions in our country today. This great nation will endure as it has endured, will revive and will prosper.

So first of all let me assert my firm belief that the only thing we have to fear is fear itself—nameless, unreasoning, unjustified terror which paralyzes needed efforts to convert retreat into advance.

In every dark hour of our national life a leadership of frankness and vigor has met with that understanding and support of the people themselves which is essential to victory. I am convinced that you will again give that support to leadership in these critical days.

In such a spirit on my part and on yours we face our common difficulties. They concern, thank God, only material things. Values have shrunken to fantastic levels; taxes have risen; our ability to pay has fallen; government of all kinds is faced by serious curtailment of income; the means of exchange are frozen in the currents of trade; the withered leaves of industrial enterprise lie on every side; farmers find no markets for their produce; the savings of many years in thousands of families are gone.

More important, a host of unemployed citizens face the grim problem of existence, and an equally great number toil with little return. Only a foolish optimist can deny the dark realities of the moment.

Yet our distress comes from no failure of substance. We are stricken by no plague of locusts. Compared with the perils which our forefathers conquered because they believed and were not afraid, we have still much to be thankful for. Nature still offers her bounty and human efforts have multiplied it. Plenty is at our doorstep, but a generous use of it languishes in the very sight of the supply.

Primarily, this is because rulers of the exchange of mankind's goods have failed through their own stubbornness and their own incompetence, have admitted their failure and have abdicated. Practices of the unscrupulous money changers stand indicted in the court of public opinion, rejected by the hearts and minds of men.

True, they have tried, but their efforts have been cast in the pattern of an outworn tradition. Faced by failure of credit, they have proposed only the lending of more money.

Stripped of the lure of profit by which to induce our people to follow their false leadership, they have resorted to exhortations, pleading tearfully for restored confidence. They know only the rules of a generation of self-seekers.

They have no vision, and when there is no vision the people perish.

The money changers have fled from their high seats in the temple of our civilization. We may now restore that temple to the ancient truths.

The measure of the restoration lies in the extent to which we apply social values more noble than mere monetary profits.

Happiness lies not in the mere possession of money; it lies in the joy of achievement, in the thrill of creative effort.

The joy and moral stimulation of work no longer must be forgotten in the mad chase of evanescent profits. These dark days will be worth all they cost us if they teach us that our true destiny is not to be ministered unto but to minister to ourselves and to our fellow men.

Recognition of the falsity of material wealth as the standard of success goes hand in hand with the abandonment of the false belief that public office and high political position are to be valued only by the standards of pride of place and personal profit; and there must be an end to a conduct in banking and in business which too often has given to a sacred trust the likeness of callous and selfish wrongdoing.

Small wonder that confidence languishes, for it thrives only on honesty, on honor, on the sacredness of obligations, on faithful protection, on unselfish performance. Without them it cannot live.

Restoration calls, however, not for changes in ethics alone. This nation asks for action, and action now.

Our greatest primary task is to put people to work. That is no unsolvable problem if we face it wisely and courageously.

It can be accomplished in part by direct recruiting by the Government itself, treating the task as we would treat the emergency of a war, but at the same time, through this employment, accomplishing greatly needed projects to stimulate and reorganize the use of our natural resources.

Hand in hand with this, we must frankly recognize the overbalance of population in our industrial centers and, by engaging on a national scale in a redistribution, endeavor to provide a better use of the land for those best fitted for the land.

The task can be helped by definite efforts to raise the values of agricultural products and with this the power to purchase the output of our cities.

It can be helped by preventing realistically the tragedy of the growing loss, through foreclosure, of our small homes and our farms.

It can be helped by insistence that the federal, state, and local governments act forthwith on the demand that their cost be drastically reduced.

It can be helped by the unifying of relief activities which today are often scattered, uneconomical, and unequal. It can be helped by national planning for and supervision of all forms of transportation and of communications and other utilities which have a definitely public character.

There are many ways in which it can be helped, but it can never be helped merely by talking about it. We must act, and act quickly.

Finally, in our progress toward a resumption of work we require two safeguards against a return of the evils of the old order: there must be a strict supervision of all banking and credits and investments so that there will be an end to speculation with other people's money; and there must be provision for an adequate but sound currency.

These are the lines of attack. I shall presently urge upon a new Congress in special session detailed measures for their fulfillment, and I shall seek the immediate assistance of the several states.

Through this program of action we address ourselves to putting our own national house in order and making income balance outgo.

Our international trade relations, though vastly important, are, in point of time and necessity, secondary to the establishment of a sound national economy.

I favor as a practical policy the putting of first things first. I shall spare no effort to restore world trade by international economic readjustment, but the emergency at home cannot wait on that accomplishment.

The basic thought that guides these specific means of national recovery is not narrowly nationalistic.

It is the insistence, as a first consideration, upon the interdependence of the various elements in and parts of the United States—a recognition of the old and permanently important manifestation of the American spirit of the pioneer.

It is the way to recovery. It is the immediate way. It is the strongest assurance that the recovery will endure.

In the field of world policy, I would dedicate this nation to the policy of the good neighbor—the neighbor who resolutely respects himself and, because he does so, respects the rights of others—the neighbor who respects his obligations and respects the sanctity of his agreements in and with a world of neighbors.

If I read the temper of our people correctly, we now realize, as we have never realized before, our interdependence on each other; that we cannot merely take, but we must give as well; that if we are to go forward we must move as a trained and loyal army willing to sacrifice for the good of a common discipline, because, without such discipline, no progress is made, no leadership becomes effective.

We are, I know, ready and willing to submit our lives and property to such discipline, because it makes possible a leadership which aims at a larger good.

This I propose to offer, pledging that the larger purposes will bind upon us all as a sacred obligation with a unity of duty hitherto evoked only in time of armed strife.

With this pledge taken, I assume unhesitatingly the leadership of this great army of our people, dedicated to a disciplined attack upon our common problems.

Action in this image and to this end is feasible under the form of government which we have inherited from our ancestors.

Our Constitution is so simple and practical that it is possible always to meet extraordinary needs by changes in emphasis and arrangement without loss of essential form.

That is why our constitutional system has proved itself the most superbly enduring political mechanism the modern world has produced. It has met every stress of vast expansion of territory, of foreign wars, of bitter internal strife, of world relations.

It is to be hoped that the normal balance of executive and legislative authority may be wholly adequate to meet the unprecedented task before us. But it may be that an unprecedented demand and need for undelayed action may call for temporary departure from that normal balance of public procedure.

I am prepared under my constitutional duty to recommend the measures that a stricken nation in the midst of a stricken world may require.

These measures, or such other measures as the Congress may build out of its experience and wisdom, I shall seek, within my constitutional authority, to bring to speedy adoption.

But in the event that the Congress shall fail to take one of these two courses, and in the event that the national emergency is still critical, I shall not evade the clear course of duty that will then confront me.

I shall ask the Congress for the one remaining instrument to meet the crisis—broad executive power to wage a war against the emergency as great as the power that would be given to me if we were in fact invaded by a foreign foe.

For the trust reposed in me I will return the courage and the devotion that befit the time. I can do no less.

We face the arduous days that lie before us in the warm courage of national unity; with the clear consciousness of seeking old and precious moral values; with the clean satisfaction that comes from the stern performance of duty by old and young alike.

We aim at the assurance of a rounded and permanent national life.

We do not distrust the future of essential democracy. The people of the United States have not failed. In their need they have registered a mandate that they want direct, vigorous action.

They have asked for discipline and direction under leadership. They have made me the present instrument of their wishes. In the spirit of the gift I take it.

In this dedication of a nation we humbly ask the blessing of God. May He protect each and every one of us. May He guide me in the days to come.

(First Inaugural Address, March 4, 1933)

THE LAW OF THE YUKON

Robert W. Service

This is the law of the Yukon, and ever she makes it plain:
"Send not your foolish and feeble, send me your strong and your sane—
Strong for the red rage of battle; sane, for I harry them sore;
Send me men girt for the combat, men who are grit to the core;
Swift as the panther in triumph, fierce as the bear in defeat,
Sired of a bulldog parent, steeled in the furnace heat.
Send me the best of your breeding, lend me your chosen ones;
Them will I take to my bosom, them will I call my sons;
Them will I gild with my treasure, them will I glut with my meat;
But the others—the misfits, the failures—I trample under my feet.
Dissolute, damned and despairful, crippled and palsied and slain,
Ye would send me the spawn of your gutters— Go! take back your spawn again.

"Wild and wide are my borders, stern as death is my sway;
From my ruthless throne I have ruled alone for a million years and a day;
Hugging my mighty treasure, waiting for man to come,
Till he swept like a turbid torrent, and after him swept—the scum.
The pallid pimp of the dead-line, the enervate of the pen,
One by one I weeded them out, for all that I sought was—Men.
One by one I dismayed them, frighting them sore with my glooms;
One by one I betrayed them unto my manifold dooms.
Drowned them like rats in my rivers, starved them like curs on my plains,
Rotted the flesh that was left them, poisoned the blood in their veins;
Burst with my winter upon them, searing forever their sight,
Lashed them with fungus-white faces, whimpering wild in the night;

"Staggering blind through the storm-whirl, stumbling mad through the snow,
Frozen stiff in the ice-pack, brittle and bent like a bow;
Featureless, formless, forsaken, scented by wolves in their flight,
Left for the wind to make music through ribs that are glittering white;
Gnawing the black crust of failure, searching the pit of despair,

Crooking the toe in the trigger, trying to patter a prayer;
Going outside with an escort, raving with lips all afoam,
Writing a cheque for a million, driveling feebly of home;
Lost like a louse in the burning . . . or else in the tented town
Seeking a drunkard's solace, sinking and sinking down;
Steeped in the slime at the bottom, dead to a decent world,
Lost 'mid the human flotsam, far on the frontier hurled;
In the camp at the bend of the river, with its dozen saloons aglare,
Its gambling dens ariot, its gramophones all ablare;
Crimped with the crimes of a city, sin-ridden and bridled with lies,
In the hush of my mountained vastness, in the flush of the midnight skies.
Plague-spots, yet tools of my purpose, so natheless I suffer them thrive,
Crushing my Weak in their clutches, that only my Strong may survive.

"But the others, the men of my mettle, the men who would 'stablish my fame
Unto its ultimate issue, winning me honor, not shame;
Searching my uttermost valleys, fighting each step as they go,
Shooting the wrath of my rapids, scaling my ramparts of snow;
Ripping the guts of my mountains, looting the beds of my creeks,
Them will I take to my bosom, and speak as a mother speaks.
I am the land that listens, I am the land that broods;
Steeped in eternal beauty, crystalline waters and woods.
Long have I waited lonely, shunned as a thing accurst,
Monstrous, moody, pathetic, the last of the lands and the first;
Visioning camp-fires at twilight, sad with a longing forlorn,
Feeling my womb's o'er-pregnant with the seed of cities unborn.
Wild and wide are my borders, stern as death is my sway,
And I wait for the men who will win me—and I will not be won in a day;
And I will not be won by weaklings, subtle, suave and mild,
But by men with the hearts of vikings, and the simple faith of a child;
Desperate, strong and resistless, unthrottled by fear or defeat,
Them will I gild with my treasure, them will I glut with my meat.

"Lofty I stand from each sister land, patient and wearily wise,
With the weight of a world of sadness in my quiet, passionless eyes;
Dreaming alone of a people, dreaming alone of a day,
When men shall not rape my riches, and curse me and go away;

Making a bawd of my bounty, fouling the hand that gave—
Till I rise in my wrath and I sweep on their path and I stamp them
  into a grave.
Dreaming of men who will bless me, of women esteeming me good,
Of children born in my borders of radiant motherhood,
Of cities leaping to stature, of fame like a flag unfurled,
As I pour the tide of my riches in the eager lap of the world."

This is the Law of the Yukon, that only the Strong shall thrive;
That surely the Weak shall perish, and only the Fit survive.
Dissolute, damned and despairful, crippled and palsied and slain,
This is the Will of the Yukon.—Lo, how she makes it plain!

MARY AND HER LAMB

Sarah Josepha Hale

Mary had a little lamb,
Its fleece was white as snow,
And everywhere that Mary went
The lamb was sure to go;
He followed her to school one day—
That was against the rule.
It made the children laugh and play
To see a lamb at school.

And so the teacher turned him out,
But still he lingered near,
And waited patiently about
Till Mary did appear;
And then he ran to her, and laid
His head upon her arm,
As if he said, "I'm not afraid—
You'll keep me from all harm."

"What makes the lamb love Mary so?"
The eager children cry.
"Oh, Mary loves the lamb, you know,"
The teacher did reply;
"And you each gentle animal
In confidence may bind
And make them follow at your call,
If you are always kind."

LINCOLN TO COLONEL ELLSWORTH'S PARENTS

Washington, D.C., May 25, 1861

My Dear Sir and Madam: In the untimely loss of your noble son, our affliction here is scarcely less than your own. So much of promised usefulness to one's country, and of bright hopes for one's self and friends, have rarely been so suddenly dashed as in his fall. In size, in years, and in youthful appearance a boy only, his power to command men was surpassingly great. This power, combined with a fine intellect, an indomitable energy, and a taste altogether military, constituted in him, as seemed to me, the best natural talent in that department I ever knew.

And yet he was singularly modest and deferential in social intercourse. My acquaintance with him began less than two years ago; yet through the latter half of the intervening period it was as intimate as the disparity of our ages and my engrossing engagements would permit. To me he appeared to have no indulgences or pastimes; and I never heard him utter a profane or intemperate word. What was conclusive of his good heart, he never forgot his parents. The honors he labored for so laudably, and for which in the sad end he so gallantly gave his life, he meant for them no less than for himself.

In the hope that it may be no intrusion upon the sacredness of your sorrow, I have ventured to address you this tribute to the memory of my young friend and your brave and early fallen child.

May God give you that consolation which is beyond all earthly power.

A. Lincoln

"I KNOW THAT MY REDEEMER LIVES"

Charles Wesley

I know that my Redeemer lives,
And ever prays for me;
A token of his love he gives,
A pledge of liberty.

I find him lifting up my head;
He brings salvation near;
His presence makes me free indeed,
And he will soon appear.

He wills that I should holy be;
  What can withstand his will?
The counsel of his grace in me
  He surely shall fulfill.

When God is mine, and I am his,
  Of paradise possessed,
I taste unutterable bliss,
  And everlasting rest.

THE SIDEWALKS OF NEW YORK *

Charles B. Lawlor

Down in front of Casey's old brown wooden stoop,
On a summer's evening we formed a merry group.
Boys and girls together, we would sing and waltz
While the Ginnie played the organ on the sidewalks of New York.

Chorus:
East-side, West-side, all around the town,
The tots sang Ring-a-Rosie, London Bridge is falling down.
Boys and girls together, me and Mamie Rorke,
Tripped the light fantastic on the sidewalks of New York.

That's where Johnny Casey and little Jimmy Crowe,
With Jakey Krause, the baker, who always had the dough,
Pretty Nelly Shannon with a dude as light as cork,
First picked up the waltz-step on the sidewalks of New York.

Things have changed since those times; some are up in G.
Others, they are on the hog, but they all feel just like me.
They would part with all they've got could they but once more
  walk
With their best girl and have a twirl on the sidewalks of New York.

CASSIUS POISONS BRUTUS' MIND

William Shakespeare

Well, honour is the subject of my story.
I cannot tell what you and other men
Think of this life, but, for my single self,
I had as lief not be as live to be
In awe of such a thing as I myself.
I was born free as Caesar; so were you:
We both have fed as well, and we can both
Endure the winter's cold as well as he:
For once, upon a raw and gusty day,
The troubled Tiber chafing with her shores,
Caesar said to me "Darest thou, Cassius, now
Leap in with me into this angry flood,
And swim to yonder point?" Upon the word,
Accoutred as I was, I plunged in
And bade him follow: so indeed he did.
The torrent roar'd, and we did buffet it
With lusty sinews, throwing it aside
And stemming it with hearts of controversy;
But ere we could arrive the point proposed,
Caesar cried "Help me, Cassius, or I sink!"
I, as Aeneas our great ancestor
Did from the flames of Troy upon his shoulder
The old Anchises bear, so from the waves of Tiber
Did I the tired Caesar. And this man
Is now become a god, and Cassius is
A wretched creature, and must bend his body
If Caesar carelessly but nod on him.
He had a fever when he was in Spain,
And when the fit was on him, I did mark
How he did shake: 'tis true, this god did shake;
His coward lips did from their colour fly,
And that same eye whose bend doth awe the world
Did lose his lustre: I did hear him groan:
Ay, and that tongue of his that bade the Romans
Mark him and write his speeches in their books,
Alas, it cried "Give me some drink, Titinius,"
As a sick girl. Ye gods, it doth amaze me
A man of such a feeble temper should
So get the start of the majestic world

And bear the palm alone. . . .
Why, man, he doth bestride the narrow world
Like a Colossus, and we petty men
Walk under his huge legs and peep about
To find ourselves dishonourable graves.
Men at some time are masters of their fates:
The fault, dear Brutus, is not in our stars,
But in ourselves, that we are underlings.
Brutus, and Caesar: what should be in that Caesar?
Why should that name be sounded more than yours?
Write them together, yours is as fair a name;
Sound them, it doth become the mouth as well;
Weigh them, it is as heavy; conjure with 'em,
Brutus will start a spirit as soon as Caesar.
Now, in the names of all the gods at once,
Upon what meat doth this our Caesar feed,
That he is grown so great?

(From Julius Caesar)

LEPANTO

G. K. Chesterton

White founts falling in the Courts of the sun,
And the Soldan of Byzantium is smiling as they run;
There is laughter like the fountains in that face of all men feared,
It stirs the forest darkness, the darkness of his beard,
It curls the blood-red crescent, the crescent of his lips,
For the inmost sea of all the earth is shaken with his ships.
They have dared the white republics up the capes of Italy,
They have dashed the Adriatic round the Lion of the Sea,
And the Pope has cast his arms abroad for agony and loss,
And called the kings of Christendom for swords about the Cross.
The cold queen of England is looking in the glass;
The shadow of the Valois is yawning at the Mass;
From evening isles fantastical rings faint the Spanish gun,
And the Lord upon the Golden Horn is laughing in the sun.

Dim drums throbbing, in the hills half heard,
Where only on a nameless throne a crownless prince has stirred,
Where, risen from a doubtful seat and half-attainted stall,

The last knight of Europe takes weapons from the wall,
The last and lingering troubadour to whom the bird has sung,
That once went singing southward when all the world was young.
In that enormous silence, tiny and unafraid,
Comes up along a winding road the noise of the Crusade.

Strong gongs groaning as the guns boom far,
Don John of Austria is going to the war,
Stiff flags straining the night-blast cold
In the gloom black-purple, in the glint old-gold,
Torchlight crimson on the copper kettle-drums,
Then the tuckets, then the trumpets, then the cannon, and he comes.
Don John laughing in the brave beard curled,
Spurning of his stirrups like the thrones of all the world,
Holding his head up for a flag of all the free.
Love-light of Spain—hurrah!
Death-light of Africa!
Don John of Austria
Is riding to the sea.

Mahound is in his paradise above the evening star,
(Don John of Austria is going to the war.)
He moves a mighty turban on the timeless houri's knees,
His turban that is woven of the sunsets and the seas.
He shakes the peacock gardens as he rises from his ease,
And he strides among the tree-tops and is taller than the trees,
And his voice through all the garden is a thunder sent to bring
Black Azrael and Ariel and Ammon on the wing.
Giants and the Genii,
Multiplex of wing and eye,
Whose strong obedience broke the sky
When Solomon was king.

They rush in red and purple from the red clouds of the morn,
From temples where the yellow gods shut up their eyes in scorn;
They rise in green robes roaring from the green hells of the sea
Where fallen skies and evil hues and eyeless creatures be;
On them the sea-valves cluster and the grey sea-forests curl,
Splashed with a splendid sickness, the sickness of the pearl;
They swell in sapphire smoke out of the blue cracks of the ground,—
They gather and they wonder and give worship to Mahound.

And he saith, "Break up the mountains where the hermit-folk can hide,
And sift the red and silver sands lest bone of saint abide,
And chase the Giaours flying night and day, not giving rest,
For that which was our trouble comes again out of the west.
We have set the seal of Solomon on all things under sun,
Of knowledge and of sorrow and endurance of things done,
But a noise is in the mountains, in the mountains, and I know
The voice that shook our palaces—four hundred years ago:
It is he that saith not 'Kismet'; it is he that knows not Fate;
It is Richard, it is Raymond, it is Godfrey in the gate!
It is he whose loss is laughter when he counts the wager worth,
Put down your feet upon him, that our peace be on the earth."
For he heard drums groaning and heard guns jar,
(Don John of Austria is going to the war.)
Sudden and still—hurrah!
Bolt from Iberia!
Don John of Austria
Is gone by Alcalar.

St. Michael's on his Mountain in the sea-roads of the north
(Don John of Austria is girt and going forth.)
Where the grey seas glitter and the sharp tides shift
And the sea-folk labour and the red sails lift.
He shakes his lance of iron and he claps his wings of stone;
The noise is gone through Normandy; the noise is gone alone;
The North is full of tangled things and texts and aching eyes
And dead is all the innocence of anger and surprise,
And Christian killeth Christian in a narrow dusty room,
And Christian dreadeth Christ that hath a newer face of doom,
And Christian hateth Mary that God kissed in Galilee,—
But Don John of Austria is riding to the sea.
Don John calling through the blast and the eclipse
Crying with the trumpet, with the trumpet to his lips,
Trumpet that sayeth *ha!*
Domino gloria!
Don John of Austria
Is shouting to the ships.

King Philip's in his closet with the Fleece about his neck
(Don John of Austria is armed upon the deck.)
The walls are hung with velvet that is black and soft as sin,
And little dwarfs creep out of it and little dwarfs creep in.
He holds a crystal phial that has colours like the moon,

He touches, and it tingles, and he trembles very soon,
And his face is as a fungus of a leprous white and grey
Like plants in the high houses that are shuttered from the day,
And death is in the phial and the end of noble work,
But Don John of Austria has fired upon the Turk.
Don John's hunting, and his hounds have bayed—
Booms away past Italy the rumour of his raid.
Gun upon gun, ha! ha!
Gun upon gun, hurrah!
Don John of Austria
Has loosed the cannonade.

The Pope was in his chapel before day or battle broke,
(Don John of Austria is hidden in the smoke.)
The hidden room in man's house where God sits all the year,
The secret window whence the world looks small and very dear.
He sees as in a mirror on the monstrous twilight sea
The crescent of his cruel ships whose name is mystery;
They fling great shadows foe-wards, making Cross and Castle dark,
They veil the plumèd lions in the galleys of St. Mark;
And above the ships are palaces of brown, black-bearded chiefs,
And below the ships are prisons, where with multitudinous griefs,
Christian captives, sick and sunless, all a labouring race repines
Like a race in sunken cities, like a nation in the mines.
They are lost like slaves that sweat, and in the skies of morning hung
The stair-ways of the tallest gods when tyranny was young.
They are countless, voiceless, hopeless as those fallen or fleeing on
Before the high Kings' horses in the granite of Babylon.
And many a one grows witless in his quiet room in hell
Where a yellow face looks inward through the lattice of his cell,
And he finds his God forgotten, and he seeks no more a sign—
(But Don John of Austria has burst the battle-line!)
Don John pounding from the slaughter-painted poop,
Purpling all the ocean like a bloody pirate's sloop,
Scarlet running over on the silvers and the golds,
Breaking of the hatches up and bursting of the holds,
Thronging of the thousands up that labour under sea
White for bliss and blind for sun and stunned for liberty.
Vivat Hispania!
Domino Gloria!
Don John of Austria
Has set his people free!

Cervantes on his galley sets the sword back in the sheath
(Don John of Austria rides homeward with a wreath.)
And he sees across a weary land a straggling road in Spain,
Up which a lean and foolish knight for ever rides in vain,
And he smiles, but not as Sultans smile, and settle back the blade . . .
(But Don John of Austria rides home from the Crusade.)

THE DEATH OF CAPTAIN WASKOW

Ernie Pyle

AT THE FRONT LINES IN ITALY, Jan. 10 [1944] (by Wireless).—In this war I have known a lot of officers who were loved and respected by the soldiers under them. But never have I crossed the trail of any man as beloved as Capt. Henry T. Waskow of Belton, Tex.

Capt. Waskow was a company commander in the 36th Division. He was very young, only in his middle twenties, but he carried in him a sincerity and gentleness that made people want to be guided by him.

"After my own father, he comes next," a sergeant told me.

"He always looked after us," a soldier said. "He'd go to bat for us every time."

"I've never known him to do anything unkind," another one said.

I was at the foot of the mule trail the night they brought Capt. Waskow down. The moon was nearly full, and you could see far up the trail, and even part way across the valley. Soldiers made shadows as they walked.

Dead men had been coming down the mountain all evening, lashed onto the backs of mules. They came lying belly down across the wooden packsaddles, their heads hanging down on the left side of the mules, their stiffened legs sticking awkwardly from the other side, bobbing up and down as the mule walked.

The Italian mule skinners were afraid to walk beside the dead men, so Americans had to lead the mules down that night. Even the Americans were reluctant to unlash and lift off the bodies when they got to the bottom, so an officer had to do it himself and ask others to help.

The first one came early in the morning. They slid him down from the mule, and stood him on his feet for a moment. In the half light he might have been merely a sick man standing there leaning on the other. Then they laid him on the ground in the shadow of the stone wall alongside the road.

I don't know who that first one was. You feel small in the presence of dead men and you don't ask silly questions.

We left him there beside the road, that first one, and we all went back into the cowshed and sat on watercans or lay on the straw, waiting for the next batch of mules.

Somebody said the dead soldier had been dead for four days, and then nobody said anything more about him. We talked for an hour or more; the dead man lay all alone, outside in the shadow of the wall.

Then a soldier came into the cowshed and said there were some more bodies outside. We went out into the road. Four mules stood there in the moonlight, in the road where the trail came down off the mountain. The soldiers who led them stood there waiting.

"This one is Capt. Waskow," one of them said quickly.

Two men unlashed his body from the mule and lifted it off and laid it in the shadow beside the stone wall. Other men took the other bodies off. Finally there were five lying end to end in a long row. You don't cover up dead men in the combat zone. They just lie there in the shadows until somebody else comes after them.

The uncertain mules moved off to their olive groves. The men in the road seemed reluctant to leave. They stood around, and gradually I could sense them moving, one by one, close to Capt. Waskow's body. Not so much to look, I think, as to say something in finality to him and to themselves. I stood close by and I could hear.

One soldier came and looked down, and he said out loud:

"God damn it!"

That's all he said, and then he walked away.

Another one came, and he said, "God damn it to hell, anyway!" He looked down for a few last moments and then turned and left.

Another man came. I think he was an officer. It was hard to tell officers from men in the dim light, for everybody was grimy and dirty. The man looked down into the dead captain's face and then spoke directly to him, as though he were alive:

"I'm sorry, ol' man."

Then a soldier came in and stood beside the officer and bent over, and he too spoke to his dead captain, not in a whisper but awfully tenderly, and he said:

"I sure am sorry, sir."

Then the first man squatted down, and he reached down and

took the captain's hand, and he sat there for a full five minutes holding the dead hand in his own and looking intently into the dead face. And he never uttered a sound all the time he sat there.

Finally he put the hand down. He reached up and gently straightened the points of the captain's shirt collar, and then he sort of rearranged the tattered edges of his uniform around the wound, and then he got up and walked away down the road in the moonlight, all alone.

The rest of us went back into the cowshed, leaving the five dead men lying in a line end to end in the shadow of the low stone wall. We lay down on the straw in the cowshed, and pretty soon we were all asleep.

THE SWEETEST STORY EVER TOLD

R. M. Stults

O, answer me a question, Love, I pray;
My heart for thee is pining day by day.
O, answer me, my dearest, answer true;
Hold me close as you were wont to do.
Whisper once again, the story old,
The dearest, sweetest story ever told;
Whisper once again the story old;
The dearest, sweetest story ever told.

Chorus:

Tell me, do you love me?
Tell me softly, sweetly, as of old!
Tell me that you love me,
For that's the sweetest story ever told.
Tell me, do you love me?
Whisper softly, sweetly, as of old!
Tell me that you love me,
For that's the sweetest story ever told.

O, tell me that your heart to me is true;
Repeat to me the story, ever new.
O, take my hand in yours and tell me, dear,
Is it joy to thee when I am near?
Whisper o'er and o'er the story old,

The dearest, sweetest story ever told.
Whisper o'er and o'er the story old,
The dearest, sweetest story ever told.

NOW THANK WE ALL OUR GOD

Martin Rinkart

(Translator: Catherine Winkworth)

Now thank we all our God,
With heart, and hands and voices,
Who wondrous things hath done,
In whom his world rejoices;
Who from our mother's arms
Hath blessed us on our way
With countless gifts of love,
And still is ours today.

O may this bounteous God
Through all our life be near us!
With ever-joyful hearts
And blessed peace to cheer us;
And keep us in his grace,
And guide us when perplexed,
And free us from all ills
In this world and the next.

RUSSIA

Winston S. Churchill

I cannot forecast to you the action of Russia. It is a riddle wrapped in a mystery inside an enigma; but perhaps there is a key. That key is Russian national interest.
(October 1, 1939, four days after Russia occupied Eastern Poland)

* * *

Most of the shadows of this life are caused by standing in one's own sunshine.—Ralph Waldo Emerson

THE BUILDERS

Henry Wadsworth Longfellow

All are architects of Fate,
 Working in these walls of Time;
Some with massive deeds and great,
 Some with ornaments of rhyme.

Nothing useless is, or low;
 Each thing in its place is best;
And what seems but idle show
 Strengthens and supports the rest.

For the structure that we raise,
 Time is with materials filled;
Our to-days and yesterdays
 Are the blocks with which we build.

Truly shape and fashion these;
 Leave no yawning gaps between;
Think not, because no man sees,
 Such things will remain unseen.

In the elder days of Art,
 Builders wrought with greatest care
Each minute and unseen part;
 For the Gods see everywhere.

Let us do our work as well,
 Both the unseen and the seen;
Make the house, where Gods may dwell,
 Beautiful, entire, and clean.

Else our lives are incomplete,
 Standing in these walls of Time,
Broken stairways, where the feet
 Stumble as they seek to climb.

Build to-day, then, strong and sure,
 With a firm and ample base;
And ascending and secure
 Shall to-morrow find its place.

Thus alone can we attain
   To those turrets, where the eye
Sees the world as one vast plain,
   And one boundless reach of sky.

THE GOOD SHEPHERD

Holy Bible, John 10:7–18

Then said Jesus unto them again, Verily, verily, I say unto you, I am the door of the sheep. All that ever came before me are thieves and robbers: but the sheep did not hear them. I am the door: by me if any man enter in, he shall be saved, and shall go in and out, and find pasture. The thief cometh not, but for to steal, and to kill, and to destroy: I am come that they might have life, and that they might have it more abundantly. I am the good shepherd: the good shepherd giveth his life for the sheep. But he that is an hireling, and not the shepherd, whose own the sheep are not, seeth the wolf coming, and leaveth the sheep, and fleeth; and the wolf catcheth them, and scattereth the sheep. The hireling fleeth, because he is an hireling, and careth not for the sheep. I am the good shepherd, and know my sheep, and am known of mine. As the Father knoweth me, even so know I the Father: and I lay down my life for the sheep. And other sheep I have, which are not of this fold: them also I must bring, and they shall hear my voice; and there shall be one fold, and one shepherd. Therefore doth my Father love me, because I lay down my life, that I might take it again. No man taketh it from me, but I lay it down of myself. I have power to lay it down, and I have power to take it again. This commandment have I received of my Father.

TO NIGHT

Percy Bysshe Shelley

Swiftly walk o'er the western wave,
            Spirit of Night!
Out of the misty eastern cave,
Where, all the long and lone daylight,
Thou wovest dreams of joy and fear,
Which make thee terrible and dear,—
            Swift be thy flight!

Wrap thy form in a mantle gray,
Star-in-wrought!
Blind with thine hair the eyes of Day;
Kiss her until she be wearied out,
Then wander o'er city, and sea, and land,
Touching all with thine opiate wand—
Come, long-sought!

When I arose and saw the dawn,
I sighed for thee;
When light rode high, and the dew was gone,
And noon lay heavy on flower and tree,
And the weary Day turned to his rest,
Lingering like an unloved guest,
I sighed for thee.

Thy brother Death came, and cried,
Wouldst thou me?
Thy sweet child Sleep, the filmy-eyed,
Murmured like a noontide bee,
Shall I nestle near thy side?
Wouldst thou me?—And I replied,
No, not thee!
Death will come when thou art dead,
Soon, too soon—
Sleep will come when thou art fled;
Of neither would I ask the boon
I ask of thee, beloved Night—
Swift be thine approaching flight.
Come soon, soon!

PROSPECTUS OF THE FAMOUS LACON, ILLINOIS, CAT-AND-RAT RANCH

Anonymous

GLORIOUS OPPORTUNITY TO GET RICH—We are starting a cat ranch in Lacon with 100,000 cats. Each cat will average twelve kittens a year. The cat skins will sell for thirty cents each. One hundred men can skin 5,000 cats a day. We figure a daily net profit of over $10,000. Now what shall we feed the cats? We will start a rat ranch next door with 1,000,000 rats. The rats will breed twelve times faster than the cats. So we will have four rats to feed each day to each cat. Now what shall we feed the rats? We will feed the rats the carcasses of the cats after they have been skinned. Now Get This! We feed the rats to the cats and the cats to the rats and get the skins for nothing.

(This hoax was carried by every newspaper in the United States, in 1875)

THE DEATH OF DEATH

William Shakespeare

Poor soul, the centre of my sinful earth,
Press'd by these rebel powers that thee array,
Why dost thou pine within and suffer dearth,
Painting thy outward walls so costly gay?
Why so large cost, having so short a lease,
Dost thou upon thy fading mansion spend?
Shall worms, inheritors of this excess,
Eat up thy charge? is this thy body's end?

Then, soul, live thou upon thy servant's loss,
And let that pine to aggravate thy store;
Buy terms divine in selling hours of dross;
Within be fed, without be rich no more;
So shalt thou feed on Death, that feeds on men,
And Death once dead, there's no more dying then.

THE AHKOOND OF SWAT

"The Ahkoond of Swat is dead."—London papers of Jan. 22, 1878.

George Thomas Lanigan

What, what, what,
What's the news from Swat?
Sad news,
Bad news,
Comes by the cable led

Through the Indian Ocean's bed,
Through the Persian Gulf, the Red
Sea and the Med-
Iterranean—he's dead;
The Ahkoond is dead!

For the Ahkoond I mourn,
  Who wouldn't?
He strove to disregard the message stern,
  But he Ahkoodn't.
Dead, dead, dead:
  (Sorrow, Swats!)
Swats wha hae wi' Ahkoond bled,
Swats whom he hath often led
Onward to a gory bed,
  Or to victory,
  As the case might be.
    Sorrow, Swats!
Tears shed,
  Shed tears like water.
Your great Ahkoond is dead!
  That Swat's the matter!

Mourn, city of Swat,
Your great Ahkoond is not,
But laid 'mid worms to rot.
His mortal part alone, his soul was caught
  (Because he was a good Ahkoond)
  Up to the bosom of Mahound.
Though earthly walls his frame surround
(Forever hallowed by the ground!)

And skeptics mock the lowly mound
And say "He's now of no Ahkoond!"
  His soul is in the skies—
The azure skies that bend above his loved
  Metropolis of Swat.
  He sees with larger, other eyes,
  Athwart all earthly mysteries—
  He knows what's Swat.

Let Swat bury the great Ahkoond
  With a noise of mourning and of lamentation!

Let Swat bury the great Ahkoond
With the noise of the mourning of the Swattish nation!
Fallen is at length
Its tower of strength;
Its sun is dimmed ere it had nooned;
Dead lies the great Ahkoond,
The great Ahkoond of Swat
Is not!

LUCY GRAY

William Wordsworth

Oft I had heard of Lucy Gray;
And, when I cross'd the wild,
I chanced to see at break of day
The solitary child.

No mate, no comrade Lucy knew;
She dwelt on a wide moor,—
The sweetest thing that ever grew
Beside a human door!

You yet may spy the fawn at play,
The hare upon the green,
But the sweet face of Lucy Gray
Will never more be seen.

"To-night will be a stormy night;
You to the town must go,
And take a lantern, child, to light
Your mother through the snow."

"That, father, will I gladly do;
'Tis scarcely afternoon;
The minster clock has just struck two,
And yonder is the moon."

At this the father raised his hook,
And snapp'd a faggot-band;
He plied his work; and Lucy took
The lantern in her hand.

Not blither is the mountain roe:
  With many a wanton stroke
Her feet disperse the powdery snow,
  That rises up like smoke.

The storm came on before its time:
  She wander'd up and down,
And many a hill did Lucy climb,
  But never reach'd the town.

The wretched parents all that night
  Went shouting far and wide,
But there was neither sound nor sight
  To serve them for a guide.

At daybreak on a hill they stood
  That overlook'd the moor,
And thence they saw the bridge of wood,
  A furlong from their door.

They wept—and, turning homeward, cried,
  "In heaven we all shall meet:"
—When in the snow the mother spied
  The print of Lucy's feet.

Then downwards from the steep hill's edge
  They track'd the foot-marks small,
And through the broken hawthorn-hedge,
  And by the long stone wall,

And then an open field they cross'd:
  The marks were still the same;
They track'd them on, nor ever lost,
  And to the bridge they came.

They follow'd from the snowy bank
  Those foot-marks one by one,
Into the middle of the plank,
  And further there were none.

—Yet some maintain that to this day
  She is a living child;
That you may see sweet Lucy Gray
  Upon the lonesome wild.

O'er rough and smooth she trips along,
  And never looks behind;
And sings a solitary song
  That whistles in the wind.

PETER PIPER

Peter Piper's Practical Principles of Plain and Perfect Pronunciation to Please the Palates of Pretty Prattling Playfellows. Pray Parents to Purchase this Playful Performance, Partly to Pay him for his Patience and Pains; Partly to Provide for the Printers and Publishers; but Principally to Prevent the Pernicious Prevalence of Perverse Pronunciation.

Peter Piper picked a peck of pickled peppers;
Did Peter Piper pick a peck of pickled peppers?
If Peter Piper picked a peck of pickled peppers,
Where's the peck of pickled peppers Peter Piper picked?

LIVING

Anonymous

To touch the cup with eager lips and taste, not drain it;
To woo and tempt and court a bliss—and not attain it;
To fondle and caress a joy, yet hold it lightly,
Lest it become necessity and cling too tightly;
To watch the sun set in the west without regretting;
To hail its advent in the east—the night forgetting;
To smother care in happiness and grief in laughter;
To hold the present close—not questioning hereafter;
To have enough to share—to know the joy of giving;
To thrill with all the sweets of life—is living.

* * *

The greatest pleasure I know is to do a good action by stealth, and to have it found out by accident.—Charles Lamb

GOD SAVE THE KING

Henry Carey

God save our gracious King,
Long live our noble King,
God save the King!
Send him victorious,
Happy and glorious,
Long to reign over us,
God save the King!

O Lord and God arise,
Scatter his enemies,
And make them fall.
Confound their politics,
Frustrate their knavish tricks,
On Thee our hopes we fix,
God save the King!

Thy choicest gifts in store
On him be pleased to pour,
Long may he reign!
May he defend our laws
And ever give us cause
To sing with heart and voice,
God save the King!

Nor on this land alone,
But be God's mercies known
From shore to shore.
Lord, make the nations see
That men should brothers be,
And form one family
The wide world o'er.

Note: In 1946 King George gave his approval to the removal of the second stanza as shown above, replacing that stanza with the above third stanza, and using last as a new third stanza, which was written many years ago by Rev. W. E. Hickson but never accepted.

DERELICT

A Reminiscence of "Treasure Island"
(Cap'n Billy Bones his song)

Young E. Allison

Fifteen men on the dead man's chest—
  Yo-ho-ho and a bottle of rum!
Drink and the devil had done for the rest—
  Yo-ho-ho and a bottle of rum!
The mate was fixed by the bos'n's pike,
The bos'n brained with a marlinspike
    It had been gripped
      By fingers ten;
    And there they lay,
      All good dead men,
Like break-o'-day in a boozing-ken—
  Yo-ho-ho and a bottle of rum!

Fifteen men of a whole ship's list—
  Yo-ho-ho and a bottle of rum!
All of 'em down from the devil's own fist—
  Yo-ho-ho and a bottle of rum!
The skipper lay with his nob in gore
Where the scullion's axe his cheek had shore—
And the scullion he was stabbed times four.
    And there they lay,
      And the soggy skies
    Dripped all day long
      In up-staring eyes—
At murk sunset and at foul sunrise—
  Yo-ho-ho and a bottle of rum!

Fifteen men of 'em stiff and stark—
  Yo-ho-ho and a bottle of rum!
Ten of the crew had the murder mark—
  Yo-ho-ho and a bottle of rum!
'Twas a cutlass swipe, or an ounce of lead,
Or a yawing hole in a battered head—
And the scuppers glut with a rotting red.
    And there they lay—
      Aye, damn my eyes!—

All lookouts clapped
On paradise—
All souls bound just contrariwise—
Yo-ho-ho and a bottle of rum!

Fifteen men of 'em good and true—
Yo-ho-ho and a bottle of rum!
Every man jack could ha' sailed with old Pew—
Yo-ho-ho and a bottle of rum!
There was chest on chest full of Spanish gold,
With a ton of plate in the middle hold,
And the cabins riot of stuff untold,
And they lay there
That had took the plum,
With sightless glare
And their lips struck dumb,
While we shared all by the rule of thumb—
Yo-ho-ho and a bottle of rum!

More was seen through the sternlight screen—
Yo-ho-ho and a bottle of rum!
Chartings ondoubt where a woman had been—
Yo-ho-ho and a bottle of rum!
A flimsy shift on a bunker cot,
With a thin dirk slot through the bosom spot
And the lace stiff-dry in a purplish blot.
Or was she wench . . .
Or some shuddering maid . . ?
That dared the knife
And that took the blade!
By God! she was stuff for a plucky jade—
Yo-ho-ho and a bottle of rum!

Fifteen men on the dead man's chest—
Yo-ho-ho and a bottle of rum!
Drink and the devil had done for the rest—
Yo-ho-ho and a bottle of rum!
We wrapped 'em all in a mains'l tight,
With twice ten turns of the hawser's bight,
And we heaved 'em over and out of sight—
With a yo-heave-ho!
And a fare-you-well!
And a sullen plunge

In the sullen swell
Ten fathoms deep on the road to hell—
Yo-ho-ho and a bottle of rum!

THE PEACE OF CHRIST

Holy Bible, John 14:1–27

Let not your heart be troubled: ye believe in God, believe also in me. In my Father's house are many mansions: if it were not so, I would have told you. I go to prepare a place for you. And if I go and prepare a place for you, I will come again, and receive you unto myself; that where I am, there ye may be also. And whither I go ye know, and the way ye know. Thomas saith unto him, Lord, we know not whither thou goest; and how can we know the way? Jesus saith unto him, I am the way, the truth, and the life: no man cometh unto the Father, but by me. If ye had known me, ye should have known my Father also: and from henceforth ye know him, and have seen him. Philip saith unto him, Lord, shew us the Father, and it sufficeth us. Jesus saith unto him, Have I been so long time with you, and yet hast thou not known me, Philip? he that seen me hath seen the Father; and how sayest thou then, Shew us the Father? Believest thou not that I am in the Father, and the Father in me? the words that I speak unto you I speak not of myself: but the Father that dwelleth in me, he doeth the works. Believe me that I am in the Father, and the Father in me: or else believe me for the very works' sake. Verily, verily, I say unto you, He that believeth on me, the works that I do shall he do also; and greater works than these shall he do; because I go unto my Father. And whatsoever ye shall ask in my name, that will I do, that the Father may be glorified in the Son. If ye shall ask any thing in my name, I will do it.

If ye love me, keep my commandments. And I will pray the Father, and he shall give you another Comforter, that he may abide with you for ever; Even the Spirit of truth; whom the world cannot receive, because it seeth him not, neither knoweth him; but ye know him; for he dwelleth with you, and shall be in you. I will not leave you comfortless; I will come to you. Yet a little while, and the world seeth me no more; but ye see me: because I live, ye shall live also. At that day ye shall know that I am in my Father, and ye in me, and I in you. He that hath my commandments, and keepeth them, he it is that loveth me. And he that loveth me shall be loved of my Father, and I will love him, and will manifest myself in him. Judas saith unto him, not Iscariot, Lord, how is it that thou wilt manifest thyself unto us, and not unto the world? Jesus answered and said unto him, If a man love me, he will keep my words: and my Father will love him, and we will come unto him, and make our abode with him. He that loveth me not keepeth not my sayings: and the word which ye hear is not mine, but the Father's which sent me. These things have I spoken unto you, being yet present with you. But the Comforter, which is the Holy Ghost, whom the Father will send in my name, he shall teach you all things, and bring all things to your remembrance, whatsoever I have said unto you. Peace I leave with you, my peace I give unto you: not as the world giveth, give I unto you. Let not your heart be troubled, neither let it be afraid.

FOR ANNIE

Edgar Allan Poe

Thank Heaven! the crisis—
  The danger is past,
And the lingering illness
  Is over at last—
And the fever called "Living"
  Is conquered at last.

Sadly, I know,
  I am shorn of my strength,
And no muscle I move
  As I lie at full length—
But no matter!—I feel
  I am better at length.

And I rest so composedly,
  Now in my bed,
That any beholder
  Might fancy me dead—
Might start at beholding me,
  Thinking me dead.

The moaning and groaning,
  The sighing and sobbing,
Are quieted now,
  With that horrible throbbing
At heart:—ah, that horrible,
  Horrible throbbing!

The sickness—the nausea—
  The pitiless pain—
Have ceased, with the fever
  That maddened my brain—
With the fever called "Living"
  That burned in my brain.

And oh! of all tortures
  That torture the worst
Has abated—the terrible
  Torture of thirst,
For the naphthaline river
  Of Passion accurst:—
I have drank of a water
  That quenches all thirst:—

Of a water that flows,
  With a lullaby sound,
From a spring but a very few
  Feet under ground—
From a cavern not very far
  Down under ground.

And ah! let it never
  Be foolishly said
That my room it is gloomy
  And narrow my bed—
For man never slept
  In a different bed;
And, to *sleep*, you must slumber
  In just such a bed.

My tantalized spirit
  Here blandly reposes,
Forgetting, or never
  Regretting its roses—
Its old agitations
  Of myrtles and roses:

For now, while so quietly
  Lying, it fancies
A holier odor
  About it, of pansies—
A rosemary odor,
  Commingled with pansies—
With rue and the beautiful
  Puritan pansies.

And so it lies happily,
  Bathing in many
A dream of the truth
  And the beauty of Annie—
Drowned in a bath
  Of the tresses of Annie.

She tenderly kissed me,
  She fondly caressed,
And then I fell gently
  To sleep on her breast—
Deeply to sleep
  From the heaven of her breast.

When the light was extinguished,
  She covered me warm,
And she prayed to the angels
  To keep me from harm—
To the queen of the angels
  To shield me from harm.

And I lie so composedly,
  Now in my bed,
(Knowing her love)
  That you fancy me dead—
And I rest so contentedly,
  Now in my bed,
(With her love at my breast)
  That you fancy me dead—
That you shudder to look at me,
  Thinking me dead.

But my heart it is brighter
  Than all of the many

Stars in the sky,
For it sparkles with Annie—
It glows with the light
  Of the love of my Annie—
With the thought of the light
  Of the eyes of my Annie.

DANNY DEEVER

Rudyard Kipling

"What are the bugles blowin' for?" said Files-on-Parade.
"To turn you out, to turn you out," the Colour-Sergeant said.
"What makes you look so white, so white?" said Files-on-Parade.
"I'm dreadin' what I've got to watch," the Colour-Sergeant said.
  For they're hangin' Danny Deever, you can hear the Dead March
    play,
  The regiment's in 'ollow square—they're hangin' him today;
  They've taken of his buttons off an' cut his stripes away.
  An' they're hangin' Danny Deever in the mornin'.

"What makes the rear-rank breathe so 'ard?" said Files-on-Parade.
"It's bitter cold, it's bitter cold," the Colour-Sergeant said.
"What makes that front-rank man fall down?" says Files-on-Parade.
"A touch o' sun, a touch o' sun," the Colour-Sergeant said.
  They are hangin' Danny Deever, they are marchin' of 'im round,
  They 'ave 'alted Danny Deever by 'is coffin on the ground;
  An' 'e'll swing in 'arf a minute for a sneakin' shootin' hound—
  O they're hangin' Danny Deever in the mornin'!

"'Is cot was right-'and cot to mine," said Files-on-Parade.
"'E's sleepin' out an' far to-night," the Colour-Sergeant said.
"I've drunk 'is beer a score o' times," said Files-on-Parade.
"'E's drinkin' bitter beer alone," the Colour-Sergeant said.
  They are hangin' Danny Deever, you must mark 'im to 'is place,
  For 'e shot a comrade sleepin'—you must look 'im in the face;
  Nine 'undred of 'is county an' the regiment's disgrace,
  While they're hangin' Danny Deever in the mornin'.

"What's that so black agin the sun?" said Files-on-Parade.
"It's Danny fightin' 'ard for life," the Colour-Sergeant said.
"What's that that whimpers over'ead?" said Files-on-Parade.

"It's Danny's soul that's passin' now," the Colour-Sergeant said.
For they're done with Danny Deever, you can 'ear the quickstep play,
The regiment's in column, an' they're marchin' us away;
Ho! the young recruits are shakin', an' they'll want their beer to-day,
After hangin' Danny Deever in the mornin'.

INSCRIPTION ON THE CHRIST OF THE ANDES

(Erected on the Chile-Argentina Border)

Sooner shall these mountains crumble into dust
than the people of Argentina and Chile break the
peace they have sworn to maintain at the feet of
Christ the Redeemer

SITTIN' ON THE PORCH *

Edgar A. Guest

Sittin' on the porch at night when all the tasks are done,
Just restin' there and talkin', with my easy slippers on,
An' my shirt band thrown wide open an' my feet upon the rail,
Oh, it's then I'm at my richest, with a wealth that cannot fail;
For the scent of early roses seems to flood the evening air,
An' a throne of downright gladness is my wicker rocking-chair.

The dog asleep beside me, an' the children rompin' round,
With their shrieks of merry laughter, oh, there is no gladder sound
To the ears o' weary mortals spite of all the scoffers say,
Or a grander bit of music than the children at their play!
An' I tell myself times over, when I'm sittin' there at night,
That the world in which I'm livin' is a place o' real delight.

Then the moon begins its climbin' an' the stars shine overhead,
An' the mother calls the children an' she takes 'em up to bed,
An' I smoke my pipe in silence an' I think o' many things,

* From *Collected Verse of Edgar A. Guest.* Copyright, 1934, by The Reilly & Lee Co., Chicago, Ill.

An' balance up my riches with the lonesomeness o' kings,
An' I come to this conclusion, an' I'll wager that I'm right—
That I'm happier than they are sittin' on my porch at night.

"TO THE VICTOR BELONGS THE SPOILS"

U. S. Senator William L. Marcy, of New York

It may be, sir, that the politicians of New York are not so fastidious as some gentlemen are, as to disclosing the principles on which they act. They boldly preach what they practice. When they are contending for victory, they avow their intentions of enjoying the fruits of it. If they are defeated, they expect to retire from office. If they are successful, they claim, as a matter of right, the advantages of success. They see nothing wrong in the rule that to the VICTOR belongs the spoils of the ENEMY.

(Defending Van Buren's appointment
as Minister to England, 1832.)

AUX ITALIENS

Edward Robert Bulwer Lytton (Owen Meredith)

At Paris it was, at the opera there;—
  And she look'd like a queen in a book that night,
With the wreath of pearl in her raven hair,
  And the brooch on her breast so bright.

Of all the operas that Verdi wrote,
  The best, to my taste, is the Trovatore;
And Mario can soothe, with a tenor note,
  The souls in purgatory.

The moon on the tower slept soft as snow;
  And who was not thrill'd in the strangest way,
As we heard him sing, while the gas burn'd low,
  "Non ti scordar di me"? *

* Do not forget me.

The emperor there, in his box of state,
  Look'd grave, as if he had just then seen
The red flag wave from the city gate,
  Where his eagles in bronze had been.

The empress, too, had a tear in her eye:
  You'd have said that her fancy had gone back again,
For one moment, under the old blue sky,
  To the old glad life in Spain.

Well, there in our front-row box we sat
  Together, my bride-betroth'd and I;
My gaze was fixed on my opera hat,
  And hers on the stage hard by.

And both were silent, and both were sad;
  Like a queen she lean'd on her full white arm,
With that regal, indolent air she had,
  So confident of her charm!

I have not a doubt she was thinking then
  Of her former lord, good soul that he was,
Who died the richest and roundest of men,
  The Marquis of Carabas.

I hope that, to get to the kingdom of heaven,
  Through a needle's eye he had not to pass;
I wish him well, for the jointure given
  To my lady of Carabas.

Meanwhile, I was thinking of my first love,
  As I had not been thinking of aught for years,
Till over my eyes there began to move
  Something that felt like tears.

I thought of the dress that she wore last time,
  When we stood 'neath the cypress trees together,
In that lost land, in that soft clime,
  In the crimson evening weather;

Of that muslin dress (for the eve was hot),
  And her warm white neck in its golden chain,
And her full, soft hair, just tied in a knot,
  And falling loose again;

And the jasmine flower in her fair young breast,
  (Oh, the faint, sweet smell of that jasmine flower!)
And the one bird singing alone to his nest,
  And the one star over the tower.

I thought of our little quarrels and strife,
  And the letter that brought me back my ring;
And it all seem'd then, in the waste of life,
  Such a very little thing!

For I thought of her grave below the hill,
  Which the sentinel cypress tree stands over,
And I thought, "Were she only living still,
  How I could forgive her, and love her!"

And I swear, as I thought of her thus, in that hour,
  And of how, after all, old things were best,
That I smelt the smell of that jasmine flower
  Which she used to wear in her breast.

It smelt so faint, and it smelt so sweet,
  It made me creep, and it made me cold;
Like the scent that steals from the crumbling sheet
  Where a mummy is half unroll'd.

And I turn'd and look'd: she was sitting there,
  In a dim box over the stage, and drest
In that muslin dress, with that full, soft hair,
  And that jasmine in her breast!

I was here: and she was there:
  And the glittering horseshoe curved between:—
From my bride-betroth'd, with her raven hair,
  And her sumptuous, scornful mien,

To my early love, with her eyes downcast,
  And over her primrose face the shade
(In short, from the future back to the past)
  There was but a step to be made.

To my early love from my future bride
  One moment I look'd. Then I stole to the door,
I traversed the passage; and down at her side
  I was sitting, a moment more.

My thinking of her, or the music's strain,
  Or something which never will be exprest,
Had brought her back from the grave again,
  With the jasmine in her breast.

She is not dead, and she is not wed,
  But she loves me now, and she loved me then!
And the very first word that her sweet lips said,
  My heart grew youthful again.

The marchioness there, of Carabas,
  She is wealthy, and young, and handsome still,
And but for her . . . well, we'll let that pass;
  She may marry whomever she will.

But I will marry my own first love,
  With her primrose face: for old things are best,
And the flower in her bosom, I prize it above
  The brooch in my lady's breast.

The world is filled with folly and sin,
  And love must cling where it can, I say:
For beauty is easy enough to win;
  But one isn't loved every day.

And I think, in the lives of most women and men,
  There's a moment when all would go smooth and even,
If only the dead could find out when
  To come back and be forgiven.

But O the smell of that jasmine flower!
  And O that music! and O the way
That voice rang out from the donjon tower,
  Non ti scordar di me,
    Non ti scordar di me!

JOHN RANDOLPH'S OPINION OF HENRY CLAY

This being, so brilliant yet so corrupt, like a rotten mackerel by moonlight, shines and stinks.

THE EMPEROR'S NEW CLOTHES*

Hans Christian Andersen

(Translator: Mrs. Edgar Lucas)

Many years ago there was an Emperor who was so excessively fond of new clothes that he spent all his money on them. He cared nothing about his soldiers, nor for the theatre, nor for driving in the woods except for the sake of showing off his new clothes. He had a costume for every hour in the day, and instead of saying as one does about any other King or Emperor, "He is in his council chamber," here one always said, "The Emperor is in his dressing-room."

Life was very gay in the great town where he lived; hosts of strangers came to visit it every day, and among them one day two swindlers. They gave themselves out as weavers, and said that they knew how to weave the most beautiful stuffs imaginable. Not only were the colours and patterns unusually fine, but the clothes that were made of these stuffs had the peculiar quality of becoming invisible to every person who was not fit for the office he held, or if he was impossibly dull.

"Those must be splendid clothes," thought the Emperor. "By wearing them I should be able to discover which men in my kingdom are unfitted for their posts. I shall distinguish the wise men from the fools. Yes, I certainly must order some of that stuff to be woven for me."

He paid the two swindlers a lot of money in advance so that they might begin their work at once.

They did put up two looms and pretended to weave, but they had nothing whatever upon their shuttles. At the outset they asked for a quantity of the finest silk and the purest gold thread, all of which they put into their own bags while they worked away at the empty looms far into the night.

"I should like to know how those weavers are getting on with the stuff," thought the Emperor; but he felt a little queer when he reflected that any one who was stupid or unfit for his post would not be able to see it. He certainly thought that he need have no fears for himself, but still he thought he would send somebody else first to see how it was getting on. Everybody in the town knew what wonderful power the stuff possessed, and every one was anxious to see how stupid his neighbour was.

* From *Fairy Tales by Hans Christian Andersen,* Everyman's Library and E. P. Dutton & Co., New York, and J. M. Dent & Sons, Ltd.

"I will send my faithful old minister to the weavers," thought the Emperor. "He will be best able to see how the stuff looks, for he is a clever man and no one fulfills his duties better than he does!"

So the good old minister went into the room where the two swindlers sat working at the empty loom.

"Heaven preserve us!" thought the old minister, opening his eyes very wide. "Why, I can't see a thing!" But he took care not to say so.

Both the swindlers begged him to be good enough to step a little nearer, and asked if he did not think it a good pattern and beautiful coloring. They pointed to the empty loom, and the poor old minister stared as hard as he could, but he could not see anything, for of course there was nothing to see.

"Good heavens!" thought he, "is it possible that I am a fool. I have never thought so and nobody must know it. Am I not fit for my post? It will never do to say that I cannot see the stuffs."

"Well, sir, you don't say anything about the stuff," said the one who was pretending to weave.

"Oh, it is beautiful! quite charming!" said the old minister looking through his spectacles; "this pattern and these colours! I will certainly tell the Emperor that the stuff pleases me very much."

"We are delighted to hear you say so," said the swindlers, and then they named all the colours and described the peculiar pattern. The old minister paid great attention to what they said, so as to be able to repeat it when he got home to the Emperor.

Then the swindlers went on to demand more money, more silk, and more gold, to be able to proceed with the weaving; but they put it all into their own pockets—not a single strand was ever put into the loom, but they went on as before weaving at the empty loom.

The Emperor soon sent another faithful official to see how the stuff was getting on, and if it would soon be ready. The same thing happened to him as to the minister; he looked and looked, but as there was only the empty loom, he could see nothing at all.

"Is not this a beautiful piece of stuff?" said both the swindlers, showing and explaining the beautiful pattern and colours which were not there to be seen.

"I know I am not a fool!" thought the man, "so it must be that I am unfit for my good post! It is very strange though! however one must not let it appear!" So he praised the stuff he did not see, and assured them of his delight in the beautiful colours and the originality of the design. "It is absolutely charming!" he said to the Emperor. Everybody in the town was talking about this splendid stuff.

Now the Emperor thought he would like to see it while it was still on the loom. So, accompanied by a number of selected courtiers, among whom were the two faithful officials who had already seen the imaginary stuff, he went to visit the crafty impostors, who were working away as hard as ever they could at the empty loom.

"It is magnificent!" said both the honest officials. "Only see, your majesty, what a design! What colours!" And they pointed to the empty loom, for they thought that no doubt the others could see the stuff.

"What!" thought the Emperor; "I see nothing at all! This is terrible! Am I a fool? Am I not fit to be Emperor? Why, nothing worse could happen to me!"

"Oh, it is beautiful!" said the Emperor. "It has my highest approval!" and he nodded his satisfaction as he gazed at the empty loom. Nothing would induce him to say that he could not see anything.

The whole suite gazed and gazed, but saw nothing more than all the others. However, they all exclaimed with his majesty, "It is very beautiful!" and they advised him to wear a suit made of this wonderful cloth on the occasion of a great procession which was just about to take place. "It is magnificent! gorgeous! excellent!" went from mouth to mouth; they were all equally delighted with it. The Emperor gave each of the rogues an order of knighthood to be worn in their buttonholes and the title of "Gentlemen weavers."

The swindlers sat up the whole night before the day on which the procession was to take place, burning sixteen candles, so that people might see how anxious they were to get the Emperor's new clothes ready. They pretended to take the stuff off the loom. They cut it out in the air with a huge pair of scissors, and they stitched away with needles without any thread in them. At last they said: "Now the Emperor's new clothes are ready!"

The Emperor, with his grandest courtiers, went to them himself, and both the swindlers raised one arm in the air, as if they were holding something, and said: "See, these are the trousers, this is the coat, here is the mantle!" and so on. "It is as light as a spider's web. One might think one had nothing on, but that is the very beauty of it."

"Yes!" said all the courtiers, but they could not see anything, for there was nothing to see.

"Will your imperial majesty be graciously pleased to take off your clothes," said the impostors, "so that we may put on the new ones, along here before the great mirror."

The Emperor took off all his clothes, and the impostors pretended to give him one article of dress after the other of the new ones which they had pretended to make. They pretended to fasten something round his waist and to tie on something; this was the train, and the Emperor turned round and round in front of the mirror.

"How well his majesty looks in the new clothes! How becoming they are!" cried all the people round. "What a design, and what colours! They are the most gorgeous robes!"

"The canopy is waiting outside which is to be carried over your majesty in the procession," said the master of the ceremonies.

"Well, I am quite ready," said the Emperor. "Don't the clothes fit well?" and then he turned round again in front of the mirror, so that he should seem to be looking at his grand things.

The chamberlains who were to carry the train stooped and pretended to lift it from the ground with both hands, and they walked along with their hands in the air. They dared not let it appear that they could not see anything.

Then the Emperor walked along in the procession under the gorgeous canopy, and everybody in the streets and at the windows exclaimed, "How beautiful the Emperor's new clothes are! What a splendid train! And they fit to perfection!" Nobody would let it appear that he could see nothing, for then he would not be fit for his post, or else he was a fool.

None of the Emperor's clothes had been so successful before.

"But he has got nothing on," said a little child.

"Oh, listen to the innocent," said its father; and one person whispered to the other what the child had said. "He has nothing on, a child says he has nothing on!"

The Emperor writhed, for he knew it was true, but he thought "the procession must go on now." So he held himself stiffer than ever, and the chamberlains held up the invisible train.

* * *

Who killed Kildare? Who dared Kildare to kill?
Death killed Kildare—who dare kill whom he will.

Jonathan Swift

CONVERSION

Frances Angermayer

Look, God, I have never spoken to You.
But now I want to say: "How do You do?"
You see, God, they told me You didn't exist—
And like a fool I believed all this.
Last night from a shellhole I saw Your sky
And figured right then they told me a lie.
Had I taken time to see things You made,
I'd have known they weren't calling a spade a spade.
I wonder, God, if You'd shake my hand.
Somehow I feel that You'll understand.
Funny I had to come to this hellish place
Before I had time to see Your face.
Well, I guess there isn't much more to say;
But I'm sure glad, God, I met You today.
I guess the zero hour will soon be here,
But I'm not afraid, since I know You're here.
The signal! Well, God, I'll have to go—
I like You lots, this I want You to know.
Look now! This will be a horrible fight;
Who knows, I may come to Your house tonight.
Tho' I wasn't friendly to You before,
I wonder, God, if You'd wait at Your door?
Look, I'm crying—me shedding tears!
I wish I had known You these many years.
Well, God, I have to go now—good-bye—
Strange, since I met You I'm not afraid to die.

CRABBÈD AGE AND YOUTH

Anonymous

Crabbèd Age and Youth
Cannot live together:
Youth is full of pleasance,
Age is full of care;
Youth like summer morn,
Age like winter weather;

Youth like summer brave,
Age like winter bare.
Youth is full of sport,
Age's breath is short;
Youth is nimble, Age is lame;
Youth is hot and bold,
Age is weak and cold;
Youth is wild, and Age is tame.
Age, I do abhor thee;
Youth, I do adore thee;
O, my Love, my Love is young!
Age, I do defy thee:
O, sweet shepherd, hie thee!
For methinks thou stay'st too long.
(Usually attributed to William Shakespeare)

OATH TAKEN BY U.S. SUPREME COURT JUSTICES

I do solemnly swear that I will administer justice without respect to persons, and do equal right to the poor and to the rich; and that I will faithfully discharge all the duties incumbent on me as Judge, according to the best of my abilities and understanding, agreeably to the Constitution and laws of the United States.

STUPIDITY STREET

Ralph Hodgson

I saw with open eyes
Singing birds sweet
Sold in the shops
For the people to eat,
Sold in the shops of
Stupidity Street.

I saw in a vision
The worm in the wheat,
And in the shops nothing
For people to eat:
Nothing for sale in
Stupidity Street.

ROLL ON, SAD WORLD!

Frederick Goddard Tuckerman

Roll on, sad world! Not Mercury or Mars
Could swifter speed or slower round the sun
Than in this year of variance thou hast done
For me. Yet pain, fear, heart-break, woes and wars
Have natural limit; from his dread eclipse
The swift sun hastens, and the night debars
The day but to bring in the day more bright;
The flowers renew their odorous fellowships;
The moon runs round and round; the slow earth dips,
True to her poise, and lifts; the planet-stars
Roll and return from circle to ellipse;
The day is dull and soft, the eave-trough drips.
And yet I know the splendor of the light
Will break anon. Look, where the gray is white!

LOCH LOMOND

Lady John Scott

By yon bonnie banks and by yon bonnie braes,
Where the sun shines bright on Loch Lomond,
Where me and my true love were ever wont to be,
On the bonnie, bonnie banks of Loch Lomond.

Chorus:
Oh, you'll take the high road
And I'll take the low road,
And I'll be in Scotland before you:
But me and my true love will never meet again,
On the bonnie, bonnie banks of Loch Lomond.

I mind where we parted in yon shady glen,
On the steep, steep side of Ben Lomond,
Where in deep purple hue the Highland hills we view,
And the moon coming out in the gloaming.

The wee birdies sing and the wild flowers spring,
And in sunshine the waters are sleeping,
But the broken heart will ken no second spring again,
And the world does not know how we are greeting.

AT THE MID HOUR OF NIGHT

Thomas Moore

At the mid hour of night, when stars are weeping, I fly
To the lone vale we loved, when life shone warm in thine eye;
And I think oft if spirits can steal from the regions of air,
To revisit past scenes of delight, thou wilt come to me there,
And tell me our love is remembered, even in the sky!

Then I sing the wild song 't was once such pleasure to hear,
When our voices, commingling, breathed, like one, on the ear;
And, as Echo far off through the vale my sad orison rolls,
I think, O my love! 't is thy voice from the Kingdom of Souls,
Faintly answering still the notes that once were so dear.

WOLSEY'S REGRETS

William Shakespeare

Cromwell, I did not think to shed a tear
In all my miseries; but thou hast forced me,
Out of thy honest truth, to play the woman.
Let's dry our eyes: and thus far hear me, Cromwell;
And, when I am forgotten, as I shall be,
And sleep in dull cold marble, where no mention
Of me more must be heard of, say, I taught thee;
Say, Wolsey, that once trod the ways of glory,
And sounded all the depths and shoals of honour,
Found thee a way, out of his wreck, to rise in;
A sure and safe one, though thy master miss'd it.
Mark but my fall and that that ruin'd me.
Cromwell, I charge thee, fling away ambition:
By that sin fell the angels; how can man then,
The image of his Maker, hope to win by it?
Love thyself last: cherish those hearts that hate thee;
Corruption wins not more than honesty.
Still in thy right hand carry gentle peace,
To silence envious tongues. Be just, and fear not:
Let all the ends thou aim'st at be thy country's,
Thy God's, and truth's; then if thou fall'st, O Cromwell,
Thou fall'st a blessed martyr! Serve the king;

And prithee, lead me in:
There take an inventory of all I have,
To the last penny; 'tis the king's: my robe,
And my integrity to heaven, is all
I dare now call mine own. O Cromwell, Cromwell!
Had I but served my God with half the zeal
I served my king, he would not in mine age
Have left me naked to mine enemies.
(From King Henry VIII)

SO NIGH IS GRANDEUR

Ralph Waldo Emerson

In an age of fops and toys,
Wanting wisdom, void of right,
Who shall nerve heroic boys
To hazard all in Freedom's fight,—
Break sharply off their jolly games,
Forsake their comrades gay
And quit proud homes and youthful dames
For famine, toil and fray?
Yet on the nimble air benign
Speed nimbler messages,
That waft the breath of grace divine
To hearts in sloth and ease.
So nigh is grandeur to our dust,
So near is God to man,
When Duty whispers low, *Thou must,*
The youth replies, *I can.*

FAITH OF OUR FATHERS

Frederick W. Faber

Faith of our fathers, living still
In spite of dungeon, fire and sword,
O how our hearts beat high with joy
Whene'er we hear that glorious word!
Faith of our fathers, holy faith,
We will be true to thee till death.

Our fathers, chained in prisons dark,
  Were still in heart and conscience free,
And blest would be their children's fate,
  If they, like them, should die for thee:
Faith of our fathers, holy faith,
  We will be true to thee till death.

Faith of our fathers, we will strive
  To win all nations unto thee;
And through the truth that comes from God
  Mankind shall then indeed be free:
Faith of our fathers, holy faith,
  We will be true to thee till death.

Faith of our fathers, we will love
  Both friend and foe in all our strife,
And preach thee, too, as love knows how,
  By kindly words and virtuous life:
Faith of our fathers, holy faith,
  We will be true to thee till death.

MARTHA

Walter de la Mare

"Once . . . once upon a time . . ."
  Over and over again,
Martha would tell us stories,
  In the hazel glen.

Hers were those clear grey eyes
  You watch, and the story seems
Told by their beautifulness
  Tranquil as dreams.

She would sit with her two slim hands
  Clasped round her bended knees;
While we on our elbows lolled,
  And stared at ease.

Her voice and her narrow chin,
  Her grave small lovely head,
Seemed half the meaning
  Of the words she said.

"Once . . . once upon a time . . ."
  Like a dream you dream in the night,
Fairies and gnomes stole out
  In the leaf-green light.

And her beauty far away
  Would fade, as her voice ran on,
Till hazel and summer sun
  And all were gone:

All fordone and forgot;
  And like clouds in the height of the sky,
Our hearts stood still in the hush
  Of an age gone by.

THE LAUGHTER OF A CHILD

Robert G. Ingersoll

The laugh of a child will make the holiest day more sacred still. Strike with hand of fire, O weird musician, thy harp strung with Apollo's golden hair; fill the vast cathedral aisles with symphonies sweet and dim, deft toucher of the organ keys; blow, bugler, blow, until thy silver notes do touch and kiss the moonlit waves, and charm lovers wandering 'mid the vine-clad hills. But know, your sweetest strains are discords all, compared with childhood's happy laugh—the laugh that fills the eyes with light and every heart with joy. O rippling river of laughter, thou art the blessed boundary line between the beasts and men; and every forward wave of thine doth drown some fretful fiend of care. O Laughter, rose-lipped daughter of joy, there are dimples enough in thy cheeks to catch and hold and glorify all the tears of grief.

THE SLUGGARD

Isaac Watts

'Tis the voice of the sluggard; I heard him complain,
"You have wak'd me too soon, I must slumber again."
As the door on its hinges, so he on his bed,
Turns his sides and his shoulders and his heavy head.

"A little more sleep, and a little more slumber;"
Thus he wastes half his days and his hours without number;
And when he gets up, he sits folding his hands,
Or walks about saunt'ring, or trifling he stands.

I pass'd by his garden, and saw the wild briar,
The thorn and the thistle grow broader and higher;
The clothes that hang on him are turning to rags;
And his money still wastes, till he starves or he begs.

I made him a visit, still hoping to find
He had took better care for improving his mind;
He told me his dreams, talk'd of eating and drinking;
But he scarce reads his Bible, and never loves thinking.

ONE MORE RIVER

Anonymous

Old Noah once he built the Ark,
And sealed it up with hickory bark,

Chorus:
There's one more river to cross,
And that's the river Jordan,
One more river,
There's one more river to cross.

He went to work to load his stock,
He anchored the Ark on a great big rock,

The animals went in one by one,
The elephant chewing a caraway bun,

The animals went in two by two,
The lion and the kangaroo,

The animals went in three by three,
The skunk, the flea and the bumble bee,

The animals went in four by four,
Old Noah got mad and yelled for more,

The animals went in five by five,
Noah asked when the rain would arrive,

The animals went in six by six,
The hyena laughed at the monkey's tricks,

The animals went in seven by seven,
Said the rabbit to the elephant, "Who are you a-shovin'?"

The animals went in eight by eight,
They came with a rush 'cause it was late,

The animals went in nine by nine,
Old Noah hollered "Cut that line!"—

The animals went in ten by ten,
The Ark she blew her whistle then,

And then the voyage did begin,
Old Noah pulled the gang-plank in,

They never knew where they were at,
Till the old Ark bumped on Ararat.

THE WORDS OF THE PREACHER

Holy Bible, Ecclesiastes 1:2–11

Vanity of vanities, saith the Preacher, vanity of vanities; all is vanity. What profit hath a man of all his labour which he taketh under the sun? One generation passeth away, and another generation cometh: but the earth abideth for ever. The sun also ariseth, and the sun goeth down, and hasteth to his place where he arose. The wind goeth toward the south, and turneth about unto the north; it whirleth about continually, and the wind returneth again according to his circuits. All the rivers run into the sea; yet the sea is not full; unto the place from whence the rivers come, thither they return again. All things are full of labour; man cannot utter it: the eye is not satisfied with seeing, nor the ear filled with hearing. The thing that hath been, it is that which shall be; and that which is done is that which shall be done: and there is no new thing under the sun. Is there any thing whereof it may be said, See, this is new? It hath been already of old time, which was before us. There is no remembrance of former things; neither shall there be any remembrance of things that are to come with those that shall come after.

SONG OF THE OPEN ROAD

Ogden Nash

I think that I shall never see
A billboard lovely as a tree.
Indeed, unless the billboards fall
I'll never see a tree at all.

ODE ON MELANCHOLY

John Keats

No, no! go not to Lethe, neither twist
Wolf's-bane, tight-rooted, for its poisonous wine;
Nor suffer thy pale forehead to be kiss'd
By nightshade, ruby grape of Proserpine;
Make not your rosary of yew-berries,
Nor let the beetle, nor the death-moth be
Your mournful Psyche, nor the downy owl
A partner in your sorrow's mysteries;
For shade to shade will come too drowsily,
And drown the wakeful anguish of the soul.

But when the melancholy fit shall fall
Sudden from heaven like a weeping cloud,
That fosters the droop-headed flowers all,
And hides the green hill in an April shroud;
Then glut thy sorrow on a morning rose,
Or on the rainbow of the salt sand-wave,
Or on the wealth of globed peonies;
Or if thy mistress some rich anger shows,
Emprison her soft hand, and let her rave,
And feed deep, deep upon her peerless eyes.

She dwells with Beauty—Beauty that must die;
  And Joy, whose hand is ever at his lips
Bidding adieu; and aching Pleasure nigh,
  Turning to poison while the bee-mouth sips:
Aye, in the very temple of Delight
  Veil'd Melancholy has her sovran shrine,
    Though seen of none save him whose strenuous tongue
Can burst Joy's grape against his palate fine;
  His soul shall taste the sadness of her might,
    And be among her cloudy trophies hung.

THE MULTIPLICATION OF BOOKS

Samuel Johnson

One of the peculiarities which distinguish the present age is the multiplication of books. Every day brings new advertisements of literary undertakings, and we are flattered with repeated promises of growing wise on easier terms than our progenitors.

How much either happiness or knowledge is advanced by this multitude of authors, is not very easy to decide. He that teaches us anything which we knew not before, is undoubtedly to be reverenced as a master. He that conveys knowledge by more pleasing ways, may very properly be loved as a benefactor; and he that supplies life with innocent amusement will be certainly caressed as a pleasing companion. But few of those who fill the world with books have any pretensions to the hope either of pleasing or instructing. They often have no other task than to lay two books before them, out of which they compile a third, without any new materials of their own, and with very little application of judgment to those which former authors have supplied.

THE ISLE OF LONG AGO

B. F. Taylor

O, a wonderful stream is the river Time,
  As it runs through the realm of tears,
With a faultless rhythm and a musical rhyme,
And a boundless sweep and a surge sublime,
  As it blends with the Oceans of Years.

How the winters are drifting, like flakes of snow,
And the summers, like buds between;
And the year in the sheaf—so they come and they go,
On the river's breast, with its ebb and flow,
As it glides in the shadow and sheen.

There's a magical isle up the river of Time,
Where the softest of airs are playing;
There's a cloudless sky and a tropical clime,
And a song as sweet as a vesper chime,
And the Junes with the roses are staying.

And the name of that Isle is the Long Ago,
And we bury our treasures there;
There are brows of beauty and bosoms of snow—
There are heaps of dust—but we loved them so!
There are trinkets and tresses of hair;

There are fragments of song that nobody sings,
And a part of an infant's prayer;
There's a lute unswept, and a harp without strings,
There are broken vows and pieces of rings,
And the garments that she used to wear.

There are hands that are waved, when the fairy shore
By the mirage is lifted in air;
And we sometimes hear, through the turbulent roar,
Sweet voices we heard in the days gone before,
When the wind down the river is fair.

O, remembered for aye, be the blessed Isle,
All the day of our life till night—
When the evening comes with its beautiful smile,
And our eyes are closing to slumber awhile,
May that "Greenwood" of Soul be in sight!

* * *

No man e'er felt the halter draw
With good opinion of the law.

John Trumbull's "M'Fingal"

ENGLISH AIR-RAID SHELTER PRAYER

Anonymous

Increase, O God, the spirit of neighborliness among us, that in peril we may uphold one another, in calamity serve one another, in suffering tend one another and in homelessness and loneliness in exile befriend one another. Grant us brave and enduring hearts that we may strengthen one another, till the disciplines and testing of these days be ended, and Thou dost give again peace in our time, through Jesus Christ, our Lord, Amen.

THE HAUNTED PALACE

Edgar Allan Poe

In the greenest of our valleys
  By good angels tenanted,
Once a fair and stately palace—
Radiant palace—reared its head.
In the monarch Thought's dominion—
  It stood there!
Never seraph spread a pinion
  Over fabric half so fair!

Banners yellow, glorious, golden,
  On its roof did float and flow,
(This—all this—was in the olden
  Time long ago),
And every gentle air that dallied,
  In that sweet day,
Along the ramparts plumed and pallid,
  A wingèd odor went away.

Wanderers in that happy valley,
  Through two luminous windows, saw
Spirits moving musically
  To a lute's well-tunèd law,
Round about a throne, where sitting
  (Porphyrogene!)
In state his glory well befitting,
  The ruler of the realm was seen.

And all with pearl and ruby glowing
Was the fair palace door,
Through which came flowing, flowing, flowing,
And sparkling evermore,
A troop of Echoes, whose sweet duty
Was but to sing,
In voices of surpassing beauty,
The wit and wisdom of their king.

But evil things, in robes of sorrow,
Assailed the monarch's high estate.
(Ah, let us mourn! for never morrow
Shall dawn upon him desolate!)
And round about his home the glory
That blushed and bloomed,
Is but a dim-remembered story
Of the old time entombed.

And travellers, now, within that valley,
Through the red-litten windows see
Vast forms, that move fantastically
To a discordant melody,
While, like a ghastly rapid river,
Through the pale door
A hideous throng rush out forever
And laugh—but smile no more.

THE HIGHWAYMAN *

Alfred Noyes

Part One

The wind was a torrent of darkness among the gusty trees,
The moon was a ghostly galleon tossed upon cloudy seas,
The road was a ribbon of moonlight over the purple moor,
And the highwayman came riding—
Riding—riding—
The highwayman came riding, up to the old inn-door.

* From *Collected Poems* in One Volume of Alfred Noyes. Copyright, 1906, 1934, by Alfred Noyes. Reprinted by permission of J. B. Lippincott Co.

He'd a French cock-hat on his forehead, a bunch of lace at his chin,
A coat of the claret velvet, and breeches of brown doe-skin;
They fitted with never a wrinkle: his boots were up to the thigh!
And he rode with a jeweled twinkle,
His pistol butts a-twinkle,
His rapier hilt a-twinkle, under the jeweled sky.

Over the cobbles he clattered and clashed in the dark inn-yard,
And he tapped with his whip on the shutters, but all was locked and barred;
He whistled a tune to the window, and who should be waiting there
But the landlord's black-eyed daughter,
Bess, the landlord's daughter,
Plaiting a dark red love-knot into her long black hair.

And dark in the dark old inn-yard, a stable-wicket creaked
Where Tim the ostler listened; his face was white and peaked;
His eyes were hollows of madness, his hair like mouldy clay,
But he loved the landlord's daughter,
The landlord's red-lipped daughter,
Dumb as a dog he listened, and he heard the robber say—

"One kiss, my bonny sweetheart, I'm after a prize to-night,
But I shall be back with the yellow gold before the morning light;
Yet, if they press me sharply, and harry me through the day,
Then look for me by moonlight,
Watch for me by moonlight,
I'll come to thee by moonlight, though hell should bar the way."

He rose upright in his stirrups; he scarce could reach her hand,
But she loosened her hair i' the casement! His face burnt like a brand
As the black cascade of perfume came tumbling over his breast;
And he kissed its waves in the moonlight,
(Oh, sweet black waves in the moonlight!)
Then he tugged at his reins in the moonlight, and galloped away to the West.

Part Two

He did not come in the dawning; he did not come at noon;
And out o' the tawny sunset, before the rise o' the moon,

When the road was a gipsy's ribbon, looping the purple moor,
A red-coat troop came marching—
   Marching—marching—
King George's men came marching, up to the old inn-door.

They said no word to the landlord, they drank his ale instead,
But they gagged his daughter and bound her to the foot of her narrow bed;
Two of them knelt at her casement, with muskets at their side!
There was death at every window;
   And hell at one dark window;
For Bess could see, through her casement, the road that *he* would ride.

They had tied her up to attention, with many a sniggering jest;
They had bound a musket beside her, with the barrel beneath her breast!
"Now keep good watch!" and they kissed her.
   She heard the dead man say—
Look for me by moonlight;
   Watch for me by moonlight;
I'll come to thee by moonlight, though hell should bar the way!

She twisted her hands behind her; but all the knots held good!
She writhed her hands till her fingers were wet with sweat or blood!
They stretched and strained in the darkness, and the hours crawled by like years,
Till, now, on the stroke of midnight,
   Cold, on the stroke of midnight,
The tip of one finger touched it! The trigger at least was hers!

The tip of one finger touched it; she strove no more for the rest!
Up, she stood up to attention, with the barrel beneath her breast,
She would not risk their hearing; she would not strive again;
For the road lay bare in the moonlight;
And the blood of her veins in the moonlight throbbed to her love's refrain.

Tlot-tlot; tlot-tlot! Had they heard it? The horse-hoofs ringing clear;
Tlot-tlot, tlot-tlot, in the distance? Were they deaf that they did not hear?

Down the ribbon of moonlight, over the brow of the hill,
The highwayman came riding,
  Riding, riding!
The red-coats looked to their priming! She stood up, straight and
    still!

Tlot-tlot, in the frosty silence! *Tlot-tlot,* in the echoing night!
Nearer he came and nearer! Her face was like a light!
Her eyes grew wide for a moment; she drew one last deep breath,
Then her finger moved in the moonlight,
  Her musket shattered the moonlight,
Shattered her breast in the moonlight and warned him—with her
    death.

He turned; he spurred to the West; he did not know who stood
Bowed, with her head o'er the musket, drenched with her own red
    blood!
Not till the dawn he heard it, his face grew gray to hear
How Bess, the landlord's daughter,
  The landlord's black-eyed daughter,
Had watched for her love in the moonlight, and died in the dark-
    ness there.

Back he spurred like a madman, shrieking a curse to the sky,
With the white road smoking behind him and his rapier bran-
    dished high!
Blood-red were his spurs i' the golden noon; wine-red was his
    velvet coat,
When they shot him down in the highway,
  Down like a dog in the highway,
And he lay in his blood on the highway, with the bunch of lace at
    his throat.

. . . .

And still of a winter's night, they say, when the wind is in the
    trees,
When the moon is a ghostly galleon tossed upon cloudy seas,
When the road is a ribbon of moonlight over the purple moor,
A highwayman comes riding—
  Riding—riding—
A highwayman comes riding, up to the old inn-door.

Over the cobbles he clatters and clangs in the dark inn-yard;
He taps with his whip on the shutters, but all is locked and barred;

He whistles a tune at the window, and who should be waiting there
But the landlord's black-eyed daughter,
  Bess, the landlord's daughter,
Plaiting a dark red love-knot into her long black hair.

"FULL MANY A GLORIOUS MORNING HAVE I SEEN"

William Shakespeare

Full many a glorious morning have I seen
Flatter the mountain-tops with sovereign eye,
Kissing with golden face the meadows green,
Gilding pale streams with heavenly alchemy;
Anon permit the basest clouds to ride
With ugly rack on his celestial face,
And from the forlorn world his visage hide,
Stealing unseen to west with his disgrace:
Even so my sun one early morn did shine
With all-triumphant splendour on my brow;
But, out, alack! he was but one hour mine,
The region cloud hath mask'd him from me now.
  Yet him for this my love no whit disdaineth;
  Suns of the world may stain when heaven's sun staineth.
(Sonnet XXXIII)

JEFFERSON DAVIS'S FAREWELL TO THE U.S. SENATE

I rise, Mr. President, for the purpose of announcing to the Senate that I have satisfactory evidence that the State of Mississippi, by a solemn ordinance of her people, in convention assembled, has declared her separation from the United States. Under these circumstances, of course, my functions are terminated here. It has seemed to me proper, however, that I should appear in the Senate to announce that fact to my associates, and I will say but very little more. The occasion does not invite me to go into argument, and my physical condition would not permit me to do so, if it were otherwise; and yet it seems to become me to say something on the part of the State I here represent on an occasion so solemn as this.

It is known to Senators who have served with me here that I

have for many years advocated, as an essential attribute of State-sovereignty, the right of a State to secede from the Union. Therefore, if I had not believed there was justifiable cause, if I had thought that Mississippi was acting without sufficient provocation, or without an existing necessity, I should still, under my theory of the government, because of my allegiance to the State of which I am a citizen, have been bound by her action. I, however, may be permitted to say that I do think she has justifiable cause, and I approve of her act. I conferred with her people before the act was taken, counseled them then that, if the state of things which they apprehended should exist when their convention met, they should take the action which they have now adopted. . . .

We recur to the principles upon which our Government was founded; and when you deny them, and when you deny us the right to withdraw from the Government which, thus perverted, threatens to be destructive to our rights, we but tread in the paths of our fathers when we proclaim our independence and take the hazard. This is done, not in hostility to others, not to injure any section of the country, not even for our own pecuniary benefit, but from the high and solemn motive of defending and protecting the rights we inherited, and which it is our duty to transmit unshorn to our children. I find in myself, perhaps, a type of the general feeling of my constituents toward yourselves. I am sure I feel no hostility towards you, Senators from the North. I am sure there is no one of you, whatever sharp discussion there may have been between us, to whom I cannot now say, in the presence of my God, I wish you well; and such, I am sure, is the feeling of the people whom I represent toward those whom you represent. I, therefore, feel that I but express their desire when I say I hope and they hope for peaceable relations with you, though we must part. They may be mutually beneficial to us in the future, as they have been in the past, if you so will it. The reverse may bring disaster on every portion of the country, and if you will have it thus, we will invoke the God of our fathers, who delivered them from the power of the lion, to protect us from the ravages of the bear; and, thus putting our trust in God and in our firm hearts and strong arms, we will vindicate the right as best we may.

In the course of my service here, associated at different times with a great variety of Senators, I see now around me some with whom I have served long; there have been points of collision, but whatever of offense there has been to me, I leave here. I carry with me no hostile remembrance. Whatever offense I have given which has not been redressed, or for which satisfaction has not been demanded, I have, Senators, in this hour of our parting, to offer you my apology for any pain which, in the heat of discussion, I have inflicted. I go hence unencumbered by the remembrance of any injury received, and having discharged the duty of making the only reparation in my power for any injury offered. Mr. President and Senators, having made the announcement which the occasion seemed to me to require, it only remains for me to bid you final adieu.

January 21, 1861

LITTLE LOST PUP *

Arthur Guiterman

He was lost!—not a shade of doubt of that;
For he never barked at a slinking cat,
But stood in the square where the wind blew raw
With a drooping ear and a trembling paw
And a mournful look in his pleading eye
And a plaintive sniff at the passer-by
That begged as plain as a tongue could sue,
"O Mister! please may I follow you?"
A lorn wee waif of a tawny brown
Adrift in the roar of a heedless town.
Oh, the saddest of sights in a world of sin
Is a little lost pup with his tail tucked in!

Now he shares my board and he owns my bed,
And he fairly shouts when he hears my tread;
Then, if things go wrong, as they sometimes do,
And the world is cold and I'm feeling blue,
He asserts his right to assuage my woes
With a warm, red tongue and a nice, cold nose
And a silky head on my arm or knee
And a paw as soft as a paw can be.

When we rove the woods for a league about
He's as full of pranks as a school let out;
For he romps and frisks like a three months' colt,

* From *Death and General Putnam and 101 Poems,* by Arthur Guiterman. Copyright, 1935, by E. P. Dutton & Co., Inc., New York.

And he runs me down like a thunderbolt.
Oh, the blithest of sights in the world so fair
Is a gay little pup with his tail in the air!

CYRANO DE BERGERAC DISCUSSES HIS NOSE

Edmond Rostand

Translator: Brian Hooker

VALVERT

(*Looks round*)

Observe. I myself will proceed
To put him in his place.

(*He walks up to* CYRANO, *who has been watching him, and stands there, looking him over with an affected air.*)

Ah . . . your nose . . . hem!
Your nose is . . . rather large!

CYRANO

(*Gravely*)

Rather.

VALVERT

(*Simpering*)

Oh well—

CYRANO

(*Coolly*)

Is that all?

VALVERT

(*Turns away, with a shrug*)

Well, of course—

CYRANO

Ah, no, young sir!
You are too simple. Why, you might have said—
Oh, a great many things! Mon dieu, why waste
Your opportunity? For example, thus:—
AGGRESSIVE: I, sir, if that nose were mine,
I'd have it amputated—on the spot!
FRIENDLY: How do you drink with such a nose?
You ought to have a cup made specially.
DESCRIPTIVE: 'Tis a rock—a crag—a cape—
A cape? say rather, a peninsula!
INQUISITIVE: What is that receptacle—
A razor-case or a portfolio?

KINDLY: Ah, do you love the little birds
So much that when they come and sing to you,
You give them this to perch on? INSOLENT:
Sir, when you smoke, the neighbors must suppose
Your chimney is on fire. CAUTIOUS: Take care—
A weight like that might make you topheavy.
THOUGHTFUL: Somebody fetch my parasol—
Those delicate colors fade so in the sun!
PEDANTIC: Does not Aristophanes
Mention a mythologic monster called
Hippocampelephantoscamelos?
Surely we have here the original!
FAMILIAR: Well, old torchlight! Hang your hat
Over that chandelier—it hurts my eyes.
ELOQUENT: When it blows, the typhoon howls,
And the clouds darken. DRAMATIC: When it bleeds—
The Red Sea! ENTERPRISING: What a sign
For some perfumer! LYRIC: Hark—the horn
Of Roland calls to summon Charlemagne!—
SIMPLE: When do they unveil the monument?
RESPECTFUL: Sir, I recognize in you
A man of parts, a man of prominence—
RUSTIC: Hey? What? Call that a nose? Na, na—
I be no fool like what you think I be—
That there's a blue cucumber! MILITARY:
Point against cavalry! PRACTICAL: Why not
A lottery with this for the grand prize?
Or—parodying FAUSTUS in the play—
"Was this the nose that launched a thousand ships
And burned the topless towers of Ilium?"
These, my dear sir, are things you might have said
Had you some tinge of letters, or of wit
To color your discourse. But wit,—not so,
You never had an atom—and of letters,
You need but three to write you down—an Ass.
Moreover,—if you had the invention, here
Before these folk to make a jest of me—
Be sure you would not then articulate
The twentieth part of half a syllable
Of the beginning! For I say these things
Lightly enough myself, about myself,
But I allow none else to utter them.

(From the play Cyrano de Bergerac)

TRAMP! TRAMP! TRAMP!

George F. Root

In the prison cell I sit, thinking, mother dear, of you,
And our bright and happy home so far away;
And the tears they fill my eyes, spite of all that I can do,
And I try to cheer my comrades and be gay.

Chorus:

Tramp, tramp, tramp, the boys are marching,
Cheer up, comrades, they will come,
And beneath the starry flag,
We will breathe the air again
Of the free land of our own beloved home.

In the battle front we stood when their fiercest charge they made,
And they swept us off a hundred men or more.
But before we reached their lines, they were driven back dismayed,
And we heard the cry of victory o'er and o'er.

So within the prison cell we are waiting for the day
That shall come to open wide the iron door.
And the hollow eye grows bright and the poor heart almost gay,
As we think of seeing homes and friends once more.

THERE IS NO UNBELIEF

Lizzie York Case

There is no unbelief;
Whoever plants a seed beneath the sod
And waits to see it push away the clod,
He trusts in God.

There is no unbelief;
Whoever says, when clouds are in the sky,
"Be patient, heart; light breaketh by and by,"
Trusts the Most High.

There is no unbelief;
Whoever sees 'neath winter's field of snow,
The silent harvest of the future grow—
God's power must know.

There is no unbelief;
Whoever lies down on his couch to sleep,
Content to lock each sense in slumber deep,
Knows God will keep.

There is no unbelief;
Whoever says, "to-morrow," "the unknown,"
"The future," trusts that power alone
He dares disown.

There is no unbelief;
The heart that looks on when dear eyelids close,
And dares to live when life has only woes,
God's comfort knows.

There is no unbelief;
For thus by day and night unconsciously
The heart lives by the faith the lips deny.
God knoweth why.

ROBERT E. LEE'S RESIGNATION FROM THE U.S. ARMY

Arlington, Va., April 20, 1861

General:

Since my interview with you on the 18th inst. I have felt that I ought no longer to retain my commission in the Army. I therefore tender my resignation, which I request you will recommend for acceptance. I would have presented it at once, but for the struggle it has cost me to separate myself from a service to which I have devoted all the best years of my life and all the ability I possessed.

During the whole of that time—more than a quarter of a century—I have experienced nothing but kindness from my superiors and a most cordial friendship from my comrades. To no one, General, have I been so much indebted as to yourself for uniform kindness and consideration, and it has always been my ardent desire to meet your approbation. I shall carry to the grave the most grateful recollections of your kind consideration, and your name and fame will always be dear to me.

Save in defense of my native State, I never desire again to draw my sword.

Be pleased to accept my most earnest wishes for the continuance of your happiness and prosperity, and believe me, most truly yours,

R. E. Lee

(Letter to Gen. Winfield Scott)

DEATH BE NOT PROUD

John Donne

Death be not proud, though some have called thee
Mighty and dreadfull, for thou art not soe,
For those whom thou think'st thou dost overthrow
Die not, poore death, nor yet canst thou kill mee.
From rest and sleepe, which but thy pictures bee,
Much pleasure, then from thee, much more must flow,
And soonest our best men with thee doe goe,
Rest of their bones, and soules deliverie.
Thou art slave to Fate, Chance, kings, and desperate men,
And dost with poyson, warre, and sicknesse dwell,
And poppie, or charmes can make us sleepe as well,
And better than thy stroake; why swell'st thou then?
One short sleepe past, wee wake eternally,
And death shall be no more; death, thou shalt die.

"I AM THE BREAD OF LIFE"

Holy Bible, John 6:35–40

And Jesus said unto them, I am the bread of life: he that cometh to me shall never hunger; and he that believeth on me shall never thirst. But I said unto you, That ye also have seen me, and believe not. All that the Father giveth me shall come to me; and him that cometh to me I will in no wise cast out. For I came down from heaven, not to do mine own will, but the will of him that sent me.

And this is the Father's will which hath sent me, that of all which he hath given me I should lose nothing, but should raise it up again at the last day. And this is the will of him that sent me, that every one which seeth the Son, and believeth on him, may have everlasting life: and I will raise him up at the last day.

FAITHLESS SALLY BROWN

Thomas Hood

Young Ben he was a nice young man,
  A carpenter by trade;
And he fell in love with Sally Brown,
  That was a lady's maid.

But as they fetched a walk one day,
  They met a press-gang crew;
And Sally she did faint away,
  Whilst Ben he was brought to.

The boatswain swore with wicked words,
  Enough to shock a saint,
That though she did seem in a fit,
  'Twas nothing but a feint.

"Come, girl," said he, "hold up your head,
  He'll be as good as me;
For when your swain is in our boat,
  A boatswain he will be."

So when they'd made their game of her,
  And taken off her elf,
She roused, and found she only was
  A coming to herself.

"And he is gone, and is he gone?"
  She cried and wept outright:
"Then I will to the water side,
  And see him out of sight."

A waterman came up to her,—
  "Now, young woman," said he,
"If you weep on so, you will make
  Eye-water in the sea."

"Alas! they've taken my beau, Ben,
  To sail with old Benbow;"
And her woe began to run afresh,
  As if she'd said, "Gee woe!"

Says he, "They've only taken him
  To the Tender-ship, you see;"
"The Tender-ship," cried Sally Brown,
  "What a hard-ship that must be!"

"O! would I were a mermaid now,
  For then I'd follow him;
But, O!—I'm not a fish-woman,
  And so I cannot swim.

"Alas! I was not born beneath
  The virgin and the scales,
So I must curse my cruel stars,
  And walk about in Wales."

Now Ben had sailed to many a place
  That's underneath the world;
But in two years the ship came home,
  And all her sails were furled.

But when he called on Sally Brown,
  To see how she got on,
He found she'd got another Ben,
  Whose Christian name was John.

"O, Sally Brown, O, Sally Brown,
  How could you serve me so?
I've met with many a breeze before,
  But never such a blow!"

Then reading on his 'bacco-box,
  He heaved a heavy sigh,
And then began to eye his pipe,
  And then to pipe his eye.

And then he tried to sing, "All's Well,"
  But could not, though he tried;
His head was turned, and so he chewed
  His pigtail till he died.

His death, which happened in his berth,
  At forty-odd befell:
They went and told the sexton, and
  The sexton tolled the bell.

SELF-ESTIMATE

Sir Isaac Newton

I do not know what I may appear to the world; but to myself I seem to have been only like a boy playing on the seashore, and diverting myself in now and then finding a smoother pebble or a prettier shell than ordinary, whilst the great ocean of truth lay all undiscovered before me.

"THE PROPER STUDY OF MAN"

Alexander Pope

Know then thyself, presume not God to scan;
The proper study of Mankind is Man.
Plac'd on this isthmus of a middle state,
A Being darkly wise, and rudely great:
With too much knowledge for the Sceptic side,
With too much weakness for the Stoic's pride,
He hangs between; in doubt to act, or rest;
In doubt to deem himself a God, or Beast;
In doubt his Mind or Body to prefer;
Born but to die, and reas'ning but to err;
Alike in ignorance, his reason such,
Whether he thinks too little, or too much:
Chaos of Thought and Passion, all confus'd;
Still by himself abus'd, or disabus'd;
Created half to rise, and half to fall;
Great lord of all things, yet a prey to all;
Sole judge of Truth, in endless Error hurl'd:
The glory, jest, and riddle of the world!

(From An Essay on Man)

HOME ON THE RANGE

Anonymous

Oh, give me a home where the buffalo roam,
Where the deer and the antelope play;
Where seldom is heard a discouraging word,
And the skies are not cloudy all day.

Chorus:

Home, home on the range;
Where the deer and the antelope play;
Where seldom is heard a discouraging word,
And the skies are not cloudy all day.

Where the air is so pure, the zephyrs so free,
The breezes so balmy and light,
That I would not exchange my home on the range
For all the cities so bright.

The red man was pressed from this part of the West,
He's likely no more to return
To the banks of the Red River where seldom if ever
Their flickering campfires burn.

How often at night when the heavens are bright
With the light of the glittering stars,
Have I stood here amazed and asked as I gazed
If their glory exceeds that of ours.

Oh, I love these wild flowers in this dear land of ours;
The curlew I love to hear scream;
And I love the white rocks and the antelope flocks
That graze on the mountain-tops green.

Oh, give me a land where the bright diamond sand
Flows leisurely down the stream;
Where the graceful white swan goes gliding along
Like a maid in a heavenly dream.

Then I would not exchange my home on the range,
Where the deer and the antelope play;
Where seldom is heard a discouraging word,
And the skies are not cloudy all day.

THE FACE AGAINST THE PANE

Thomas Bailey Aldrich

Mabel, little Mabel,
With her face against the pane,
Looks out across the night,
And sees the beacon light
A trembling in the rain.
She hears the sea bird screech,
And the breakers on the beach
Making moan, making moan,
And the wind about the eaves
Of the cottage sobs and grieves,
And the willow tree is blown
To and fro, to and fro,
Till it seems like some old crone
Standing out there all alone with her woe,
Wringing as she stands
Her gaunt and palsied hands;
While Mabel, timid Mabel,
With her face against the pane,
Looks out across the night
And sees the beacon light
A trembling in the rain.

Set the table, maiden Mabel,
And make the cabin warm,
Your little fisher lover
Is out there in the storm;
And your father, you are weeping,
O Mabel, timid Mabel,
Go spread the supper table,
And set the tea a steeping;
Your lover's heart is brave,
His boat is staunch and tight,
And your father knows
The perilous reef,
That makes the water white.
But Mabel, Mabel darling,
With her face against the pane,
Looks out across the night
At the beacon in the rain.

The heavens are veined with fire!
And the thunder how it rolls!
In the lullings of the storm
The solemn church bell tolls
  For lost souls!
But no sexton sounds the knell;
In that belfry old and high,
Unseen fingers sway the bell
As the wind goes tearing by!
How it tolls, for the souls
Of the sailors on the sea.
God pity them! God pity them!
Wherever they may be.
God pity wives and sweethearts
Who wait and wait in vain,
And pity little Mabel,
With her face against the pane!
A boom! the light house gun,
How it echoes, rolls and rolls,
'Tis to warn home bound ships
  Off the shoals.
See, a rocket cleaves the sky
From the fort, a shaft of light!
See, it fades, and fading leaves
Golden furrows on the night!
What makes Mabel's cheeks so pale?
What makes Mabel's lips so white?
Did she see the helpless sail
That tossing here and there
Like a feather in the air,
Went down and out of sight,
Down, down and out of sight?
O, watch no more, no more,
With face against the pane—
You cannot see the men that drown
By the beacon in the rain!

From a shoal of richest rubies
Breaks the morning clear and cold,
And the angel on the village spire,
Frost touched, is bright as gold.
Four ancient fishermen
In the pleasant autumn air,

Come toiling up the sands,
With something in their hands.
Two bodies stark and white,
Ah! so ghastly in the light,
With sea weed in their hair.
O ancient fishermen
Go up to yonder cot!
You'll find a little child
With face against the pane,
Who looks towards the beach
And looking sees it not.
She will never watch again,
Never watch and wake at night,
For those pretty saintly eyes
Look beyond the stormy skies,
And they see the beacon light.

A MEDITATION UPON A BROOMSTICK

Jonathan Swift

This single stick, which you now behold ingloriously lying in that neglected corner, I once knew in a flourishing state in a forest; it was full of sap, full of leaves, and full of boughs; but now, in vain does the busy art of man pretend to vie with nature, by tying that withered bundle of twigs to its sapless trunk; it is now, at best, but the reverse of what it was, a tree turned upside down, the branches on the earth, and the root in the air; it is now handled by every dirty wench, condemned to do her drudgery, and by a capricious kind of fate, destined to make other things clean, and be nasty itself; at length worn to the stumps in the service of the maids, it is either thrown out of doors, or condemned to the last use, of kindling a fire. When I beheld this, I sighed, and said within myself, *Surely Man is a Broomstick!* Nature sent him into the world strong, and lusty, in a thriving condition, wearing his own hair on his head, the proper branches of this reasoning vegetable, until the ax of intemperance has lopped off his green boughs, and left him a withered trunk; he then flies to art, and puts on a periwig, valuing himself upon an unnatural bundle of hairs (all covered with powder) that never grew on his head; but now, should this our broomstick pretend to enter the scene, proud of those birchen spoils it never bore, and all covered with dust, though the sweepings of the finest lady's chamber, we should be apt to ridicule and despise its vanity. Partial judges that we are of our own excellencies, and other men's defaults!

But a broomstick, perhaps you will say, is an emblem of a tree standing on its head; and pray what is man, but a topsy-turvy creature, his animal faculties perpetually mounted on his rational, his head where his heels should be, groveling on the earth! And yet, with all his faults, he sets up to be a universal reformer and corrector of abuses, a remover of grievances, rakes into every slut's corner of nature, bringing hidden corruption to the light, and raises a mighty dust where there was none before; sharing deeply all the while in the very same pollutions he pretends to sweep away; his last days are spent in slavery to women, and generally the least deserving; till worn out to the stumps, like his brother's besom, he is either kicked out of doors, or made use of to kindle flames for others to warm themselves by.

SLIDE, KELLY, SLIDE

J. W. Kelly

I played a game of baseball, I belong to Casey's Nine,
The crowd was feeling jolly, and the weather it was fine;
A nobler lot of players I think were never found.
When the omnibuses landed that day upon the ground,
The game was quickly started, they sent me to the bat;
I made two strikes. Says Casey, "What are you striking at?"
I made the third, the catcher muffed, and to the ground it fell;
I run like a devil to first base, when the gang began to yell:

Chorus:

Slide, Kelly, slide! Your running's a disgrace!
Slide, Kelly, slide! Stay there, hold your base!
If someone doesn't steal you, and your batting doesn't fail you,
They'll take you to Australia! Slide, Kelly, slide!

'Twas in the second inning they called me in, I think,
To take the catcher's place, while he went to take a drink;
But something was the matter, sure I couldn't see the ball;
And the second one that came in, broke my muzzle, nose and all.

The crowd up in the grandstand they yelled with all their might,
I ran towards the club house. I thought there was a fight.
'Twas the most unpleasant feeling I ever felt before,
I knew they had me rattled, when the gang began to roar: *(Chorus)*

They sent me out to center field, I didn't want to go,
The way my nose was swelling up, I must have been a show;
They said on me depended victory or defeat.
If a blind man were to look at us he'd know that we were beat.
"Sixty-four to nothing!" was the score when we got done,
And ev'rybody there but me said they had lots of fun.
The news got home ahead of me, they heard I was knocked out,
The neighbors carried me in the house, and then began to shout:
(Chorus)

AN EPITAPH UPON HUSBAND AND WIFE WHO DIED AND WERE BURIED TOGETHER

Richard Crashaw

To these whom death again did wed
This grave's the second marriage-bed.
For though the hand of Fate could force
'Twixt soul and body a divorce,
It could not sever man and wife,
Because they both lived but one life.
Peace, good reader, do not weep;
Peace, the lovers are asleep.
They, sweet turtles, folded lie
In the last knot that love could tie.
Let them sleep, let them sleep on,
Till the stormy night be gone,
And the eternal morrow dawn;
Then the curtains will be drawn,
And they wake into a light
Whose day shall never die in night.

* * *

The heart has its reasons, which reason does not know.
—Blaise Pascal

ACRES OF DIAMONDS

Russell H. Conwell

When going down the Tigris and Euphrates rivers many years ago with a party of English travelers I found myself under the direction of an old Arab guide whom we hired up at Bagdad, and I have often thought how that guide resembled our barbers in certain mental characteristics. He thought that it was not only his duty to guide us down those rivers, and do what he was paid for doing, but also to entertain us with stories curious and weird, ancient and modern, strange and familiar. Many of them I have forgotten, and I am glad I have, but there is one I shall never forget. . . .

The old guide told me that there once lived not far from the River Indus an ancient Persian by the name of Ali Hafed. He said that Ali Hafed owned a very large farm, that he had orchards, grain-fields, and gardens; that he had money at interest, and was a wealthy and contented man. He was contented because he was wealthy, and wealthy because he was contented. One day there visited that old Persian farmer one of those ancient Buddhist priests, one of the wise men of the East. He sat down by the fire and told the old farmer how this world of ours was made. He said that this world was once a mere bank of fog and that the Almighty thrust His finger into this bank of fog, and began slowly to move His finger around, increasing the speed until at last He whirled this bank of fog into a solid ball of fire. Then it went rolling through the universe, burning its way through other banks of fog, and condensed the moisture without, until it fell in floods of rain upon its hot surface, and cooled the outward crust. Then the internal fires bursting outward through the crust threw up the mountains and hills, the valleys, the plains and prairies of this wonderful world of ours. If this internal molten mass came bursting out and cooled very quickly it became granite; less quickly copper, less quickly silver, less quickly gold, and, after gold, diamonds were made.

Said the old priest, "A diamond is a congealed drop of sunlight." Now that is literally scientifically true, that a diamond is an actual deposit of carbon from the sun. The old priest told Ali Hafed that if he had one diamond the size of his thumb he could purchase the county, and if he had a mine of diamonds he could place his children upon thrones through the influence of their great wealth.

Ali Hafed heard all about diamonds, how much they were

worth, and went to his bed that night a poor man. He had not lost anything, but he was poor because he was discontented, and discontented because he feared he was poor. He said, "I want a mine of diamonds," and he lay awake all night.

Early in the morning he sought out the priest. I know by experience that a priest is very cross when awakened early in the morning, and when he shook the old priest out of his dreams, Ali Hafed said to him:

"Will you tell me where I can find diamonds?"

"Diamonds! What do you want with diamonds?" "Why, I wish to be immensely rich." "Well, then, go along and find them. That is all you have to do; go and find them, and then you have them." "But I don't know where to go." "Well, if you will find a river that runs through white sand, between high mountains, in those white sands you will always find diamonds." "I don't believe there is any such river." "Oh, yes, there are plenty of them. All you have to do is to go and find them, and then you have them." Said Ali Hafed, "I will go."

So he sold his farm, collected his money, left his family in charge of a neighbor, and away he went in search of diamonds. He began his search, very properly to my mind, at the Mountains of the Moon. Afterwards he came around into Palestine, and then wandered on into Europe, and at last when his money was all spent and he was in rags, wretchedness, and poverty, he stood on the shore of that bay at Barcelona, in Spain, when a great tidal wave came rolling in between the pillars of Hercules, and the poor, afflicted, suffering, dying man could not resist the awful temptation to cast himself into that incoming tide, and he sank beneath its foaming crest, never to rise in this life again. . . .

The man who purchased Ali Hafed's farm one day led his camel into the garden to drink, and as that camel put its nose into the shallow water of that garden brook, Ali Hafed's successor noticed a curious flash of light from the white sands of the stream. He pulled out a black stone having an eye of light reflecting all the hues of the rainbow. He took the pebble into the house and put it on the mantel which covers the central fires, and forgot all about it.

A few days later this same old priest came in to visit Ali Hafed's successor, and the moment he opened that drawing-room door he saw that flash of light on the mantel, and he rushed up to it, and shouted: "Here is a diamond! Has Ali Hafed returned?" "Oh no, Ali Hafed has not returned, and that is not a diamond. That is nothing but a stone we found right out here in our own garden." "But," said the priest, "I tell you I know a diamond when I see it. I know positively that is a diamond."

Then together they rushed out into that old garden and stirred up the white sands with their fingers, and lo! there came up other more beautiful and valuable gems than the first. "Thus," said the guide to me, and, friends, it is historically true, "was discovered the diamond-mine of Golconda, the most magnificent diamond-mine in all the history of mankind, excelling the Kimberley itself. The Kohinoor, and the Orloff of the crown jewels of England and Russia, the largest on earth, came from that mine."

When that old Arab guide told me the second chapter of his story, he then took off his Turkish cap and swung it around in the air again to get my attention to the moral. Those Arab guides have morals to their stories, although they are not always moral. As he swung his hat, he said to me, "Had Ali Hafed remained at home and dug in his own cellar, or underneath his own wheatfields, or in his own garden, instead of wretchedness, starvation, and death by suicide in a strange land, he would have had 'acres of diamonds.' For every acre of that old farm, yes, every shovelful, afterwards revealed gems which since have decorated the crowns of monarchs."

When he added the moral to his story I saw why he had reserved it for "his particular friends." But I did not tell him I could see it. It was that mean old Arab's way of going around a thing like a lawyer, to say indirectly what he did not dare say directly, that "in his private opinion there was a certain young man then traveling down the Tigris River that might better be at home in America."

* * * *

Let every man or woman here, if you never hear me again, remember this, that if you wish to be great at all, you must begin where you are and what you are—now. He that can give to his city any blessing, he who can be a good citizen while he lives here, he that can make better homes, he that can be a blessing whether he works in a shop or sits behind the counter or keeps house, whatever be his life, he who would be great anywhere must first be great in his own town.

* * *

Be thine own palace, or the world's thy gaol.—John Donne

THE AFRICAN CHIEF

William Cullen Bryant

Chained in the market-place he stood,
  A man of giant frame,
Amid the gathering multitude
  That shrunk to hear his name—
All stern of look and strong of limb,
  His dark eye on the ground:—
And silently they gazed on him,
  As on a lion bound.

Vainly, but well, that chief had fought,
  He was a captive now,
Yet pride, that fortune humbles not,
  Was written on his brow.
The scars his dark broad bosom wore
  Showed warrior true and brave;
A prince among his tribe before,
  He could not be a slave.

Then to his conqueror he spake—
  "My brother is a king;
Undo this necklace from my neck,
  And take this bracelet ring,
And send me where my brother reigns,
  And I will fill thy hands
With store of ivory from the plains,
  And gold-dust from the sands."

"Not for thy ivory nor thy gold
  Will I unbind thy chain;
That bloody hand shall never hold
  The battle-spear again.
A price thy nation never gave,
  Shall yet be paid for thee;
For thou shalt be the Christian's slave,
  In lands beyond the sea."

Then wept the warrior chief, and bade
  To shred his locks away;
And, one by one, each heavy braid

Before the victor lay.
Thick were the platted locks, and long,
And deftly hidden there
Shone many a wedge of gold among
The dark and crisped hair.

"Look, feast thy greedy eye with gold
Long kept for sorest need;
Take it—thou askest sums untold,
And say that I am freed.
Take it—my wife, the long, long day
Weeps by the cocoa-tree,
And my young children leave their play,
And ask in vain for me."

"I take thy gold—but I have made
Thy fetters fast and strong,
And ween that by the cocoa shade
Thy wife will wait thee long."
Strong was the agony that shook
The captive's frame to hear,
And the proud meaning of his look
Was changed to mortal fear.

His heart was broken—crazed his brain;
At once his eye grew wild;
He struggled fiercely with his chain,
Whispered, and wept, and smiled;
Yet wore not long those fatal bands,
And once, at shut of day,
They drew him forth upon the sands,
The foul hyena's prey.

NO SECT IN HEAVEN

Elizabeth H. Jocelyn Cleaveland

Talking of sects till late one eve,
Of the various doctrines the saints believe,
That night I stood in a troubled dream,
By the side of a darkly-flowing stream.

And a "Churchman" down to the river came,
When I heard a strange voice call his name,
"Good father, stop; when you cross this tide,
You must leave your robes on the other side."

But the aged father did not mind,
And his long gown floated out behind,
As down to the stream his way he took,
His pale hands clasping a gilt-edged book.

"I'm bound for Heaven, and when I'm there
I shall want my book of Common Prayer;
And though I put on a starry crown,
I should feel quite lost without my gown."

Then he fixed his eyes on the shining track,
But his gown was heavy, and held him back;
And the poor old father tried in vain,
A single step in the flood to gain.

I saw him once on the other side,
But his silk gown floated on the tide;
And no one asked in that blissful spot,
Whether he belonged to "*the* Church" or not.

When down to the river a Quaker strayed,
His dress of a sober hue was made;
"My coat and hat must all be gray,
I cannot go any other way."

Then he buttoned his coat straight up to his chin,
And staidly, solemnly, waded in,
And his broad-brimmed hat he pulled down tight
Over his forehead, so cold and white.

But a strong wind carried away his hat;
A moment he silently sighed over that,
And then, as he gazed on the farther shore,
The coat slipped off, and was seen no more.

As he entered Heaven, his suit of gray
Went quietly sailing away, away,
And none of the angels questioned him
About the width of his beaver's brim.

Next came Dr. Watts with a bundle of Psalms,
Tied nicely up in his aged arms,
And hymns as many, a very wise thing,
That the people in Heaven, "all round," might sing.

But I thought that he heaved an anxious sigh,
As he saw that the river ran broad and high,
And looked rather surprised as, one by one
The Psalms and Hymns in the wave went down.

And after him with his MSS.,
Came Wesley, the pattern of godliness;
But he cried, "Dear me, what shall I do?
The water has soaked them through and through."

And there on the river, far and wide,
Away they went down the swollen tide,
And the saint astonished passed through alone,
Without his manuscripts up to the throne.

Then gravely walking, two saints by name,
Down to the stream together came;
But as they stopped by the river's brink,
I saw one saint from the other shrink.

"Sprinkled or plunged, may I ask you, friend,
How you attained to life's great end?"
"*Thus,* with a few drops on my brow;"
"But *I* have been dipped, as you'll see me now.

"And I really think it will hardly do,
As I'm 'close communion,' to cross with you;
You're bound, I know, to the realms of bliss,
But you must go that way, and I'll go this."

Then straightway plunging with all his might,
Away to the left—his friend at the right,
Apart they went from this world of sin,
But at last together they entered in.

And, now, when the river is rolling on,
A Presbyterian Church went down;
Of women there seemed an innumerable throng,
But the men I could count as they passed along.

And concerning the road, they could never agree,
The *old* or the *new way,* which it could be,
Nor even a moment paused to think
That both would lead to the river's brink.
And a sound of murmuring long and loud
Came ever up from the moving crowd,
"You're in the old way, and I'm in the new,
That is the false, and this is the true";
Or, "I'm in the old way, and you're in the new,
That is the false, and *this* is the true."

But the *brethren* only seemed to speak,
Modest the sisters walked, and meek,
And if ever one of them chanced to say
What troubles she met with on the way,
How she longed to pass to the other side,
Nor feared to cross over the swelling tide,
A voice arose from the brethren then:
"Let no one speak but the 'holy men'!
For have ye not heard the words of Paul,
'O let the women keep silence all'?"

I watched them long in my curious dream,
Till they stood by the borders of the stream,
Then, just as I thought, the two ways met,
But all the brethren were talking yet,
And would talk on, till the heaving tide
Carried them over side by side;
Side by side, for the way was one,
The toilsome journey of life was done,
And all who in Christ the Saviour died
Came out alike on the other side;
No forms, or crosses, or books had they,
No gowns of silk, or suits of gray,
No creeds to guide them, or MSS.,
For all had put on Christ's righteousness.

* * *

Society flourishes by the antagonism of its atoms.—Herbert Spencer

"WHEN TO THE SESSIONS OF SWEET SILENT THOUGHT"

William Shakespeare

When to the sessions of sweet silent thought
I summon up remembrance of things past,
I sigh the lack of many a thing I sought,
And with old woes new wail my dear time's waste:
Then can I drown an eye, unused to flow,
For precious friends hid in death's dateless night,
And weep afresh love's long since cancell'd woe,
And moan the expense of many a vanish'd sigh:
Then can I grieve at grievances foregone,
And heavily from woe to woe tell o'er
The sad account of fore-bemoaned moan,
Which I new pay as if not paid before.
But if the while I think on thee, dear friend,
All losses are restored and sorrows end.

(Sonnet XXX)

"THE TIMES THAT TRIED MEN'S SOULS ARE OVER"

Thomas Paine

"The times that tried men's souls" are over—and the greatest and completest revolution the world has ever known, gloriously and happily accomplished.

But to pass from the extremes of danger to safety—from the tumult of war to the tranquillity of peace, though sweet in contemplation, requires a gradual composure of senses to receive it. Even calmness has the power of stunning, when it opens too instantly upon us. The long and raging hurricane that should cease in a moment, would leave us in a state rather of wonder than enjoyment; and some moments of recollection must pass, before we could be capable of tasting the felicity of repose. There are but few instances, in which the mind is fitted for sudden transitions: it takes in its pleasures by reflection and comparison and those must have time to act, before the relish for new scenes is complete. . . .

To see it in our power to make a world happy—to teach mankind in the art of being so—to exhibit, on the theater of the universe, a character hitherto unknown—and to have, as it were, a new creation intrusted to our hands, are honours that command reflection, and can neither be too highly estimated, nor too gratefully received.

(From Thoughts on Peace)

LET DOGS DELIGHT TO BARK AND BITE

Isaac Watts

Let dogs delight to bark and bite,
  For God hath made them so;
Let bears and lions growl and fight,
  For 'tis their nature, too.

But, children, you should never let
  Such angry passions rise;
Your little hands were never made
  To tear each other's eyes.

L'ALLEGRO

John Milton

Hence loathed Melancholy
  Of *Cerberus,* and blackest midnight born,
In *Stygian* Cave forlorn
  'Mongst horrid shapes, and shrieks, and sights unholy,
Find out som uncouth cell,
  Where brooding darknes spreads his jealous wings,
And the night-Raven sings;
  There under *Ebon* shades, and low-brow'd Rocks,
As ragged as thy Locks,
  In dark *Cimmerian* desert ever dwell.
But com thou Goddes fair and free,
In Heav'n yclep'd *Euphrosyne,*
And by men, heart-easing Mirth,
Whom lovely *Venus* at a birth
With two sister Graces more

To ivy-crowned *Bacchus* bore;
Or whether (as som Sager sing)
The frolick Wind that breathes the Spring,
Zephir with *Aurora* playing,
As he met her once a Maying,
There on Beds of Violets blew,
And fresh-blown Roses washt in dew,
Fill'd her with thee a daughter fair,
So bucksom, blith, and debonair.
Haste thee nympth, and bring with thee
Jest and youthful Jollity,
Quips and Cranks, and wanton Wiles,
Nods, and Becks, and Wreathed Smiles,
Such as hang on *Hebe's* cheek,
And love to live in dimple sleek;
Sport that wrincled Care derides,
And Laughter holding both his sides.
Com, and trip it as ye go
On the light fantastick toe,
And in thy right hand lead with thee,
The Mountain Nympth, sweet Liberty;
And if I give thee honour due,
Mirth, admit me of thy crue
To live with her, and live with thee,
In unreproved pleasures free;
To hear the Lark begin his flight,
And singing startle the dull night,
From his watch-towre in the skies,
Till the dappled dawn doth rise;
Then to com in spight of sorrow,
And at my window bid good morrow,
Through the Sweet-Briar, or the Vine,
Or the twisted Eglantine.
While the Cock with lively din,
Scatters the rear of darknes thin,
And to the stack, or the Barn dore,
Stoutly struts his Dames before,
Oft list'ning how the Hounds and horn
Chearly rouse the slumbring morn,
From the side of som Hoar Hill,
Through the high wood echoing shrill.
Som time walking not unseen
By Hedge-row Elms, on Hillocks green,

Right against the Eastern gate,
Wher the great Sun begins his state,
Rob'd in flames, and Amber light,
The clouds in thousand Liveries dight.
While the Plowman neer at hand,
Whistles ore the Furrow'd Land,
And the Milkmaid singeth blithe,
And the Mower whets his sithe,
And every Shepherd tells his tale
Under the Hawthorn in the dale.
Streit mine eye hath caught new pleasures
Whilst the Lantskip round it measures,
Russet Lawns, and Fallows Gray,
Where the nibbling flocks do stray,
Mountains on whose barren brest
The labouring clouds do often rest:
Meadows trim with Daisies pide,
Shallow Brooks, and Rivers wide.
Towers, and Battlements it sees
Boosom'd high in tufted Trees,
Wher perhaps som beauty lies,
The Cynosure of neighbouring eyes.
Hard by, a Cottage chimney smokes,
From betwixt two aged Okes,
Where *Corydon* and *Thyrsis* met,
Are at their savory dinner set
Of Hearbs, and other Country Messes,
Which the neat-handed *Phillis* dresses;
And then in haste her Bowre she leaves,
With *Thestylis* to bind the Sheaves;
Or if the earlier season lead
To the tann'd Haycock in the Mead,
Som times with secure delight
The up-land Hamlets will invite,
When the merry Bells ring round,
And the jocond rebecks sound
To many a youth, and many a maid,
Dancing in the Chequer'd shade;
And young and old com forth to play
On a Sunshine Holyday,
Till the live-long day-light fail,
Then to the Spicy Nut-brown Ale,
With stories told of many a feat,

How *Faery Mab* the junkets eat,
She was pincht, and pull'd she sed
And he by Friars Lanthorn led
Tells how the drudging *Goblin* swet,
To ern his Cream-bowle duly set,
When in one night, ere glimps of morn,
His shadowy Flale hath thresh'd the Corn
That ten day-labourers could not end,
Then lies him down the Lubbar Fend.
And stretch'd out all the Chimney's length,
Basks at the fire his hairy strength;
And Crop-full out of dores he flings,
Ere the first Cock his Mattin rings.
Thus don the Tales, to bed they creep,
By whispering Windes soon lull'd asleep.
Towred Cities please us then,
And the busie humm of men,
Where throngs of Knights and Barons bold,
In weeds of Peace high triumphs hold,
With store of Ladies, whose bright eies
Rain influence, and judge the prise
Of Wit, or Arms, while both contend
To win her Grace, whom all commend.
There let *Hymen* oft appear
In Saffron robe, with Taper clear,
And pomp, and feast, and revelry,
With mask, and antique Pageantry,
Such sights as youthfull Poets dream
On Summer eeves by haunted stream.
Then to the well-trod stage anon,
If *Jonsons* learned Sock be on,
Or sweetest *Shakespear* fancies childe,
Warble his native Wood-notes wilde,
And ever against eating Cares,
Lap me in soft *Lydian* Aires,
Married to immortal verse
Such as the meeting soul may pierce
In notes, with many a winding bout
Of lincked sweetnes long drawn out,
With wanton heed, and giddy cunning,
The melting voice through mazes running;
Untwisting all the chains that ty
The hidden soul of harmony.

That *Orpheus* self may heave his head
From golden slumber on a bed
Of heapt *Elysian* flowres, and hear
Such streins as would have won the ear
Of *Pluto,* to have quite set free
His half regain'd *Eurydice.*
These delights, if thou canst give,
Mirth with thee, I mean to live.

EPITAPH TO A NEWFOUNDLAND DOG

Lord Byron

Near this spot
Are deposited the Remains of one
Who possessed Beauty without Vanity,
Strength without Insolence,
Courage without Ferocity,
And all the Virtues of Man, without his Vices.
This Praise, which would be unmeaning Flattery
If inscribed over human ashes,
Is but a just Tribute to the Memory of
BOATSWAIN, a Dog,
Who was born at Newfoundland, May, 1803,
And died at Newstead Abbey, Nov. 18, 1808.

THE BALLAD OF THE OYSTERMAN

Oliver Wendell Holmes

It was a tall young oysterman lived by the river-side,
His shop was just upon the bank, his boat was on the tide;
The daughter of a fisherman, that was so straight and slim,
Lived over on the other bank, right opposite to him.

It was the pensive oysterman that saw a lovely maid,
Upon a moonlight evening, a-sitting in the shade;
He saw her wave her handkerchief, as much as if to say,
"I'm wide awake, young oysterman, and all the folks away."

Then up arose the oysterman, and to himself said he,
"I guess I'll leave the skiff at home, for fear that folks should see;
I read it in the story-book, that, for to kiss his dear,
Leander swam the Hellespont,—and I will swim this here."

And he has leaped into the waves, and crossed the shining stream,
And he has clambered up the bank, all in the moonlight gleam;
Oh there were kisses sweet as dew, and words as soft as rain,—
But they have heard her father's step, and in he leaps again!

Out spoke the ancient fisherman,—"Oh what was that, my daughter?"
" 'Twas nothing but a pebble, sir, I threw into the water."
"And what is that, pray tell me, love, that paddles off so fast?"
"It's nothing but a porpoise, sir, that's been a-swimming past."

Out spoke the ancient fisherman,—"Now bring me my harpoon!
I'll get into my fishing boat, and fix the fellow soon."
Down fell that pretty innocent, as falls a snow-white lamb,
Her hair drooped round her pallid cheeks, like seaweed on a clam.

Alas for those two loving ones! she waked not from her swound,
And he was taken with the cramp, and in the waves was drowned;
But Fate has metamorphosed them, in pity of their woe,
And now they keep an oyster-shop for mermaids down below.

DAVID AND GOLIATH

Holy Bible, I Samuel 16;17:1–51

And the Lord said unto Samuel, How long wilt thou mourn for Saul, seeing I have rejected him from reigning over Israel? Fill thine horn with oil, and go, I will send thee to Jesse the Bethlehemite: for I have provided me a king among his sons. And Samuel said, How can I go? if Saul hear it, he will kill me. And the Lord said, Take an heifer with thee, and say, I am come to sacrifice to the Lord. And call Jesse to the sacrifice, and I will shew thee what thou shalt do: and thou shalt anoint unto me him whom I name unto thee. And Samuel did that which the Lord spake, and came to Bethlehem. And the elders of the town trembled at his coming, and said, Comest thou peaceably? And he said, Peaceably: I am come to sacrifice unto the Lord: sanctify yourselves, and come with me to the sacrifice. And he sanctified Jesse and his sons, and called them to the sacrifice.

And it came to pass, when they were come, that he looked on Eliab, and said, Surely the Lord's anointed is before him. But the Lord said unto Samuel, Look not on his countenance, or on the height of his stature; because I have refused him: for the Lord seeth not as man seeth; for man looketh on the outward appearance, but the Lord looketh on the heart. Then Jesse called Abinadab, and made him pass before Samuel. And he said, Neither hath the Lord chosen this. Then Jesse made Shammah to pass by. And he said, Neither hath the Lord chosen this. Again, Jesse made seven of his sons to pass before Samuel. And Samuel said unto Jesse, The Lord hath not chosen these. And Samuel said unto Jesse, Are here all thy children? And he said, There remaineth yet the youngest, and, behold, he keepeth the sheep. And Samuel said unto Jesse, Send and fetch him: for we will not sit down till he come hither. And he sent, and he brought him in. Now he was ruddy, and withal of a beautiful countenance, and goodly to look to. And the Lord said, Arise, anoint him: for this is he. Then Samuel took the horn of oil, and anointed him in the midst of his brethren: and the Spirit of the Lord came upon David from that day forward. So Samuel rose up, and went to Ramah.

But the Spirit of the Lord departed from Saul, and an evil spirit from the Lord troubled him. And Saul's servants said unto him, Behold now, an evil spirit from God troubleth thee. Let our lord now command thy servants, which are before thee, to seek out a man, who is a cunning player on an harp: and it shall come to pass, when the evil spirit from God is upon thee, that he shall play with his hand, and thou shalt be well. And Saul said unto his servants, Provide me now a man that can play well, and bring him to me. Then answered one of the servants, and said, Behold, I have seen a son of Jesse the Bethlehemite, that is cunning in playing, and a mighty valiant man, and a man of war, and prudent in matters, and a comely person, and the Lord is with him.

Wherefore Saul sent messengers unto Jesse, and said, Send me David thy son, which is with the sheep. And Jesse took an ass laden with bread, and a bottle of wine, and a kid, and sent them by David his son unto Saul. And David came to Saul, and stood before him: and he loved him greatly; and he became his armourbearer. And Saul sent to Jesse, saying, Let David, I pray thee, stand before me; for he hath found favour in my sight. And it came to pass, when the evil spirit from God was upon Saul, that David took an harp, and played with his hand: so Saul was refreshed, and was well, and the evil spirit departed from him.

Now the Philistines gathered together their armies to battle, and were gathered together at Shochoh, which belongeth to Judah, and pitched between Shochoh and Azekah, in Ephesdammim. And Saul and the men of Israel were gathered together, and pitched by the valley of Elah, and set the battle in array against the Philistines. And the Philistines stood on a mountain on the one side, and Israel stood on a mountain on the other side: and there was a valley between them.

And there went out a champion out of the camp of the Philistines, named Goliath, of Gath, whose height was six cubits and a span. And he had an helmet of brass upon his head, and he was armed with a coat of mail; and the weight of the coat was five thousand shekels of brass. And he had greaves of brass upon his legs, and a target of brass between his shoulders. And the staff of his spear was like a weaver's beam; and his spear's head weighed six hundred shekels of iron: and one bearing a shield went before him. And he stood and cried unto the armies of Israel, and said unto them, Why are ye come out to set your battle in array? am not I a Philistine, and ye servants to Saul? choose you a man for you, and let him come down to me. If he be able to fight with me, and to kill me, then will we be your servants: but if I prevail against him, and kill him, then shall ye be our servants, and serve us. And the Philistine said, I defy the armies of Israel this day; give me a man, that we may fight together. When Saul and all Israel heard those words of the Philistine, they were dismayed, and greatly afraid.

Now David was the son of that Ephrathite of Bethlehem-judah, whose name was Jesse; and he had eight sons: and the man went among men for an old man in the days of Saul. And the three eldest sons of Jesse went and followed Saul to the battle: and the names of his three sons that went to the battle were Eliab the firstborn, and next unto him Abinadab, and the third Shammah. And David was the youngest: and the three eldest followed Saul. But David went and returned from Saul to feed his father's sheep at Bethlehem. And the Philistine drew near morning and evening, and presented himself forty days. And Jesse said unto David his son, Take now for thy brethren an ephah of this parched corn, and these ten loaves, and run to the camp of thy brethren; and carry these ten cheeses unto the captain of their thousand, and look how thy brethren fare, and take their pledge. Now Saul, and they, and all the men of Israel, were in the valley of Elah, fighting with the Philistines.

And David rose up early in the morning, and left the sheep with a keeper, and took, and went, as Jesse had commanded him; and he came to the trench, as the host was going forth to the fight, and shouted for the battle. For Israel and the Philistines had put the battle in array, army against army. And David left his carriage in the hand of the keeper of the carriage, and ran into the army, and came and saluted his brethren. And as he talked with them, behold, there came up the champion, the Philistine of Gath, Goliath by name, out of the armies of the Philistines, and spake according to the same words: and David heard them. And all the men of Israel, when they saw the man, fled from him, and were sore afraid. And the men of Israel said, Have ye seen this man that has come up? surely to defy Israel is he come up: and it shall be, that the man who killeth him, the king will enrich him with great riches, and will give him his daughter, and make his father's house free in Israel. And David spake to the men that stood by him, saying, What shall be done to the man that killeth this Philistine, and taketh away the reproach from Israel? for who is this uncircumcised Philistine, that he should defy the armies of the living God? And the people answered him after this manner, saying, So shall it be done to the man that killeth him.

And Eliab his eldest brother heard when he spake unto the men; and Eliab's anger was kindled against David, and he said, Why camest thou down hither? and with whom hast thou left those few sheep in the wilderness? I know thy pride, and the naughtiness of thine heart; for thou art come down that thou mightest see the battle. And David said, What have I now done? Is there not a cause?

And he turned from him toward another, and spake after the same manner: and the people answered him again after the former manner. And when the words were heard which David spake, they rehearsed them before Saul: and he sent for him.

And David said to Saul, Let no man's heart fail because of him: thy servant will go and fight with this Philistine. And Saul said to David, Thou art not able to go against this Philistine to fight with him: for thou art but a youth, and he a man of war from his youth. And David said unto Saul, Thy servant kept his father's sheep, and there came a lion, and a bear, and took a lamb out of the flock: and I went out after him, and smote him, and delivered it out of his mouth: and when he arose against me, I caught him by his beard, and smote him, and slew him. Thy servant slew both the lion and the bear: and this uncircumcised Philistine shall be as one of them, seeing he hath defied the armies of the living God.

David said moreover, The Lord that delivered me out of the paw of the lion, and out of the paw of the bear, he will deliver me out of the hand of this Philistine. And Saul said unto David, Go, and the Lord be with thee.

And Saul armed David with his armour, and he put an helmet of brass upon his head; also he armed him with a coat of mail. And David girded his sword upon his armour, and he assayed to go; for he had not proved it. And David said unto Saul, I cannot go with these; for I have not proved them. And David put them off him. And he took his staff in his hand, and he chose him five smooth stones out of the brook, and put them in a shepherd's bag which he had, even in a scrip; and his sling was in his hand; and he drew near to the Philistine. And the Philistine came on and drew near unto David; and the man that bare the shield went before him. And when the Philistine looked about, and saw David, he disdained him; for he was but a youth, and ruddy, and of a fair countenance. And the Philistine said unto David, Am I a dog, that thou comest to me with staves? And the Philistine cursed David by his gods. And the Philistine said to David, Come to me, and I will give thy flesh unto the fowls of the air, and to the beasts of the field. Then said David to the Philistine, Thou comest to me with a sword, and with a spear, and with a shield: but I come to thee in the name of the Lord of hosts, the God of the armies of Israel, whom thou hast defied. This day will the Lord deliver thee into mine hand: and I will smite thee, and take thine head from thee; and I will give the carcasses of the host of the Philistines this day unto the fowls of the air, and to the wild beasts of the earth; that all the earth may know that there is a God in Israel. And all this assembly shall know that the Lord saveth not with sword and spear: for the battle is the Lord's, and he will give you into our hands. And it came to pass, when the Philistine arose, and came and drew nigh to meet David, that David hasted, and ran toward the army to meet the Philistine. And David put his hand in his bag, and took thence a stone, and slang it, and smote the Philistine in his forehead, that the stone sunk into his forehead; and he fell upon his face to the earth. So David prevailed over the Philistine with a sling and with a stone, and smote the Philistine, and slew him; but there was no sword in the hand of David. Therefore David ran, and stood upon the Philistine, and took his sword, and drew it out of the sheath thereof, and slew him, and cut off his head therewith. And when the Philistines saw their champion was dead they fled.

THE SHADOWS OF THE EVENING HOURS

Adelaide A. Procter

The shadows of the evening hours
Fall from the darkening sky;
Upon the fragrance of the flowers
The dews of evening lie:
Before Thy throne, O Lord of heaven,
We kneel at close of day;
Look on Thy children from on high,
And hear us while we pray.

Slowly the rays of daylight fade:
So fade within our heart
The hopes in earthly love and joy,
That one by one depart.
Slowly the bright stars, one by one
Within the heavens shine:
Give us, O Lord, fresh hopes in heav'n,
And trust in things divine.

Let peace, O Lord, Thy peace, O God,
Upon our souls descend;
From midnight fears and perils, Thou
Our trembling hearts defend.
Give us a respite from our toil,
Calm and subdue our woes;
Through the long day we labor, Lord,
O give us now repose.

INSCRIPTION ON STONE OVER SHAKESPEARE'S GRAVE

Good frend for Jesus sake forbeare,
To digg the dust encloased heare!
Bleste be ye man y^t spares thes stones,
And curst be he y^t moves my bones.

THE BLUE BELLS OF SCOTLAND

Anonymous

Oh where, and oh where is your Highland laddie gone?
Oh where, and oh where is your Highland laddie gone?
He's gone to fight the foe for King George upon the throne,
And it's oh, in my heart, I wish him safe at home.

Oh where, and oh where did your Highland laddie dwell?
Oh where, and oh where did your Highland laddie dwell?
He dwelt in merry Scotland at the sign of the Blue Bell,
And it's oh, in my heart, I love my laddie well.

Suppose, and suppose your Highland laddie should die?
Suppose, and suppose your Highland laddie should die?
The bagpipes shall play o'er him and I'll lay me down to cry,
But it's oh, in my heart, I wish he may not die.

THE LESSON OF THE WATER-MILL

Sarah Doudney

Listen to the water-mill;
  Through the livelong day,
How the clicking of its wheel
  Wears the hours away!
Languidly the autumn wind,
  Stirs the forest leaves,
From the field the reapers sing,
  Binding up their sheaves;
And a proverb haunts my mind
  As a spell is cast—
"The mill cannot grind
  With the water that is past."

Autumn winds revive no more
  Leaves that once are shed,
And the sickle cannot reap
  Corn once gathered;
Flows the ruffled streamlet on,
  Tranquil, deep, and still;

Never gliding back again
To the water-mill;
Truly speaks the proverb old
With a meaning vast—
"The mill cannot grind
With the water that is past."

Take the lesson to thyself,
True and loving heart;
Golden youth is fleeting by,
Summer hours depart;
Learn to make the most of life,
Lose no happy day;
Time will never bring thee back
Chances swept away!
Leave no tender word unsaid,
Love while love shall last—
"The mill cannot grind
With the water that is past."

Work while yet the daylight shines,
Man of strength and will!
Never does the streamlet glide
Useless by the mill;
Wait not till to-morrow's sun
Beams upon thy way,
All that thou canst call thine own
Lies in thy "To-day";
Power, intellect and health
May not always last—
"The mill cannot grind
With the water that is past."

Oh, the wasted hours of life
That have drifted by!
Oh, the good that might have been—
Lost, without a sigh!
Love that we might once have saved
By a single word,
Thoughts conceived, but never penned,
Perishing unheard,—
Take the proverb to thine heart,
Take and hold it fast—
"The mill cannot grind
With the water that is past."

AN IRISH BULL

"Why should we put ourselves out of the way to do anything for posterity? for what has posterity done for us?" When laughter followed this remark the speaker added, "By posterity I do not mean all of our ancestors, but those who were to come immediately after them."

(Attributed to Sir Boyle Roche, member of
the Irish House in the eighteenth century)

ONCE IN A SAINTLY PASSION

James Thomson

Once in a saintly passion
 I cried with desperate grief,
"O Lord, my heart is black with guile,
 Of sinners I am chief."
Then stooped my guardian angel
 And whispered from behind,
"Vanity, my little man,
 You're nothing of the kind."

SWEET MARIE

Cy Warman

I've a secret in my heart, sweet Marie,
A tale I would impart, love, to thee.
Every daisy in the dell
Knows my secret, knows it well.
And yet I dare not tell sweet Marie.
When I hold your hand in mine, sweet Marie,
A feeling most divine comes to me;
All the world is full of spring,
Full of warblers on the wing,
And I listen while they sing, sweet Marie.

Cho.: Come to me, sweet Marie, sweet Marie, come to me;
Not because your face is fair, love, to see,
But your soul, so pure and sweet,
Makes my happiness complete;
Makes me falter at your feet, sweet Marie.

In the morn when I awake, sweet Marie,
Seems to me my heart will break, love, for thee,
Every wave that shakes the shore
Seems to sing it o'er and o'er,
Seems to say that I adore sweet Marie.
When the sun tints the west, sweet Marie,
And I sit down to rest, love, with thee;
Every star that studs the sky
Seems to stand and wonder why,
They're so dimmer than your eye, sweet Marie.

DULUTH!

Representative J. Proctor Knott, of Kentucky

Years ago, when I first heard that there was somewhere in the vast *terra incognita,* somewhere in the bleak regions of the great North-west, a stream of water known to the nomadic inhabitants of the neighborhood as the river St. Croix, I became satisfied that the construction of a railroad from that raging torrent to some point in the civilized world was essential to the happiness and prosperity of the American people, if not absolutely indispensable to the perpetuity of republican institutions on this continent. I felt instinctively that the boundless resources of that prolific region of sand and pine-shrubbery would never be fully developed without a railroad constructed and equipped at the expense of the Government, and perhaps not then. I had an abiding presentiment that, some day or other, the people of this whole country, irrespective of party affiliations, regardless of sectional prejudices, and "without distinction of race, color, or previous condition of servitude," would rise in their majesty and demand an outlet for the enormous agricultural productions of those vast and fertile pine-barrens, drained in the rainy season by the surging waters of the turbid St. Croix.

Now, sir, who, after listening to this emphatic and unequivocal testimony of these intelligent, competent, and able-bodied witnesses; who that is not as incredulous as St. Thomas himself, will doubt for a moment that the Goshen of America is to be found in the sandy valleys and upon the pine-clad hills of the St. Croix? Who will have the hardihood to rise in his seat on this floor and assert that, excepting the pine bushes, the entire region would not produce vegetation enough in ten years to fatten a grasshopper? Where is the patriot who is willing that his country shall incur the peril of remaining another day without the amplest railroad connection with such an inexhaustible mine of agricultural wealth?

Duluth! The word fell upon my ear with a peculiar and indescribable charm, like the gentle murmur of a low fountain stealing forth in the midst of roses, or the soft, sweet accents of an angel's whisper in the bright, joyous dream of sleeping innocence. Duluth! 'Twas the name for which my soul had panted for years, as the hart panteth for the water-brooks. But where was Duluth? Never in all my limited reading had my vision been gladdened by seeing the celestial word in print. And I felt a profounder humiliation in my ignorance that its dulcet syllables had never before ravished my delighted ear. I was certain the draughtsman of this bill had never heard of it, or it would have been designated as one of the termini of this road. I asked my friends about it, but they knew nothing of it. I rushed to the library and examined all the maps I could find. I discovered in one of them a delicate, hair-like line, diverging from the Mississippi near a place marked Prescott, which I supposed was intended to represent the river St. Croix, but I could nowhere find Duluth.

Nevertheless, I was confident it existed somewhere, and that its discovery would constitute the crowning glory of the present century, if not of all modern times. I knew it was bound to exist, in the very nature of things; that the symmetry and perfection of our planetary system would be incomplete without it; that the elements of material nature would long since have resolved themselves back into original chaos if there had been such a hiatus in creation as would have resulted from leaving out Duluth. In fact, sir, I was overwhelmed with the conviction that Duluth not only existed somewhere, but that, wherever it was, it was a great and glorious place. I was convinced that the greatest calamity that ever befell the benighted nations of the ancient world was in their having passed away without a knowledge of the actual existence of Duluth; that their fabled Atlantis, never seen save by the hallowed vision of inspired poetry, was, in fact, but another name for Duluth; that the golden orchard of the Hesperides was but a poetical synonym for the beer-gardens in the vicinity of Duluth. I was certain that Herodotus had died a miserable death because in all his travels and with all his geographical research he had never heard of Duluth. I knew that if the immortal spirit of Homer could look down from another heaven than that created by his own celestial genius upon the long lines of pilgrims from every nation of the earth to the gushing fountain of poesy opened by the touch of his magic wand, if he could be permitted to behold the vast assemblage of grand and glorious productions of the lyric art called into being by his own inspired strains, he would weep tears of bitter anguish that, instead of lavishing all the stores of his mighty genius upon the fall of Illion, it had not been his more blessed lot to crystallize in deathless song the rising glories of Duluth. Yet, sir, had it not been for this map, kindly furnished me by the Legislature of Minnesota, I might have gone down to my obscure and humble grave in an agony of despair because I could nowhere find Duluth. Had such been my melancholy fate, I have no doubt that with the last feeble pulsation of my breaking heart, with the last faint exhalation of my fleeting breath, I should have whispered, "Where is Duluth?"

But, thanks to the beneficence of that band of ministering angels who have their bright abodes in the far-off capital of Minnesota, just as the agony of my anxiety was about to culminate in the frenzy of despair, this blessed map was placed in my hands; and as I unfolded it a resplendent scene of ineffable glory opened before me, such as I imagine burst upon the enraptured vision of the wandering peri through the opening gates of paradise. There, there for the first time, my enchanted eye rested upon the ravishing word "Duluth." . . .

If gentlemen will examine it, they will find Duluth not only in the centre of the map, but represented in the centre of a series of concentric circles one hundred miles apart, and some of them as much as four thousand miles in diameter, embracing alike in their tremendous sweep the fragrant savannas of the sunlit South and the eternal solitudes of snow that mantle the ice-bound North. How these circles were produced is perhaps one of those primordial mysteries that the most skilled paleologist will never be able to explain. But the fact is, sir, Duluth is pre-eminently a central place, for I have been told by gentlemen who have been so reckless of their own personal safety as to venture away into those awful regions where Duluth is supposed to be, that it is so exactly in the centre of the visible universe that the sky comes down at precisely the same distance all around it.

I find by reference to this map that Duluth is situated somewhere near the western end of Lake Superior, but as there is no dot or other mark indicating its exact location I am unable to say whether it is actually confined to any particular spot, or whether "it is just lying around there loose." I really cannot tell whether it is one of those ethereal creations of intellectual frostwork, more intangible than the rose-tinted clouds of a summer sunset; one of those airy exhalations of the speculator's brain, which I am told are ever flitting in the form of towns and cities along those lines of railroad, built with Government subsidies, luring the unwary settler as the mirage of the desert lures the famishing traveler on, and ever on, until it fades in the darkening horizon, or whether it is a real, *bona fide,* substantial city, all "staked off," with the lots marked with their owners' names, like that proud commercial metropolis recently discovered on the desirable shores of San Domingo. But, however that may be, I am satisfied Duluth is there, or thereabout, for I see it stated here on this map that it is exactly thirty-nine hundred and ninety miles from Liverpool; though I have no doubt, for the sake of convenience, it will be moved back ten miles, so as to make the distance an even four thousand.

(In the House of Representatives, January 27, 1871)

INSCRIPTION ON THE STATUE OF LIBERTY

THE NEW COLOSSUS

Not like the brazen giant of Greek fame,
With conquering limbs astride from land to land,
Here at our sea-washed, sunset gates shall stand
A mighty woman with a torch, whose flame
Is the imprisoned lightning, and her name
Mother of Exiles. From her beacon-hand
Glows world-wide welcome; her mild eyes command
The air-bridged harbor that twin cities frame.
"Keep, ancient lands, your storied pomp!" cries she
With silent lips. "Give me your tired, your poor,
Your huddled masses yearning to breathe free,
The wretched refuse of your teeming shore.
Send these, the homeless, tempest-tost to me,
I lift my lamp beside the golden door!"

This tablet, with her Sonnet to the Bartholdi Statue
of Liberty engraved upon it, is placed upon these walls
in loving memory of
Emma Lazarus
born in New York City, July 22, 1849
Died November 18, 1887

THE COURTIN'

James Russell Lowell

God makes sech nights, all white an' still
  Fur'z you can look or listen.
Moonshine an' snow on field an' hill,
  All silence an' all glisten.

Zekle crep' up quite unbeknown
  An' peeked in thru' the winder,
An' there sot Huldy all alone,
  'ith no one nigh to hender.

A fireplace filled the room's one side
  With half a cord o' wood in—
There warn't no stoves (tell comfort died)
  To bake ye to a puddin'.

The wa'nut logs shot sparkles out
  Towards the pootiest, bless her,
An' leetle flames danced all about
  The chiny on the dresser.

Agin the chimbley crook-necks hung,
  An' in amongst 'em rusted
The ole queen's-arm thet gran'ther Young
  Fetched back from Concord busted.

The very room, coz she was in,
  Seemed warm from floor to ceilin',
An' she looked full ez rosy agin
  Ez the apples she was peelin'.

'Twas kin' o' kingdom-come to look
  On sech a blessed cretur,
A dogrose blushin' to a brook
  Ain't modester nor sweeter.

He was six foot o' man, A 1,
  Clear grit an' human natur';
None couldn't quicker pitch a ton
  Nor dror a furrer straighter.

He'd sparked it with full twenty gals,
He'd squired 'em, danced 'em, druv 'em,
Fust this one, an' then thet, by spells—
All is, he couldn't love 'em.

But long o' her his veins 'ould run
All crinkly like curled maple,
The side she breshed felt full o' sun
Ez a south slope in Ap'il.

She thought no v'ice hed sech a swing
Ez hisn in the choir;
My! when he made Ole Hunderd ring,
She *knowed* the Lord was nigher.

An' she'd blush scarlit, right in prayer,
When her new meetin'-bunnet
Felt somehow thru' its crown a pair
O' blue eyes sot upon it.

Thet night, I tell ye, she looked *some!*
She seemed to 've gut a new soul,
For she felt sartin-sure he'd come,
Down to her very shoe-sole.

She heered a foot, an' knowed it tu,
A-raspin' on the scraper,—
All ways to once her feelins flew
Like sparks in burnt-up paper.

He kin' o' l'itered on the mat,
Some doubtfle o' the sekle,
His heart kep' goin' pity-pat,
But hern went pity Zekle.

An' yit she gin her cheer a jerk
Ez though she wished him furder,
An' on her apples kep' to work,
Parin' away like murder.

"You want to see my Pa, I s'pose?"
"Wal . . . no . . . I come dasignin'—"
"To see my Ma? She's sprinklin' clo'es
Agin to-morrer's i'nin'."

To say why gals act so or so,
  Or don't, 'ould be presumin';
Mebby to mean *yes* an' say *no*
  Comes nateral to women.

He stood a spell on one foot fust,
  Then stood a spell on t' other,
An' on which one he felt the wust
  He couldn't ha' told ye nuther.

Says he, "I'd better call agin";
  Says she, "Think likely, Mister":
Thet last word pricked him like a pin,
  An' . . . Wal, he up an' kist her.

When Ma bimeby upon 'em slips,
  Huldy sot pale ez ashes,
All kin' o' smily roun' the lips
  An' teary roun' the lashes.

For she was jes' the quiet kind
  Whose naturs never vary,
Like streams that keep a summer mind
  Snowhid in Jenooary.

The blood clost roun' her heart felt glued
  Too tight for all expressin',
Tell mother see how metters stood,
  An' gin em both her blessin'.

Then her red come back like the tide
  Down to the Bay o' Fundy,
An' all I know is they was cried
  In meetin' come nex' Sunday.

THE DEATH OF CLEOPATRA

William Shakespeare

Cleopatra. Give me my robe, put on my crown; I have
Immortal longings in me: now no more
The juice of Egypt's grape shall moist this lip:
Yare, yare, good Iras; quick. Methinks I hear
Antony call; I see him rouse himself
To praise my noble act; I hear him mock
The luck of Caesar, which the gods give men
To excuse their after wrath. Husband, I come:
Now to that name my courage prove my title!
I am fire and air; my other elements
I give to baser life. So; have you done?
Come then and take the last warmth of my lips.
Farewell, kind Charmian; Iras, long farewell.
[*Kisses them. Iras falls and dies.*
Have I the aspic in my lips? Dost fall?
If thou and nature can so gently part,
The stroke of death is as a lover's pinch,
Which hurts, and is desired. Dost thou lie still?
If thus thou vanishest, thou tell'st the world
It is not worth leave-taking.
Charmian. Dissolve, thick cloud, and rain, that I may say
The gods themselves do weep!
Cleopatra. This proves me base:
If she first meet the curled Antony,
He'll make demand of her, and spend that kiss
Which is my heaven to have. Come, thou mortal wretch,
[*To an asp which she applies to her breast*
With thy sharp teeth this knot intrinsicate
Of life at once untie: poor venomous fool,
Be angry, and dispatch. O, couldst thou speak,
That I might hear thee call great Caesar ass
Unpolicied!
Charmian. O eastern star!
Cleopatra. Peace, peace!
Dost thou not see my baby at my breast,
That sucks the nurse asleep?

(From Antony and Cleopatra)

LEND A HAND

Edward Everett Hale

Look up! and not down;
Out! and not in;
Forward! and not back;
And lend a hand.

THREE LITTLE KITTENS

Anonymous

The three little kittens, they lost their mittens,
And they began to cry,
"Oh, Mammy dear, we sadly fear,
Our mittens we have lost!"
"What! lost your mittens, you naughty kittens?
Then you shall have no pie!"
"Mi-ew, mi-ew,
We shall have no pie!"

The three little kittens, they found their mittens,
And they began to cry,
"Oh, Mammy dear, see here, see here,
Our mittens we have found."
"What! found your mittens, you good little kittens?
Then you shall have some pie."
"Purr, purr, purr, purr,
We shall have some pie."

The three little kittens put on their mittens,
And soon ate up the pie.
"Oh, Mammy dear, we greatly fear,
Our mittens we have soiled."
"What! soiled your mittens, you naughty kittens?"
Then they began to sigh,
"Mi-ew, mi-ew,"
They began to sigh.

The three little kittens, they washed their mittens,
And hung them up to dry.
"Oh, Mammy dear, look here, look here,
Our mittens we have washed."
"What! washed your mittens, you darling kittens?
But I smell a rat close by!
Hush, hush, hush, hush!
I smell a rat close by!"

LOGAN'S SPEECH

I appeal to any white man to say if ever he entered Logan's cabin hungry, and he gave him not meat; if he ever came cold and naked, and he clothed him not. During the course of the last long and bloody war, Logan remained idle in his cabin, an advocate for peace. Such was my love for the whites, that my countrymen pointed as they passed, and said, "Logan is the friend of the white men." I had even thought to live with you, but for the injuries of one man. Colonel Cresap, last spring, in cold blood, and unprovoked, murdered all the relatives of Logan, not sparing even my women and children. There runs not a drop of my blood in the veins of any living creature. This called on me for revenge. I have sought it. I have killed many. I have fully glutted my vengeance. For my country, I rejoice at the beam of peace: but do not harbor a thought that mine is the joy of fear. Logan never felt fear. He will not turn on his heel to save his life. Who is there to mourn for Logan? Not one.

(Logan, a Mingo chief, to Lord Dunmore, Governor of Virginia, in 1774. Colonial forces had defeated several Indian tribes. Logan refused to join the pleas for peace, but sent this speech to be read to the Governor lest his absence harm the negotiations.)

* * *

I never could believe that Providence sent a few men into the world, ready booted and spurred to ride, and millions ready saddled and bridled to be ridden.—Richard Rumbold, on the scaffold, 1685.

THE OLD TESTAMENT

Thomas Russell

The great Jehovah speaks to us
In Genesis and Exodus;
Leviticus and Numbers see,
Followed by Deuteronomy.
Joshua and Judges sway the land,
Ruth gleans a sheaf with trembling hand,
Samuel and numerous Kings appear,
Whose Chronicles we wondering hear;
Ezra and Nehemiah now
Esther, the beauteous mourner, show;
Job speaks in sighs, David in Psalms,
The Proverbs teach to scatter alms.
Ecclesiastes then comes on
And the sweet Song of Solomon.
Isaiah, Jeremiah then,
With Lamentations takes his pen.
Ezekiel, Daniel, Hosea's lyres
Swell Joel, Amos, Obadiah's.
Next Jonah, Micah, Nahum come,
And lofty Habakkuk finds room.
While Zephaniah, Haggai call,
Rapt Zechariah builds his wall,
And Malachi with garments rent,
Concludes the ancient Testament.

"O ELOQUENT, JUST AND MIGHTY DEATH!"

Sir Walter Raleigh

O eloquent, just and mighty Death! whom none could advise, thou hast persuaded; what none hath dared, thou hast done; and whom all the world hath flattered, thou only hast cast out of the world and despised; thou hast drawn together all the far-stretched greatness, all the pride, cruelty, and ambition of man, and covered it all over with these two narrow words, *Hic jacet.*

(From The History of the World)

THE DIVERTING HISTORY OF JOHN GILPIN

SHOWING HOW HE WENT FARTHER THAN HE INTENDED AND CAME SAFE HOME AGAIN

William Cowper

John Gilpin was a citizen
  Of credit and renown,
A train-band captain eke was he
  Of famous London town.

John Gilpin's spouse said to her dear,
  "Though wedded we have been
These twice ten tedious years, yet we
  No holiday have seen.

"To-morrow is our wedding-day,
  And we will then repair
Unto the Bell at Edmonton,
  All in a chaise and pair.

"My sister, and my sister's child,
  Myself, and children three,
Will fill the chaise; so you must ride
  On horseback after we."

He soon replied, "I do admire
  Of womankind but one,
And you are she, my dearest dear,
  Therefore it shall be done.

"I am a linen-draper bold,
  As all the world doth know,
And my good friend the calender
  Will lend his horse to go."

Quoth Mrs. Gilpin, "That's well said;
  And for that wine is dear,
We will be furnished with our own,
  Which is both bright and clear."

John Gilpin kissed his loving wife;
O'erjoyed was he to find,
That though on pleasure she was bent,
She had a frugal mind.

The morning came, the chaise was brought,
But yet was not allowed
To drive up to the door, lest all
Should say that she was proud.

So three doors off the chaise was stayed,
Where they did all get in;
Six precious souls, and all agog
To dash through thick and thin.

Smack went the whip, round went the wheels,
Were never folk so glad,
The stones did rattle underneath,
As if Cheapside were mad.

John Gilpin at his horse's side
Seized fast the flowing mane,
And up he got, in haste to ride,
But soon came down again;

For saddle-tree scarce reached had he,
His journey to begin,
When, turning round his head, he saw
Three customers come in.

So down he came; for loss of time,
Although it grieved him sore,
Yet loss of pence, full well he knew,
Would trouble him much more.

'Twas long before the customers
Were suited to their mind,
When Betty screaming came downstairs,
"The wine is left behind!"

"Good lack!" quoth he—"yet bring it me,
My leathern belt likewise,
In which I bear my trusty sword,
When I do exercise."

Now Mistress Gilpin (careful soul!)
  Had two stone bottles found,
To hold the liquor that she loved,
  And keep it safe and sound.

Each bottle had a curling ear,
  Through which the belt he drew,
And hung a bottle on each side,
  To make his balance true.

Then over all, that he might be
  Equipped from toe to toe,
His long red cloak, well brushed and neat,
  He manfully did throw.

Now see him mounted once again
  Upon his nimble steed,
Full slowly pacing o'er the stones,
  With caution and good heed.

But finding soon a smoother road
  Beneath his well-shod feet,
The snorting beast began to trot,
  Which galled him in his seat.

So, "Fair and softly," John he cried,
  But John he cried in vain;
That trot became a gallop soon,
  In spite of curb and rein.

So stooping down, as needs he must
  Who cannot sit upright,
He grasped the mane with both his hands,
  And eke with all his might.

His horse, who never in that sort
  Had handled been before,
What thing upon his back had got
  Did wonder more and more.

Away went Gilpin, neck or nought;
  Away went hat and wig;
He little dreamt, when he set out,
  Of running such a rig.

The wind did blow, the cloak did fly,
Like streamer long and gay,
Till loop and button failing both,
At last it flew away.

Then might all people well discern
The bottles he had slung;
A bottle swinging at each side,
As hath been said or sung.

The dogs did bark, the children screamed,
Up flew the windows all;
And every soul cried out, "Well done!"
As loud as he could bawl.

Away went Gilpin—who but he?
His fame soon spread around;
"He carries weight!" "He rides a race!"
" 'Tis for a thousand pound!"

And still, as fast as he drew near,
'Twas wonderful to view
How in a trice the turnpike-men
Their gates wide open threw.

And now, as he went bowing down
His reeking head full low,
The bottles twain behind his back
Were shattered at a blow.

Down ran the wine into the road,
Most piteous to be seen,
Which made his horse's flanks to smoke
As they had basted been.

But still he seemed to carry weight,
With leathern girdle braced;
For all might see the bottle-necks
Still dangling at his waist.

Thus all through merry Islington
These gambols he did play,
Until he came unto the Wash
Of Edmonton so gay;

And there he threw the Wash about
  On both sides of the way,
Just like unto a trundling mop,
  Or a wild goose at play.

At Edmonton his loving wife
  From the balcony spied
Her tender husband, wondering much
  To see how he did ride.

"Stop, stop, John Gilpin!—Here's the house!"
  They all at once did cry:
"The dinner waits, and we are tired;"—
  Said Gilpin—"So am I!"

But yet his horse was not a whit
  Inclined to tarry there!
For why?—his owner had a house
  Full ten miles off, at Ware,

So like an arrow swift he flew,
  Shot by an archer strong;
So did he fly—which brings me to
  The middle of my song.

Away went Gilpin, out of breath,
  And sore against his will,
Till at his friend the calender's
  His horse at last stood still.

The calender, amazed to see
  His neighbor in such trim,
Laid down his pipe, flew to the gate,
  And thus accosted him:

"What news? what news? your tidings tell;
  Tell me you must and shall—
Say why bareheaded you are come,
  Or why you come at all?"

Now Gilpin had a pleasant wit
  And loved a timely joke;
And thus unto the calender
  In merry guise he spoke:

"I came because your horse would come,
And, if I well forebode,
My hat and wig will soon be here,—
They are upon the road."

The calender, right glad to find
His friend in merry pin,
Returned him not a single word
But to the house went in;

Whence straight he came with hat and wig;
A wig that flowed behind,
A hat not much the worse for wear,
Each comely in its kind.

He held them up, and in his turn
Thus showed his ready wit,
"My head is twice as big as yours,
They therefore needs must fit.

"But let me scrape the dirt away
That hangs upon your face;
And stop and eat, for well you may
Be in a hungry case."

Said John, "It is my wedding-day,
And all the world would stare,
If wife should dine at Edmonton,
And I should dine at Ware."

So turning to his horse, he said,
"I am in haste to dine;
'Twas for your pleasure you came here,
You shall go back for mine."

Ah, luckless speech, and bootless boast!
For which he paid full dear;
For, while he spake, a braying ass
Did sing most loud and clear;

Whereat his horse did snort, as he
Had heard a lion roar,
And galloped off with all his might
As he had done before.

Away went Gilpin, and away
  Went Gilpin's hat and wig:
He lost them sooner than at first;
  For why?—they were too big.

Now Mistress Gilpin, when she saw
  Her husband posting down
Into the country far away,
  She pulled out half-a-crown;

And thus unto the youth she said
  That drove them to the Bell,
"This shall be yours, when you bring back
  My husband safe and well."

The youth did ride, and soon did meet
  John coming back amain:
Whom in a trice he tried to stop,
  By catching at his rein;

But not performing what he meant,
  And gladly would have done,
The frighted steed he frighted more,
  And made him faster run.

Away went Gilpin, and away
  Went postboy at his heels,
The postboy's horse right glad to miss
  The lumbering of the wheels.

Six gentlemen upon the road,
  Thus seeing Gilpin fly,
With postboy scampering in the rear,
  They raised the hue and cry:

"Stop thief! stop thief!—a highwayman!"
  Not one of them was mute;
And all and each that passed that way
  Did join in the pursuit.

And now the turnpike gates again
  Flew open in short space;
The toll-men thinking, as before,
  That Gilpin rode a race.

And so he did, and won it too,
  For he got first to town;
Nor stopped till where he had got up
  He did again get down.

Now let us sing, Long live the King!
  And Gilpin, long live he!
And when he next doth ride abroad
  May I be there to see!

PRAYER IN THE MORNING

From *The Book of Common Prayer*

O God, the King Eternal, who dividest the day from the darkness, and turnest the shadow of death into the morning; Drive far off from us all wrong desires, incline our hearts to keep thy law, and guide our feet into the way of peace; that having done thy will with cheerfulness while it was day, we may, when the night cometh, rejoice to give thee thanks; through Jesus Christ our Lord. *Amen.*

Almighty God, who alone gavest us the breath of life, and alone canst keep alive in us the holy desires thou dost impart; We beseech thee, for thy compassion's sake, to sanctify all our thoughts and endeavours; that we may neither begin an action without a pure intention nor continue it without thy blessing. And grant that, having the eyes of the mind opened to behold things invisible and unseen, we may in heart be inspired by thy wisdom, and in work be upheld by thy strength, and in the end be accepted of thee as thy faithful servants; through Jesus Christ our Saviour. *Amen.*

OH, BREATHE NOT HIS NAME!

(Robert Emmet)

Thomas Moore

Oh, breathe not his name! let it sleep in the shade,
Where cold and unhonored his relics are laid;
Sad, silent, and dark be the tears that we shed,
As the night-dew that falls on the grass o'er his head.

But the night-dew that falls, though in silence it weeps,
Shall brighten with verdure the grave where he sleeps;
And the tear that we shed, though in secret it rolls,
Shall long keep his memory green in our souls.

CINDY

Anonymous

I wish I was an apple, a-hangin' on a tree,
And ev'ry time my Cindy passed, she'd take a bite of me.
She told me that she loved me, she called me sugar-plum,
She throwed 'er arms around me, I thought my time had come.

Chorus:

Get along home Cindy, Cindy, Get along home, Cindy, Cindy,
Get along home Cindy, Cindy, I'll marry you some time.

She took me to the parlor, she cooled me with her fan,
She swore that I's the purtiest thing in the shape of mortal man.
Oh where did you get your liquor, oh where did you get your dram?
I got it from a nigger, away down in Birmingham.

Cindy got religion, she had it once before,
When she heard my old banjo, she 'uz the first one on the floor.
I wish I had a needle, as fine as I could sew,
I'd sew that girl to my coat tail, and down the road we'd go.

Cindy in the springtime, Cindy in the fall,
If I can't have my Cindy girl, I'll have no girl at all.
Cindy went to the meetin', she swung around and around,
She got so full of glory, she knocked the parson down.

FLAG DAY—1940

What's a flag? What's the love of country for which it stands? Maybe it begins with love of the land itself. It is the fog rolling in with the tide at Eastport, or through the Golden Gate and among the towers of San Francisco. It is the sun coming up behind the

White Mountains, over the Green, throwing a shining glory on Lake Champlain and above the Adirondacks. It is the storied Mississippi rolling swift and muddy past St. Louis, rolling past Cairo, pouring down past the levees of New Orleans. It is lazy noontide in the pines of Carolina, it is a sea of wheat rippling in Western Kansas, it is the San Francisco peaks far north across the glowing nakedness of Arizona, it is the Grand Canyon and a little stream coming down out of a New England ridge, in which are trout.

It is men at work. It is the storm-tossed fishermen coming into Gloucester and Provincetown and Astoria. It is the farmer riding his great machine in the dust of harvest, the dairyman going to the barn before sunrise, the lineman mending the broken wire, the miner drilling for the blast. It is the servants of fire in the murky splendor of Pittsburgh, between the Allegheny and the Monongahela, the trucks rumbling through the night, the locomotive engineer bringing the train in on time, the pilot in the clouds, the riveter running along the beam a hundred feet in the air. It is the clerk in the office, the housewife doing the dishes and sending the children off to school. It is the teacher, doctor and parson tending and helping, body and soul, for small reward.

It is small things remembered, the little corners of the land, the houses, the people that each one loves. We love our country because there was a little tree on a hill, and grass thereon, and a sweet valley below; because the hurdy-gurdy man came along on a sunny morning in a city street; because a beach or a farm or a lane or a house that might not seem much to others were once, for each of us, made magic. It is voices that are remembered only, no longer heard. It is parents, friends, the lazy chat of street and store and office, and the ease of mind that makes life tranquil. It is Summer and Winter, rain and sun and storms. These are flesh of our flesh, bone of our bone, blood of our blood, a lasting part of what we are, each of us and all of us together.

It is stories told. It is the Pilgrims dying in their first dreadful Winter. It is the minute man standing his ground at Concord Bridge, and dying there. It is the army in rags, sick, freezing, starving at Valley Forge. It is the wagons and the men on foot going westward over Cumberland Gap, floating down the great rivers, rolling over the great plains. It is the settler hacking fiercely at the primeval forest on his new, his own lands. It is Thoreau at Walden Pond, Lincoln at Cooper Union, and Lee riding home from Appomattox. It is corruption and disgrace, answered always by men who would not let the flag lie in the dust, who have stood up in every generation to fight for the old ideals and the old rights, at risk of ruin or of life itself.

It is a great multitude of people on pilgrimage, common and ordinary people, charged with the usual human failings, yet filled with such a hope as never caught the imaginations and the hearts of any nation on earth before. The hope of liberty. The hope of justice. The hope of a land in which a man can stand straight, without fear, without rancor.

The land and the people and the flag—the land a continent, the people of every race, the flag a symbol of what humanity may aspire to when the wars are over and the barriers are down: to these each generation must be dedicated and consecrated anew, to defend with life itself, if need be, but, above all, in friendliness, in hope, in courage, to live for.

(Editorial from the *New York Times,* June 14, 1940)

A GOOD NAME

William Shakespeare

Iago. Good name in man and woman, dear my lord,
Is the immediate jewel of their souls:
Who steals my purse steals trash; 'tis something, nothing;
'Twas mine, 'tis his, and has been slave to thousands.
But he that filches from me my good name
Robs me of that which not enriches him
And makes me poor indeed.

(From Othello)

"THERE IS NO GOD," THE WICKED SAITH

Arthur Hugh Clough

"There is no God," the wicked saith,
"And truly it's a blessing,
For what He might have done with us
It's better only guessing."

"There is no God," a youngster thinks,
"Or really, if there may be,
He surely did not mean a man
Always to be a baby."

"There is no God, or if there is,"
The tradesman thinks, " 'twere funny
If He should take it ill in me
To make a little money."

"Whether there be," the rich man says,
"It matters very little,
For I and mine, thank somebody,
Are not in want of victual."

Some others, also, to themselves,
Who scarce so much as doubt it,
Think there is none, when they are well
And do not think about it.

But country folks who live beneath
The shadow of the steeple;
The parson and the parson's wife,
And mostly married people;

Youths green and happy in first love,
So thankful for illusion;
And men caught out in what the world
Calls guilt, in first confusion;

And almost everyone when age,
Disease, or sorrows strike him,
Inclines to think there is a God,
Or something very like Him.

* * *

The rung of a ladder was never meant to rest upon, but only to hold a man's foot long enough to enable him to put the other somewhat higher.—Thomas Henry Huxley

JIM BLUDSO

John Hay

Wall, no! I can't tell whar he lives,
Bekase he don't live, you see;
Leastways, he's got out of the habit
Of livin' like you an' me.
Whar have you been for the last three year
That you haven't heard folks tell
How Jimmy Bludso passed in his checks
The night of the Prairie Belle?

He weren't no saint—them engineers
Is all pretty much alike,—
One wife in Natchez-under-the-Hill
And another one here, in Pike;
A keerless man in his talk was Jim,
And an awkward hand in a row,
But he never flunked, an' he never lied—
I reckon he never knowed how.

And this was all the religion he had,—
To treat his engine well;
Never be passed on the river;
To mind the pilot's bell;
And if ever the Prairie Belle took fire,—
A thousand times he swore
He'd hold her nozzle agin the bank
Till the last soul got ashore.

All boats has their day on the Mississip,
And her day come at last,—
The Movastar was a better boat,
But the Belle she *wouldn't* be passed.
And so she come tearin' along that night—
The oldest craft on the line—
With a nigger squat on her safety-valve,
And her furnace crammed, rosin and pine.

The fire bust out as she clared the bar
And burnt a hole in the night,
And quick as a flash she turned, and made

For that willer-bank on the right.
There was runnin' an' cursin', but Jim yelled out,
Over all the infernal roar,
"I'll hold her nozzle agin the bank
Till the last galoot's ashore!"

Through the hot black breath of the burnin' boat
Jim Bludso's voice was heard,
An' they all had trust in his cussedness,
And knowed he would keep his word.
And, sure's you're born, they all got off
Afore the smokestacks fell,—
And Bludso's ghost went up alone
In the smoke of the Prairie Belle.

He weren't no saint—but at Jedgment
I'd run my chance with Jim,
'Longside of some pious gentlemen
That wouldn't shook hands with him.
He seen his duty, a dead-sure thing,—
And went for it, thar an' then:
And Christ ain't a-goin' to be too hard
On a man that died for men.

"DO WHAT THY MANHOOD BIDS THEE DO"

Richard Burton

Do what thy manhood bids thee do, from none but self expect applause;
He noblest lives and noblest dies who makes and keeps his self-made laws.

All other living is living death, a world where none but phantoms dwell,
A breath, a wind, a sound, a voice, a tinkling of the camel-bell.

* * *

Where law ends tyranny begins.—William Pitt

THE TWO MATCHES

Robert Louis Stevenson

One day there was a traveller in the woods in California, in the dry season, when the Trades were blowing strong. He had ridden a long way, and was tired and hungry, and dismounted from his horse to smoke a pipe. But when he felt in his pocket he found but two matches. He struck the first, and it would not light.

"Here is a pretty state of things!" said the traveller. "Dying for a smoke; only one match left; and that certain to miss fire!

"Was there ever so unfortunate a creature? And yet," thought the traveller, "suppose I light this match, and smoke my pipe, and shake out the dottle here in the grass—the grass might catch on fire, for it is dry like tinder; and while I snatch out the flames in front, they might evade and run behind me, and seize upon yon bush of poison oak; before I could reach it, that would have blazed up; over the bush I see a pine tree hung with moss; that too would fly in fire upon the instant to its topmost bough; and the flame of that long torch—how would that trade wind take and brandish that through the inflammable forest! I hear this dell roar in a moment with the joint voice of wind and fire, I see myself gallop for my soul, and the flying conflagration chase and outflank me through the hills; I see this pleasant forest burn for days, and the cattle roasted, and the springs dried up, and the farmer ruined, and his children cast upon the world. What a world hangs upon this moment!"

With that he struck the match and it missed fire.

"Thank God!" said the traveller, and put his pipe in his pocket.

O COME ALL YE FAITHFUL

(ADESTE FIDELES)

Anonymous

O come, all ye faithful, joyful and triumphant;
O come ye, O come ye to Bethlehem.
Come and behold Him, born the King of angels;
O come, let us adore Him, O come, let us adore Him,
O come, let us adore Him, Christ the Lord.

Sing, choirs of angels, sing in exultation,
Sing, all ye citizens of heav'n above:
Glory to God, in the highest:
O come, etc.

Yea, Lord, we greet Thee, born this happy morning,
Jesus, to Thee be glory giv'n;
Word of the Father, now in flesh appearing:
O come, etc.

In Latin
Adeste fideles, laeti triumphantes;
Venite, venite in Bethlehem;
Natum videte, Regem angelorum;
Venite adoremus, Venite adoremus,
Venite adoremus, Dominum.

"GO FROM ME. YET I FEEL THAT I SHALL STAND"

Elizabeth Barrett Browning

Go from me. Yet I feel that I shall stand
Henceforward in thy shadow. Nevermore
Alone upon the threshold of my door
Of individual life, I shall command
The uses of my soul, nor lift my hand
Serenely in the sunshine as before,
Without the sense of that which I forbore—
Thy touch upon the palm. The widest land
Doom takes to part us, leaves thy heart in mine
With pulses that beat double. What I do
And what I dream include thee, as the wine
Must taste of its own grapes. And when I sue
God for myself, He hears that name of thine,
And sees within my eyes the tears of two.

* * *

Shadow owes its birth to light.—John Gay

EULOGY OF THE DOCTOR

Robert Louis Stevenson

There are men and classes of men that stand above the common herd; the soldier, the sailor, and the shepherd not unfrequently; the artist rarely; rarelier still, the clergyman; the physician almost as a rule. He is the flower (such as it is) of our civilization; and when that stage of man is done with, and only remembered to be marvelled at in history, he will be thought to have shared as little as any in the defects of the period, and most notably exhibited the virtues of the race. Generosity he has, such as is possible to those who practice an art, never to those who drive a trade; discretion, tested by a hundred secrets; tact, tried in a thousand embarrassments; and what are more important, Heraclean cheerfulness and courage. So it is that he brings air and cheer into the sick-room, and often enough, though not so often as he wishes, brings healing.

LIFE

Anna Letitia Barbauld

Life! I know not what thou art,
But know that thou and I must part;
And when, or how, or where we met,
I own to me's a secret yet.
But this I know, when thou art fled,
Where'er they lay these limbs, this head,
No cloud so valueless shall be
As all that then remains of me.

* * *

Life! we've been long together,
Through pleasant and through cloudy weather;
'Tis hard to part when friends are dear;
Perhaps 'twill cost a sigh, a tear;—
Then steal away, give little warning,
Choose thine own time;
Say not Good-night, but in some brighter clime
Bid me Good-morning!

HAMLET BROODS OVER THE DEATH OF HIS FATHER

William Shakespeare

O, that this too too solid flesh would melt,
Thaw and resolve into a dew!
Or that the Everlasting had not fix'd
His canon 'gainst self-slaughter! O God! God!
How weary, stale, flat and unprofitable
Seem to me all the uses of this world!
Fie on 't! ah fie! 'Tis an unweeded garden,
That grows to seed; things rank and gross in nature
Possess it merely. That it should come to this!
But two months dead! nay, not so much, not two:
So excellent a king; that was, to this,
Hyperion to a satyr: so loving to my mother,
That he might not beteem the winds of heaven
Visit her face too roughly. Heaven and earth!
Must I remember? why, she would hang on him,
As if increase of appetite had grown
By what it fed on: and yet, within a month—
Let me not think on 't—Frailty, thy name is woman!—
A little month, or ere those shoes were old
With which she follow'd my poor father's body,
Like Niobe, all tears:—why she, even she,—
O God! a beast that wants discourse of reason
Would have mourn'd longer,—married with my uncle,
My father's brother, but no more like my father
Than I to Hercules: within a month;
Ere yet the salt of most unrighteous tears
Had left the flushing in her galled eyes,
She married.

(From Hamlet)

PARABLE OF THE ISMS

Anonymous

Socialism: If you have two cows, you give one to your neighbor.

Communism: If you have two cows, you give them to the government and then the government gives you some milk.

Fascism: If you have two cows, you keep the cows and give the milk to the government; then the government sells you some milk.
New Dealism: If you have two cows, you shoot one and milk the other; then you pour the milk down the drain.
Nazism: If you have two cows, the government shoots you and keeps the cows.
Capitalism: If you have two cows, you sell one and buy a bull.

(From *Supervision*)

CALVARY

Edwin Arlington Robinson

Friendless and faint, with martyred steps and slow,
Faint for the flesh, but for the spirit free,
Stung by the mob that came to see the show,
The Master toiled along to Calvary;
We gibed him, as he went, with houndish glee,
Till his dimmed eyes for us did overflow;
We cursed his vengeless hands thrice wretchedly—
And this was nineteen hundred years ago.

But after nineteen hundred years the shame
Still clings, and we have not made good the loss
That outraged faith has entered in his name.
Ah, when shall come love's courage to be strong!
Tell me, O Lord—tell me, O Lord, how long
Are we to keep Christ writhing on the cross!

A WOMAN'S LAST WORD

Robert Browning

Let's contend no more, Love,
  Strive nor weep:
All be as before, Love,
  —Only sleep!

What so wild as words are?
  I and thou
In debate, as birds are,
  Hawk on bough!

See the creature stalking
While we speak!
Hush and hide the talking,
Cheek on cheek!

What so false as truth is,
False to thee?
Where the serpent's tooth is
Shun the tree—

Where the apple reddens
Never pry—
Lest we lose our Edens,
Eve and I.

Be a god and hold me
With a charm!
Be a man and fold me
With thine arm!

Teach me, only teach, Love!
As I ought
I will speak thy speech, Love.
Think thy thought—

Meet, if thou require it,
Both demands,
Laying flesh and spirit
In thy hands.

That shall be to-morrow,
Not to-night:
I must bury sorrow
Out of sight:

—Must a little weep, Love,
(Foolish me!)
And so fall asleep, Love,
Loved by thee.

TRAY'S EPITAPH

Peter Pindar (John Wolcot)

Here rest the relics of a friend below,
Blest with more sense than half the folks I know:
Fond of his ease, and to no parties prone,
He damn'd no sect, but calmly gnaw'd his bone;
Perform'd his functions well in ev'ry way—
Blush, *Christians,* if you can, and copy *Tray.*

BARTER

Sara Teasdale

Life has loveliness to sell,
  All beautiful and splendid things,
Blue waves whitened on a cliff,
  Soaring fire that sways and sings,
And children's faces looking up
Holding wonder like a cup.

Life has loveliness to sell,
  Music like a curve of gold,
Scent of pine trees in the rain,
  Eyes that love you, arms that hold,
And for your spirit's still delight,
Holy thoughts that star the night.

Spend all you have for loveliness,
  Buy it and never count the cost;
For one white singing hour of peace
  Count many a year of strife well lost,
And for a breath of ecstasy
Give all you have been, or could be.

* * *

Do good by stealth and blush to find it fame.—Alexander Pope

BOSWELL DESCRIBES HIS FIRST MEETING WITH SAMUEL JOHNSON

Mr. Thomas Davies the actor, who then kept a bookseller's shop in Russell Street, Covent Garden, told me that Johnson was very much his friend, and came frequently to his house, where he more than once invited me to meet him; but by some unlucky accident or other he was prevented from coming to us.

Mr. Thomas Davies was a man of good understanding and talents, with the advantage of a liberal education. Though somewhat pompous, he was an entertaining companion; and his literary performances have no inconsiderable share of merit. He was a friendly and very hospitable man. Both he and his wife (who had been celebrated for her beauty), though upon the stage for many years, maintained an uniform decency of character; and Johnson esteemed them, and lived in as easy an intimacy with them as with any family which he used to visit. Mr. Davies recollected several of Johnson's remarkable sayings, and was one of the best of the many imitators of his voice and manner, while relating them. He increased my impatience more and more to see the extraordinary man whose work I highly valued, and whose conversation was reported to be so peculiarly excellent.

At last, on Monday the 16th of May, when I was sitting in Mr. Davies' back-parlor, after having drunk tea with him and Mrs. Davies, Johnson unexpectedly came into the shop; and Mr. Davies having perceived him through the glass door in the room in which we were sitting, advancing towards us, he announced his awful approach to me, somewhat in the manner of an actor in the part of Horatio, when he addresses Hamlet on the appearance of his father's ghost, "Look, my Lord, it comes." I found that I had a very perfect idea of Johnson's figure, from the portrait of him painted by Sir Joshua Reynolds soon after he had published his *Dictionary,* in the attitude of sitting in his easy chair in deep meditation; which was the first picture his friend did for him, which Sir Joshua very kindly presented to me, and from which an engraving has been made for this work. Mr. Davies mentioned my name, and respectfully introduced me to him. I was much agitated; and recollecting his prejudice against the Scotch, of which I had heard much, I said to Davies, "Don't tell where I come from."—"From Scotland," cried Davies, roguishly. "Mr. Johnson," said I, "I do indeed come from Scotland, but I cannot help it." I am willing to flatter myself that I meant this as light pleasantry to soothe and conciliate him, and not as an humiliating abasement at the expense of my country. But however that might be, this speech was somewhat unlucky; for with that quickness of wit for which he was so remarkable, he seized the expression "come from Scotland," which I used in sense of being of that country; and, as if I had said that I had come away from it, or left it, retorted, "That, Sir, I find is what a very great many of your countrymen cannot help." This stroke stunned me a good deal; and when we had sat down, I felt myself not a little embarrassed, and apprehensive of what might come next. He then addressed himself to Davies: "What do you think of Garrick? He has refused me an order for the play for Miss Williams, because he knows the house will be full, and that an order would be worth three shillings." Eager to take any opening to get into conversation with him, I ventured to say, "O Sir, I cannot think Mr. Garrick would grudge such a trifle to you." "Sir," said he, with a stern look, "I have known David Garrick longer than you have done; and I know no right you have to talk to me on the subject." Perhaps I deserved this check; for it was rather presumptuous in me, an entire stranger, to express any doubt of the justice of his animadversion upon his old acquaintance and pupil. I now felt myself much mortified, and began to think that the hope which I had long indulged of obtaining his acquaintance was blasted. And, in truth, had not my ardor been uncommonly strong, and my resolution uncommonly persevering, so rough a reception might have deterred me forever from making any further attempts. Fortunately, however, I remained upon the field not wholly discomfited; and was soon rewarded by hearing some of his conversation. . . .

I was highly pleased with the extraordinary vigor of his conversation, and regretted that I was drawn away from it by an engagement at another place. I had, for a part of the evening, been left alone with him, and had ventured to make an observation now and then, which he received very civilly; so that I was satisfied that though there was a roughness in his manner, there was no ill-nature in his disposition. Davies followed me to the door, and when I complained to him a little of the hard blows which the great man had given me, he kindly took upon him to console me by saying, "Don't be uneasy. I can see he likes you very well."

* * *

Censure is the tax a man pays to the public for being eminent.

—Jonathan Swift

LITTLE BREECHES

John Hay

I don't go much on religion,
  I never ain't had no show;
But I've got a middlin' tight grip, sir,
  On the handful o' things I know.
I don't pan out on the prophets
  An' free-will, an' that sort of thing—
But I b'lieve in God an' the angels,
  Ever sence one night last spring.

I come to town with some turnips,
  An' my little Gabe come along—
No four-year-old in the country
  Could beat him for pretty an' strong,
Peart an' chipper an' sassy.
  Always ready to swear and fight,—
And I'd l'arnt him to chaw terbacker,
  Jest to keep his milk-teeth white.

The snow come down like a blanket
  As I passed by Taggart's store;
I went in for a jug of molasses
  An' left the team at the door.
They scared at something an' started—
  I heard one little squall,
An' hell-to-split over the prairie
  Went team, Little Breeches an' all.

Hell-to-split over the prairie!
  I was almost froze with skeer;
But we rousted up some torches,
  An' s'arched for 'em far and near.
At last we struck horse an' wagon,
  Snowed under a soft white mound,
Upsot, dead beat—but of little Gabe
  No hide nor hair was found.

And here all hope soured on me,
  Of my feller-critter's aid—
I jest flopped down on my marrow-bones

Crotch-deep in the snow, an' prayed . . .
By this, the torches wuz played out,
An' me an' Isrul Parr
Went off for some wood to a sheepfold
That he said wuz somewhar thar.

We found it at last, an' a little shed
Where they shut up the lamb at night.
We looked in an' seen them huddled thar,
So warm an' sleepy an' white;
An' THAR sot Little Breeches an' chirped,
As peart as ever you see,
"I wants a chaw of terbacky,
An' that's what's the matter of me."

How did he git thar? Angels.
He could never have walked in that storm.
They jest scooped down an' toted him
To whar it was safe an' warm.
An' I think that savin' a little child,
An' bringin' him to his own,
Is a derned sight better business
Than loafin' around The Throne.

"NO COWARD SOUL IS MINE"

Emily Brontë

No coward soul is mine,
No trembler in the world's storm-troubled sphere:
I see Heaven's glories shine,
And Faith shines equal, arming me from Fear.

O God within my breast,
Almighty, ever-present Deity!
Life, that in me has rest,
As I, undying Life, have power in Thee!

Vain are the thousand creeds
That move men's hearts, unutterably vain,
Worthless as withered weeds,
Or idle froth amid the boundless main,

To waken doubt in one
Holding so fast by Thine infinity,
So surely anchored on
The steadfast rock of Immortality.

With wide-embracing love
Thy spirit animates eternal years,
Pervades and broods above,
Changes, sustains, dissolves, creates, and rears.

Though earth and moon were gone,
And suns and universes ceased to be,
And Thou were left alone,
Every existence would exist in Thee.

There is not room for Death,
Nor atom that his might could render void:
Thou—THOU art Being and Breath,
And what THOU art may never be destroyed.

BREAK THE NEWS TO MOTHER *

Charles K. Harris

While the shot and shell were screaming on the battlefield,
The boys in blue were fighting their noble flag to shield;
Came a cry from their brave captain, "Look, boys! our flag is down;
Who'll volunteer to save it from disgrace?"
"I will," a young voice shouted, "I'll bring it back or die,"
Then sprang into the thickest of the fray,
Saved the flag but gave his young life; all for his country's sake.
They brought him back and softly heard him say:

Chorus:
"Just break the news to mother,
She knows how dear I love her,
And tell her not to wait for me,
For I'm not coming home;
Just say there is no other

Can take the place of mother;
Then kiss her dear, sweet lips for me,
And break the news to her."

From afar a noted general had witnessed this brave deed.
"Who saved our flag? Speak up, lads; 'twas noble, brave, indeed!"
"There he lies, sir," said the captain, "he's sinking very fast,"
Then slowly turned away to hide a tear.
The general, in a moment, knelt down beside the boy;
Then gave a cry that touch'd all hearts that day.
"It's my son, my brave, young hero; I thought you safe at home."
"Forgive me, Father, for I ran away."

THE GOLDEN CITY

John Bunyan

Now, when they were come up to the gate, there was written over it, in letters of gold,

"BLESSED ARE THEY THAT DO HIS COMMANDMENTS, THAT THEY MAY HAVE RIGHT TO THE TREE OF LIFE, AND MAY ENTER IN THROUGH THE GATES INTO THE CITY"

Then I saw in my dream, that the shining men bid them call at the gate; the which when they did, some from above looked over the gate, to wit, Enoch, Moses, and Elijah, &c; to whom it was said, These pilgrims are come from the city of Destruction, for the love that they bear to the King of this place: and then the pilgrims gave in unto them each man his certificate, which they had received in the beginning: those, therefore, were carried in unto the King, who, when he had read them, said, Where are the men? To whom it was answered, They are standing without the gate. The King then commanded to open the gate, "that the righteous nation (said he) that keepeth the truth may enter in."

Now I saw in my dream, that these two men went in at the gate, and, lo! as they entered, they were transfigured; and they had raiment put on, that shone like gold. There were also that met them with harps and crowns, and gave them to them; the harps to praise withal, and the crowns in token of honour. Then I heard in my dream, that all the *bells* in the City rang again for joy, and that it was said unto them, ENTER YE INTO THE JOY OF

OUR LORD. I also heard the men themselves, that they sang with a loud voice, saying,

> "BLESSING, AND HONOUR, AND GLORY, AND POWER BE UNTO HIM THAT SITTETH UPON THE THRONE, AND UNTO THE LAMB, FOR EVER AND EVER."

Now, just as the gates were opened to let in the men, I looked in after them, and behold the City shone like the sun; the streets also were paved with gold; and in them walked many men with crowns on their heads, palms in their hands, and golden harps, to sing praises withal.

There were also of them that had wings, and they answered one another without intermission, saying, "Holy, holy, holy is the Lord." And after that they shut up the gates; which when I had seen, I wished myself among them.

Now, while I was gazing upon all these things, I turned my head to look back, and saw Ignorance come up the river-side: but he soon got over, and that without half the difficulty which the other two men met with. For it happened that there was then in that place one Vain-hope, a ferryman, that with his boat helped him over: so he, as the others I saw, did ascend the hill, to come up to the gate; only he came alone neither did any man meet him with the least encouragement. When he was come up to the gate, he looked up to the writing that was above, and then began to knock, supposing that entrance should have been quickly administered to him: but he was asked by the men that looked over the top of the gate, Whence come you? and what would you have? He answered, I have eat and drunk in the presence of the King, and he has taught in our streets. Then they asked him for his certificate, that they might go in and show it to the King: so he fumbled in his bosom for one, and found none. Then said they, Have you none? but the man answered never a word. So they told the King, but he would not come down to see him, but commanded the two shining ones, that conducted Christian and Hopeful to the City, to go out, and take Ignorance, and bind him hand and foot, and have him away. Then they took him up, and carried him through the air to the door that I saw in the side of the hill, and put him in there. Then I saw that there was a way to hell, even from the gates of heaven, as well as from the city of Destruction. So I awoke, and behold it was a dream.

(The concluding paragraphs of
Part One of The Pilgrim's Progress)

BASEBALL'S SAD LEXICON

Franklin P. Adams

These are the saddest of possible words:
  "Tinker to Evers to Chance."
Trio of bear cubs, and fleeter than birds,
  Tinker and Evers and Chance.
Ruthlessly pricking our gonfalon bubble,
Making a Giant hit into a double—
Words that are heavy with nothing but trouble:
  "Tinker to Evers to Chance."

LORD LOVEL

Anonymous

Lord Lovel he stood at his castle gate,
  A-combing his milk-white steed;
When along came Lady Nancy Bell,
  A-wishing her lover good speed, speed, speed,
  A-wishing her lover good speed.

"Oh where are you going, Lord Lovel?" she said,
  "Oh where are you going?" said she.
"I'm going, my dear Lady Nancy Bell,
  Strange countries for to see, see, see,
  Strange countries for to see."

"When will you be back, Lord Lovel?" she said;
  "When will you be back?" said she.
"In a year or two or three at the most
  I'll return to my Lady Nancee—cee, cee,
  I'll return to my Lady Nancee."

He'd not been gone but a year and a day,
  Strange countries for to see,
When languishing thoughts came into his mind
  Lady Nancy Bell he would see.

He rode and he rode on his milk-white steed,
Till he reached fair London town;
And there he heard St. Varney's bell
And the people all mourning around.

"Is any one dead?" Lord Lovel he said;
"Is any one dead?" said he.
"A lady is dead," the people all said,
"And they call her Lady Nancy."

He ordered the grave to be opened forthwith,
The shroud to be folded down;
And then he kissed her clay-cold lips
Till the tears came trickling down.

Lady Nancy she died as it might be today,
Lord Lovel he died tomorrow.
Lady Nancy she died of pure, pure grief,
Lord Lovel he died of sorrow.

Lady Nancy was laid in St. Clement's churchyard,
Lord Lovel was buried close by her;
And out of her bosom there grew a red rose,
And out of his backbone a briar.

They grew and they grew on the old church tower,
Till they couldn't grow up any higher;
And there they tied in a true lover's knot,
For all true lovers to admire.

THE MELTING POT

Israel Zangwill

There she lies, the great Melting Pot—listen! Can't you hear the roaring and bubbling? There gapes her mouth—the harbor where a thousand mammoth feeders come from the ends of the world to pour in their human freight. Ah, what a stirring and a seething! Celt and Latin, Slav and Teuton, Greek and Syrian—black and yellow—Jew and Gentile. Yes, East and West, North and South, the palm and the pine, the pole and the equator, the crescent and the cross—how the great alchemist melts and fuses them with his purging flame! Here shall they all unite to build the Republic of Man and the Kingdom of God. Ah, what is the glory of Rome and Jerusalem, where all nations and races come to worship and look back, compared with the glory of America, where all races and nations come to labor and look forward!

America is God's crucible, the great Melting Pot, where all the races of Europe are melting and re-forming! Here you stand, good folk, think I, when I see them at Ellis Island, here you stand in your fifty groups, with your fifty languages and histories, and your fifty blood hatreds and rivalries. But you won't be long like that, brothers, for these are the fires of God you've come to—these are the fires of God. A fig for your feuds and vendettas! German and Frenchman, Irishman and Englishman, Jews and Russians—into the crucible with you all! God is making the American. The real American has not yet arrived. He is only in the crucible. I tell you—he will be the fusion of all races, the common superman.

OPPORTUNITY

Edward Rowland Sill

This I beheld, or dreamed it in a dream:—
There spread a cloud of dust along a plain;
And underneath the cloud, or in it, raged
A furious battle, and men yelled, and swords
Shocked upon swords and shields. A prince's banner
Wavered, then staggered backward, hemmed by foes.
A craven hung along the battle's edge,
And thought, "Had I a sword of keener steel—
That blue blade that the king's son bears,—but this
Blunt thing—!" he snapt and flung it from his hand,
And lowering crept away and left the field.
Then came the king's son, wounded, sore bestead,
And weaponless, and saw the broken sword,
Hilt-buried in the dry and trodden sand,
And ran and snatched it, and with battle-shout
Lifted afresh he hewed his enemy down,
And saved a great cause that heroic day.

ONE WORLD

Woodrow Wilson

We are participants, whether we would or not, in the life of the world. The interests of all nations are our own also. What affects mankind is inevitably our affair, as well as the affair of the nations of Europe and Asia.

(From Speech, May 1916)

"IT IS A BEAUTEOUS EVENING"

William Wordsworth

It is a beauteous evening, calm and free,
The holy time is quiet as a Nun
Breathless with adoration; the broad sun
Is sinking down in its tranquillity;
The gentleness of heaven broods o'er the Sea:
Listen! the mighty Being is awake,
And doth with his eternal motion make
A sound like thunder—everlastingly.
Dear Child! dear Girl! that walkest with me here,
If thou appear untouched by solemn thought,
Thy nature is not therefore less divine:
Thou liest in Abraham's bosom all the year;
And worship'st at the Temple's inner shrine,
God being with thee when we know it not.

JULIET'S YEARNING

William Shakespeare

Spread thy close curtain, love-performing night,
That runaways' eyes may wink, and Romeo
Leap to these arms, untalk'd of and unseen.
Lovers can see to do their amorous rites
By their own beauties; or, if love be blind,
It best agrees with night. Come, civil night,
Thou sober-suited matron, all in black,
And learn me how to lose a winning match,

Play'd for a pair of stainless maidenhoods:
Hood my unmann'd blood bating in my cheeks
With thy black mantle, till strange love grown bold
Think true love acted simple modesty.
Come, night, come, Romeo, come, thou day in night;
For thou wilt lie upon the wings of night
Whiter than new snow on a raven's back.
Come, gentle night, come, loving, black-brow'd night,
Give me my Romeo; and, when he shall die,
Take him and cut him out in little stars,
And he will make the face of heaven so fine,
That all the world will be in love with night,
And pay no worship to the garish sun.
O, I have bought the mansion of a love,
But not possess'd it, and, though I am sold,
Not yet enjoy'd; so tedious is this day
As is the night before some festival
To an impatient child that hath new robes
And may not wear them.

(From Romeo and Juliet)

THEODORE ROOSEVELT STANDS AT ARMAGEDDON

What happens to me is not of the slightest consequence; I am to be used, as in a doubtful battle any man is used, to his hurt or not, so long as he is useful and is then cast aside and left to die. I wish you to feel this. I mean it; and I shall need no sympathy when you are through with me. . . . It would be far better to fail honorably for the cause we champion than it would be to win by foul methods the foul victory for which our opponents hope. But the victory shall be ours, and it shall be . . . clean and honest fighting for the loftiest of causes. We fight in honorable fashion for the good of mankind; unheeding of our individual fates; with unflinching hearts and undimmed eyes; we stand at Armageddon, and we battle for the Lord.

(Before the Republican National
Convention, Chicago, 1912)

* * *

In a calm sea every man is a pilot.—Anonymous

GOOD KING WENCESLAS

John Mason Neale

Good King Wenceslas looked out,
  On the Feast of Stephen,
When the snow lay round about,
  Deep, and crisp, and even:
Brightly shone the moon that night,
  Though the frost was cruel,
When a poor man came in sight,
  Gathering winter fuel.

"Hither, page, and stand by me,
  If thou know'st it, telling,
Yonder peasant, who is he?
  Where and what his dwelling?"
"Sire, he lives a good league hence,
  Underneath the mountain;
Right against the forest fence,
  By Saint Agnes' fountain."

"Bring me flesh and bring me wine,
  Bring me pine logs hither;
Thou and I will see him dine,
  When we bear them thither."
Page and monarch forth they went,
  Forth they went together;
Through the rude wind's wild lament,
  And the bitter weather.

"Sire, the night is darker now,
  And the wind blows stronger;
Fails my heart, I know not how,
  I can go no longer."
"Mark my footsteps, good my page!
  Tread thou in them boldly;
Thou shalt find the winter's rage
  Freeze thy blood less coldly."

In his master's steps he trod,
  Where the snow lay dinted;
Heat was in the very sod

Which the saint had printed.
Therefore, Christian men, be sure,
Wealth or rank possessing,
Ye who now will bless the poor,
Shall yourselves find blessing.

"THE WORLD'S GREAT AGE BEGINS ANEW"

Percy Bysshe Shelley

The world's great age begins anew,
The golden years return,
The earth doth like a snake renew
Her winter weeds outworn;
Heaven smiles, and faiths and empires gleam,
Like wrecks of a dissolving dream.

A brighter Hellas rears its mountains
From waves serener far;
A new Peneus rolls his fountains
Against the morning star.
Where fairer Tempes bloom, there sleep
Young Cyclads on a sunnier deep,

A loftier Argo cleaves the main,
Fraught with a later prize;
Another Orpheus sings again,
And loves, and weeps, and dies.
A new Ulysses leaves once more
Calypso for his native shore.

Oh, write no more the tale of Troy,
If earth Death's scroll must be!
Nor mix with Laian rage the joy
Which dawns upon the free:
Although a subtler Sphinx renew
Riddles of death Thebes never knew.

Another Athens shall arise,
And to remoter time
Bequeath, like sunset to the skies,

The splendour of its prime;
And leave, if naught so bright may live,
All earth can take or Heaven can give.

Saturn and Love their long repose
Shall burst, more bright and good
Than all who fell, than One who rose,
Than many unsubdued:
Not gold, not blood, their altar dowers,
But votive tears and symbol flowers.

Oh, cease! must hate and death return?
Cease! must men kill and die?
Cease! drain not to its dregs the urn
Of bitter prophecy.
The world is weary of the past,
Oh, might it die or rest at last!

(From Hellas)

IS EPIMENIDES A LIAR?

Epimenides the Cretan says, "All Cretans are liars." But Epimenides is himself a Cretan; therefore he is a liar himself. But if he is a liar, his statements are lies, and consequently the Cretans are veracious. But Epimenides is a Cretan, and, since they are veracious, what he says is true; and it follows after all that all the Cretans are liars.

GIVE ALL TO LOVE

Ralph Waldo Emerson

Give all to love;
Obey thy heart;
Friends, kindred, days,
Estate, good-fame,
Plans, credit and the Muse,—
Nothing refuse.

'Tis a brave master;
Let it have scope;
Follow it utterly,
Hope beyond hope;
High and more high
It dives into noon,
With wing unspent,
Untold intent;
But it is a god,
Knows its own path
And the outlets of the sky.

It was never for the mean;
It requireth courage stout.
Souls above doubt,
Valor unbending,
It will reward,—
They shall return
More than they were,
And ever ascending.

Leave all for love;
Yet, hear me, yet,
One word more thy heart behoved,
One pulse more of firm endeavor,—
Keep thee to-day,
To-morrow, forever,
Free as an Arab
Of thy beloved.

Cling with life to the maid;
But when the surprise,
First vague shadow of surmise
Flits across her bosom young,
Of a joy apart from thee,
Free be she, fancy-free;
Nor thou detain her vesture's hem,
Nor the palest rose she flung
From her summer diadem.

Though thou loved her as thyself,
As a self of purer clay,
Though her parting dims the day,

Stealing grace from all alive;
Heartily know,
When half-gods go,
The gods arrive.

the song of mehitabel

Don Marquis

this is the song of mehitabel
of mehitabel the alley cat
as i wrote you before boss
mehitabel is a believer
in the pythagorean
theory of the transmigration
of the soul and she claims
that formerly her spirit
was incarnated in the body
of cleopatra
that was a long time ago
and one must not be
surprised if mehitabel
has forgotten some of her
more regal manners

i have had my ups and downs
but wotthehell wotthehell
yesterday sceptres and crowns
fried oysters and velvet gowns
and today i herd with bums
but wotthehell wotthehell
i wake the world from sleep
as i caper and sing and leap
when i sing my wild free tune
wotthehell wotthehell
under the blear eyed moon
i am pelted with cast off shoon
but wotthehell wotthehell

do you think I would change
my present freedom to range

for a castle or moated grange
wotthehell wotthehell
cage me and i d go frantic
my life is so romantic
capricious and corybantic
and i m toujours gai toujours gai

i know that i am bound
for a journey down the sound
in the midst of a refuse mound
but wotthehell wotthehell
oh i should worry and fret
death and i will coquette
there s a dance in the dame yet
toujours gai toujours gai

i once was an innocent kit
wotthehell wotthehell
with a ribbon my neck to fit
and bells tied onto it
o wotthehell wotthehell
but a maltese cat came by
with a come hither look in his eye
and a song that soared to the sky
and wotthehell wotthehell
and i followed adown the street
the pad of his rhythmical feet
o permit me again to repeat
wotthehell wotthehell

my youth i shall never forget
but there s nothing i really regret
wotthehell wotthehell
there s a dance in the old dame yet
toujours gai toujours gai

the thing that i had not ought to
i do because i ve gotto
wotthehell wotthehell
and i end with my favorite motto
toujours gai toujours gai

DUTY

Ellen S. Hooper

I slept and dreamed that life was Beauty:
I woke and found that life was Duty:
Was my dream then a shadowy lie?
Toil on, sad heart, courageously,
And thou shalt find thy dream to be
A noonday light and truth to thee.

MY BED IS A BOAT

Robert Louis Stevenson

My bed is like a little boat;
  Nurse helps me when I embark;
She girds me in my sailor's coat
  And starts me in the dark.

At night, I go on board and say
  Good-night to all my friends on shore;
I shut my eyes and sail away
  And see and hear no more.

And sometimes things to bed I take,
  As prudent sailors have to do;
Perhaps a slice of wedding cake,
  Perhaps a toy or two.

HIAWATHA'S WOOING

Henry Wadsworth Longfellow

"As unto the bow the cord is,
So unto the man is woman;
Though she bends him, she obeys him,
Though she draws him, yet she follows;
Useless each without the other!"
  Thus the youthful Hiawatha

Said within himself and pondered,
Much perplexed by various feelings,
Listless, longing, hoping, fearing,
Dreaming still of Minnehaha,
Of the lovely Laughing Water,
In the land of the Dacotahs.
"Wed a maiden of your people,"
Warning said the old Nokomis;
"Go not eastward, go not westward,
For a stranger, whom we know not!
Like a fire upon the hearth-stone
Is a neighbor's homely daughter,
Like the starlight or the moonlight
Is the handsomest of strangers!"
Thus dissuading spake Nokomis:
And my Hiawatha answered
Only this: "Dear old Nokomis,
Very pleasant is the firelight,
But I like the starlight better,
Better do I like the moonlight!"
Gravely then said old Nokomis:
"Bring not here an idle maiden,
Bring not here a useless woman,
Hands unskilful, feet unwilling:
Bring a wife with nimble fingers,
Heart and hand that move together,
Feet that run on willing errands!"
Smiling answered Hiawatha:
"In the land of the Dacotahs
Lives the Arrow-maker's daughter,
Minnehaha, Laughing Water,
Handsomest of all the women.
I will bring her to your wigwam,
She shall run upon your errands,
Be your starlight, moonlight, firelight,
Be the sunlight of my people!"
Still dissuading said Nokomis:
"Bring not to my lodge a stranger
From the land of the Dacotahs!
Very fierce are the Dacotahs,
Often is there war between us,
There are feuds yet unforgotten,
Wounds that ache and still may open!"

Laughing answered Hiawatha:
"For that reason, if no other,
Would I wed the fair Dacotah,
That our tribes might be united,
That old feuds might be forgotten,
And old wounds be healed forever!"
Thus departed Hiawatha
To the lands of the Dacotahs,
To the land of handsome women;
Striding over moor and meadow,
Through interminable forests,
Through uninterrupted silence.
With his moccasins of magic,
At each stride a mile he measured;
Yet the way seemed long before him,
And his heart outran his footsteps;
And he journeyed without resting,
Till he heard the cataract's laughter,
Heard the Falls of Minnehaha
Calling to him through the silence,
"Pleasant is the sound!" he murmured,
"Pleasant is the voice that calls me!"
On the outskirts of the forests,
'Twixt the shadow and the sunshine,
Herds of fallow deer were feeding,
But they saw not Hiawatha;
To his bow, he whispered, "Fail not!"
To his arrow whispered, "Swerve not!"
Sent it singing on its errand,
To the red heart of the roebuck;
Threw the deer across his shoulder,
And sped forward without pausing.
At the doorway of his wigwam
Sat the ancient Arrow-maker,
In the land of the Dacotahs,
Making arrow-heads of jasper,
Arrow-heads of chalcedony.
At his side, in all her beauty,
Sat the lovely Minnehaha,
Sat his daughter, Laughing Water,
Plaiting mats of flags and rushes;
Of the past the old man's thoughts were,
And the maiden's of the future.

He was thinking, as he sat there.
Of the days when with such arrows
He had struck the deer and bison,
On the Muskoday, the meadow;
Shot the wild goose, flying southward,
On the wing, the clamorous Wawa;
Thinking of the great war-parties,
How they came to buy his arrows,
Could not fight without his arrows.
Ah, no more such noble warriors
Could be found on earth as they were!
Now the men were all like women,
Only used their tongues for weapons!
She was thinking of a hunter,
From another tribe and country,
Young and tall and very handsome,
Who one morning, in the Spring-time,
Came to buy her father's arrows,
Sat and rested in the wigwam,
Lingered long about the doorway,
Looking back as he departed.
She had heard her father praise him,
Praise his courage and his wisdom;
Would he come again for arrows
To the Falls of Minnehaha?
On the mat her hands lay idle,
And her eyes were very dreamy.
Through their thoughts they heard a footstep,
Heard a rustling in the branches,
And with glowing cheek and forehead,
With the deer upon his shoulders,
Suddenly from out the woodlands
Hiawatha stood before them.
Straight the ancient Arrow-maker
Looked up gravely from his labor,
Laid aside the unfinished arrow,
Bade him enter at the doorway,
Saying as he rose to meet him.
"Hiawatha, you are welcome!"
At the feet of Laughing Water
Hiawatha laid his burden,
Threw the red deer from his shoulders;
And the maiden looked up at him,

Looked up from her mat of rushes,
Said with gentle look and accent,
"You are welcome, Hiawatha!"
   Very spacious was the wigwam,
Made of deer-skins dressed and whitened,
With the Gods of the Dacotahs
Drawn and painted on its curtains,
And so tall the doorway, hardly
Hiawatha stooped to enter,
Hardly touched his eagle-feathers
As he entered at the doorway.
   Then uprose the Laughing Water,
From the ground fair Minnehaha,
Laid aside her mat unfinished,
Brought forth food and set before them,
Water brought them from the brooklet,
Gave them food in earthen vessels,
Gave them drink in bowls of basswood,
Listened while the guest was speaking,
Listened while her father answered,
But not once her lips she opened,
Not a single word she uttered.
   Yes, as in a dream she listened
To the words of Hiawatha,
As he talked of old Nokomis,
Who had nursed him in his childhood,
As he told of his companions,
Chibiabos, the musician,
And the very strong man, Kwasind,
And of happiness and plenty
In the land of the Ojibways,
In the pleasant land and peaceful.
   "After many years of warfare,
Many years of strife and bloodshed,
There is peace between the Ojibways
And the tribe of the Dacotahs."
Thus continued Hiawatha,
And then added, speaking slowly,
"That this peace may last forever,
And our hands be clasped more closely,
And our hearts be more united,
Give me as my wife this maiden,
Minnehaha, Laughing Water,

Loveliest of Dacotah women!"
  And the ancient Arrow-maker
Paused a moment ere he answered,
Smoked a little while in silence,
Looked at Hiawatha proudly.
Fondly looked at Laughing Water,
And made answer very gravely:
"Yes, if Minnehaha wishes;
Let your heart speak, Minnehaha!"
  And the lovely Laughing Water
Seemed more lovely as she stood there,
Neither willing nor reluctant,
As she went to Hiawatha,
Softly took the seat beside him,
While she said, and blushed to say it,
"I will follow you, my husband!"
  This was Hiawatha's wooing!
Thus it was he won the daughter
Of the ancient Arrow-maker.
In the land of the Dacotahs!
  From the wigwam he departed,
Leading with him Laughing Water;
Hand in hand they went together,
Through the woodland and the meadow,
Left the old man standing lonely
At the doorway of his wigwam,
Heard the Falls of Minnehaha
Calling to them from the distance,
Crying to them from afar off,
"Fare thee well, O Minnehaha!"
  And the ancient Arrow-maker
Turned again unto his labor,
Sat down by his sunny doorway,
Murmuring to himself, and saying:
"Thus it is our daughters leave us,
Those we love, and those who love us!
Just when they have learned to help us,
When we are old and lean upon them,
Comes a youth with flaunting feathers,
With his flute of reeds, a stranger
Wanders piping through the village,
Beckons to the fairest maiden,
And she follows where he leads her,

Leaving all things for the stranger!"
  Pleasant was the journey homeward,
Through interminable forests,
Over meadow, over mountain,
Over river, hill, and hollow.
Short it seemed to Hiawatha,
Though they journeyed very slowly,
Though his pace he checked and slackened
To the steps of Laughing Water.
  Over wide and rushing rivers
In his arms he bore the maiden;
Light he thought her as a feather,
As the plume upon his head-gear;
Cleared the tangled pathway for her.
Bent aside the swaying branches,
Made at night a lodge of branches,
And a bed with boughs of hemlock,
And a fire before the doorway
With the dry cones of the pine-tree.
  All the travelling winds went with them,
O'er the meadows, through the forest;
All the stars of night looked at them,
Watched with sleepless eyes their slumber;
From his ambush in the oak-tree
Peeped the squirrel, Adjidaumo,
Watched with eager eyes the lovers;
And the rabbit, the Wabasso,
Scampered from the path before them,
Peering, peeping from his burrow,
Sat erect upon his haunches,
Watched with curious eyes the lovers.
  Pleasant was the journey homeward!
All the birds sang loud and sweetly
Songs of happiness and heart's-ease;
Sang the bluebird, the Owaissa,
"Happy are you, Hiawatha,
Having such a wife to love you!"
Sang the robin, the Opechee,
"Happy are you, Laughing Water,
Having such a noble husband!"
  From the sky the sun benignant
Looked upon them through the branches,
Saying to them, "O my children,

Love is sunshine, hate is shadow,
Life is checkered shade and sunshine,
Rule by love, O Hiawatha!"
  From the sky the moon looked at them,
Filled the lodge with mystic splendors,
Whispered to them, "O my children,
Day is restless, night is quiet,
Man imperious, woman feeble;
Half is mine, although I follow;
Rule by patience, Laughing Water!"
  Thus it was they journeyed homeward;
Thus it was that Hiawatha
To the lodge of old Nokomis
Brought the moonlight, starlight, firelight,
Brought the sunshine of his people,
Minnehaha, Laughing Water,
Handsomest of all the women
In the land of the Dacotahs,
In the land of handsome women.

LIZZIE BORDEN

Anonymous

Lizzie Borden took an axe
And gave her mother forty whacks;
When she saw what she had done,
She gave her father forty-one.

THE FEDERAL UNION

Daniel Webster

I profess, Sir, in my career hitherto, to have kept steadily in view the prosperity and honor of the whole country, and the preservation of our Federal Union. It is to that Union we owe our safety at home, and our consideration and dignity abroad. It is to that Union that we are chiefly indebted for whatever makes us most proud of our country. That Union we reached only by the discipline of our virtues in the severe school of adversity. It had its origin in the necessities of disordered finance, prostrate commerce, and ruined credit. Under its benign influences, these great interests immediately awoke, as from the dead, and sprang forth with newness of life. Every year of its duration has teemed with fresh proofs of its utility and its blessings; and although our territory has stretched out wider and wider, and our population spread farther and farther, they have not outrun its protection or its benefits. It has been to us all a copious fountain of national, social, and personal happiness.

I have not allowed myself, Sir, to look beyond the Union, to see what might lie hidden in the dark recess behind. I have not coolly weighed the chances of preserving liberty when the bonds that unite us together shall be broken asunder. I have not accustomed myself to hang over the precipice of disunion, to see whether, with my short sight, I can fathom the depth of the abyss below; nor could I regard him as a safe counselor in the affairs of this government, whose thoughts should be mainly bent on considering not how the Union may be best preserved, but how tolerable might be the condition of the people when it should be broken up and destroyed.

While the Union lasts, we have high, exciting, gratifying prospects spread out before us, for us and our children. Beyond that I seek not to penetrate the veil. God grant that, in my day at least, that curtain may not rise! God grant that on my vision never may be opened what lies behind! When my eyes shall be turned to behold for the last time the sun in heaven, may I not see him shining on the broken and dishonored fragments of a once glorious Union; on States dissevered, discordant, belligerent; on a land rent with civil feuds, or drenched, it may be, in fraternal blood! Let their last feeble and lingering glance rather behold the gorgeous ensign of the republic, now known and honored throughout the earth, still full high advanced, its arms and trophies streaming in their original lustre, not a stripe erased or polluted, nor a single star obscured, bearing for its motto no such miserable interrogatory as "What is all this worth?" nor those other words of delusion and folly, "Liberty first and Union afterwards"; but everywhere, spread all over in characters of living light, blazing on all its ample folds, as they float over the sea and over the land, and in every wind under the whole heavens, that other sentiment, dear to every true American heart,—Liberty and Union, now and for ever, one and inseparable!

(Conclusion to the Second Reply to Hayne, Jan. 26, 1830)

TO AGE

Walter Savage Landor

Welcome, old friend! These many years
Have we lived door by door;
The Fates have laid aside their shears
Perhaps for some few more.

I was indocile at an age
When better boys were taught,
But thou at length hast made me sage,
If I am sage in aught.

Little I know from other men,
Too little they from me,
But thou hast pointed well the pen
That writes these lines to thee.

Thanks for expelling Fear and Hope,
One vile, the other vain;
One's scourge, the other's telescope,
I shall not see again:

Rather what lies before my feet
My notice shall engage—
He who hath braved Youth's dizzy heat
Dreads not the frost of Age.

JESSE JAMES

Anonymous

Jesse James was a lad that killed a-many a man;
He robbed the Danville train.
But that dirty little coward that shot Mr. Howard *
Has laid poor Jesse in his grave.

* The name under which Jesse James was living at the time Ford killed him.

Poor Jesse had a wife to mourn for his life,
Three children, they were brave;
But that dirty little coward that shot Mr. Howard
Has laid poor Jesse in his grave.

It was Robert Ford, that dirty little coward,
I wonder how he does feel,
For he ate of Jesse's bread and he slept in Jesse's bed,
Then laid poor Jesse in his grave.

Jesse was a man, a friend to the poor,
He never would see a man suffer pain;
And with his brother Frank he robbed the Chicago bank,
And stopped the Glendale train.

It was his brother Frank that robbed the Gallatin bank,
And carried the money from the town;
It was in this very place that they had a little race,
For they shot Captain Sheets to the ground.

They rallied out West for to live upon the best,
The Fletchers asked their names;
They laughed and smiled as they made their reply,
"We are Frank and Jesse James."

It was on a Wednesday night, the moon was shining bright,
They robbed the Glendale train;
The people they did say, for many miles away,
It was robbed by Frank and Jesse James.

It was on Saturday night, Jesse James was at home
Talking to his family brave,
Robert Ford came along like a thief in the night
And laid poor Jesse in his grave.

The people held their breath when they heard of Jesse's death,
And wondered how he ever came to die.
It was one of the gang called little Robert Ford,
He shot poor Jesse on the sly.

Jesse went to his rest with his hand on his breast;
The devil will be upon his knee.
He was born one day in the County of Clay
And came from a solitary race.

Jesse went down to the old man town,
Thinking he would do as he'd please;
But he will dwell in the City of Hell
And he'll go to the devil on his knees.

This song was made by Billy Gashade,
As soon as the news did arrive;
He said there was no man with the law in his hand
Who could take Jesse James when alive.

"NOW IS THE HIGH-TIDE OF THE YEAR"

James Russell Lowell

Now is the high-tide of the year,
  And whatever of life hath ebbed away
Comes flooding back with a ripply cheer,
  Into every bare inlet and creek and bay;
Now the heart is so full that a drop overfills it,
We are happy now because God wills it;
No matter how barren the past may have been,
'Tis enough for us now that the leaves are green;
We sit in the warm shade and feel right well
How the sap creeps up and the blossoms swell;
We may shut our eyes, but we cannot help knowing
That skies are clear and grass is growing;
The breeze comes whispering in our ear,
That dandelions are blossoming near,
  That maize has sprouted, that streams are flowing,
That the river is bluer than the sky,
That the robin is plastering his house hard by;
And if the breeze kept the good news back,
For other couriers we should not lack;
  We could guess it all by yon heifer's lowing,—
And hark! how clear bold chanticleer,
Warmed with the new wine of the year,
  Tells all in his lusty crowing!

Joy comes, grief goes, we know not how;
Everything is happy now,
  Everything is upward striving;

'Tis as easy now for the heart to be true
As for grass to be green or skies to be blue,—
  'Tis the natural way of living:
Who knows whither the clouds have fled?
  In the unscarred heaven they leave no wake;
And the eyes forget the tears they have shed,
  The heart forgets its sorrow and ache;
The soul partakes the season's youth,
  And the sulphurous rifts of passion and woe
Lie deep 'neath a silence pure and smooth,
  Like burnt-out craters healed with snow.

(From the Prelude to Part First,
The Vision of Sir Launfal)

THE FOUR FREEDOMS

Franklin D. Roosevelt

In the future days, which we seek to make secure, we look forward to a world founded upon four essential human freedoms.

The first is freedom of speech and expression—everywhere in the world.

The second is freedom of every person to worship God in his own way—everywhere in the world.

The third is freedom from want—which, translated into world terms, means economic understandings which will secure to every nation a healthy peacetime life for its inhabitants—everywhere in the world.

The fourth is freedom from fear—which, translated into world terms, means a world-wide reduction of armaments to such a point and in such a thorough fashion that no nation will be in a position to commit an act of physical aggression against any neighbor—anywhere in the world.

That is no vision of a distant millennium. It is a definite basis for a kind of world attainable in our own time and generation. That kind of world is the very antithesis of the so-called new order of tyranny which the dictators seek to create with the crash of a bomb.

(From the speech of January 6, 1941)

THE VAGABONDS

John Townsend Trowbridge

We are two travelers, Roger and I,
  Roger's my dog:—come here, you scamp!
Jump for the gentlemen—mind your eye!
  Over the table—look out for the lamp!—
The rogue is growing a little old;
  Five years we've tramped through wind and weather,
And slept out-doors when nights were cold,
  And ate and drank—and starved together.

We've learned what comfort is, I tell you!
  A bed on the floor, a bit of rosin,
A fire to thaw our thumbs (poor fellow!
  The paw he holds up there's been frozen),
Plenty of catgut for my fiddle
  (This out-door business is bad for the strings),
Then a few nice buckwheats hot from the griddle,
  And Roger and I set up for kings!

No, thank ye, sir,—I never drink;
  Roger and I are exceedingly moral—
Aren't we, Roger?—see him wink!—
  Well, something hot, then—we won't quarrel.
He's thirsty too—see him nod his head?
  What a pity, sir, that dogs can't talk!
He understands every word that's said—
  And he knows good milk from water-and-chalk.

The truth is, sir, now I reflect,
  I've been so sadly given to grog,
I wonder I've not lost the respect
  (Here's to you, sir!) even of my dog.
But he sticks by through thick and thin;
  And this old coat, with its empty pockets,
And rags that smell of tobacco and gin,
  He'll follow while he has eyes in his sockets.

There isn't another creature living
  Would do it, and prove, through every disaster,
So fond, so faithful, and so forgiving

To such a miserable, thankless master!
No, sir!—see him wag his tail and grin!
By George! it makes my old eyes water—
That is, there's something in this gin
That chokes a fellow. But no matter!

We'll have some music, if you're willing,
And Roger (hem! what a plague a cough is, sir!)
Shall march a little. Start, you villain!
Stand straight! 'Bout face! Salute your officer!
Put up that paw! Dress! Take your rifle!
(Some dogs have arms, you see!) Now hold your
Cap while the gentlemen give a trifle,
To aid a poor old patriot soldier!

March! Halt! Now show how the rebel shakes
When he stands up to hear his sentence.
Now tell us how many drams it takes
To honor a jolly new acquaintance.
Five yelps—that's five; he's mighty knowing!
The night's before us, fill the glasses!—
Quick, sir! I'm ill—my brain is going!
Some brandy—thank you—there!—it passes!

Why not reform? That's easily said,
But I've gone through such wretched treatment,
Sometimes forgetting the taste of bread,
And scarce remembering what meat meant,
That my poor stomach's past reform;
And there are times when, mad with thinking,
I'd sell out heaven for something warm
To prop a horrible inward sinking.

Is there a way to forget to think?
At your age, sir, home, fortune, friends,
A dear girl's love—but I took to drink—
The same old story; you know how it ends.
If you could have seen these classic features—
You needn't laugh, sir; they were not then
Such a burning libel on God's creatures;
I was one of your handsome men!

If you had seen her, so fair and young,
  Whose head was happy on this breast!
If you could have heard the songs I sung
  When the wine went round, you wouldn't have guessed
That ever I, sir, should be straying
  From door to door, with fiddle and dog
Ragged and penniless, and playing
  To you to-night for a glass of grog!

She's married since—a parson's wife;
  'Twas better for her that we should part—
Better the soberest, prosiest life
  Than a blasted home and a broken heart.
I have seen her? Once: I was weak and spent
  On the dusty road, a carriage stopped;
But little she dreamed, as on she went,
  Who kissed the coin that her fingers dropped!

You've set me talking, sir; I'm sorry;
  It makes me wild to think of the change!
What do you care for a beggar's story?
  Is it amusing? you find it strange?
I had a mother so proud of me!
  'Twas well she died before— Do you know
If the happy spirits in heaven can see
  The ruin and wretchedness here below?

Another glass, and strong, to deaden
  This pain; then Roger and I will start.
I wonder, has he such a lumpish, leaden,
  Aching thing in place of a heart?
He is sad sometimes, and would weep if he could,
  No doubt, remembering things that were—
A virtuous kennel, with plenty of food,
  And himself a sober, respectable cur.

I'm better now; that glass was warming.
  You rascal! limber your lazy feet!
We must be fiddling and performing
  For supper and bed, or starve in the street.
Not a very gay life to lead, you think?
  But soon we shall go where lodgings are free,
And the sleepers need neither victuals nor drink—
  The sooner the better for Roger and me!

MONEY

Richard Armour

Workers earn it,
Spendthrifts burn it,
Bankers lend it,
Women spend it,
Forgers fake it,
Taxes take it,
Dying leave it,
Heirs receive it,
Thrifty save it,
Misers crave it,
Robbers seize it,
Rich increase it,
Gamblers lose it . . .
I could use it.

THE MAD HATTER'S TEA-PARTY

Lewis Carroll

There was a table set out under a tree in front of the house, and the March Hare and the Hatter were having tea at it: a Dormouse was sitting between them, fast asleep, and the other two were using it as a cushion, resting their elbows on it, and talking over its head. 'Very uncomfortable for the Dormouse,' thought Alice; 'only as it's asleep, I suppose it doesn't mind.'

The table was a large one, but the three were all crowded together at one corner of it. 'No room! No room!' they cried out when they saw Alice coming. 'There's *plenty* of room!' said Alice indignantly, and she sat down in a large arm-chair at one end of the table.

'Have some wine,' the March Hare said in an encouraging tone.

Alice looked all round the table, but there was nothing on it but tea. 'I don't see any wine,' she remarked.

'There isn't any,' said the March Hare.

'Then it wasn't very civil of you to offer it,' said Alice angrily.

'It wasn't very civil of you to sit down without being invited,' said the March Hare.

'I didn't know it was *your* table,' said Alice; 'it's laid for a great many more than three.'

'Your hair wants cutting,' said the Hatter. He had been looking at Alice for some time with great curiosity, and this was his first speech.

'You shouldn't make personal remarks,' Alice said with some severity; 'it's very rude.'

The Hatter opened his eyes very wide on hearing this; but all he *said* was: 'Why is a raven like a writing-desk?'

'Come, we shall have some fun now!' thought Alice. 'I'm glad they've begun asking riddles.—I believe I can guess that,' she added aloud.

'Do you mean that you think you can find out the answer to it?' said the March Hare.

'Exactly so,' said Alice.

'Then you should say what you mean,' the March Hare went on.

'I do,' Alice hastily replied; 'at least—at least I mean what I say—that's the same thing, you know.'

'Not the same thing a bit!' said the Hatter. 'You might just as well say that "I see what I eat" is the same thing as "I eat what I see"!'

'You might just as well say,' added the March Hare, 'that "I like what I get" is the same thing as "I get what I like"!'

'You might just as well say,' added the Dormouse, which seemed to be talking in its sleep, 'that "I breathe when I sleep" is the same thing as "I sleep when I breathe"!'

'It *is* the same thing with you,' said the Hatter, and here the conversation dropped, and the party sat silent for a minute, while Alice thought over all she could remember about ravens and writing-desks, which wasn't much.

The Hatter was the first to break the silence. 'What day of the month is it?' he said, turning to Alice: he had taken his watch out of his pocket, and was looking at it uneasily, shaking it every now and then, and holding it to his ear.

Alice considered a little, and then said: 'The fourth.'

'Two days wrong!' sighed the Hatter, 'I told you butter wouldn't suit the works!' he added, looking angrily at the March Hare.

'It was the *best* butter,' the March Hare meekly replied.

'Yes, but some crumbs must have got in as well,' the Hatter grumbled: 'you shouldn't have put it in with the bread-knife.'

The March Hare took the watch and looked at it gloomily: then he dipped it into his cup of tea, and looked at it again: but he could think of nothing better to say than his first remark: 'It was the *best* butter, you know.'

Alice had been looking over his shoulder with some curiosity.

'What a funny watch!' she remarked. 'It tells the day of the month, and doesn't tell what o'clock it is!'

'Why should it?' muttered the Hatter. 'Does *your* watch tell you what year it is?'

'Of course not,' Alice replied very readily: 'but that's because it stays the same year for such a long time together.'

'Which is just the case with *mine,*' said the Hatter.

Alice felt dreadfully puzzled. The Hatter's remark seemed to her to have no sort of meaning in it, and yet it was certainly English. 'I don't quite understand you,' she said, as politely as she could.

'The Dormouse is asleep again,' said the Hatter, and he poured a little hot tea upon its nose.

The Dormouse shook its head impatiently, and said, without opening its eyes: 'Of course, of course; just what I was going to remark myself.'

'Have you guessed the riddle yet?' the Hatter said, turning to Alice again.

'No, I give it up,' Alice replied: 'what's the answer?'

'I haven't the slightest idea,' said the Hatter.

'Nor I,' said the March Hare.

Alice sighed wearily. 'I think you might do something better with the time,' she said, 'than waste it in asking riddles with no answers.'

'If you knew Time as well as I do,' said the Hatter, 'you wouldn't talk about wasting *it*. It's *him*.'

'I don't know what you mean,' said Alice.

'Of course you don't!' the Hatter said, tossing his head contemptuously. 'I dare say you never even spoke to Time!'

'Perhaps not,' Alice cautiously replied: 'but I know I have to beat time when I learn music.'

'Ah! that accounts for it,' said the Hatter. 'He won't stand beating. Now, if you only kept on good terms with him, he'd do almost anything you liked with the clock. For instance, suppose it were nine o'clock in the morning, just time to begin lessons: you'd only have to whisper a hint to Time, and round goes the clock in a twinkling! Half-past one, time for dinner!'

('I only wish it was,' the March Hare said to itself in a whisper.)

'That would be grand, certainly,' said Alice thoughtfully: 'but then—I shouldn't be hungry for it, you know.'

'Not at first, perhaps,' said the Hatter: 'but you could keep it to half-past one as long as you liked.'

'Is that the way *you* manage?' Alice asked.

The Hatter shook his head mournfully. 'Not I!' he replied. 'We quarrelled last March—just before *he* went mad, you know—' (pointing with his teaspoon at the March Hare) '—it was at the great concert given by the Queen of Hearts, and I had to sing

Twinkle, twinkle, little bat!
How I wonder what you're at!

You know the song, perhaps?'

'I've heard something like it,' said Alice.

'It goes on, you know,' the Hatter continued, 'in this way:

Up above the world you fly,
Like a tea-tray in the sky.
Twinkle, twinkle—'

Here the Dormouse shook itself, and began singing in its sleep: 'Twinkle, twinkle, twinkle, twinkle—' and went on so long that they had to pinch it to make it stop.

'Well, I'd hardly finished the first verse,' said the Hatter, 'when the Queen jumped up and bawled out: "He's murdering the time! Off with his head!" '

'How dreadfully savage!' exclaimed Alice.

'And ever since that,' the Hatter went on in a mournful tone, 'he won't do a think I ask! It's always six o'clock now.'

A bright idea came into Alice's head. 'Is that the reason so many tea-things are put out here?' she asked.

'Yes, that's it,' said the Hatter with a sigh: 'it's always tea-time, and we've no time to wash the things between whiles.'

'Then you keep moving round, I suppose?' said Alice.

'Exactly so,' said the Hatter: 'as the things get used up.'

'But what happens when you come to the beginning again?' Alice ventured to ask.

'Suppose we change the subject,' the March Hare interrupted, yawning. 'I'm getting tired of this. I vote the young lady tells us a story.'

'I'm afraid I don't know one,' said Alice, rather alarmed at the proposal.

'Then the Dormouse shall!' they both cried. 'Wake up, Dormouse!' And they pinched it on both sides at once.

The Dormouse slowly opened its eyes. 'I wasn't asleep,' it said in a hoarse, feeble voice: 'I heard every word you fellows were saying.'

'Tell us a story!' said the March Hare.

'Yes, please do!' pleaded Alice.

'And be quick about it,' added the Hatter, 'or you'll be asleep again before it's done.'

'Once upon a time there were three little sisters,' the Dormouse began in a great hurry; 'and their names were Elsie, Lacie, and Tillie; and they lived at the bottom of a well—'

'What did they live on?' said Alice, who always took a great interest in questions of eating and drinking.

'They lived on treacle,' said the Dormouse, after thinking a minute or two.

'They couldn't have done that, you know,' Alice gently remarked; 'they'd have been ill.'

'So they were,' said the Dormouse: '*very* ill.'

Alice tried to fancy to herself what such an extraordinary way of living would be like, but it puzzled her too much, so she went on: 'But why did they live at the bottom of a well?'

'Take some more tea,' the March Hare said to Alice, very earnestly.

'I've had nothing yet,' Alice replied in an offended tone, 'so I can't take more.'

'You mean you can't take *less,*' said the Hatter: 'it's very easy to take *more* than nothing.'

'Nobody asked *your* opinion,' said Alice.

'Who's making personal remarks now?' the Hatter asked triumphantly.

Alice did not quite know what to say to this: so she helped herself to some tea and bread-and-butter, and then turned to the Dormouse, and repeated her question: 'Why did they live at the bottom of a well?'

The Dormouse again took a minute or two to think about it, and then said: 'It was a treacle-well.'

'There's no such thing!' Alice was beginning very angrily, but the Hatter and the March Hare went 'Sh! sh!' and the Dormouse sulkily remarked: 'If you can't be civil, you'd better finish the story for yourself.'

'No, please go on!' Alice said. 'I won't interrupt again. I dare say there may be *one.*'

'One, indeed!' said the Dormouse indignantly. However, it consented to go on. 'And so, these three little sisters—they were learning to draw, you know—'

'What did they draw?' said Alice, quite forgetting her promise.

'Treacle,' said the Dormouse, without considering at all this time.

'I want a clean cup,' interrupted the Hatter: 'let's all move one place on.'

He moved on as he spoke, and the Dormouse followed him: the March Hare moved into the Dormouse's place, and Alice rather unwillingly took the place of the March Hare. The Hatter was the only one who got any advantage from the change: and Alice was a good deal worse off, as the March Hare had just upset the milk-jug into his plate.

Alice did not wish to offend the Dormouse again, so she began very cautiously: 'But I don't understand. Where did they draw the treacle from?'

'You can draw water out of a water-well,' said the Hatter; 'so I should think you could draw treacle out of a treacle-well—eh, stupid?'

'But they were *in* the well,' Alice said to the Dormouse, not choosing to notice this last remark.

'Of course they were,' said the Dormouse; '—well in.'

This answer so confused poor Alice that she let the Dormouse go on for some time without interrupting it.

'They were learning to draw,' the Dormouse went on, yawning and rubbing its eyes, for it was getting very sleepy: 'and they drew all manner of things—everything that begins with an M—'

'Why with an M?' said Alice.

'Why not?' said the March Hare.

Alice was silent.

The Dormouse had closed its eyes by this time, and was going off into a doze; but, on being pinched by the Hatter, it woke up again with a little shriek, and went on: '—that begins with an M, such as mouse-traps, and the moon, and memory, and muchness—you know you say things are "much of a muchness"—did you ever see such a thing as a drawing of a muchness?'

'Really, now you ask me,' said Alice, very much confused, 'I don't think—'

'Then you shouldn't talk,' said the Hatter.

This piece of rudeness was more than Alice could bear: she got up in great disgust, and walked off; the Dormouse fell asleep instantly, and neither of the others took the least notice of her going, though she looked back once or twice, half hoping that they would call after her: the last time she saw them, they were trying to put the Dormouse into the teapot.

'At any rate I'll never go *there* again!' said Alice as she picked her way through the wood. 'It's the stupidest tea-party I ever was at in all my life!'

(From Alice's Adventures in Wonderland)

THE WIDOW MALONE

Charles Lever

Did you hear of the Widow Malone
O hone!
Who lived in the town of Athlone
Alone?
O, she melted the hearts
Of the swain in them parts;
So lovely the widow Malone,
O hone!
So lovely the Widow Malone.

Of lovers she had a full score
Or more;
And fortunes they all had galore
In store;
From the minister down
To the clerk of the Crown,
All were courting the Widow Malone
O hone!
All were courting the Widow Malone.

But so modest was Mrs. Malone
'Twas known,
That no one could see her alone,
O hone!
Let them ogle and sigh,
They could ne'er catch her eye;
So bashful the Widow Malone,
O hone!
So bashful the Widow Malone.

Till one Mister O'Brien from Clare,
How quare!

'Tis little for blushing they care
Down there;
Put his arm round her waist,
Gave ten kisses at laste,
And says he, "You're my Molly Malone,
My own."
Says he, "You're my Molly Malone."

And the widow they all thought so shy—
My eye!
Never thought of a simper or sigh;
For why?
"O Lucius," said she,
"Since you've now made so free,
You may marry your Mary Malone,
Your own;
You may marry your Mary Malone."

There's a moral contained in my song,
Not wrong;
And one comfort it's not very long,
But strong:—
If for widows you die,
Learn to kiss—not to sigh,
For they're all like sweet Mistress Malone!
O hone!
O they're all like sweet Mistress Malone!

ISRAFEL

Edgar Allan Poe

And the angel Israfel, whose heart-strings are a lute, and who has the sweetest voice of all of God's creatures.—*Koran*

In Heaven a spirit doth dwell
"Whose heart-strings are a lute";
None sing so wildly well
As the angel Israfel,
And the giddy Stars (so legends tell)
Ceasing their hymns, attend the spell
Of his voice, all mute.

Tottering above
   In her highest noon,
   The enamored Moon
Blushes with love,
   While, to listen, the red levin
   (With the rapid Pleiads, even,
   Which were seven),
   Pauses in Heaven.

And they say (the starry choir
   And the other listening things)
That Israfeli's fire
Is owing to that pyre
   By which he sits and sings—
The trembling living wire
   Of those unusual strings.

But the skies that angels trod,
   Where deep thoughts are a duty—
Where Love's a grown-up God—
   Where the Houri glances are
Imbued with all the beauty
   Which we worship in a star.

Therefore, thou art not wrong,
   Israfeli, who despisest
An unimpassioned song;
To thee the laurels belong,
   Best bard, because the wisest:
Merrily live and long!

The ecstasies above
   With thy burning measures suit—
Thy grief, thy joy, thy hate, thy love,
   With the fervor of thy lute—
   Well may the stars be mute!

Yes, Heaven is thine; but this
   Is a world of sweets and sours;
   Our flowers are merely—flowers,
And the shadow of thy perfect bliss
   Is the sunshine of ours.

If I could dwell
Where Israfel
  Hath dwelt, and he where I,
He might not sing so wildly well
  A mortal melody,
While a bolder note than this might swell
  From my lyre within the sky.

From ALUMNUS FOOTBALL

Grantland Rice

You'll find the road is long and rough, with soft spots far apart,
Where only those can make the grade who have the Uphill Heart,
And when they stop you with a thud or jolt you with a crack,
Let Courage call the signals as you keep on coming back.
Keep coming back, and though the world may romp across your spine,
Let every game's end find you still upon the battling line:
For when the One Great Scorer comes to mark against your name,
He writes—not that you won or lost—but how you played the game.

TURKEY IN THE STRAW

Anonymous

As I was a-gwine down the road,
Tired team and a heavy load,
Crack my whip and the leader sprung;
I says day—day to the wagon tongue.
  Turkey in the straw, turkey in the hay,
  Roll 'em up and twist 'em up a high tuckahaw,
  And hit 'em up a tune called Turkey in the Straw.

Went out to milk and I didn't know how,
I milked the goat instead of the cow.
A monkey sittin' on a pile of straw
A-winkin' at his mother-in-law.
  Turkey in the straw, *etc.*

Met Mr. Catfish comin' down the stream,
Says Mr. Catfish, "What does you mean?"
Caught Mr. Catfish by the snout
And turned Mr. Catfish wrong side out.
Turkey in the straw, *etc.*

Came to the river and I couldn't get across
Paid five dollars for an old blind hoss
Wouldn't go ahead, nor he wouldn't stand still
So he went up and down like an old saw mill.
Turkey in the straw, *etc.*

As I came down the new cut road
Met Mr. Bullfrog, met Miss Toad,
And every time Miss Toad would sing
Ole Bullfrog cut a pigeon wing.
Turkey in the straw, *etc.*

O I jumped in the seat, and I gave a little yell,
The horses run away, broke the wagon all to hell;
Sugar in the gourd and honey in the horn,
I never was so happy since the hour I was born.
Turkey in the straw, *etc.*

THE NEW TESTAMENT

Thomas Russell

Matthew and Mark, and Luke and John,
The Holy Gospels wrote,
Describing how the Saviour died—
His life—and all He taught;
Acts prove how God the Apostles owned
With signs in every place;
St. Paul, in Romans, teaches us
How man is saved by grace;
The Apostle, in Corinthians,
Instructs, exhorts, reproves;
Galatians shows that faith in Christ
Alone the Father loves.
Ephesians and Philippians tell

What Christians ought to be;
Colossians bids us live to God
And for eternity.
In Thessalonians we are taught
The Lord will come from Heaven;
In Timothy and Titus
A bishop's rule is given.
Philemon marks a Christian's love,
Which only Christians know;
Hebrews reveals the Gospel
Prefigured by the law;
James teaches without holiness
Faith is but vain and dead;
St. Peter points the narrow way
In which the saints are led;
John, in his three Epistles,
On love delights to dwell;
St. Jude gives awful warning
Of judgment, wrath, and hell;
The Revelation prophesies
Of that tremendous day
When Christ, and Christ alone, shall be
The trembling sinner's stay.

HAIL COLUMBIA

Joseph Hopkinson

Hail, Columbia! happy land!
Hail, ye heroes! heaven-born band!
Who fought and bled in freedom's cause,
Who fought and bled in freedom's cause,
And when the storm of war was gone,
Enjoyed the peace your valor won.
Let independence be our boast,
Ever mindful what it cost;
Ever grateful for the prize,
Let its altar reach the skies.

Cho.: Firm, united, let us be,
Rallying round our liberty;
As a band of brothers joined,
Peace and safety we shall find.

Immortal patriots! rise once more:
Defend your rights, defend your shore:
  Let no rude foe, with impious hand,
  Let no rude foe, with impious hand,
Invade the shrine where sacred lies
Of toil and blood the well-earned prize.
  While offering peace sincere and just,
  In Heaven we place a manly trust,
  That truth and justice will prevail,
  And every scheme of bondage fail.

Sound, sound the trumpet of fame!
Let Washington's great name
  Ring through the world with loud applause;
  Ring through the world with loud applause;
Let every clime to freedom dear,
Listen with joyful ear.
  With equal skill, and godlike power,
  He governed in the fearful hour
  Of horrid war; or guides, with ease,
  The happier times of honest peace.

Behold the chief who now commands,
Once more to serve his country, stands—
  The rock on which the storm will beat,
  The rock on which the storm will beat;
But, armed in virtue firm and true,
His hopes are fixed on Heaven and you.
  When hope was sinking in dismay,
  And glooms obscured Columbia's day,
  His steady mind, from changes free,
  Resolved on death or liberty.

THE ASS AND THE LAP-DOG

Aesop
(Translator: Thomas James)

There was an Ass and a Lap-dog that belonged to the same master. The Ass was tied up in the stable, and had plenty of corn and hay to eat, and was as well off as Ass could be. The little Dog was always sporting and gamboling about, caressing and fawning upon his master in a thousand amusing ways, so that he became a great favorite, and was permitted to lie in his master's lap. The Ass, indeed, had enough to do; he was drawing wood all day, and had to take his turn at the mill at night. But while he grieved over his own lot, it galled him more to see the Lap-dog living in such ease and luxury; so thinking that if he acted a like part to his master, he should fare the same, he broke one day from his halter, and rushing into the hall began to kick and prance about in the strangest fashion; then swishing his tail and mimicking the frolics of the favorite, he upset the table where his master was at dinner, breaking it in two and smashing all the crockery; nor would he leave off till he jumped upon his master, and pawed him with his rough-shod feet. The servants, seeing their master in no little danger, thought it was now high time to interfere, and having released him from the Ass's caresses, they so belabored the silly creature with sticks and staves, that he never got up again; and as he breathed his last, exclaimed: "Why could not I have been satisfied with my natural position, without attempting, by tricks and grimaces, to imitate one who was but a puppy after all!"

RICHARD II'S DEJECTION

William Shakespeare

Let's talk of graves, of worms and epitaphs;
Make dust our paper and with rainy eyes
Write sorrow on the bosom of the earth.
Let's choose executors and talk of wills:
And yet not so, for what can we bequeath
Save our deposed bodies to the ground?
Our lands, our lives and all are Bolingbroke's,
And nothing can we call our own but death,
And that small model of the barren earth
Which serves as paste and cover to our bones.
For God's sake, let us sit upon the ground
And tell sad stories of the death of kings:
How some have been deposed; some slain in war;
Some haunted by the ghosts they have deposed;
Some poison'd by their wives; some sleeping kill'd;
All murder'd: for within the hollow crown

That rounds the mortal temples of a king
Keeps Death his court, and there the antic sits,
Scoffing his state and grinning at his pomp,
Allowing him a breath, a little scene,
To monarchize, be fear'd and kill with looks,
Infusing him with self and vain conceit,
As if this flesh which walls about our life
Were brass impregnable, and humour'd thus
Comes at the last and with a little pin
Bores through his castle wall, and farewell king!
Cover your heads and mock not flesh and blood
With solemn reverence: throw away respect,
Tradition, form and ceremonious duty,
For you have but mistook me all this while:
I live with bread like you, feel want,
Taste grief, need friends: subjected thus,
How can you say to me, I am a king?

(From King Richard II)

THE KING'S RING

Theodore Tilton

Once in Persia reigned a king,
Who upon his signet ring
Graved a maxim true and wise,
Which, if held before his eyes,
Gave him counsel, at a glance,
Fit for every change or chance:
Solemn words, and these are they:
"Even this shall pass away!"

Trains of camels through the sand
Brought him gems from Samarcand;
Fleets of galleys through the seas
Brought him pearls to rival these.
But he counted little gain
Treasures of the mine or main.
"What is wealth?" the king would say;
"Even this shall pass away."

In the revels of his court,
At the zenith of his sport,
When the palms of all his guests
Burned with clapping at his jests,
He, amid his figs and wine,
Cried, "O loving friends of mine!
Pleasure comes, but does not stay;
'Even this shall pass away.' "

Lady fairest ever seen
Was the bride he crowned his queen.
Pillowed on the marriage-bed,
Whispering to his soul, he said,
"Though a bridegroom never pressed
Dearer bosom to his breast,
Mortal flesh must come to clay:
'Even this shall pass away.' "

Fighting on a furious field,
Once a javelin pierced his shield.
Soldiers with a loud lament
Bore him bleeding to his tent.
Groaning from his tortured side,
"Pain is hard to bear," he cried,
"But with patience day by day,
'Even this shall pass away.' "

Towering in the public square
Twenty cubits in the air,
Rose his statue carved in stone,
Then the king, disguised, unknown,
Gazing at his sculptured name,
Asked himself, "And what is fame?
Fame is but a slow decay:
'Even this shall pass away.' "

Struck with palsy, sere and old,
Waiting at the Gates of Gold,
Spake he with his dying breath,
"Life is done, but what is Death?"
Then, in answer to the king,
Fell a sunbeam on his ring,
Showing by a heavenly ray—
"Even this shall pass away."

THE IRON CURTAIN

Winston S. Churchill

From Stettin to the Baltic to Trieste in the Adriatic, an iron curtain has descended across the Continent. Behind that line lie all the capitals of the ancient states of central and eastern Europe. Warsaw, Berlin, Prague, Vienna, Budapest, Belgrade, Bucharest and Sofia, all of these famous cities and the populations around them lie in what I might call the Soviet Sphere, and all are subject, in one form or another, not only to Soviet influence but to very high and in some cases increasing measure of control from Moscow.

Police governments are pervading from Moscow. But Athens alone, with its immortal glories, is free to decide its future at an election under British, American and French observation. . . .

This is certainly not the liberated Europe we fought to build up. Nor is it one which contains the essentials of permanent peace.

The safety of the world requires a unity in Europe from which no nation should be permanently outcast.

(From the address at Fulton, Mo., March 5, 1946)

TO A MOUSE, ON TURNING HER UP IN HER NEST WITH THE PLOUGH, NOVEMBER, 1785

Robert Burns

Wee, sleekit, cow'rin, tim'rous beastie,
O, what a panic's in thy breastie!
Thou need na start awa sae hasty,
        Wi' bickering brattle!
I wad be laith to rin an' chase thee,
        Wi' murd'ring pattle!

I'm truly sorry man's dominion
Has broken Nature's social union,
An' justifies that ill opinion,
        Which makes thee startle,
At me, thy poor, earth-born companion
        An' fellow-mortal!

I doubt na, whiles, but thou may thieve;
What then? poor beastie, thou maun live!
A daimen-icker in a thrave
'S a sma' request;
I'll get a blessin wi' the lave,
And never miss't!

Thy wee housie, too, in ruin!
Its silly wa's the win's are strewin!
An' naething, now, to big a new ane,
O' foggage green!
An' bleak December's winds ensuin,
Baith snell an' keen!

Thou saw the fields laid bare and waste,
An' weary winter comin fast,
An' cozie here, beneath the blast,
Thou thought to dwell,
Till crash! the cruel coulter past,
Out thro' thy cell.

That wee bit heap o' leaves an' stibble,
Has cost thee mony a weary nibble!
Now thou's turn'd out, for a' thy trouble,
But house or hald,
To thole the winter's sleety dribble,
An' cranreuch cauld!

But, Mousie, thou art no thy lane,
In proving foresight may be vain:
The best laid schemes o' mice an' men
Gang aft a-gley,
An' lea'e us naught but grief an' pain,
For promis'd joy.

Still thou art blest, compar'd wi' me!
The present only toucheth thee:
But, Och! I backward cast my e'e
On prospects drear!
An' forward, tho' I canna see,
I guess an' fear!

SWEET IS CHILDHOOD

Jean Ingelow

Sweet is childhood—childhood's over,
Kiss and part.
Sweet is youth; but youth's a river—
So's my heart.
Sweet is rest; but by all showing
Toil is nigh.
We must go. Alas! the going,
Say "good-bye."

LINDBERGH FLIES ALONE

Harold MacDonald Anderson

Alone?

Is he alone at whose right side rides Courage, with Skill within the cockpit and Faith upon the left? Does solitude surround the brave when Adventure leads the way and Ambition reads the dials? Is there no company with him, for whom the air is cleft by Daring and the darkness made light by Emprise?

True, the fragile bodies of his fellows do not weigh down his plane; true, the fretful minds of weaker men are lacking from his crowded cabin; but as his airship keeps her course he holds communion with those rare spirits that inspire to intrepidity and by their sustaining potency give strength to arm, resource to mind, content to soul.

Alone? With what other companions would man fly to whom the choice were given?

(Editorial in the New York Sun, 1927)

DOVER BEACH

Matthew Arnold

The sea is calm to-night.
The tide is full, the moon lies fair
Upon the straits;—on the French coast the light

Gleams and is gone; the cliffs of England stand,
Glimmering and vast, out in the tranquil bay.
Come to the window, sweet is the night-air!
Only, from the long line of spray
Where the sea meets the moon-blanch'd land,
Listen! you hear the grating roar
Of pebbles which the waves draw back, and fling,
At their return, up the high strand,
Begin, and cease, and then again begin,
With tremulous cadence slow, and bring
The eternal note of sadness in.

Sophocles long ago
Heard it on the Aegean, and it brought
Into his mind the turbid ebb and flow
Of human misery; we
Find also in the sound a thought,
Hearing it by this distant northern sea.

The Sea of Faith
Was once, too, at the full, and round earth's shore
Lay like the folds of a bright girdle furl'd.
But now I only hear
Its melancholy, long, withdrawing roar,
Retreating, to the breath
Of the night-wind, down the vast edges drear
And naked shingles of the world.

Ah, love, let us be true
To one another! for the world, which seems
To lie before us like a land of dreams,
So various, so beautiful, so new,
Hath really neither joy, nor love, nor light,
Nor certitude, nor peace, nor help for pain;
And we are here as on a darkling plain
Swept with confused alarms of struggle and flight,
Where ignorant armies clash by night.

* * *

A Philosopher is a fool who torments himself while he is alive, to be talked of after he is dead.—Jean D'Alembert

POETICAL ECONOMY

Harry Graham

What hours I spent of precious time,
  What pints of ink I used to waste,
Attempting to secure a rhyme
  To suit the public taste,
Until I found a simple plan
  Which makes the lamest lyric scan!

When I've a syllable *de trop,*
  I cut it off, without apol.:
This verbal sacrifice, I know,
  May irritate the schol.;
But all may praise my dev'lish cunn.
  Who realize that Time is Mon.

My sense remains as clear as cryst.,
  My style as pure as any Duch.
Who does not boast a bar sinist.
  Upon her fam. escutch.;
And I can treat with scornful pit.
  The sneers of ev'ry captious crit.

We gladly publish to the pop.
  A scheme of which I make no myst.;
And beg my fellow scribes to cop.
  This labor-saving syst.
I offer it to the consid.
  Of ev'ry thoughtful individ.

The author, working like a beav.,
  His readers' pleasure could redoub.
Did he but now and then abbrev.
  The work he gives his pub.
(This view I most partic. suggest
  To A. C. Bens. and G. K. Chest.)

If Mr. Caine rewrote *The Scape.,*
  And Miss Corell. condensed Barabb.,
What could they save in foolscap pape.
  Did they but cult. the hab.
Which teaches people to suppress
  All syllables that are unnec.!

If playwrights would but thus dimin.
  The length of time each drama takes,
(*The Second Mrs. Tanq.* by Pin.
  Or even *Ham.* by Shakes.),
We could maintain a watchful att.
  When at a mat. on Wed. or Sat.

Have done, ye bards, with dull monot.!
  Foll. my examp., O Stephen Phill.,
O Owen Seam., O William Wat.,
  O Ella Wheeler Wil.,
And share with me the grave respons.
  Of writing this amazing nons.!

RIENZI TO THE ROMANS

Mary R. Mitford

Friends!
I came not here to talk. Ye know too well
The story of our thraldom. We are slaves!
The bright sun rises to his course, and lights
A race of slaves! he sets, and his last beam
Falls on a slave! Not such as, swept along
By the full tide of power, the conqueror leads
To crimson glory and undying fame,
But base, ignoble slaves!—slaves to a horde
Of petty tyrants, feudal despots; lords
Rich in some dozen paltry villages,
Strong in some hundred spearmen, only great
In that strange spell,—a name! Each hour, dark fraud,
Or open rapine, or protected murder,
Cries out against them. But this very day
An honest man, my neighbor,—there he stands—
Was struck—struck like a dog—by one who wore
The badge of Ursini! because, forsooth,
He tossed not high his ready cap in air,
Nor lifted up his voice in servile shouts,
At sight of that great ruffian! Be we men,
And suffer such dishonor? men, and wash not
The stain away in blood? such shames are common.

I have known deeper wrongs. I, that speak to ye—
I had a brother once, a gracious boy,
Full of gentleness, of calmest hope,
Of sweet and quiet joy; there was the look
Of Heaven upon his face which limners give
To the beloved disciple. How I loved
That gracious boy! younger by fifteen years,
Brother at once and son! He left my side,—
A summer bloom on his fair cheeks, a smile
Parting his innocent lips. In one short hour
The pretty, harmless boy was slain! I saw
The corse, the mangled corse, and then I cried
For vengeance! Rouse ye, Romans! Rouse ye, slaves!
Have ye brave sons?—Look in the next fierce brawl
To see them die! Have ye fair daughters?—Look
To see them live, torn from your arms, distained,
Dishonored; and, if ye dare call for justice,
Be answered by the lash! Yet this is Rome,
That sate on her seven hills, and from her throne
Of beauty ruled the world! Yet we are Romans!
Why, in that elder day, to be a Roman
Was greater than a king! And once again—
Hear me, ye walls, that echoed to the tread
Of either Brutus!—once again, I swear,
The eternal city shall be free! her sons shall walk with princes.

PLATONIC LOVE

From *Plato's "The Symposium"*

Translator: Benjamin Jowett

"When a man loves the beautiful, what does he love?" I answered her, "That the beautiful may be his." "Still," she said, "the answer suggests a further question, which is this: What is given by the possession of beauty?" "That," I replied, "is a question to which I have no answer ready." "Then," she said, "let me put the word 'good' in the place of the beautiful, and repeat the question: What does he who loves the good desire?" "The possession of the good," I said. "What does he gain who possesses the good?" "Happiness," I replied; "there is no difficulty in answering that." "Yes," she said, "the happy are made happy by the acquisition of good things. Nor is there any need to ask why a man desires happiness; the answer is already final." "That is true," I said. "And is this wish and this desire common to all? and do all men always desire their own good, or only some men?—what think you?" "All men," I replied; "the desire is common to all." "But all men, Socrates," she rejoined, "are not said to love, but only some of them; and you say that all men are always loving the same thing." "I myself wonder," I said, "why that is." "There is nothing to wonder at," she replied: "the reason is that only one part of love is separated off and receives the name of the whole, but the other parts have other names." "Give an example," I said. She answered me as follows: "There is poetry, which, as you know, is complex and manifold. And all creation or passage of non-being into being is poetry or making, and the processes of all art are creative; and the masters of art are all poets or makers." "Very true." "Still," she said, "you know that they are not called poets, but have other names; the generic term 'poetry' is confined to that specific art which is separated off from the rest of poetry, and is concerned with music and metre, this is what is called poetry, and they who possess this kind of poetry are called poets." "Very true," I said. "And the same holds of love. For you may say generally that all desire of good and happiness is due to the great and subtle power of Love; but those who, having their affections set upon him, are yet diverted into the paths of money-making or gymnastic philosophy, are not called lovers—the name of the genus reserved for those whose devotion takes one form only—they alone are said to love, or to be lovers." "In that," I said, "I am of the opinion that you are right." "Yes," she said, "and you hear people say that lovers are seeking neither for the half, nor for the whole, unless the half or whole be also a good. And they will cut off their own hands and feet and cast them away, if they are evil; for they love them not because they are their own, but because they are good, and dislike them not because they are another's, but because they are evil. There is nothing which men love but the good. Do you think that there is?" "Indeed," I answered, "I should say not." "Then," she said, "the conclusion of the whole matter is that men love the good." "Yes," I said. "To which may be added that they love the possession of the good?" "Yes, that may be added." "And not only the possession, but the everlasting possession of the good?" "That may be added, too." "Then love," she said, "may be described generally as the love of the everlasting possession of the good?" "That is most true," I said.

(From Socrates' speech on Love)

TO AUTUMN

John Keats

Season of mists and mellow fruitfulness,
  Close bosom-friend of the maturing sun;
Conspiring with him how to load and bless
  With fruit the vines that round the thatch-eaves run;
To bend with apples the moss'd cottage-trees,
  And fill all fruit with ripeness to the core;
    To swell the gourd, and plump the hazel shells
  With a sweet kernel; to set budding more,
And still more, later flowers for the bees,
Until they think warm days will never cease,
    For Summer has o'er-brimmed their clammy cells.

Who hath not seen thee oft amid thy store?
  Sometimes whoever seeks abroad may find
Thee sitting careless on a granary floor,
  Thy hair soft-lifted by the winnowing wind;
Or on a half-reap'd furrow sound asleep,
  Drows'd with the fume of poppies, while thy hook
    Spares the next swath and all its twined flowers:
And sometimes like a gleaner thou dost keep
  Steady thy laden head across a brook;
  Or by a cider-press, with patient look,
    Thou watchest the last oozings hours by hours.

Where are the songs of Spring? Ay, where are they?
  Think not of them, thou hast thy music too,—
While barred clouds bloom the soft-dying day,
  And touch the stubble-plains with rosy hue;
Then in a wailful choir the small gnats mourn
  Among the river sallows, borne aloft
    Or sinking as the light wind lives or dies;
And full-grown lambs loud bleat from hilly bourn;
  Hedge-crickets sing; and now with treble soft
  The red-breast whistles from a garden-croft;
    And gathering swallows twitter in the skies.

* * *

Nothing except a battle lost can be half so melancholy as a battle won.—Duke of Wellington

"O LORD, HOW EXCELLENT IS THY NAME"

Holy Bible, Psalm 8

O Lord our Lord, how excellent is thy name in all the earth! who hast set thy glory above the heavens.
Out of the mouths of babes and sucklings hast thou ordained strength because of thine enemies, that thou mightest still the enemy and the avenger.
When I consider thy heavens, the work of thy fingers, the moon and the stars, which thou hast ordained;
What is man, that thou art mindful of him? and the son of man, that thou visitest him?
For thou hast made him a little lower than the angels, and hast crowned him with glory and honour.
Thou madest him to have dominion over the works of thy hands: thou hast put all things under his feet:
All sheep and oxen, yea, and the beasts of the field;
The fowl of the air, and the fish of the sea, and whatsoever passeth through the paths of the seas.
O Lord our Lord, how excellent is thy name in all the earth!

WHY DID THEY DIG MA'S GRAVE SO DEEP?

George Cooper

Poor little Nellie is weeping tonight,
Thinking of days that were full of delight,
Lonely she sits by the old kitchen grate,
Sighing for Mother, but now 'tis too late.
Under the daisies now cover'd with snow,
Rests the fond mother, away from life's woe;
Nellie is left now to murmur and weep:

Chorus:

Why did they dig Ma's grave so deep?
Why did they dig Ma's grave so deep?
Down in the clay so deep?
Why did they leave me here to weep?
Why did they dig Ma's grave so deep?

Only sweet mem'ries of gladness and love,
Come to the child of the dear one above,
Shadows are creeping around the lone room,
Early and late there's a feeling of gloom.
Out in the churchyard the wild breezes blow,
Seeming to echo her heart's grief and woe;
Softly she murmurs, while chills o'er her creep: (*Chorus*)

Poor little Nellie in slumber's sweet rest,
Dreams all the night of the mother so blest,
Sees her again in a vision of light,
Praying, "God bless little Nellie tonight!"
Smiling upon her with glorified face,
Calling her home to that bright resting place;
Poor little Nellie oft sighs in her sleep: (*Chorus*)

FROM PARADISE LOST

John Milton

Invocation to the Heavenly Muse

Of Man's first disobedience, and the fruit
Of that forbidden tree whose mortal taste
Brought death into the World, and all our woe,
With loss of Eden, till one greater Man
Restore us, and regain the blissful Seat,
Sing, Heavenly Muse, that, on the secret top
Of Oreb, or of Sinai, didst inspire
That Shepherd who first taught the chosen seed
In the beginning how the heavens and earth
Rose out of Chaos: or, if Sion hill
Delight thee more, and Siloa's brook that flowed
Fast by the oracle of God, I thence
Invoke thy aid to my adventrous song,
That with no middle flight intends to soar
Above the Aonian mount, while it pursues
Things unattempted yet in prose or rhyme.
And chiefly Thou, O Spirit, that dost prefer
Before all temples the upright heart and pure,
Instruct me, for Thou know'st; Thou from the first

Wast present, and, with mighty wings outspread,
Dove-like sat'st brooding on the vast Abyss,
And mad'st it pregnant: what in me is dark
Illumine, what is low raise and support;
That, to the highth of this great argument,
I may assert Eternal Providence,
And justify the ways of God to men.

Satan Ponders His Fallen State

"Is this the region, this the soil, the clime,"
Said then the lost Archangel, "this the seat
That we must change for Heaven?—this mournful gloom
For that celestial light? Be it so, since he
Who now is sovran can dispose and bid
What shall be right: fardest from him is best,
Whom reason hath equalled, force hath made supreme
Above his equals. Farewell, happy fields,
Where joy for ever dwells! Hail, horrors! hail,
Infernal World! and thou, profoundest Hell,
Receive thy new possessor—one who brings
A mind not to be changed by place or time.
The mind is its own place, and in itself
Can make a Heaven of Hell, a Hell of Heaven.
What matter where, if I be still the same,
And what I should be, all but less than he
Whom thunder hath made greater? Here at least
We shall be free; the Almighty hath not built
Here for his envy, will not drive us hence:
Here we may reign secure; and, in my choice,
To reign is worth ambition, though in Hell:
Better to reign in Hell than serve in Heaven.

Pandemonium and Its Architect

Anon out of the earth a fabric huge
Rose like an exhalation, with the sound
Of dulcet symphonies and voices sweet—
Built like a temple, where pilasters round
Were set, and Doric pillars overlaid
With golden architrave; nor did there want
Cornice or frieze, with bossy sculptures graven:
The roof was fretted gold. Not Babilon

Nor great Alcairo such magnificence
Equalled in all their glories, to inshrine
Belus or Serapis their gods, or seat
Their kings, when Aegypt with Assyria strove
In wealth and luxury. The ascending pile
Stood fixed her stately highth; and straight the doors,
Opening their brazen folds, discover, wide
Within, her ample spaces o'er the smooth
And level pavement: from the archèd roof,
Pendent by subtle magic, many a row
Of starry lamps and blazing cressets, fed
With naphtha and asphaltus, yielded light
As from a sky. The hasty multitude
Admiring entered; and the work some praise,
And some the architect. His hand was known
In Heaven by many a towered structure high,
Where sceptred Angels held their residence,
And sat as Princes, whom the supreme King
Exalted to such power, and gave to rule,
Each in his hierarchy, the Orders bright.
Nor was his name unheard or unadored
In ancient Greece; and in Ausonian land
Men called him Mulciber; and how he fell
From Heaven they fabled, thrown by angry Jove
Sheer o'er the crystal battlements: from morn
To noon he fell, from noon to dewy eve,
A summer's day, and with the setting sun
Dropt from the zenith, like a falling star,
On Lemnos, the Aegaean isle.

Satan Looks upon Adam and Eve in Paradise

Two of far nobler shape, erect and tall,
God-like erect, with native honour clad
In naked majesty, seemed lords of all,
And worthy seemed; for in their looks divine
The image of their glorious Maker shon,
Truth, wisdom, sanctitude severe and pure—
Severe, but in true filial freedom placed,
Whence true authority in men: though both
Not equal, as their sex not equal seemed;
For contemplation he and valour formed,

For softness she and sweet attractive grace;
He for God only, she for God in him.
His fair large front and eye sublime declared
Absolute rule; and Hyacinthin locks
Round from his parted forelock manly hung
Clustering, but not beneath his shoulders broad:
She, as a veil down to the slender waist,
Her unadornèd golden tresses wore
Dishevelled, but in wanton ringlets waved
As the vine curls her tendrils—which implied
Subjection, but required with gentle sway,
And by her yielded, by him best received
Yielded, with coy submission, modest pride,
And sweet, reluctant, amorous delay.
Nor those mysterious parts were then concealed;
Then was not guilty shame. Dishonest shame
Of Nature's works, honour dishonourable,
Sin-bred, how have ye troubled all mankind
With shews instead, mere shews of seeming pure,
And banished from man's life his happiest life,
Simplicity and spotless innocence!
So passed they naked on, nor shunned the sight
Of God or Angel, for they thought no ill:
So hand in hand they passed, the loveliest pair
That ever since in love's imbraces met—
Adam the goodliest man of men since born
His sons; the fairest of her daughters Eve.

Night Falls on Eden

Now came still Evening on, and Twilight gray
Had in her sober livery all things clad;
Silence accompanied; for beast and bird,
They to their grassy couch, these to their nests
Were slunk, all but the wakeful nightingale.
She all night long her amorous descant sung:
Silence was pleased. Now glowed the firmament
With living Saphirs; Hesperus, that led
The starry host, rode brightest, till the Moon,
Rising in clouded majesty, at length
Apparent queen, unveiled her peerless light,
And o'er the dark her silver mantle threw.

Eve to Adam

"With thee conversing, I forget all time,
All seasons, and their change; all please alike.
Sweet is the breath of Morn, her rising sweet,
With charm of earliest birds; pleasant the Sun,
When first on this delightful land he spreads
His orient beams, on herb, tree, fruit, and flower,
Glistering with dew; fragrant the fertil Earth
After soft showers; and sweet the coming on
Of grateful Evening mild, then silent Night,
With this her solemn bird, and this fair Moon,
And these the gems of Heaven, her starry train:
But neither breath of Morn, when she ascends
With charm of earliest birds; nor rising Sun
On this delighful land; nor herb, fruit, flower,
Glistering with dew; nor fragrance after showers;
Nor grateful Evening mild; nor silent Night,
With this her solemn bird; nor walk by moon,
Or glittering star-light, without thee is sweet."

Banishment from Paradise

Descended, Adam to the bower where Eve
Lay sleeping ran before, but found her waked;
And thus with words not sad she him received:—
"Whence thou return'st and whither went'st I know;
For God is also in sleep, and dreams advise,
Which he hath sent propitious, some great good
Presaging, since, with sorrow and heart's distress
Wearied, I fell asleep. But now lead on;
In me is no delay; with thee to go
Is to stay here; without thee here to stay
Is to go hence unwilling; thou to me
Art all things under Heaven, all places thou,
Who for my wilful crime art banished hence.
This further consolation yet secure
I carry hence: though all by me is lost,
Such favour I unworthy am voutsafed,
By me the Promised Seed shall all restore."
So spake our mother Eve; and Adam heard
Well pleased, but answered not; for now too nigh
The Archangel stood, and from the other hill

To their fixed station, all in bright array,
The Cherubim descended, on the ground
Gliding metéorous, as evening mist
Risen from a river o'er the marish glides,
And gathers ground fast at the labourer's heel
Homeward returning. High in front advanced,
The brandished sword of God before them blazed,
Fierce as a comet; which with torrid heat,
And vapour as the Libyan air adust,
Began to parch that temperate clime; whereat
In either hand the hastening Angel caught
Our lingering Parents, and to the eastern gate
Led them direct, and down the cliff as fast
To the subjected plain—then disappeared.
They, looking back, all the eastern side beheld
Of Paradise, so late their happy seat,
Waved over by that flaming brand; the gate
With dreadful faces thronged and fiery arms.
Some natural tears they dropped, but wiped them soon;
The world was all before them, where to choose
Their place of rest, and Providence their guide.
They, hand in hand, with wandering steps and slow,
Through Eden took their solitary way.

ROBERT LOUIS STEVENSON GIVES HIS BIRTHDAY TO A LITTLE GIRL

Robert Louis Stevenson, Advocate of the Scots Bar, author of *The Master of Ballantrae* and *Moral Emblems,* stuck civil engineer, sole owner and potentate of the Palace and Plantation known as Vailima on the island of Upolu, Samoa, a British subject, being in sound mind, and pretty well, I thank you, in body:

In consideration that Miss Annie H. Ide, daughter of H. C. Ide, the town of Saint Johnsbury; in the county of Caledonia, in the State of Vermont, United States of America, was born, out of all reason, upon Christmas Day, and is therefore out of all justice denied the consolation and profit of a proper birthday;

And, considering that I, the said Robert Louis Stevenson, having attained an age when Oh, we never mention it, and that I have now no further use for a birthday of any description;

And, in consideration that I have met H. C. Ide, the father of the said Annie H. Ide, and found him about as white a land commissioner as I require: *Have transferred, and do hereby transfer,* to the said Annie H. Ide, *all and whole* my rights and privileges in the thirteenth day of November, formerly my birthday, now, hereby and henceforth, the birthday of the said Annie H. Ide, to have, to hold, exercise, and enjoy the same in the customary manner, by the sporting of fine raiment, eating of rich meats, and receipt of gifts, compliments, and copies of verse, according to the manner of our ancestors;

And I direct, the said Annie H. Ide to add to the same name of Annie H. Ide the name Louisa—at least in private; and I charge her to use my said birthday with moderation and humanity *et tamquam bona filia familiae,* the said birthday not being so young as it once was, and having carried me in a very satisfactory manner since I can remember;

And in case the said Annie H. Ide shall neglect or contravene either of the above conditions, I hereby revoke the donation and transfer my rights in the said birthday to the President of the United States of America for the time being;

In witness whereof I have hereto set my hand and seal this nineteenth day of June in the year of grace eighteen hundred and ninety-one.

ROBERT LOUIS STEVENSON

Witness, Lloyd Osbourne
Witness, Harold Watts.

AN OLD WOMAN OF THE ROADS

Padraic Colum

O, to have a little house!
  To own the hearth and stool and all!
The heaped-up sods upon the fire,
  The pile of turf against the wall!

To have a clock with weights and chains
  And pendulum swinging up and down!
A dresser filled with shining delph,
  Speckled and white and blue and brown!

I could be busy all the day
  Clearing and sweeping hearth and floor,
And fixing on their shelf again
  My white and blue and speckled store!

I could be quiet there at night
  Beside the fire and by myself,
Sure of a bed and loath to leave
  The ticking clock and the shining delph!

Och! but I'm weary of mist and dark,
  And roads where there's never a house or bush,
And tired I am of bog and road
  And the crying wind and the lonesome hush!

And I am praying to God on high,
  And I am praying Him night and day,
For a little house—a house of my own—
  Out of the wind's and the rain's way.

THE BETTER PATH

Holy Bible, Ecclesiastes 7:1–5

A good name is better than precious ointment; and the day of death better than the day of one's birth. It is better to go to the house of mourning, than to go to the house of feasting: for that is the end of all men; and the living will lay it to his heart. Sorrow is better than laughter: for by the sadness of the countenance the heart is made better. The heart of the wise is in the house of mourning; but the heart of fools is in the house of mirth. It is better to hear the rebuke of the wise, than for a man to hear the song of fools.

MAKE WAY FOR LIBERTY

James Montgomery

"Make way for Liberty!" he cried;
Made way for Liberty, and died!

In arms the Austrian phalanx stood,
A living wall, a human wood!
A wall, where every conscious stone
Seemed to its kindred thousands grown;
A rampart all assaults to bear,
Till time to dust their frames should wear;
A wood like that enchanted grove,
In which, with fiends, Rinaldo strove,
Where every silent tree possessed
A spirit prisoned in its breast,
Which the first stroke of coming strife
Would startle into hideous life:
So dense, so still, the Austrians stood,
A living wall, a human wood!

Impregnable their front appears,
All horrent with projected spears,
Whose polished points before them shine,
From flank to flank, one brilliant line,
Bright as the breakers' splendors run
Along the billows to the sun.

Opposed to these, a hovering band,
Contending for their native land;
Peasants, whose new-found strength had broke
From manly necks the ignoble yoke,
And forged their fetters into swords,
On equal terms to fight their lords;
And what insurgent rage had gained,
In many a mortal fray maintained;
Marshaled once more at Freedom's call,
They came to conquer or to fall,
Where he who conquered, he who fell,
Was deemed a dead or living Tell!

And now the work of life and death
Hung on the passing of a breath;
The fire of conflict burned within;
The battle trembled to begin;
Yet, while the Austrians held their ground,
Point for attack was nowhere found;
Where'er the impatient Switzers gazed,
The unbroken line of lances blazed;

That line 'twere suicide to meet,
And perish at their tyrants' feet;
How could they rest within their graves,
And leave their homes the homes of slaves?
Would they not feel their children tread
With clanking chains above their head?

It must not be: this day, this hour,
Annihilates the oppressor's power;
All Switzerland is in the field,
She will not fly, she can not yield;
Few were the numbers she could boast,
But every freeman was a host,
And felt as though himself were he
On whose sole arm hung victory.

It did depend on *one,* indeed:
Behold him! Arnold Winkelried!
There sounds not to the trump of fame
The echo of a nobler name.
Unmarked he stood among the throng,
In rumination deep and long,
Till you might see with sudden grace,
The very thought come o'er his face;
And by the motion of his form,
Anticipate the bursting storm;
And by the uplifting of his brow,
Tell where the bolt would strike, and how.
But 'twas no sooner thought than done;
The field was in a moment won.

"Make way for Liberty!" he cried:
Then ran, with arms extended wide,
As if his dearest friend to clasp;
Ten spears he swept within his grasp:
"Make way for Liberty!" he cried,
Their keen points met from side to side;
He bowed among them like a tree,
And thus made way for Liberty.

Swift to the breach his comrades fly;
"Make way for Liberty!" they cry,
And through the Austrian phalanx dart,

As rushed the spears through Arnold's heart;
While instantaneous as his fall,
Rout, ruin, panic, scattered all.
An earthquake could not overthrow
A city with a surer blow.

Thus Switzerland again was free,
Thus Death made way for Liberty!

OLD GRIMES

Albert Gorton Greene

Old Grimes is dead; that good old man
  We never shall see more:
He used to wear a long black coat,
  All buttoned down before.

His heart was open as the day,
  His feelings all were true;
His hair was some inclined to gray—
  He wore it in a queue.

Whene'er he heard the voice of pain,
  His breast with pity burned;
The large, round head upon his cane
  From ivory was turned.

Kind words he had for all;
  He knew no base design:
His eyes were dark and rather small,
  His nose was aquiline.

He lived at peace with all mankind,
  In friendship he was true;
His coat had pocket-holes behind,
  His pantaloons were blue.

Unharmed, the sin which earth pollutes
  He passed securely o'er,
And never wore a pair of boots
  For thirty years or more.

But good old Grimes is now at rest,
  Nor fears misfortune's frown:
He wore a double-breasted vest—
  The stripes ran up and down.

He modest merit sought to find,
  And pay it its desert:
He had no malice in his mind,
  No ruffles on his shirt.

His neighbors he did not abuse—
  Was sociable and gay:
He wore large buckles on his shoes,
  And changed them every day.

His knowledge, hid from public gaze,
  He did not bring to view,
Nor made a noise, town-meeting days,
  As many people do.

His worldly goods he never threw
  In trust to fortune's chances,
But lived (as all his brothers do)
  In easy circumstances.

Thus undisturbed by anxious cares,
  His peaceful moments ran;
And everybody said he was
  A fine old gentleman.

"LORD, MAKE ME AN INSTRUMENT OF YOUR PEACE"

St. Francis of Assisi

Lord, make me an instrument of Your peace; where there is hatred, let me sow love; where there is injury, pardon; where there is discord, union; where there is doubt, faith; where there is despair, hope; where there is darkness, light; and where there is sadness, joy.

O Divine Master, grant that I may not so much seek to be consoled as to console, to be understood as to understand, to be loved as to love; for it is in giving that we receive, it is in pardoning that we are pardoned, and it is in dying that we are born to eternal life

THE FEMALE OF THE SPECIES

Rudyard Kipling

When the Himalayan peasant meets the he-bear in his pride,
He shouts to scare the monster, who will often turn aside,
But the she-bear thus accosted rends the peasant tooth and nail.
For the female of the species is more deadly than the male.

When Nag the basking cobra hears the careless foot of man,
He will sometimes wriggle sideways and avoid it if he can.
But his mate makes no such motion where she camps beside the trail.
For the female of the species is more deadly than the male.

When the early Jesuit fathers preached to Hurons and Choctaws,
They prayed to be delivered from the vengeance of the squaws.
'Twas the women, not the warriors, turned those stark enthusiasts pale.
For the female of the species is more deadly than the male.

Man's timid heart is bursting with the things he must not say,
For the Woman that God gave him isn't his to give away;
But when hunter meets with husband, each confirms the other's tale—
The female of the species is more deadly than the male.

Man, a bear in most relations—worm and savage otherwise,—
Man propounds negotiations, Man accepts the compromise.
Very rarely will he squarely push the logic of a fact
To its ultimate conclusion in unmitigated act.

Fear, or foolishness, impels him, ere he lay the wicked low,
To concede some form of trial even to his fiercest foe.
Mirth obscene diverts his anger—Doubt and Pity oft perplex
Him in dealing with an issue—to the scandal of The Sex!

But the Woman that God gave him, every fibre of her frame
Proves her launched for one sole issue, armed and engined for the same;
And to serve that single issue, lest the generations fail,
The female of the species must be deadlier than the male.

She who faces Death by torture for each life beneath her breast
May not deal in doubt or pity—must not swerve for fact or jest.
These be purely male diversions—not in these her honor dwells.
She the Other Law we live by, is that Law and nothing else.

She can bring no more to living than the powers that make her great
As the Mother of the Infant and the Mistress of the Mate.
And when Babe and Man are lacking and she strides unclaimed to claim
Her right as femme (and baron), her equipment is the same.

She is wedded to convictions—in default of grosser ties:
Her contentions are her children, Heaven help him who denies!
He will meet no suave discussion, but the instant, white-hot, wild,
Wakened female of the species warring as for spouse and child.

Unprovoked and awful charges—even so the she-bear fights,
Speech that drips, corrodes, and poisons—even so the cobra bites,
Scientific vivisection of one nerve till it is raw
And the victim writhes in anguish—like the Jesuit with the squaw!

So it comes that Man, the coward, when he gathers to confer
With his fellow-braves in council, dare not leave a place for her
Where, at war with Life and Conscience, he uplifts his erring hands
To some God of Abstract Justice—which no woman understands.

And Man knows it! Knows, moreover, that the Woman that God gave him
Must command but may not govern—shall enthral but not enslave him.
And *She* knows, because She warns him, and Her instincts never fail,
That the Female of Her Species is more deadly than the Male.

BEN JONSON SENDS A MESSAGE TO JAMES I

He despises me, I suppose, because I live in an alley; tell him his soul lives in an alley.

CORONATION

Edward Perronet

All hail the Power of Jesus' name!
  Let angels prostrate fall;
Bring forth the royal diadem,
  And crown Him Lord of all!

Crown Him, ye martyrs of our God,
  Who from His altar call;
Extol the stem of Jesse's rod,
  And crown Him Lord of all.

Ye seed of Israel's chosen race,
  Ye ransomed from the Fall,
Hail Him who saves you by His grace,
  And crown Him Lord of all.

Sinners, whose love can ne'er forget
  The wormwood and the gall,
Go, spread your trophies at His feet,
  And crown Him Lord of all.

Let every kindred, every tribe,
  On this terrestrial ball,
To Him all majesty ascribe,
  And crown Him Lord of all.

Oh that with yonder sacred throng
  We at His feet may fall,
Join in the everlasting song,
  And crown Him Lord of all!

AMERICAN LAUGHTER

Kenneth Allan Robinson

Oh, the men who laughed the American laughter
Whittled their jokes from the tough bull-pines;
They were tall men, sharpened before and after;
They studied the sky for the weather-signs;
They tilted their hats and they smoked long-nines!

Their laughter was ladled in Western flagons
And poured down throats that were parched for more;
This was the laughter of democrat wagons
And homely men at the crossroads store
—It tickled the shawl that a lawyer wore!

It hurt the ears of the dainty and pretty
But they laughed the louder and laughed their fill,
A laughter made for Virginia City,
Springfield, and Natchez-under-the-Hill,
And the river that flows past Hannibal still!

American laughter was lucky laughter,
A coonskin tune by a homespun bard;
It tasted of hams from the smokehouse rafter
And locust trees from the courthouse yard,
And Petroleum Nasby and Artemus Ward!

They laughed at the Mormons and Mike Fink's daughter,
And the corncob tale of Sut Lovingood's dog,
Till the ague fled from the fever-water
And the damps deserted the tree-stump bog,
—They laughed at the tale of the jumping frog!

They laughed at the British, they laughed at Shakers,
At Horace Greeley, and stovepipe hats;
They split their fences and ploughed their acres,
And treed their troubles like mountain-cats;
—They laughed calamity out of the flats!

Now the Boston man, according to rumor,
Said, as he turned in his high-backed bed,
"This doesn't conform to my rules for humor,"
And he settled his nightcap over his head,
-But it shook the earth like the buffalo-tread!

And the corn grew tall and the fields grew wider,
And the land grew sleek with the mirth they sowed;
They laughed the fat-meat into the spider,
They laughed the blues from the Wilderness Road,
—They crossed hard times to the Comstock Lode!

GO, LOVELY ROSE!

Edmund Waller

Go, lovely rose!
Tell her that wastes her time and me,
That now she knows,
When I resemble her to thee,
How sweet and fair she seems to be.

Tell her that's young,
And shuns to have her graces spied,
That hadst thou sprung
In deserts, where no men abide,
Thou must have uncommended died.

Small is the worth
Of beauty from the light retired;
Bid her come forth,
Suffer herself to be desired,
And not blush so to be admired.

Then die! that she
The common fate of all things rare
May read in thee;
How small a part of time they share
That are so wondrous sweet and fair!

THANKSGIVING PROCLAMATION

State of Connecticut

By His Excellency Wilbur L. Cross, Governor

Time out of mind at this turn of the seasons when the hardy oak leaves rustle in the wind and the frost gives a tang to the air and the dusk falls early and the friendly evenings lengthen under the heel of Orion, it has seemed good to our people to join together in praising the Creator and Preserver, who has brought us by a way that we did not know to the end of another year. In observance of this custom, I appoint Thursday, the twenty-sixth of November as a day of

PUBLIC THANKSGIVING

for the blessings that have been our common lot and have placed our beloved State with the favored regions of earth—for all the creature comforts; the yield of the soil that has fed us and the richer yield from labor of every kind that has sustained our lives—and for all those things, as dear as breath to the body, that quicken man's faith in his manhood, that nourish and strengthen his spirit to do the great work still before him: for the brotherly word and act; for honor held above price; for steadfast courage and zeal in the long, long search after truth; for liberty and for justice freely granted by each to his fellow and so as freely enjoyed; and for the crowning glory and mercy of peace upon our land—that we may humbly take heart of these blessings as we gather once again with solemn and festive rites to keep our Harvest Home.

Given under my hand and seal of the State at the Capitol, in Hartford, this twelfth day of November, in the year of our Lord one thousand nine hundred and thirty-six and of the independence of the United States the one hundred and sixty-first.

WILBUR L. CROSS

THANKSGIVING DAY

Lydia Maria Child

Over the river and through the wood,
To grandfather's house we go;
The horse knows the way
To carry the sleigh
Through the white and drifted snow.

Over the river and through the wood—
Oh, how the wind doth blow!
It stings the toes
And bites the nose
As over the ground we go.

Over the river and through the wood,
To have a first-rate play.
Hear the bells ring,
"Ting-a-ling-ling!"
Hurrah for Thanksgiving Day!

Over the river and through the wood,
Trot fast, my dapple-gray!
    Spring over the ground
    Like a hunting-hound,
For this is Thanksgiving Day!

Over the river and through the wood,
And straight through the barnyard gate.
    We seem to go
    Extremely slow—
It is so hard to wait.

Over the river and through the wood—
Now grandmother's cap I spy!
    Hurrah for the fun!
    Is the pudding done?
Hurrah for the pumpkin pie!

A CHINESE EDITOR REJECTS A MANUSCRIPT

Anonymous

Illustrious brother of the sun and moon—Behold thy servant prostrate before thy feet. I kow-tow to thee and beg of thy graciousness thou mayest grant that I may speak and live. Thy honored manuscript has deigned to cast the light of its august countenance upon me. With raptures I have pursued it. By the bones of my ancestors, never have I encountered such wit, such pathos, such lofty thoughts. With fear and trembling I return the writing. Were I to publish the treasure you sent me, the Emperor would order that it should be made the standard, and that none be published except such as equalled it. Knowing literature as I do, and that it would be impossible in ten thousand years to equal what you have done, I send your writing back. Ten thousand times I crave your pardon. Behold my head is at your feet. Do what you will.

Your servant's servant,
The Editor.

THE RHODORA: ON BEING ASKED WHENCE IS THE FLOWER?

Ralph Waldo Emerson

In May, when sea-winds pierced our solitudes,
I found the fresh Rhodora in the woods,
Spreading its leafless blooms in a damp nook,
To please the desert and the sluggish brook.
The purple petals, fallen in the pool,
Made the black water with their beauty gay;
Here might the red-bird come his plumes to cool,
And court the flower that cheapens his array.
Rhodora! if the sages ask thee why
This charm is wasted on the earth and sky,
Tell them, dear, that if eyes were made for seeing,
Then Beauty is its own excuse for being:
Why thou wert there, O rival of the rose!
I never thought to ask, I never knew:
But, in my simple ignorance, suppose
The self-same Power that brought me there brought you.

PRAYER AT NIGHT

From The Book of Common Prayer

O Lord, support us all the day long, until the shadows lengthen and the evening comes, and the busy world is hushed, and the fever of life is over, and our work is done. Then in thy mercy grant us a safe lodging, and a holy rest, and peace at the last. Amen.

O God, who art the life of mortal men, the light of the faithful, the strength of those who labour, and the repose of the dead; We thank thee for the timely blessings of the day, and humbly supplicate thy merciful protection all this night. Bring us, we beseech thee, in safety to the morning hours; through him who died for us and rose again, thy Son, our Saviour Jesus Christ. Amen.

THE MODERN HIAWATHA

Anonymous

He killed the noble Mudjokivis.
Of the skin he made him mittens,
Made them with the fur side inside,
Made them with the skin side outside.
He, to get the warm side inside,
Put the inside skin outside;
He, to get the cold side outside,
Put the warm side fur side inside.
That's why he put the fur side inside,
Why he put the skin side outside,
Why he turned them inside outside.

THOMAS JEFFERSON'S DECALOGUE FOR THE PRACTICAL LIFE

1. Never put off till to-morrow what you can do to-day.
2. Never trouble another for what you can do yourself.
3. Never spend your money before you have it.
4. Never buy what you do not want, because it is cheap; it will be dear to you.
5. Pride costs us more than hunger, thirst and cold.
6. We never repent of having eaten too little.
7. Nothing is troublesome that we do willingly.
8. How much pain have cost us the evils which have never happened.
9. Take things always by their smooth handle.
10. When angry, count ten, before you speak; if very angry, an hundred.

(From a Letter to Thomas Jefferson Smith, dated from Monticello, February 21, 1825)

* * *

Imitation is the sincerest flattery.—Charles Caleb Colton

"WITH WHOM IS NO VARIABLENESS, NEITHER SHADOW OR TURNING"

Arthur Hugh Clough

It fortifies my soul to know
That, though I perish, Truth is so:
That, howso'er I stray and range,
Whate'er I do Thou dost not change.
I steadier step when I recall
That, if I slip, Thou dost not fall.

"LO, THE POOR INDIAN!"

Alexander Pope

Lo, the poor Indian! whose untutor'd mind
Sees God in clouds, or hears him in the wind;
His soul proud Science never taught to stray
Far as the solar walk or milky way;
Yet simple nature to his hope has giv'n,
Behind the cloud-topt hill, an humbler Heav'n,
Some safer world in depth of woods embraced,
Some happier island in the wat'ry waste,
Where slaves once more their native land behold,
No fiends torment, no Christians thirst for gold.
To be, contents his natural desire;
He asks no Angel's wing, no Seraph's fire;
But thinks, admitted to that equal sky,
His faithful dog shall bear him company.

(From An Essay on Man)

SHELLEY

Francis Thompson

Enchanted child, born into a world unchildlike; spoiled darling of Nature, playmate of her elemental daughters; 'pard-like spirit, beautiful and swift,' laired amidst the burning fastnesses of his own fervid mind; bold foot along the verges of precipitous dream; light leaper from crag to crag of inaccessible fancies; towering Genius, whose soul rose like a ladder between heaven and earth with the angels of song ascending and descending it;—he is shrunken into the little vessel of death, and sealed with the unshatterable seal of doom, and cast down deep below the rolling tides of Time.

Mighty meat for little guests, when the heart of Shelley was laid in the cemetery of Caius Cestius! Beauty, music, sweetness, tears—the mouth of the worm has fed them all. Into that sacred bridal-gloom of death where he holds his nuptials with eternity let not our rash speculations follow him; let us hope rather that as, amidst material nature, where our dull eyes see only ruin, the finer eye of science has discovered life in putridity and vigour in decay, seeing dissolution even and disintegration, which in the mouth of man symbolize disorder, to be in the works of God undeviating order, and the manner of our corruption to be no less wonderful than the manner of our health,—so, amidst the supernatural universe, some tender undreamed surprise of life in doom awaited that wild nature, which, worn by warfare with itself, its Maker, and all the world, now

> Sleeps, and never palates more the dug,
> The beggar's nurse, and Caesar's.

EPITAPH

> As I was, so be ye;
> As I am, ye shall be;
> That I gave, that I have;
> That I spent, that I had;
> Thus I end all my cost;
> What I left, that I lost.

(Churchyard, Leek, Derbyshire, England, on the grave of Thomas Osborne, died 1749)

* * *

Here's to the banker, who lends you an umbrella when the sun is shining and demands it back as soon as it starts to rain.

—Anonymous

ODE ON SOLITUDE

Alexander Pope

Happy the man whose wish and care
  A few paternal acres bound,
Content to breathe his native air
    In his own ground.

Whose herds with milk, whose fields with bread,
  Whose flocks supply him with attire,
Whose trees in summer yield him shade,
    In winter fire.

Bless'd who can unconcern'dly find
  Hours, days, and years slide soft away,
In health of body, peace of mind,
    Quiet by day;

Sound sleep by night: study and ease
  Together mix'd; sweet recreation;
And innocence, which most does please,
    With meditation.

Thus let me live, unseen, unknown,
  Thus unlamented let me die;
Steal from the world, and not a stone
    Tell where I lie.

DARLING NELLY GRAY

B. R. Hanby

There's a lone green valley by the old Kentucky shore
  Where we've whiled many happy hours away;
A-sitting and singing by the little cottage door
  Where dwelt my lovely Nelly Gray.

Refrain:
  Oh! my poor Nelly Gray, they have taken you away,
    And I'll never see my darling any more;
  I am sitting by the river and I'm weeping all the day,
    For you're gone from the old Kentucky shore.

Where the moon had climbed the mountain and the stars were
shining too,
Then I took my lovely Nelly Gray.
And I travelled down the river in my little red canoe
While the banjo so sweetly I did play.

Oh! my eyes are getting blinded and I cannot see my way;
Hark! there's somebody knocking at the door.
I hear the angels calling and I see my Nelly Gray,
Farewell to my old Kentucky shore.

Oh! my darling Nelly Gray, up in heaven there, they say,
That they'll never take you from me any more;
I'm coming, coming, coming, as the angels clear the way,
Farewell to the old Kentucky shore.

WHAT THE GOVERNOR OF NORTH CAROLINA SAID TO THE GOVERNOR OF SOUTH CAROLINA

A few miles from Raleigh, North Carolina, is the Nancy Jones House, built in 1805. The diary of Mrs. Nancy Anne Jones describes . . . [how] on a hot summer day in 1838, Governor Edward B. Dudley of North Carolina and Governor Pierce Mason Butler of South Carolina arrived at the same time, were ushered into the parlor and served tall cool mint juleps. Lany, the maid, and the houseboy ran to mix more juleps, but not quickly enough for the thirsty governors. Lany reentered the room as the Governor of North Carolina was saying to the Governor of South Carolina: "It's a damned long time between drinks." "Damn long!" his companion replied. When Mrs. Jones heard of the remark from the scandalized maid, she was shocked and embarrassed at the implied reflection on her hospitality.

Another version has been handed down in the family of John Motley Morehead, Minister to Sweden (1930–33), whose grandfather was Governor of North Carolina (1841–45). After futile correspondence between Governor Morehead, a Whig, and Governor J. H. Hammond of South Carolina, a Democrat, concerning the extradition of a political offender, the two officials met with their staffs and legal advisers for a conference on the State line, not far from Charlotte. During the discussion Governor Hammond became excited and finally announced that further refusal would result in his sending a military force into North Carolina to seize the fugitive. "Now sir," he shouted, crashing his fist upon the table, "what is your answer?" "My reply, sir," answered Governor Morehead with great deliberation, "is this: It's a damned long time between drinks." This unexpected answer had the effect of so relieving the tension that the two Governors were able to talk dispassionately and eventually to reach a settlement satisfactory to both States.

(From North Carolina: A Guide
to the Old North State)

RUTH

Thomas Hood

She stood breast high among the corn,
Clasped by the golden light of morn,
Like the sweetheart of the sun,
Who many a glowing kiss had won.

On her cheek an autumn flush,
Deeply ripened;—such a blush
In the midst of brown was born,
Like red poppies grown with corn.

Round her eyes her tresses fell,
Which were blackest none could tell.
But long lashes veiled a light,
That had else been all too bright.

And her hat, with shady brim,
Made her tressy forehead dim;
Thus she stood amid the stooks,
Praising God with sweetest looks.—

Sure, I said, Heav'n did not mean,
Where I reap thou shouldst but glean,
Lay thy sheaf adown and come,
Share my harvest and my home.

From THE DESERTED VILLAGE

Oliver Goldsmith

Sweet Auburn! loveliest village of the plain;
Where health and plenty cheered the laboring swain,
Where smiling spring its earliest visit paid,
And parting summer's lingering blooms delayed:
Dear lovely bowers of innocence and ease,
Seats of my youth when every sport could please,
How often have I loitered o'er thy green,
Where humble happiness endeared each scene!
How often have I paused on every charm—
The sheltered cot, the cultivated farm,
The never-failing brook, the busy mill,
The decent church that topped the neighboring hill,
The hawthorn bush, with seats beneath the shade,
For talking age and whispering lovers made!
How often have I blessed the coming day,
When toil remitting lent its turn to play,
And all the village train, from labor free,
Led up their sports beneath the spreading tree,
While many a pastime circled in the shade,
The young contending as the old surveyed;
And many a gambol frolicked o'er the ground,
And sleights of art and feats of strength went round.
And still, as each repeated pleasure tired,
Succeeding sports the mirthful band inspired:
The dancing pair that simply sought renown
By holding out to tire each other down;
The swain mistrustless of his smutted face,
While secret laughter tittered round the place;
The bashful virgin's sidelong looks of love,
The matron's glance that would those looks reprove.
These were thy charms, sweet village! sports like these,
With sweet succession, taught e'en toil to please;
These, round thy bowers their cheerful influence shed.

* * *

Sweet was the sound, when oft, at evening's close,
Up yonder hill the village murmur rose;
There as I passed with careless steps and slow,
The mingling notes came softened from below;
The swain responsive as the milkmaid sung,

The sober herd that lowed to meet their young,
The noisy geese that gabbled o'er the pool,
The playful children just let loose from school,
The watch-dog's voice that bayed the whispering wind,
And the loud laugh that spoke the vacant mind,—
These all in sweet confusion sought the shade,
And filled each pause the nightingale had made.

ARMED FORCES SLOGAN—WORLD WAR II

If it moves, salute it.
If it doesn't move, pick it up.
If you can't pick it up, paint it.

NORTH AMERICAN INDIANS

Charles Sprague

Not many generations ago, where you now sit, encircled with all that exalts and embellishes civilized life, the rank thistle nodded in the wind and the wild fox dug his hole unscared. Here lived and loved another race of beings. Beneath the same sun that rolls over your heads, the Indian hunter pursued the panting deer; gazing on the same moon that smiles for you, the Indian lover wooed his dusky mate. Here the wigwam blaze beamed on the tender and helpless, and the council-fire glared on the wise and daring. Now they dipped their noble limbs in your sedgy lakes, and now they paddled the light canoe along your rocky shores. Here they warred; the echoing whoop, the bloody grapple, the defying death-song, all were here; and when the tiger-strife was over, here curled the smoke of peace.

Here, too, they worshiped; and from many a dark bosom went up a fervent prayer to the Great Spirit. He had not written his laws for them on tables of stone, but he had traced them on the tables of their hearts. The poor child of nature knew not the God of Revelation, but the God of the universe he acknowledged in every thing around. He beheld him in the star that sank in beauty behind his lonely dwelling; in the sacred orb that flamed on him from his midday throne; in the flower that snapped in the morning breeze; in the lofty pine that defied a thousand whirlwinds; in the timid warbler that never left its native grove; in the fearless eagle, whose untired pinion was wet in clouds; in the worm that crawled at his feet; and in his own matchless form, glowing with a spark of that light, to whose mysterious source he bent in humble though blind adoration.

And all this has passed away. Across the ocean came a pilgrim bark, bearing the seeds of life and death. The former were sown for you; the latter sprang up in the path of the simple native. Two hundred years have changed the character of a great continent, and blotted forever from its face a whole, peculiar people. Art has usurped the bowers of nature, and the anointed children of education have been too powerful for the tribes of the ignorant. Here and there a stricken few remain; but how unlike their bold, untamable progenitors. The Indian of falcon glance and lion bearing, the theme of the touching ballad, the hero of the pathetic tale is gone, and his degraded offspring crawls upon the soil where he walked in majesty, to remind us how miserable is man when the foot of the conqueror is on his neck.

As a race they have withered from the land. Their arrows are broken, their springs are dried up, their cabins are in the dust. Their council-fire has long since gone out on the shore, and their war-cry is fast fading to the untrodden west. Slowly and sadly they climb the distant mountains, and read their doom in the setting sun. They are shrinking before the mighty tide which is pressing them away; they must soon hear the roar of the last wave which will settle over them forever. Ages hence, the inquisitive white man, as he stands by some growing city, will ponder on the structure of their disturbed remains, and wonder to what manner of persons they belonged. They will live only in the songs and chronicles of their exterminators. Let these be faithful to their rude virtues as men, and pay due tribute to their unhappy fate as a people.

(From an address delivered in Boston, Mass., 1825)

THE WRECK OF THE "JULIE PLANTE"

A Legend of Lac St. Pierre

William Henry Drummond

On wan dark night on Lac St. Pierre,
De win' she blow, blow, blow,
An' de crew of de wood scow *Julie Plante*
Got scar't an' run below—

For de win' she blow lak hurricane
Bimeby she blow some more,
An' de scow bus' up on Lac St. Pierre
Wan arpent from de shore.

De captinne walk on de fronte deck,
An' walk de hin' deck too—
He call de crew from up de hole
He call de cook also.
De cook she's name was Rosie,
She come from Montreal,
Was chambre maid on lumber barge,
On de Grande Lachine Canal.

De win' she blow from nor'-eas'-wes',—
De sout' win' she blow too,
W'en Rosie cry "Mon cher captinne,
Mon cher, w'at I shall do?"
Den de captinne t'row de big ankerre,
But still the scow she dreef,
De crew he can't pass on de shore,
Becos' he los' hees skeef.

De night was dark lak wan black cat,
De wave run high an' fas',
W'en de captinne tak de Rosie girl
An' tie her to de mas'.
Den he also tak' de life preserve,
An' jomp off on de lak',
An' say, "Good-bye, ma Rosie dear,
I go drown for your sak'."

Nex' morning very early
'Bout ha'f-pas' two-t'ree-four—
De captinne—scow—an' de poor Rosie
Was corpses on de shore,
For de win' she blow lak hurricane
Bimeby she blow some more,
An' de scow bus' up on Lac St. Pierre,
Wan arpent from de shore.

Moral

Now all good wood scow sailor man
Tak' warning by dat storm

An' go an' marry some nice French girl
An' leev on wan beeg farm.
De win' can blow lak hurricane
An' s'pose she blow some more,
You can't get drown on Lac St. Pierre
So long you stay on shore.

SELF-DEPENDENCE

Matthew Arnold

Weary of myself, and sick of asking
What I am, and what I ought to be,
At this vessel's prow I stand, which bears me
Forwards, forwards, o'er the starlit sea.

And a look of passionate desire
O'er the sea and to the stars I send:
"Ye who from my childhood up have calm'd me,
Calm me, ah, compose me to the end!

"Ah, once more," I cried, "ye stars, ye waters,
On my heart your mighty charm renew;
Still, still let me, as I gaze upon you,
Feel my soul becoming vast like you!"

From the intense, clear, star-sown vault of heaven,
Over the lit sea's unquiet way,
In the rustling night-air came the answer:
"Wouldst thou *be* as these are? *Live* as they.

"Unaffrighted by the silence round them,
Undistracted by the sights they see,
These demand not that the things without them
Yield them love, amusement, sympathy.

"And with joy the stars perform their shining,
And the sea its long moon-silver'd roll;
For self-poised they live, nor pine with noting
All the fever of some differing soul.

"Bounded by themselves, and unregardful
In what state God's other work may be,
In their own tasks all their powers pouring,
These attain the mighty life you see."

O air-born voice! long since, severely clear,
A cry like thine in mine own heart I hear:
"Resolve to be thyself; and know that he,
Who finds himself, loses his misery!"

I SING OF A MAIDEN

Anonymous (Fifteenth Century)

I sing of a maiden that
  Matchless is,
King of all Kings is her son
  I wis.

He came all so still
  Where his mother was
As dew in April
  That falleth on grass.

He came all so still
  To his mother's bower
As dew in April
  That falleth on shower.

He came all so still
  Where his mother lay
As dew in April
  That falleth on spray.

Mother and maiden
  Was ne'er none but she
Well may such a lady
  God's mother be.

"HERE LIES JULIET"

William Shakespeare

Romeo. For here lies Juliet, and her beauty makes
This vault a feasting presence full of light.
Death, lie thou there, by a dead man interr'd.
How oft when men are at the point of death
Have they been merry! which their keepers call
A lightning before death: O, how may I
Call this a lightning? O my love! my wife!
Death, that hath suck'd the honey of thy breath,
Hath had no power yet upon thy beauty:
Thou art not conquer'd; beauty's ensign yet
Is crimson in thy lips and in thy cheeks,
And death's pale flag is not advanced there.
Tybalt, liest thou there in thy bloody sheet?
O, what more favour can I do to thee
Than with that hand that cut thy youth in twain
To sunder his that was thine enemy?
Forgive me, cousin! Ah, dear Juliet,
Why art thou yet so fair? shall I believe
That unsubstantial death is amorous,
And that the lean abhorred monster keeps
Thee here in dark to be his paramour?
For fear of that, I still will stay with thee;
And never from this dim palace of dim night
Depart again: here, here will I remain
With worms that are thy chamber-maids; O, here
Will I set up my everlasting rest,
And shake the yoke of inauspicious stars
From this world-wearied flesh. Eyes, look your last!
Arms, take your last embrace! and lips, O you
The doors of breath, seal with a righteous kiss
A dateless bargain to engrossing death!
Come, bitter conduct, come, unsavoury guide!
Thou desperate pilot, now at once run on
The dashing rocks thy sea-sick weary bark.
Here's to my love! (*Drinks*) O true apothecary!
Thy drugs are quick. Thus with a kiss I die.

(From Romeo and Juliet)

KIT CARSON'S RIDE

Joaquin Miller

ROOM! room to turn round in, to breathe and be free,
To grow to be giant, to sail as at sea
With the speed of the wind on a steed with his mane
To the wind, without pathway or route or a rein.
Room! room to be free where the white border'd sea
Blows a kiss to a brother as boundless as he;
Where the buffalo come like a cloud on the plain,
Pouring on like the tide of a storm-driven main,
And the lodge of the hunter to friend or to foe
Offers rest; and unquestion'd you come or you go.
My plains of America! Seas of wild lands!
From a land in the seas in a raiment of foam,
That has reached to a stranger the welcome of home,
I turn to you, lean to you, lift you my hands.

Run! Run! See this flank, sir, and I do love him so!
But he's blind, badger blind. Whoa, Pache boy, whoa,
No, you wouldn't believe it to look at his eyes,
But he's blind, badger blind, and it happen'd this wise:

"We lay in the grass and sunburnt clover
That spread on the ground like a great brown cover
Northward and southward, and west and away
To the Brazos, where our lodges lay,
One broad and unbroken level of brown.
We were waiting the curtains of night to come down
To cover us trio and conceal our flight
With my brown bride, won from an Indian town
That lay in the rear the full ride of a night.

"We lounged in the grass—her eyes were in mine,
And her hands on my knee, and her hair was as wine
In its wealth and its flood, pouring on and all over
Her bosom wine red, and press'd never by one.
Her touch was as warm as the tinge of the clover
Burnt brown as it reach'd to the kiss of the sun.
Her words they were low as the lute-throated dove,
And as laden with love as the heart when it beats
In its hot, eager answer to earliest love,
Or the bee hurried home by its burthen of sweets.

"We lay low in the grass on the broad plain levels,
Old Revels and I, and my stolen brown bride;
'Forty full miles if a foot to ride!
Forty full miles if a foot, and the devils
Of red Comanches are hot on the track
When once they strike it. 'Let the sun go down
Soon, very soon,' muttered bearded old Revels
As he peer'd at the sun, lying low on his back,
Holding fast to his lasso. Then he jerk'd at his steed
And he sprang to his feet, and glanced swiftly around,
And then dropp'd, as if shot, with an ear to the ground;
Then again to his feet, and to me, to my bride,
While his eyes were like flame, his face like a shroud,
His form like a king, and his beard like a cloud,
And his voice loud and shrill, as both trumpet and reed,—
'Pull, pull in your lassoes, and bridle to steed,
And speed you if ever for life you would speed.
Aye, ride for your lives, for your lives you must ride!
For the plain is aflame, the prairie on fire,
And the feet of wild horses hard flying before
I heard like a sea breaking high on the shore,
While the buffalo comes like a surge of the sea,
Driven far by the flame, driving fast on us three
As a hurricane comes, crushing palms in his ire.'

"We drew in the lassoes, seized saddle and rein,
Threw them on, cinched them on, cinched them over again,
And again drew the girth; and spring we to horse,
With head to the Brazos, with a sound in the air
Like the surge of a sea, with a flash in the eye,
From that red wall of flame reaching up to the sky;
A red wall of flame and a black rolling sea
Rushing fast upon us, as the wind sweeping free
And afar from the desert blown hollow and hoarse.

"Not a word, not a wail from a lip was let fall,
We broke not a whisper, we breathed not a prayer,
There was work to be done, there was death in the air,
And the chance was one to a thousand for all.

"Twenty miles! . . . thirty miles! . . . a dim distant speck . . .
Then a long reaching line, and the Brazos in sight!
And I rose in my seat with a shout of delight.

I stood in my stirrup, and look'd to my right—
But Revels was gone; I glanced by my shoulder
And saw his horse stagger; I saw his head drooping
Hard down on his breast, and his naked breast stooping
Low down to the mane, as so swifter and bolder
Ran reaching out for us the red-footed fire.
He rode neck to neck with a buffalo bull,
That made the earth shake where he came in his course,
The monarch of millions, with a shaggy mane full
Of smoke and of dust, and it shook with desire
Of battle, with rage and with bellowings hoarse.
His keen, crooked horns, through the storm of his mane,
Like black lances lifted and lifted again;
And I looked but this once, for the fire licked through,
And Revels was gone, as we rode two and two.

"I look'd to my left then—and nose, neck, and shoulder
Sank slowly, sank surely, till back to my thighs,
And up through the black blowing veil of her hair
Did beam full in mine her two marvelous eyes,
With a longing and love yet a look of despair
And of pity for me, as she felt the smoke fold her,
And flames leaping far for her glorious hair.
Her sinking horse falter'd, plunged, fell and was gone
As I reach'd through the flame and I bore her still on.
On! into the Brazos, she, Pache and I—
Poor burnt, blinded Pache. I love him . . .
That's why."

GRADATIM

Josiah Gilbert Holland

Heaven is not reached at a single bound;
But we build the ladder by which we rise
From the lowly earth to the vaulted skies,
And we mount to its summit round by round.

I count this thing to be grandly true,
That a noble deed is a step toward God,
Lifting the soul from the common sod
To a purer air and a broader view.

We rise by things that are 'neath our feet;
  By what we have mastered of good and gain,
  By the pride deposed and the passion slain,
And the vanquished ills that we hourly meet.

We hope, we aspire, we resolve, we trust,
  When the morning calls us to life and light;
  But our hearts grow weary, and ere the night,
Our lives are trailing the sordid dust.

We hope, we resolve, we aspire, we pray,
  And we think that we mount the air on wings
  Beyond the recall of sensual things,
While our feet still cling to the heavy clay.

Wings for angels, but feet for men!
  We may borrow the wings to find the way;
  We may hope, and resolve, and aspire, and pray;
But our feet must rise, or we fall again.

Only in dreams is a ladder thrown
  From the weary earth to the sapphire walls,
  But the dreams depart, and the vision falls,
And the sleeper wakes on his pillow of stone.

Heaven is not reached at a single bound;
  But we build the ladder by which we rise
  From the lowly earth to the vaulted skies,
And we mount to its summit round by round.

GOD AND THE SOLDIER

God and the soldier
All men adore
In time of trouble,
And no more;
For when war is over
And all things righted,
God is neglected—
The old soldier slighted.

(Said to have been found on an old stone sentry-box at Gibraltar. Sometimes the lines are adapted to read "God and the doctor.")

BRIGHT STAR, WOULD I WERE STEADFAST AS THOU ART!

John Keats

Bright star, would I were steadfast as thou art!
  Not in lone splendour hung aloft the night,
And watching, with eternal lids apart,
  Like Nature's patient, sleepless Eremite,
The moving waters at their priestlike task
  Of pure ablution round earth's human shores,
Or gazing on the new soft fallen mask
  Of snow upon the mountains and the moors:
No—yet still steadfast, still unchangeable,
  Pillow'd upon my fair love's ripening breast,
To feel for ever its soft fall and swell,
  Awake for ever in a sweet unrest,
Still, still to hear her tender-taken breath,
And so live ever—or else swoon to death.

BETH GÊLERT

William Robert Spencer

The Spearmen heard the bugle sound,
  And cheerily smiled the morn;
And many a brach, and many a hound,
  Obeyed Llewellyn's horn.

And still he blew a louder blast,
  And gave a lustier cheer,
"Come, Gêlert, come, wert never last
  Llewellyn's horn to hear.

"O, where does faithful Gêlert roam,
  The flower of all his race?
So true, so brave,—a lamb at home,
  A lion in the chase!"

'Twas only at Llewellyn's board
  The faithful Gêlert fed;
He watch'd, he serv'd, he cheer'd his lord,
  And sentinell'd his bed.

In sooth, he was a peerless hound,
The gift of royal John;
But now no Gêlert could be found,
And all the chase rode on.

And now, as o'er the rocks and dells
The gallant chidings rise,
All Snowdon's craggy chaos yells
The many-mingled cries!

That day Llewellyn little loved
The chase of hart and hare;
And scant and small the booty proved,
For Gêlert was not there.

Unpleased, Llewellyn homeward hied,
When, near the portal seat,
His truant Gêlert he espied
Bounding his lord to greet.

But, when he gained his castle-door,
Aghast the chieftain stood;
The hound all o'er was smeared with gore
His lips, his fangs, ran blood.

Llewellyn gazed with fierce surprise;
Unused such looks to meet,
His favorite checked his joyful guise,
And crouched, and licked his feet.

Onward, in haste, Llewellyn passed,
And on went Gêlert too;
And still where'er his eyes he cast,
Fresh blood-gouts shocked his view.

O'erturned his infant's bed he found,
With blood-stained covert rent;
And all around the walls and ground
With recent blood besprent.

He called his child,—no voice replied,—
He searched with terror wild;
Blood, blood he found on every side,
But nowhere found his child.

"Hell-hound! my child's by thee devoured!"
  The frantic father cried;
And to the hilt his vengeful sword
  He plunged in Gêlert's side.

His suppliant looks as prone he fell,
  No pity could impart;
But still his Gêlert's dying yell
  Pass'd heavy o'er his heart.

Aroused by Gêlert's dying yell,
  Some slumberer wakened nigh:
What words the parent's joy could tell
  To hear his infant's cry!

Concealed beneath a tumbled heap
  His hurried search had missed,
All glowing from his rosy sleep,
  The cherub boy he kissed.

Nor scathe had he, nor harm, nor dread,
  But, the same couch beneath,
Lay a gaunt wolf, all torn and dead,
  Tremendous still in death.

Ah, what was then Llewellyn's pain!
  For now the truth was clear;
His gallant hound the wolf had slain
  To save Llewellyn's heir.

Vain, vain was all Llewellyn's woe:
  "Best of thy kind, adieu!
The frantic blow, which laid thee low,
  This heart shall ever rue."

And now a gallant tomb they raise,
  With costly sculpture deckt;
And marbles, storied with his praise,
  Poor Gêlert's bones protect.

There never could the spearman pass,
  Or forester, unmoved;
There oft the tear-besprinkled grass
  Llewellyn's sorrow proved.

And there he hung his sword and spear,
  And there as evening fell,
In Fancy's ear he oft would hear
  Poor Gêlert's dying yell.

And till great Snowdon's rocks grow old,
  And cease the storm to brave,
The consecrated spot shall hold
  The name of "Gêlert's Grave."

From THE AMERICAN CRISIS

Thomas Paine

I have as little suspicion in me as any man living, but my secret opinion has ever been, and still is, that God Almighty will not give up a people to military destruction, or leave them unsupported to perish, who have so earnestly and so repeatedly sought to avoid the calamities of war, by every decent method which wisdom could invent. Neither have I so much of the infidel in me, as to suppose that He has relinquished the government of the world, and given us up to the care of devils.

(From The American Crisis, No. 1)

CORONACH *

By Sir Walter Scott

He is gone on the mountain,
  He is lost to the forest,
Like a summer-dried fountain,
  When our need was the sorest.
The font, reappearing,
  From the rain-drops shall borrow,
But to us comes no cheering,
  To Duncan no morrow!

* A dirge.

The hand of the reaper
  Takes the ears that are hoary,
But the voice of the weeper
  Wails manhood in glory.
The autumn winds rushing
  Waft the leaves that are searest,
But our flower was in flushing,
  When blighting was nearest.

Fleet foot on the correi,
  Sage counsel in cumber,
Red hand in the foray,
  How sound is thy slumber!
Like the dew on the mountain,
  Like the foam on the river,
Like the bubble on the fountain,
  Thou art gone, and for ever!
(From The Lady of the Lake)

CHAUCER

Artemus Ward

Some kind person has sent me Chaucer's poems. Mr. C. had talent, but he couldn't spel. No man has a right to be a lit-rary man onless he knows how to spel. It is a pity that Chaucer, who had a geneyus, was so unedicated. He's the wus speller I know of.

UP-HILL

Christina Georgina Rossetti

Does the road wind up-hill all the way?
  Yes, to the very end.
Will the day's journey take the whole long day?
  From morn to night, my friend.

But is there for the night a resting-place?
  A roof for when the slow dark hours begin.
May not the darkness hide it from my face?
  You cannot miss that inn.

Shall I meet other way-farers at night?
Those who have gone before.
Then must I knock, or call when just in sight?
They will not keep you standing at that door.

Shall I find comfort, travel-sore and weak?
Of labour you shall find the sum.
Will there be beds for me and all who seek?
Yea, beds for all who come.

GO WEST, YOUNG MAN

Horace Greeley

If any young man is about to commence the world, with little in his circumstances to prepossess him in favor of one section above another, we say to him publicly and privately: Go to the West; there your capacities are sure to be appreciated and your industry and energy rewarded.

AGAINST OBLIVION

Percy Bysshe Shelley

Peace, peace! he is not dead, he doth not sleep—
He hath awaken'd from the dream of life—
'Tis we, who, lost in stormy visions, keep
With phantoms an unprofitable strife,
And in mad trance strike with our spirit's knife
Invulnerable nothings.—*We* decay
Like corpses in a charnel; fear and grief
Convulse us and consume us day by day,
And cold hopes swarm like worms within our living clay.

He has outsoar'd the shadow of our night;
Envy and calumny, and hate and pain,
And that unrest which men miscall delight,
Can touch him not and torture not again;
From the contagion of the world's slow stain
He is secure, and now can never mourn

A heart grown cold, a head grown grey in vain;
Nor, when the spirit's self has ceased to burn,
With sparkless ashes load an unlamented urn. . . .

He is made one with Nature; there is heard
His voice in all her music, from the moan
Of thunder, to the song of night's sweet bird;
He is a presence to be felt and known
In darkness and in light, from herb and stone,
Spreading itself where'er that Power may move
Which has withdrawn its being to its own;
Which wields the world with never-wearied love,
Sustains it from beneath, and kindles it above.

He is a portion of the loveliness
Which once he made more lovely; he doth bear
His part, while the one Spirit's plastic stress
Sweeps through the dull dense world, compelling there
All new successions to the forms they wear;
Torturing th' unwilling dross that checks its flight
To its own likeness, as each mass may bear;
And bursting in its beauty and its might
From trees and beasts and men into the Heaven's light.

The splendours of the firmament of time
May be eclipsed but are extinguish'd not;
Like stars to their appointed height they climb,
And death is a low mist which cannot blot
The brightness it may veil. When lofty thought
Lifts a young heart above its mortal lair,
And love and life contend in it, for what
Shall be its earthly doom, the dead live there
And move like winds of light on dark and stormy air. . . .

Or go to Rome, which is the sepulchre,
O, not of him, but of our joy; 'tis nought
That ages, empires, and religions there
Lie buried in the ravage they have wrought;
For such as he can lend,—they borrow not
Glory from those who made the world their prey;
And he is gather'd to the kings of thought
Who waged contention with their time's decay,
And of the past are all that cannot pass away.

Go thou to Rome,—at once the Paradise,
The grave, the city, and the wilderness;
And where its wrecks like shatter'd mountains rise,
And flowering weeds, and fragrant copses dress
The bones of Desolation's nakedness,
Pass, till the Spirit of the spot shall lead
Thy footsteps to a slope of green access,
Where, like an infant's smile, over the dead
A light of laughing flowers along the grass is spread.

And grey walls moulder round, on which dull Time
Feeds, like slow fire upon a hoary brand;
And one keen pyramid with wedge sublime,
Pavilioning the dust of him who plann'd
This refuge for his memory, doth stand
Like flame transform'd to marble; and beneath,
A field is spread, on which a newer band
Have pitch'd in Heaven's smile their camp of death,
Welcoming him we lose with scarce extinguish'd breath.

Here pause: these graves are all too young as yet
To have outgrown the sorrow which consign'd
Its charge to each; and if the seal is set,
Here, on one fountain of a mourning mind,
Break it not thou! too surely shalt thou find
Thine own well full, if thou returnest home,
Of tears and gall. From the world's bitter wind
Seek shelter in the shadow of the tomb.
What Adonais is, why fear we to become?

The One remains, the many change and pass;
Heaven's light for ever shines, Earth's shadows fly;
Life, like a dome of many-colour'd glass,
Stains the white radiance of Eternity,
Until Death tramples it to fragments.—Die,
If thou wouldst be with that which thou dost seek!
Follow where all is fled!—Rome's azure sky,
Flowers, ruins, statues, music, words, are weak
The glory they transfuse with fitting truth to speak. . . .

The breath whose might I have invoked in song
Descends on me; my spirit's bark is driven
Far from the shore, far from the trembling throng

Whose sails were never to the tempest given;
The massy earth and sphered skies are riven!
I am borne darkly, fearfully, afar;
Whilst burning through the inmost veil of Heaven,
The soul of Adonais, like a star,
Beacons from the abode where the Eternal are.

(From Adonais)

GOING TO THE DOGS

Anonymous

My granddad, viewing earth's worn cogs,
Said things were going to the dogs;
His granddad in his house of logs,
Said things were going to the dogs;
His granddad in the Flemish bogs,
Said things were going to the dogs;
His granddad in his old skin togs,
Said things were going to the dogs;
There's one thing that I have to state—
The dogs have had a good long wait.

THE RISING

Thomas Buchanan Read

Out of the North the wild news came,
Far flashing on its wings of flame,
Swift as the boreal light which flies
At midnight through the startled skies.

And there was tumult in the air,
The fife's shrill note, the drum's loud beat,
And through the wide land everywhere
The answering tread of hurrying feet,
While the first oath of Freedom's gun
Came on the blast from Lexington.
And Concord, roused, no longer tame,

Forgot her old baptismal name,
Made bare her patriot arm of power,
And swelled the discord of the hour.

The yeoman and the yeoman's son,
  With knitted brow and sturdy dint,
Renewed the polish of each gun,
  Reoiled the lock, reset the flint;
And oft the maid and matron there,
While kneeling in the firelight glare,
Long poured, with half-suspended breath,
The lead into the molds of death.

The hands by Heaven made silken soft
  To soothe the brow of love or pain,
Alas! are dulled and soiled too oft
  By some unhallowed earthly stain;
But under the celestial bound
No nobler picture can be found
Than woman, brave in word and deed,
Thus serving in her nation's need:
Her love is with her country now,
Her hand is on its aching brow.

Within its shade of elm and oak
  The church of Berkley Manor stood:
There Sunday found the rural folk,
  And some esteemed of gentle blood.
In vain their feet with loitering tread
  Passed 'mid the graves where rank is naught:
  All could not read the lesson taught
In that republic of the dead.

The pastor rose: the prayer was strong;
The psalm was warrior David's song;
The text, a few short words of might,—
"The Lord of hosts shall arm the right."

He spoke of wrongs too long endured,
Of sacred rights to be secured;
Then from his patriot tongue of flame
The startling words for Freedom came.
The stirring sentences he spake

Compelled the heart to glow or quake,
And, rising on his theme's broad wing,
  And grasping in his nervous hand
  The imaginary battle brand,
In face of death he dared to fling
Defiance to a tyrant king.

Even as he spoke, his frame, renewed
In eloquence of attitude,
Rose, as it seemed, a shoulder higher;
Then swept his kindling glance of fire
From startled pew to breathless choir;
When suddenly his mantle wide
His hands impatient flung aside,
And, lo! he met their wondering eyes
Complete in all a warrior's guise.

A moment there was awful pause,—
  When Berkley cried, "Cease, traitor! cease!
  God's temple is the house of peace!"
The other shouted, "Nay, not so,
When God is with our righteous cause:
  His holiest places then are ours,
  His temples are our forts and towers
That frown upon the tyrant foe:
In this the dawn of Freedom's day
There is a time to fight and pray!"

And now before the open door—
  The warrior priest had ordered so—
The enlisting trumpet's sudden soar
Rang through the chapel, o'er and o'er,
  Its long reverberating blow,
So loud and clear, it seemed the ear
Of dusty death must wake and hear.
And there the startling drum and fife
Fired the living with fiercer life;
While overhead with wild increase,
Forgetting its ancient toll of peace,
  The great bell swung as ne'er before:
It seemed as it would never cease;
And every word its ardor flung
From off its jubilant iron tongue
  Was, "WAR! WAR! WAR!"

"Who dares"—this was the patriot's cry,
As striding from the desk he came—
"Come out with me, in Freedom's name,
For her to live, for her to die?"
A hundred hands flung up reply,
A hundred voices answered "I."

THE SPIRIT OF LIBERTY

Judge Learned Hand

We have gathered here to affirm a faith, a faith in a common purpose, a common conviction, a common devotion. Some of us have chosen America as the land of our adoption; the rest have come from those who did the same. For this reason we have some right to consider ourselves a picked group, a group of those who had the courage to break from the past and brave the dangers and loneliness of a strange land.

What was the object that nerved us, or those who went before us, to this choice? We sought liberty; freedom from oppression, freedom from want, freedom to be ourselves. This we then sought. This we now believe that we are by way of winning.

What do we mean when we say that first of all we seek liberty? I often wonder whether we do not rest our hopes too much upon constitutions, upon laws and upon courts. These are false hopes; believe me, these are false hopes. Liberty lies in the hearts of men and women. When it dies there, no constitution, no law, no court can save it. No constitution, no law, no court can even do much to help it. While it lies there, it needs no constitution, no law, no court to save it.

And what is this liberty which must lie in the hearts of men and women? It is not the ruthless, the unbridled will. It is not freedom to do as one likes. That is the denial of liberty, and leads straight to its overthrow. A society in which men recognize no check upon their freedom soon becomes a society where freedom is the possession of only a savage few; as we have learned to our sorrow.

What then is the spirit of liberty? I cannot define it; I can only tell you my own faith. The spirit of liberty is the spirit which is not too sure that it is right. The spirit of liberty is the spirit which seeks to understand the minds of other men and women. The spirit of liberty is the spirit which weighs their interests alongside its own without bias. The spirit of liberty remembers that not even a sparrow falls to earth unheeded. The spirit of liberty is the spirit of Him who, near two thousand years ago, taught mankind that lesson it has never learned, but has never quite forgotten: that there may be a kingdom where the least shall be heard and considered side by side with the greatest.

And now in that spirit, that spirit of an America which has never been, and which may never be; nay, which never will be, except as the conscience and courage of Americans create it; yet in the spirit of that America which lies hidden in some form in the aspirations of us all; in the spirit of that America for which our young men are at this moment fighting and dying; in that spirit of liberty and of America I ask you to rise and with me to pledge our faith in the glorious *destiny* of our beloved country—with liberty and justice for all.

(Address on "I Am an American Day"—
Central Park, New York City, May, 1944)

WHY SO PALE AND WAN, FOND LOVER?

Sir John Suckling

Why so pale and wan, fond lover?
  Prithee, why so pale?
Will, when looking well can't move her,
  Looking ill prevail?
  Prithee, why so pale?

Why so dull and mute, young sinner?
  Prithee, why so mute?
Will, when speaking well can't win her,
  Saying nothing do 't?
  Prithee, why so mute?

Quit, quit for shame! This will not move,
  This cannot take her.
If of herself she will not love,
  Nothing can make her:
  The devil take her!

PATTERNS

Amy Lowell

I walk down the garden-paths,
And all the daffodils
Are blowing, and the bright blue squills.
I walk down the patterned garden-paths
In my stiff, brocaded gown.
With my powdered hair and jewelled fan,
I too am a rare
Pattern. As I wander down
The garden-paths.

My dress is richly figured,
And the train
Makes a pink and silver stain
On the gravel, and the thrift
Of the Borders.
Just a plate of current fashion,
Tripping by in high-heeled, ribboned shoes.
Not a soft anywhere about me,
Only whale-bone and brocade.
And I sink on a seat in the shade
Of a lime-tree. For my passion
Wars against the stiff brocade.
The daffodils and squills
Flutter in the breeze
As they please.
And I weep;
For the lime-tree is in blossom
And one small flower has dropped upon my bosom.

And the plashing of waterdrops
In the marble fountain
Comes down the garden-paths.
The dripping never stops.
Underneath my stiffened gown
Is the softness of a woman bathing in a marble basin,
A basin in the midst of hedges grown
So thick, she cannot see her lover hiding.
But she guesses he is near,
And the sliding of the water

Seems the stroking of a dear
Hand upon her.
What is Summer in a fine brocaded gown!
I should like to see it lying in a heap upon the ground.
All the pink and silver crumpled upon the ground.

I would be the pink and silver as I ran along the paths,
And he would stumble after,
Bewildered by my laughter.
I should see the sun flashing from his sword-hilt and the buckles
on his shoes.
I would choose
To lead him in a maze along the patterned paths,
A bright and laughing maze for my heavy-booted lover,
Till he caught me in the shade,
And the buttons of his waistcoat bruised my body as he clasped me,
Aching, melting, unafraid.
With the shadows of the leaves and the sundrops,
And the plopping of the waterdrops,
All about us in the open afternoon—
I am very like to swoon
With the weight of this brocade,
For the sun shifts through the shade.

Underneath the fallen blossom
In my bosom,
Is a letter I have hid.
It was brought to me this morning by a rider from the Duke,
"Madam, we regret to inform you that Lord Hartwell
Died in action Thursday se'nnight."
As I read it in the white, morning sunlight,
The letters squirmed like snakes.
"Any answer, Madam?" said my footman.
"No," I told him.
"See that the messenger take some refreshment.
No, no answer."
And I walked into the garden,
Up and down the patterned paths,
In my stiff, correct brocade.
The blue and yellow flowers stood up proudly in the sun,
Each one.
I stood upright too,
Held rigid to the pattern

By the stiffness of my gown.
Up and down I walked,
Up and down.

In a month he would have been my husband.
In a month, here, underneath this lime,
We would have broke the pattern;
He for me, and I for him,
He as Colonel, I as Lady,
On this shady seat.
He had a whim
That sunlight carried blessing.
And I answered, "It shall be as you have said."
Now he is dead.

In Summer and in Winter I shall walk
Up and down
The patterned garden-paths
In my stiff, brocaded gown.
The squills and daffodils
Will give place to pillared roses, and to asters, and to snow.
I shall go
Up and down,
In my gown.
Gorgeously arrayed,
Boned and stayed.
And the softness of my body will be guarded from embrace
By each button, hook and lace.
For the man who should loose me is dead,
Fighting with the Duke in Flanders,
In a pattern called a war.
Christ! What are patterns for?

MR. DOOLEY ON NEW YEAR'S RESOLUTIONS

Finley Peter Dunne

Mr. Hennessy looked out at the rain dripping down in Archey Road, and sighed, "A-ha, 'tis a bad spell iv weather we're havin' ".

"Faith, it is," said Mr. Dooley, "or else we mind it more thin we did. I can't remimber wan day fr'm another. Whin I was young,

I niver thought iv rain or snow, cold or heat. But now th' heat stings and th' cold wrenches me bones; an', if I go out in th' rain with less on me thin a ton iv rubber, I'll pay dear f'r it in achin' j'ints, so I will. That's what old age means; an' now another year has been put on to what we had befur, an' we're expected to be gay. 'Ring out th' old, ring in th' new,' says a guy at th' Brothers' School. 'Ring out th' old, ring in th' new,' he says. 'Ring out th' false, ring in th' true,' says he. It's a pretty sintimint, Hinnissy; but how ar-re we goin' to do it? Nawthin'd please me betther thin to turn me back on th' wicked an' ingloryous past, rayform me life, an' live at peace with th' wurruld to th' end iv me days. But how th' divvle can I do it? As th' fellow says, 'Can the leopard change his spots,' or can't he?

"You know Dorsey, iv coorse, th' cross-eyed May-o man that comes to this counthry about wan day in advance iv a warrant f'r stealin'? Ye know what he done to me, tellin' people I was caught in me cellar poorin' wather into a bar'l? Well, last night says I to mesilf, thinkin' iv Dorsey, I says: 'I swear that henceforth I'll keep me temper with me fellow-men. I'll not let anger or jealousy get the betther iv me,' I says. 'I'll lave off all me old feuds; an' if I meet me inimy goin' down th' sthreet, I'll go up an' shake him by th' hand, if I'm sure he hasn't a brick in th' other hand.' Oh, I was mighty compliminthry to mesilf. I set by th' stove dhrinkin' hot wans, an' ivry wan I dhrunk made me more iv a pote. 'Tis th' way with th' stuff. Whin I'm in dhrink, I have a fine thought; an' if I wasn't too comfortable to go an' look f'r th' ink-bottle, I cud write pomes that'd make Shakespeare an' Mike Scanlan think they were wur-rkin' on a dredge. 'Why,' says I, 'carry into th' new year th' hathreds iv th' old?' I says. 'Let the dead past bury its dead,' says I. 'Tur-rn ye'er lamps up to th' blue sky,' I says. (It was rainin' like the divvile, an' th' hour was midnight, but I give no heed to that, bein' comfortable with the hot wans.) An' I wint to th' dure, an', whin Mike Duffy came by on number wan hundherd an' five, ringin' th' gong iv th' ca-ar, I hollered to him: 'Ring out th' old, ring in th' new.' 'Go back into ye-er stall,' he says, 'an' wring ye-ersilf out,' he says. 'Ye-er wet through,' he says.

"Whin I woke up this mornin', th' pothry had all disappeared, an' I begun to think th' las' hot wan I took had something wrong with it. Besides, th' lumbago was grippin' me till I cud hardly put wan foot befure th' other. But I remimbered me promises to mesilf, an' wint out on th' sthreet, intindin' to wish ivry wan a 'Happy New Year!' an' hopin' in me hear-rt that th' first wan I wished it to'd tell me to go to th' divvle, so I cud hit him in th' eye. I hadn't gone half a block befure I spied Dorsey acrost the sthreet. I picked up half a brick an' put it in me pocket, an' Dorsey done th' same. Thin we wint up to each other. 'A Happy New Year,' says I. 'Th' same to you!' says he. 'An' manny iv thim,' he says. 'Ye have a brick in ye-er hand,' says I. 'I was thinkin' iv givin' ye a New Year's gift,' says he. 'Th' same to you, an' manny iv thim,' says I, fondlin' me own ammunition. ' 'Tis even all around,' says he. 'It is,' says I. 'I was thinkin' las' night I'd give up me gredge again ye,' says he. 'I had th' same thought mesilf,' says I. 'But, since I seen ye-er face,' he says, 'I've concluded that I'd be more comfortable hatin' ye thin havin' ye f'r a frind,' says he. 'Ye-er a man iv taste,' says I. An' we backed away fr'm each other. He's a Tip, an' can throw a stone like a rifleman; an' Hinnissy, I'm somethin' iv an amachoor shot with a half-brick mesilf.

"Well, I've been thinkin' it over, and I've argied it out that life'd not be worth livin' if we didn't keep our inimies. I can have all th' frinds I need. Anny man can that keeps a liquor sthore. But a rale sthrong inimy, specially a May-o inimy—wan that hates ye ha-ard, an' that ye'd take th' coat off yer back to do a bad tur-rn to—is a luxury that I can't go without in me ol' days. Dorsey is the right sort. I can't go by his house without bein' in fear he'll spill the chimbly down on me head; an', whin he passes my place, he walks in th' middle iv th' sthreet, an' crosses himsilf. I'll swear off anything but Dorsey. He's a good man, an' I despise him. Here's long life to him."

WHEN I HAVE FEARS THAT I MAY CEASE TO BE

John Keats

When I have fears that I may cease to be
  Before my pen has glean'd my teeming brain,
Before high pilèd books, in charactry,
  Hold like rich garners the full-ripen'd grain;
When I behold, upon the night's starr'd face,
  Huge cloudy symbols of a high romance,
And think that I may never live to trace
  Their shadows, with the magic hand of chance;
And when I feel, fair creature of an hour!
  That I shall never look upon thee more,
Never have relish in the faery power
  Of unreflecting love;—then on the shore

Of the wide world I stand alone, and think
Till Love and Fame to nothingness do sink.

HAPPY THOUGHT

Robert Louis Stevenson

The world is so full of a number of things,
I'm sure we should all be as happy as kings.

ON A GIRDLE

Edmund Waller

That which her slender waist confined
Shall now my joyful temples bind;
No monarch but would give his crown,
His arms might do what this has done.

It was my heaven's extremest sphere,
The pale which held that lovely dear;
My joy, my grief, my hope, my love,
Did all within this circle move.

A narrow compass! and yet there
Dwelt all that's good, and all that's fair;
Give me but what this ribband bound,
Take all the rest the sun goes round!

I SHALL NOT PASS THIS WAY AGAIN

Anonymous

Through this toilsome world, alas!
Once and only once I pass;
If a kindness I may show,
If a good deed I may do
To a suffering fellow man,
Let me do it while I can.
No delay, for it is plain
I shall not pass this way again.

POOR GINGER

Anna Sewell

One day, while our cab and many others were waiting outside one of the parks where music was playing, a shabby old cab drove up beside ours. The horse was an old worn-out chestnut, with an ill-kept coat, and bones that showed plainly through it, the knees buckled over, and the fore-legs were very unsteady. I had been eating some hay, and the wind rolled a little lock of it that way, and the poor creature put out her long thin neck and picked it up, and then turned and looked about for more. There was a hopeless look in the dull eye that I could not help noticing, and then, as I was thinking where I had seen that horse before, she looked full at me and said, "Black Beauty, is that you?"

It was Ginger! but how changed! The beautifully arched and glossy neck was now straight, and lank, and fallen in; the clean straight legs and delicate fetlocks were swelled; the joints were grown out of shape with hard work; the face, that once was so full of spirit and life, was now full of suffering, and I could tell by the heaving of her sides, and her frequent cough, how bad her breathing was.

Our drivers were standing together a little way off, so I sidled up to her a step or two, that we might have a little quiet talk. It was a sad tale that she had to tell.

After a twelvemonths' run off at Earlshall, she was considered to be fit for work again, and was sold to a gentleman. For a little while she got on very well, but after a longer gallop than usual the old strain returned, and after being rested and doctored she was again sold. In this way she changed hands several times, but always getting lower down.

"And so at last," said she, "I was bought by a man who keeps a number of cabs and horses, and lets them out. You look well off, and I am glad of it, but I could not tell you what my life has been. When they found out my weakness they said I was not worth what they gave for me, and that I must go into one of the low cabs, and just be used up; that is what they are doing, and whipping and working with never one thought of what I suffer—they paid for me, and must get it out of me, they say. The man who hires me now pays a good deal of money to the owner every day, and so he has to get it out of me, too; and so it's all the week round and round, with never a Sunday rest."

I said, "You used to stand up for yourself if you were ill-used."

"Ah!" she said, "I did once, but it's no use; men are strongest, and if they are cruel and have no feeling, there is nothing we can do, but just bear it—bear it on and on to the end. I wish the end was come, I wish I was dead. I have seen dead horses, and I am sure they do not suffer pain; I wish I may drop down my head at my work, and not be sent off to the knackers."

I was very much troubled, and I put my nose up to hers, but I could say nothing to comfort her. I think she was pleased to see me, for she said, "You are the only friend I ever had."

Just then her driver came up, and with a tug at her mouth backed her out of the line and drove off, leaving me very sad indeed.

A short time after this a cart with a dead horse in it passed our cab-stand. The head hung out of the cart-tail, the lifeless tongue was slowly dropping with blood; and the sunken eyes! but I can't speak of them, the sight was too dreadful. It was a chestnut horse with a long, thin neck. I saw a white streak on the forehead. I believe it was Ginger; I hoped it was, for then her troubles would be over. Oh! if men were more merciful they would shoot us before we came to such misery.

(From Black Beauty)

THE FIRST NOWELL

Anonymous

The first Nowell the angel did say,
Was to certain poor shepherds in fields as they lay;
In fields where they lay keeping their sheep,
On a cold winter's night that was so deep.
Nowell, Nowell, Nowell, Nowell,
Born is the King of Israel.

They looked up and saw a star
Shining in the East beyond them far,
And to the earth it gave great light,
And so it continued both day and night.

This star drew nigh to the northwest,
O'er Bethlehem it took its rest.
And there it did both stop and stay
Right over the place where Jesus lay.

Then enter'd in those wise men three,
Full rev'rently upon their knee,
And offer'd there in His presence,
Their gold, and myrrh, and frankincense.

Then let us all with one accord
Sing praises to our heavenly Lord,
That hath made heaven and earth of nought,
And with His blood mankind hath bought.

BARNEY McGEE

Richard Hovey

Barney McGee, there's no end of good luck in you,
Will-o'-the-wisp, with a flicker of Puck in you,—
Wild as a bull-pup and all of his pluck in you—
Let a man tread on your coat and he'll see!—
Eyes like the lakes of Killarney for clarity,
Nose that turns up without any vulgarity,
Smile like a cherub, and hair that is carroty,—
Wow, you're a rarity, Barney McGee!
Mellow as Tarragon,
Prouder than Aragon—
Hardly a paragon,
You will agree—
Here's all that's fine to you!
Books and old wine to you!
Girls be divine to you!
Barney McGee!

Lucky the day when I met you unwittingly,
Dining where vagabonds came and went flittingly.
Here's some *Barbera* to drink it befittingly,
That day at Silvio's, Barney McGee!
Many's the time we have quaffed our Chianti there,
Listened to Silvio quoting us Dante there,—
Once more to drink *Nebiolo spumante* there,
How we'd pitch Pommery into the sea!
There where the gang of us
Met ere Rome rang of us,
They had the hang of us

To a degree.
How they would trust to you!
That was but just to you.
Here's o'er their dust to you,
Barney McGee!

Barney McGee, when you're sober you scintillate,
But when you're in drink you're the pride of the intellect;
Divil a one of us ever came in till late,
Once at the bar, where you happened to be,—
Every eye there like a spoke in you centering,
You with your eloquence, blarney, and bantering—
All Vagabondia shouts at your entering,
King of the Tenderloin, Barney McGee!
There's no satiety
In your society,
With the variety
Of your *esprit*.
Here's a long purse to you,
And a great thirst to you!
Fate be no worse to you,
Barney McGee!

Och, and the girls whose poor hearts you deracinate,
Whirl and bewilder and flutter and fascinate!
Faith, it's so killing you are, you assassinate,—
Murder's the word for you, Barney McGee!
Bold when they're sunny and smooth when they're showery,—
Oh, but the style of you, fluent and flowery!
Chesterfield's way, with a touch of the Bowery!
How would they silence you, Barney *machree?*
Nought can your gab allay,
Learned as Rabelais
(You in his abbey lay
Once on the spree).
Here's to the smile of you,
(Oh, but the guile of you!)
And a long while to you,
Barney McGee!

Facile with phrases of length and Latinity,
Like *honorificabilitudinity*.
Where is the maid could resist your vicinity,

Wiled by the impudent grace of your plea?
Then your vivacity and pertinacity,
Carry the day with the divil's audacity;
No mere veracity robs your sagacity
Of perspicacity, Barney McGee!
When all is new to them,
What will you do to them?
Will you be true to them?
Who shall decree?
Here's a fair strife to you!
Health and long life to you!
And a great wife to you,
Barney McGee!

Barney McGee, you're the pick of gentility;
Nothing can phase you, you've such a facility;
Nobody ever yet found your utility,—
That is the charm of you, Barney McGee;
Under conditions that others would stammer in,
Still unperturbed as a cat or a Cameron,
Polished as somebody in the Decameron,
Putting the glamour on prince or Pawnee!
In your meanderin',
Love and philanderin',
Calm as a mandarin
Sipping his tea!
Under the art of you,
Parcel and part of you,
Here's to the heart of you,
Barney McGee!

You who were ever alert to befriend a man,
You who were ever the first to defend a man,
You who had always the money to lend a man,
Down on his luck and hard up for a V!
Sure, you'll be playing a harp in beatitude
(And a quare sight you will be in that attitude)—
Some day, where gratitude seems but a platitude,
You'll find your latitude,
Barney McGee.
That's no flim-flam at all,
Frivol or sham at all,
Just the plain— Damn it all,

Have one on me!
Here's luck and more to you,
Friends by the score to you,
True to the core of you
Barney McGee!

ON PRINCE FREDERICK

Anonymous

Here lies Fred
Who was alive and is dead.
Had it been his father,
I had much rather;
Had it been his brother,
Still better than another;
Had it been his sister,
No one would have missed her;
Had it been the whole generation,
So much the better for the nation;
But since 'tis only Fred
Who was alive and is dead,
Why, there's no more to be said.

THE TOYS

Coventry Patmore

My Little Son, who look'd from thoughtful eyes
And moved and spoke in quiet grown-up wise,
Having my law the seventh time disobey'd,
I struck him and dismiss'd
With hard words and unkiss'd,
—His Mother, who was patient, being dead.
Then, fearing lest his grief should hinder sleep,
I visited his bed,
But found him slumbering deep,
With darken'd eyelids, and their lashes yet
From his late sobbing wet.
And I, with moan,
Kissing away his tears, left others of my own;

For, on a table drawn beside his head,
He had put, within his reach,
A box of counters and a red-vein'd stone,
A piece of glass abraded by the beach,
And six or seven shells,
A bottle with bluebells,
And two French copper coins, ranged there with careful art,
To comfort his sad heart.

So when that night I pray'd
To God, I wept, and said:
Ah, when at last we lie with trancèd breath,
Not vexing Thee in death,
And Thou rememberest of what toys
We made our joys,
How weakly understood
Thy great commanded good,
Then, fatherly not less
Than I whom Thou hast moulded from the clay,
Thou'lt leave Thy wrath, and say,
"I will be sorry for their childishness."

JUST FOLKS *

Edgar A. Guest

We're queer folks here.
We'll talk about the weather,
The good times we've had together,
The good times near,
The roses buddin', an' the bees
Once more upon their nectar sprees;
The scarlet fever scare, an' who
Came mighty near not pullin' through,
An' who had light attacks, an' all
The things that int'rest, big or small;
But here you'll never hear of sinnin'
Or any scandal that's beginnin'.
We've got too many other labors
To scatter tales that harm our neighbors.

* From *Collected Verse of Edgar A. Guest.* Copyright, 1934, by The Reilly & Lee Co., Chicago, Ill.

We're strange folks here.
We're tryin' to be cheerful,
An' keep this home from gettin' tearful.
We hold it dear;
Too dear for pettiness an' meanness,
An' nasty tales of men's uncleanness.
Here you shall come to joyous smilin',
Secure from hate and harsh revilin';
Here, where the wood fire brightly blazes,
You'll hear from us our neighbor's praises.
Here, that they'll never grow to doubt us,
We keep our friends always about us;
An' here, though storms outside may pelter
Is refuge for our friends, an' shelter.

We've one rule here,
An' that is to be pleasant.
The folks we know are always present,
Or very near.
An' though they dwell in many places,
We think we're talkin' to their faces;
An' that keeps us from only seein'
The faults in any human bein',
An' checks our tongues when they'd go trailin'
Into the mire of mortal failin'.
Flaws aren't so big when folks are near you;
You don't talk mean when they can hear you.
An' so no scandal here is started,
Because from friends we're never parted.

A BOOK

Emily Dickinson

There is no frigate like a book
   To take us lands away,
Nor any coursers like a page
   Of prancing poetry.

This traverse may the poorest take
   Without oppress of toll;
How frugal is the chariot
   That bears a human soul!

THE FIRST LORD'S SONG

W. S. Gilbert

When I was a lad I served a term
As office boy to an Attorney's firm;
I cleaned the windows and I swept the floor,
And I polished up the handle of the big front door.
    I polished up that handle so successfulee,
    That now I am the Ruler of the Queen's Navee!

As office boy I made such a mark
That they gave me the post of a junior clerk;
I served the writs with a smile so bland,
And I copied all the letters in a big round hand.
    I copied all the letters in a hand so free,
    That now I am the Ruler of the Queen's Navee!

In serving writs I made such a name
That an articled clerk I soon became;
I wore clean collars and a brand-new suit
For the Pass Examination at the Institute:
    And that Pass Examination did so well for me,
    That now I am the Ruler of the Queen's Navee!

Of legal knowledge I acquired such a grip
That they took me into the partnership,
And that junior partnership, I ween,
Was the only ship that I ever had seen:
    But that kind of ship so suited me,
    That now I am the Ruler of the Queen's Navee!

I grew so rich that I was sent
By a pocket borough into Parliament;
I always voted at my Party's call,
And I never thought of thinking for myself at all.
    I thought so little they rewarded me,
    By making me the Ruler of the Queen's Navee!

Now, landsmen all, whoever you may be,
If you want to rise to the top of the tree—
If your soul isn't fettered to an official stool,
Be careful to be guided by this golden rule—
    Stick close to your desks and *never go to sea,*
    And you all may be Rulers of the Queen's Navee!

THE OWL CRITIC

James T. Fields

"Who stuffed that white owl?" No one spoke in the shop;
The barber was busy, and he couldn't stop;
The customers, waiting their turns, were all reading
The "Daily," the "Herald," the "Post," little heeding
The young man who blurted out such a blunt question;
Not one raised a head, or even made a suggestion;
  And the barber kept on shaving.

"Don't you see, Mister Brown,"
Cried the youth with a frown,
"How wrong the whole thing is,
How preposterous each wing is,
How flattened the head is, how jammed down the neck is—
In short, the whole owl, what an ignorant wreck 'tis!
I make no apology;
I've learned owleology.

"I've passed days and nights in a hundred collections,
And cannot be blinded to any deflections
Arising from unskilful fingers that fail
To stuff a bird right, from his beak to his tail.
Mister Brown! Mister Brown!
Do take that bird down,
Or you'll soon be the laughing stock all over town!"
  And the barber kept on shaving.

"I've *studied* owls,
And other night fowls,
And I tell you
What I know to be true!
An owl cannot roost
With his limbs so unloosed;
No owl in this world
Ever had his claws curled,
Ever had his legs slanted,
Ever had his bill canted,
Ever had his neck screwed
Into that attitude.
He can't *do* it, because

'Tis against all bird laws.
Anatomy teaches,
Ornithology preaches,
An owl has a toe
That *can't* turn out so!
I've made the white owl my study for years,
And to see such a job almost moves me to tears!

"Mister Brown, I'm amazed
You should be so gone crazed
As to put up a bird
In that posture absurd!
To look at that owl really brings on a dizziness;
The man who stuffed *him* don't half know his business!"
And the barber kept on shaving.

"Examine those eyes.
I'm filled with surprise
Taxidermists should pass
Off on you such poor glass;
So unnatural they seem
They'd make Audubon scream,
And John Burroughs laugh
To encounter such chaff.
Do take that bird down;
Have him stuffed again, Brown!"
And the barber kept on shaving.

"With some sawdust and bark
I could stuff in the dark
An owl better than that.
I could make an old hat
Look more like an owl
Than that horrid fowl,
Stuck up there so stiff like a side of coarse leather.
In fact, about *him* there's not one natural feather."

Just then, with a wink and a sly normal lurch,
The owl, very gravely, got down from his perch,
Walked round, and regarded his fault-finding critic
(Who thought he was stuffed) with a glance analytic,
And then fairly hooted, as if he should say:
"Your learning's at fault *this* time, anyway;

Don't waste it again on a live bird, I pray.
I'm an owl; you're another. Sir Critic, good day!"
And the barber kept on shaving.

WHY BOOKS ARE WRITTEN

Robert J. Burdette

The appearance of a new book is an indication that another man has found a mission, has entered upon the performance of a lofty duty, activated by the noblest impulses that can spur the soul of man to action. It is the proudest boast of the profession of literature, that no man ever published a book for selfish purposes or with ignoble aim. Books have been published for the consolation of the distressed; for the guidance of the wandering; for the relief of the destitute; for the hope of the penitent; for uplifting the burdened soul above its sorrows and fears; for the general amelioration of the condition of all mankind; for the right against wrong; for the good against bad; for the truth. This book is published for two dollars per volume.

(Preface to The Rise and Fall of the Mustache, 1877)

TO NIGHT

Joseph Blanco White

Mysterious Night! when our first parent knew
Thee from report divine, and heard thy name,
Did he not tremble for this lovely frame,
This glorious canopy of light and blue?
Yet 'neath the curtain of translucent dew,
Bathed in the rays of the great setting flame,
Hesperus with the host of heaven came,
And lo! creation widened on man's view.
Who could have thought such darkness lay concealed
Within thy beams, O Sun! or who could find,
While fly, and leaf, and insect stood revealed,
That to such countless orbs thou mad'st us blind!
Why do we, then, shun Death with anxious strife?—
If Light can thus deceive, wherefore not Life?

GEORGE WASHINGTON

Inscription at Mount Vernon, Virginia

Washington, the brave, the wise, the good,
Supreme in war, in council, and in peace.
Valiant without ambition, discreet without fear, confident without assumption.
In disaster calm; in success moderate; in all, himself.
The hero, patriot, the Christian.
The father of nations, the friend of mankind,
Who, when he had won all, renounced all, and sought in the bosom of his family and of nature, retirement, and in the hope of religion, immortality.

TEXAS JUDGE ROY BEAN SENTENCES A MAN TO DEATH

Anonymous

"Hear ye! Hear ye! This honorable court's now in session; and if any galoot wants a snort afore we start, let him step up to the bar and name his pizen. Oscar, serve the gentlemen." . . .

"Carlos Robles, it is the findin' of this court that you are charged with a grave offense against the peace and dignity of the law West of the Pecos and the State of Texas, to wit: cattle-rustlin'. Guilty or not guilty?"

Not being able to speak or comprehend English, Robles merely grunted.

"Court accepts yore plea of guilt. The jury will now deliberate; and if it brings a verdict short of hangin' it'll be declared in contempt. Gentlemen, is yore verdict ready?"

The twelve nondescript citizens cleared their throats in unison. "It is, your honor," several spoke.

"Thank you, gentlemen. Stand up, Carlos Robles, and receive yore sentence. You got anything to say why judgment shouldn't be passed on you in this court?"

Of course Carlos had not, in view of the fact he had only the vaguest idea of what was transpiring.

"Carlos Robles," Judge Roy continued, his voice almost quaking with the solemnity of the occasion, "you been tried by twelve true and good men, not men of yore peers, but as high above you as heaven is of hell; and they've said you're guilty of rustlin' cattle.

"Time will pass and seasons will come and go; Spring with its wavin' green grass and heaps of sweet-smellin' flowers on every hill and in every dale. Then will come sultry Summer, with her shimmerin' heat-waves on the baked horizon; and Fall, with her yeller harvest-moon and the hills growin' brown and golden under a sinkin' sun; and finally Winter, with its bitin' whinin' wind, and all the land will be mantled with snow. But you won't be here to see any of 'em, Carlos Robles; not by a dam' sight, because it's the order of this court that you be took to the nearest tree and hanged by the neck till you're dead, dead, dead, you olive-colored son-of-a-billy-goat."

EVENTIDE

Caroline Atherton Briggs Mason

At cool of day, with God I walk
  My garden's grateful shade;
I hear His voice among the trees,
  And I am not afraid.

He speaks to me in every wind,
  He smiles from every star;
He is not deaf to me, nor blind,
  Nor absent, nor afar.

His hand that shuts the flowers to sleep,
  Each in its dewy fold,
Is strong my feeble life to keep,
  And competent to hold.

The powers below and powers above,
  Are subject to His care—
I cannot wander from His love
  Who loves me everywhere.

Thus dowered, and guarded thus, with Him
  I walk this peaceful shade;
I hear His voice among the trees,
  And I am not afraid.

RED RIVER VALLEY

Anonymous

From this valley they say you are going,
I shall miss your sweet face and your smile;
Because you are weary and tired,
You are changing your range for a while.
I've been thinking a long time, my darling,
Of the sweet words you never would say;
Now, alas, must my fond hopes all vanish?
For they say you are going away.

Chorus:

Then come sit here awhile e'er you leave us,
Do not hasten to bid us adieu,
Just remember the Red River Valley
And the cowboy who loves you so true.

I have promised you, darling, that never
Will words from my lips cause you pain;
And my life it will be yours forever,
If you only will love me again.
Must the past with its joys all be blighted
By the future of sorrow and pain?
Must the vows that were spoken be slighted?
Don't you think you could love me again?

There never could be such a longing
In the heart of a poor cowboy's breast,
As dwells in the heart you are breaking,
As I wait in my home in the West.
Do you think of the valley you're leaving?
Oh, how lonely and dreary it'll be!
Do you think of the kind hearts you're hurting,
And the pain you are causing to me?

* * *

Give me the avowed, the erect, the manly foe,
Bold I can meet,—perhaps may turn his blow!
But of all plagues, good Heaven, thy wrath can send,
Save, save, oh save me from the *candid friend!*

George Canning

A BRIEF SERMON

Anonymous

Man's ingress into the world is naked and bare;
His progress through the world is trouble and care;
His egress out of the world is nobody knows where;
If we do well here we shall do well there;
I can tell you no more if I preach for a year.

CALIBAN IN THE COAL MINES

Louis Untermeyer

God, we don't like to complain,
We know that the mine is no lark,
But—there's the pools from the rain;
But—there's the cold and the dark.

God, You don't know what it is—
You, in Your well-lighted sky—
Watching the meteors whizz;
Warm, with the sun always by.

God, if You had but the moon
Stuck in Your cap for a lamp,
Even You'd tire of it soon,
Down in the dark and the damp.

Nothing but blackness above
And nothing that moves but the cars . . .
God, if You wish for our love,
Fling us a handful of stars!

TO THE VIRGINS TO MAKE MUCH OF TIME

Robert Herrick

Gather ye rosebuds while ye may,
Old Time is still a-flying;
And this same flower that smiles today,
Tomorrow will be dying.

The glorious lamp of heaven, the sun,
  The higher he's a-getting,
The sooner will his race be run,
  And nearer he's to setting.

That age is best which is the first,
  When youth and blood are warmer;
But being spent, the worse and worst
  Times still succeed the former.

Then be not coy, but use your time,
  And while ye may, go marry;
For, having lost but once your prime,
  You may forever tarry.

GENERAL EISENHOWER'S D DAY ORDER OF THE DAY

June 6, 1944

Soldiers, sailors, and airmen of the Allied expeditionary force: You are about to embark upon a great crusade toward which we have striven these many months. The eyes of the world are upon you. The hopes and prayers of liberty-loving peoples everywhere march with you.

You will bring about the destruction of the German war machine, the elimination of Nazi tyranny over the oppressed peoples of Europe, and security for ourselves in a free world.

Your task will not be an easy one. Your enemy is well trained, well equipped, and battle-hardened. He will fight savagely.

But this is the year 1944. Much has happened since the Nazi triumphs of 1940–41.

The United Nations have inflicted upon the Germans great defeat in open battle man to man. Our air offensive has seriously reduced their strength in the air and their capacity to wage war on the ground.

Our home fronts have given us an overwhelming superiority in weapons and munitions of war and placed at our disposal great reserves of trained fighting men.

The tide has turned.

The free men of the world are marching together to victory. I have full confidence in your courage, devotion to duty, and skill in battle.

We will accept nothing less than full victory.

Good luck, and let us all beseech the blessings of Almighty God upon this great and noble undertaking.

DWIGHT D. EISENHOWER

LINES ON THE MERMAID TAVERN

John Keats

Souls of Poets dead and gone,
What Elysium have ye known,
Happy field or mossy cavern,
Choicer than the Mermaid Tavern?
Have ye tippled drink more fine
Than mine host's Canary wine?
Or are fruits of Paradise
Sweeter than those dainty pies
Of venison? O generous food!
Drest as though bold Robin Hood
Would, with his maid Marian,
Sup and bowse from horn and can.

I have heard that on a day
Mine host's sign-board flew away,
Nobody knew whither, till
An astrologer's old quill
To a sheepskin gave the story,
Said he saw you in your glory,
Underneath a new-old sign
Sipping beverage divine,
And pledging with contented smack
The Mermaid in the Zodiac.

Souls of Poets dead and gone,
What Elysium have ye known,
Happy field or mossy cavern,
Choicer than the Mermaid Tavern?

THE COWBOY'S LAMENT

Anonymous

As I walked out in the streets of Laredo,
As I walked out in Laredo one day,
I spied a poor cowboy wrapped up in white linen,
Wrapped up in white linen as cold as the clay.

"Oh, beat the drum slowly and play the fife lowly,
Play the dead march as you carry me along;
Take me to the green valley, there lay the sod o'er me,
For I'm a young cowboy and I know I've done wrong.

"I see by your outfit that you are a cowboy"—
These words he did say as I boldly stepped by.
"Come sit down beside me and hear my sad story;
I am shot in the breast and I know I must die.

"Let sixteen gamblers come handle my coffin,
Let sixteen cowboys come sing me a song.
Take me to the graveyard and lay the sod o'er me,
For I'm a poor cowboy and I know I've done wrong.

"My friends and relations they live in the Nation,
They know not where their boy has gone.
He first came to Texas and hired to a ranchman,
Oh, I'm a young cowboy and I know I've done wrong.

"It was once in the saddle I used to go dashing;
It was once in the saddle I used to go gay;
First to the dram-house and then to the card-house;
Got shot in the breast and I am dying today.

"Get six jolly cowboys to carry my coffin;
Get six pretty maidens to bear up my pall.
Put bunches of roses all over my coffin,
Put roses to deaden the sods as they fall.

"Then swing your rope slowly and rattle your spurs lowly,
And give a wild whoop as you carry me along;
And in the grave throw me and roll the sod o'er me
For I'm a young cowboy and I know I've done wrong.

"Oh, bury beside me my knife and six-shooter,
My spurs on my heel, my rifle by my side,
And over my coffin put a bottle of brandy
That the cowboys may drink as they carry me along.

"Go bring me a cup, a cup of cold water,
To cool my parched lips," the cowboy then said;
Before I returned his soul had departed,
And gone to the round-up—the cowboy was dead.

We beat the drum slowly and played the fife lowly,
And bitterly wept as we bore him along;
For we all loved our comrade, so brave, young, and handsome,
We all loved our comrade although he'd done wrong.

Where men lived raw, in the desert's maw,
And hell was nothing to shun;
Where they buried 'em neat, without preacher or sheet,
And writ on their foreheads, crude but sweet,
"This Jasper was slow with a gun."

OLD AGE

Marcus Tullius Cicero

(Translator: William Melmoth)

No portion of time can justly be deemed long that will necessarily have an end, since the longest, when once it is elapsed, leaves not a trace behind, and nothing valuable remains with us but the conscious satisfaction of having employed it well. Thus, hours and days, months and years glide imperceptibly away—the past never to return, the future involved in impenetrable obscurity. But whatever the extent of our present duration may prove, a wise and good man ought to be contented with the allotted measure, remembering that it is in life as it is on the stage, where it is not necessary in order to be approved, that the actor's part should continue to the conclusion of the drama; it is sufficient, in whatever scene he shall make his final exit, that he support the character assigned him with deserved applause. . . .

Every event agreeable to the course of nature ought to be looked upon as a real good, and surely none can be more natural than for an old man to die. It is true, youth likewise stands exposed to the same dissolution, but it is a dissolution contrary to Nature's evident intentions, and in direct opposition to her strongest efforts. In the latter instance, the privation of life may be resembled to a fire forcibly extinguished by a deluge of water; in the former, to a fire spontaneously and gradually going out from a total consumption of its fuel. Or to have recourse to another illustration, as fruit before it is ripe cannot, without some degree of force, be separated from the stalk, but drops of itself when perfectly mature, so the disunion of the soul and body is effected in the young by dint of violence, but is wrought in the old by a mere fullness and completion of years. This ripeness for death I perceive in myself, with much satisfaction; and I look forward to my dissolution as to a secure haven, where I shall at length find a happy repose from the fatigues of a long voyage.

Every stage of human life, except the last, is marked out by certain and definite limits; old age alone has no precise and determinate boundary. It may well therefore be sustained to any period, how far soever it may be extended, provided a man is capable of performing those offices which are suited to this season of life, and preserves at the same time a perfect indifference with respect to its continuance. Old age under these circumstances, and with these sentiments, may be animated with more courage and fortitude than is usually found even in the prime of life. . . .

Tell me, my friends, whence it is that those men who have made the greatest advances in true wisdom and genuine philosophy are observed to meet death with the most perfect equanimity; while the ignorant and unimproved part of our species generally see its approach with the utmost discomposure and reluctance? Is it not because the more enlightened the mind is, and the farther it extends its view, the more clearly it discerns in the hour of its dissolution (what narrow and vulgar souls are too short-sighted to discover) that it is taking its flight into some happier region?

* * *

It is the common fate of the indolent to see their rights become a prey to the active. The condition upon which God hath given liberty to man is eternal vigilance, which condition if he break, servitude is at once the consequence of his crime and the punishment of his guilt.—John Philpot Curran (from Speech, 1790)

WINTER

William Shakespeare

When icicles hang by the wall,
  And Dick the shepherd blows his nail,
And Tom bears logs into the hall,
  And milk comes frozen home in pail,
When blood is nipp'd and ways be foul,
Then nightly sings the staring owl,
        Tu-whit;
To-who, a merry note,
While greasy Joan doth keel the pot.

When all aloud the wind doth blow,
  And coughing drowns the parson's saw,
And birds sit brooding in the snow,
  And Marian's nose looks red and raw,
When roasted crabs hiss in the bowl,
Then nightly sings the staring owl,
        Tu-whit;
To-who, a merry note,
While greasy Joan doth keel the pot.
    (From Love's Labour's Lost)

WHAT MY LOVER SAID

Homer Greene

By the merest chance, in the twilight gloom,
  In the orchard path he met me;
In the tall, wet grass, with its faint perfume,
And I tried to pass, but he made no room,
  Oh, I tried, but he would not let me.
So I stood and blushed till the grass grew red,
  With my face bent down above it,
While he took my hand as he whispering said—
  (How the clover lifted each pink, sweet head,
To listen to all that my lover said:
  Oh, the clover in bloom, I love it!)

In the high, wet grass went the path to hide,
  And the low, wet leaves hung over;
But I could not pass upon either side,
For I found myself, when I vainly tried,
  In the arms of my steadfast lover.
And he led me there and he raised my head,
  While he closed the path before me,
And he looked down into my eyes and said—
  (How the leaves bent down from the boughs o'erhead,
To listen to all that my lover said:
  Oh, the leaves hanging lowly o'er me!)

Had he moved aside but a little way,
  I could surely then have passed him;
And he knew I never could wish to stay,
And would not have heard what he had to say,
  Could I only aside have cast him.
It was almost dark, and the moments sped,
  And the searching night wind found us,
But he drew me nearer and softly said—
  (How the pure, sweet wind grew still, instead,
To listen to all that my lover said:
  Oh, the whispering wind around us!)

I am sure that he knew when he held me fast,
  That I must be all unwilling;
For I tried to go, and I would have passed,
As the night was come with its dew, at last,
  And the sky with its stars was filling.
But he clasped me close when I would have fled,
  And he made me hear his story,
And his soul came out from his lips and said—
  (How the stars crept out where the white moon led,
To listen to all that my lover said:
  Oh, the moon and the stars in glory!)

I know that the grass and the leaves will not tell,
  And I'm sure that the wind, precious rover,
Will carry my secret so safely and well
  That no being shall ever discover
One word of the many that rapidly fell
  From the soul-speaking lips of my lover;
  And the moon and the stars that looked over

Shall never reveal what a fairy-like spell
They wove round about us that night in the dell,
  In the path through the dew-laden clover,
Nor echo the whispers that made my heart swell
  As they fell from the lips of my lover.

THE LAND OF STORY-BOOKS

Robert Louis Stevenson

At evening when the lamp is lit,
Around the fire my parents sit;
They sit at home and talk and sing,
And do not play at anything.

Now, with my little gun, I crawl
All in the dark along the wall,
And follow round the forest track
Away behind the sofa back.

There, in the night, where none can spy,
All in my hunter's camp I lie,
And play at books that I have read
Till it is time to go to bed.

These are the hills, these are the woods,
These are my starry solitudes;
And there the river by whose brink
The roaring lions come to drink.

I see the others far away
As if in firelit camp they lay,
And I, like to an Indian scout,
Around their party prowled about.

So, when my nurse comes in for me,
Home I return across the sea,
And go to bed with backward looks
At my dear land of Story-books.

SECRET LAUGHTER *

Christopher Morley

There is a secret laughter
That often comes to me,
And though I go about my work
As humble as can be,
There is no prince or prelate
  I envy—no, not one.
No evil can befall me—
  By God, I have a son!

GOD REST YOU MERRY, GENTLEMEN

Anonymous

God rest you merry, gentlemen,
  Let nothing you dismay,
For Jesus Christ, our Saviour,
  Was born upon this day,
To save us all from Satan's power
  When we were gone astray.
    O tidings of comfort and joy!
    For Jesus Christ, our Saviour,
    Was born on Christmas Day.

In Bethlehem, in Jewry,
  This blessèd babe was born,
And laid within a manger,
  Upon this blessèd morn;
The which His mother, Mary,
  Nothing did take in scorn.

From God our Heavenly Father,
  A blessèd angel came;
And unto certain shepherds
  Brought tidings of the same:
How that in Bethlehem was born
  The Son of God by name.

* From *Songs for a Little House.* Copyright, 1917, 1945, by Christopher Morley. Published by J. B. Lippincott Co.

"Fear not," then said the angel,
  "Let nothing you affright,
This day is born a Saviour
  Of virtue, power, and might,
So frequently to vanquish all
  The friends of Satan quite."

The shepherds at these tidings
  Rejoicèd much in mind,
And left their flock a-feeding
  In tempest, storm, and wind,
And went to Bethlehem straightway,
  This blessèd babe to find.

But when to Bethlehem they came,
  Whereat this infant lay,
They found Him in a manger,
  Where oxen feed on hay,
His mother Mary kneeling,
  Unto the Lord did pray.

Now to the Lord sing praises,
  All you within this place,
And with true love and brotherhood
  Each other now embrace;
This holy tide of Christmas
  All others doth deface.
    O tidings of comfort and joy!
    For Jesus Christ, our Saviour,
    Was born on Christmas Day.

THE BILL OF RIGHTS

(Adopted as the first ten amendments to the Constitution)

1. Congress shall make no law respecting an establishment of religion, or prohibiting the free exercise thereof; or abridging the freedom of speech, or of the press; or the right of the people peaceably to assemble, and to petition the Government for a redress of grievances.

2. A well regulated Militia, being necessary to the security of a free State, the right of the people to keep and bear Arms, shall not be infringed.

3. No Soldier shall, in time of peace be quartered in any house, without the consent of the Owner, nor in time of war, but in a manner to be prescribed by law.

4. The right of the people to be secure in their persons, houses, papers, and effects, against unreasonable searches and seizures, shall not be violated, and no Warrants shall issue, but upon probable cause, supported by Oath or affirmation, and particularly describing the place to be searched, and the persons or things to be seized.

5. No person shall be held to answer for a capital, or otherwise infamous crime, unless on a presentment or indictment of a Grand Jury, except in cases arising in the land or naval forces, or in the Militia, when in actual service in time of War or public danger; nor shall any person be subject for the same offense to be twice put in jeopardy of life or limb; nor shall be compelled in any criminal case to be a witness against himself, nor be deprived of life, liberty, or property, without due process of law; nor shall private property be taken for public use, without just compensation.

6. In all criminal prosecutions, the accused shall enjoy the right to a speedy and public trial, by an impartial jury of the State and district wherein the crime shall have been committed, which district shall have been previously ascertained by law, and to be informed of the nature and cause of the accusation; to be confronted with the witnesses against him; to have compulsory process for obtaining witnesses in his favor, and to have the Assistance of Counsel for his defense.

7. In Suits at common law, where the value in controversy shall exceed twenty dollars, the right of trial by jury shall be preserved, and no fact tried by a jury shall be otherwise re-examined in any Court of the United States, than according to the rules of the common law.

8. Excessive bail shall not be required, nor excessive fines imposed, nor cruel and unusual punishments inflicted.

9. The enumeration in the Constitution of certain rights shall not be construed to deny or disparage others retained by the people.

10. The powers not delegated to the United States by the Constitution, nor prohibited by it to the States, are reserved to the States respectively, or to the people.

WAR

John Dryden

War, he sung, is Toil and Trouble;
Honour but an empty Bubble.
  Never ending, still beginning,
Fighting still, and still destroying,
  If the World be worth thy Winning,
Think, O think, it worth Enjoying.
(From Alexander's Feast)

ON THE COUNTESS OF PEMBROKE

William Browne

Underneath this sable hearse
Lies the subject of all verse:
Sidney's sister, Pembroke's mother:
Death, ere thou hast killed another,
Fair, and learn'd, and good as she,
Time shall throw a dart at thee.

AN AMERICAN

Daniel Webster

I was born an American; I will live an American; I shall die an American; and I intend to perform the duties incumbent upon me in that character to the end of my career. I mean to do this with absolute disregard of personal consequences. What are the personal consequences? What is the individual man, with all the good or evil that may betide him, in comparison with the good or evil which may befall a great country, and in the midst of great transactions which concern that country's fate? Let the consequences be what they will, I am careless. No man can suffer too much, and no man can fall too soon, if he suffer, or if he fall, in the defense of the liberties and constitution of his country.

(July 17, 1850)

COME WHERE MY LOVE LIES DREAMING

Stephen C. Foster

Come where my love lies dreaming,
  Dreaming the happy hours away,
In visions bright redeeming
  The fleeting joys of day;
Dreaming the happy hours,
Dreaming the happy hours away.

Come where my love lies dreaming,
  Come with a lute-toned lay;
Come where my love lies dreaming,
  Dreaming the happy hours away;
Come with a lute, come with a lay,
Dreaming the happy hours away.

Soft is her slumber, thoughts bright and free
Dance through her dreams like a gushing melody,
Light is her young heart, light may it be,
Come where my love lies dreaming,
Dreaming the happy hours away.

THE TRICKS OF IMAGINATION

William Shakespeare

The lunatic, the lover and the poet
Are of imagination all compact:
One sees more devils than vast hell can hold,
That is, the madman: the lover, all as frantic,
Sees Helen's beauty in a brow of Egypt:
The poet's eye, in a fine frenzy rolling,
Doth glance from heaven to earth, from earth to heaven;
And as imagination bodies forth
The forms of things unknown, the poet's pen
Turns them to shapes, and gives to airy nothing
A local habitation and a name.
Such tricks hath strong imagination,
That, if it would but apprehend some joy,

It comprehends some bringer of that joy;
Or in the night, imagining some fear,
How easy is a bush supposed a bear!
(From A Midsummer-Night's Dream)

A CREED

Edwin Markham

There is a destiny that makes us brothers;
None goes his way alone:
All that we send into the lives of others
Comes back into our own.

I care not what his temples or his creeds,
One thing holds firm and fast—
That into his fateful heap of days and deeds
The soul of man is cast.

DIOGENES TO ALEXANDER THE GREAT

ARISTIPPUS:

You send me word that Alexander, King of Macedonia, has a great desire to see me. You did well to give him that title, for whatever the Macedonians may be, you know I am subject to nobody. If that prince has a mind to be acquainted with me, and my manner of life, let him come hither, for I shall always think Athens as far distant from Macedon as Macedon is from Athens.

Farewell.

EPIGRAM

ENGRAVED ON THE COLLAR OF A DOG WHICH I GAVE TO HIS ROYAL HIGHNESS

Alexander Pope

I am his Highness' dog at Kew;
Pray tell me, sir, whose dog are you?

SKIPPER IRESON'S RIDE

John Greenleaf Whittier

Of all the rides since the birth of time,
Told in story or sung in rhyme,—
On Apuleius's Golden Ass,
Or one-eyed Calender's horse of brass,
Witch astride of a human back,
Islam's prophet on Al-Borák,—
The strangest ride that ever was sped
Was Ireson's, out from Marblehead!
  Old Floyd Ireson, for his hard heart,
  Tarred and feathered and carried in a cart
    By the women of Marblehead!

Body of turkey, head of owl,
Wings a-droop like a rained-on fowl,
Feathered and ruffled in every part,
Skipper Ireson stood in the cart.
Scores of women, old and young,
Strong of muscle, and glib of tongue,
Pushed and pulled up the rocky lane,
Shouting and singing the shrill refrain:
  "Here's Flud Oirson, fur his horrd horrt,
  Torr'd an' futherr'd an' corr'd in a corrt
    By the women o' Morble'ead!"

Wrinkled scolds with hands on hips,
Girls in bloom of cheek and lips,
Wild-eyed, free-limbed, such as chase
Bacchus round some antique vase,
Brief of skirt, with ankles bare,
Loose of kerchief, and loose of hair,
With conch-shells blowing and fish-horns' twang,
Over and over the Maenads sang:
  "Here's Flud Oirson, fur his horrd horrt,
  Torr'd an' futherr'd an' corr'd in a corrt
    By the women o' Morble'ead!"

Small pity for him!—He sailed away
From a leaking ship in Chaleur Bay,—
Sailed away from a sinking wreck,

With his own town's-people on her deck!
"Lay by! lay by!" they called to him.
Back he answered, "Sink or swim!
Brag of your catch of fish again!"
And off he sailed through the fog and rain!
  Old Floyd Ireson, for his hard heart,
  Tarred and feathered and carried in a cart
    By the women of Marblehead!

Fathoms deep in a dark Chaleur
That wreck shall lie for evermore.
Mother and sister, wife and maid,
Looked from the rocks of Marblehead
Over the moaning and rainy sea,—
Looked for the coming that might not be!
What did the winds and the sea-birds say
Of the cruel captain who sailed away?—
  Old Floyd Ireson, for his hard heart,
  Tarred and feathered and carried in a cart
    By the women of Marblehead!

Through the street, on either side,
Up flew windows, doors swung wide;
Sharp-tongued spinsters, old wives gray,
Treble lent the fish-horn's bray.
Sea-worn grandsires, cripple-bound,
Hulks of old sailors run aground,
Shook head, and fist, and hat, and cane,
And cracked with curses the hoarse refrain:
  "Here's Flud Oirson, fur his horrd horrt,
  Torr'd an' futherr'd an' corr'd in a corrt
    By the women o' Morble'ead!"

Sweetly along the Salem road
Bloom of orchard and lilac showed.
Little the wicked skipper knew
Of the fields so green and the sky so blue.
Riding there in his sorry trim,
Like an Indian idol glum and grim,
Scarcely he seemed the sound to hear
Of voices shouting, far and near:
  "Here's Flud Oirson, fur his horrd horrt,
  Torr'd an' futherr'd an' corr'd in a corrt
    By the women o' Morble'ead!"

"Hear me, neighbors!" at last he cried,—
"What to me is this noisy ride?
What is the shame that clothes the skin
To the nameless horror that lives within?
Waking or sleeping, I see a wreck,
And hear a cry from a reeling deck!
Hate me and curse me,—I only dread
The hand of God and the face of the dead!"
  Said old Floyd Ireson, for his hard heart,
  Tarred and feathered and carried in a cart
    By the women of Marblehead!

Then the wife of the skipper lost at sea
Said, "God has touched him! why should we!"
Said an old wife mourning for her only son,
"Cut the rogue's tether and let him run!"
So with soft relentings and rude excuse,
Half scorn, half pity, they cut him loose,
And gave him a cloak to hide him in,
And left him alone with his shame and sin.
  Poor old Floyd Ireson, for his hard heart,
  Tarred and feathered and carried in a cart
    By the women of Marblehead!

DAVID CROCKETT'S COON-SKIN CURRENCY

I started off to the Cross Roads dressed in my hunting shirt, and my rifle on my shoulder. Many of our constituents had assembled there to get a taste of the quality of the candidates at orating. Job Snelling, a gander-shanked Yankee, who had been caught somewhere about Plymouth Bay, and been shipped to the West with a cargo of codfish and rum, erected a large shantee, and set up shop for the occasion. A large posse of the voters had assembled before I arrived, and my opponent had already made considerable headway with his speechifying and his treating, when they spied me about a rifle shot from camp, sauntering along as if I was not a party in business. "There comes Crockett," cried one. "Let us hear the colonel," cried another; and so I mounted the stump that had been cut down for the occasion, and began to bushwack in the most approved style.

I had not been up long before there was such an uproar in the crowd that I could not hear my own voice, and some of my constituents let me know that they could not listen to me on such a dry subject as the welfare of the nation until they had something to drink, and that I must treat them. Accordingly I jumped down from the rostrum, and led the way to the shantee, followed by my constituents, shouting, "Huzza for Crockett!" and "Crockett forever!"

When we entered the shantee Job was busy dealing out his rum in a style that showed he was making a good day's work of it, and I called for a quart of the best; but the crooked crittur returned no other answer than by pointing to a board over the bar, on which he had chalked in large letters, *"Pay to-day and trust tomorrow."* Now that idea brought me up all standing; it was a sort of cornering in which there was no back-out, for ready money in the West, in those times, was the shyest thing in all natur, and it was most particularly shy with me on that occasion.

The voters, seeing my predicament, fell off to the other side, and I was left deserted and alone, as the Government will be, when he no longer has any offices to bestow. I saw as plain as day that the tide of popular opinion was against me, and that unless I got some rum speedily I should lose my election as sure as there are snakes in Virginny; and it must be done soon, or even burnt brandy wouldn't save me. So I walked away from the shantee, but in another guess sort from the way I entered it, for on this occasion I had no train after me, and not a voice shouted, "Huzza for Crockett!" Popularity sometimes depends on a very small matter indeed; in this particular it was worth a quart of New England rum, and no more.

Well, knowing that a crisis was at hand, I struck into the woods, with my rifle on my shoulder, my best friend in time of need; and, as good fortune would have it, I had not been out more than a quarter of an hour before I treed a fat coon, and in the pulling of a trigger he lay dead at the foot of the tree. I soon whipped his hairy jacket off his back, and again bent my steps toward the shantee, and walked up to the bar, but not alone, for this time I had half a dozen of my constituents at my heels. I threw down the coon-skin upon the counter, and called for a quart, and Job, though busy dealing out rum, forgot to point at his chalked rules and regulations; for he knew that a coon was as good as legal tender for a quart in the West as a New York shilling any day.

My constituents now flocked about me, and cried "Huzza for Crockett!" "Crockett forever!" and finding the tide had taken a turn, I told them several yarns to get them in good humor; and having soon dispatched the value of the coon, I went out and mounted the stump without opposition, and a clear majority of the voters followed me to hear what I had to offer for the good of the nation. Before I was half through one of my constituents moved that they would hear the balance of my speech after they had washed down the first part with some more of Job Snelling's extract of cornstalk and molasses, and the question being put, it was carried unanimously. It wasn't considered necessary to tell the yeas and nays, so we adjourned to the shantee, and on the way I began to reckon that the fate of the nation pretty much depended upon my shooting another coon.

While standing at the bar, feeling sort of bashful while Job's rules and regulations stared me in the face, I cast down my eyes, and discovered one end of the coon-skin sticking between the logs that supported the bar. Job had slung it there in the hurry of business. I gave it a sort of quick jerk, and it followed my hand as natural as if I had been the rightful owner. I slapped it on the counter, and Job, little dreaming that he was barking up the wrong tree, shoved along another bottle, which my constituents quickly disposed of with great good humor, for some of them saw the trick; and then we withdrew to the rostrum to discuss the affairs of the nation.

I don't know how it was, but the voters soon became dry again, and nothing would do but we must adjourn to the shantee; and as luck would have it, the coon-skin was still sticking between the logs, as if Job had flung it there on purpose to tempt me. I was not slow in raising it to the counter, the rum followed, of course, and I wish that I may be shot if I didn't, before the day was over, get ten quarts for the same identical skin, and from a fellow, too, who in those parts was considered as sharp as a steel trap and as bright as a pewter button.

This joke secured me my election, for it soon circulated like smoke among my constituents, and they allowed, with one accord, that the man who could get the whip hand of Job Snelling in fair trade, could outwit Old Nick himself, and was the real grit for them in Congress.

(From the Life of Colonel David Crockett, written by himself, 1860)

* * *

All the world is queer save thee and me, and even thou art a little queer.—Robert Owen (in letter to William Allen, 1828)

WHAT I LIVE FOR

George Linnaeus Banks

I live for those who love me,
  Whose hearts are kind and true;
For the Heaven that smiles above me,
  And awaits my spirit too;
For all human ties that bind me,
For the task by God assigned me,
For the bright hopes yet to find me,
  And the good that I can do.

I live to learn their story
  Who suffered for my sake;
To emulate their glory,
  And follow in their wake;
Bards, patriots, martyrs, sages,
The heroic of all ages,
Whose deeds crowd History's pages,
  And Time's great volume make.

I live to hold communion
  With all that is divine,
To feel there is a union
  Twixt Nature's heart and mine;
To profit by affliction,
Reap truth from fields of fiction,
Grow wiser from conviction,
  And fulfil God's grand design.

I live to hail that season
  By gifted ones foretold,
When men shall live by reason,
  And not alone by gold;
When man to man united,
And every wrong thing righted,
The whole world shall be lighted
  As Eden was of old.

I live for those who love me,
  For those who know me true,
For the Heaven that smiles above me,

And awaits my spirit too;
For the cause that lacks assistance,
For the wrong that needs resistance,
For the future in the distance,
And the good that I can do.

MIA CARLOTTA

T. A. Daly

Giuseppe, da barber, ees greata for "mash,"
He gotta da bigga, da blacka moustache,
Good clo'es an' good styla an' playnta good cash.

W'enevra Giuseppe ees walk on da street,
Da peopla dey talka, "How nobby! how neat!
How softa da handa, how smalla da feet."

He leefta hees hat an' he shaka hees curls,
An' smila weeth teetha so shiny like pearls;
Oh, manny da heart of da seelly young girls

He gotta.
Yes, playnta he gotta—
But notta
Carlotta!

Giuseppe, da barber, he maka da eye,
An' lika da steam engine puffa an' sigh,
For catch Carlotta w'en she ees go by.

Carlotta she walka weeth nose in da air,
An' look through Giuseppe weeth far-away stare,
As eef she no see dere ees som'body dere.

Giuseppe, da barber, he gotta da cash,
He gotta da clo'es an' da bigga moustache,
He gotta da seelly young girl for da "mash,"

But notta—
You bat my life, notta—
Carlotta
I gotta!

ABRAHAM LINCOLN ON LABOR AND CAPITAL

I am glad to see that a system of labor prevails in New England under which laborers can strike when they want to, where they are not obliged to work under all circumstances, and are not tied down and obliged to labor whether you pay them or not! I like the system which lets a man quit when he wants to, and wish it might prevail everywhere. One of the reasons why I am opposed to slavery is just here. What is the true condition of the laborer? I take it that it is best for all to leave each man free to acquire property as fast as he can. Some will get wealthy. I don't believe in a law to prevent a man from getting rich; it would do more harm than good. So while we do not propose any war upon capital, we do wish to allow the humblest man an equal chance to get rich with everybody else. When one starts poor, as most do in the race of life, free society is such that he knows he can better his condition; he knows that there is no fixed condition of labor for his whole life. I am not ashamed to confess that twenty-five years ago I was a hired laborer, mauling rails, at work on a flatboat—just what might happen to any poor man's son. I want every man to have a chance—and I believe a black man is entitled to it—in which he can better his condition—when he may look forward and hope to be a hired laborer this year and the next, work for himself afterward, and finally to hire men to work for him. That is the true system.

(From a speech at New Haven, Conn., March 6, 1860.)

WHILE SHEPHERDS WATCHED THEIR FLOCKS BY NIGHT

Nahum Tate

While shepherds watched their flocks by night,
All seated on the ground,
The angel of the Lord came down,
And glory shone around.

"Fear not," said he, for mighty dread
Had seized their troubled mind;
"Glad tidings of great joy I bring
To you and all mankind.

"To you, in David's town, this day
Is born, of David's line,
The Saviour, who is Christ the Lord,
And this shall be the sign:

"The heavenly babe you there shall find
To human view displayed,
All meanly wrapped in swaddling bands,
And in a manger laid."

Thus spake the seraph; and forthwith
Appeared a shining throng
Of angels, praising God, who thus
Addressed their joyful song:

"All glory be to God on high,
And to the earth be peace;
Good-will henceforth from Heaven to men
Begin and never cease."

JOE BOWERS

Anonymous

My name it is Joe Bowers, I've got a brother Ike;
I came here from Missouri, yes, all the way from Pike;
I'll tell you why I left there and how I came to roam,
To leave my poor old mammy, so far away from home.

I used to love a gal there, her name was Sallie Black,
I asked her for to marry me, she said it was a whack;
She says to me, "Joe Bowers, before you hitch for life,
You ought to have a little home to keep your little wife."

Says I, "My dearest Sallie, O Sallie, for your sake,
I'll go to California and try to raise a stake."
Says she to me: "Joe Bowers, you are the chap to win.
Give me a kiss to seal the bargain"—and I throwed a dozen in.

I'll never forget my feelings when I bid adieu to all.
Sal, she cotched me round the neck and I began to bawl.
When I begun they all commenced, you never heard the like,
How they all took on and cried the day I left old Pike.

When I got to this here country, I hadn't nary a red,
I had such wolfish feelings I wished myself most dead.
But the thoughts of my dear Sallie soon made these feelings git;
And whispered hopes to Bowers— Lord, I wish I had 'em yit.

At last I went to mining, put in my biggest licks,
Came down upon boulders just like a thousand bricks.
I worked both late and early in rain and sun and snow,
But I was working for my Sallie; it was all the same to Joe.

I made a very lucky strike, as the gold itself did tell,
For I was working for my Sallie, the girl I loved so well.
I saved it for my Sallie that I might pour it at her feet;
That she might hug and kiss me and call me something sweet.

But one day I got a letter from my dear, kind brother Ike;
It came from old Missouri, yes, all the way from Pike;
It told me the gol-darndest news that ever you did hear,
My heart it is a-bustin', so please excuse this tear.

I'll tell you what it was, boys—you'll bust your sides, I know;
For when I read that letter you ought to seen poor Joe.
My knees gave way beneath me, and I pulled out half my hair;
And if you ever tell this now, you bet you'll hear me swear.

It said my Sallie was fickle, her love for me had fled,
That she had married a butcher, whose hair was awful red;
It told me more than that, it's enough to make me swear—
It said that Sallie had a baby and the baby had red hair.

Now I've told you all that I can tell about this said affair,
'Bout Sallie marrying a butcher and the baby had red hair
But whether it was a boy or girl the letter never said;
It only said its cussed hair was inclined to be red.

* * *

And so no force, however great, can stretch a cord, however fine, into a horizontal line which shall be absolutely straight.—William Whewell (Elementary Treatise on Mechanics)

ROSE AYLMER

Walter Savage Landor

Ah, what avails the sceptred race,
  Ah, what the form divine!
What every virtue, every grace!
  Rose Aylmer, all were thine.

Rose Aylmer, whom these wakeful eyes
  May weep, but never see,
A night of memories and of sighs
  I consecrate to thee.

From AUGURIES OF INNOCENCE

William Blake

To see a World in a Grain of Sand
And a Heaven in a Wild Flower,
Hold Infinity in the palm of your hand
And Eternity in an hour.

THE HEART OF THE MONROE DOCTRINE

James Monroe

The occasion has been judged proper for asserting, as a principle in which the rights and interests of the United States are involved, that the American continents, by the free and independent condition which they have assumed and maintain, are henceforth not to be considered as subjects for future colonization by any Euro pean powers. . . .

. . . In the wars of the European powers in matters relating to themselves we have never taken any part, nor does it comport with our policy so to do. It is only when our rights are invaded or seriously menaced that we resent injuries or make preparation for our defense. With the movements in this hemisphere we are, of necessity, more immediately connected, and by causes which must be obvious to all enlightened and impartial observers. . . .

We owe it, therefore, to candor and to the amicable relations existing between the United States and those powers to declare that we should consider any attempt on their part to extend their system to any portion of this hemisphere as dangerous to our peace and safety. With the existing colonies or dependencies of any European power we have not interfered and shall not interfere.

But with the Governments who have declared their independence and maintained it, and whose independence we have, on great consideration and on just principles, acknowledged, we could not view any interposition for the purpose of oppressing them, or controlling in any other manner their destiny, by any European power in any other light than as the manifestation of an unfriendly disposition toward the United States.

TO THE MEMORY OF MY BELOVED MASTER, WILLIAM SHAKESPEARE

Ben Jonson

To draw no envy, Shakespeare, on thy name,
Am I thus ample to thy book and fame;
While I confess thy writings to be such
As neither man, nor muse, can praise too much.
'Tis true, and all men's suffrage. But these ways
Were not the paths I meant unto thy praise;
For silliest ignorance on these may light,
Which, when it sounds at best, but echoes right;
Or blind affection, which doth ne'er advance
The truth, but gropes, and urgeth all by chance;
Or crafty malice might pretend this praise,
And think to ruin, where it seemed to raise.
These are, as some infamous bawd or whore
Should praise a matron. What could hurt her more?
But thou art proof against them, and indeed,
Above the ill fortune of them, or the need.
I therefore will begin. Soul of the age!
The applause, delight, the wonder of our stage!
My Shakespeare, rise! I will not lodge thee by
Chaucer, or Spenser, or bid Beaumont lie
A little further, to make thee a room;

Thou art a monument without a tomb,
And art alive still while thy book doth live
And we have wits to read and praise to give.
That I not mix thee so, my brain excuses,
I mean with great, but disproportioned Muses;
For if I thought my judgement were of years,
I should commit thee surely with thy peers,
And tell how far thou didst our Lyly outshine,
Or sporting Kyd, or Marlowe's mighty line.
And though thou hadst small Latin and less Greek,
From thence to honor thee, I would not seek
For names; but call forth thundering Aeschylus,
Euripides, and Sophocles to us;
Pacuvius, Accius, him of Cordova dead,
To life again, to hear thy buskin tread,
And shake a stage; or, when thy socks were on,
Leave thee alone for the comparison
Of all that insolent Greece or haughty Rome
Sent forth, or since did from their ashes come.
Triumph, my Britain, thou hast one to show
To whom all scenes of Europe homage owe.
He was not of an age, but for all time!
And all the Muses still were in their prime,
When, like Apollo, he came forth to warm
Our ears, or like a Mercury to charm!
Nature herself was proud of his designs
And joyed to wear the dressing of his lines!
Which were so richly spun, and woven so fit,
As, since, she will vouchsafe no other wit.
The merry Greek, tart Aristophanes,
Neat Terence, witty Plautus, now not please,
But antiquated and deserted lie,
As they were not of nature's family.
Yet must I not give nature all; thy art,
My gentle Shakespeare, must enjoy a part.
For though the poet's matter nature be,
His art doth give the fashion; and, that he
Who casts to write a living line, must sweat
(Such as thine are) and strike the second heat
Upon the Muses' anvil; turn the same
(And himself with it) that he thinks to frame,
Or, for the laurel, he may gain a scorn;
For a good poet's made, as well as born.

And such wert thou! Look how the father's face
Lives in his issue; even so the race
Of Shakespeare's mind and manners brightly shines
In his well turnéd, and true filéd lines;
In each of which he seems to shake a lance,
As brandished at the eyes of ignorance.
Sweet Swan of Avon! what a sight it were
To see thee in our waters yet appear,
And to make those flights upon the banks of Thames,
That so did take Eliza, and our James!
But stay, I see thee in the hemisphere
Advanced, and made a constellation there!
Shine forth, thou Star of poets, and with rage
Or influence, chide or cheer the drooping stage,
Which, since thy flight from hence, hath mourned like night,
And despairs day, but for thy volume's light.

THE FIRST CHRISTMAS TREE

Eugene Field

Once upon a time the forest was in a great commotion. Early in the evening the wise old cedars had shaken their heads ominously and predicted strange things. They had lived in the forest many, many years; but never had they seen such marvellous sights as were to be seen now in the sky, and upon the hills, and in the distant village.

"Pray tell us what you see," pleaded a little vine; "we who are not as tall as you can behold none of these wonderful things. Describe them to us, that we may enjoy them with you."

"I am filled with such amazement," said one of the cedars, "that I can hardly speak. The whole sky seems to be aflame, and the stars appear to be dancing among the clouds. Angels walk down from heaven to the earth, and enter the village or talk with the shepherds upon the hills."

The vine listened in mute astonishment. Such things never before had happened. The vine trembled with excitement. Its nearest neighbor was a tiny tree so small it scarcely ever was noticed; yet it was a very beautiful little tree, and the vines and ferns and mosses and other humble residents of the forest loved it dearly.

"How I should like to see the angels!" sighed the little tree, "and how I should like to see the stars dancing among the clouds! It must be very beautiful!"

As the vine and the little tree talked of these things, the cedars watched with increasing interest the wonderful scenes over and beyond the confines of the forest. Presently they thought they heard music, and they were not mistaken, for soon the whole air was full of the sweetest harmonies ever heard upon earth.

"What beautiful music!" cried the little tree. "I wonder whence it comes."

"The angels are singing," said a cedar; "for none but angels could make such sweet music."

"But the stars are singing, too," said another cedar. "Yes, and the shepherds on the hills join in the song, and what a strangely glorious song it is!"

The trees listened to the singing, but they did not understand its meaning: it seemed to be an anthem, and it was of a Child that had been born; but further than this they did not understand. The strange and glorious song continued all the night; and all that night the angels walked to and fro, and the shepherd-folk talked with the angels, and the stars danced and carolled in high heaven. And it was nearly morning when the cedar cried out, "They are coming to the forest! the angels are coming to the forest!" And, surely enough, this was true. The vine and the little tree were very terrified, and they begged their older and stronger neighbors to protect them from harm. But the cedars were too busy with their own fears to pay any heed to the faint pleadings of the humble vine and the little tree. The angels came into the forest, singing the same glorious anthem about the Child, and the stars sang in chorus with them, until every part of the woods rang with echoes of that wondrous song. There was nothing in the appearance of this angel host to inspire fear; they were clad all in white, and there were crowns upon their fair heads, and golden harps in their hands; love, hope, charity, compassion and joy beamed from their beautiful faces, and their presence seemed to fill the forest with a divine peace. The angels came through the forest to where the little tree stood, and gathering round it, they touched it with their hands, and kissed its little branches, and sang even more sweetly than before. And their song was about the Child, the Child, the Child that had been born. Then the stars came down from the skies and danced and hung upon the branches of the tree, and they, too, sang that song,—the song of the Child. And all the other trees and the vines and the ferns and mosses beheld in wonder; nor could they understand why all these things were being done, and why this exceeding honor should be shown the little tree.

When the morning came the angels left the forest,—all but one angel, who remained behind and lingered near the little tree. Then a cedar asked: "Why do you tarry with us, holy angel?" And the angel answered: "I stay to guard this little tree, for it is sacred, and no harm shall come to it."

The little tree felt quite relieved by this assurance, and it held up its head more confidently than ever before. And how it thrived and grew, and walked in strength and beauty! The cedars said they had never seen the like. The sun seemed to lavish its choicest rays upon the little tree, heaven dropped its sweetest dew upon it, and the winds never came to the forest that they did not forget their rude manners and sing it their prettiest songs. No danger ever menaced it, no harm threatened; for the angel never slept,—through the day and through the night the angel watched the little tree and protected it from all evil. Often times the trees talked with the angel; but of course they understood little of what he said, for he spoke always of the Child who was to become the Master; and always when thus he talked, he caressed the little tree and stroked its branches and leaves, moistened them with his tears. It was all so very very strange that none in the forest could understand.

So the years passed, the angel watching his blooming charge. Sometimes the beasts strayed toward the little tree and threatened to devour its tender foliage; sometimes the woodman came with his axe, intent upon hewing down the straight and comely thing; sometimes the hot, consuming breath of drought swept from the south, and sought to blight the forest and all its verdure; the angel kept them all from the little tree. Serene and beautiful it grew, until now it was no longer a little tree, but the pride and glory of the forest.

One day the tree heard some one coming through the forest. Hitherto the angel had hastened to its side when men approached; but now the angel strode away and stood under the cedars yonder.

"Dear angel," cried the tree, "can you not hear the footsteps of some one approaching? Why do you leave me?"

"Have no fear," said the angel; "for He who comes is the Master."

The Master came to the tree and beheld it. He placed His hands upon its smooth trunk and branches, and the tree was thrilled with a strange and glorious delight. Then He stooped and kissed the tree, and then He turned and went away.

Many times after that the Master came to the forest, and when He came it always was to where the tree stood. Many times He rested beneath the tree and enjoyed the shade of its foliage, and listened to the music of the wind as it swept through the rustling leaves. Many times He slept there, and the tree watched over Him, and the forest was still, and all its voices were hushed. And the angel hovered near like a faithful sentinel.

Ever and anon men came with the Master to the forest, and sat with Him in the shade of the tree, and talked with Him of matters which the tree never could understand; only it heard that the talk was of love and charity and gentleness, and it saw that the Master was beloved and venerated by the others. It heard them tell of the Master's goodness and humility,—how He had healed the sick and raised the dead and bestowed inestimable blessings wherever He walked. And the tree loved the Master for His beauty and His goodness; and when He came to the forest it was full of joy, but when He came not it was sad. And the other trees of the forest joined in its happiness and its sorrow, for they, too, loved the Master. And the angel always hovered near.

The Master came one night alone into the forest, and His face was pale with anguish and wet with tears, and He fell upon His knees and prayed. The tree heard Him, and all the forest was still, as if it were standing in the presence of death. And when the morning came, lo! the angel had gone.

Then there was a great confusion in the forest. There was a sound of rude voices, and a clashing of swords and staves. Strange men appeared, uttering loud oaths and cruel threats, and the tree was filled with terror. It called aloud for the angel, but the angel came not.

"Alas," cried the vine, "they have come to destroy the tree, the pride and glory of the forest!"

The forest was sorely agitated, but it was in vain. The strange men plied their axes with cruel vigor, and the tree was hewn to the ground. Its beautiful branches were cut away and cast aside, and its soft, thick foliage was strewn to the tenderer mercies of the winds.

"They are killing me!" cried the tree; "why is not the angel here to protect me?"

But no one heard the piteous cry,—none but the other trees of the forest; and they wept, and the little vine wept, too.

Then the cruel men dragged the despoiled and hewn tree from the forest, and the forest saw that beauteous thing no more.

But the night wind that swept down from the City of the Great King that night to ruffle the bosom of distant Galilee, tarried in the forest awhile to say that it had seen that day a cross upraised on Calvary,—the tree on which was stretched the body of the dying Master.

COME, SLEEP

Sir Philip Sidney

Come, Sleep! O Sleep, the certain knot of peace,
The baiting-place of wit, the balm of woe,
The poor man's wealth, the prisoner's release,
The indifferent judge between the high and low;
With shield of proof shield me from out the prease
Of those fierce darts Despair at me doth throw;
O make in me those civil wars to cease.
I will good tribute pay, if thou do so.
Take thou of me smooth pillows, sweetest bed,
A chamber deaf to noise and blind to light,
A rosy garland and a weary head;
And if these things, as being thine by right,
Move not thy heavy grace, thou shalt in me,
Livelier than elsewhere, Stella's image see.

(From Astrophel and Stella)

DOWN IN A COAL MINE

J. B. Geoghegan

I am a jovial collier lad, and blithe as blithe can be,
For let the times be good or bad, they're all the same to me;
For where the dog-star never glows, I wear away my days.

Chorus:

Down in a coal mine, underneath the ground,
Where a gleam of sunshine never can be found;
Digging dusky diamonds all the season round,
Down in a coal mine, underneath the ground.

My hands are horny, hard and black, with working on the vein,
And, like the clothes upon my back, my speech is rough and plain;
Well, if I stumble with my tongue, I've one excuse to say,
'Tis not the collier's heart that's wrong, 'tis the head that goes astray.

At every shift bit soon or late, I haste my bread to earn,
And anxiously my kindred wait and watch for my return;
For Death, that levels all alike, whate'er their rank may be,
Amid the fire and damp may strike, and fling his darts at me.

How little do the great ones care, who sit at home secure,
What hidden dangers colliers dare, what hardships they endure;
The very fire their mansions boast to cheer themselves and wives,
Mayhap were kindled at the cost of jovial colliers' lives.

Then cheer up, lads, and make ye much of every joy ye can,
But let your mirth be always such as best becomes a man;
However Fortune turns about, we'll still be jovial souls,
What would our country be without the lads that look for coals?

SOUND THE CLARION

Sir Walter Scott

Sound, sound the clarion, fill the fife!
To all the sensual world proclaim,
One crowded hour of glorious life
Is worth an age without a name.

ON THE ROAD TO EMMAUS

Holy Bible, Luke 24:13–36

And, behold, two of them [that is, two of the disciples on the day of Christ's resurrection] went that same day to a village called Emmaus, which was from Jerusalem about threescore furlongs. And they talked together of all these things which had happened. And it came to pass, that, while they communed together and reasoned, Jesus himself drew near, and went with them. But their eyes were holden that they should not know him. And he said unto them, What manner of communications are these that ye have one to another, as ye walk, and are sad? And the one of them, whose name was Cleopas, answering said unto him, Art thou only a stranger in Jerusalem, and hast not known the things which are come to pass there in these days? And he said unto them, What things? And they said unto him, Concerning Jesus of Nazareth, which was a prophet mighty in deed and word before God and all the people: And how the chief priests and our rulers delivered him to be condemned to death, and have crucified him. But we trusted that it had been he which should have redeemed Israel: and beside all this, today is the third day since these things were done. Yea, and certain women also of our company made us astonished, which were early at the sepulchre; And when they found not his body, they came, saying, that they had also seen a vision of angels, which said that he was alive. And certain of them which were with us went to the sepulchre, and found it even so as the women had said: but him they saw not. Then he said unto them, O fools, and slow of heart to believe all that the prophets have spoken: Ought not Christ to have suffered these things, and to enter into his glory? And beginning at Moses and all the prophets, he expounded unto them in all the scriptures the things concerning himself. And they drew nigh unto the village, whither they went: and he made as though he would have gone further. But they constrained him, saying, Abide with us: for it is toward evening, and the day is far spent. And he went in to tarry with them. And it came to pass, as he sat at meat with them, he took bread, and blessed it, and brake, and gave to them. And their eyes were opened, and they knew him; and he vanished out of their sight. And they said one to another, Did not our heart burn within us, while he talked with us by the way, and while he opened to us the scriptures? And they rose up the same hour, and returned to Jerusalem, and found the eleven gathered together, and them that were with them, saying, The Lord is risen indeed, and hath appeared to Simon. And they told what things were done in the way, and how he was known of them in breaking of bread. And as they thus spake, Jesus himself stood in the midst of them, and saith unto them, Peace be unto you.

* * *

Every man complains of his memory but no man complains of his judgment.—Anonymous

THE ARAB TO HIS FAVORITE STEED

Caroline Norton

My Beautiful! my beautiful! that standest meekly by,
With thy proudly arched and glossy neck, and dark and fiery eye,
Fret not to roam the desert now, with all thy wingèd speed;
I may not mount on thee again,—thou'rt sold, my Arab steed!
Fret not with that impatient hoof—snuff not the breezy wind,—
The farther that thou fliest now, so far am I behind;
The stranger hath thy bridle-rein,—thy master hath *his* gold,—
Fleet-limbed and beautiful, farewell; thou'rt sold, my steed, thou'rt sold.

Farewell! those free, untired limbs full many a mile must roam,
To reach the chill and wintry sky which clouds the stranger's home;
Some other hand, less fond, must now thy corn and bed prepare,
The silky mane, I braided once, must be another's care!
The morning sun shall dawn again, but nevermore with thee
Shall I gallop through the desert paths, where we were wont to be;
Evening shall darken on the earth, and o'er the sandy plain
Some other steed, with slower step, shall bear me home again.

Yes, thou must go! the wild, free breeze, the brilliant sun and sky,
The master's house,—from all of these my exiled one must fly;
The proud dark eye will grow less proud, thy step become less fleet,
And vainly shalt thou arch thy neck, thy master's hand to meet.
Only in sleep shall I behold that dark eye, glancing bright;—
Only in sleep shall hear again that step so firm and light;
And when I raise my dreaming arm to check or cheer thy speed,
Then must I, starting, wake to feel,—thou'rt *sold,* my Arab steed!

Ah! rudely then, unseen by me, some cruel hand may chide,
Till foam-wreaths lie, like crested waves, along thy panting side:
And the rich blood that's in thee swells, in thy indignant pain,
Till careless eyes, which rest on thee, may count each starting vein.
Will they ill-use thee? If I thought—but no, it cannot be,—
Thou art so swift, yet easy curbed; so gentle, yet so free:
And yet, if haply, when thou'rt gone, my lonely heart should yearn,—
Can the hand which casts thee from it now command thee to return?

Return! alas! my Arab steed! what shall thy master do,
When thou, who wast his all of joy, hast vanished from his view?
When the dim distance cheats mine eye, and through the gathering
  tears
Thy bright form, for a moment, like the false mirage appears;
Slow and unmounted shall I roam, with weary step alone,
Where, with fleet step and joyous bound, thou oft hast borne me
  on;
And sitting down by that green well, I'll pause and sadly think,
"It was here he bowed his glossy neck when last I saw him drink!"

When last I saw thee drink!—Away! the fevered dream is o'er,—
I could not live a day, and *know* that we should meet no more!
They tempted me, my beautiful!—for hunger's power is strong,—
They tempted me, my beautiful! but I have loved too long.
Who said that I had given thee up? who said that thou wast sold?
'Tis false,—'tis false, my Arab steed! I fling them back their gold!
Thus, *thus,* I leap upon thy back, and scour the distant plains;
Away! who overtakes us now shall claim thee for his pains!

NOW THE LABORER'S TASK IS O'ER

John Ellerton

Now the laborer's task is o'er;
  Now the battle day is past;
Now upon the farther shore
  Lands the voyager at last.
Father, in thy gracious keeping
Leave we now thy servant sleeping.

There the tears of earth are dried;
  There its hidden things are clear;
There the work of life is tried
  By a juster Judge than here.
Father, in thy gracious keeping
Leave we now thy servant sleeping.

There the sinful souls, that turn
  To the cross their dying eyes,
All the love of Christ shall learn
  At his feet in Paradise.
Father, in thy gracious keeping
Leave we now thy servant sleeping.

"Earth to earth, and dust to dust,"
  Calmly now the words we say;
Left behind, we wait in trust
  For the resurrection day.
Father, in thy gracious keeping
Leave we now thy servant sleeping.

FANCY

William Shakespeare

Tell me where is fancy bred,
Or in the heart or in the head?
How begot, how nourished?
  Reply, reply,
It is engender'd in the eyes,
With gazing fed; and fancy dies
In the cradle where it lies.
  Let us all ring fancy's knell;
  I'll begin it,—Ding, dong, bell.
    (From The Merchant of Venice)

REQUIESCAT

Matthew Arnold

Strew on her roses, roses,
  And never a spray of yew.
In quiet she reposes:
  Ah! would that I did too.

Her mirth the world required:
  She bathed it in smiles of glee.
But her heart was tired, tired,
  And now they let her be.

Her life was turning, turning,
  In mazes of heat and sound.
But for peace her soul was yearning,
  And now peace laps her round.

Her cabin'd, ample spirit,
It flutter'd and fail'd for breath.
Tonight it doth inherit
The vasty Hall of Death.

THE FIGHT

William Hazlitt

Reader, have you ever seen a fight? If not, you have a pleasure to come, at least if it is a fight like that between the Gas-man and Bill Neate. The crowd was very great when we arrived on the spot; open carriages were coming up, with streamers flying and music playing, and the country-people were pouring in over hedge and ditch in all directions, to see their hero beat or be beaten. The odds were still on Gas, but only about five to four. . . . About £200,000 were pending. . . .

Few but those who had bet on him wished Gas to win. With my own prepossessions on the subject, the result of the 11th of December appeared to me as fine a piece of poetical justice as I had ever witnessed. The difference of weight between the two combatants (14 stone to 12) was nothing to the sporting men. Great, heavy, clumsy, long-armed Bill Neate kicked the beam in the scale of the Gas-man's vanity. The amateurs were frightened at his big words, and thought they would make up for the difference of six feet and five feet nine. . . .

The day, as I have said, was fine for a December morning. The grass was wet and the ground miry, and ploughed up with multitudinous feet, except that, within the ring itself, there was a spot of virgin-green, closed in and unprofaned by vulgar tread, that shone with dazzling brightness in the mid-day sun. For it was now noon, and we had an hour to wait. This is the trying time. It is then the heart sickens, as you think what the two champions are about, and how short a time will determine their fate. After the first blow is struck, there is no opportunity for nervous apprehensions; you are swallowed up in the immediate interest of the scene—but

Between the acting of a dreadful thing
And the first motion, all the interim is
Like a phantasma, or a hideous dream.

I found it so as I felt the sun's rays clinging to my back, and saw the white wintry clouds sink below the verge of the horizon. "So," I thought, "my fairest hopes have faded from my sight!—so will the Gas-man's glory, or that of his adversary, vanish in an hour." The *swells* were parading in their white box-coats, the other ring was cleared with some bruises on the heads and shins of the rustic assembly (for the *cockneys* had been distanced by the sixty-five miles); the time drew near; I had got a good stand; a bustle, a buzz, ran through the crowd; and from the opposite entered Neate, between his second and bottle-holder. He rolled along, swathed in his loose greatcoat, his knock-knees bending under his huge bulk; and, with a modest, cheerful air, threw his hat into the ring. He then just looked around, and began quietly to undress; when from the other side there was a similar rush and an opening made, and the Gas-man came forward with a conscious air of anticipated triumph, too much like the cock-of-the-walk. He strutted about more than became a hero, sucked oranges with a supercilious air, and threw away the skin with a toss of his head, and went up and looked at Neate, which was an act of supererogation. The only sensible thing he did was, as he strode away from the modern Ajax, to fling out his arms, as if he wanted to try whether they would do their work that day. By this time they had stripped and presented a strong contrast in appearance. If Neate was like Ajax, "with Atlantean shoulders, fit to bear" the pugilistic reputation of all Bristol, Hickman might be compared to Diomed, light, vigorous, elastic, and his back glistened in the sun, as he moved about, like a panther's hide. There was a dead pause—attention was awe-struck. Who at that moment, big with a great event, did not draw his breath short—did not feel his heart throb? All was ready. They tossed for the sun, and the Gas-man won. They were led up to the *scratch*—shook hands, and went at it.

In the first round every one thought it was all over. After making play a short time, the Gas-man flew at his adversary like a tiger, struck five blows in as many seconds, three first, and then following him as he staggered back, two more, right and left, and down he fell, a mighty ruin. There was a shout, and I said, "There is no standing this." Neate seemed like a lifeless lump of flesh and bone, round which the Gas-man's blows played with the rapidity of electricity or lightning, and you imagined he would only be lifted up to be knocked down again. It was as if Hickman held a sword or a fire in that right hand of his, and directed it against an unarmed body. They met again, and Neate seemed, not cowed, but particularly cautious. I saw his teeth clenched together and his brows knit close against the sun. He held out both his arms at full length straight before him, like two sledge hammers, and raised his left an inch or two higher. The Gas-man could not get over his guard—they struck mutually and fell, but without advantage on either side. It was the same in the next round; but the balance of power was thus restored—the fate of the battle was suspended. No one could tell how it would end. This was the only moment in which opinion was divided; for, in the next, the Gas-man aimed a mortal blow at his adversary's neck, with his right hand, and failing from the length he had to reach, the other returned it with his left at full swing, planted a tremendous blow on his cheek-bone and eyebrow, and made a red ruin of that side of his face. The Gas-man went down, and there was another shout—a roar of triumph as the waves of fortune rolled tumultuously from side to side. This was a settler. Hickman got up, and "grinned horrible a ghastly smile," yet he was evidently dashed in his opinion of himself; it was the first time he had ever been so punished; all one side of his face was perfect scarlet, and his right eye was closed in dingy blackness, as he advanced to the fight, less confident, but still determined. After one or two rounds, not receiving another such remembrancer, he rallied and went at it with his former impetuosity. But in vain. His strength had been weakened—his blows could not tell at such a distance—he was obliged to fling himself at his adversary, and could not strike from his feet; and almost as regularly as he flew at him with his right hand, Neate warded the blow, or drew back out of its reach, and felled him with the return of his left. There was little cautious sparring—no half-hits—no tapping and trifling, none of the *petit-maitreship* of the art—they were almost all knock-down blows: the fight was a good stand-up fight. The wonder was the half-minute time. If there had been a minute or more allowed between each round, it would have been intelligible how they should by degrees recover strength and resolution: but to see two men smashed to the ground, smeared with gore. stunned, senseless, the breath beaten out of their bodies; and then. before you recover from the shock, to see them rise up with new strength and courage, stand ready to inflict or receive mortal offence, and rush upon each other "like two clouds over the Caspian"—this is the most astonishing thing of all:—this is the high and heroic state of man! From this time forward the event became more certain every round; and about the twelfth it seemed as if it must have been over. Hickman generally stood with his back to me; but

In the scuffle, he had changed positions, and Neate just then made a tremendous lunge at him, and hit him full in the face. It was doubtful whether he would fall backwards or forwards; he hung suspended for a second or two, and then fell back, throwing his hands in the air, and with his face lifted up to the sky. I never saw anything more terrific than his aspect just before he fell. All traces of life, of natural expression, were gone from him. His face was like a human skull, a death's head spouting blood. The eyes were filled with blood, the nose streamed with blood, the mouth gaped blood. He was not like an actual man, but like a preternatural, spectral appearance, or like one of the figures in Dante's *Inferno*. Yet he fought on after this for several rounds, still striking the first desperate blow, and Neate standing on the defensive, and using the same cautious guard to the last, as if he had still all his work to do; and it was not till the Gas-man was so stunned in the seventeenth or eighteenth round, that his senses forsook him, and he could not come to time, that the battle was declared over.[1] Ye who despise the FANCY, do something to show as much *pluck*, or as much self-possession as this, before you assume a superiority which you have never given a single proof of by any one action in the whole course of your lives!—When the Gas-man came to himself, the first words he uttered were, "Where am I? What is the matter?" "Nothing is the matter, Tom,—you have lost the battle, but you are the bravest man alive." And Jackson whispered to him, "I am collecting a purse for you, Tom."—Vain sounds and unheard at that moment! Neate instantly went up and shook him cordially by the hand, and seeing some old acquaintance, began to flourish with his fists, calling out, "Ah, you always said I couldn't fight—what do you think now?" But all in good humour, and without any appearance of arrogance; only it was evident Bill Neate was pleased that he had won the fight. When it was over, I asked Cribb if he did not think it was a good one? He said, *"Pretty well!"* The carrier-pigeons now mounted into the air, and one of them flew with the news of her husband's victory to the bosom of Mrs. Neate. Alas for Mrs. Hickman!

[1] Scroggins said of the Gas-man, that he thought he was a man of that courage, that if his hands were cut off he would still fight on with the stumps—like that of Widdrington—

—In doleful dumps,
Who, when his legs were smitten off,
Still fought upon his stumps.

"PIPING DOWN THE VALLEYS WILD"

William Blake

Piping down the valleys wild,
Piping songs of pleasant glee,
On a cloud I saw a child,
And he laughing said to me:

"Pipe a song about a Lamb!"
So I piped with a merry chear.
"Piper, pipe that song again":
So I piped: he wept to hear.

"Drop thy pipe. thy happy pipe;
Sing thy songs of happy chear":
So I sung the same again,
While he wept with joy to hear.

"Piper, sit thee down and write
In a book, that all may read."
So he vanish'd from my sight,
And I pluck'd a hollow reed,

And I made a rural pen,
And I stain'd the water clear,
And I wrote my happy songs
Every child may joy to hear.

IF THIS BE TREASON

Patrick Henry

Caesar had his Brutus; Charles the First his Cromwell; and George the Third ("Treason!" cried the Speaker)—may profit by their example. If *this* be treason, make the most of it!

(In the Virginia Convention, 1765)

THE BLACK HOLE OF CALCUTTA

Thomas Babington Macaulay

From a child Surajah Dowlah had hated the English. It was his whim to do so, and his whims were never opposed. He had also formed a very exaggerated notion of the wealth which might be obtained by plundering them; and his feeble and uncultivated mind was incapable of perceiving that the riches of Calcutta, had they been even greater than he imagined, would not compensate him for what he must lose, if the European trade, of which Bengal was a chief seat, should be driven by his violence to some other quarter. Pretexts for a quarrel were readily found. The English, in expectation of a war with France, had begun to fortify their settlement without permission from the Nabob. A rich native, whom he longed to plunder, had taken refuge at Calcutta, and had not been delivered up. On such grounds as these Surajah Dowlah marched with a great army against Fort William.

The servants of the Company at Madras had been forced by Dupleix to become statesmen and soldiers. Those in Bengal were still mere traders, and were terrified and bewildered by the approaching danger. The governor, who had heard much of Surajah Dowlah's cruelty, was frightened out of his wits, jumped into a boat, and took refuge in the nearest ship. The military commandant thought that he could do no better than to follow so good an example. The fort was taken after a feeble resistance, and great numbers of the English fell into the hands of the Conqueror. The Nabob seated himself with regal pomp in the principal hall of the factory, and ordered Mr. Holwell, the first in rank among the prisoners, to be brought before him. His Highness talked about the insolence of the English, and grumbled at the smallness of the treasure which he had found; but promised to spare their lives, and retired to rest.

Then was committed that great crime, memorable for its singular atrocity, memorable for the tremendous retribution by which it was followed. The English captives were left at the mercy of their guards, and the guards determined to secure them for the night in the prison of the garrison, a chamber known by the fearful name of the Black Hole. Even for a single European malefactor, that dungeon would, in such a climate, have been too close and narrow. The air-holes were small and obstructed. It was the summer solstice, the season when the fierce heat of Bengal can scarcely be rendered tolerable to natives of England by lofty halls and by the constant waving of fans. The number of the prisoners was one hundred and forty-six. When they were ordered to enter the cell, they imagined that the soldiers were joking; and, being in high spirits on account of the promise of the Nabob to spare their lives, they laughed and jested at the absurdity of the notion. They soon discovered their mistake. They expostulated; they entreated: but in vain. The guards threatened to cut down all who hesitated. The captives were driven into the cell at the point of the sword, and the door was instantly shut and locked upon them.

Nothing in history or fiction, not even the story which Ugolino told in the sea of everlasting ice, after he had wiped his bloody lips on the scalp of his murderer, approaches the terrors which were recounted by the few survivors of that night. They cried for mercy. They strove to burst the door. Holwell who, even in that extremity, retained some presence of mind, offered large bribes to the gaolers. But the answer was that nothing could be done without the Nabob's order, that the Nabob was asleep, and that he would be angry if anybody woke him. Then the prisoners went mad with despair. They trampled each other down, fought for the places at the windows, fought for the pittance of water with which the cruel mercy of the murderers mocked their agonies, raved, prayed, blasphemed, implored the guards to fire among them. The gaolers in the mean time held lights to the bars, and shouted with laughter at the frantic struggles of their victims. At length the tumult died away in low gaspings and moanings. The day broke. The Nabob had slept off his debauch, and permitted the door to be opened. But it was some time before the soldiers could make a lane for the survivors, by piling on each side the heaps of corpses on which the burning climate had already begun to do its loathsome work. When at length a passage was made, twenty-three ghastly figures, such as their own mothers would not have known, staggered one by one out of the charnal-house. A pit was instantly dug. The dead bodies, a hundred and twenty-three in number, were flung into it promiscuously, and covered up.

(From the essay on Clive)

EPITAPH ON A DENTIST

Stranger, approach this spot with gravity;
John Brown is filling his last cavity.

"COMFORT YE MY PEOPLE"

Holy Bible, Isaiah 40:1–11

Comfort ye, comfort ye my people, saith your God.
Speak ye comfortably to Jerusalem, and cry unto her, that her warfare is accomplished, that her iniquity is pardoned: for she hath received of the Lord's hand double for all her sins.
The voice of him that crieth in the wilderness, Prepare ye the way of the Lord, make straight in the desert a highway for our God.
Every valley shall be exalted, and every mountain and hill shall be made low; and the crooked shall be made straight, and the rough places plain:
And the glory of the Lord shall be revealed, and all flesh shall see it together: for the mouth of the Lord hath spoken it.
The voice said, Cry. And he said, What shall I cry? All flesh is grass, and all the goodliness thereof is as the flower of the field:
The grass withereth, the flower fadeth: because the spirit of the Lord bloweth upon it: surely the people is grass.
The grass withereth, the flower fadeth: but the word of our God shall stand for ever.
O Zion, that bringest good tidings, get thee up into the high mountain; O Jerusalem, that bringest good tidings, lift up thy voice with strength; lift it up, be not afraid; say unto the cities of Judah, Behold your God!
Behold, the Lord God will come with strong hand, and his arm shall rule for him; behold, his reward is with him, and his work before him.
He shall feed his flock like a shepherd, he shall gather the lambs with his arm, and carry them in his bosom, and shall gently lead those that are with young.

THE BLIND BOY

Colley Cibber

O say what is that thing called Light,
Which I must ne'er enjoy;
What are the blessings of the sight,
O tell your poor blind boy!

You talk of wondrous things you see,
  You say the sun shines bright;
I feel him warm, but how can he
  Or make it day or night.

My day or night myself I make
  Whene'er I sleep or play;
And could I ever keep awake
  With me 'twere always day.

With heavy sighs I often hear
  You mourn my hapless woe;
But sure with patience I can bear
  A loss I ne'er can know.

Then let not what I cannot have
  My cheer of mind destroy;
Whilst thus I sing, I am a king,
  Although a poor blind boy.

JUST TELL THEM THAT YOU SAW ME *

Paul Dresser

While strolling down the street one eve upon mere pleasure bent,
'Twas after business worries of the day,
I saw a girl who shrank from me in whom I recognized
My school mate in a village far away.
"Is that you, Madge?" I said to her. She quickly turned away.
"Don't turn away, Madge, I am still your friend.
Next week I'm going back to see the old folks and I thought
Perhaps some message you would like to send."

Chorus

"Just tell them that you saw me,"
She said; "they'll know the rest.
Just tell them I was looking well you know.
Just whisper if you get a chance to mother dear, and say
I love her as I did long, long ago."

"Your cheeks are pale, your face is thin, come tell me were you ill.
When last we met your eye shone clear and bright.
Come home with me when I go, Madge, the change will do you good,
Your mother wonders where you are to-night!"
"I long to see them all again, but not just yet," she said.
" 'Tis pride alone that's keeping me away.
Just tell them not to worry, for I'm all right, don't you know,
Tell mother I am coming home some day."

SWEET PERIL

George Macdonald

Alas, how easily things go wrong!
A sigh too much, or a kiss too long,
And there follows a mist and a weeping rain,
And life is never the same again.

Alas, how hardly things go right!
'Tis hard to watch in a summer night,
For the sigh will come, and the kiss will stay,
And the summer night is a wintry day.

And yet how easily things go right,
If the sight and a kiss of a summer's night
Come deep from the soul in the stronger ray
That is born in the light of the winter's day.

And things can never go badly wrong
If the heart be true and the love be strong,
For the mist, if it comes, and the weeping rain
Will be changed by the love into the sunshine again.

* * *

There is in every true woman's heart a spark of heavenly fire, which lies dormant in the broad daylight of prosperity; but which kindles up, and beams and blazes in the dark hour of adversity.
—Washington Irving (The Sketch-Book)

WAS SOLOMON WISE?

Mark Twain

I read considerable to Jim about kings and dukes and earls and such, and how gaudy they dressed, and how much style they put on, and called each other your majesty, and your grace, and your lordship, and so on, 'stead of mister; and Jim's eyes bugged out, and he was interested. He says: "I didn' know dey was so many un um. I hain't hearn 'bout none un um, skasely, but ole King Sollermun, onless you counts dem kings dat's in a pack er k'yards. How much do a king git?"

"Get?" I says; "why they get a thousand dollars a month if they want it; they can have just as much as they want; everything belongs to them."

"*Ain'* dat gay? En what dey got to do, Huck?"

"*They* don't do nothing! Why, how you talk! They just set around."

"No; is dat so?"

"Of course it is. They just set around—except, maybe, when there's a war; then they go to the war. But other times they just lazy around; or go hawking—just hawking and sp— Sh!—d'you hear a noise?"

We skipped out and looked; but it warn't nothing but the flutter of a steamboat's wheel away down, coming around the point; so we come back.

"Yes," says I, "and other times, when things is dull, they fuss with the parlyment; and if everybody don't go just so he whacks their heads off. But mostly they hang round the harem."

"Roun' de which?"

"Harem."

"What's de harem?"

"The place where he keeps his wives. Don't you know about the harem? Solomon had one; he had about a million wives."

"Why, yes, dat's so; I—I'd done forgot it. A harem's a bo'd'n house, I reck'n. Mos' likely dey has rackety times in de nussery. En I reck'n de wives quarrels considable; en dast 'crease de racket. Yit dey say Sollermun de wises' man dat ever live'. I doan' take no stock in dat. Bekase why: would a wise man want to live in de mids' er sich a blim-blammin' all de time? No—'deed he wouldn't. A wise man 'ud take en buil' a biler-factry; en den he could shet *down* de biler-factry when he want to res'."

"Well, but he *was* the wisest man, anyway; because the widow she told me so, her own self."

"I doan' k'yer what de widder say, he *warn't* no wise man nuther. He had some er de dad-fetchedes' ways I ever see. Does you know 'bout dat chile dat he 'uz gwyne to chop in two?"

"Yes, the widow told me all about it."

"*Well,* den! Warn' dat de beatenes' notion in de worl'? You jes' take en look at it a minute. Dah's de stump, dah—dat's one er de women; heah's you—dat's de yuther one; I's Sollermun; en dish yer dollar bill's de chile. Bofe un you claims it. What does I do? Does I shin aroun' mongs' de neighbors en fine out which un you de bill *do* b'long to, en han' it over to de right one, all safe en soun', de way dat anybody dat had any gumption would? No; I take en whack de bill in *two,* en give half un it to you, en de yuther half to de yuther woman. Dat's de way Sollermun was gwyne to do wid de chile. Now I want to ast you: what's de use er dat half a bill?—can't buy noth'n wid it. En what use is a half a chile? I wouldn't give a dern for a million un um."

"But hang it, Jim, you've clean missed the point—blame it, you've missed it a thousand mile."

"Who? Me? Go 'long. Doan' talk to *me* 'bout yo' pints. I reck'n I knows sense when I sees it; en dey ain' no sense in sich doin's as dat. De 'spute warn't 'bout a half a chile, de 'spute was 'bout a whole chile; en de man dat think he kin settle a 'spute 'bout a whole chile wid a half a chile doan' know enough to come in out'n de rain. Doan' talk to me 'bout Sollermun, Huck, I knows him by de back."

"But I tell you you don't get the point."

"Blame de point? I reck'n I knows what I knows. En mine you, de *real* pint is down furder—it's down deeper. It lays in de way Sollermun was raised. You take a man dat's got on'y one or two chillen; is dat man gwyne to be waseful o' chillen? No, he ain't; he can't 'ford it. *He* know how to value 'em. But you take a man dat's got 'bout five million chillen runnin' roun' de house, en it's diffunt. *He* as soon chop a chile in two as a cat. Dey's plenty mo'. A chile er two, mo' er less, warn't no consekens to Sollermun, dad fetch him!"

I never see such a nigger. If he got a notion in his head once, there warn't no getting it out again. He was the most down on Solomon of any nigger I ever see. So I went to talking about other kings, and let Solomon slide. I told about Louis Sixteenth that got his head cut off in France long time ago; and about his little boy the dolphin, that would 'a' been a king, but they took and shut him up in jail, and some say he died there.

"Po' little chap."

"But some says he got out and got away, and come to America."

"Dat's good! But he'll be pooty lonesome—day ain' no kings here, is dey, Huck?"

"No."

"Den he can't git no situation. What he gwyne to do?"

"Well, I don't know. Some of them gets on the police, and some of them learns people how to talk French."

"Why, Huck, doan' de French people talk de same way we does?"

"*No,* Jim; you couldn't understand a word they said—not a single word."

"Well, now, I be ding-busted! How do dat come?"

"I don't know; but it's so. I got some of their jabber out of a book. S'pose a man was to come to you and say Polly-voo-franzy—what would you think?"

"I wouldn' think nuffn; I'd take en bust him over de head—dat is, if he warn't white. I wouldn't 'low no nigger to call me dat."

"Shucks, it ain't calling you anything. It's only saying, do you know how to talk French?"

"Well, den, why couldn't he say it?"

"Why, he *is* a-saying it. That's a Frenchman's *way* of saying it."

"Well, it's a blame ridicklous way, en I doan' want to hear no mo' 'bout it. Dey ain' no sense in it."

"Looky here, Jim; does a cat talk like we do?"

"No, a cat don't."

"Well, does a cow?"

"No, a cow don't, nuther."

"Does a cat talk like a cow, or a cow talk like a cat?"

"No, dey don't."

"It's natural and right for 'em to talk different from each other, ain't it?"

"Course."

"And ain't it natural and right for a cat and a cow to talk different from *us*?"

"Why, mos' sholy it is."

"Well, then why ain't it natural and right for a *Frenchman* to talk different from us? You answer me that."

"Is a cat a man, Huck?"

"No."

"Well, den, dey ain't no sense in a cat talkin' like a man. Is a cow a man?—er is a cow a cat?"

"No, she ain't either of them."

"Well, den, she ain't got no business to talk like either one er the yuther of 'em. Is a Frenchman a man?"

"Yes."

"*Well,* den! Dad blame it, why don' he *talk* like a man? You answer me *dat*!"

I see it warn't no use wasting words—you can't learn a nigger to argue. So I quit.

(From The Adventures of Huckleberry Finn)

EPITAPH ON CHARLES II

John Wilmot, Earl of Rochester

Here lies our Sovereign Lord the King,
Whose word no man relies on,
Who never said a foolish thing,
Nor ever did a wise one.

ANGELS WE HAVE HEARD ON HIGH

Anonymous

Angels we have heard on high,
Sweetly singing o'er the plains,
And the mountains in reply,
Echoing their joyous strains:

Gloria in excelsis Deo,
Gloria in excelsis Deo.

Shepherds, why this jubilee?
Why your joyous strains prolong?
What the gladsome tidings be
Which inspire your heavenly song?

Come to Bethlehem and see
Him Whose birth the angels sing;
Come, adore on bended knee,
Christ the Lord, the new-born King.

See him in a manger laid,
Whom the choirs of angels praise;
Mary, Joseph, lend your aid,
While our hearts in love we raise.

THE PARTING OF HECTOR AND ANDROMACHE *

Homer

(Translators: William B. Smith and Walter Miller)

"I to my home shall be going,
There to see my dear wife and my infant son and my housefolk.
Truly I know not whether to them I shall have a returning
Or now, under the hands of Achaeans, the gods will subdue me."
Thus he spake and departed, the shimmering-helmeted Hector.
Quickly anon he arrived at his own well-stablishèd mansion,
Yet found not in her halls his Andromache, her of the white arms,
Since she had gone with her babe and a handmaid in beautiful raiment
Unto the tow'r and had taken her place there, weeping and wailing.
Hector, on finding his faultless wife not there in her chamber,
Came to the inner threshold and stood and spake 'mid the servants:
"Come now, servants of mine, and tell me the truth with exactness,
Where is the white-armed lady Andromache gone from the palace?
Gone to my sisters' perchance, or the fair-robed wives of my brothers?
Or, it may be to the shrine of Athena along with the others,
Ilium's fair-haired daughters, t' appease the obdurate goddess?"
Him then in turn with a word a busy housekeeper answered:
"Hector, seeing thou strictly biddest that truth shall be told thee,
Neither went she to a sister nor fair-robed wife of a brother,

* From Book VI of The Iliad. Copyright, 1944, by The Macmillan Company.

Neither is gone to the shrine of Athena along with the others,
Ilium's fair-haired daughters, t' appease the obdurate goddess—
Nay, but to Ilium's tower, the great one, hearing the Argives
Press on the Trojans hard and victory crowns the Achaeans.
So in precipitate haste she is gone ev'n now to the rampart.
Like unto one that is mad; and a nurse bears with her her infant."
Thus made answer the woman, the housekeeper. Hector, departing,
Hastened the same way back through the well-built streets of the city.
When he had passed through the wide-walled town and arrived at the Scaean
Gateway—there he was minded to fare forth into the battle—
Lo! came running to meet him Andromache, wife of his bosom,
Bountiful daughter of King Eëtion, great-hearted Eëtion—
Him who dwelt at the foot of the forested mountain of Placus,
Habiting Thebè of Placus and ruling the men of Cilicia.
That king's daughter was wife to the bronzen-harnessèd Hector.
She now met him; and with her her handmaid came; on her bosom
Nestled the light-hearted boy—for as yet he was only an infant—
Dear-loved scion of Hector and like to a star in his beauty.
Hector would call him Scamandrius, th' others Astyanax named him,
Seeing that Hector alone was protector of Ilium city.
He, as he stood there, smiled on his offspring, gazing in silence.
Close by his side stood his wife, Andromache, letting a tear fall;
Laying her hand in his own, she spake a word and addressed him:
"Good man of mine, this courage of thine will undo thee, nor pity
Moveth *thee* for thy infant boy or for me, the unhappy,
Soon to be widowed of thee—the Achaeans will certainly kill thee,
Setting upon thee in mass; and for me it were verily better
Earth should enwrap me, bereavèd of thee; since no other comfort
Bideth for me, grief only, when Destiny cometh to meet thee,
Seeing (alas!) I have no father nor worshipful mother.
Yea, thou knowest our father was slain by the doughty Achilles,
What time he utterly sacked Cilicia's well-builded city,
Thebè, lofty of gates. And he slew the royal Eëtion,
Yet he despoiled him not—for awe in his spirit forbade it—
Rather he burned him along with his inlaid armor, and o'er him
Builded a barrow; around it the nymphs of the mountain have planted
Elms in a ring—fair daughters of Zeus who beareth the aegis.

Then seven brothers of mine—all dwelt in the halls of the palace—
All on the selfsame day went down to the mansion of Hades.
He it was slaughtered them all, the divine fleet-footed Achilles,
As they were keeping their white-fleeced sheep and their kine, trailing-footed.
Also he carried the queen, who reigned 'neath Placus the wooded,
Carried my mother away along with our other possessions;
Later, indeed, on payment of untold ransom he freed her.
Artemis, rainer of darts, slew *her* in the halls of her father.—
Thou art alone unto me both father and worshipful mother.
Hector, and brother thou art, and my husband, blooming in manhood.
Come then, pity me now, and abide right here on the tower,
Lest thou widow thy wife and make thy child but an orphan.
Station the host along at the fig-tree; there is the city
Easiest far to be scaled, and the rampart assailable also.
Thrice came thither the bravest, indeed, and attempted to enter,
Led by the Ajaxes twain and Idomeneus, highly renownèd,
Tydeus' valorous son, and the warrior children of Atreus—
Whether, perhaps, it was someone who knew well oracles told them,
Or if their own heart rather commands them, urges them onward."
Then in his turn great shimmering-helmeted Hector addressed her:
"Verily all these things are my care, dear wife, but believe me,
I were despised of the Trojans, the men and the trailing-robed women,
Were I to skulk, as a craven, aloof and apart from the battle.
Yea, my own spirit forbids, since I have learned to be valiant
Always, ever to fight in the fore front along with the Trojans,
Winning a wid'ning renown no less for myself than my father.
This do I know full well in my heart, in my soul do I know it:
Cometh the day when the city of Ilium holy shall perish,
Priam, too, of the ashen spear, and the people of Priam.
Yet it afflicteth me not, that anguish to come of the Trojans,
Neither of Hecabe's self, not even of Priam, our sovereign,
Nor of my hero-brothers, the many perchance and the valiant
Fated to fall in the dust 'neath the hands of the foemen in battle,
Like unto anguish of thine, when a bronze-clad son of Achaia,
Victor, shall lead thee away in tears and bereave thee of freedom.
Haply in Argos the loom thou'lt ply at the hest of another,
Bring in water from found Hypereia, perchance, or Messeïs,
Sorely reluctant, with the heavy necessity pressing upon thee.

Ay, mayhap he will say, some wight that beholds thee a-weeping:
'This was the wife of Hector, the foremost chief of the Trojans,
Tamers of steeds, when aforetime men fought round Ilium's ramparts.'
So shall someone speak and anguish requicken within thee
Lacking a husband as thine is, to ward off slavery's hour.
Me let the mantle of death and the heaped-up earth have enfolded,
Ere I shall hear thy wail, thy dragging away into thralldom."
So spake glorious Hector and reached out after the infant;
Backward it shrank with a cry, and it clung to the beauteous-girdled
Nursemaid's breast, affrighted at sight of its father belovèd,
Fearstruck both at the bronze and the horsehair crest that it noted
Dreadfully nodding on high from the topmost ridge of the helmet.
Thereat they laughed out loud, both father and worshipful mother.
Straightway glorious Hector removed the helm from his forehead,
Laying it down on the ground, wide-flashing its splendor about it.
When he had kissed his dear son, in his arms had dandled him fondly,
Thus he bespake in prayer both Zeus and the other immortals:
"Vouchsafe, Zeus and ye other immortals, that even as I am,
This, my son, may prove in the eyes of the Trojans outstanding,
Even as valiant in might, o'er Ilium mightily reigning.
Then may someone say 'Far better this man than his father,'
As he returneth from war; may he bring home trophies encrimsoned,
Harness of enemy slain, and gladden the heart of his mother."
Thus he spake and placed his child in the arms of its mother,
Hector's beloved, and she on her fragrant bosom received it,
Smiling through her tears, and her husband beheld her in pity,
Gently caressed with his hand, then spake a word and addressed her:
"Good wife, be not distressed past measure in spirit, I pray thee.
No man hurls me to Hades, unless whom Fate hath appointed;
Yet, as I ween, no man hath evaded his destiny ever,
Once he is born—no, never a one, whether coward or valiant.
Go thou home and attend to thy tasks, the loom and the distaff,
Works that beseem thee well, and bid thy maidens in waiting
Ply at the duties assigned them. But war unto men is appointed,
All men—chiefly to me—that dwell in Ilium city."
Thus spake glorious Hector and took up his shimmering helmet,
Bronzen, horsetail-crested. His dear wife homeward departed,

Turning again and again, while big tears fell in abundance.
Quickly anon she reached the well-stablished home of her husband,
Hector, slayer of men, and she found there waiting within it
Many a handmaid. In all she stirred up loud lamentation.
So they lamented for Hector, while yet he lived, in his palace,
Seeing that never again they deemed he would come from the battle
Safe to his home, escaped from the hands and the fury Achaean.

THE VACANT CHAIR

H. S. Washburn

We shall meet, but we shall miss him,
There will be one vacant chair;
We shall linger to caress him,
When we breathe our evening prayer.
When a year ago we gathered,
Joy was in his mild blue eye,
But a golden cord is severed,
And our hopes in ruin lie.

Chorus:
We shall meet, but we shall miss him,
There will be one vacant chair;
We shall linger to caress him,
When we breathe our evening prayer.

At our fireside, sad and lonely,
Often will the bosom swell
At remembrance of the story
How our noble Willie fell;
How he strove to bear our banner
Through the thickest of the fight;
And uphold our country's honor,
In the strength of manhood's might.

True, they tell us wreaths of glory
Evermore will deck his brow,
But this soothes the anguish only
Sweeping o'er our heartstrings now.

Sleep today, O early fallen,
In thy green and narrow bed,
Dirges from the pine and cypress
Mingle with the tears we shed.

THE HAPPIEST HEART

John Vance Cheney

Who drives the horses of the sun
  Shall lord it but a day;
Better the lowly deed were done,
  And kept the humble way.

The rust will find the sword of fame,
  The dust will hide the crown;
Aye, none shall nail so high his name
  Time will not tear it down.

The happiest heart that ever beat
  Was in some quiet breast
That found the common daylight sweet,
  And left to Heaven the rest.

THE DEATH OF "THE MAN WITHOUT A COUNTRY"

Edward Everett Hale

Levant, 2° 2′ S. @ 131° W.

Dear Fred: I try to find heart and life to tell you that it is all over with dear old Nolan. I have been with him on this voyage more than I ever was, and I can understand wholly now the way in which you used to speak of the dear old fellow. I could see that he was not strong, but I had no idea the end was so near. The doctor has been watching him very carefully, and yesterday morning came to me and told me that Nolan was not so well, and had not left his stateroom—a thing I never remember before. He had let the doctor come and see him as he lay there—the first time the doctor had been in the stateroom—and he said he should like to see me. Oh, dear! do you remember the mysteries we boys used to invent about his room in the old *Intrepid* days? Well, I went in, and there, to be sure, the poor fellow lay in his berth, smiling pleasantly, as he gave me his hand, but looking very frail. I could not help a glance round, which showed me what a little shrine he had made of the box he was lying in. The Stars and Stripes were triced up above and around a picture of Washington, and he had painted a majestic eagle, with lightnings blazing from his beak and his foot just clasping the whole globe, which his wings overshadowed. The dear old boy saw my glance, and said, with a sad smile, "Here, you see, I have a country!" And then he pointed to the foot of his bed, where I had not seen before a great map of the United States, as he had drawn it from memory, and which he had there to look upon as he lay. Quaint, queer old names were on it, in large letters; "Indiana Territory" "Mississippi Territory," and "Louisiana Territory," as I suppose our fathers learned such things. But the old fellow had patched in Texas, too; he had carried his western boundary all the way to the Pacific, but on that shore he had defined nothing.

"Oh, Danforth," he said, "I know I am dying. I cannot get home. Surely you will tell me something now? Stop! Stop! Do not speak till I say what I am sure you know, that there is not in this ship, that there is not in America—God bless her!—a more loyal man than I. There cannot be a man who loves the old flag as I do, or prays for it as I do, or hopes for it as I do. There are thirty-four stars in it now, Danforth. I thank God for that, though I do not know what their names are. There has never been one taken away; I thank God for that. I know by that that there has never been any successful Burr. Oh, Danforth, Danforth," he sighed out, "how like a wretched night's dream a boy's idea of personal fame or of separate sovereignty seems, when one looks back on it after such a life as mine! But tell me—tell me something—tell me everything, Danforth, before I die!"

Ingham, I swear to you that I felt like a monster that I had not told him everything before. Danger or no danger, delicacy or no delicacy, who was I, that I should have been acting the tyrant all this time over this dear, sainted old man, who had years ago expiated, in his whole manhood's life, the madness of a boy's treason? "Mr. Nolan," said I, "I will tell you everything you ask about. Only, where shall I begin?"

Oh, the blessed smile that crept over his white face! And he pressed my hand and said, "God bless you! Tell me their names," he said, and he pointed to the stars on the flag. "The last I know is Ohio. My father lived in Kentucky. But I have guessed Michigan and Indiana and Mississippi—that was where Fort Adams is. They make twenty. But where are your other fourteen? You have not cut up any of the old ones, I hope?"

Well, that was not a bad text, and I told him the names in as good order as I could, and he bade me take down his beautiful map and draw them in as I best could with my pencil. He was wild with delight about Texas—told me how his cousin died there; he had marked a gold cross near where he supposed his grave was; and he had guessed at Texas. Then he was delighted as he saw California and Oregon. That, he said, he had suspected partly, because he had never been permitted to land on that shore, though the ships were there so much. "And the men," said he, laughing, "brought off a good deal besides furs." Then he went back—heavens, how far!—to ask about the *Chesapeake,* and what was done to Barron for surrendering her to the *Leopard* and whether Burr ever tried again—and he ground his teeth with the only passion he showed. But in a moment that was over, and he said, "God forgive me, for I am sure I forgive him." Then he asked about the old war—told me the true story of his serving the gun the day we took the *Java*—asked about dear old David Porter, as he called him. Then he settled down more quietly, and very happily, to hear me tell in an hour the history of fifty years.

How I wished it had been somebody who knew something! But I did as well as I could. I told him of the English war. I told him about Fulton and the steamboat beginning. I told him about old Scott, and Jackson—told him all I could think of about the Mississippi, and New Orleans, and Texas and his own old Kentucky. And what do you think he asked? "Who was in command of the Legion of the West!" I told him it was a very gallant officer named Grant, and that, by our last news, he was about to establish his headquarters at Vicksburg. Then, "Where was Vicksburg?" I worked that out on the map; it was about a hundred miles, more or less, above his old Fort Adams, and I thought Fort Adams must be a ruin now. "It must be at old Vick's plantation, at Walnut Hills," said he; "well, that is a change!"

I tell you, Ingham, it was a hard thing to condense the history of half a century into that talk with a sick man. And I do not know what I told him—of emigration, and the means of it—of steamboats, and railroads, and telegraphs—of inventions, and books, and literature—of the colleges, and West Point, and the Naval School—but with the queerest interruptions that ever you heard. You see, it was Robinson Crusoe asking all the accumulated questions of fifty-six years!

I remember he asked, all of a sudden, who was President now.

And when I told him, he asked if Old Abe was General Benjamin Lincoln's son. He said he met old General Lincoln, when he was quite a boy himself, at some Indian treaty. I said no, that Old Abe was a Kentuckian like himself, but I could not tell him of what family; he had worked up from the ranks. "Good for him!" cried Nolan; "I am glad of that. As I have brooded and wondered, I have thought our danger was in keeping up those regular successions in the first families." Then I got talking about my visit to Washington. I told him of meeting the Oregon Congressman, Harding; I told him about the Smithsonian, and the Exploring Expedition; I told him about the Capitol, and the statues for the pediment, and Crawford's Liberty, and Greenough's Washington. Ingham, I told him everything I could think of that would show the grandeur of his country and its prosperity; but I could not make up my mouth to tell him a word about this infernal rebellion!

And he drank it in and enjoyed it as I cannot tell you. He grew more and more silent, yet I never thought he was tired or faint. I gave him a glass of water, but he just wet his lips, and told me not to go away. Then he asked me to bring the Presbyterian "Book of Public Prayer," which lay there, and said, with a smile, that it would open at the right place—and so it did. There was his double red mark down the page. And I knelt down and read, and he repeated with me, "For ourselves and our country, Oh, gracious God, we thank Thee, that, notwithstanding our manifold transgressions of Thy holy laws, Thou hast continued to us Thy marvellous kindness"—and so to the end of that thanksgiving. Then he turned to the end of the same book, and I read the words more familiar to me: "Most heartily we beseech Thee with Thy favour to behold and bless Thy servant, the President of the United States, and all others in authority"—and the rest of the Episcopal collect. "Danforth," said he, "I have repeated those prayers night and morning, it is now fifty-five years." And then he said he would go to sleep.

He bent me down over him and kissed me, and he said, "Look in my Bible, Danforth, when I am gone." And I went away.

But I had no thought it was the end. I thought he was tired and would sleep. I knew he was happy, and I wanted him to be alone.

But in an hour, when the doctor went in gently, he found Nolan had breathed his life away with a smile. He had something pressed closed to his lips. It was his father's badge of the Order of the Cincinnati.

We looked in his Bible, and there was a slip of paper at the place where he had marked the text:

"They desire a country, even a heavenly: wherefore God is not ashamed to be called their God: for He hath prepared for them a city."

On this slip of paper he had written: "Bury me in the sea; it has been my home, and I love it. But will not some one set up a stone for my memory at Fort Adams or at Orleans, that my disgrace may not be more than I ought to bear? Say on it:

In Memory of
PHILIP NOLAN
Lieutenant in the Army of the United States.

He loved his country as no other man has loved her;
but no man deserved less at her hands!

THE GARDENER

Robert Louis Stevenson

The gardener does not love to talk,
He makes me keep the gravel walk;
And when he puts his tools away,
He locks the door and takes the key.

Away behind the currant row
Where no one else but cook may go,
Far in the plots, I see him dig,
Old and serious, brown and big.

He digs the flowers, green, red, and blue,
Nor wishes to be spoken to.
He digs the flowers and cuts the hay,
And never seems to want to play.

Silly gardener! summer goes,
And winter comes with pinching toes,
When in the garden bare and brown
You must lay your barrow down.

Well now, and while the summer stays,
To profit by these garden days,
O how much wiser you would be
To play at Indian wars with me!

THE NEAREST FRIEND

Frederic W. Faber

Dear Jesus! ever at my side,
  How loving must Thou be,
To leave Thy home in heaven to guard
  A little child like me!

Thy beautiful and shining face
  I see not, though so near;
The sweetness of Thy soft, low voice
  I am too deaf to hear.

I cannot feel Thee touch my hand
  With pressure light and mild,
To check me, as my mother did
  When I was but a child;

But I have felt Thee in my thoughts,
  Fighting with sin for me;
And when my heart loves God, I know
  The sweetness is from Thee.

Yes! when I pray, Thou prayest too;
  Thy prayer is all for me;
But when I sleep, Thou sleepest not,
  But watchest patiently.

ON GROWING OLD

John Masefield

Be with me, Beauty, for the fire is dying,
My dog and I are old, too old for roving,
Man, whose young passion sets the spindrift flying,
Is soon too lame to march, too cold for loving.
I take the book and gather to the fire,
Turning old yellow leaves; minute by minute,
The clock ticks to my heart; a withered wire
Moves a thin ghost of music in the spinet.

I cannot sail your seas, I cannot wander,
Your cornland, nor your hill-land nor your valleys,
Ever again, nor share the battle yonder
Where the young knight the broken squadron rallies.
Only stay quiet while my mind remembers
The beauty of fire from the beauty of embers.

Beauty, have pity, for the strong have power,
The rich their wealth, the beautiful their grace,
Summer of man its sunlight and its flower,
Spring-time of man all April in a face.
Only, as in the jostling in the Strand,
Where the mob thrusts or loiters or is loud,
The beggar with the saucer in his hand
Asks only a penny from the passing crowd.
So, from this glittering world with all its fashion,
Its fire and play of men, its stir, its march,
Let me have wisdom, Beauty, wisdom and passion,
Bread to the soul, rain where the summers parch.
Give me but these, and though the darkness close
Even the night will blossom as the rose.

COME BACK TO ERIN

Charlotte Alington Barnard ("Claribel")

Come back to Erin, Mavourneen, Mavourneen,
Come back, Aroon, to the land of thy birth;
Come with the shamrocks and springtime, Mavourneen,
And it's Killarney shall ring with our mirth.
Sure when you left us, our beautiful darling,
Little we thought of the lone winter days,
Little we thought of the hush of the starling,
Over the mountain, the bluffs, and the brays!

Chorus:

Then come back to Erin, Mavourneen, Mavourneen,
Come back, Aroon, to the land of thy birth;
Come back to Erin, Mavourneen, Mavourneen,
And it's Killarney shall ring with our mirth.

Over the green sea, Mavourneen, Mavourneen,
Long shone the white sail that bore thee away;
Riding the white waves that fair summer morning,
Just like a May flower afloat on the bay,
Oh, but my heart sank when clouds came between us,
Like a gray curtain the rain falling down
Hid from my sad eyes the path o'er the ocean,
Far, far away where my Colleen had flown.

Oh, may the angels while waking or sleeping,
Watch o'er my bird in the land far away,
And it's my prayers will consign to their keeping,
Care o' my jewel by night and by day.
When by the fireside I watch the bright embers,
Then all my heart flies o'er the sea,
Craving to know if my darling remembers,
Or if her thoughts may be crossing to me.

AN EPITAPH AND A REPLY

Remember man that passeth by,
As thou art now so once was I;
And as I so must thou be;
Prepare thyself to follow me.

On a grave, Linton, England, 1825.

Under this inscription someone wrote:

To follow you is not my intent,
Unless I know which way you went.

MISS YOU

David Cory

Miss you, miss you, miss you;
Everything I do
Echoes with the laughter
And the voice of you.
You're on every corner,
Every turn and twist,
Every old familiar spot
Whispers how you're missed.

Miss you, miss you, miss you.
Everywhere I go
There are poignant memories
Dancing in a row,
Silhouette and shadow
Of your form and face
Substance and reality
Everywhere displace.

Oh, I miss you, miss you!
How I miss you, Girl!
There's a strange, sad silence
'Mid the busy whirl,
Just as tho' the ordinary,
Daily things I do
Wait with me, expectant,
For a word from you.

Miss you, miss you, miss you!
Nothing now seems true,
Only that 'twas Heaven
Just to be with you.

MY FINANCIAL CAREER

Stephen Leacock

When I go into a bank I get rattled. The clerks rattle me; the wickets rattle me; the sight of the money rattles me; everything rattles me.

The moment I cross the threshold of a bank and attempt to transact business there, I become an irresponsible idiot.

I knew this beforehand, but my salary had been raised to fifty dollars a month and I felt that the bank was the only place for it.

So I shambled in and looked timidly round at the clerks. I had an idea that a person about to open an account must needs consult the manager.

I went up to a wicket marked "Accountant." The accountant was a tall, cool devil. The very sight of him rattled me. My voice was sepulchral.

"Can I see the manager?" I said, and added solemnly, "alone." I don't know why I said "alone."

"Certainly," said the accountant, and fetched him.

The manager was a grave, calm man. I held my fifty-six dollars clutched in a crumpled ball in my pocket.

"Are you the manager?" I said. God knows I didn't doubt it.

"Yes," he said.

"Can I see you," I asked, "alone?" I didn't want to say "alone" again, but without it the thing seemed self-evident.

The manager looked at me in some alarm. He felt that I had an awful secret to reveal.

"Come in here," he said, and led the way to a private room. He turned the key in the lock.

"We are safe from interruption here," he said; "sit down."

We both sat down and looked at each other. I found no voice to speak.

"You are one of Pinkerton's men, I presume," he said.

He had gathered from my mysterious manner that I was a detective. I knew what he was thinking, and it made me worse.

"No, not from Pinkerton's," I said, seeming to imply that I came from a rival agency.

"To tell the truth," I went on, as if I had been prompted to lie about it, "I am not a detective at all. I have come to open an account. I intend to keep all my money in this bank."

The manager looked relieved but still serious; he concluded now that I was a son of Baron Rothschild or a young Gould.

"A large account, I suppose," he said.

"Fairly large," I whispered. "I propose to deposit fifty-six dollars now and fifty dollars a month regularly."

The manager got up and opened the door. He called to the accountant.

"Mr. Montgomery," he said unkindly loud, "this gentleman is opening an account, and he will deposit fifty-six dollars. Good morning."

I rose.

A big iron door stood open at the side of the room.

"Good morning," I said, and stepped into the safe.

"Come out," said the manager coldly, and showed me the other way.

I went up to the accountant's wicket and poked the ball of money at him with a quick convulsive movement as if I were doing a conjuring trick.

My face was ghastly pale.

"Here," I said, "deposit it." The tone of the words seemed to mean, "Let us do this painful thing while the fit is on us."

He took the money and gave it to another clerk.

He made me write the sum on a slip and sign my name in a book I no longer knew what I was doing. The bank swam before my eyes.

"Is it deposited?" I asked in a hollow, vibrating voice.

"It is," said the accountant.

"Then I want to draw a cheque."

My idea was to draw out six dollars of it for present use. Some one gave me a cheque book through a wicket and some one else began telling me how to write it out. The people in the bank had the impression that I was an invalid millionaire. I wrote something on the cheque and thrust it in at the clerk. He looked at it.

"What! Are you drawing it all out again?" he asked in surprise. Then I realized I had written fifty-six instead of six. I was too far gone to reason now. I had a feeling that it was impossible to explain the thing. All the clerks had stopped writing to look at me.

Reckless with misery, I made a plunge.

"Yes, the whole thing."

"You withdraw your money from the bank?"

"Every cent of it."

"Are you not going to deposit any more?" said the clerk, astonished.

"Never."

An idiot hope struck me that they might think something had insulted me while I was writing the cheque and that I had changed my mind. I made a wretched attempt to look like a man with a fearfully quick temper.

The clerk prepared to pay the money.

"How will you have it?" he said.

"What?"

"How will you have it?"

"Oh—I caught his meaning and answered without even trying to think—in fifties."

He gave me a fifty dollar bill.

"And the six?" he asked dryly.

"In sixes," I said.

He gave it to me and I rushed out.

As the big door swung behind me I caught the echo of a roar of laughter that went up to the ceiling of the bank. Since then I bank no more. I keep my money in cash in my trousers and my savings in silver dollars in a sock.

THE LITTLE BLACK BOY

William Blake

My mother bore me in the southern wild,
And I am black, but O! my soul is white;
White as an angel is the English child,
But I am black, as if bereav'd of light.

My mother taught me underneath a tree,
And sitting down before the heat of day,
She took me on her lap and kissed me,
And pointing to the east, began to say:

"Look on the rising sun: there God does live,
And gives his light, and gives his heat away;
And flowers and trees and beasts and men receive
Comfort in morning, joy in the noonday.

"And we are put on earth a little space,
That we may learn to bear the beams of love;
And these black bodies and this sunburnt face
Are but a cloud, and like a shady grove.

"For when our souls have learn'd the heat to bear.
The cloud will vanish; we shall hear his voice,
Saying: 'Come out from the grove, my love and care,
And round my golden tent like lambs rejoice.' "

Thus did my mother say, and kissed me;
And thus I say to little English boy:
When I from black and he from white cloud free,
And round the tent of God like lambs we joy,

I'll shade him from the heat, till he can bear
To lean in joy upon our father's knee;
And then I'll stand and stroke his silver hair,
And be like him, and he will then love me.

* * *

The happiness of man in this life does not consist in the absence but in the mastery of his passions.—Alfred, Lord Tennyson

"I WILL BE HEARD"

William Lloyd Garrison

I *will* be as harsh as truth, and as uncompromising as justice. On this subject, I do not wish to think, or speak, or write, with moderation. No! No! Tell a man whose house is on fire, to give a moderate alarm; tell him to moderately rescue his wife from the hands of the ravisher; tell the mother to gradually extricate her babe from the fire into which it has fallen;—but urge me not to use moderation in a cause like the present. I am in earnest—I will not equivocate—I will not excuse—I will not retreat a single inch—AND I WILL BE HEARD.

(Vol. 1, No. 1, The Liberator, January 1, 1831)

HIGHLAND MARY

Robert Burns

Ye banks, and braes, and streams around
  The castle o' Montgomery,
Green be your woods, and fair your flowers,
  Your waters never drumlie!
There simmer first unfauld her robes
  And there the langest tarry;
For there I took the last fareweel
  O' my sweet Highland Mary.

How sweetly bloom'd the gay green birk,
  How rich the hawthorn's blossom,
As underneath their fragrant shade
  I clasp'd her to my bosom!
The golden hours, on angel wings,
  Flew o'er me and my dearie;
For dear to me, as light and life,
  Was my sweet Highland Mary.

Wi' monie a vow, and lock'd embrace,
  Our parting was fu' tender;
And, pledging aft to meet again,
  We tore oursels asunder;

But oh! fell death's untimely frost
  That nipt my flower sae early!
Now green's the sod, and cauld's the clay,
  That wraps my Highland Mary!

O pale, pale now, those rosy lips,
  I aft hae kiss'd sae fondly!
And closed for ay the sparking glance
  That dwelt on me sae kindly!
And mold'ring now in silent dust,
  That heart that lo'ed me dearly!
But still within my bosom's core
  Shall live my Highland Mary.

BROADCAST ON HIS NINETIETH BIRTHDAY

Oliver Wendell Holmes, Jr.

In this symposium my part is only to sit in silence. To express one's feelings as the end draws near is too intimate a task.

But I may mention one thought that comes to me as a listener-in. The riders in a race do not stop short when they reach the goal. There is a little finishing canter before coming to a standstill. There is time to hear the kind voice of friends and to say to one's self: "The work is done."

But just as one says that, the answer comes: "The race is over, but the work never is done while the power to work remains."

The canter that brings you to a standstill need not be only coming to rest. It cannot be while you still live. For to live is to function. That is all there is in living.

And so I end with a line from a Latin poet who uttered the message more than fifteen hundred years ago:

"Death plucks my ears and says, Live—
  I am coming."

(March 7, 1931)

* * *

A good constitution is infinitely better than the best despot.
—Thomas Babington Macaulay

A POISON TREE

William Blake

I was angry with my friend:
I told my wrath, my wrath did end.
I was angry with my foe:
I told it not, my wrath did grow.

And I water'd it in fears,
Night and morning with my tears;
And I sunned it with smiles,
And with soft deceitful wiles.

And it grew both day and night,
Till it bore an apple bright;
And my foe beheld it shine,
And he knew that it was mine,

And into my garden stole
When the night had veil'd the pole:
In the morning glad I see
My foe outstretch'd beneath the tree.

THE DEMAND FOR LIGHT LABOR

Robert J. Burdette

One morning, just as the rush of housecleaning day was beginning to abate, a robust tramp called at a house on Barnes Street, and besought the inmates to give him something to eat, averring that he had not tasted food for nine days.

"Why don't you go to work?" asked the lady to whom he proffered his petition.

"Work!" he ejaculated. "Work! And what have I been doing since the middle of May but hunting work? Who will give me work? When did I ever refuse work?"

"Well," said the woman, "I guess I can find you some employment. What can you do?"

"Anything!" he shouted in a kind of delirious joy. "Anything that any man can do. I'm sick for something to fly at. Why, only yesterday I worked all day, carrying water in an old sieve from Flint River an' emptying it into the Mississippi, just because I was so tired of having nothing to do, that I had to work at something or I would have gone ravin' crazy. I'll do anything, from cleaning house to building a steamboat. Jest give me work, ma'am, an' you'll never hear me ask for bread agin."

The lady was pleased at the willingness and anxiety of this industrious man to do something, and she led him to the wood pile.

"Here," she said, "you can saw and split the wood, and if you are a good, industrious worker, I will find work for you to do nearly all winter."

"Well, now," said the tramp, while a look of disappointment stole over his face, "that's just my luck. Only three days ago I was pullin' a blind cow out of a well for a poor widow who had nothin' in the world but that cow to support her, an' I spraint my wrist till I hain't been able to lift a pound with it sinst. You kin jest put your hand on it now and feel it throb, it's so painful and inflamed. I could jest cry of disappointment, but it's a Bible fact, ma'am, that I couldn't lift that ax above my head ef I died fur it, and I'd jest as lief let you pull my arm out by the roots as to try to pull that saw through a lath. Jest set me at something I kin do, though, if you want to see the dust fly."

"Very well," said the lady, "then you can take these flower beds, which have been very much neglected, and weed them very carefully for me. You can do that with your well hand, but I want you to be very particular with them, and get them very clean, and not injure any of the plants, for they are all very choice and I am very proud of them."

The look of disappointment that had been chased away from the industrious man's face when he saw a prospect of something else to do, came back deeper than ever as the lady described the new job, and when she concluded, he had to remain quiet for a moment before he could control his emotions sufficiently to speak.

"If I ain't the most onfortinit man in Ameriky," he sighed. "I'm jest dyin' for work, crazy to get somethin' to do, and I'm blocked out of work at every turn. I jest love to work among flowers, and dig in the ground, but I never dassent do it fur I'm jest blue ruin among the posies. Nobody ever cared to teach me anything about flowers and it's a Gospel truth, ma'am, I can't tell a violet from a sunflower nor a red rose from a dog fennel. Last place I tried to get work at, woman of the house set me to work weedin' the garden, an' I worked about a couple of hours, monstrous glad to get work, now you bet, an' I pulled up every last livin' green thing in that yard. Hope I may die ef I didn't. Pulled up all the grass, every blade of it. Pulled up a vine worth seventy-five dollars, that had roots reachin' cl'ar under the cellar and into the cistern, and I yanked 'em right up, every fiber of 'em. Woman was so heart broke when she came out and see the yard that they had to put her to bed. Bible's truth, they did, ma'am; and I had to work for that house for three months for nothin' and find my own board, to pay for the damage I done. Hope to die ef I didn't. Jest gimme suthin' I kin do, I'll show you what work is, but I wouldn't dare to go foolin' around no flowers. You've got a kind heart, ma'am, gimme some work; don't send a despairin' man away hungry for work."

"Well," said the lady, "you can beat my carpets for me. They have just been taken up, and you can beat them thoroughly, and by the time they are done, I will have something else ready for you."

The man made a gesture of despair and sat down on the ground, the picture of abject helplessness and disappointed aspirations.

"Look at me now," he exclaimed. "What is goin' to become of me? Did you ever see a man so down on his luck as me? I tell you, ma'am, you must give me somethin' I can do. I wouldn't no more dare for to tech them carpets than nothin' in the world. I'd tear 'em to pieces. I'm a awful hard hitter, an' the last time I beat any carpets was for a woman out at Creston, and I just welted them carpets into strings and carpet rags. I couldn't help it. I can't hold in my strength. I'm too glad to get to work, that's the trouble with me, ma'am, it's a Bible fact. I'll beat them carpets if you say so, but I won't be responsible fur 'em; no makin' me work for nothin' fur five or six weeks to pay fur tearin' 'em into slits yer know. I'll go at 'em ef you'll say the word and take the responsibility, but the fact is, I'm too hard a worker to go foolin' around carpets, that's just what I am."

The lady excused the energetic worker from going at the carpets, but was puzzled what to set him at. Finally she asked him what there was he would like to do and could do, with safety to himself and the work.

"Well, now," he said, "that's considerit in ye. That's real considerit, and I'll take a hold and do something that'll give ye the wuth of your money, and won't give me no chance to destroy nothin' by workin' too hard at it. If ye'll jest kindly fetch me out a rockin' chair, I'll set down in the shade and keep the cows from liftin' the latch off the front gate and gettin' into the yard. I'll do it well and only charge you reasonable for it, fur the fact is I'm so dead crazy fur work that it isn't big pay I want so much as a steady job."

And when he was rejected and sent forth, jobless and breakfastless, to wander up and down the cold, unfeeling world in search of work, he cast stones at the house and said, in dejected tones,

"There, now, that's jest the way. They call us a bad lot, and say we're lazy and thieves, and won't work, when a feller is just crazy to work and nobody won't give him nary a job he can do. Won't work! Land alive, they won't give us work, an' when we want to an' try to, they won't let us work. There ain't a man in Ameriky that 'ud work as hard an' as stiddy as I would if they'd gimme a chance."

"I TASTE A LIQUOR NEVER BREWED"

Emily Dickinson

I taste a liquor never brewed,
From tankards scooped in pearl;
Not all the vats upon the Rhine
Yield such an alcohol!

Inebriate of air am I,
And debauchee of dew,
Reeling, through endless summer days,
From inns of molten blue.

When landlords turn the drunken bee
Out of the foxglove's door,
When butterflies renounce their drams,
I shall but drink the more!

Till seraphs swing their snowy hats,
And saints to windows run,
To see the little tippler
Leaning against the sun!

* * *

She wears her clothes as if they were thrown on her with a pitchfork.—Jonathan Swift

THE FESTAL BOARD

Anonymous

Come to the festal board to-night,
  For bright-eyed beauty will be there,
Her coral lips in nectar steeped,
  And garlanded her hair.

Come to the festal board to-night,
  For there the joyous laugh of youth
Will ring those silvery peals, which speak
  Of bosom pure and stainless truth.

Come to the festal board to-night,
  For friendship, there, with stronger chain,
Devoted hearts already bound
  For good or ill, will bind again.
I went.

Nature and art their stores outpoured;
  Joy beamed in every kindling glance;
Love, friendship, youth, and beauty smiled;
  What could that evening's bliss enhance?
We parted.

And years have flown; but where are now
  The guests who round that table met?
Rises their sun as gloriously
  As on the banquet's eve it set?

How holds the chain which friendship wove?
  It broke; and soon the hearts it bound
Were widely sundered; and for peace,
  Envy and strife and blood were found.

The merriest laugh which then was heard
  Has changed its tones to maniac screams,
As half-quenched memory kindles up
  Glimmerings of guilt in feverish dreams.

And where is she whose diamond eyes
  Golconda's purest gems outshone?
Whose roseate lips of Eden breathed?
  Say, where is she, the beauteous one?

Beneath yon willow's drooping shade,
  With eyes now dim, and lips all pale,
She sleeps in peace. Read on her urn,
  "A broken heart." This tells her tale.

And where is he, that tower of strength,
  Whose fate with hers for life was joined?
How beats his heart, once honor's throne?
  How high has soared his daring mind?

Go to the dungeon's gloom to-night;
  His wasted form, his aching head,
And all that now remains of him,
  Lies, shuddering, on a felon's bed.

Ask you of all these woes the cause—
  The festal board, the enticing bowl,
More often came, and reason fled,
  And maddened passions spurned control.

Learn wisdom, then. The frequent feast
  Avoid; for there, with stealthy tread
Temptation walks, to lure you on,
  Till death, at last, the banquet spread.

And shun, oh, shun the enchanted cup!
  Though now its draught like joy appears,
Ere long it will be fanned by sighs,
  And sadly mixed with blood and tears.

* * *

Hypocrisy is a homage vice pays to virtue.—François, Duc de la Rochefoucauld

A LIFE ON THE OCEAN WAVE

Epes Sargent

A life on the ocean wave,
  A home on the rolling deep,
Where the scattered waters rave,
  And the winds their revels keep!
Like an eagle caged, I pine,
  On this dull, unchanging shore;
Oh! give me the flashing brine,
  The spray and the tempest's roar!

Once more on the deck I stand
  Of my own swift-gliding craft,
Set sail! sail farewell to the land,
  The gale follows far a-baft.
We shoot through the sparkling foam,
  Like an ocean bird set free;
Like the ocean bird, our home,
  We'll find far out on the sea!

The land is no longer in view,
  The clouds have begun to frown,
But with a stout vessel and crew
  We'll say "Let the storm come down!"
And the song of our heart shall be,
  While the winds and the waters rave,
A life on the heaving sea,
  A home on the bounding wave!

OF DEATH

Francis Bacon

Men fear death as children fear to go in the dark. And as that natural fear in children is increased with tales, so is the other. Certainly, the contemplation of death, as the wages of sin and passage to another world, is holy and religious. But the fear of it, as a tribute due unto Nature, is weak. . . . It is worthy of the observing that there is no passion in the mind of man so weak but it mates and masters the fear of death. And, therefore, death is no such terrible enemy when a man hath so many attendants about him that can win the combat of him. Revenge triumphs over death. Love slights it. Honor aspireth to it. Grief fleeth to it. Fear preoccupateth it. . . . A man would die, though he were neither valiant nor miserable, only upon a weariness to do the same thing so oft over and over. It is no less worthy to observe how little alteration in good spirits the approach of death make. For they appear to be the same men till the last instant. . . . It is as natural to die as to be born; but to a little infant, perhaps, the one is as painful as the other. He that dies in an earnest pursuit is like one that is wounded in hot blood, who, for the time, scarce feels the hurt. And, therefore, a mind fixed and bent upon somewhat that is good doth avert the dolors of death. But above all, believe it, the sweetest canticle is, *Nunc dimittis;* when a man hath obtained worthy ends and expectations. Death hath this also: that it openeth the gate to good fame and extinguisheth envy.

GRAMMAR IN A NUTSHELL

Anonymous

Three little words you often see
Are Articles—A, An, and The.

A Noun's the name of anything,
As School, or Garden, Hoop or Swing.

Adjectives tell the kind of Noun,
As Great, Small, Pretty, White or Brown.

Instead of Nouns the Pronouns stand—
Her head, His face, Your arm, My hand.

Verbs tell something being done—
To Read, Count, Laugh, Sing, Jump or Run.

How things are done the Adverbs tell,
As Slowly, Quickly, Ill, or Well.

Conjunctions join the words together,
As men And women, wind Or weather.

The preposition stands before
A Noun, as In or Through a door.

The Interjection shows surprise,
As Oh! how pretty! Ah! how wise!

The Whole are called Nine Parts of Speech,
Which reading, writing, speaking teach.

MONEY

My friends, money is not all. It is not money that will mend a broken heart or reassemble the fragments of a dream. Money cannot brighten the hearth nor repair the portals of a shattered home. I refer, of course, to Confederate money.

(Attributed to Judge Kelly of Chicago)

A PRAYER FOUND IN CHESTER CATHEDRAL

Anonymous

Give me a good digestion, Lord,
And also something to digest;
Give me a healthy body, Lord,
With sense to keep it at its best.

Give me a healthy mind, Lord,
To keep the good and pure in sight;
Which, seeing sin, is not appalled,
But finds a way to set it right.

Give me a mind that is not bored,
That does not whimper, whine or sigh;
Don't let me worry overmuch,
About the fussy thing called "I."

Give me a sense of humour, Lord;
Give me the grace to see a joke;
To get some happiness from life,
And pass it on to other folk.

CHANGE THE NAME OF ARKANSAS?

Mr. Speaker: The man who would CHANGE THE NAME OF ARKANSAS is the original iron-jawed, brass-mounted, copper-bellied corpse-maker from the wilds of the Ozarks! Sired by a hurricane, dammed by an earthquake, half-brother to the cholera, nearly related to the small-pox on his mother's side, he is the man they call Sudden Death and General Desolation! Look at him! He takes nineteen alligators and a barrel of whiskey for breakfast, when he is in robust health; and a bushel of rattlesnakes and a dead body when he is ailing. He splits the everlasting rocks with his glance, and quenches the thunder when he speaks!

Change the name of Arkansas! Hell, no! stand back and give him room according to his strength. Blood's his natural drink! and the wail of the dying is music to his ears! Cast your eyes on the gentleman, and lay low and hold your breath, for he's 'bout to turn himself loose! He's the bloodiest son of a wild-cat that lives, who would change the name of Arkansas! Hold him down to earth, for he is a child of sin! Don't attempt to look at him with your naked eye, gentlemen; use smoked glass. The man who would change the name of Arkansas, by gosh, would use the meridians of longitude and the parallels of latitude for a seine, and drag the Atlantic Ocean for whales! He would scratch himself awake with the lightning, and purr himself asleep with the thunder! When he's cold, he would "bile" the Gulf of Mexico and bathe in it! When he's hot, he would fan himself with an equinoctial storm! When he's thirsty, he would reach up and suck a cloud dry like a sponge! When he's hungry, famine follows in his wake! You may put your hand on the sun's face, and make it night on the earth; bite a piece out of the moon, and hurry the seasons; shake yourself and rumble the mountains; but, sir, you will never change the name of Arkansaw!

The man who would change the name of Arkansaw would massacre isolated communities as a pastime. He would destroy nationalities as a serious business! He would use the boundless vastness of the Great American Desert for his private grave-yard! He would attempt to extract sunshine from cucumbers! Hide the stars in a nail-keg, put the sky to soak in a gourd, hang the Arkansas River on a clothesline, unbuckle the belly-band of Time, and turn the sun and moon out to pasture; but you will never change the name of Arkansaw! The world will again pause and wonder at the audacity of the lop-eared, lantern-jawed, half-breed, half-born, whiskey-soaked hyena who has proposed to change the name of

Arkansaw! He's just starting to climb the political banister, and wants to knock the hay-seed out of his hair, pull the splinters out of his feet, and push on and up to the governorship. *But change the name of Arkansaw, hell, no!*

Note: There are numerous versions of this speech, each attributed to a different person. The above version is attributed to Cassius M. Johnson. Even the date of the speech, if it was actually ever delivered, is undetermined.

LINCOLN, THE MAN OF THE PEOPLE

Edwin Markham

When the Norn Mother saw the Whirlwind Hour
Greatening and darkening as it hurried on,
She left the Heaven of Heroes and came down
To make a man to meet the mortal need.
She took the tried clay of the common road—
Clay warm yet with the ancient heat of Earth,
Dashed through it all a strain of prophecy;
Tempered the heap with thrill of human tears;
Then mixed a laughter with the serious stuff.
Into the shape she breathed a flame to light
That tender, tragic, ever-changing face.
Here was a man to hold against the world,
A man to match the mountains and the sea.

The color of the ground was in him, the red earth;
The smell and smack of elemental things:
The rectitude and patience of the cliff;
The good-will of the rain that loves all leaves;
The friendly welcome of the wayside well;
The courage of the bird that dares the sea;
The gladness of the wind that shakes the corn;
The mercy of the snow that hides all scars;
The secrecy of streams that make their way
Beneath the mountain to the rifted rock;
The undelaying justice of the light
That gives as freely to the shrinking flower
As to the great oak flaring to the wind—
To the grave's low hill as to the Matterhorn
That shoulders out the sky.

Sprung from the West,
The strength of virgin forests braced his mind,
The hush of spacious prairies stilled his soul.
Up from log cabin to the Capitol,
One fire was on his spirit, one resolve—
To send the keen ax to the root of wrong,
Clearing a free way for the feet of God.
And evermore he burned to do his deed
With the fine stroke and gesture of a king:
He built the rail-pile as he built the State,
Pouring his splendid strength through every blow,
The conscience of him testing every stroke,
To make his deed the measure of a man.

So came the Captain with the thinking heart;
And when the judgment thunders split the house,
Wrenching the rafters from their ancient rest,
He held the ridgepole up, and spiked again
The rafters of the Home. He held his place—
Held the long purpose like a growing tree—
Held on through blame and faltered not at praise.
And when he fell in whirlwind, he went down
As when a lordly cedar, green with boughs,
Goes down with a great shout upon the hills,
And leaves a lonesome place against the sky.

HOW DOTH THE LITTLE CROCODILE

Lewis Carroll

How doth the little crocodile
  Improve his shining tail,
And pour the waters of the Nile
  On every golden scale!

How cheerfully he seems to grin,
  How neatly spreads his claws,
And welcomes little fishes in
  With gently smiling jaws!

JOHN RUSKIN, ART CRITIC AND AUTHOR, AND JAMES McNEILL WHISTLER, ARTIST, EXCHANGE INSULTS

For Mr. Whistler's own sake, no less than for the protection of the purchaser, Sir Coutts Lindsay ought not to have admitted works into the gallery in which the ill-educated conceit of the artist so nearly approached the aspect of willful imposture. I have seen, and heard, much of cockney impudence before now; but never expected to hear a coxcomb ask two hundred guineas for flinging a pot of paint in the public's face.

* * *

Over and over again did the Attorney-General cry out aloud, in the agony of his cause, "What is to become of painting if the critics withhold their lash?"

As well might he ask what is to become of mathematics under similar circumstances, were they possible. I maintain that two and two the mathematician would continue to make four, in spite of the whine of the amateur for three, or the cry of the critic for five. We are told that Mr. Ruskin has devoted his long life to art, and as a result is "Slade Professor" at Oxford. In the same sentence we have thus his position and its worth. It suffices not, Messieurs! A life passed among pictures makes not a painter—else the policeman in the National Gallery might assert himself. As well allege that he who lives in a library must needs die like a poet. Let not Mr. Ruskin flatter himself that more education makes the difference between himself and the policeman when both stand gazing in the Gallery. There they might remain until the end of time; the one decently silent, the other saying, in good English, many high-sounding empty things, like the crackling of thorns under a pot—undismayed by the presence of the Masters with whose names he is sacrilegiously familiar; whose intentions he interprets, whose vices he discovers with the facility of the incapable, and whose virtues he descants upon with a verbosity and flow of language that would, could he hear it, give Titian the same shock of surprise that was Balaam's, when the first great critic proffered his opinion.

* * *

An expert is one who knows more and more about less and less.

—Nicholas Murray Butler

ODE TO DUTY

William Wordsworth

Stern Daughter of the Voice of God!
O Duty! if that name thou love
Who art a light to guide, a rod
To check the erring, and reprove;
Thou, who art victory and law
When empty terrors overawe;
From vain temptations dost set free;
And calm'st the weary strife of frail humanity!

There are who ask not if thine eye
Be on them; who, in love and truth,
Where no misgiving is, rely
Upon the genial sense of youth:
Glad Hearts! without reproach or blot
Who do thy work, and know it not:
Oh! if through confidence misplaced
They fail, thy saving arms, dread Power! around them cast.

Serene will be our days and bright,
And happy will our nature be,
When love is an unerring light,
And joy its own security.
And they a blissful course may hold
Even now, who, not unwisely bold,
Live in the spirit of this creed;
Yet seek thy firm support, according to their need.

I, loving freedom, and untried;
No sport of every random gust,
Yet being to myself a guide,
Too blindly have reposed my trust:
And oft, when in my heart was heard
Thy timely mandate, I deferred
The task, in smoother walks to stray;
But thee I now would serve more strictly, if I may.

Through no disturbance of my soul,
Or strong compunction in me wrought,
I supplicate for thy control;

But in the quietness of thought:
Me this unchartered freedom tires;
I feel the weight of chance-desires:
My hopes no more must change their name,
I long for a repose that ever is the same.

Stern Lawgiver! yet thou dost wear
The Godhead's most benignant grace;
Nor know we anything so fair
As is the smile upon thy face:
Flowers laugh before thee on their beds
And fragrance in thy footing treads;
Thou dost preserve the stars from wrong;
And the most ancient heavens, through Thee, are fresh and strong.

To humbler functions, awful Power!
I call thee: I myself commend
Unto thy guidance from this hour;
Oh, let my weakness have an end!
Give unto me, made lowly wise,
The spirit of self-sacrifice;
The confidence of reason give;
And in the light of truth thy Bondman let me live!

PLATO'S CAVE ALLEGORY

(Translator: Benjamin Jowett)

I said, imagine the enlightenment or ignorance of our nature in a figure:—Behold! human beings living in a sort of underground den, which has a mouth open towards the light and reaching across the den; they have been here from their childhood, and have their legs and necks chained so that they cannot move, and can only see before them; for the chains are arranged in such a manner as to prevent them from turning round their heads. At a distance above and behind them the light of a fire is blazing, and between the fire and the prisoners there is a raised way; and you will see, if you look, a low wall built along the way, like the screen which marionette players have before them, over which they show the puppets.

I see.

And do you see, I said, men passing along the wall carrying vessels which appear over the wall; also figures of men and animals made of wood and stone and various materials; and some of the passengers, as you would expect, are talking, and some are silent?

That is a strange image, he said, and they are strange prisoners.

Like ourselves, I replied; and they see only their own shadows, or the shadows of one another, which the fire throws on the opposite wall of the cave?

True, he said; how could they see anything but the shadows if they were never allowed to move their heads?

And of the subjects which are being carried in like manner they would only see the shadows?

Yes, he said.

And if they were able to converse with one another, would they not suppose that they were naming what was actually before them?

Very true.

And suppose further that the prison had an echo which came from the other side, would they not be sure to fancy that the voice which they heard was that of a passing shadow?

No question, he replied.

There can be no question, I said, that the truth would be to them just nothing but the shadows of the images.

That is certain.

And now look again, and see how they are released and cured of their folly. At first, when any of them is liberated and compelled suddenly to go up and turn his neck round and walk and look at the light, he will suffer sharp pains; the glare will distress him, and he will be unable to see the realities of which in his former state he had seen the shadows; and then imagine some one saying to him, that what he saw before was an illusion, but that now, he is approaching real being and has a truer sight and vision of more real things,—what will be his reply? And you may further imagine that his instructor is pointing to the objects as they pass and requiring him to name them,—will he not be in a difficulty? Will he not fancy that the shadows which he formerly saw are truer than the objects which are now shown to him?

Far truer.

And if he is compelled to look at the light, will he not have a pain in his eyes which will make him turn away to take refuge in the object of vision which he can see, and which he will conceive to be clearer than the things which are now being shown to him?

True, he said.

And suppose once more, that he is reluctantly dragged up a steep and rugged ascent, and held fast and forced into the presence of the sun himself, do you not think he will be pained and irritated, and when he approaches the light he will have his eyes dazzled, and will not be able to see any of the realities which are now affirmed to be the truth?

Not all in a moment, he said.

He will require to get accustomed to the sight of the upper world. And first he will see the shadows best, next the reflections of men and other objects in the water, and then the objects themselves; then he will gaze upon the light of the moon and the stars; and he will see the sky and the stars by night, better than the sun, or the light of the sun, by day?

Certainly.

And at last he will be able to see the sun, and not mere reflections of him in the water, but he will see him as he is in his own proper place, and not in another; and he will contemplate his nature.

Certainly.

And after that he will reason that the sun is he who gives the seasons and the years, and is the guardian of all that is in the visible world, and in a certain way the cause of all things which he and his fellows have been accustomed to behold?

Clearly, he said, he would come to the other first and to this afterwards.

And when he remembered his old habitation, and the wisdom of the den and his fellow-prisoners, do you not suppose that he would felicitate himself on the change, and pity them?

Certainly, he would.

And if they were in the habit of conferring honors on those who were quickest to observe and remember and foretell which of the passing shadows went before, and which followed after, and which were together, do you think that he would care for such honors and glories, or envy the possessors of them? Would he not say with Homer,

> "Better to be a poor man, and not have a poor master,"

and endure anything, rather than to think and live after their manner?

Yes, he said, I think he would rather suffer anything than live after their manner.

Imagine once more, I said, that such an one coming suddenly out of the sun were to be replaced in his old situation, is he not certain to have his eyes full of darkness?

Very true, he said.

And if there were a contest, and he had to compete in measuring the shadows with the prisoners who had never moved out of the den during the time that his sight was weak, and before his eyes are steady (and the time which would be needed to acquire this new habit of sight might be very considerable), would he not be ridiculous? Men would say of him that he went up and down he came without his eyes, and that there was no use in even thinking of ascending; and if anyone tried to loose another and lead him up to the light, let them only catch the offender in the act, and they would put him to death.

No question, he said.

This allegory, I said, you may now append to the previous argument; the prison is the world of sight, the light of the fire is the sun, the ascent and vision of the things above you may truly regard as the upward progress of the soul into the intellectual world; that is my poor belief, to which, at your desire, I have given expression. Whether I am right or not God only knows; but, whether true or false, my opinion is that in the world of knowledge the idea of good appears last of all, and is seen only with an effort; and, when seen, is also inferred to be the universal author of all things beautiful and right, parent of light and lord of light in this world, and the source of truth and reason in the other: this is the first great cause which he who would act rationally either in public or private life must behold.

I agree, he said, as far as I am able to understand you. . . .

I said, I would not have you marvel that those who attain to this beatific vision are unwilling to descend to human affairs; but their souls are ever hastening into the upper world in which they desire to dwell; and this is very natural, if our allegory may be trusted.

Certainly, that is quite natural.

And is there anything surprising in one who passes from divine contemplation to human things, misbehaving himself in ridiculous manner; if, while his eyes are blinking and before he has become accustomed to the visible darkness, he is compelled to fight in courts of law, or in other places, about the images or the shadows of images of justice, and is endeavoring to meet the conceptions of those who have never yet seen the absolute justice?

There is nothing surprising in that, he replied.

Any one who has common sense will remember that the bewilderments of the eyes are of two kinds, and arise from two causes, either from coming out of the light or from going into the light, which is true of the mind's eye, quite as much as of the bodily eye; and he who remembers this when he sees the soul of any one is perplexed and weak, will not be too ready to laugh; he will first ask whether that soul of man has come out of the brighter life, and is unable to see because unaccustomed to the dark, or having turned from darkness to the day is dazzled by excess of light. And he will count the one happy in his condition and state of being, and he will pity the other; or, if he have a mind to laugh at the soul which comes from below into the light, there will be more reason in this than in the laugh which greets the other from the den.

(From Book Seven of Plato's The Republic)

THE YARN OF THE *NANCY BELL*

W. S. Gilbert

'Twas on the shores that round our coast
  From Deal to Ramsgate span,
That I found alone on a piece of stone
  An elderly naval man.

His hair was weedy, his beard was long,
  And weedy and long was he,
And I heard this wight on the shore recite,
  In a singular minor key:

"Oh, I am a cook and a captain bold,
  And the mate of the *Nancy* brig,
And a bo'sun tight, and a midshipmite,
  And the crew of the captain's gig."

And he shook his fists and he tore his hair,
  Till I really felt afraid,
For I couldn't help thinking the man had been drinking,
  And so I simply said:

"Oh, elderly man, it's little I know
  Of the duties of men of the sea,
But I'll eat my hand if I understand
  How you can possibly be

"At once a cook, and a captain bold,
  And the mate of the *Nancy* brig,
And a bo'sun tight, and a midshipmite,
  And the crew of the captain's gig."

Then he gave a hitch to his trousers, which
  Is a trick all seamen larn,
And having got rid of a thumping quid,
  He spun this painful yarn:

"'Twas in the good ship *Nancy Bell*
  That we sailed to the Indian sea,
And there on a reef we come to grief,
  Which has often occurred to me.

"And pretty nigh all o' the crew was drowned
  (There was seventy-seven o' soul),
And only ten of the *Nancy's* men
  Said 'Here!' to the muster-roll.

"There was me and the cook and the captain bold,
  And the mate of the *Nancy* brig,
And the bo'sun tight, and a midshipmite,
  And the crew of the captain's gig.

"For a month we'd neither wittles nor drink,
  Till a-hungry we did feel,
So we drawed a lot, and accordin' shot
  The captain for our meal.

"The next lot fell to the *Nancy's* mate,
  And a delicate dish he made;
Then our appetite with the midshipmite
  We seven survivors stayed.

"And then we murdered the bo'sun tight,
  And he much resembled pig;
Then we wittled free, did the cook and me,
  On the crew of the captain's gig.

"Then only the cook and me was left,
  And the delicate question, 'Which
Of us two goes to the kettle?' arose
  And we argued it out as sich.

"For I loved that cook as a brother, I did,
  And the cook he worshipped me;
But we'd both be blowed if we'd either be stowed
  In the other chap's hold, you see.

" 'I'll be eat if you dines off me,' says Tom,
  'Yes, that,' says I, 'you'll be,'—
'I'm boiled if I die, my friend,' quoth I,
  And 'Exactly so,' quoth he.

"Says he, 'Dear James, to murder me
  Were a foolish thing to do,
For don't you see that you can't cook *me,*
  While I can—and will—cook *you*!'

"So he boils the water, and takes the salt
  And the pepper in portions true
(Which he never forgot), and some chopped shalot,
  And some sage and parsley too.

" 'Come here,' says he, with a proper pride,
  Which his smiling features tell,
' 'Twill soothing be if I let you see,
  How extremely nice you'll smell.'

"And he stirred it round and round and round,
  And he sniffed at the foaming froth;
When I ups with his heels, and smothers his squeals
  In the scum of the boiling broth.

"And I eat that cook in a week or less,
  And—as I eating be
The last of his chops, why, I almost drops,
  For a wessel in sight I see!

* * *

"And I never grin, and I never smile,
  And I never larf nor play,
But I sit and croak, and a single joke
  I have—which is to say:

"Oh, I am a cook and a captain bold,
  And the mate of the *Nancy* brig,
And a bo'sun tight, *and* a midshipmite,
  And the crew of the captain's gig!"

HARK! THE HERALD ANGELS SING

Charles Wesley

Hark! the herald angels sing,
"Glory to the new-born King;
Peace on earth, and mercy mild,
God and sinners reconciled!"
Joyful all ye nations rise,
Join the triumph of the skies;
With the angelic host proclaim,
"Christ is born in Bethlehem!"

Christ, by the highest heaven adored;
Christ, the everlasting Lord;
Come, Desire of Nations, come,
Fix in us Thy humble home.
Veiled in flesh the God-head see;
Hail the Incarnate Deity,
Pleased as man with men to dwell,
Jesus, our Emmanuel.

Mild He lays His glory by,
Born that man no more may die;
Born to raise the sons of earth,
Born to give them second birth.
Ris'n with healing in His wings,
Light and life to all He brings,
Hail, the Son of Righteousness!
Hail, the heav'n-born Prince of Peace!

THE BATTLE CRY OF FREEDOM

George F. Root

Yes, we'll rally round the flag, boys, we'll rally once again,
Shouting the battle cry of Freedom,
We'll rally from the hillside, we'll gather from the plain,
Shouting the battle cry of Freedom!

Chorus:

The Union forever, hurrah! boys, hurrah!
Down with the traitor, up with the star,
While we rally round the flag, boys, rally once again,
Shouting the battle cry of Freedom!

We are springing to the call of our brothers gone before,
Shouting the battle cry of Freedom,
And we'll fill the vacant ranks with a million freemen more.
Shouting the battle cry of Freedom!

We will welcome to our numbers the loyal, true, and brave,
Shouting the battle cry of Freedom;
And although they may be poor, not a man shall be a slave,
Shouting the battle cry of Freedom!

So we're springing to the call from the East and from the West,
Shouting the battle cry of Freedom;
And we'll hurl the rebel crew from the land we love the best,
Shouting the battle cry of Freedom!

GRANDPA VANDERHOF SAYS GRACE

Moss Hart and George S. Kaufman

Quiet, everybody! Quiet!

Well, Sir, we've been getting along pretty good for quite a while now, and we're certainly much obliged. Remember, all we ask is just to go along and be happy in our own sort of way. Of course we want to keep our health, but as far as anything else is concerned, we'll leave it to You. Thank You.

(From the play You Can't Take It With You)

* * *

I knew a very wise man that believed that if a man were permitted to make all the ballads, he need not care who should make the laws of a nation.—Andrew Fletcher of Saltoun, in Letter to Marquis of Montrose

IT COULDN'T BE DONE *

Edgar A. Guest

Somebody said it couldn't be done,
 But he with a chuckle replied
That "maybe it couldn't," but he would be one
 Who wouldn't say so until he had tried.
So he buckled right in with a trace of a grin
 On his face. If he worried he hid it.
He started to sing as he tackled the thing
 That couldn't be done, and he did it.

Somebody scoffed: "Oh, you'll never do that;
 At least no one ever has done it";
But he took off his coat and he took off his hat,
 And the first thing we knew he'd begun it.
With a lift of his chin and a bit of a grin,
 Without any doubting or quiddit,
He started to sing as he tackled the thing
 That couldn't be done, and he did it.

There are thousands to tell you it cannot be done,
 There are thousands to prophesy failure;
There are thousands to point out to you, one by one,
 The dangers that wait to assail you.
But just buckle in with a bit of a grin,
 Just take off your coat and go to it;
Just start to sing as you tackle the thing
 That "cannot be done," and you'll do it.

"SOLDIER, REST"

Sir Walter Scott

Soldier, rest! thy warfare o'er,
 Sleep the sleep that knows not breaking:
Dream of battled fields no more,
 Days of danger, nights of waking.

* From Collected Verse of Edgar A. Guest. Copyright, 1934, by The Reilly & Lee Co., Chicago, Ill.

In our isle's enchanted hall,
  Hands unseen thy couch are strewing,
Fairy strains of music fall,
  Every sense in slumber dewing.
Soldier, rest! thy warfare o'er,
Dream of fighting fields no more:
Sleep the sleep that knows not breaking,
Morn of toil, nor night of waking.

No rude sound shall reach thine ear,
  Armor's clang or war-steed champing,
Trump nor pibroch summon here
  Mustering clan, or squadron tramping.
Yet the lark's shrill fife may come
  At the daybreak from the fallow,
And the bittern sound his drum,
  Booming from the sedgy shallow.
Ruder sounds shall none be near,
Guards nor warders challenge here,
Here's no war-steed's neigh and champing,
Shouting clans or squadron's stamping.

THE SPIDER AND THE FLY

Mary Howitt

"Will you walk into my parlor?" said the Spider to the Fly,
" 'Tis the prettiest little parlor that ever you did spy;
The way into my parlor is up a winding stair,
And I have many curious things to show when you are there."
"Oh no, no," said the little Fly, "to ask me is in vain;
For who goes up your winding stair can ne'er come down again."

"I'm sure you must be weary, dear, with soaring up so high;
Will you rest upon my little bed?" said the Spider to the Fly.
"There are pretty curtains drawn around, the sheets are fine and thin;
And if you like to rest awhile, I'll snugly tuck you in!"
"Oh no, no," said the little Fly, "for I've often heard it said
They never wake again, who sleep upon your bed!"

Said the cunning Spider to the Fly, "Dear friend, what can I do
To prove the warm affection I've always felt for you?
I have within my pantry, good store of all that's nice;
I'm sure you're very welcome—will you please to take a slice?"
"Oh no, no," said the little Fly, "kind sir, that cannot be,
I've heard what's in your pantry, and I do not wish to see!"

"Sweet creature," said the Spider, "you're witty and you're wise;
How handsome are your gauzy wings, how brilliant are your eyes!
I have a little looking-glass upon my parlor shelf;
If you'll step in one moment, dear, you shall behold yourself."
"I thank you, gentle sir," she said, "for what you're pleased to say,
And bidding you good-morning now, I'll call another day."

The Spider turned him round about, and went into his den,
For well he knew the silly Fly would soon be back again;
So he wove a subtle web in a little corner sly,
And set his table ready to dine upon the Fly.
Then he came out to his door again, and merrily did sing,
"Come hither, hither, pretty Fly, with the pearl and silver wing;
Your robes are green and purple, there's a crest upon your head;
Your eyes are like the diamond bright, but mine are dull as lead."

Alas, alas! how very soon this silly little Fly,
Hearing his wily, flattering words, came slowly flitting by;
With buzzing wings she hung aloft, then near and nearer drew,—
Thinking only of her brilliant eyes, and green and purple hue;
Thinking only of her crested head—poor foolish thing! At last,
Up jumped the cunning Spider, and fiercely held her fast.
He dragged her up his winding stair, into his dismal den
Within his little parlor—but she ne'er came out again!

And now, dear little children, who may this story read,
To idle, silly, flattering words, I pray you ne'er give heed;
Unto an evil counsellor close heart, and ear, and eye,
And take a lesson from this tale of the Spider and the Fly.

JUSTICE HOLMES UPHOLDS FREEDOM OF SPEECH

Persecution for the expression of opinions seems to me perfectly logical. If you have no doubt of your premises or your power and want a certain result with all your heart you naturally express your wishes in law and sweep away all opposition. To allow opposition by speech seems to indicate that you think the speech impotent, as when a man says that he has squared the circle, or that you do not care whole-heartedly for the result, or that you doubt either your power or your premises. But when men have realized that time has upset many fighting faiths, they may come to believe even more than they believe the very foundations of their own conduct that the ultimate good desired is better reached by free trade in ideas—that the best test of truth is the power of the thought to get itself accepted in the competition of the market, and that truth is the only ground upon which their wishes safely can be carried out. That at any rate is the theory of our Constitution. It is an experiment, as all life is an experiment. Every year if not every day we have to wager our salvation upon some prophecy based upon imperfect knowledge. While that experiment is part of our system I think that we should be eternally vigilant against attempts to check the expression of opinions that we loathe and believe to be fraught with death, unless they so imminently threaten immediate interference with the lawful and pressing purposes of the law that an immediate check is required to save the country.

(Dissenting Opinion, Abrams vs.
United States, 250 U.S. 616, 1919)

"THREE YEARS SHE GREW"

William Wordsworth

Three years she grew in sun and shower,
Then Nature said, "A lovelier flower
On earth was never sown;
This Child I to myself will take;
She shall be mine, and I will make
A Lady of my own.

"Myself will to my darling be
Both law and impulse; and with me
The Girl, in rock and plain,
In earth and heaven, in glade and bower,
Shall feel an overseeing power
To kindle or restrain.

"She shall be sportive as the fawn
That wild with glee across the lawn,
Or up the mountain springs;
And her's shall be the breathing balm,
And her's the silence and the calm
Of mute insensate things.

"The floating clouds their state shall lend
To her; for her the willow bend;
Nor shall she fail to see
Even in the motions of the Storm
Grace that shall mould the Maiden's form
By silent sympathy.

"The stars of midnight shall be dear
To her; and she shall lean her ear
In many a secret place
Where rivulets dance their wayward round,
And beauty born of murmuring sound
Shall pass into her face.

"And vital feelings of delight
Shall rear her form to stately height,
Her virgin bosom swell;
Such thoughts to Lucy I will give
While she and I together live
Here in this happy dell."

Thus Nature spake—the work was done—
How soon my Lucy's race was run!
She died, and left to me
This heath, this calm and quiet scene;
The memory of what has been,
And never more will be.

"A SLUMBER DID MY SPIRIT SEAL"

William Wordsworth

A slumber did my spirit seal;
I had no human fears:
She seemed a thing that could not feel
The touch of earthly years.

No motion has she now, no force;
She neither hears nor sees;
Rolled round in earth's diurnal course,
With rocks, and stones, and trees.

SWEETES' LI'L' FELLER

Frank L. Stanton

Sweetes' li'l' feller,
Everybody knows;
Dunno what to call him,
But he mighty lak' a rose!
Lookin' at his Mammy
Wid eyes so shiny blue,
Mek' you think that heav'n
Is comin' clost ter you!
W'en he's dar a-sleepin',
In his li'l' place,
Think I see de angels
Lookin' through de place.
W'en de dark is fallin',
W'en de shadders creep,
Den dey comes on tiptoe
Ter kiss 'im in his sleep.
Sweetes' li'l' feller,
Everybody knows;
Dunno what to call 'im,
But he mighty lak' a rose!
Lookin' at his Mammy
Wid eyes so shiny blue,
Mek' you think that heav'n
Is comin' clost ter you!

OBLIVION

Sir Thomas Browne

Oblivion is not to be hired: the greater part must be content to be as though they had not been; to be found in the register of God, not in the record of man. Twenty-seven names make up the first story before the flood, and the recorded names ever since contain not one living century. The number of the dead long exceedeth all that shall live. The night of time far surpasseth the day, and who knows when was the equinox? Every hour adds unto that current arithmetick, which scarce stands one moment. And since death must be the Lucina of life, and even Pagans could doubt whether thus to live were to die; since our longest sun sets at right descensions, and makes but winter arches, and therefore it cannot be long before we lie down in darkness, and have our light in ashes; since the brother of death daily haunts us with dying mementos, and time, that grows old in itself, bids us hope no long duration: Diuturnity is a dream and folly of expectation.

Darkness and light divide the course of time, and oblivion shares with memory a great part even of our living beings; we slightly remember our felicities, and the smartest strokes of affliction leave but short smart upon us. Sense endureth no extremities, and sorrows destroy us or themselves. To weep into stones are fables. Afflictions induce callosities; miseries are slippery, or fall like snow upon us, which notwithstanding is no unhappy stupidity. To be ignorant of evils to come, and forgetful of evils past, is a merciful provision in nature, whereby we digest the mixture of our few and evil days; and our delivered senses not relapsing into cutting remembrances, our sorrows are not kept raw by the edge of repetitions. A great part of antiquity contented their hopes of subsistency with a transmigration of their souls: a good way to continue their memories, while, having the advantage of plural successions, they could not but act something remarkable in such variety of beings, and enjoying the fame of their past selves, make accumulation of glory unto their last durations. Others, rather than be lost in the uncomfortable night of nothing, were content to recede into the common being, and make one particle of the public soul of all things, which was no more than to return into their unknown and divine original again. Egyptian ingenuity was more unsatisfied, contriving their bodies in sweet consistencies to attend the return of their souls. But all was vanity, feeding the wind, and folly. The Egyptian mummies, which Cambyses or time hath spared, avarice now consumeth. Mummy is become merchandise, Mizraim cures wounds, and Pharaoh is sold for balsams.

(From Urn Burial)

* * *

Love thy neighbor but do not pull down thy hedge.—Anonymous

MORNING HYMN

Thomas Ken

Awake, my soul, and with the sun
Thy daily stage of duty run;
Shake off dull sloth, and joyful rise
To pay thy morning sacrifice.

Wake, and lift up thyself, my heart,
And with the angels bear thy part,
Who all night long unwearied sing
High praise to the Eternal King.

All praise to Thee, Who safe hast kept
And hast refreshed me while I slept!
Grant, Lord, when I from death shall wake,
I may of endless life partake!

Lord, I my vows to Thee renew;
Disperse my sins as morning dew:
Guard my first springs of thought and will,
And with Thyself my spirit fill.

Direct, control, suggest this day
All I design, or do, or say;
That all my powers, with all their might,
In Thy sole glory may unite.

Praise God, from Whom all blessings flow!
Praise Him, all creatures here below!
Praise Him above, ye heavenly host!
Praise Father, Son, and Holy Ghost!

TOMMY

Rudyard Kipling

I went into a public-'ouse to get a pint o' beer,
The publican 'e up an' sez, "We serve no red-coats here."
The girls be'ind the bar they laughed an' giggled fit to die,
I outs into the street again an' to myself sez I:

O it's Tommy this, an' Tommy that, an' "Tommy, go away";
But it's "Thank you, Mister Atkins," when the band begins to play—
The band begins to play, my boys, the band begins to play,
O it's "Thank you, Mister Atkins," when the band begins to play.

I went into a theatre as sober as could be,
They gave a drunk civilian room, but 'ad n't none for me;
They sent me to the gallery or round the music-'alls,
But when it comes to fightin', Lord! they'll shove me in the stalls!
For it's Tommy this, an' Tommy that, an' "Tommy, wait outside";
But it's "Special train for Atkins" when the trooper's on the tide.
The troopship's on the tide, my boys, the troopship's on the tide,
O it's "Special train for Atkins" when the trooper's on the tide.

Yes, makin' mock o' uniforms that guard you while you sleep
Is cheaper than them uniforms, an' they're starvation cheap;
An' hustlin' drunken soldiers when they're goin' large a bit
Is five times better business than paradin' in full kit.
Then it's Tommy this, an' Tommy that, an' "Tommy, 'ow's yer soul?"
But it's "Thin red line of 'eroes" when the drums begin to roll—
The drums begin to roll, my boys, the drums begin to roll,
O it's "Thin red line of 'eroes" when the drums begin to roll.

We are n't no thin red 'eroes, nor we are n't no blackguards too,
But single men in barricks, most remarkable like you;
An' if sometimes our conduck is n't all your fancy paints,
Why, single men in barricks don't grow into plaster saints;
While it's Tommy this, and Tommy that, an' "Tommy, fall be'ind,"
But it's "Please to walk in front, sir," when there's trouble in the wind—
There's trouble in the wind, my boys, there's trouble in the wind,
O it's "Please to walk in front, sir," when there's trouble in the wind.

You talk o' better food for us, an' schools, an' fires, an' all:
We'll wait for extry rations if you treat us rational.
Don't mess about the cook-room slops, but prove it to our face
The Widow's Uniform is not the soldier-man's disgrace.

For it's Tommy this, an' Tommy that, an' "Chuck him out, the brute!"
But it's "Saviour of 'is country" when the guns begin to shoot;
An' it's Tommy this, an' Tommy that, an' anything you please;
An' Tommy ain't a bloomin' fool—you bet that Tommy sees!

AS I'D NOTHING ELSE TO DO

Herbert Fry

'Twas a pleasant summer's morning—
Just the day I like t' enjoy,
When I woke, and looked out early,
Puzzled how my time t' employ;
In such fine and splendid weather
I don't care for work—do you?
So I went to see my sweetheart,
As I'd nothing else to do.

Off I started thro' the meadow,
Where the dew-beads pearled the pray,
And responsive to the song-birds,
I kept singing all the way;
Quite surprised she was to see me
Come so early there to woo,
Till I said I'd just walked over,
'Cause I'd nothing else to do.

Then we rambled forth together,
Down the lane beneath the trees,
While so gentle stirred the shadow
Of their branches in the breeze;
And whenever our conversation
Languished for a word or two,
Why, of course I kindly kissed her,
As I'd nothing else to do.

But before the day was over,
I'd somehow made up my mind,
That I'd pop the question to her,
If to me her heart inclined;

So I whispered "Sweet, my darling,
Will you have me, Yes or No?"
"Well," said she, "perhaps I may my dear,
When I've nothing else to do."

"LET US MOVE FORWARD . . . INTO THE STORM AND THROUGH THE STORM"

Winston S. Churchill

Tonight I speak to you at home, I speak to you in Australia and New Zealand, for whose safety we will strain every nerve; to our loyal friends in India and Burma; to our gallant allies, the Dutch and Chinese; and to our kith and kin in the United States. I speak to you all under the shadow of a heavy and far-reaching military defeat.

It is a British and Imperial defeat. Singapore has fallen. All the Malay Peninsula has been overrun. Other dangers gather about out there and none of the dangers which we have hitherto successfully withstood at home and in the East are in any way diminished.

This, therefore, is one of those moments when the British race and nation can show their quality and their genius. This is one of those moments when they can draw from the heart of misfortune the vital impulses of victory.

Here is the moment to display that calm and poise combined with grim determination which not so long ago brought us out of the very jaws of death. Here is another occasion to show, as so often in our long story, that we can meet reverses with dignity and with renewed accessions of strength.

We must remember that we are no longer alone. We are in the midst of a great company. Three quarters of the human race are now moving with us. The whole future of mankind may depend upon our conduct. So far we have not failed. We shall not fail now. Let us move forward steadfastly together into the storm and through the storm.

(February 1942)

* * *

He who lies down with dogs rises with fleas.—Anonymous

THE MARSEILLAISE

Claude Joseph Rouget de Lisle

(Translator: Charles H. Kerr)

Ye sons of freedom, wake to glory!
  Hark! Hark! what myriads bid you rise!
Your children, wives, and grandsires hoary,
  Behold their tears and hear their cries!
Shall hateful tyrants, mischief breeding,
  With hireling hosts, a ruffian band,
  Affright and desolate the land,
While peace and liberty lie bleeding?

Chorus:
    To arms! to arms, ye brave!
    The avenging sword unsheathe;
    March on! march on! all hearts resolved
      On victory or death.

Now, now the dangerous storm is rolling,
  With treacherous kings, confederate, raise;
The dogs of war, let loose, are howling,
  And lo! our fields and cities blaze;
And shall we basely view the ruin,
  While lawless force, with guilty stride,
  Spreads desolation far and wide,
With crimes and blood his hands imbruing?

With luxury and pride surrounded,
  The vile, insatiate despots dare,
Their thirst of power and gold unbounded,
  To meet and vend the light and air;
Like beasts of burden would they load us,
  Like gods would bid their slaves adore;
  But man is man, and who is more?
Then, shall they longer lash and goad us?

O Liberty! can man resign thee,
  Once having felt thy generous flame?
Can dungeons, bolts, or bars confine thee?
  Or whips the noble spirit tame?

Too long the world has wept, bewailing
That falsehood's dagger tyrants wield,
But freedom is our sword and shield,
And all their arts are unavailing.

THE BABY

Sir William Jones

On parent knees, a naked, new-born child,
Weeping thou sat'st when all around thee smiled;
So live that, sinking to thy last long sleep,
Thou then mayst smile while all around thee weep.
(From the Sanskrit of Kalidasa)

IN TENEBRIS (1)

Thomas Hardy

"Percussus sum sicut foenum, et aruit cor meum."—Ps. ci.

Wintertime nighs;
But my bereavement-pain
It cannot bring again:
Twice no one dies.

Flower-petals flee;
But, since it once hath been,
No more that severing scene
Can harrow me.

Birds faint in dread:
I shall not lose old strength
In the lone frost's black length:
Strength long since fled!

Leaves freeze to dun;
But friends can not turn cold
This season as of old
For him with none.

Tempests may scath;
But love can not make smart
Again this year his heart
Who no heart hath.

Black is night's cope;
But death will not appal
One who, past doubtings all,
Waits in unhope.

"A LITTLE GROUP OF WILLFUL MEN"

Woodrow Wilson

In the immediate presence of a crisis fraught with more subtle and far-reaching possibilities of national danger than any other the Government has known within the whole history of its international relations, the Congress has been unable to act either to safeguard the country or to vindicate the elementary rights of its citizens. More than 500 of the 531 members of the two houses were ready and anxious to act; the House of Representatives had acted by an overwhelming majority; but the Senate was unable to act because a little group of eleven Senators had determined that it should not. The Senate of the United States is the only legislative body which cannot act when its majority is ready for action. A little group of willful men, representing no opinion but their own, have rendered the great Government of the United States helpless and contemptible.

(From the Address to the Country, March 4, 1917, when eleven Senators blocked a bill, passed by the House, for the arming of merchant ships)

IT'S THE SYME THE WHOLE WORLD OVER

Anonymous

It's the syme the whole world over,
It's the poor what gets the blyme,
W'ile the rich 'as all the plysures.
Now a'nt that a blinkin' shyme?

She was just a parson's daughter,
Pure, unstyned was 'er fyme;
Till a country squire came courtin'—
And the poor girl lorst 'er nyme.

So she went aw'y to Lunnon,
Just to 'ide 'er guilty shyme.
There she met another squire;
Once agine, she lorst her nyme.

Look at 'im with all 'is 'orses,
Drinking champyne in 'is club,
W'ile the wictim of 'is passions
Drinks 'er Guinness in a pub.

Now 'e's in 'is ridin' britches,
'Untin' foxes in the chyse,
W'ile the wictim of 'is folly
Mykes 'er livin' by 'er wice.

So she settled down in Lunnon,
Sinkin' deeper in 'er shyme,
Till she met a lybor leader
And agine she lorst 'er nyme.

Now 'e's in the 'Ouse of Commons
Mykin' laws to put down crime,
W'ile the wictim of 'is plysure
Walks the street each night in shyme.

Then there cyme a bloated bishop.
Marriage was the tyle 'e told.
There was no one else to tyke 'er
So she sold her soul for gold.

See 'er in 'er 'orse and carriage,
Drivin' d'ily through the park.
Though she's myde a wealthy marriage
Still she 'ides a brykin' 'eart.

In a cottage down in Sussex
Lives 'er payrents old and lyme.
And they drink the wine she sends 'em.
But they never speak 'er nyme.

In their poor and humble dwellin',
There 'er grievin' payrents live,
Drinkin' champyne as she sends 'em
But they never can forgive.

It's the syme the whole world over,
It's the poor what gets the blyme,
W'ile the rich 'as all the plysures;
Now, a'nt that a blinkin' shyme!

A MAN OF WORDS

Anonymous

A man of words and not of deeds,
Is like a garden full of weeds;
And when the weeds begin to grow,
It's like a garden full of snow;
And when the snow begins to fall,
It's like a bird upon the wall;
And when the bird away does fly,
It's like an eagle in the sky;
And when the sky begins to roar,
It's like a lion at the door;
And when the door begins to crack,
It's like a stick across your back;
And when your back begins to smart,
It's like a penknife in your heart;
And when your heart begins to bleed,
You're dead, and dead, and dead indeed.

THE MONARCH

William Cowper

I am monarch of all I survey,
  My right there is none to dispute,
From the center all round to the sea,
  I am lord of the fowl and the brute.

LINCOLN'S LETTER TO EDWARD EVERETT, WRITTEN THE DAY AFTER THE GETTYSBURG ADDRESS

(Everett, a noted orator of his day, spoke for two hours and ostensibly made the principal address. He was followed by Lincoln who spoke only a few but immortal words)

Executive Mansion, Washington, November 20, 1863.

HON. EDWARD EVERETT:

MY DEAR SIR: Your kind note of to-day is received. In our respective parts yesterday, you could not have been excused to make a short address, nor I a long one. I am pleased to know that, in your judgment, the little I did say was not entirely a failure. Of course I knew Mr. Everett would not fail, and yet, while the whole discourse was eminently satisfactory, and will be of great value, there were passages in it which transcended my expectations. The point made against the theory of the General Government being only an agency whose principals are the States, was new to me, and, as I think, is one of the best arguments for the national supremacy. The tribute to our women for their angel ministering to the suffering soldiers surpasses in its way, as do the subjects of it, whatever has gone before.

Our sick boy, for whom you kindly inquire. we hope is past the worst.

Your obedient servant,
A. Lincoln

O, MAY I JOIN THE CHOIR INVISIBLE

George Eliot (Marian Evans Cross)

O, may I join the choir invisible
Of those immortal dead who live again
In minds made better by their presence; live
In pulses stirred to generosity,
In deeds of daring rectitude, in scorn
Of miserable aims that end with self,

In thoughts sublime that pierce the night like stars,
And with their mild persistence urge men's minds
To vaster issues.

So to live is heaven:
To make undying music in the world,
Breathing a beauteous order, that controls
With growing sway the growing life of man.
So we inherit that sweet purity
For which we struggled, failed, and agonized
With widening retrospect that bred despair.
Rebellious flesh that would not be subdued,
A vicious parent shaming still its child,
Poor anxious penitence, is quick dissolved;
Its discords, quenched by meeting harmonies,
Die in the large and charitable air.
And all our rarer, better, truer self,
That sobbed religiously in yearning song,
That watched to ease the burden of the world,
Laboriously tracing what must be,
And what may yet be better,—saw within
A worthier image for the sanctuary,
And shaped it forth before the multitude,
Divinely human, raising worship so
To higher reverence more mixed with love,
That better self shall live till human Time
Shall fold its eyelids, and the human sky
Be gathered like a scroll within the tomb,
Unread forever.

This is life to come,
Which martyred men have made more glorious
For us, who strive to follow.

May I reach
That purest heaven,—be to other souls
The cup of strength in some great agony,
Enkindle generous ardor, feed pure love,
Beget the smiles that have no cruelty,
Be the sweet presence of a good diffused,
And in diffusion ever more intense!
So shall I join the choir invisible,
Whose music is the gladness of the world.

THE HISTORY OF MANKIND

Anatole France

(Translator: Mrs. Wilfrid Jackson)

When the young Prince Zémire succeeded his father on the throne of Persia, he called all the academicians of his kingdom together, and said:

"The learned Zeb, my instructor, has taught me that monarchs would be liable to fewer errors if they were enlightened by past experience. Therefore I wish to study the history of nations. I order you to compose a universal history, and to neglect nothing to make it complete."

The wise men promised to carry out the prince's desire, and having withdrawn, they set to work immediately. At the end of twenty years they appeared before the king, followed by a caravan composed of twelve camels, each bearing 500 volumes. The secretary of the academy, having prostrated himself on the steps of the throne, spoke in these terms:

"Sire, the academicians of your kingdom have the honour to place at your feet the universal history that they have compiled at your majesty's behest. It comprises 6,000 volumes, and contains all that we could possibly collect regarding the customs of nations and the vicissitudes of empires. We have inserted the ancient chronicles which have been luckily preserved, and we have illustrated them with abundant notes on geography, chronology, and diplomacy. The prolegomena are alone one camel's load, and the paralipomena are borne with great difficulty by another camel."

The king answered:

"Gentlemen, I thank you for the trouble you have taken. But I am very busy with the cares of state. Moreover, I have aged while you worked. I am arrived, as says the Persian poet, half-way along the road of life, and even supposing I die full of years, I cannot reasonably hope to have the time to read such a lengthy history. It shall be placed in the archives of the kingdom. Be good enough to make me a summary better fitted to the brevity of human life."

The Persian academicians worked another twenty years; then they brought to the king 1,500 volumes on three camels.

"Sire," said the permanent secretary, in a weakened voice, "here is our new work. We believe we have omitted nothing essential."

"That may be," answered the king, "but I shall not read it. I am old; lengthy undertakings do not suit my years; abridge it further, and do not be long about it."

They lingered so little that at the end of ten years they returned followed by a young elephant bearing 500 volumes.

"I flatter myself I have been succinct," said the permanent secretary.

"You have not been sufficiently so," answered the king.

"I am at the end of my life. Abridge, abridge, if you want me to know the history of mankind ere I die."

The permanent secretary reappeared before the palace at the end of five years. Walking with crutches, he held by the bridle a small donkey which bore a big book on its back.

"Hasten," said the officer to him, "the king is dying."

The king in fact was on his death-bed. He turned on the academician and his big book his nearly expiring gaze, and said with a sigh:

"I shall die, then, without knowing the history of mankind!"

"Sire," replied the learned man, who was almost as near death himself, "I will sum it up for you in three words: *They were born, they suffered, they died!*"

Thus did the king of Persia learn the history of mankind in the evening of his life.

(From The Opinions of Jerome Coignard)

"HOW SWEET THE MOONLIGHT SLEEPS UPON THIS BANK!"

William Shakespeare

Lorenzo. How sweet the moonlight sleeps upon this bank!
Here will we sit, and let the sounds of music
Creep in our ears: soft stillness and the night
Become the touches of sweet harmony.
Sit, Jessica. Look how the floor of heaven
Is thick inlaid with patines of bright gold:
There's not the smallest orb which thou behold'st
But in his motion like an angel sings,
Still quiring to the young-eyed cherubins;
Such harmony is in immortal souls;
But whilst this muddy vesture of decay
Doth grossly close it in, we cannot hear it.
[*Enter Musicians*]

Come, ho, and wake Diana with a hymn!
With sweetest touches pierce your mistress' ear,
And draw her home with music.

Jessica. I am never merry when I hear sweet music.

Lorenzo. The reason is, your spirits are attentive:
For do but note a wild and wanton herd,
Or race of youthful and unhandled colts,
Fetching mad bounds, bellowing and neighing loud,
Which is the hot condition of their blood;
If they but hear perchance a trumpet sound,
Or any air of music touch their ears,
You shall perceive them make a mutual stand,
Their savage eyes turn'd to a modest gaze
By the sweet power of music: therefore the poet
Did feign that Orpheus drew trees, stones and floods;
Since nought so stockish, hard and full of rage,
But music for the time doth change his nature.
The man that hath no music in himself,
Nor is not moved with concord of sweet sounds,
Is fit for treasons, stratagems and spoils;
The motions of his spirit are dull as night,
And his affections dark as Erebus:
Let no such man be trusted. Mark the music.

(From The Merchant of Venice)

ESCAPE AT BEDTIME

Robert Louis Stevenson

The lights from the parlour and kitchen shone out
Through the blinds and the windows and bars;
And high overhead and all moving about,
There were thousands of millions of stars.
There ne'er were such thousands of leaves on a tree,
Nor of people in church or the Park.
As the crowds of the stars that looked down upon me,
And that glittered and winked in the dark.

The Dog, and the Plough, and the Hunter, and all,
And the star of the sailor, and Mars,
These shone in the sky, and the pail by the wall
Would be half full of water and stars.

They saw me at last, and they chased me with cries,
  And they soon had me packed into bed;
But the glory kept shining and bright in my eyes,
  And the stars going round in my head.

THE JOLLY OLD PEDAGOGUE

George Arnold

'Twas a jolly old pedagogue, long ago,
  Tall, and slender, and sallow, and dry;
His form was bent, and his gait was slow,
And his long, thin hair was white as snow,
  But a wonderful twinkle shone in his eye:
And he sang every night as he went to bed,
  "Let us be happy down here below;
The living should live, though the dead be dead,"
  Said the jolly old pedagogue, long ago.

He taught the scholars the Rule of Three,
  Reading, and writing, and history, too;
He took the little ones on his knee,
For a kind old heart in his breast had he,
  And the wants of the littlest child he knew.
"Learn while you're young," he often said,
  "There is much to enjoy down here below;
Life for the living, and the rest for the dead!"
  Said the jolly old pedagogue, long ago.

With the stupidest boys, he was kind and cool,
  Speaking only in gentlest tones;
The rod was scarcely known in his school—
Whipping to him was a barbarous rule,
  And too hard work for his poor old bones;
Besides it was painful, he sometimes said:
  "We should make life pleasant down here below—
The living need charity more than the dead,"
  Said the jolly old pedagogue, long ago.

He lived in the house by the hawthorn lane,
  With roses and woodbine over the door;
His rooms were quiet, and neat, and plain,

But a spirit of comfort there held reign,
And made him forget that he was old and poor.
"I need so little," he often said;
"And my friends and relatives here below
Won't litigate over me when I am dead,"
Said the jolly old pedagogue, long ago.

But the pleasantest times of all he had,
Were the sociable hours he used to pass,
With his chair tipped back to a neighbor's wall,
Making an unceremonious call,
Over a pipe and a friendly glass:
This was the finest pleasure, he said,
Of the many he tasted here below.
"Who had no cronies had better be dead,"
Said the jolly old pedagogue, long ago.

The jolly old pedagogue's wrinkled face
Melted all over in sunshiny smiles;
He stirred his glass with an old-school grace,
Chuckled, and sipped, and prattled apace,
Till the house grew merry from cellar to tiles.
"I'm a pretty old man," he gently said,
"I've lingered a long time here below;
But my heart is fresh, if my youth is fled!"
Said the jolly old pedagogue, long ago.

He smoked his pipe in the balmy air
Every night, when the sun went down;
And the soft wind played in his silvery hair,
Leaving its tenderest kisses there,
On the jolly old pedagogue's jolly old crown;
And feeling the kisses, he smiled, and said:
" 'Tis a glorious world down here below;
Why wait for happiness till we are dead?"
Said this jolly pedagogue, long ago.

He sat at his door one midsummer night,
After the sun had sunk in the west,
And the lingering beams of golden light
Made his kindly old face look warm and bright,
While the odorous night-winds whispered, "Rest!"

Gently, gently, he bowed his head;
There were angels waiting for him, I know;
He was sure of his happiness, living or dead;
This jolly old pedagogue, long ago!

EARTH IS ENOUGH

Edwin Markham

We men of Earth have here the stuff
Of Paradise—we have enough!
We need no other stones to build
The stairs into the Unfulfilled—
No other ivory for the doors—
No other marble for the floors—
No other cedar for the beam
And dome of man's immortal dream.

Here on the paths of every-day—
Here on the common human way
Is all the stuff the gods would take
To build a Heaven, to mold and make
New Edens. Ours the stuff sublime
To build Eternity in time!

DOWN BY THE OLD MILL STREAM

John Read

You must know that my uncle is a farmer,
Keeps a large farm in the West,
While staying there I met a little charmer,
And many a time I caress'd
That girl so fair, with nut-brown hair,
Her equal ne'er was seen,
And where I met this charming little pet,
Was down by the old mill stream. Ah!

Chorus:

Down by the old mill stream,
There many happy hours I've seen,
Strolling day by day,
We passed the time away,
Down by the old mill stream.

Her father was the owner of a dairy,
Her brother worked the plough,
And while I used to roam with little Mary,
Her mother would milk the cow;
But her father said we should not wed,
Which I thought rather mean.
As she could not be my wife, she said
She'd end her life,
By drowning in the old mill stream.

Now the old man laughed at his daughter,
Saying, "I don't believe a word you say."
But when he saw her struggling in the water,
He exclaimed, "Do save her, pray!"
But it was too late, she had met her fate,
Oh, what a terrible scene!
The old man cried, as the neighbors tried
To pull her out of the stream.

"SIGH NO MORE, LADIES"

William Shakespeare

Sigh no more, ladies, sigh no more,
Men were deceivers ever,
One foot in sea and one on shore,
To one thing constant never:
Then sigh not so, but let them go,
And be you blithe and bonny,
Converting all your sounds of woe
Into Hey nonny, nonny.

Sing no more ditties, sing no more,
Of dumps so dull and heavy;
The fraud of men was ever so,

Since summer first was leavy:
Then sigh not so, *etc.*
(From Much Ado About Nothing)

ONE-THIRD OF A NATION

Franklin D. Roosevelt

Here is the challenge to our democracy: In this nation I see tens of millions of its citizens—a substantial part of its whole population—who at this very moment are denied the greater part of what the very lowest standards of today call the necessities of life.

I see millions of families trying to live on incomes so meager that the pall of family disaster hangs over them day by day.

I see millions whose daily lives in city and on farm continue under conditions labeled indecent by a so-called polite society half a century ago.

I see millions denied education, recreation, and the opportunity to better their lot and the lot of their children.

I see millions lacking the means to buy the products of farm and factory and by their poverty denying work and productiveness to many other millions.

I see one-third of a nation ill-housed, ill-clad, ill-nourished.

It is not in despair that I paint you that picture. I paint it for you in hope—because the Nation, seeing and understanding the injustice in it, proposes to paint it out. We are determined to make every American citizen the subject of his country's interest and concern; and we will never regard any faithful, law-abiding group within our borders as superfluous. The test of our progress is not whether we add more to the abundance of those who have much; it is whether we provide enough for those who have too little.

(From Second Inaugural Address, January 20, 1937)

* * *

The man who has not anything to boast of but his illustrious ancestors is like a potato—the only good belonging to him is underground.—Sir Thomas Overbury

LINES COMPOSED A FEW MILES ABOVE TINTERN ABBEY

William Wordsworth

Five years have past; five summers, with the length
Of five long winters! and again I hear
These waters, rolling from their mountain-springs
With a soft inland murmur.—Once again
Do I behold these steep and lofty cliffs,
That on a wild secluded scene impress
Thoughts of more deep seclusion; and connect
The landscape with the quiet of the sky.
The day is come when I again repose
Here, under this dark sycamore, and view
These plots of cottage-ground, these orchard-tufts,
Which at this season, with their unripe fruits,
Are clad in one green hue, and lose themselves
'Mid groves and copses. Once again I see
These hedge-rows, hardly hedge-rows, little lines
Of sportive wood run wild: these pastoral farms,
Green to the very door; and wreaths of smoke
Sent up, in silence, from among the trees!
With some uncertain notice, as might seem
Of vagrant dwellers in the houseless woods,
Or of some Hermit's cave, where by his fire
The Hermit sits alone.
These beauteous forms,
Through a long absence, have not been to me
As is a landscape to a blind man's eye:
But oft, in lonely rooms, and 'mid the din
Of towns and cities, I have owed to them
In hours of weariness, sensations sweet,
Felt in the blood, and felt along the heart,
And passing even into my purer mind,
With tranquil restoration:—feelings too
Of unremembered pleasure: such, perhaps,
As have no slight or trivial influence
On that best portion of a good man's life,
His little, nameless, unremembered acts
Of kindness and of love. Nor less, I trust,
To them I may have owed another gift,
Of aspect more sublime; that blessed mood,

In which the burthen of the mystery,
In which the heavy and the weary weight
Of all this unintelligible world,
Is lightened:—that serene and blessed mood,
In which the affections gently lead us on,—
Until, the breath of this corporeal frame
And even the motion of our human blood
Almost suspended, we are laid asleep
In body, and become a living soul:
While with an eye made quiet by the power
Of harmony, and the deep power of joy,
We see into the life of things.
                                                    If this
Be but a vain belief, yet, oh! how oft—
In darkness and amid the many shapes
Of joyless daylight; when the fretful stir
Unprofitable, and the fever of the world,
Have hung upon the beatings of my heart—
How oft in spirit, have I turned to thee,
O sylvan Wye! thou wanderer thro' the woods,
How often has my spirit turned to thee!
   And now, with gleams of half-extinguished thought,
With many recognitions dim and faint,
And somewhat of a sad perplexity,
The picture of the mind revives again:
While here I stand, not only with the sense
Of present pleasure, but with pleasing thoughts
That in this moment there is life and food
For future years. And so I dare to hope,
Though changed, no doubt, from what I was when first
I came among these hills; when like a roe
I bounded o'er the mountains, by the sides
Of the deep rivers, and the lonely streams,
Wherever nature led: more like a man
Flying from something that he dreads, than one
Who sought the thing he loved. For nature then
(The coarser pleasures of my boyish days,
And their glad animal movements all gone by)
To me was all in all.—I cannot paint
What then I was. The sounding cataract
Haunted me like a passion: the tall rock,
The mountain, and the deep and gloomy wood,
Their colours and their forms, were then to me

An appetite; a feeling and a love,
That had no need of a remoter charm,
By thought supplied, nor any interest
Unborrowed from the eye.—That time is past,
And all its aching joys are now no more,
And all its dizzy raptures. Not for this
Faint I, nor mourn nor murmur; other gifts
Have followed; for such loss, I would believe,
Abundant recompense. For I have learned
To look on nature, not as in the hour
Of thoughtless youth; but hearing often-times
The still, sad music of humanity,
Nor harsh, nor grating, though of ample power
To chasten and subdue. And I have felt
A presence that disturbs me with the joy
Of elevated thoughts; a sense sublime
Of something far more deeply interfused,
Whose dwelling is the light of setting suns,
And the round ocean and the living air,
And the blue sky, and in the mind of man;
A motion and a spirit, that impels
All thinking things, all objects of all thought,
And rolls through all things. Therefore am I still
A lover of the meadows and the woods,
And mountains; and of all that we behold
From this green earth; of all the mighty world
Of eye, and ear,—both what they half create,
And what perceive; well pleased to recognise
In nature and the language of the sense,
The anchor of my purest thoughts, the nurse,
The guide, the guardian of my heart, and soul
Of all my moral being.

Nor perchance,
If I were not thus taught, should I the more
Suffer my genial spirits to decay:
For thou art with me here upon the banks
Of this fair river; thou my dearest Friend.
My dear, dear Friend; and in thy voice I catch
The language of my former heart, and read
My former pleasures in the shooting lights
Of thy wild eyes. Oh! yet a little while
May I behold in thee what I was once,
My dear, dear Sister! and this prayer I make,

Knowing that Nature never did betray
The heart that loved her; 'tis her privilege,
Through all the years of this our life, to lead
From joy to joy: for she can so inform
The mind that is within us, so impress
With quietness and beauty, and so feed
With lofty thoughts, that neither evil tongues,
Rash judgments, nor the sneers of selfish men,
Nor greetings where no kindness is, nor all
The dreary intercourse of daily life,
Shall e'er prevail against us, or disturb
Our cheerful faith, that all which we behold
Is full of blessings. Therefore let the moon
Shine on thee in thy solitary walk;
And let the misty mountain-winds be free
To blow against thee: and, in after years,
When these wild ecstasies shall be matured
Into a sober pleasure; when thy mind
Shall be a mansion for all lovely forms,
Thy memory be as a dwelling-place
For all sweet sounds and harmonies; oh! then,
If solitude, or fear, or pain, or grief,
Should be thy portion, with what healing thoughts
Of tender joy wilt thou remember me,
And these my exhortations! Nor, perchance—
If I should be where I no more can hear
Thy voice, nor catch from thy wild eyes these gleams
Of past existence—wilt thou then forget
That on the banks of this delightful stream
We stood together; and that I, so long
A worshipper of Nature, hither came
Unwearied in that service: rather say
With warmer love—oh! with far deeper zeal
Of holier love. Nor wilt thou then forget,
That after many wanderings, many years
Of absence, these steep woods and lofty cliffs,
And this green pastoral landscape, were to me
More dear, both for themselves and for thy sake!

* * *

Adam and Eve had many advantages, but the principal one was that they escaped teething.—Mark Twain

THE LITTLE LOST CHILD *

Edward B. Marks

A passing policeman found a little child,
She walked beside him, dried her tears and smiled.
Said he to her kindly, "Now you must not cry,
I will find your mama for you by and by."
At the station when he asked her for her name,
And she answered "Jennie," it made him exclaim,
"At last of your mother I have now a trace;
Your little features bring back her sweet face."

Chorus:

"Do not fear, my little darling,
And I will take you right home.
Come and sit down close beside me,
No more from me you shall roam.
For you were a babe in arms,
When your mother left me one day,
Left me at home deserted, alone, and took,
And took you, my child, away."

" 'Twas all through a quarrel madly jealous she,
Vowed then to leave me, woman-like you see.
Oh, how I loved her, grief near drove me wild."
"Papa, you are crying," lisped the little child.
Suddenly the door of the station opened wide.
"Have you seen my darling?" an anxious mother cried.
Husband and wife then meeting face to face,
All is soon forgiven in one fond embrace.

MARIE ANTOINETTE

Edmund Burke

It is now sixteen or seventeen years since I saw the Queen of France, then the dauphiness, at Versailles; and surely never lighted on this orb, which she hardly seemed to touch, a more delightful

* Copyright, Edward B. Marks Music Corporation, Radio City, New York, N. Y. Used by permission.

vision. I saw her just above the horizon, decorating and cheering the elevated sphere she just began to move in—glittering like the morning-star, full of life, and splendour, and joy. Oh! what a revolution! and what a heart must I have, to contemplate without emotion that elevation and that fall! Little did I dream when she added titles of veneration to those of enthusiastic, distant, respectful love, that she should ever be obliged to carry the sharp antidote against disgrace concealed in that bosom; little did I dream that I should live to see such disasters fallen upon her in a nation of gallant men, in a nation of men of honour, and of cavaliers. I thought ten thousand swords must have leaped from their scabbards to avenge even a look that threatened her with insult. But the age of chivalry is gone. That of sophisters, economists, and calculators has succeeded; and the glory of Europe is extinguished for ever. Never, never more shall we behold that generous loyalty to rank and sex, that proud submission, that dignified obedience, that subordination of the heart, which kept alive, even in servitude itself, the spirit of an exalted freedom. The unbought grace of life, the cheap defence of nations, the nurse of manly sentiment and heroic enterprise is gone! It is gone, that sensibility of principle, that chastity of honour, which felt a stain like a wound, which inspired courage whilst it mitigated ferocity, which ennobled whatever it touched, and under which vice itself lost half its evil, by losing all its grossness.

(From Reflections on the Revolution in France)

SO, WE'LL GO NO MORE A-ROVING

Lord Byron

So, we'll go no more a-roving
  So late into the night,
Though the heart be still as loving,
  And the moon be still as bright.

For the sword outwears its sheath,
  And the soul wears out the breast,
And the heart must pause to breathe,
  And love itself have rest.

Though the night was made for loving,
And the day returns too soon,
Yet we'll go no more a-roving
By the light of the moon.

COME, LET US KISS AND PART

Michael Drayton

Since there's no help, come, let us kiss and part,
Nay, I have done; you get no more of me.
And I am glad, yea, glad with all my heart
That thus so cleanly I myself can free.
Shake hands for ever; cancel all our vows;
And when we meet at any time again,
Be it not seen in either of our brows
That we one jot of former love retain.
Now at the last gasp of Love's latest breath,
When, his pulse failing, Passion speechless lies,
When Faith is kneeling by his bed of death,
And Innocence is closing up his eyes—
Now, if thou wouldst, when all have given him over,
From death to life thou might'st him yet recover.

ON POLITICIANS

Jonathan Swift

And he gave it for his opinion that whoever could make two ears of corn, or two blades of grass, to grow upon a spot of ground where only one grew before, would deserve better of mankind, and do more essential service to his country, than the whole race of politicians put together.

(From Gulliver's Travels)

* * *

The imagination gallops but judgment goes on foot.—Anonymous

PROPOSAL

Anonymous

"Go ask Papa," the maiden said.
The young man knew Papa was dead;
He knew the life Papa had led;
He understood when the maiden said,
"Go ask Papa."

A SOLDIER: HIS PRAYER

Gerald Kersch

Stay with me, God. The night is dark,
The night is cold; my little spark
Of courage dies. The night is long;
Be with me, God, and make me strong.

I love a game. I love a fight.
I hate the dark; I love the light.
I love my child; I love my wife.
I am no coward; I love life—

Life with its change of mood and shade.
I want to live. I'm not afraid,
But me and mine are hard to part;
O unknown God, lift up my heart.

You stilled the waters at Dunkirk
And saved Your servants. All Your work
Is wonderful, dear God. You strode
Before us down that dreadful road.

We were alone, and hope had fled;
We loved our country and our dead,
And could not shame them, so we stayed
The course, and were not much afraid.

Dear God, that nightmare road! And then
That sea! We got there—we were men;
My eyes were blind, my feet were torn,
My soul sang like a bird at dawn!

I knew that death is but a door.
I knew what we were fighting for;
Peace for the kids, our brothers freed,
A kinder world, a cleaner breed.

I'm but the son my mother bore,
A simple man, and nothing more.
But—God of strength and gentleness,
Be pleased to make me nothing less.

Help me, O God, when death is near
To mock the haggard face of fear,
That when I fall—if fall I must—
My soul may triumph in the dust.

THE CATARACT OF LODORE

Robert Southey

"How does the water
Come down at Lodore?"
My little boy asked me
Thus, once on a time;
And moreover he tasked me
To tell him in rhyme.
Anon at the word,
There first came one daughter.
And then came another,
To second and third
The request of their brother,
And to hear how the water
Comes down at Lodore,
With its rush and its roar,
As many a time
They had seen it before.
So I told them in rhyme,
For of rhymes I had store;
And 'twas in my vocation
For their recreation
That so I should sing;
Because I was Laureate
To them and the King.

From its sources which well
In the tarn on the fell;
From its fountains
In the mountains,
Its rills and its gills;
Through moss and through brake,
It runs and it creeps
For a while, till it sleeps
In its own little lake.
And thence at departing,
Awakening and starting,
It runs through the reeds,
And away it proceeds,
Through meadows and glade,
In sun and in shade,
And through the wood-shelter,
Among crags in its flurry,
Helter-skelter,
Hurry-skurry.
Here it comes sparkling,
And there it lies darkling;
Now smoking and frothing
Its tumult and wrath in,
Till in this rapid race
On which it is bent,
It reaches the place
Of its steep descent.

The cataract strong
Then plunges along,
Striking and raging
As if a war waging
Its caverns and rocks among;
Rising and leaping,
Sinking and creeping,
Swelling and sweeping,
Showering and springing,
Flying and flinging,
Writhing and ringing,
Eddying and whisking,
Spouting and frisking,
Turning and twisting,
Around and around

With endless rebound:
Smiting and fighting,
A sight to delight in;
Confounding, astounding,
Dizzying and deafening the ear with its sound.

Collecting, projecting,
Receding and speeding,
And shocking and rocking,
And darting and parting,
And threading and spreading,
And whizzing and hissing,
And dripping and skipping,
And hitting and splitting,
And shining and twining,
And rattling and battling,
And shaking and quaking,
And pouring and roaring,
And waving and raving,
And tossing and crossing,
And flowing and going,
And running and stunning,
And foaming and roaming,
And dinning and spinning,
And dropping and hopping,
And working and jerking,
And guggling and struggling,
And heaving and cleaving,
And moaning and groaning;

And glittering and frittering,
And gathering and feathering,
And whitening and brightening,
And quivering and shivering,
And hurrying and skurrying,
And thundering and floundering;

Dividing and gliding and sliding,
And falling and brawling and sprawling,
And driving and riving and striving,
And sprinkling and twinkling and wrinkling,
And sounding and bounding and rounding,

And bubbling and troubling and doubling,
And grumbling and rumbling and tumbling,
And clattering and battering and shattering;

Retreating and beating and meeting and sheeting,
Delaying and straying and playing and spraying,
Advancing and prancing and glancing and dancing,
Recoiling, turmoiling and toiling and boiling,
And gleaming and streaming and steaming and beaming,
And rushing and flushing and brushing and gushing,
And flapping and rapping and clapping and slapping,
And curling and whirling and purling and twirling,
And thumping and plumping and bumping and jumping,
And dashing and flashing and splashing and clashing,
And so never ending, but always descending,
Sounds and motions forever and ever are blending,
All at once and all o'er, with a mighty uproar,
And this way the water comes down at Lodore.

QUANDARY

Mrs. Edward Craster

The centipede was happy quite
Until a toad in fun
Said, "Pray, which leg goes after which?"
That worked her mind to such a pitch,
She lay distracted in a ditch,
Considering how to run.

THE SURRENDER OF GENERAL ROBERT E. LEE

General U. S. Grant

I found Lee at the house of a Mr. McLean, at Appomattox Court House, with Colonel Marshall, one of his staff officers, awaiting my arrival. The head of his column was occupying a hill, on a portion of which was an apple orchard, beyond a little valley which separated it from that on the crest of which Sheridan's forces were drawn up in line of battle to the south.

I had known General Lee in the old army, and had served with him in the Mexican War; but did not suppose, owing to the difference in our age and rank that he would remember me; while I would more naturally remember him distinctly, because he was the chief of staff of General Scott in the Mexican War.

When I had left camp that morning, I had not expected so soon the result that was then taking place, and consequently was in rough garb. I was without a sword, as I usually was when on horseback in the field, and wore a soldier's blouse for a coat, with the shoulder straps of my rank to indicate to the army who I was. When I went into the house I found General Lee. I had my staff with me, a good portion of whom were in the room during the whole of the interview.

What General Lee's feelings were I do not know. As he was a man of much dignity, with an impassible face, it was impossible to say whether he felt inwardly glad that the end had finally come, or felt sad over the result, and was too manly to show it. Whatever his feelings, they were entirely concealed from my observation; but my own feelings, which had been quite jubilant on the receipt of his letter, were sad and depressed. I felt like anything rather than rejoicing at the downfall of a foe who had fought so long and valiantly.

General Lee was dressed in a full uniform which was entirely new, and was wearing a sword of considerable value, very likely the sword which had been presented by the State of Virginia; at all events, it was an entirely different sword from the one that would ordinarily be worn in the field. In my rough traveling suit, the uniform of a private with the straps of a lieutenant-general, I must have contrasted very strangely with a man so handsomely dressed, six feet high and of faultless form. But this was not a matter that I thought of until afterwards.

We soon fell into a conversation about old army times. He remarked that he remembered me very well in the old army; and I told him that as a matter of course I remembered him perfectly, but from the difference in our ranks and years (there being about sixteen years difference in our ages), I had thought it very likely that I had not attracted his attention sufficiently to be remembered by him after such a long interval. Our conversation grew so pleasant that I almost forgot the object of our meeting. After the conversation had run on in this style for some time, General Lee called my attention to the object of our meeting, and said he had asked for this interview for the purpose of getting from me the terms I had proposed to give his army. I said that I meant merely that his army should lay down its arms, not to take them up again during the continuance of the war unless duly and properly exchanged. He said that he had so understood my letter.

Then we gradually fell off again into conversation about matters foreign to the subject which had brought us together. This continued for some little time, when General Lee again interrupted the course of the conversation by suggesting that the terms I proposed to give his army ought to be written out. I called to General Parker, secretary on my staff, for writing materials, and commenced writing out the terms.

When I put my pen to the paper I did not know the first word that I should make use of in writing the terms. I only knew what was in my mind, and I wished to express it clearly, so that there could be no mistaking it. As I wrote on, the thought occurred to me that the officers had their own private horses and effects, which were important to them, but of no value to us; also that it would be an unnecessary humiliation to call upon them to deliver their side arms.

No conversation, not one word, passed between General Lee and myself, either about private property, side arms or kindred subjects. He appeared to have no objections to the terms first proposed; or if he had a point to make against them he wished to wait until they were in writing to make it. When he had read over that part of the terms about side arms, horses, and private property of the officers, he remarked, with some feeling, I thought, that this would have a happy effect upon his army.

Then, after a little further conversation, General Lee remarked to me again that their army was organized a little differently from the army of the United States (still maintaining by implication that we were two countries); that in their army the cavalry-men and artillerists owned their own horses; and he asked if he was to understand that the men who so owned their horses were to be permitted to retain them. I told him that as the terms were written they would not; that only the officers were permitted to take their private property. He then, after reading over the terms a second time, remarked that that was clear.

I then said to him that I thought this would be about the last battle of the war—I sincerely hoped so; and I said further I took it that most of the men in the ranks were small farmers. The whole country had been so raided by the two armies that it was doubtful whether they would be able to put in a crop to carry themselves and their families through the next winter without the aid of the horses they were then riding. The United States did not want them and I would, therefore, instruct the officers I left behind to receive the paroles of his troops to let every man of the Confederate army who claimed to own a horse or mule take the animal to his home. Lee remarked again that this would have a happy effect upon his army.

The much talked of surrendering of Lee's sword and my handing it back, this and much more that has been said about it is the purest romance. The word sword or side arms was not mentioned by either of us until I wrote it in the terms. There was no premeditation, and it did not occur to me until the moment I wrote it down. If I had happened to omit it, and General Lee had called my attention to it, I should have put it in the terms precisely as I acceded to the provision about the soldiers retaining their horses.

General Lee, after all was completed and before taking his leave, remarked that his army was in a very bad condition for want of food, and they were without forage; that his men had been living for some days on parched corn exclusively, and that he would have to ask me for rations and forage. I told him "certainly" and asked for how many men he wanted rations. His answer was "about twenty-five thousand"; and I authorized him to send his own commissary and quartermaster to Appomattox Station, two or three miles away, where he could have, out of the trains we had stopped, all the provisions wanted. As for forage, we had ourselves depended almost entirely upon the country for that.

When news of the surrender first reached our lines our men commenced firing a salute of a hundred guns in honor of the victory. I at once sent word, however, to have it stopped. The Confederates were now our prisoners, and we did not want to exult over their downfall.

I determined to return to Washington at once, with a view to putting a stop to the purchase of supplies, and what I now deemed other useless outlay of money. Before leaving, however, I thought I would like to see General Lee again; so next morning I rode out beyond our lines toward his headquarters, preceded by a bugler and a staff-officer carrying a white flag.

Lee soon mounted his horse, seeing who it was, and met me. We had there between the lines, sitting on horseback, a very pleasant conversation of over half an hour, in the course of which Lee said to me that the South was a big country and that we might have to march over it three or four times before the war entirely ended, but that we would now be able to do it as they could no longer resist us. He expressed it as his earnest hope, however, that we would not be called upon to cause more loss and sacrifice of life;

but he could not foretell the result. I then suggested to General Lee that there was not a man in the Confederacy whose influence with the soldiery and the whole people was as great as his, and that if he would now advise the surrender of all the armies I had no doubt his advice would be followed with alacrity. But Lee said, that he could not do that without consulting the President first. I knew there was no use to urge him to do anything against his idea of what was right.

BEFORE SEDAN

Austin Dobson

"The dead hand clasped a letter."
—Special Correspondence

Here in this leafy place
  Quiet he lies,
Cold with his sightless face
  Turned to the skies;
'Tis but another dead;
All you can say is said.

Carry his body hence,—
  Kings must have slaves;
Kings climb to eminence
  Over men's graves:
So this man's eye is dim;—
Throw the earth over him.

What was the white you touched,
  There, at his side?
Paper his hand had clutched
  Tight ere he died;—
Message or wish, may be;
Smooth the folds out and see.

Hardly the worst of us
  Here could have smiled!
Only the tremulous
Prattle, that has for stops
Just a few ruddy drops.

Look. She is sad to miss,
  Morning and night,
His—her dead father's—kiss;
  Tries to be bright,
Good to mamma, and sweet.
That is all. "Marguerite."

Ah, if beside the dead
  Slumbered the pain!
Ah, if the hearts that bled
  Slept with the slain!
If the grief died;—but no,
Death will not have it so.

GENTLE JESUS

Charles Wesley

Gentle Jesus, meek and mild,
Look upon a little child;
Pity my simplicity,
Suffer me to come to Thee.

Lamb of God, I look to Thee:
Thou shalt my example be;
Thou art gentle, meek and mild;
Thou wast once a little child.

Fain I would be as Thou art;
Give me Thy obedient heart.
Thou art pitiful and kind,
Let me have Thy loving mind.

Loving Jesus, gentle Lamb,
In Thy gracious hands I am:
Make me, Saviour, what Thou art;
Live Thyself within my heart.

WHOLE DUTY OF CHILDREN

Robert Louis Stevenson

A child should always say what's true,
And speak when he is spoken to,
And behave mannerly at table;
At least as far as he is able.

CHRISTOPHER COLUMBUS DESCRIBES THE DISCOVERY OF AMERICA

(Translator: Samuel Kettell)

Thursday, October 11th. 1492 Steered W.S.W.; and encountered a heavier sea than they had met with before in the whole voyage. Saw *pardelas* and a green rush near the vessel. The crew of the Pinta saw a cane and a log; they also picked up a stick which appeared to have been carved with an iron tool, a piece of cane, a plant which grows on land, and a board. The crew of the Nina saw other signs of land, and a stalk loaded with roseberries. These signs encouraged them, and they all grew cheerful. Sailed this day till sunset, twenty-seven leagues.

After sunset steered their original course W. and sailed twelve miles an hour till two hours after midnight, going ninety miles, which are twenty-two leagues and a half; and as the Pinta was the swifter sailer, and kept ahead of the Admiral, she discovered land and made the signals which had been ordered. The land was first seen by a sailor called Rodrigo de Triana, although the Admiral at ten o'clock that evening, standing on the quarter-deck, saw a light, but so small a body that he could not affirm it to be land; calling to Pero Gutierrez, groom of the King's wardrobe, he told him he saw a light, and bid him look that way, which he did and saw it; he did the same to Rodrigo Sanchez of Segovia, whom the King and Queen had sent with the squadron as comptroller, but he was unable to see it from his situation. The Admiral again perceived it once or twice, appearing like the light of a wax candle moving up and down, which some thought an indication of land. But the Admiral held it for certain that land was near; for which reason, after they had said the *Salve* which the seamen are accustomed to repeat and chant after their fashion, the Admiral directed them to keep a strict watch upon the forecastle and look out diligently for land, and to him who should first discover it he promised a silken jacket, besides the reward which the King and Queen had offered, which was an annuity of ten thousand maravedis. At two o'clock in the morning the land was discovered, at two leagues distance; they took in sail and remained under the square-sail lying to till day, which was Friday, when they found themselves near a small island, one of the Lucayos, called in the Indian language Guanahani. Presently they descried people, naked, and the Admiral landed in the boat, which was armed, along with Martin Alonzo Pinzon, and Vincent Yanez his brother, captain of the Nina. The Admiral bore the royal standard, and the two captains each a banner of the Green Cross, which all the ships had carried; this contained the initials of the names of the King and Queen each side of the cross, and a crown over each letter. Arrived on shore, they saw trees very green, many streams of water, and diverse sorts of fruit. The Admiral called upon the two captains, and the rest of the crew who landed, as also to Rodrigo de Escovedo notary of the fleet, and Rodrigo Sanchez, of Segovia, to bear witness that he before all others took possession (as in fact he did) of that island for the King and Queen his sovereigns.

TENTING ON THE OLD CAMP GROUND

Walter Kittredge

We're tenting tonight on the old Camp ground,
  Give us a song to cheer
Our weary hearts, a song of home
  And friends we love so dear.

Chorus:
    Many are the hearts that are weary tonight,
      Wishing for the war to cease;
    Many are the hearts that are looking for the right
      To see the dawn of peace.
    Tenting tonight, tenting tonight, tenting on the old Camp ground.

We've been tenting tonight on the old Camp ground,
  Thinking of days gone by,
Of the loved ones at home that gave us the hand,
  And the tear that said, "Good-bye."

We are tired of war on the old Camp ground,
  Many are dead and gone,
Of the brave and true who've left their homes,
  Others have been wounded long.

We've been fighting today on the old Camp ground,
  Many are lying near;
Some are dead, and some are dying,
  Many are in tears.

"I GAVE HER CAKES; I GAVE HER ALE"

Anonymous

I gave her cakes; I gave her ale,
  I gave her sack and sherry;
I kissed her once, I kissed her twice,
  And we were wondrous merry.

I gave her beads and bracelets fine,
  And I gave her gold down derry;
I thought she was afeard till she stroked my beard,
  And we were wondrous merry.

Merry my heart, merry my cocks, merry my sprights.
  Merry my hey down derry;
I kissed her once and I kissed her twice,
  And we were wondrous merry.

OF MARRIAGE AND THE SINGLE LIFE

Francis Bacon

He that hath wife and children hath given hostages to fortune, for they are impediments to great enterprise, either of virtue or mischief. Certainly, the best works, and of greatest merit for the public, have proceeded from the unmarried, or childless men, which, both in affection and means have married and endowed the public. Yet it were great reason that those that have children should have greatest care of future times, unto which they know they must transmit their dearest pledges. Some there are who, though they lead a single life, yet their thoughts do end with themselves and account future times impertinences. Nay, there are some other that account wife and children but as bills of charges. Nay more, there are some foolish rich, covetous men that take a pride in having no children because they may be thought so much the richer. . . . Certainly, wife and children are a kind of discipline of humanity. And single men, though they be many times more charitable because their means are less exhaust, yet on the other side, they are more cruel and hard hearted (good to make severe inquisitors) because their tenderness is not so oft called upon. Grave natures, led by custom and therefore constant, are commonly loving husbands. . . . It is one of the best bonds both of chastity and obedience in the wife if she think her husband wise; which she will never do if she find him jealous. Wives are young men's mistresses; companions for middle age, and old men's nurses. So as a man may have a quarrel to marry, when he will. But yet, he was reputed one of the wise men that made answer to the question: When a man should marry? *A young man not yet, an elder man not at all.*

THE SOLDIER'S DREAM

Thomas Campbell

Our bugles sang truce,—for the night-cloud had lowered,
And the sentinel stars set their watch in the sky;
And thousands had sunk on the ground over-powered,
The weary to sleep, and the wounded to die.

When reposing that night on my pallet of straw,
By the wolf-scaring fagot that guarded the slain;
At the dead of the night a sweet vision I saw,
And thrice ere the morning I dreamt it again.

Methought from the battle-field's dreadful array,
Far, far I had roamed on a desolate track:
'Twas autumn,—and sunshine arose on the way
To the home of my fathers, that welcomed me back.

I flew to the pleasant fields traversed so oft
  In life's morning march, when my bosom was young;
I heard my own mountain-goats bleating aloft,
  And knew the sweet strain that the corn-reapers sung.

Then pledged we the wine-cup, and fondly I swore,
  From my home and my weeping friends never to part;
My little ones kissed me a thousand times o'er,
  And my wife sobbed aloud in her fulness of heart.

"Stay, stay with us,—rest, thou art weary and worn!"
  And fain was their war-broken soldier to stay;
But sorrow return'd with the dawning of morn,
  And the voice in my dreaming ear melted away.

JESUS ANSWERS THE PHARISEES

Holy Bible, John 8:12–32

Then spake Jesus again unto them, saying, I am the light of the world: he that followeth me shall not walk in darkness, but shall have the light of life. The Pharisees therefore said unto him, Thou bearest record of thyself; thy record is not true. Jesus answered and said unto them, Though I bear record of myself, yet my record is true: for I know whence I came, and whither I go; but ye cannot tell whence I come, and whither I go. Ye judge after the flesh; I judge no man. And yet if I judge, my judgment is true: for I am not alone, but I and the Father that sent me. It is also written in your law, that the testimony of two men is true. I am one that bear witness of myself, and the Father that sent me beareth witness of me. Then said they unto him, Where is thy Father? Jesus answered, Ye neither know me, nor my Father: if ye had known me, ye should have known my Father also. These words spake Jesus in the treasury, as he taught in the temple: and no man laid hands on him; for his hour was not yet come. Then said Jesus again unto them, I go my way, and ye shall seek me, and shall die in your sins: whither I go, ye cannot come. Then said the Jews, Will he kill himself? because he saith, Whither I go, ye cannot come. And he said unto them, Ye are from beneath; I am from above: ye are of this world; I am not of this world. I said therefore unto you, that ye shall die in your sins: for if ye believe not that I am he, ye shall die in your sins. Then said they unto him, Who art thou? And Jesus saith unto them, Even the same that I said unto you from the beginning. I have many things to say and to judge of you: but he that sent me is true; and I speak to the world those things which I have heard of him. They understood not that he spake to them of the Father. Then said Jesus unto them, When ye have lifted up the Son of man, then shall ye know that I am he, and that I do nothing of myself; but as my Father hath taught me, I speak these things. And he that sent me is with me: the Father hath not left me alone; for I do always those things that please him. As he spake these words, many believed on him. Then said Jesus to those Jews which believed on him, If ye continue in my word, then ye are my disciples indeed; And ye shall know the truth, and the truth shall make you free.

LOVE IS A SICKNESS

Samuel Daniel

Love is a sickness full of woes,
All remedies refusing;
A plant that with most cutting grows,
Most barren with best using.
Why so?
More we enjoy it, more it dies;
If not enjoy'd, it sighing cries—
Heigh ho!

Love is a torment of the mind,
A tempest everlasting;
And Jove hath made it of a kind
Not well, nor full nor fasting.
Why so?
More we enjoy it, more it dies;
If not enjoy'd, it sighing cries—
Heigh ho!

* * *

Give me a lever long enough, and a fulcrum strong enough, and single-handed I can move the world.—Archimedes

SAMUEL PEPYS HAS A MERRY EVENING

After dinner, with my wife and Mercer to the Bear Garden; where I have not been, I think, of many years, and saw some good sport of the bull's tossing the dogs—one into the very boxes. But it is a very rude and nasty pleasure. We had a great many hectors in the same box, and one very fine went into the pit, and played his dog for a wager; which was a strange sport for a gentleman; where they drank wine, and drank Mercer's health first; which I pledged with my hat off. We supped at home, and very merry. And then about nine to Mrs. Mercer's gate, where the fire and boys expected us, and her son had provided abundance of serpents and rockets; and there mighty merry, my Lady Pen and Peggy going thither with us, and Nan Wright, till about twelve at night, flinging our fireworks, and burning one another, and the people over the way.

And, at last, our business being most spent, we went into Mrs. Mercer's, and there mighty merry, smutting one another with candle grease and soot, then we broke up, and to my house; and there I made them drink, and upstairs we went, and then fell into dancing, W. Batelier dancing well; and dressing him and I, and one Mr. Banister, who, with my wife, came over also with us, like women; and Mercer put on a suit of Tom's, like a boy, and mighty mirth we had, and Mercer danced a jig; and Nan Wright and my wife and Peggy Pen put on perriwigs. Thus we spent till three or four in the morning, mighty merry; and then parted, and so to bed.

(From the Diary, August, 1666)

MARK ANTONY'S LAMENT

William Shakespeare

O mighty Caesar! dost thou lie so low?
Are all thy conquests, glories, triumphs, spoils,
Shrunk to this little measure? Fare thee well.
I know not, gentlemen, what you intend,
Who else must be let blood, who else is rank:
If I myself, there is no hour so fit
As Caesar's death hour, nor no instrument
Of half that worth as those your swords, made rich
With the most noble blood of all this world.

I do beseech ye, if you bear me hard,
Now, whilst your purpled hands do reek and smoke,
Fulfil your pleasure. Live a thousand years,
I shall not find myself so apt to die:
No place will please me so, no mean of death,
As here by Caesar, and by you cut off,
The choice and master spirits of this age.

* * *

O, pardon me, thou bleeding piece of earth,
That I am meek and gentle with these butchers!
Thou art the ruins of the noblest man
That ever lived in the tide of times.
Woe to the hand that shed this costly blood!
Over thy wounds now do I prophesy,—
Which, like dumb mouths, do ope their ruby lips,
To beg the voice and utterance of my tongue—
A curse shall light upon the limbs of men;
Domestic fury and fierce civil strife
Shall cumber all the parts of Italy;
Blood and destruction shall be so in use,
And dreadful objects so familiar,
That mothers shall but smile when they behold
Their infants quarter'd with the hands of war;
All pity choked with custom of fell deeds;
And Caesar's spirit ranging for revenge,
With Ate by his side come hot from hell,
Shall in these confines with a monarch's voice
Cry "Havoc," and let slip the dogs of war
That this foul deed shall smell above the earth
With carrion men, groaning for burial.

(From Julius Caesar)

STOPPING BY WOODS ON A SNOWY EVENING

Robert Frost

Whose woods these are I think I know.
His house is in the village though;
He will not see me stopping here
To watch his woods fill up with snow.

The little horse must think it queer
To stop without a farmhouse near
Between the woods and frozen lake
The darkest evening of the year.

He gives his harness bells a shake
To ask if there is some mistake.
The only other sound's the sweep
Of easy wind and downy flake.

The woods are lovely, dark and deep.
But I have promises to keep,
And miles to go before I sleep,
And miles to go before I sleep.

LITTLE WILLIE

Anonymous

Little Willie hung his sister;
She was dead before we missed her.
Willie's always up to tricks!
Ain't he cute? He's only six!

PRESIDENT FRANKLIN D. ROOSEVELT'S "STAB IN THE BACK" SPEECH

Every generation of young men and women in America has questions to ask the world. Most of the time they are the simple but nevertheless difficult questions, questions of work to do, opportunities to find, ambitions to satisfy.

But every now and again in the history of the Republic a different kind of question presents itself—a question that asks, not about the future of an individual or even of a generation, but about the future of the country, the future of the American people. . . .

There is such a time again today. Again today the young men and the young women of America ask themselves with earnestness and with deep concern this same question: "What is to become of the country we know?"

Now they ask it with even greater anxiety than before. They ask, not only what the future holds for this Republic, but what the future holds for all peoples and all nations that have been living under democratic forms of Government—under the free institutions of a free people. . . .

Perception of danger to our institutions may come slowly or it may come with a rush and a shock as it has to the people of the United States in the past few months. This perception of danger has come to us clearly and overwhelmingly; and we perceive the peril in a world-wide arena—an arena that may become so narrowed that only the Americas will retain the ancient faiths. . . .

Let us not hesitate—all of us—to proclaim certain truths. Overwhelmingly we, as a nation—and this applies to all the other American nations—are convinced that military and naval victory for the gods of force and hate would endanger the institutions of democracy in the western world, and that equally, therefore, the whole of our sympathies lies with those nations that are giving their life blood in combat against these forces.

The people and the Government of the United States have seen with the utmost regret and with grave disquiet the decision of the Italian Government to engage in the hostilities now raging in Europe. . . .

I have . . . of course, felt it necessary in my communications to Signor Mussolini to express the concern of the Government of the United States because of the fact that any extension of the war in the region of the Mediterranean would inevitably result in great prejudice to the ways of life and Government and to the trade and commerce of all the American Republics.

The Government of Italy has now chosen to preserve what it terms its "freedom of action" and to fulfill what it states are its promises to Germany. In so doing it has manifested disregard for the rights and security of other nations, disregard for the lives of the peoples of those nations which are directly threatened by the spread of the war; and has evidenced its unwillingness to find the means through pacific negotiations for the satisfaction of what it believes are its legitimate aspirations.

On this tenth day of June, 1940, the hand that held the dagger has struck it into the back of its neighbor.

On this tenth day of June, 1940, in this University founded by the first great American teacher of democracy, we send forth our prayers and our hopes to those beyond the seas who are maintaining with magnificent valor their battle for freedom.

In our American unity, we will pursue two obvious and simultaneous courses; we will extend to the opponents of force the material resources of this nation; and, at the same time, we will harness and speed up the use of those resources in order that we ourselves in the Americas may have equipment and training equal to the task of any emergency and every defense.

All roads leading to the accomplishment of these objectives must be kept clear of obstructions. We will not slow down or detour. Signs and signals call for speed—full speed ahead.

It is right that each new generation should ask questions. But in recent months the principal question has been somewhat simplified. Once more the future of the nation and of the American people is at stake.

We need not and we will not, in any way, abandon our continuing effort to make democracy work within our borders. We still insist on the need for vast improvements in our own social and economic life.

But that is a component part of national defense itself.

The program unfolds swiftly and into that program will fit the responsibility and the opportunity of every man and woman in the land to preserve his and her heritage in days of peril.

I call for effort, courage, sacrifice, devotion. Granting the love of freedom, all of these are possible.

And the love of freedom is still fierce and steady in the nation today.

(Charlottesville, Va., June 10, 1940,
the day after Italy entered the War)

THE BRIDGE BUILDER

(Miss) Will Allen Dromgoole

An old man, going a lone highway,
Came at the evening, cold and gray,
To a chasm, vast and deep and wide,
Through which was flowing a sullen tide.
The old man crossed in the twilight dim—
That sullen stream had no fears for him;
But he turned, when he reached the other side,
And built a bridge to span the tide.

"Old man," said a fellow pilgrim near,
"You are wasting strength in building here.
Your journey will end with the ending day;
You never again must pass this way.
You have crossed the chasm, deep and wide,
Why build you the bridge at the eventide?"

The builder lifted his old gray head.
"Good friend, in the path I have come," he said,
"There followeth after me today
A youth whose feet must pass this way.
This chasm that has been naught to me
To that fair-haired youth may a pitfall be.
He, too, must cross in the twilight dim;
Good friend, I am building the bridge for *him*."

JUST BEFORE THE BATTLE, MOTHER

George F. Root

Just before the battle, Mother,
  I am thinking most of you,
While upon the field we're watching,
  With the enemy in view.
Comrades brave are round me lying,
  Filled with thoughts of home and God;
For well they know that on the morrow,
  Some will sleep beneath the sod.

Chorus:
Farewell, Mother, you may never
  Press me to your heart again;
But oh, you'll not forget me, Mother,
  If I'm numbered with the slain.

Hark! I hear the bugles sounding,
  'Tis the signal for the fight;
Now may God protect us, Mother,
  As He ever does the right.
Hear the "Battle Cry of Freedom,"
  How it swells upon the air;
Oh, yes, we'll rally round the standard,
  Or we'll perish nobly there.

AT LAST

John Greenleaf Whittier

When on my day of life the night is falling,
  And, in the winds from unspanned space blown,
I hear far voices out of darkness calling
  My feet to paths unknown,

Thou who hast made my home of life so pleasant,
  Leave not its tenant when its walls decay;
O Love Divine, O Helper ever present,
  Be Thou my strength and stay!

Be near me when all else is from me drifting;
  Earth, sky, home's pictures, days of shade and shine,
And kindly faces to my own uplifting
  The love which answers mine.

I have but Thee, my Father! let Thy spirit
  Be with me then to comfort and uphold;
No gate of pearl, no branch of palm I merit,
  Nor street of shining gold.

Suffice it if—my good and ill unreckoned,
  And both forgiven through Thy abounding grace—
I find myself by hands familiar beckoned
  Unto my fitting place.

Some humble door among Thy many mansions,
  Some sheltering shade where sin and striving cease,
And flows forever through heaven's green expansions
  The river of Thy peace.

There, from the music round about me stealing,
  I fain would learn the new and holy song,
And find at last, beneath Thy trees of healing,
  The life for which I long.

* * *

Learning without wisdom is a load of books on an ass's back.
—Anonymous

THE AMERICAN BOY

Theodore Roosevelt

What we have a right to expect of the American boy is that he shall turn out to be a good American man. The boy can best become a good man by being a good boy—not a goody-goody boy, but just a plain good boy. I do not mean that he must love only the negative virtues; I mean that he must love the positive virtues also. "Good," in the largest sense, should include whatever is fine, straightforward, clean, brave, and manly. The best boys I know—the best men I know—are good at their studies or their business, fearless and stalwart, hated and feared by all that is wicked and depraved; incapable of submitting to wrongdoing, and equally incapable of being aught but tender to the weak and helpless. Of course the effect that a thoroughly manly, thoroughly straight and upright boy can have upon the companions of his own age, and upon those who are younger, is incalculable. If he is not thoroughly manly, then they will not respect him, and his good qualities will count for but little; while, of course, if he is mean, cruel or wicked, then his physical strength and force of mind merely make him so much the more objectionable a member of society. He can not do good work if he is not strong and does not try with his whole heart and soul to count in any contest; and his strength will be a curse to himself and to every one else if he does not have a thorough command over himself and over his own evil passions, and if he does not use his strength on the side of decency, justice and fair dealing.

In short, in life, as in a football game, the principle to follow is: Hit the line hard; don't foul and don't shirk, but hit the line hard.

SLEEP

William Shakespeare

Methought I heard a voice cry "Sleep no more!
Macbeth does murder sleep"—the innocent sleep,
Sleep that knits up the ravell'd sleave of care,
The death of each day's life, sore labour's bath,
Balm of hurt minds, great nature's second course,
Chief nourisher in life's feast.

(From Macbeth)

THE OWL AND THE PUSSY-CAT

Edward Lear

The Owl and the Pussy-cat went to sea
  In a beautiful pea-green boat:
They took some honey, and plenty of money
  Wrapped up in a five-pound note.
The Owl looked up to the stars above,
  And sang to a small guitar,
"O lovely Pussy, O Pussy, my love,
  What a beautiful Pussy you are!"

Pussy said to the Owl, "You elegant fowl,
  How charmingly sweet you sing!
Oh! let us be married; too long we have tarried:
  But what shall we do for a ring?"
They sailed away, for a year and a day,
  To the land where the bong-tree grows;
And there in a wood a Piggy-wig stood,
  With a ring at the end of his nose.

"Dear Pig, are you willing to sell for one shilling
  Your ring?" Said the Piggy, "I will."
So they took it away, and were married next day
  By the turkey who lives on the hill.
They dined on mice and slices of quince,
  Which they ate with a runcible spoon;
And hand in hand, on the edge of the sand,
  They danced by the light of the moon.

ABRAHAM LINCOLN ON DOING RIGHT

I do the very best I know how—the very best I can; and I mean to keep doing so until the end. If the end brings me out all right, what is said against me won't amount to anything. If the end brings me out wrong, ten angels swearing I was right would make no difference.

"O, WOMAN!"

Sir Walter Scott

O, Woman! in our hours of ease,
Uncertain, coy, and hard to please,
And variable as the shade
By the light quivering aspen made;
When pain and anguish wring the brow,
A ministering angel thou!

(From *Marmion*)

ST. FRANCIS AND POVERTY

Anonymous

(Translator: T. W. Arnold)

The wonderful servant and follower of Christ, to wit Saint Francis, to the end that he might in all things conform himself perfectly unto Christ, who, as the Gospel saith, sent His disciples forth by two and two unto all the cities and places where He was himself purposing to go; seeing that after the pattern of Christ he had gathered together twelve companions, sent them forth by two and two to preach throughout the world. And to give them an ensample of true obedience, he was himself the first to go, after the pattern of Christ who began to do before He taught. Wherefore having allotted to his companions the other parts of the world, he with Brother Masseo as his companion took the road that led to the land of France. And coming one day to a town sore hungered, they went according to the rule, begging their bread for the love of God; and Saint Francis went by one street, and Brother Masseo by another. But because Saint Francis was mean to look upon and small of stature, and was deemed thereby a vile beggar by whoso knew him not, he got by his begging naught save a few mouthfuls and scraps of dry bread; but to Brother Masseo, in that he was tall and fair of form, were given good pieces, large and in plenty, and of fresh bread.

When they had done their begging, they met together to eat in a place without the city, where was a fair fountain and, hard by, a fine, broad stone; upon the which each set the alms that he had begged. And Saint Francis, seeing that Brother Masseo's pieces of bread were more and finer and larger than his own, rejoiced with great joy, and said: "O Brother Masseo, we are not worthy of such vast treasure": and when he repeated many times these self-same words, Brother Masseo made answer: "Father, how can one speak of treasure where is such poverty and lack of all things whereof there is need? Here is nor cloth, nor knife, nor plate, nor porringer, nor house, nor table, nor man-servant, nor maid-servant." Quoth Saint Francis: "And this it is that I account vast treasure, wherein is no thing at all prepared by human hands, but whatsoe'er we have is given by God's own providence, as manifestly doth appear in the bread that we have begged, in the table of stone so fine, and in the fount so clear; wherefore I will that we pray unto God that He make us love with all our heart the treasure of holy poverty which is so noble, that thereunto did God Himself become a servitor."

(From The Little Flowers of St. Francis)

SONG

Hartley Coleridge

She is not fair to outward view
  As many maidens be,
Her loveliness I never knew
  Until she smiled on me;
O, then I saw her eye was bright,
A well of love, a spring of light!

But now her looks are coy and cold,
  To mine they ne'er reply,
And yet I cease not to behold
  The love-light in her eye:
Her very frowns are fairer far
Than smiles of other maidens are.

ARITHMETIC

Multiplication is vexation,
Division is as bad;
The Rule of Three doth puzzle me,
And Practice drives me mad.

THE DESPERADO

Anonymous

I'm a howler from the prairies of the West.
If you want to die with terror, look at me.
I'm chain-lightning—if I ain't may I be blessed.
I'm the snorter of the boundless prairie.

He's a killer and a hater!
He's the great annihilator!
He's a terror of the boundless prairie.

I'm the snoozer from the upper trail!
I'm the reveler in murder and in gore!
I can bust more Pullman coaches on the rail
Than any one who's worked the job before.

He's a snorter and a snoozer,
He's the great trunk-line abuser.
He's the man who puts the sleeper on the rail.

I'm the double-jawed hyena from the East,
I'm the blazing, bloody blizzard of the States.
I'm the celebrated slugger; I'm the Beast.
I can snatch a man bald-headed while he waits.

He's a double-jawed hyena!
He's the villain of the scena!
He can snatch a man bald-headed while he waits.

THE CHARIOT

Emily Dickinson

Because I could not stop for Death,
He kindly stopped for me;
The carriage held but just ourselves
And Immortality.

We slowly drove, he knew no haste,
And I had put away
My labor, and my leisure too,
For his civility.

We passed the school where children played
At wrestling in a ring;
We passed the field of grazing grain,
We passed the setting sun.

We paused before a house that seemed
A swelling of the ground;
The roof was scarcely visible,
The cornice but a mound.

Since then 'tis centuries; but each
Feels shorter than the day
I first surmised the horses' heads
Were toward eternity.

CATHERINE OF ARAGON'S LAST LETTER TO HENRY VIII

My most dear lord, king, and husband,

The hour of my death now approaching, I cannot choose but out of the love I bear you to advise you of your soul's health, which you ought to prefer before all considerations of the world or flesh whatsoever. For which yet you have cast me into many calamities, and yourself into many troubles. But I forgive you all; and pray God to do so likewise. For the rest I commend unto you Mary, our daughter, beseeching you to be a good father unto her, as I have heretofore desired. I must intreat you also, to respect my maids, and give them in marriage, which is not much, they being but three; and to all my other servants a year's pay, besides their due, lest otherwise they should be unprovided for; lastly I make this vow, that mine eyes desire you above all things. Farewell.

(1536)

* * *

Let us endeavor so to live that when we come to die even the undertaker will be sorry.—Mark Twain

KUBLA KHAN

Samuel Taylor Coleridge

In Xanadu did Kubla Khan
A stately pleasure-dome decree:
Where Alph, the sacred river, ran
Through caverns measureless to man
  Down to a sunless sea.
So twice five miles of fertile ground
With walls and towers were girdled round:
And here were gardens bright with sinuous rills,
Where blossom'd many an incense-bearing tree;
And here were forests ancient as the hills,
Enfolding sunny spots of greenery.

But oh! that deep romantic chasm which slanted
Down the green hill athwart a cedarn cover!
A savage place! as holy and enchanted
As e'er beneath a waning moon was haunted
By woman wailing for her demon-lover!
And from this chasm, with ceaseless turmoil seething,
As if this earth in fast thick pants were breathing,
A mighty fountain momently was forced;
Amid whose swift half-intermitted burst
Huge fragments vaulted like rebounding hail,
Or chaffy grain beneath the thresher's flail:
And 'mid these dancing rocks at once and ever
It flung up momently the sacred river.
Five miles meandering with a mazy motion
Through wood and dale the sacred river ran,
Then reach'd the caverns measureless to man,
And sank in tumult to a lifeless ocean:
And 'mid this tumult Kubla heard from far
Ancestral voices prophesying war!

  The shadow of the dome of pleasure
  Floated midway on the waves;
  Where was heard the mingled measure
  From the fountain and the caves.
It was a miracle of rare device,
A sunny pleasure-dome with caves of ice!

A damsel with a dulcimer
In a vision once I saw:
It was an Abyssinian maid,
And on her dulcimer she play'd,
Singing of Mount Abora.
Could I revive within me,
Her symphony and song,

To such a deep delight 'twould win me,
That with music loud and long,
I would build that dome in air,
That sunny dome! those caves of ice!
And all who heard should see them there,
And all should cry, Beware! Beware!
His flashing eyes, his floating hair!
Weave a circle round him thrice,
And close your eyes with holy dread,
For he on honey-dew hath fed,
And drunk the milk of Paradise.

A WAND'RING MINSTREL

W. S. Gilbert

A wand'ring minstrel I,
A thing of shreds and patches,
Of ballads, songs and snatches,
And dreamy lullaby!

My catalogue is long,
Through ev'ry passion ranging,
And to your humours changing
I tune my supple song!
I tune my supple song!

Are you in sentimental mood?
I'll sigh with you, Oh, sorrow!
On maiden's coldness do you brood?
I'll do so too, Oh, sorrow, sorrow!
I'll charm your willing ears
With songs of lovers' fears,
While sympathetic tears
My cheeks bedew, Oh, sorrow, sorrow!

But if patriotic sentiment is wanted,
I've patriotic ballads cut and dried;
For where'er our country's banner may be planted,
All other local banners are defied!
Our warriors, in serried ranks assembled,
Never quail, or they conceal it if they do,
And I shouldn't be surprised if nations trembled
Before the mighty troops, the troops of Titipu!

And if you call for a song of the sea,
We'll heave the capstan round,
With a yeo heave-ho, for the wind is free,
Her anchor's a-trip and her helm's a-lee,
Hurrah for the homeward bound!
Yeo heave-ho, hurrah for the homeward bound!

To lay aloft in a howling breeze
May tickle a landsman's taste,
But the happiest hour a sailor sees
Is when he's down at an inland town,
With his Nancy on his knees, yeo-ho!
And his arm around her waist!

A wand'ring minstrel I,
A thing of shreds and patches,
Of ballads, songs and snatches,
And dreamy lullaby,
And dreamy lulla-lullaby, lullaby!

THE ATLANTIC CHARTER

The President of the United States of America and the Prime Minister, Mr. Churchill, representing His Majesty's Government in the United Kingdom, being met together, deem it right to make known certain common principles in the national policies of their respective countries on which they base their hopes for a better future for the world.

FIRST, their countries seek no aggrandizement, territorial or other;

SECOND, they desire to see no territorial changes that do not accord with the freely expressed wishes of the peoples concerned;

THIRD, they respect the right of all peoples to choose the form of government under which they will live; and they wish to see sovereign rights and self-government restored to those who have been forcibly deprived of them;

FOURTH, they will endeavor, with due respect for their existing obligations, to further the enjoyment by all States, great or small, victor or vanquished, of access, on equal terms, to the trade and to the raw materials of the world which are needed for their economic prosperity;

FIFTH, they desire to bring about the fullest collaboration between all nations in the economic field with the object of securing, for all, improved labor standards, economic adjustment and social security;

SIXTH, after the final destruction of the Nazi tyranny, they hope to see established a peace which will afford to all nations the means of dwelling in safety within their own boundaries, and which will afford assurance that all the men in all the lands may live out their lives in freedom from fear and want;

SEVENTH, such a peace should enable all men to traverse the high seas and oceans without hindrance;

EIGHTH, they believe that all the nations of the world, for realistic as well as spiritual reasons, must come to the abandonment of the use of force. Since no future peace can be maintained if land, sea or air armaments continue to be employed by nations which threaten, or may threaten, aggression outside of their frontiers, they believe, pending the establishment of a wider and permanent system of general security, that the disarmament of such nations is essential. They will likewise aid and encourage all other practicable measures which will lighten for peace-loving peoples the crushing burden of armaments.

Franklin D. Roosevelt
Winston S. Churchill
(August, 1941)

GOD BE WITH YOU TILL WE MEET AGAIN

J. E. Rankin

God be with you till we meet again,
By his counsels guide, uphold you,
With his sheep securely fold you,
God be with you till we meet again.

Chorus:

Till we meet, till we meet,
Till we meet at Jesus' feet,
Till we meet, till we meet,
God be with you till we meet again.

God be with you till we meet again;
'Neath his wings protecting hide you;
Daily manna still provide you,
God be with you till we meet again.

God be with you till we meet again;
When life's perils thick confound you;
Put his arms unfailing round you,
God be with you till we meet again.

God be with you till we meet again;
Keep love's banner floating o'er you;
Smite death's threat'ning wave before you;
God be with you till we meet again.

LIBERTY AND INDEPENDENCE

July 4, 1776

Anonymous

There was tumult in the city,
In the quaint old Quaker town,
And the streets were rife with people
Pacing restless up and down;
People gathering at corners,
Where they whispered each to each,
And the sweat stood on their temples,
With the earnestness of speech.

As the bleak Atlantic currents
Lash the wild Newfoundland shore,
So they beat against the State House,
So they surged against the door;

And the mingling of their voices
  Made a harmony profound,
Till the quiet street of Chestnut
  Was all turbulent with sound.

"Will they do it?" "Dare they do it?"
  "Who is speaking?" "What's the news?"
"What of Adams?" "What of Sherman?"
  "Oh! God grant they won't refuse."
"Make some way there!" "Let me nearer!"
  "I am stifling!" "Stifle, then!
When a nation's life's at hazard,
  We've no time to think of men."
So they beat against the portal,
  Man and woman, maid and child;
And the July sun in heaven
  On the scene looked down and smiled.
The same sun that saw the Spartan
  Shed his patriot blood in vain,
Now beheld the soul of freedom,
  All unconquered rise again.

See! see! the dense crowd quivers
  Through all its lengthy line,
As the boy beside the portal
  Looks forth to give the sign;
With his little hands uplifted,
  Breezes dallying with his hair,
Hark! with deep, clear intonation
  Breaks his young voice on the air.

Hushed the people's swelling murmur,
  List the boy's exulting cry!
"Ring!" he shouts, "ring! grandpa,
  Ring! oh, ring for LIBERTY!"
Quickly at the given signal
  The old bellman lifts his hand,
Forth he sends the good news, making
  Iron music through the land.

How they shouted! what rejoicing!
  How the old bell shook the air,
Till the clang of freedom ruffled
  The calmly gliding Delaware.

How the bonfires and the torches
  Lighted up the night's repose,
And from flames, like fabled Phoenix,
  Our glorious liberty arose.

That old State House bell is silent,
  Hushed is now its clamorous tongue;
But the spirit it awakened
  Still is living—ever young;
And when we greet the smiling sunlight,
  On the fourth of each July,
We will ne'er forget the bellman,
  Who, betwixt the earth and sky,
Rang out loudly "INDEPENDENCE,"
  Which, please God, shall never die.

EPITAPH BENJAMIN FRANKLIN WROTE FOR HIMSELF

The Body
of
Benjamin Franklin, Printer
(Like the cover of an old book,
Its contents torn out,
And stripped of its lettering and gilding,)
Lies here food for worms.
Yet the work itself shall not be lost,
For it will (as he believes) appear once
more
In a new
And more beautiful Edition
Corrected and Amended
By
The Author

* * *

There are three kinds of lies: lies, damned lies, and statistics. —Variously attributed, among others to Disraeli, Henry Labouchère and Abraham Hewitt.

RED SKY AT MORNING

Gilbert Thomas

I drew the blind on Christmas Morn.
The sky was one wild riot of red.
Its glory told me Christ was born,
Yet filled my soul with dread.

Against the dawn's too radiant light,
There stood a solitary Tree.
Its naked arms were black as night,
And grim with prophecy.

EDWARD, EDWARD

Anonymous

"Why does your brand sae drop wi' blude,
Edward, Edward?
Why does your brand sae drop wi' blude,
And why sae sad gang ye, O?"—
"O I hae kill'd my hawk sae gude,
Mither, mither;
O I hae kill'd my hawk sae gude,
And I hae nae mair but he, O."

"Your hawk's blude was never sae red,
Edward, Edward;
Your hawk's blude was never sae red,
My dear son, I tell thee, O."—
"O I hae kill'd my red-roan steed,
Mither, mither;
O I hae kill'd my red-roan steed
That erst was sae fair and free, O."

"Your steed was auld, and ye hae got mair,
Edward, Edward;
Your steed was auld, and ye hae got mair,
Some other dule [1] ye dree,[2] O."

[1] Woe.
[2] Suffer.

"O I hae kill'd my father dear,
Mither, mither;
O I hae kill'd my father dear,
Alas, and wae is me, O!"

"And whatten penance will ye dree for that,
Edward, Edward?
Whatten penance will ye dree for that?
My dear son, now tell me, O."—
"I'll set my feet in yonder boat,
Mither, mither;
I'll set my feet in yonder boat,
And I'll fare over the sea, O."

"And what will ye do wi' your tow'rs and your ha',
Edward, Edward?
And what will ye do wi' your tow'rs and your ha',
That were sae fair to see, O?"—
"I'll let them stand till they doun fa',
Mither, mither;
I'll let them stand till they doun fa',
For here never mair maun I be, O."

"And what will ye leave to your bairns and your wife,
Edward, Edward?
And what will ye leave to your bairns and your wife,
When ye gang owre the sea, O."—
"The warld's room: let them beg through life,
Mither, mither;
The warld's room: let them beg through life;
For them never mair will I see, O."

"And what will ye leave to your ain mither, dear,
Edward, Edward?
And what will ye leave to your ain mither, dear,
My dear son, now tell me, O."—
"The curse of hell, frae me sall ye bear,
Mither, mither;
The curse of hell, frae me sall ye bear:
Sic counsels ye gave to me, O!"

OATH TAKEN BY NATURALIZED CITIZENS OF THE UNITED STATES

I hereby declare, on oath, that I absolutely and entirely renounce and abjure all allegiance and fidelity to any foreign prince, potentate, state, or sovereignty of whom or which I have heretofore been a subject or citizen; that I will support and defend the Constitution and laws of the United States of America against all enemies, foreign and domestic; that I will bear true faith and allegiance to the same; and that I take this obligation freely without any mental reservation or purpose of evasion; so help me God. In acknowledgment whereof I have hereunto affixed my signature.

THE LOVER'S RESOLUTION

George Wither

Shall I, wasting in despair,
Die because a woman's fair?
Or make pale my cheeks with care
'Cause another's rosy are?
Be she fairer than the day,
Or the flow'ry meads in May,
  If she think not well of me,
  What care I how fair she be?

Shall my silly heart be pined
'Cause I see a woman kind?
Or a well-disposèd nature
Joinèd with a lovely feature?
Be she meeker, kinder, than
Turtle-dove or pelican,
  If she be not so to me,
  What care I how kind she be?

Shall a woman's virtues move
Me to perish for her love?
Or her well-deservings known
Make me quite forget my own?

Be she with that goodness blest
Which may merit name of Best,
  If she be not such to me,
  What care I how good she be?

'Cause her fortune seems too high,
Shall I play the fool and die?
She that bears a noble mind,
If not outward helps she find,
Thinks what with them he would do
That without them dares her woo;
  And unless that mind I see,
  What care I how great she be?

Great, or good, or kind, or fair,
I will ne'er the more despair;
If she love me, this believe,
I will die ere she shall grieve;
If she slight me when I woo,
I can scorn and let her go;
  For if she be not for me,
  What care I for whom she be?

MY FAMILIAR

John Godfrey Saxe

Again I hear that creaking step—
  He's rapping at the door!
Too well I know the boding sound
  That ushers in a bore.
I do not tremble when I meet
  The stoutest of my foes,
But Heaven defend me from the friend
  Who comes—but never goes!

He drops into my easy-chair,
  And asks about the news;
He peers into my manuscript,
  And gives his candid views;

He tells me where he likes the line,
And where he's forced to grieve;
He takes the strangest liberties—
But never takes his leave!

He reads my daily paper through
Before I've seen a word;
He scans the lyric (that I wrote)
And thinks it quite absurd;
He calmly smokes my last cigar,
And coolly asks for more;
He opens everything he sees—
Except the entry door!

He talks about his fragile health,
And tells me of the pains
He suffers from a score of ills
Of which he ne'er complains;
And how he struggled once with death
To keep the fiend at bay;
On themes like those away he goes—
But never goes away!

He tells me of the carping words
Some shallow critic wrote;
And every precious paragraph
Familiarly can quote;
He thinks the writer did me wrong;
He'd like to run him through!
He says a thousand pleasant things—
But never says, "Adieu!"

Whene'er he comes, that dreadful man,
Disguise it as I may,
I know that, like an Autumn rain,
He'll last throughout the day.
In vain I speak of urgent tasks;
In vain I scowl and pout;
A frown is no extinguisher—
It does not put him out!

I mean to take the knocker off,
  Put crape upon the door,
Or hint to John that I am gone
  To stay a month or more.
I do not tremble when I meet
  The stoutest of my foes,
But Heaven defend me from the friend
  Who never, never goes!

THE PURPLE COW

Gelett Burgess

Reflections on a Mythic Beast,
Who's Quite Remarkable, at Least.

I never saw a Purple Cow,
I never Hope to See One.
But I can Tell You Anyhow,
I'd rather See than Be One.

Years later Mr. Burgess added to the plethora of parodies of "The Purple Cow" by writing "Cinq Ans Après":

(Confession: and a Portrait, too,
Upon a Background that I Rue!)

Ah, Yes! I Wrote the Purple Cow—
I'm Sorry, now, I Wrote It!
But I can Tell You Anyhow,
I'll Kill You if You Quote It!

THE FORGOTTEN MAN

William Graham Sumner

Wealth comes from production, and all that the wrangling grabbers, loafers, and robbers get to deal with comes from somebody's toil and sacrifice. Who, then, is he who provides it all? Go and find him, and you will have once more before you the Forgotten Man. You will find him hard at work because he has a great many to support. Nature has done a great deal for him in giving him a fertile soil and an excellent climate, and he wonders why it is that, after all, his scale of comfort is so moderate. He has to get out of the soil enough to pay all his taxes, and that means the cost of all the jobs and the fund for all the plunder. The Forgotten Man is delving away in patient industry, supporting his family, paying his taxes, casting his vote, supporting the church and school, reading his newspaper, and cheering for the politician of his admiration, but he is the only one for whom there is no provision in the great scramble and the big divide. Such is the Forgotten Man. He works, he votes, generally he prays—but he always pays—yes, above all, he pays.

THE USES OF ADVERSITY

William Shakespeare

Now, my co-mates and brothers in exile,
Hath not old custom made this life more sweet
Than that of painted pomp? Are not these woods
More free from peril than the envious court?
Here feel we but the penalty of Adam,
The season's difference, as the icy fang
And churlish chiding of the winter's wind,
Which, when it bites and blows upon my body,
Even till I shrink with cold, I smile and say
"This is no flattery: these are counsellors
That feelingly persuade me what I am."
Sweet are the uses of adversity,
Which, like the toad, ugly and venomous,
Wears yet a precious jewel in his head,
And this our life exempt from public haunt
Finds tongues in trees, books in the running brooks,
Sermons in stones and good in every thing.
I would not change it.

(From As You Like It)

OLD BLACK JOE

Stephen C. Foster

Gone are the days when my heart was young and gay,
Gone are my friends from the cotton fields away;
Gone from the earth to a better land I know,
I hear their gentle voices calling "Old Black Joe."

Chorus:
I'm coming, I'm coming, for my head is bending low;
I hear their gentle voices calling "Old Black Joe."

Why do I weep when my heart should feel no pain?
Why do I sigh that my friends come not again?
Grieving for forms now departed long ago,
I hear their gentle voices calling "Old Black Joe."

Where are the hearts once so happy and so free?
The children so dear that I held upon my knee?
Gone to the shore where my soul has longed to go,
I hear their gentle voices calling "Old Black Joe."

EXCHANGE OF LETTERS BETWEEN LINCOLN AND McCLELLAN

President Abraham Lincoln
Washington, D. C.
We have just captured six cows. What shall we do with them?
George B. McClellan

General George B. McClellan
Army of the Potomac
As to the six cows captured—milk them.
A. Lincoln

* * *

The Puritans hated bear-baiting, not because it gave pain to the bear, but because it gave pleasure to the spectators.—Thomas Babington Macaulay

A HEALTH

Edward Coote Pinkney

I fill this cup to one made up of loveliness alone,
A woman, of her gentle sex the seeming paragon;
To whom the better elements and kindly stars have given
A form so fair, that, like the air, 'tis less of earth than heaven.

Her every tone is music's own, like those of morning birds,
And something more than melody dwells ever in her words;
The coinage of her heart are they, and from her lips each flows
As one may see the burthened bee forth issue from the rose.

Affections are as thoughts to her, the measure of her hours;
Her feelings have the fragrancy, the freshness of young flowers;
And lovely passions, changing oft, so fill her, she appears
The image of themselves by turns,—the idol of past years!

Of her bright face one glance will trace a picture on the brain,
And of her voice in echoing hearts a sound must long remain,
But memory such as mine of her so very much endears,
When death is nigh my latest sigh will not be life's but hers.

I fill this cup to one made up of loveliness alone,
A woman, of her gentle sex the seeming paragon—
Her health! and would on earth there stood some more of such a
  frame,
That life might be all poetry, and weariness a name.

WHEN WE TWO PARTED

Lord Byron

When we two parted
  In silence and tears,
Half broken-hearted
  To sever for years,
Pale grew thy cheek and cold,
  Colder thy kiss;
Truly that hour foretold
  Sorrow to this.

The dew of the morning
  Sunk chill on my brow—
It felt like the warning
  Of what I feel now.
Thy vows are all broken,
  And light is thy fame:
I hear thy name spoken,
  And share in its shame.

They name thee before me,
  A knell to mine ear;
A shudder comes o'er me—
  Why wert thou so dear?
They know not I knew thee,
  Who knew thee too well:
Long, long shall I rue thee,
  Too deeply to tell.

In secret we met—
  In silence I grieve,
That thy heart could forget,
  Thy spirit deceive.
If I should meet thee
  After long years,
How should I greet thee?
  With silence and tears.

"THE RIGHT IS MORE PRECIOUS THAN PEACE"

Woodrow Wilson

It is a fearful thing to lead this great peaceful people into war, into the most terrible and disastrous of wars, civilization itself seeming to be in the balance. But the right is more precious than peace, and we shall fight for the things which we have always carried nearest our hearts—for democracy, for the right of those who submit to authority to have a voice in their own governments, for the rights and liberties of small nations, for a universal dominion of right by such a concert of free peoples as shall bring peace and safety to all nations and make the world itself at last free. To such a task we can dedicate our lives and our fortunes, everything that we are and everything that we have, with the pride of those who know that the day has come when America is privileged to spend her blood and her might for the principles that gave her birth and the peace which she has treasured. God helping her, she can do no other.

(From a message to Congress, April 2, 1917, asking for Declaration of War Against Germany)

CATO'S SOLILOQUY

Joseph Addison

It must be so—Plato, thou reason'st well—
Else whence this pleasing hope, this fond desire,
This longing after immortality?
Or whence this secret dread, and inward horror
Of falling into nought? Why shrinks the Soul
Back on herself, and startles at destruction?
'Tis the Divinity, that stirs within us;
'Tis Heav'n itself, that points out a hereafter,
And intimates eternity to man.
Eternity! thou pleasing, dreadful thought!
Through what variety of untried being,
Through what new scenes and changes must we pass!
The wide, th' unbounded prospect lies before me;
But shadows, clouds, and darkness rest upon it.
Here will I hold. If there's a power above us,
(And that there is, all Nature cries aloud
Through all her works,) He must delight in virtue;
And that which He delights in must be happy.
But when or where? This world was made for Caesar.
I'm weary of conjectures—this must end 'em.
  Thus am I doubly arm'd—my death and life,
My bane and antidote are both before me.
This in a moment brings me to an end;
But this informs me I shall never die.
The Soul, secured in her existence, smiles
At the drawn dagger, and defies its point;
The stars shall fade away, the Sun himself
Grow dim with age, and Nature, sink in years;
But thou shalt flourish in immortal youth,
Unhurt amidst the war of elements,
The wreck of matter and the crash of worlds.

(From Cato, Act 5, Sc. 1)

From IS LIFE WORTH LIVING?

Alfred Austin

Is life worth living? Yes, so long
  As there is wrong to right,
Wail of the weak against the strong,
  Or tyranny to fight;
Long as there lingers gloom to chase,
  Or streaming tear to dry,
One kindred woe, one sorrowing face
  That smiles as we draw nigh;
Long as a tale of anguish swells
  The heart, and lids grow wet,
And at the sound of Christmas bells
  We pardon and forget;
So long as Faith with Freedom reigns,
  And loyal Hope survives,
And gracious Charity remains
  To leaven lowly lives;
While there is one untrodden tract
  For Intellect or Will,
And men are free to think and act
  Life is worth living still.

ROBINSON CRUSOE DISCOVERS FRIDAY'S FOOTPRINT

Daniel Defoe

It happened one day, about noon, going towards my boat, I was exceedingly surprised with the print of a man's naked foot on the shore, which was very plain to be seen in the sand. I stood like one thunderstruck, or as if I had seen an apparition. I listened, I looked round me, I could hear nothing, nor see anything. I went up to a rising ground, to look farther. I went up the shore, and down the shore, but it was all one; I could see no other impression but that one. I went to it again to see if there were any more, and to observe if it might not be my fancy; but there was no room for that, for there was exactly the very print of a foot—toes, heel and every part of a foot. How it came thither I knew not, nor could in the least imagine. But after innumerable fluttering thoughts, like a man perfectly confused and out of myself, I came home to my fortification, not feeling, as we say, the ground I went on, but terrified to the last degree, looking behind me at every two or three steps, mistaking every bush and tree, and fancying every stump at a distance to be a man; nor is it possible to describe how many various shapes affrighted imagination represented things to me in, how many wild ideas were found every moment in my fancy, and what strange, unaccountable whimsies came into my thought by the way.

When I came to my castle, for so I think I called it ever after this, I fled into it like one pursued. Whether I went over by the ladder, as first contrived, or went in at the hole in the rock, which I called a door, I cannot remember; no, nor could I remember the next morning, for never frighted hare fled to cover, or fox to earth, with more terror of mind than I to this retreat.

(From Robinson Crusoe)

WANTED, A MINISTER'S WIFE

Anonymous

At length we have settled a pastor:
  I am sure I cannot tell why
The people should grow so restless,
  Or candidates grow so shy;
But after a two years searching
  For the "smartest" man in the land,
In a fit of desperation
  We took the nearest at hand.

And really, he answers nicely
  To "fill up the gap," you know,
To "run the machine," and "bring up arrears,"
  And make things generally go;
He has a few little failings,
  His sermons are common-place quite,
But his manner is very charming,
  And his teeth are perfectly white.

And so, of all the "dear people,"
  Not one in a hundred complains,
For beauty and grace of manner

Are so much better than *brains.*
But the parish have all concluded
He needs a partner for life,
To shine a gem in the parlor:
"Wanted, a minister's wife!"

Wanted, a perfect lady,
Delicate, gentle, refined,
With every beauty of person,
And every endowment of mind;
Fitted by early culture
To move in fashionable life—
Please notice our advertisement:
"Wanted," *etc.*

Wanted, a thoroughbred worker,
Who well to her household looks
(Shall we see our money wasted
By extravagant Irish cooks?);
Who cuts the daily expenses
With economy sharp as a knife;
And washes and scrubs in the kitchen:
"Wanted," *etc.*

A very "domestic person,"
To callers she must not be "out,"
It has such a bad appearance
For her to be gadding about:
Only to visit the parish
Every year of her life,
And attend the funerals and weddings:
"Wanted," *etc.*

To conduct the "ladies' meeting,"
The "sewing circle" attend;
And when we work for the soldiers,
Her ready assistance to lend.
To clothe the destitute children
When sorrow and want are rife,
And look-up Sunday-school scholars:
"Wanted," *etc.*

Careful to entertain strangers,
  Traveling agents, and "such,"
Of this kind of angel visits,
  The deacons have had so much
As to prove a perfect nuisance,
  And hope these plagues of their life
Can soon be sent to the parson's:
  "Wanted," *etc.*

A perfect pattern of prudence,
  Than all others spending less,
But never disgracing the parish
  By looking shabby in dress;
Playing the organ on Sunday
  Would aid our laudable life
To save the society money:
  "Wanted," *etc.*

And when we have found the person,
  We hope, by working the two,
To lift our debt, and build a new church,
  Then we shall know what to do;
For they will be worn and weary,
  And we'll advertise: "Wanted,
  A minister and his wife!"

I WANT A GIRL *
(Just Like the Girl That Married Dear Old Dad)

Will Dillon and Harry Von Tilzer

When I was a boy my mother often said to me,
Get married, boy, and see how happy you will be.
I have looked all over, but no girl can I find,
Who seems to be just like the little girl I have in mind;
I will have to look around until the right one I have found.

Chorus:

I want a girl, just like the girl that married dear old Dad,
She was a pearl and the only girl that Daddy ever had,
A good old-fashioned girl with heart so true,
One who loves nobody else but you.
I want a girl, just like the girl that married dear old Dad.

By the old mill stream there sits a couple old and gray,
Though years have rolled away, their hearts are young to-day;
Mother dear looks up at Dad with love light in her eye,
He steals a kiss, a fond embrace, while ev'ning breezes sigh,
They're as happy as can be, so that's the kind of love for me.

THE AMERICAN CREED

William Tyler Page

I believe in the United States of America as a government of the people, for the people, by the people; whose just powers are derived from the consent of the governed; a democracy in a republic; a sovereign Nation of many sovereign states; a perfect union, one and inseparable; established upon those principles of freedom, equality, justice, and humanity for which American patriots sacrificed their lives and fortunes.

I therefore believe it is my duty to my country to love it; to support its Constitution; to obey its laws; to respect its flag; and to defend it against all enemies.

DO THEY THINK OF ME AT HOME

Joseph Edward Carpenter

Do they think of me at home,
  Do they ever think of me?
I who shared their every grief,
  I who mingled in their glee?
Have their hearts grown cold and strange,
  To the one now doomed to roam?

I would give the world to know,
  Do they think of me at home?
I would give the world to know,
  Do they think of me at home?

Do they think of me at eve,
  Of the songs I used to sing?
Is the harp I struck untouched,
  Does a stranger wake the string?
Will no kind, forgiving word
  Come across the raging foam?
Shall I never cease to sigh,
  "Do they think of me at home?"
Shall I never cease to sigh,
  "Do they think of me at home?"

Do they think of how I loved
  In my happy, early days?
Do they think of him who came
  But could never win their praise?
I am happy by his side,
  And from mine he'll never roam,
But my heart will sadly ask,
  "Do they think of me at home?"
But my heart will sadly ask,
  "Do they think of me at home?"

CODA

Dorothy Parker

There's little in taking or giving,
There's little in water or wine;
This living, this living, this living
Was never a project of mine.
Oh, hard is the struggle, and sparse is
The gain of the one at the top,
For art is a form of catharsis,
And love is a permanent flop,
And work is the province of cattle,
And rest's for a clam in a shell,
So I'm thinking of throwing the battle—
Would you kindly direct me to hell?

DREAM-PEDLARY

Thomas Lovell Beddoes

If there were dreams to sell,
  What would you buy?
Some cost a passing bell;
  Some a light sigh,
That shakes from Life's fresh crown
Only a rose-leaf down.

If there were dreams to sell,
Merry and sad to tell,
And the crier rang the bell,
  What would you buy?

A cottage lone and still,
  With bowers nigh,
Shadowy, my woes to still,
  Until I die.
Such pearl from Life's fresh crown
Fain would I shake me down,
Were dreams to have at will,
This would best heal my ill,
  This would I buy.

A BALLOT

Benjamin R. Tucker

What is a ballot? It is neither more nor less than a paper representative of the bayonet, the billy, and the bullet. It is a labor-saving device for ascertaining on which side force lies and bowing to the inevitable. The voice of the majority saves bloodshed, but it is no less the arbitrament of force than is the decree of the most absolute of despots backed by the most powerful of armies.

* * *

Men heap together the mistakes of their lives, and create a monster they call Destiny.—Oliver Wendell Holmes

I DREAMT I DWELT IN MARBLE HALLS

Alfred Bunn

I dreamt that I dwelt in marble halls,
With vassals and serfs at my side,
And of all who assembled within those walls
That I was the hope and the pride.
I had riches too great to count; could boast
Of a high ancestral name;
But I also dreamt, which pleased me most,
That you loved me still the same.

I dreamt that suitors sought my hand;
That knights upon bended knees,
And with vow no maiden heart could withstand,
They pledged their faith to me,
And I dreamt that one of that noble host
Came forth my hand to claim;
But I also dreamt, which charmed me most,
That you loved me still the same.

REMEMBER

Christina Georgina Rossetti

Remember me when I am gone away,
Gone far away into the silent land;
When you can no more hold me by the hand,
Nor I half turn to go yet turning stay.
Remember me when no more day by day
You tell me of our future that you plann'd:
Only remember me; you understand
It will be late to counsel then or pray.
Yet if you should forget me for a while
And afterwards remember, do not grieve:
For if the darkness and corruption leave
A vestige of the thoughts that once I had,
Better by far you should forget and smile
Than that you should remember and be sad.

SHAKESPEARE

Robert G. Ingersoll

He exceeded all the sons of men in the splendor of his imagination. To him the whole world paid tribute, and Nature poured her treasures at his feet. In him all races lived again, and even those to be were pictured in his brain.

He was a man of imagination—that is to say, of genius, and having seen a leaf, and a drop of water, he could construct the forests, the rivers, and the seas. In his presence all the cataracts would fall and foam, the mists rise, the clouds form and float.

If Shakespeare knew one fact, he knew its kindred and its neighbors. Looking at a coat of mail, he instantly imagined the society, the conditions, that produced it and what it, in turn, produced. He saw the castle, the moat, the drawbridge, the lady in the tower, and the knightly lover spurring across the plain. He saw the bold baron and the rude retainer, the trampled serf, and all the glory and the grief of feudal life.

He lived the life of all. . . .

He lived all lives, and through his blood and brain there crept the shadow and the chill of every death, and his soul, like Mazeppa, was lashed naked to the wild horse of every fear and love and hate.

The Imagination had a stage in Shakespeare's brain, whereon were set all the scenes that lie between the morn of laughter and the night of tears, and where his players bodied forth the false and true, the joys and griefs, the careless shallows and the tragic deeps of universal life.

From Shakespeare's brain there poured a Niagara of gems spanned by Fancy's seven-hued arch. He was as many-sided as clouds are many-formed. To him giving was hoarding, sowing was harvest; and waste itself the source of wealth. Within his marvelous mind were the fruits of all thought past, the seeds of all to be. As a drop of dew contains the image of the earth and sky, so all there is of life was mirrored forth in Shakespeare's brain.

Shakespeare was an intellectual ocean, whose waves touched all the shores of thought; within which were all the tides and waves of destiny and will; over which swept all the storms of fate, ambition, and revenge; upon which fell the gloom and darkness of despair and death and all the sunlight of content and love, and within which was the inverted sky, lit with the eternal stars—an intellectual ocean—towards which all rivers ran, and from which now the isles and continents of thought receive their dew and rain.

A BAKER'S DUZZEN UV WIZE SAWZ

Edward Rowland Sill

Them ez wants, must choose.
Them ez hez, most lose.
Them ez knows, won't blab.
Them ez guesses, will gab.
Them ez borrows, sorrows.
Them ez lends, spends.
Them ez gives, lives.
Them ez keeps dark, is deep.
Them ez kin earn, kin keep.
Them ez aims, hits.
Them ez hez, gits.
Them ez waits, win.
Them ez *will, kin.*

MY MOTHER'S HANDS

Anonymous

Such beautiful, beautiful hands!
They're neither white nor small;
And you, I know, would scarcely think
That they are fair at all.
I've looked on hands whose form and hue
A sculptor's dream might be;
Yet are those aged, wrinkled hands
More beautiful to me.

Such beautiful, beautiful hands!
Though heart were weary and sad,
Those patient hands kept toiling on,
That the children might be glad.
I always weep, as, looking back
To childhood's distant day,
I think how those hands rested not
When mine were at their play.

Such beautiful, beautiful hands!
They're growing feeble now,

For time and pain have left their mark
  On hands and heart and brow.
Alas! alas! the nearing time,
  And the sad, sad day to me,
When 'neath the daisies, out of sight,
  These hands will folded be.

But oh! beyond this shadow land,
  Where all is bright and fair,
I know full well these dear old hands
  Will palms of victory bear;
Where crystal streams through endless years
  Flow over golden sands,
And where the old grow young again,
  I'll clasp my mother's hands.

LINCOLN'S LETTER TO GENERAL HOOKER

January 26, 1863

General:

I have placed you at the head of the Army of the Potomac. Of course I have done this upon what appears to me to be sufficient reasons, and yet I think it best for you to know that there are some things in regard to which I am not quite satisfied with you. I believe you to be a brave and skillful soldier, which of course I like. I also believe you do not mix politics with your profession, in which you are right. You have confidence in yourself, which is a valuable if not an indispensable quality. You are ambitious, which, within reasonable bounds, does good rather than harm; but I think that during General Burnside's command of the army you have taken counsel of your ambition and thwarted him as much as you could, in which you did a great wrong to the country and to a meritorious and honorable brother officer. I have heard, in such a way as to believe it, of your recently saying that both the Army and the Government needed a dictator. Of course it was not for this, but in spite of it, that I have given you the command. Only those generals who gain successes can set up dictators. What I now ask of you is military success, and I will risk the dictatorship. The Government will support you to the utmost of its ability, which is neither more nor less than it has done and will do for all commanders. I much fear that the spirit which you have aided to infuse into the army, of criticizing their commander and withholding confidence from him, will now turn upon you. I shall assist you as far as I can to put it down. Neither you nor Napoleon, if he were alive again, could get any good out of an army while such a spirit prevails in it. And now beware of rashness. Beware of rashness, but with energy and sleepless vigilance go forward and give us victories.

Yours, very truly,
A. Lincoln

UNDER THE GREENWOOD TREE

William Shakespeare

Under the greenwood tree
Who loves to lie with me,
And turn his merry note
Unto the sweet bird's throat,
Come hither, come hither, come hither:
Here shall he see
No enemy
But winter and rough weather.
(From As You Like It)

TO OUR LADY

Mary Dixon Thayer

Lovely Lady dressed in blue—
Teach me how to pray!
God was just your little Boy,
Tell me what to say!
Did you lift Him up, sometimes,
Gently, on your knee?
Did you sing to Him the way
Mother does to me?
Did you hold His hand at night?
Did you ever try
Telling stories of the world?

O! And did He cry?
Do you really think He cares
If I tell Him things—
Little things that happen? And
Do the Angels' wings
Make a noise? And can He hear
Me if I speak low?
Does He understand me now?
Tell me—for you know!
Lovely Lady dressed in blue,
Teach me how to pray!
God was just your little Boy,
And you know the way.

THE LAST MINSTREL

Sir Walter Scott

The way was long, the wind was cold,
The Minstrel was infirm and old;
His withered cheek, and tresses grey,
Seemed to have known a better day;
The harp, his sole remaining joy,
Was carried by an orphan boy.
The last of all the Bards was he,
Who sung of Border chivalry;
For, welladay! their date was fled,
His tuneful brethren all were dead;
And he, neglected and oppressed,
Wished to be with them, and at rest.
No more on prancing palfrey borne,
He carolled, light as lark at morn;
No longer courted and caressed,
High placed in hall, a welcome guest,
He poured to lord and lady gay
The unpremeditated lay:
Old times were changed, old manners gone;
A stranger filled the Stuarts' throne;
The bigots of the iron time
Had called his harmless art a crime.
A wandering Harper, scorned and poor,

He begged his bread from door to door,
And tuned, to please a peasant's ear,
The harp a king had loved to hear.
(From The Lay of the Last Minstrel)

A LONDON WAIF

Thomas De Quincey

Towards nightfall I went down to Greek Street, and found, on taking possession of my new quarters, that the house already contained one single inmate,—a poor, friendless child, apparently ten years old; but she seemed hunger-bitten; and sufferings of that sort often make children look older than they are. From this forlorn child I learned that she had slept and lived there alone for some time before I came; and great joy the poor creature expressed when she found that I was in future to be her companion through the hours of darkness. The house could hardly be called large—that is, it was not large on each separate storey; but having four storeys in all, it was large enough to impress vividly the sense of its echoing loneliness; and from the want of furniture, the noise of the rats made a prodigious uproar on the staircase and hall; so that, amidst the real fleshly ills of cold and hunger, the forsaken child had found leisure to suffer still more from the self-created one of ghosts. Against these enemies I could promise her protection; human companionship was in itself protection; but of other and more needful aid I had, alas! but little to offer. We lay upon the floor, with a bundle of law-papers for a pillow, but with no other covering than a large horseman's cloak; afterwards, however, we discovered in a garret an old sofa-cover, a small piece of rug, and some fragments of other articles, which added a little to our comfort. The poor child crept close to me for warmth, and for security against her ghostly enemies. When I was not more than usually ill, I took her into my arms, so that, in general, she was tolerably warm, and often slept when I could not. . . .

Whether this child were an illegitimate daughter of Mr. Brunnell, or only a servant, I could not ascertain; she did not herself know; but certainly she was treated altogether as a menial servant. No sooner did Mr. Brunnell make his appearance than she went below-stairs, brushed his shoes, coat, etc.; and, except when she was summoned to run upon some errand, she never emerged from the dismal Tartarus of the kitchens to the upper air until my welcome knock towards nightfall called up her little trembling footsteps to the front-door. Of her life during the day-time, however, I knew little but what I gathered from her own account at night; for, as soon as the hours of business commenced, I saw that my absence would be acceptable; and, in general, therefore, I went off and sat in the parks or elsewhere until the approach of twilight.

(From Confessions of an Opium-Eater)

SONNET ON CHILLON

Lord Byron

Eternal Spirit of the chainless Mind!
  Brightest in dungeons, Liberty! thou art,
  For there thy habitation is the heart—
The heart which love of thee alone can bind;
And when thy sons to fetters are consign'd—
  To fetters, and the damp vault's dayless gloom,
  Their country conquers with their martyrdom,
And Freedom's fame finds wings on every wind.
Chillon! thy prison is a holy place,
  And thy sad floor an altar—for 'twas trod,
Until his very steps have left a trace
  Worn, as if thy cold pavement were a sod,
By Bonnivard!—May none those marks efface!
  For they appeal from tyranny to God.

THE BANKS O' DOON

Robert Burns

Ye banks and braes o' bonnie Doon,
  How can be bloom sae fresh and fair!
How can ye chant, ye little birds,
  And I sae weary fu' o' care!
Thou'lt break my heart, thou warbling bird,
  That wantons thro' the flowering thorn:
Thou minds me o' departed joys,
  Departed—never to return.

Thou'lt break my heart, thou bonnie bird,
  That sings beside thy mate,
For sae I sat, and sae I sang,
  And wist na o' my fate.
Aft hae I rov'd by bonnie Doon,
  To see the rose and woodbine twine;
And ilka bird sang o' its luve,
  And fondly sae did I o' mine.

Wi' lightsome heart I pu'd a rose,
  Fu' sweet upon its thorny tree;
And my fause luver stole my rose,
  But ah! he left the thorn wi' me.
Wi' lightsome heart I pu'd a rose
  Upon a morn in June;
And sae I flourish'd on the morn,
  And sae was pu'd on noon.

ON CONSISTENCY

Ralph Waldo Emerson

A foolish consistency is the hobgoblin of little minds, adored by little statesmen and philosophers and divines. With consistency a great soul has simply nothing to do. He may as well concern himself with his shadow on the wall. Out upon your guarded lips! Sew them up with pack thread, do. Else, if you would be a man, speak what you think today in words as hard as cannon balls, and tomorrow speak what tomorrow thinks in hard words again, though it contradict everything you said today. . . . Fear never but what you shall be consistent in whatever variety of actions, so they be each honest and natural in their hour. For of one will, the actions will be harmonious, however unlike they seem. These varieties are lost sight of when seen at a little distance, at a little height of thought. One tendency unites them all. The voyage of the best ship is a zigzag line of a hundred tacks. This is only a microscopic criticism. See the line from a sufficient distance, and it straightens itself to the average tendency, your genuine action will explain itself and will explain your other genuine actions.

(From the essay, Self-Reliance)

ALL GOD'S CHILLUN GOT WINGS

Anonymous

I got a robe, you got a robe,
All o' God's Chillun got a robe.
When I get to heab'n I'm goin' to put on my robe,
I'm goin' to shout all ovah God's Heab'n, Heab'n, Heab'n.
Ev'rybody talkin' bout heab'n ain't goin' dere;
Heab'n, Heab'n, I'm goin' to shout all ovah God's Heab'n.

I got-a wings, you got-a wings,
All o' God's Chillun got-a wings.
When I get to heab'n I'm goin' to put on my wings,
I'm goin' to fly all ovah God's Heab'n, Heab'n, Heab'n,
Ev'rybody talkin' bout heab'n ain't goin' dere;
Heab'n, Heab'n, I'm goin' to fly all ovah God's Heab'n.

I got a harp, you got a harp,
All o' God's Chillun got harp.
When I get to heab'n I'm goin' to take up my harp,
I'm goin' to play all ovah God's Heab'n, Heab'n, Heab'n,
Ev'rybody talkin' bout heab'n ain't goin' dere;
Heab'n, Heab'n, I'm goin' to play all ovah God's Heab'n.

I got shoes, you got shoes,
All o' God's Chillun got shoes,
When I get to heab'n I'm goin' to put on my shoes,
I'm goin' to walk all ovah God's Heab'n, Heab'n, Heab'n,
Ev'rybody talkin' bout heab'n ain't goin' dere;
Heab'n, Heab'n, I'm goin' to walk all ovah God's Heab'n,
I'm goin' to walk all ovah, goin' to talk all ovah God's Heab'n,

HIGH FLIGHT

John Gillespie Magee, Jr.

Oh! I have slipped the surly bonds of Earth
And danced the skies on laughter-silvered wings;
Sunward I've climbed, and joined the tumbling mirth
Of sun-split clouds—and done a hundred things
You have not dreamed of—wheeled and soared and swung

High in the sunlit silence. Hov'ring there,
I've chased the shouting wind along, and flung
My eager craft through footless halls of air. . . .

Up, up the long, delirious, burning blue
I've topped the wind-swept heights with easy grace,
Where never lark, or even eagle, flew;
And, while with silent, lifting mind I've trod
The high untrespassed sanctity of space,
Put out my hand, and touched the face of God.

(Written by a 19-year-old American volunteer with the Royal Canadian Air Force, who was killed in training December 11, 1941)

AWAY IN A MANGER

Martin Luther

Away in a manger, no crib for a bed,
The little Lord Jesus laid down His sweet head.
The stars in the sky looked down where He lay,
The little Lord Jesus, asleep on the hay.

The cattle are lowing, the Baby awakes,
But little Lord Jesus, no crying He makes.
I love Thee, Lord Jesus, look down from the sky,
And stay by my cradle till morning is nigh.

Be near me, Lord Jesus, I ask Thee to stay
Close by me for ever, and love me, I pray.
Bless all the dear children in Thy tender care,
And fit us for heaven to live with Thee there.

SO LONG, SON

Howard Vincent O'Brien

January 8, 1942.

There was no band, no flags, no ceremonial. It wasn't even dramatic. A car honked outside and he said, "Well, I guess that's for me." He picked up his little bag, and his mother said, "You haven't forgotten your gloves?"

He kissed his mother, and held out his hand to me. "Well, so long," he said. I took his hand but all I could say was "Good luck!"

The door slammed and that was that—another boy gone to war.

I had advised waiting for the draft—waiting at least until he was required to register. I had pointed out that he was not yet of age. He had smiled at that, and assured me that his mind was made up. He wanted peace, he said. Without peace, what good was living?

There was finality in the way he said this—a finality at once grim and gentle. I said no more about waiting.

After the door closed behind him I went upstairs. I went to what had been his room. It was in worse chaos than usual. His bureau was littered—an incredible collection of things, letters, keys, invitations to parties he would not attend.

Clothing was scattered about—dancing pumps, a tennis racket, his collection of phonograph records, his trumpet gleaming in its case.

I went then to my room. On the wall was a picture of a little boy, his toothless grin framed in tawny curls—the same boy who had just taken my hand and said, "Well, so long."

Not much time, I thought, between the making of that picture and the slamming of the front door. Not much more than a decade.

Suddenly a queer thing happened. Objects came alive, whispered to me. The house was full of soft voices. They led me up to the attic—to a box of toy soldiers, a broken music rack, a football helmet, a homemade guitar, schoolbooks, class pictures, a stamp album, a penny bank with the lid pried off . . . ancient history, long hidden under dust.

The voices led me on to a filing case and a folder stuffed with pages and report cards, letters, among them the wail of an exasperated teacher: "Though he looks like an angel . . ." telegrams, passports, a baptismal certificate, a ribbon won in a track meet, faded photographs (one taken on the memorable first day of long pants), a bit of golden hair.

I sat down and thought how time had flown. Why, it was only yesterday when I held him on my arms! That, somehow, made me remember all the scoldings I had given him, the preachments, the exhortations to virtue and wisdom I did not myself possess. . . .

I thought, too, of that last inarticulate "good luck," that last perfunctory handclasp; and I wished that I had somehow been able to tell him how much I really loved him. Had he perhaps penetrated my brusque reserve? Had he perhaps guessed what was in my heart?

And then I thought, what fools we are with our children—always plotting what we shall make of them, always planning for a future that never comes, always intent on what they may be, never accepting what they are!

Well, curlyhead, you're a man now, bearing your bright new shield and spear. I hated to see you go out of my house and close the door behind you, but I think I would not have halted you if I could. I salute you, sir. I cannot pretend that I am not sad; but I am proud, too. So long.

(Some months later the son of the author of the above was killed in combat)

THE LARGER HOPE

Alfred, Lord Tennyson

Oh yet we trust that somehow good
  Will be the final goal of ill,
  To pangs of nature, sins of will,
Defects of doubt, and taints of blood;

That nothing walks with aimless feet;
  That not one life shall be destroy'd,
  Or cast as rubbish to the void,
When God hath made the pile complete;

That not a worm is cloven in vain;
  That not a moth with vain desire
  Is shrivell'd in a fruitless fire,
Or but subserves another's gain.

Behold, we know not anything;
  I can but trust that good shall fall
  At last—far off—at last, to all,
And every winter change to spring.

So runs my dream; but what am I?
  An infant crying in the night;
  An infant crying for the light,
And with no language but a cry.

(From In Memoriam)

SOLITUDE

Henry David Thoreau

This is a delicious evening, when the whole body is one sense, and imbibes delight through every pore. I go and come with a strange liberty in Nature, a part of herself. As I walk along the stony shore of the pond in my shirt sleeves, though it is cool as well as cloudy and windy, and I see nothing special to attract me, all the elements are unusually congenial to me. The bullfrogs trump to usher in the night, and the note of the whippoorwill is borne on the rippling wind from over the water. Sympathy with the fluttering alder and poplar leaves almost takes away my breath; yet, like the lake, my serenity is rippled but not ruffled. The small waves raised by the evening wind are as remote from storm as the smooth reflecting surface. Though it is now dark, the wind still blows and roars in the wood, the waves still dash, and some creatures lull the rest with their notes. The repose is never complete. The wildest animals do not repose, but seek their prey now; the fox, and skunk, and rabbit now roam the fields and woods without fear. They are Nature's watchmen—links which connect the days of animated life.

When I return to my house I find that visitors have been there and left their cards, either a bunch of flowers, or a wreath of evergreen, or a name in pencil on a yellow walnut leaf or chip. They who come rarely to the woods take some little piece of the forest into their hands to play with by the way, which they leave, either intentionally or accidentally. One has peeled a willow wand, woven it into a ring, and dropped it on my table. I could always tell if visitors had called in my absence, either by the bended twigs or grass, or the print of their shoes, and generally of what sex or age or quality they were by some slight trace left, as a flower dropped, or a bunch of grass plucked and thrown away, even as far off as the railroad, half a mile distant, or by the lingering odor of a cigar or pipe. Nay, I was frequently notified of the passage of a traveler along the highway sixty rods off by the scent of his pipe.

There is commonly sufficient space about us. Our horizon is never quite at our elbows. The thick wood is not just at our door, nor the pond, but somewhat is always clearing, familiar and worn by us, appropriated and fenced in some way, and reclaimed from Nature. For what reason have I this vast range and circuit, some square miles of unfrequented forest, for my privacy, abandoned to me by men? My nearest neighbor is a mile distant, and no house is visible from any place but the hilltops within half a mile of my own. I have my horizon bounded by woods all to myself; a distant view of the railroad where it touches the pond on the one hand, and of the fence which skirts the woodland road on the other. But for the most part it is as solitary where I live as on the prairies. It is as much Asia or Africa as New England. I have, as it were, my own sun and moon and stars, and a little world all to myself. At night there was never a traveler passed my house, or knocked at my door, more than if I were the first or last man; unless it were in the spring, when at long intervals some came from the village to fish for pouts—they plainly fished much more in the Walden Pond of their own natures, and baited their hooks with darkness—but they soon retreated, usually with light baskets, and left "the world to darkness and to me," and the black kernel of the night was never profaned by any human neighborhood.

(From Walden)

DEPARTED FRIENDS

Henry Vaughan

They are all gone into the world of light!
  And I alone sit ling'ring here;
Their very memory is fair and bright,
  And my sad thoughts doth clear:

It glows and glitters in my cloudy breast
  Like stars upon some gloomy grove,
Or those faint beams in which this hill is dress'd,
  After the sun's remove.

I see them walking in an air of glory,
  Whose light doth trample on my days:
My days which are at best but dull and hoary,
  Mere glimmering and decays.

O holy Hope! And high Humility,
  High as the heavens above!
These are your walks, and you have show'd them me
  To kindle my cold love.

Dear, beauteous Death! the jewel of the just,
  Shining nowhere but in the dark!
What mysteries do lie beyond thy dust,
  Could man outlook that mark!

He that hath found some fledg'd bird's nest may know
  At first sight if the bird be flown;
But what fair grove or dell he sings in now,
  That to him is unknown.

And yet, as angels in some brighter dreams
  Call to the soul, when man doth sleep,
So some strange thoughts transcend our wonted themes,
  And into glory peep.

If a star were confin'd into a tomb,
  The captive flames must needs burn there;
But when the hand that lock'd her up, gives room,
  She'll shine through all the sphere.

O Father of eternal life, and all
  Created glories under Thee!
Resume Thy spirit from this world of thrall
  Into true liberty.

Either disperse these mists, which blot and fill
  My perspective still as they pass;
Or else remove me hence unto that hill,
  Where I shall need no glass.

SWEET GENEVIEVE

George Cooper

O Genevieve, I'd give this world
  To live again the lovely past!
The rose of youth was dew-impearled;
  But now it withers in the blast.
I see thy face in every dream,
  My waking thoughts are full of thee;
Thy glance is in the starry beam
  That falls along the summer sea.

Chorus:

O Genevieve, sweet Genevieve,
The days may come, the days may go,
But still the hands of mem'ry weave
The blissful dreams of long ago.

Fair Genevieve, my early love,
The years but make thee dearer far!
My heart shall never, never rove:
Thou art my only guiding star.
For me the past has no regret,
Whate'er the years may bring to me;
I bless the hour when first we met,
The hour that gave me love and thee!

ROUGE BOUQUET

March 7, 1918

Joyce Kilmer

In a wood they call the Rouge Bouquet
There is a new-made grave today,
Built by never a spade nor pick
Yet covered with earth ten metres thick.
There lie many fighting men,
Dead in their youthful prime,
Never to laugh nor love again
Nor taste the Summertime.
For Death came flying through the air
And stopped his flight at the dugout stair,
Touched his prey and left them there,
Clay to clay.
He hid their bodies stealthily
In the soil of the land they fought to free
And fled away.
Now over the grave abrupt and clear
Three volleys ring;
And perhaps their brave young spirits hear
The bugle sing:
"Go to sleep!
Go to sleep!

Slumber well where the shell screamed and fell.
Let your rifles rest on the muddy floor,
You will not need them any more.
Danger's past;
Now at last,
Go to sleep!"

There is on earth no worthier grave
To hold the bodies of the brave
Than this place of pain and pride
Where they nobly fought and nobly died.
Never fear but in the skies
  Saints and angels stand
Smiling with their holy eyes
  On this new-come band.
St. Michael's sword darts through the air
And touches the aureole on his hair
As he sees them standing at salute there,
  His stalwart sons:
And Patrick, Brigid, Columkill,
Rejoice that in veins of warriors still
  The Gael's blood runs.
And up to Heaven's doorway floats,
  From the wood called Rouge Bouquet,
A delicate cloud of bugle notes
  That softly say:
"Farewell! Farewell.
Comrades true, born anew, peace to you!
Your souls shall be where the heroes are
And your memory shine like the morning-star.
Brave and dear,
Shield us here.
Farewell!"

"SPEAK SOFTLY AND CARRY A BIG STICK"

Theodore Roosevelt

There is a homely adage which runs, "Speak softly and carry a big stick; you will go far." If the American nation will speak softly and yet build and keep at a pitch of the highest training a thoroughly efficient navy, the Monroe Doctrine will go far.

(1901)

FARE THEE WELL

Lord Byron

Fare thee well! and if for ever,
  Still for ever, fare *thee well*:
Even though unforgiving, never
  'Gainst thee shall my heart rebel.
Would that breast were bared before thee
  Where thy head so oft hath lain,
While that placid sleep came o'er thee
  Which thou ne'er canst know again:
Would that breast, by thee glanced over,
  Every inmost thought could show!
Then thou wouldst at last discover
  'Twas not well to spurn it so.
Though the world for this commend thee—
  Though it smile upon the blow,
Even its praises must offend thee,
  Founded on another's woe:
Though my many faults defaced me,
  Could no other arm be found,
Than the one which once embraced me,
  To inflict a cureless wound?
Yet, oh yet, thyself deceive not—
  Love may sink by low decay,
But by sudden wrench, believe not
  Hearts can thus be torn away:
Still thine own its life retaineth—
  Still must mine, though bleeding, beat;
And the undying thought which paineth
  Is—that we no more may meet.
These are words of deeper sorrow
  Than the wail above the dead;
Both shall live—but every morrow
  Wake us from a widowed bed.
And when thou wouldst solace gather,
  When our child's first accents flow
Wilt thou teach her to say "Father!"
  Though his care she must forego?
When her little hands shall press thee,
  When her lip to thine is pressed,

Think of him whose prayer shall bless thee,
Think of him thy love *had* blessed!
Should her lineaments resemble
Those thou never more mayst see,
Then thy heart will softly tremble
With a pulse yet true to me.
All my faults perchance thou knowest,
All my madness none can know;
All my hopes—where'er thou goest—
Wither, yet with *thee* they go.
Every feeling hath been shaken;
Pride—which not a world could bow—
Bows to thee—by thee forsaken.
Even my soul forsakes me now.
But 'tis done—all words are idle—
Words from me are vainer still;
But the thoughts we cannot bridle
Force their way without the will.
Fare thee well! thus disunited,
Torn from every nearer tie,—
Sear'd in heart, and lone, and blighted,
More than this I scarce can die.

MEMORIAL DAY

Robert G. Ingersoll

These heroes are dead. They died for liberty—they died for us. They are at rest. They sleep in the land they made free, under the flag they rendered stainless, under the solemn pines, the sad hemlocks, the tearful willows, the embracing vines. They sleep beneath the shadow of the clouds, careless alike of sunshine or storm, each in the windowless palace of rest. Earth may run red with other wars—they are at peace. In the midst of battles, in the roar of conflicts, they found the serenity of death.

* * *

Don't cheer, boys; the poor devils are dying.—Capt. John W. Philip, U.S.N., at the battle of Santiago, 1898.

TO F. C.

Mortimer Collins

Fast falls the snow, O lady mine,
Sprinkling the lawn with crystals fine,
But by the gods we won't repine
    While we're together,
We'll chat and rhyme and kiss and dine,
    Defying weather.

So stir the fire and pour the wine,
And let those sea-green eyes divine
Pour their love-madness into mine:
    I don't care whether
'Tis snow or sun or rain or shine
    If we're together.

ROBERT EMMET FROM THE DOCK

I am charged with being an emissary of France! An emissary of France! And for what end? It is alleged that I wished to sell the independence of my country! And for what end? Was this the object of my ambition? And is this the mode by which a tribunal of justice reconciles contradictions? No, I am no emissary; and my ambition was to hold a place among the deliverers of my country—not in power, not in profit, but in the glory of the achievement! Sell my country's independence to France! And for what? Was it for a change of masters? No! But for ambition! O my country, was it personal ambition that could influence me? Had it been the soul of my actions, could I not by my education and fortune, by the rank and consideration of my family, have placed myself among the proudest of my oppressors? My country was my idol, to it I sacrificed every selfish, every endearing sentiment; and for it, I now offer up my life, O God! . . .

Let no man dare, when I am dead, to charge me with dishonor; let no man attaint my memory by believing that I could have engaged in any cause but that of my country's liberty and independence; or that I could have become the pliant minion of power in the oppression of the miseries of my countrymen. . . . Am I, who lived but for my country, and who have subjected myself to the dangers of the jealous and watchful oppressor, and the bondage of the grave, only to give my countrymen their rights, and my country her independence, am I to be loaded with calumny, and not suffered to resent or repel it—no, God forbid! . . .

I have but one request to ask at my departure from this world—it is the charity of its silence! Let no man write my epitaph: for as no man who knows my motives dare now vindicate them, let not prejudice or ignorance asperse them. Let them and me repose in obscurity and peace, and my tomb remain uninscribed, until other times, and other men, can do justice to my character; when my country takes her place among the nations of the earth—then, and not till then, let my epitaph be written. I have done.

(1803)

THE BROOKSIDE

Richard Monckton Milnes (Lord Houghton)

I wandered by the brookside,
  I wandered by the mill;
I could not hear the brook flow,—
  The noisy wheel was still.
There was no burr of grasshopper,
  No chirp of any bird,
But the beating of my own heart
  Was all the sound I heard.

I sat beneath the elm tree;
  I watched the long, long shade,
And, as it grew still longer,
  I did not feel afraid;
For I listened for a footfall,
  I listened for a word,
But the beating of my own heart
  Was all the sound I heard.

He came not,—no, he came not,—
  The night came on alone,—
The little stars sat, one by one,
  Each on his golden throne;

The evening air passed by my cheek,
  The leaves above were stirred,
But the beating of my own heart
  Was all the sound I heard.

Fast silent tears were flowing,
  When something stood behind;
A hand was on my shoulder,—
  I knew its touch was kind:
It drew me nearer—nearer—
  We did not speak one word,
For the beating of our own hearts
  Was all the sound we heard.

"THERE IS A LADY SWEET AND KIND"

Anonymous

There is a lady sweet and kind,
Was never face so pleased my mind;
I did but see her passing by,
And yet I love her till I die.

Her gesture, motion, and her smiles,
Her wit, her voice my heart beguiles,
Beguiles my heart, I know not why,
And yet I love her till I die.

Her free behaviour, winning looks,
Will make a lawyer burn his books;
I touched her not, alas! not I,
And yet I love her till I die.

Had I her fast betwixt mine arms,
Judge you that think such sports were harms
Were't any harm? no, no, fie, fie,
For I will love her till I die.

Should I remain confinèd there
So long as Phoebus in his sphere,
I to request, she to deny,
Yet would I love her till I die.

Cupid is wingèd and doth range,
Her country so my love doth change:
But change she earth, or change she sky,
Yet will I love her till I die.

ARTHUR'S DISILLUSIONMENT

Alfred, Lord Tennyson

"I found Him in the shining of the stars,
I mark'd Him in the flowering of His fields,
But in His ways with men I find Him not.
I waged His wars, and now I pass and die.
O me! for why is all around us here
As if some lesser god had made the world,
But had not force to shape it as he would,
Till the High God behold it from beyond,
And enter it, and make it beautiful?
Or else as if the world were wholly fair,
But that these eyes of men are dense and dim,
And have not power to see it as it is:
Perchance, because we see not to the close;—
For I, being simple, thought to work His will,
And have but stricken with the sword in vain,
And all whereon I lean'd in wife and friend
Is traitor to my peace, and all my realm
Reels back into the beast, and is no more.
My God, thou hast forgotten me in my death:
Nay—God my Christ—I pass but shall not die."
(From Idylls of the King)

THE FACE OF ABRAHAM LINCOLN

Walt Whitman

I see the President almost every day, as I happen to live where he passes to and from his lodgings out of town. He never sleeps at the White House during the hot season, but has quarters at a healthy location some three miles north of the city, the Soldiers' home, a United States military establishment. I saw him this morning about 8½ coming in to business, riding on Vermont Avenue, near L Street. He always has a company of twenty-five or thirty cavalry, with sabres drawn and held upright over their shoulders. They say this guard was against his personal wish, but he let his counselors have their way. The party makes no great show in uniform or horses. Mr. Lincoln on the saddle generally rides a good-sized, easy-going gray horse, is dressed in plain black, somewhat rusty and dusty, wears a black stiff hat, and looks about as ordinary in attire, etc. as the commonest man. A lieutenant, with yellow straps, rides at his left, and following behind, two by two, come the cavalry men, in their yellow-striped jackets. They are generally going at a slow trot, as that is the pace set them by the one they wait upon. The sabres and accoutrements clank, and the entirely unornamental *cortège* as it trots towards Lafayette Square arouses no sensation, only some curious stranger stops and gazes. I see very plainly Abraham Lincoln's dark brown face, with the deep-cut lines, the eyes, always to me with a deep latent sadness in the expression. We have got so that we exchange bows, and very cordial ones. Sometimes the President goes and comes in an open barouche. The cavalry always accompany him, with drawn sabres. Often I notice as he goes out evening—and sometimes in the morning, when he returns early—he turns off and halts at the large and handsome residence of the Secretary of War, on K Street, and holds conference there. If in his barouche, I can see from my window he does not alight, but sits in his vehicle, and Mr. Stanton comes out to attend him. Sometimes one of his sons, a boy of ten or twelve, accompanies him, riding at his right on a pony. Earlier in the summer I occasionally saw the President and his wife, toward the latter part of the afternoon, out in a barouche, on a pleasure ride through the city. Mrs. Lincoln was dressed in complete black, with a long crepe veil. The equipage is of the plainest kind, only two horses, and they nothing extra. They passed me once very close, and I saw the President in the face fully, as they were moving slowly, and his look, though abstracted, happened to be directed steadily in my eye. He bowed and smiled, but far beneath his smile I noticed well the expression I have alluded to. None of the artists or pictures has caught the deep, though subtle and indirect expression of this man's face. There is something else there. One of the great portrait painters of two or three centuries ago is needed.

(From Specimen Days)

EARLY DEATH

Hartley Coleridge

She passed away, like morning dew,
  Before the sun was high;
So brief her time, she scarcely knew
  The meaning of a sigh.

As round the rose its soft perfume,
  Sweet love around her floated;
Admired she grew—while mortal doom
  Crept on, unfeared, unnoted.

Love was her guardian Angel here,
  But love to death resigned her;
Tho' love was kind, who should we fear,
  But holy death is kinder?

SHYLOCK'S DEFENSE

William Shakespeare

Salanio. Now, what news on the Rialto?

Salarino. Why, yet it lives there unchecked that Antonio hath a ship of rich lading wrecked on the narrow seas; the Goodwins, I think they call the place; a very dangerous flat and fatal, where the carcasses of many a tall ship lie buried, as they say, if my gossip Report be an honest woman of her word.

Salanio. I would she were as lying a gossip in that as ever knapped ginger, or made her neighbours believe she wept for the death of a third husband. But it is true, without any slips of prolixity or crossing the plain highway of talk, that the good Antonio, the honest Antonio,— O that I had a title good enough to keep his name company!—

Salarino. Come, the full stop.

Salanio. Ha! what sayest thou? Why, the end is, he hath lost a ship.

Salarino. I would it might prove the end of his losses.

Salanio. Let me say "amen" betimes, lest the devil cross my prayer, for here he comes in the likeness of a Jew.

[*Enter Shylock*]

How now, Shylock! what news among the merchants?

Shylock. You knew, none so well, none so well as you, of my daughter's flight.

Salarino. That's certain: I, for my part, knew the tailor that made the wings she flew withal.

Salanio. And Shylock, for his own part, knew the bird was fledged; and then it is the complexion of them all to leave the dam.

Shylock. She is damned for it.

Salarino. That's certain, if the devil may be her judge.

Shylock. My own flesh and blood to rebel!

Salanio. Out upon it, old carrion! rebels it at these years?

Shylock. I say, my daughter is my flesh and blood.

Salarino. There is more difference between thy flesh and hers than between jet and ivory; more between your bloods than there is between red wine and rhenish. But tell us, do you hear whether Antonio have had any loss at sea or no?

Shylock. There I have another bad match: a bankrupt, a prodigal, who dare scarce show his head on the Rialto; a beggar, that was used to come so smug upon the mart; let him look to his bond: he was wont to call me usurer; let him look to his bond: he was wont to lend money for a Christian courtesy; let him look to his bond.

Salarino. Why, I am sure, if he forfeit, thou wilt not take his flesh: what's that good for?

Shylock. To bait fish withal: if it will feed nothing else, it will feed my revenge. He hath disgraced me, and hindered me half a million; laughed at my losses, mocked at my gains, scorned my nation, thwarted my bargains, cooled my friends, heated mine enemies; and what's his reason? I am a Jew. Hath not a Jew eyes? hath not a Jew hands, organs, dimensions, senses, affections, passions? fed with the same food, hurt with the same weapons, subject to the same diseases, healed by the same means, warmed and cooled by the same winter and summer, as a Christian is? If you prick us, do we not bleed? If you tickle us, do we not laugh? if you poison us, do we not die? and if you wrong us, shall we not revenge? If we are like you in the rest, we will resemble you in that. If a Jew wrong a Christian, what is his humility? Revenge. If a Christian wrong a Jew, what should his sufferance be by Christian example? Why, revenge. The villany you teach me, I will execute; and it shall go hard but I will better the instruction.

From THE EVERLASTING MERCY

John Masefield

O Christ who holds the open gate,
O Christ who drives the furrow straight,
O Christ, the plough, O Christ, the laughter
Of holy white birds flying after,
Lo, all my heart's field red and torn,
And Thou wilt bring the young green corn,
The young green corn divinely springing,
The young green corn forever singing;
And when the field is fresh and fair
Thy blessèd feet shall glitter there,
And we will walk the weeded field,
And tell the golden harvest's yield,
The corn that makes the holy bread
By which the soul of man is fed,
The holy bread, the food unpriced,
Thy everlasting mercy, Christ.

MY LAST DUCHESS

Robert Browning

That's my last Duchess painted on the wall,
Looking as if she were alive. I call
That piece a wonder, now: Frà Pandolf's hands
Worked busily a day, and there she stands.
Will 't please you sit and look at her? I said
"Frà Pandolf" by design, for never read
Strangers like you that pictured countenance,
The depth and passion of its earnest glance,
But to myself they turned (since none puts by
The curtain I have drawn for you, but I)
And seemed as they would ask me, if they durst,
How such a glance came there; so not the first
Are you to turn and ask thus. Sir, 't was not
Her husband's presence only, called that spot
Of joy into the Duchess' cheek: perhaps
Frà Pandolf chanced to say, "Her mantle laps
Over my lady's wrist too much," or "Paint

Must never hope to reproduce the faint
Half-flush that dies along her throat:" such stuff
Was courtesy, she thought, and cause enough
For calling up that spot of joy. She had
A heart—how shall I say?—too soon made glad.
Too easily impressed: she liked whate'er
She looked on, and her looks went everywhere.
Sir, 't was all one! My favor at her breast,
The dropping of the daylight in the West,
The bough of cherries some officious fool
Broke in the orchard for her, the white mule
She rode with round the terrace—all and each
Would draw from her alike the approving speech,
Or blush, at least. She thanked men,—good! but thanked
Somehow—I know not how—as if she ranked
My gift of a nine-hundred-years-old name
With anybody's gift. Who'd stoop to blame
This sort of trifling? Even had you skill
In speech—(which I have not)—to make your will
Quite clear to such an one, and say, "Just this
Or that in you disgusts me; here you miss,
Or there exceed the mark"—and if she let
Herself be lessoned so, nor plainly set
Her wits to yours, forsooth, and made excuse,
—E'en then would be some stooping; and I choose
Never to stoop. Oh, sir, she smiled, no doubt,
Whene'er I passed her; but who passed without
Much the same smile? This grew; I gave commands;
Then all smiles stopped together. There she stands
As if alive. Will 't please you rise? We'll meet
The company below, then. I repeat,
The Count your master's known munificence
Is ample warrant that no just pretense
Of mine for dowry will be disallowed;
Though his fair daughter's self, as I avowed
At starting, is my object. Nay, we'll go
Together down, sir. Notice Neptune, though,
Taming a sea-horse, thought a rarity,
Which Claus of Innsbruck cast in bronze for me!

MEMORY

Thomas Bailey Aldrich

My mind lets go a thousand things,
Like dates of wars and deaths of kings,
And yet recalls the very hour—
'T was noon by yonder village tower,
And on the last blue noon in May—
The wind came briskly up this way,
Crisping the brook beside the road;
Then, pausing here, set down its load
Of pine-scents, and shook listlessly
Two petals from that wild-rose tree.

"I REJOICE THAT AMERICA HAS RESISTED"

William Pitt

Gentlemen, sir, have been charged with giving birth to sedition in America. They have spoken their sentiments with freedom against this unhappy act, and that freedom has become their crime. Sorry I am to hear the liberty of speech in this House imputed as a crime. But the imputation shall not discourage me. It is a liberty I mean to exercise. No gentleman ought to be afraid to exercise it. It is a liberty by which the gentleman who calumniates against it might have profited. He ought to have desisted from his project. The gentleman tells us that America is obstinate; America is almost in open rebellion. I rejoice that America has resisted. Three millions of people, so dead to all the feelings of liberty as voluntarily to submit to be slaves, would have been fit instruments to make slaves of the rest.

(On the Right of Taxing America, speech in the House of Commons, January 14, 1766)

THIS IS THE KEY

Anonymous

This is the key of the kingdom:
In that kingdom there is a city.
In that city there is a town.

In that town there is a street.
In that street there is a lane.
In that lane there is a yard.
In that yard there is a house.
In that house there is a room.
In that room there is a bed.
On that bed there is a basket.
In that basket there are some flowers.

Flowers in a basket.
Basket in the bed.
Bed in the room.
Room in the house.
House in the yard.
Yard in the lane.
Lane in the street.
Street in the town.
Town in the city.
City in the kingdom.
Of the kingdom this is the key.

WHEN YOU ARE OLD

William Butler Yeats

When you are old and grey and full of sleep,
And nodding by the fire, take down this book,
And slowly read, and dream of the soft look
Your eyes had once, and of their shadows deep;

How many loved your moments of glad grace,
And loved your beauty with love false or true;
But one man loved the pilgrim soul in you,
And loved the sorrows of your changing face.

And bending down beside the glowing bars,
Murmur, a little sadly, how love fled
And paced upon the mountains overhead
And hid his face amid a crowd of stars.

A LETTER FROM FRA GIOVANNI TO THE CONTESSINA

To the Most Illustrious
The Contessina Allagia
degli Aldobrandeschi,
on the Via de' Martelli, Firenze.

Most Noble Contessina:

I salute you. Believe me your most humble servant.

The rascal who carries this letter, if he devour them not on the way, will crave your acceptance of some of the fruits of our garden. Would that the peace of heaven might reach you through such things of earth!

Contessina, forgive an old man's babble. But I am your friend, and my love for you goes deep. There is nothing I can give you which you have not got; but there is much, very much, that, while I cannot give it, you can take. No heaven can come to us unless our hearts find rest in it today. Take heaven! No peace lies in the future which is not hidden in this present little instant. Take peace!

The gloom of the world is but a shadow. Behind it, yet within our reach, is joy. There is radiance and glory in the darkness, could we but see; and to see, we have only to look. Contessina, I beseech you to look.

Life is so generous a giver, but we, judging its gifts by their covering, cast them away as ugly or heavy or hard. Remove the covering, and you will find beneath it a living splendor, woven of love, by wisdom, with power. Welcome it, grasp it, and you touch the Angel's hand that brings it to you. Everything we call a trial, a sorrow, or a duty: believe me, that Angel's hand is there; the gift is there, and the wonder of an overshadowing presence. Our joys, too: be not content with them as joys. They, too, conceal diviner gifts.

Life is so full of meaning and of purpose, so full of beauty: beneath its covering: that you will find earth but cloaks your heaven. Courage, then, to claim it: that is all! But courage you have; and the knowledge that we are pilgrims together, wending, through unknown country, home.

And so, at this Christmas time, I greet you: not quite as the world sends greetings, but with profound esteem, and with the prayer that for you, now and for ever, the day breaks and the shadows flee away.

I have the honor to be your servant, though the least of them.
Fra Giovanni.
Christmas Eve, Anno Domini MDXIII. Pontassieve.
(Actually written by Ernest Temple Hargrove, who died in 1939)

FALSE WITNESSES

Henry Ward Beecher

Life would be a perpetual flea hunt if a man were obliged to run down all the innuendos, inveracities, insinuations and misrepresentations which are uttered against him.

SOFTLY NOW THE LIGHT OF DAY

George W. Doane

Softly now the light of day
Fades upon my sight away;
Free from care, from labour free,
Lord, I would commune with Thee.

Thou, whose all-pervading eye
Naught escapes, without, within,
Pardon each infirmity,
Open fault, and secret sin

Soon, for me, the light of day
Shall for ever pass away;
Then, from sin and sorrow free,
Take me, Lord, to dwell with Thee.

Thou, who, sinless, yet hast known
All of man's infirmity;
Then, from Thine eternal throne,
Jesus, look with pitying eye.

GENERAL WILLIAM BOOTH ENTERS INTO HEAVEN

Vachel Lindsay

(To be sung to the tune of "The Blood of the Lamb"
with indicated instrument)

I

(Bass drum beaten loudly)
Booth led boldly with his big bass drum—
(Are you washed in the blood of the Lamb?)
The Saints smiled gravely and they said: "He's come."
(Are you washed in the blood of the Lamb?)
Walking lepers followed, rank on rank,
Lurching bravoes from the ditches dank,
Drabs from the alleyways and drug fiends pale—
Minds still passion-ridden, soul-powers frail:—
Vermin-eaten saints with mouldy breath,
Unwashed legions with the ways of Death—
(Are you washed in the blood of the Lamb?)

(Banjos)
Every slum had sent its half-a-score
The round world over. (Booth had groaned for more.)
Every banner that the wide world flies
Bloomed with glory and transcendent dyes.
Big-voiced lasses made their banjos bang,
Tranced, fanatical they shrieked and sang:—
"Are you washed in the blood of the Lamb?"
Hallelujah! It was queer to see
Bull-necked convicts with that land make free.
Loons with trumpets blowed a blare, blare, blare
On, on upward thro' the golden air!
(Are you washed in the blood of the Lamb?)

II

(Bass drum slower and softer)
Booth died blind and still by Faith he trod,
Eyes still dazzled by the ways of God.
Booth led boldly, and he looked the chief
Eagle countenance in sharp relief,
Beard a-flying, air of high command
Unabated in that holy land.

(Sweet flute music)
Jesus came from out the court-house door,
Stretched his hands above the passing poor.
Booth saw not, but led his queer ones there
Round and round the mighty court-house square.
Then, in an instant all that blear review
Marched on spotless, clad in raiment new.
The lame were straightened, withered limbs uncurled
And blind eyes opened on a new, sweet world.

(Bass drum louder)
Drabs and vixens in a flash made whole!
Gone was the weasel-head, the snout, the jowl!
Sages and sibyls now, and athletes clean,
Rulers of empires, and of forests green!

(Grand chorus of all instruments. Tambourines to foreground.)
The hosts were sandalled, and their wings were fire!
(Are you washed in the blood of the Lamb?)
But their noise played havoc with the angel-choir.
(Are you washed in the blood of the Lamb?)
O, shout Salvation! It was good to see
Kings and Princes by the Lamb set free.
The banjos rattled and the tambourines
Jing-jing-jingled in the hands of Queens.

(Reverently sung, no instruments)
And when Booth halted by the curb for prayer
He saw his Master thro' the flag-filled air.
Christ came gently with a robe and crown
For Booth the soldier, while the throng knelt down.
He saw King Jesus. They were face to face,
And he knelt a-weeping in that holy place.
Are you washed in the blood of the Lamb?

AS THRO' THE LAND AT EVE

Alfred, Lord Tennyson

As thro' the land at eve we went,
  And pluck'd the ripen'd ears,
We fell out, my wife and I,

O we fell out I know not why,
  And kiss'd again with tears.
And blessings on the falling out
  That all the more endears,
When we fall out with those we love
  And kiss again with tears!
For when we came where lies the child
  We lost in other years,
There above the little grave,
O there above the little grave,
  We kiss'd again with tears.
(From The Princess)

LINCOLN TO GREELEY ON SAVING THE UNION

Executive Mansion, Washington
August 22, 1862

Hon. Horace Greeley:

Dear Sir: I have just read yours of the 19th, addressed to myself through THE N.Y. TRIBUNE. If there be in it any statements or assumptions of fact which I may know to be erroneous, I do not now and here controvert them. If there be in it any inferences which I may believe to be falsely drawn, I do not now here argue against them. If there be perceptible in it an impatient and dictatorial tone, I waive it in deference to an old friend, whose heart I have always supposed to be right.

As to the policy "I seem to be pursuing," as you say, I have not meant to leave any one in doubt.

I would save the Union. I would save it in the shortest way under the Constitution. The sooner the National authority can be restored, the nearer the Union will be "the Union as it was." If there be those who would not save the Union unless they could at the same time *save* Slavery, I do not agree with them. If there be those who would not save the Union unless they could at the same time *destroy* Slavery, I do not agree with them. My paramount object in this struggle is to save the Union, and is *not* either to save or destroy Slavery. If I could save the Union without freeing *any* slave, I would do it; and if I could save it by freeing *all* the slaves, I would do it; and if I could save it by freeing some and leaving others alone, I would also do that. What I do about Slavery and the colored race, I do because I believe it helps to save this Union and what I forbear, I forbear because I do not believe it would help to save the Union. I shall do *less* whenever I shall believe what I am doing hurts the cause, and I shall do *more* whenever I shall believe doing more will help the cause. I shall try to correct errors when shown to be errors; and I shall adopt new views so fast as they shall appear to be true views. I have here stated my purpose according to my view of *official* duty; and I intend no modification of my oft-expressed *personal* wish that all men, everywhere, could be free.

Yours,
A. Lincoln

ASK AND HAVE

Samuel Lover

"Oh, 'tis time I should talk to your mother,
Sweet Mary," says I;
"Oh, don't talk to my mother," says Mary,
Beginning to cry:
"For my mother says men are deceivers,
And never, I know, will consent;
She says girls in a hurry to marry,
At leisure repent."

"Then, suppose I would talk to your father,
Sweet Mary," says I;
"Oh, don't talk to my father," says Mary,
Beginning to cry:
"For my father he loves me so dearly,
He'll never consent I should go—
If you talk to my father," says Mary,
"He'll surely say, 'No.' "

"Then how shall I get you, my jewel?
Sweet Mary," says I;
"If your father and mother's so cruel,
Most surely I'll die!"
"Oh, never say die, dear," says Mary;
"A way now to save you I see;
Since my parents are both so contrary—
You'd better ask me!"

From AN OLD SWEETHEART OF MINE

James Whitcomb Riley

As one who cons at evening o'er an album all alone,
And muses on the faces of the friends that he has known,
So I turn the leaves of Fancy, till, in shadowy design,
I find the smiling features of an old sweetheart of mine.

The lamplight seems to glimmer with a flicker of surprise,
As I turn it low—to rest me of the dazzle in my eyes,
And light my pipe in silence, save a sight that seems to yoke
Its fate with my tobacco and to vanish with the smoke.

'Tis a *fragrant* retrospection—for the loving thoughts that start
Into being are like perfume from the blossom of the heart;
And to dream the old dreams over is a luxury divine—
When my truant fancies wander with that old sweetheart of mine.

Though I hear beneath my study, like a fluttering of wings,
The voices of my children, and the mother as she sings,
I feel no twinge of conscience to deny me any theme
When Care has cast her anchor in the harbor of a dream—

In fact, to speak in earnest, I believe it adds a charm
To spice the good a trifle with a little dust of harm—
For I find an extra flavor in Memory's mellow wine
That makes me drink the deeper to that old sweetheart of mine.

* * *

A face of lily beauty, with a form of airy grace,
Floats out of my tobacco as the Genii from the vase;
And I thrill beneath the glances of a pair of azure eyes
As glowing as the summer and as tender as the skies.

I can see the pink sunbonnet and the little checkered dress
She wore when first I kissed her and she answered the caress
With the written declaration that, "as surely as the vine
Grew 'round the stump," she loved me—that old sweetheart of mine.

* * *

And again I feel the pressure of her slender little hand,
As we used to talk together of the future we had planned—
When I should be a poet, and with nothing else to do
But write the tender verses that she set the music to . . .

When we should live together in a cozy little cot
Hid in a nest of roses, with a fairy garden-spot
Where the vines were ever fruited, and the weather ever fine,
And the birds were ever singing for that old sweetheart of mine:

When I should be her lover forever and a day,
And she my faithful sweetheart till the golden hair was gray;
And we should be so happy that when either's lips were dumb
They would not smile in Heaven till the other's kiss had come.

But, ah! my dream is broken by a step upon the stair,
And the door is softy opened, and—my wife is standing there:
Yet with eagerness and rapture all my visions I resign
To greet the *living* presence of that old sweetheart of mine.

MUSIC AND POETRY

Charles Darwin

If I had my life to live over again, I would have made a rule to read some poetry and listen to some music at least once a week; for perhaps the parts of my brain now atrophied would thus have kept active through use.

The loss of these tastes is a loss of happiness, and may possibly be injurious to the intellect, and more probably the moral character, by enfeebling the emotional part of our nature.

ALL THROUGH THE NIGHT

Anonymous

Sleep, my love, and peace attend thee,
  All through the night;
Guardian angels God will lend thee,
  All through the night;
Soft the drowsy hours are creeping,
Hill and dale in slumber steeping,
Love alone his watch is keeping—
  All through the night.

Though I roam a minstrel lonely,
  All through the night,
My true harp shall praise thee only,
  All through the night;
Love's young dream, alas, is over,
Yet my strains of love shall hover
Near the presence of my lover,
  All through the night.

Hark! a solemn bell is ringing,
  Clear through the night;
Thou, my love, art heavenward winging,
  Home through the night;
Earthly dust from off thee shaken,
Soul immortal thou shalt waken,
With thy last dim journey taken
  Home through the night.

IF I SHOULD DIE TO-NIGHT

Ben King

If I should die to-night,
And you should come to my cold corpse and say,
Weeping and heartsick o'er my lifeless clay—
If I should die to-night,
And you should come in deepest grief and woe—
And say: "Here's that ten dollars that I owe,"
I might arise in my large white cravat
And say, "What's that?"

If I should die to-night,
And you should come to my cold corpse and kneel,
Clasping my bier to show the grief you feel,
I say, if I should die to-night,
And you should come to me, and there and then
Just even hint at paying me that ten,
I might arise the while,
But I'd drop dead again.

A LITTLE WHILE

Emily Brontë

A little while, a little while,
  The weary task is put away,
And I can sing and I can smile,
  Alike, while I have holiday.

Where wilt thou go, my harassed heart—
  What thought, what scene invites thee now?
What spot, or near or far apart,
  Has rest for thee, my weary brow?

There is a spot, 'mid barren hills,
  Where winter howls, and driving rain;
But, if the dreary tempest chills,
  There is a light that warms again.

The house is old, the trees are bare,
  Moonless above bends twilight's dome;
But what on earth is half so dear—
  So longed for—as the hearth of home?

The mute bird sitting on the stone,
  The dank moss dripping from the wall,
The thorn trees gaunt, the walks o'ergrown,
  I love them—how I love them all!

Still, as I mused, the naked room,
  The alien firelight died away;
And from the midst of cheerless gloom,
  I passed to bright, unclouded day.

A little and a lone green lane
  That opened on a common wide;
A distant, dreamy, dim blue chain
  Of mountains circling every side.

A heaven so clear, and earth so calm,
  So sweet, so soft, so hushed an air;
And, deepening still the dreamlike charm,
  Wild moor-sheep feeding everywhere.

That was the scene, I knew it well;
  I knew the turfy pathway's sweep,
That, winding o'er each billowy swell,
  Marked out the tracks of wandering sheep.

Could I have lingered but an hour,
  It well had paid a week of toil;
But Truth has banished Fancy's power:
  Restraint and heavy task recoil.

Even as I stood with raptured eye,
  Absorbed in bliss so deep and dear,
My hour of rest had fleeted by,
  And back came labor, bondage, care.

SAMUEL JOHNSON'S TRIBUTE TO DAVID GARRICK

I hoped to have gratified with this character of our common friend: but what are the hopes of man! I am disappointed by that stroke of death, which has eclipsed the gaiety of nations and impoverished the public stock of harmless pleasure.

MY MARY

William Cowper

The twentieth year is wellnigh past
Since first our sky was overcast;
Ah, would that this might be the last!
                My Mary!

Thy spirits have a fainter glow,
I see thee daily weaker grow;
'Twas my distress that brought thee low,
                My Mary!

Thy needles, once a shining store,
For my sake restless heretofore,
Now rust disused, and shine no more;
                My Mary!

For though thou gladly wouldst fulfil
The same kind office for me still,
Thy sight now seconds not thy will,
My Mary!

But well thou play'dst the housewife's part,
And all thy threads with magic art
Have wound themselves about this heart,
My Mary!

Thy indistinct expressions seem
Like language utter'd in a dream;
Yet me they charm, whate'er the theme,
My Mary!

Thy silver locks, once auburn bright,
Are still more lovely in my sight
Than golden beams of orient light,
My Mary!

For could I view nor them nor thee,
What sight worth seeing could I see?
The sun would rise in vain for me,
My Mary!

Partakers of thy sad decline,
Thy hands their little force resign;
Yet, gently press'd, press gently mine,
My Mary!

Such feebleness of limbs thou prov'st,
That now at every step thou mov'st
Upheld by two; yet still thou lov'st,
My Mary!

And still to love, though press'd with ill,
In wintry age to feel no chill,
With me is to be lovely still,
My Mary!

But ah! by constant heed I know
How oft of the sadness that I show
Transforms thy smiles to looks of woe,
My Mary!

And should my future lot be cast
With much resemblance of the past,
Thy worn-out heart will break at last—
My Mary!

THE WIND AND THE MOON

George Macdonald

Said the Wind to the Moon: "I will blow you out;
You stare
In the air
Like a ghost in a chair,
Always looking what I am about—
I hate to be watched; I'll blow you out."

The Wind blew hard, and out went the Moon.
So, deep
On a heap
Of clouds to sleep,
Down lay the Wind, and slumbered soon,
Muttering low, "I've done for that Moon."

He turned in his bed; she was there again!
On high
In the sky,
With her one ghost eye,
The Moon shone white and alive and plain,
Said the Wind, "I will blow you out again."

The Wind blew hard, and the Moon grew dim,
"With my sledge,
And my wedge,
I have knocked off her edge!
If only I blow right fierce and grim,
The creature will soon be dimmer than dim."

He blew and he blew, and she thinned to a thread,
"One puff
More's enough
To blow her to snuff!
One good puff more where the last was bred,
And glimmer, glimmer, glum will go the thread."

He blew a great blast, and the thread was gone.
In the air
Nowhere
Was a moonbeam bare;
Far off and harmless the shy stars shone—
Sure and certain the Moon was gone!

The Wind he took to his revels once more;
On down,
In town,
Like a merry-mad clown,
He leaped and halloed with whistle and roar—
"What's that?" The glimmering thread once more!

He flew in a rage—he danced and blew;
But in vain
Was the pain
Of his bursting brain;
For still the broader the Moon-scrap grew,
The broader he swelled his big cheeks and blew.

Slowly she grew—till she filled the night,
And shone
On her throne
In the sky alone,
A matchless, wonderful silvery light,
Radiant and lovely, the queen of the night.

Said the Wind: "What a marvel of power am I!
With my breath,
Good faith!
I blew her to death—
First blew her away right out of the sky—
Then blew her in; what strength have I!"

But the Moon she knew nothing about the affair;
For high
In the sky,
With her one white eye,
Motionless, miles above the air,
She had never heard the great Wind blare.

LIFE'S UNCERTAINTY

Holy Bible, Ecclesiastes 11

Cast thy bread upon the waters: for thou shalt find it after many days. Give a portion to seven, and also to eight; for thou knowest not what evil shall be upon the earth. If the clouds be full of rain, they empty themselves upon the earth: and if the tree fall toward the south, or toward the north, in the place where the tree falleth, there shall it be. He that observeth the wind shall not sow; and he that regardeth the clouds shall not reap. As thou knowest not what is the way of the spirit, nor how the bones do grow in the womb of her that is with child: even so thou knowest not the works of God who maketh all. In the morning sow thy seed, and in the evening withhold not thine hand: for thou knowest not whether shall prosper, either this or that, or whether they both shall be alike good. Truly the light is sweet, and a pleasant thing it is for the eyes to behold the sun: But if a man live many years, and rejoice in them all; yet let him remember the days of darkness; for they shall be many. All that cometh is vanity.

Rejoice, O young man, in thy youth; and let thy heart cheer thee in the days of thy youth, and walk in the ways of thine heart, and in the sight of thine eyes: but know thou, that for all these things God will bring thee into judgment. Therefore remove sorrow from thy heart, and put away evil from thy flesh: for childhood and youth are vanity.

LITTLE BILLEE

William Makepeace Thackeray

There were three sailors of Bristol City
Who took a boat and went to sea.
But first with beef and captain's biscuits
And pickled pork they loaded she.

There was gorging Jack and guzzling Jimmy,
And the youngest he was little Billee.
Now when they got as far as the Equator
They'd nothing left but one split pea.

Says gorging Jack to guzzling Jimmy,
"I am extremely hungaree."
To gorging Jack says guzzling Jimmy,
"We've nothing left, we must eat we."

Says gorging Jack to guzzling Jimmy,
"With one another we shouldn't agree!
There's little Bill, he's young and tender,
We're old and tough, so let's eat he.

"Oh! Billy, we're going to kill and eat you,
So undo the button of your chemie."
When Bill received this information
He used his pocket-handkerchie.

"First let me say my catechism,
Which my poor mammy taught to me."
"Make haste, make haste," says guzzling Jimmy,
While Jack pulled out his snickersnee.

So Billy went up to the main-top gallant mast,
And down he fell on his bended knee.
He scarce had come to the twelfth commandment
When up he jumps. "There's land I see!

"Jerusalem and Madagascar,
And North and South Amerikee:
There's the British flag a-riding at anchor,
With Admiral Napier, K.C.B."

So when they got aboard of the Admiral's
He hanged fat Jack and flogged Jimmee;
But as for little Bill he made him
The Captain of a Seventy-three.

PRAYER FOR A VERY NEW ANGEL

Violet Alleyn Storey

God, God, be lenient her first night there.
The crib she slept in was so near my bed;
Her blue-and-white wool blanket was so soft,
Her pillow hollowed so to fit her head.

Teach me that she'll not want small rooms or me
When she has You and Heaven's immensity!

I always left a light out in the hall.
  I hoped to make her fearless in the dark;
And yet, she was so small—one little light,
  Not in the room, it scarcely mattered. Hark!

No, no; she seldom cried! God, not too far
For her to see, this first night, light a star!

And in the morning, when she first woke up,
  I always kissed her on the left cheek where
The dimple was. And oh, I wet the brush,
  It made it easier to curl her hair.

Just, just tomorrow morning, God, I pray,
When she wakes up, do things for her my way!

"THE CRIME OF BEING A YOUNG MAN"

William Pitt

The atrocious crime of being a young man, which the honourable gentleman has, with such spirit and decency charged upon me, I shall neither attempt to palliate nor deny; but content myself with wishing that I may be one of those whose follies may cease with their youth, and not of those who continue ignorant in spite of age and experience.

(From a speech, March 3, 1741, in reply to Walpole)

THE COURSE OF TRUE LOVE

William Shakespeare

Lysander. Ay me! for aught that I could ever read,
Could ever hear by tale or history,
The course of true love never did run smooth;
But, either it was different in blood,—

Hermia. O cross! too high to be enthrall'd to low.
Lysander. Or else misgraffed in respect of years,—
Hermia. O spite! too old to be engaged to young.
Lysander. Or else it stood upon the choice of friends,—
Hermia. O hell! to choose love by another's eyes.
Lysander. Or, if there were a sympathy in choice,
War, death, or sickness did lay siege to it,
Making it momentany as a sound,
Swift as a shadow, short as any dream;
Brief as the lightning in the collied night,
That, in a spleen, unfolds both heaven and earth,
And ere a man hath power to say "Behold!"
The jaws of darkness do devour it up:
So quick bright things come to confusion.
Hermia. If then true lovers have been ever cross'd,
It stands as an edict in destiny:
Then let us teach our trial patience,
Because it is a customary cross,
As due to love as thought and dreams and sighs,
Wishes and tears, poor fancy's followers.
(From A Midsummer-Night's Dream)

IN THE EVENING BY THE MOONLIGHT

James A. Bland

In de ebening by de moonlight when dis darkie's work was over.
We would gather round de fire, till the hoe-cake it was done,
Den we all would eat our supper, after dat we'd clear de kitchen;
Dat's de only time we had to spare, to hab a little fun.
Uncle Gabe would take de fiddle down dat hung upon de wall,
While de sil'vry moon was shining clear to bright,
How de old folks would enjoy it, they would sit all night and listen,
As we sang in de ebening by de moonlight.

Chorus:

In de ebening by de moonlight, you could hear us darkies singing,
In de ebening by de moonlight, you could hear us darkies singing,
In de ebening by de moonlight you could hear de banjo ringing,

How de old folks would enjoy it,
They would sit all night and listen,
As we sang in de ebening by de moonlight.

In de ebening by de moonlight when de watch-dog would be sleeping,
In de corner near de fire-place, beside de old arm-chair,
Whar Aunt Chloe used to sit and tell de piccaninnies stories,
And de cabin would be fill'd wid merry coons from near and far,
All dem happy times we used to hab, will ne'er return again,
Eb'ry thing was den so merry, gay and bright,
And I nebber will forget it, when our daily toil was o'er,
How we sang in de ebening by de moonlight.

THE STRENUOUS LIFE

Theodore Roosevelt

In speaking to you men of the greatest city of the West, men of the State which gave to the country Lincoln and Grant, men who pre-eminently and distinctly embody all that is most American in the American character, I wish to preach, not the doctrine of ignoble ease, but the doctrine of the strenuous life, the life of toil and effort, of labor and strife; to preach that highest form of success which comes, not to the man who desires mere easy peace, but to the man who does not shrink from danger, from hardship, or from bitter toil, and who out of these wins the splendid ultimate triumph.

A life of slothful ease, a life of that peace which springs merely from lack either of desire or of power to strive after great things, is as little worthy of a nation as an individual. I ask only that what every self-respecting American demands from himself and from his sons shall be demanded of the American nation as a whole. Who among you would teach your boys that ease, that peace, is to be the first consideration in their eyes—to be the ultimate goal after which they strive? . . .

We do not admire the man of timid peace. We admire the man who embodies victorious efforts, the man who never wrongs his neighbor, who is prompt to help a friend, but who has those virile qualities necessary to win in the stern strife of actual life. It is hard to fail, but is worse never to have tried to succeed. In this life we get nothing save by effort. Freedom from effort in the present merely means that there has been effort stored up in the past. A man can be freed from the necessity of work only by the fact that he or his fathers before him have worked to good purpose. If the freedom thus purchased is used aright, and the man still does actual work, though of a different kind, whether as a writer or a general, whether in the field of politics or in the field of exploration and adventure, he shows he deserves his good fortune.

But if he treats this period of freedom from the need of actual labor as a period, not of preparation, but of mere enjoyment, even though perhaps not of vicious enjoyment, he shows that he is simply a cumberer on the earth's surface; and he surely unfits himself to hold his own place with his fellows, if the need to do so should again arise. A mere life of ease is not in the end a very satisfactory life, and, above all, it is a life which ultimately unfits those who follow it for serious work in the world.

As it is with the individual, so it is with the nation. It is a base untruth to say that happy is the nation that has no history. Thrice happy is the nation that has a glorious history. Far better it is to dare mighty things, to win glorious triumphs, even though checkered by failure, than to take rank with those poor spirits who neither enjoy much nor suffer much, because they live in the gray twilight that knows neither victory nor defeat. . . .

Let us, the children of the men who proved themselves equal to the mighty days—let us, the children of the men who carried the great civil war to a triumphant conclusion, praise the God of our fathers that the ignoble counsels of peace were rejected; that the suffering and loss, the blackness of sorrow and despair, were unflinchingly faced, and the years of strife endured, for in the end the slave was free, the Union restored, and the mighty American Republic placed once more as a helmeted queen among nations.

(1899)

EPITAPH ON HIMSELF

Nobles and heralds, by your leave,
Here lies what once was Matthew Prior,
The son of Adam and Eve;
Can Bourbon or Nassau claim higher?

COURAGE

Sydney Smith

A great deal of talent is lost in the world for want of a little courage. Every day sends to their graves obscure men whom timidity prevented from making a first effort; who, if they could have been induced to begin, would in all probability have gone great lengths in the career of fame. The fact is, that to do anything in the world worth doing, we must not stand back shivering and thinking of the cold and danger, but jump in and scramble through as well as we can. It will not do to be perpetually calculating risks and adjusting nice chances; it did very well before the Flood, when a man would consult his friends upon an intended publication for a hundred and fifty years, and live to see his success afterwards; but at present, a man waits, and doubts, and consults his brother, and his particular friends, till one day he finds he is sixty years old and that he has lost so much time in consulting cousins and friends that he has no more time to follow their advice.

PEOPLE WILL TALK

Anonymous

We may go through the world, but it will be slow,
If we listen to all that is said as we go.
We will be worried and fretted and kept in a stew;
Too meddlesome tongues must have something to do.
    For people will talk, you know, people will talk;
    Oh, yes, they must talk, you know.

If quiet and modest, you'll have it presumed
Your humble position is only assumed—
You're a wolf in sheep's clothing, or else you're a fool;
But don't get excited, keep perfectly cool,
    For people will talk, etc.

If generous and noble, they'll vent out their spleen—
You'll hear some loud hints that you're selfish and mean;
If upright and honest and fair as the day,
They'll call you a rogue in a sly, sneaking way.
    For people will talk, etc.

And then if you show the least boldness of heart,
Or slight inclination to take your own part,
They'll call you an upstart, conceited and vain;
But keep straight ahead, and don't stop to complain.
    For people will talk, etc.

If threadbare your coat, and old-fashioned your hat,
Some one of course will take notice of that,
And hint rather strong that you can't pay your way,
But don't get excited, whatever you say.
    For people will talk, etc.

If you dress in the fashion, don't think to escape,
For they will criticize then in a different shape;
You're ahead of your means, or your tailor's unpaid;
But mind your own business, there's nought to be made,
    For people will talk, etc.

They'll talk fine before you; but then at your back,
Of venom and slander there's never a lack;
How kind and polite in all that they say,
But bitter as gall when you are away.
    For people will talk, etc.

The best way to do is to do as you please,
For your mind (if you have one) will then be at ease;
Of course you will meet with all sorts of abuse,
But don't think to stop them, it isn't any use,
    For people will talk, you know, people will talk;
    Oh, yes, they must talk, you know.

THREE GATES

Beth Day

If you are tempted to reveal
A tale to you someone has told
About another, make it pass,
Before you speak, three gates of gold.
These narrow gates: First, "Is it true?"
Then, "Is it needful?" In your mind

Give truthful answer. And the next
Is last and narrowest, "Is it kind?"
And if to reach your lips at last
It passes through these gateways three,
Then you may tell the tale, nor fear
What the result of speech may be.
(From the Arabian)

AUTRES BÊTES, AUTRES MOEURS

Ogden Nash

The turtle lives 'twixt plated decks
Which practically conceals its sex.
I think it clever of the turtle
In such a fix to be so fertile.

HOME THEY BROUGHT HER WARRIOR

Alfred, Lord Tennyson

Home they brought her warrior dead;
She nor swoon'd nor utter'd cry.
All her maidens, watching, said,
"She must weep or she will die."

Then they praised him soft and low,
Call'd him worthy to be loved,
Truest friend and noblest foe;
Yet she neither spoke nor moved.

Stole a maiden from her place,
Lightly to the warrior stept,
Took the face-cloth from the face;
Yet she neither moved nor wept.

Rose a nurse of ninety years,
Set his child upon her knee—
Like summer tempest came her tears—
'Sweet my child, I live for thee.'
(From The Princess)

CITIZENSHIP

Grover Cleveland

The man who takes the oath today to preserve, protect and defend the Constitution of the United States only assumes the solemn obligation which every patriotic citizen—on the farm, in the workshop, in the busy marts of trade and everywhere—should share with him. The Constitution which prescribes his [the President's] oath, my countrymen, is yours; the government you have chosen him to administer for a time is yours; the laws and the entire scheme of our civil rule, from the town meeting to the State capitals and the national capital, is yours. Every voter, as surely as your chief magistrate, under the same high sanction, though in a different sphere, exercises a public trust. Nor is this all. Every citizen owes to the country a vigilant watch and close scrutiny of its public servants and a fair and reasonable estimate of their fidelity and usefulness. Thus is the people's will impressed upon the whole framework of our civil policy—municipal, state and federal; and this is the price of our liberty and the inspiration of our faith in the republic.

DRIVING HOME THE COWS

Kate Putnam Osgood

Out of the clover and blue-eyed grass
  He turned them into the river-lane;
One after another he let them pass,
  Then fastened the meadow bars again.

Under the willows, and over the hill,
  He patiently followed their sober pace;
The merry whistle for once was still,
  And something shadowed the sunny face.

Only a boy! and his father had said
  He never could let his youngest go;
Two already were lying dead
  Under the feet of the trampling foe.

But after the evening work was done,
  And the frogs were loud in the meadow-swamp,
Over his shoulder he slung his gun
  And stealthily followed the foot-path damp,

Across the clover and through the wheat
  With resolute heart and purpose grim,
Though cold was the dew on his hurrying feet,
  And the blind bat's flitting startled him.

Thrice since then had the lanes been white,
  And the orchards sweet with apple-bloom;
And now, when the cows came back at night,
  The feeble father drove them home.

For news had come to the lonely farm
  That three were lying where two had lain;
And the old man's tremulous, palsied arm
  Could never lean on a son's again.

The summer day grew cool and late,
  He went for the cows when the work was done;
But down the lane, as he opened the gate,
  He saw them coming one by one,—

Brindle, Ebony, Speckle, and Bess,
  Shaking their horns in the evening wind;
Cropping the buttercups out of the grass,—
  But who was it following close behind?

Loosely swung in the idle air
  The empty sleeve of army blue;
And worn and pale, from the crisping hair,
  Looked out a face that the father knew.

For Southern prisons will sometimes yawn,
  And yield their dead unto life again;
And the day that comes with a cloudy dawn
  In the golden glory at last may wane.

The great tears sprang to their meeting eyes;
  For the heart must speak when the lips are dumb;
And under the silent evening skies
  Together they followed the cattle home.

IN AFTER DAYS

Austin Dobson

In after days when grasses high
O'er-top the stone where I shall lie,
  Though ill or well the world adjust
  My slender claim to honoured dust,
I shall not question nor reply.

I shall not see the morning sky;
I shall not hear the night-wind sigh;
  I shall be mute, as all men must,
    In after days.

But yet, now living, fain were I
That some one then should testify,
  Saying—"He held his pen in trust
  To Art, not serving shame or lust."
Will none?—Then let my memory die
    In after days!

THE SEA

Bryan Waller Procter (Barry Cornwall)

The sea! the sea! the open sea!
The blue, the fresh, the ever free!
Without a mark, without a bound,
It runneth the earth's wide regions round;
It plays with the clouds; it mocks the skies;
Or like a cradled creature lies.

I'm on the sea! I'm on the sea!
I am where I would ever be;
With the blue above, and the blue below,
And silence wheresoe'er I go;
If a storm should come and awake the deep,
What matter? *I* shall ride and sleep.

I love, O, how I love to ride
On the fierce, foaming, bursting tide,
When every mad wave drowns the moon

Or whistles aloft his tempest tune,
And tells how goeth the world below,
And why the sou'west blasts do blow.

I never was on the dull, tame shore,
But I loved the great sea more and more,
And backwards flew to her billowy breast,
Like a bird that seeketh its mother's nest;
And a mother she *was,* and *is,* to me;
For I was born on the open sea!

The waves were white, and red the morn,
In the noisy hour when I was born;
And the whale it whistled, the porpoise rolled,
And the dolphins bared their backs of gold;
And never was heard such an outcry wild
As welcomed to life the ocean-child!

I've lived since then, in calm and strife,
Full fifty summers, a sailor's life,
With wealth to spend and power to range,
But never have sought nor sighed for change;
And Death, whenever he comes to me,
Shall come on the wild, unbounded sea!

"MY YOKE IS EASY"

Holy Bible, Matthew 11:28–30

Come unto me, all ye that labour and are heavy laden, and I will give you rest. Take my yoke upon you, and learn of me; for I am meek and lowly in heart; and ye shall find rest unto your souls. For my yoke is easy, and my burden is light.

OLD SUSAN

Walter de la Mare

When Susan's work was done, she would sit,
With one fat guttering candle lit,
And window opened wide to win
The sweet night air to enter in.

There, with a thumb to keep her place,
She would read, with stern and wrinkled face,
Her mild eyes gliding very slow
Across the letters to and fro,
While wagged the guttering candle flame
In the wind that through the window came.
And sometimes in the silence she
Would mumble a sentence audibly,
Or shake her head as if to say,
"You silly souls, to act this way!"
And never a sound from night I would hear,
Unless some far-off cock crowed clear;
Or her old shuffling thumb should turn
Another page; and rapt and stern,
Through her great glasses bent on me,
She would glance into reality;
And shake her round old silvery head,
With—"You!—I thought you was in bed!"—
Only to tilt her book again,
And rooted in Romance remain.

THE ISLES OF GREECE

Lord Byron

The isles of Greece! the isles of Greece!
  Where burning Sappho loved and sung,
Where grew the arts of war and peace,
  Where Delos rose and Phoebus sprung!
Eternal summer gilds them yet,
But all, except their sun, is set.

The Scian and the Teian muse,
  The hero's harp, the lover's lute,
Have found the fame your shores refuse;
  Their place of birth alone is mute
To sounds which echo further west
Than your sires' "Islands of the Blest."

The mountains look on Marathon—
  And Marathon looks on the sea;
And musing there an hour alone

I dream'd that Greece might still be free;
For, standing on the Persians' grave,
I could not deem myself a slave.

A king sate on the rocky brow
Which looks o'er sea-born Salamis;
And ships, by thousands, lay below,
And men in nations;—all were his!
He counted them at break of day—
And when the sun set where were they?

And where are they? and where art thou,
My country? On thy voiceless shore
The heroic lay is tuneless now—
The heroic bosom beats no more!
And must thy lyre, so long divine,
Degenerate into hands like mine?

'Tis something, in the dearth of fame,
Though link'd among a fetter'd race,
To feel at least a patriot's shame,
Even as I sing, suffuse my face:
For what is left the poet here?
For Greeks a blush—for Greece a tear.

Must *we* but weep o'er days more blest?
Must *we* but blush?—Our fathers bled.
Earth! render back from out thy breast
A remnant of our Spartan dead!
Of the three hundred grant but three,
To make a new Thermopylæ!

What, silent still? and silent all?
Ah, no;—the voices of the dead
Sound like a distant torrent's fall,
And answer, "Let one living head,
But one, arise—we come, we come!"
'Tis but the living who are dumb.

In vain—in vain; strike other chords;
Fill high the cup with Samian wine,
Leave battles to the Turkish hordes,

And shed the blood of Scio's vine!
Hark! rising to the ignoble call,—
How answers each bold Bacchanal!

You have the Pyrrhic dance as yet,
Where is the Pyrrhic phalanx gone?
Of two such lessons, why forget
The nobler and the manlier one?
You have the letters Cadmus gave—
Think ye he meant them for a slave?

Fill high the bowl with Samian wine!
We will not think of themes like these!
It made Anacreon's song divine:
He served—but served Polycrates—
A tyrant: but our masters then
Were still, at least, our countrymen.

The tyrant of the Chersonese
Was freedom's best and bravest friend;
That tyrant was Miltiades!
Oh, that the present hour would lend
Another despot of the kind!
Such chains as his were sure to bind.

Fill high the bowl with Samian wine!
On Suli's rock and Parga's shore,
Exists the remnant of a line
Such as the Doric mothers bore:
And there, perhaps, some seed is sown,
The Heracleidan blood might own.

Trust not for freedom to the Franks—
They have a king who buys and sells:
In native swords and native ranks,
The only hope of courage dwells;
But Turkish force and Latin fraud
Would break your shield, however broad.

Fill high the bowl with Samian wine!
Our virgins dance beneath the shade—
I see their glorious black eyes shine;
But gazing on each glowing maid,
My own the burning tear-drop laves,
To think such breasts must suckle slaves.

Place me on Sunium's marble steep,
Where nothing, save the waves and I,
May hear our mutual murmurs sweep:
There, swan-like, let me sing and die:
A land of slaves shall ne'er be mine—
Dash down yon cup of Samian wine!

(From Don Juan)

THE DEFINITION OF A GENTLEMAN

John Henry Newman

It is almost a definition of a gentleman to say he is one who never inflicts pain. This description is both refined and, as far as it goes, accurate. He is mainly occupied in merely removing the obstacles which hinder the free and unembarrassed action of those about him; and he concurs with their movements rather than takes the initiative himself. His benefits may be considered as parallel to what are called comforts or conveniences in arrangements of a personal nature: like an easy chair or a good fire, which do their part in dispelling cold and fatigue, though nature provides both means of rest and animal heat without them. The true gentleman in like manner carefully avoids whatever may cause a jar or a jolt in the minds of those with whom he is cast;—all clashing of opinion, or collision of feeling, all restraint, or suspicion, or gloom, or resentment; his great concern being to make everyone at their ease and at home. He has his eyes on all his company; he is tender towards the bashful, gentle towards the distant, and merciful towards the absurd; he can recollect to whom he is speaking; he guards against unseasonable allusions, or topics which may irritate; he is seldom prominent in conversation, and never wearisome. He makes light of favors while he does them, and seems to be receiving when he is conferring. He never speaks of himself except when compelled, never defends himself by a mere retort; he has no ears for slander or gossip, is scrupulous in imputing motives to those who interfere with him, and interprets every thing for the best. He is never mean or little in his disputes, never takes unfair advantage, never mistakes personalities or sharp sayings for arguments, or insinuates evil which he dare not say out. From a long-sighted prudence, he observes the maxim of the ancient sage, that we should ever conduct ourselves towards our enemy as if he were one day to be our friend. He has too much good sense to be affronted at insults, he is too well employed to remember injuries, and too indolent to bear malice. He is patient, forbearing, and resigned, on philosophical principles; he submits to pain, because it is inevitable, to bereavement, because it is irreparable, and to death, because it is his destiny. If he engages in controversy of any kind, his disciplined intellect preserves him from the blundering discourtesy of better, perhaps, but less educated minds; who, like blunt weapons, tear and hack instead of cutting clean, who mistake the point in argument, waste their strength on trifles, misconceive their adversary, and leave the question more involved than they find it. He may be right or wrong in his opinion, but he is too clear-headed to be unjust; he is as simple as he is forcible, and as brief as he is decisive. Nowhere shall we find greater candor, consideration, indulgence: he throws himself into the minds of his opponents, he accounts for their mistakes. He knows the weakness of human reason as well as its strength, its province and its limits. If he be an unbeliever, he will be too profound and large-minded to ridicule religion or to act against it; he is too wise to be a dogmatist or fanatic in his infidelity. He respects piety and devotion; he even supports institutions as venerable, beautiful, or useful, to which he does not assent; he honors the ministers of religion, and it contents him to decline its mysteries without assailing or denouncing them. He is a friend of religious toleration, and that, not only because his philosophy has taught him to look on all forms of faith with an impartial eye, but also from the gentleness and effeminacy of feeling, which is the attendant on civilization.

Not that he may not hold a religion too, in his own way, even when he is not a Christian. In that case his religion is one of imagination and sentiment; it is the embodiment of those ideas of the sublime, majestic, and beautiful, without which there can be no large philosophy. Sometimes he acknowledges the being of God; sometimes he invests an unknown principle or quality with the attributes of perfection. And this deduction of his reason, or creation of his fancy, he makes the occasion of such excellent thoughts, and the starting-point of so varied and systematic a teaching, that he even seems like a disciple of Christianity itself. From the very accuracy and steadiness of his logical powers, he is able to see what sentiments are consistent in those who hold any religious doctrine at all, and he appears to others to feel and to hold a whole circle of theological truths, which exist in his mind no otherwise than as a number of deductions.

THE SEA GYPSY

Richard Hovey

I am fevered with the sunset,
I am fretful with the bay,
For the wander-thirst is on me
And my soul is in Cathay.

There's a schooner in the offing,
With her topsails shot with fire,
And my heart has gone aboard her
For the Islands of Desire.

I must forth again to-morrow!
With the sunset I must be
Hull down on the trail of rapture
In the wonder of the sea.

MUSIC

William Shakespeare

If music be the food of love, play on;
Give me excess of it, that, surfeiting,
The appetite may sicken, and so die.
That strain again! it had a dying fall:
O, it came o'er my ear like the sweet sound,
That breathes upon a bank of violets,
Stealing and giving odour! Enough, no more:
'Tis not so sweet now as it was before.
O spirit of love, how quick and fresh art thou!
That, notwithstanding thy capacity
Receiveth as the sea, nought enters there,
Of what validity and pitch soe'er,
But falls into abatement and low price,
Even in a minute: so full of shapes is fancy,
That it alone is high fantastical.

(From Twelfth Night)

THE YAK

Hilaire Belloc

As a friend to the children, commend me the Yak;
You will find it exactly the thing;
It will carry and fetch, you can ride on its back,
Or lead it about with a string.

The Tartar who dwells on the plains of Thibet
(A desolate region of snow),
Has for centuries made it a nursery pet,
And surely the Tartar should know!

Then tell your papa where the Yak can be got,
And if he is awfully rich,
He will buy you the creature—or else he will not,
(I cannot be positive which).

IN THE BAGGAGE COACH AHEAD *

Gussie L. Davis

On a dark and stormy night, as the train rattled on, all the passengers had gone to bed,
Except one young man with a babe in his arms who sat there with a bowed-down head.
The innocent one began crying just then, as though its poor heart would break,
One angry man said,
"Make that child stop its noise, for it's keeping all of us awake,"—
"Put it out," said another, "Don't keep it in here,
We've paid for our berths and want rest."
But never a word said the man with the child,
As he fondled it close to his breast,
"Where is its mother, go take it to her," thus a lady then softly said.
"I wish I could," was the man's sad reply,
"But she's dead in the coach ahead."

Chorus:

While the train rolled onward
A husband sat in tears,
Thinking of the happiness,
Of just a few short years;
For baby's face brings pictures of
A cherished hope that's dead,
But baby's cries can't waken her,
In the baggage coach ahead.

MY AUNT

Oliver Wendell Holmes

My aunt! my dear unmarried aunt!
  Long years have o'er her flown;
Yet still she strains the aching clasp
  That binds her virgin zone;
I know it hurts her,—though she looks
  As cheerful as she can;
Her waist is ampler than her life,
  For life is but a span.

My aunt! my poor deluded aunt!
  Her hair is almost grey;
Why will she train that winter curl
  In such a spring-like way?
How can she lay her glasses down,
  And say she reads as well,
When through a double convex lens
  She just makes out to spell?

Her father—grandpapa! forgive
  This erring lip its smiles—
Vowed she should make the finest girl
  Within a hundred miles;
He sent her to a stylish school;
  'Twas in her thirteenth June;
And with her, as the rules required,
  "Two towels and a spoon."

They braced my aunt against a board,
  To make her straight and tall;
They laced her up, they starved her down,
  To make her light and small;
They pinched her feet, they singed her hair,
  They screwed it up with pins;—
Oh, never mortal suffered more
  In penance for her sins.

So, when my precious aunt was done,
  My grandsire brought her back;
(By daylight, lest some rabid youth
  Might follow on the track;)
"Ah!" said my grandsire, as he shook
  Some powder in his pan,
"What could this lovely creature do
  Against a desperate man!"

Alas! nor chariot, nor barouche,
  Nor bandit cavalcade,
Tore from the trembling father's arms
  His all-accomplished maid.
For her how happy had it been!
  And Heaven had spared to me
To see one sad, ungathered rose
  On my ancestral tree.

FROM ABRAHAM LINCOLN'S "HOUSE DIVIDED" SPEECH

If we could first know where we are, and whither we are tending, we could better judge what to do, and how to do it. We are now far into the fifth year since a policy was initiated with the avowed object and confident promise of putting an end to slavery agitation. Under the operation of that policy, that agitation has not only not ceased but has constantly augmented. In my opinion it will not cease until a crisis shall have been reached and passed. "A house divided against itself cannot stand." I believe this government cannot endure permanently, half-slave and half-free. I do not expect the Union to be dissolved,—I do not expect the house to fall—but I do expect it will cease to be divided. It will become all one thing, or all the other. Either the opponents of slavery will arrest the further spread of it, and place it where the public mind shall rest in the belief that it is in the course of ultimate extinction; or its advocates will push it forward till it shall become alike lawful in all the States, old as well as new, North as well as South.

(Springfield, Ill., June 17, 1858)

LOVE CONCEALED

William Shakespeare

She never told her love,
But let concealment, like a worm i' the bud,
Feed on her damask cheek: she pined in thought;
And with a green and yellow melancholy
She sat like patience on a monument,
Smiling at grief. Was not this love indeed?
We men may say more, swear more: but indeed
Our shows are more than will; for still we prove
Much in our vows, but little in our love.

(From Twelfth Night)

FOR MY BROTHER

Sgt. John Paul Merton, R.C.A.F.
Reported Missing in Action, 1943

Thomas Merton

Sweet brother, if I do not sleep
My eyes are flowers for your tomb;
And if I cannot eat my bread,
My fasts shall live like willows where you died.
If in the heat I find no water for my thirst,
My thirst shall turn to springs for you, poor traveller.

Where, in what desolate and smoky country,
Lies your poor body, lost and dead?
And in what landscape of disaster
Has your unhappy spirit lost its road?

Come, in my labor find a resting place
And in my sorrows lay your head,
Or rather take my life and blood
And buy yourself a better bed—
Or take my breath and take my death
And buy yourself a better rest.

When all the men of war are shot
And flags have fallen into dust,
Your cross and mine shall tell men still
Christ died on each, for both of us.

For in the wreckage of your April Christ lies slain,
And Christ weeps in the ruins of my spring;
The money of Whose tears shall fall
Into your weak and friendless hand,
And buy you back to your own land:
The silence of Whose tears shall fall
Like bells upon your alien tomb.
Hear them and come: they call you home.

THE CELESTIAL SURGEON

Robert Louis Stevenson

If I have faltered more or less
In my great task of happiness;
If I have moved among my race
And shown no glorious morning face;
If beams from happy human eyes
Have moved me not; if morning skies,
Books, and my food, and summer rain
Knocked on my sullen heart in vain:—
Lord, thy most pointed pleasure take
And stab my spirit broad awake;
Or, Lord, if too obdurate I,
Choose thou, before that spirit die,
A piercing pain, a killing sin,
And to my dead heart run them in!

ON HIS DECEASED WIFE

John Milton

Methought I saw my late espoused saint
  Brought to me like Alcestis from the grave,
  Whom Jove's great son to her glad husband gave,
  Rescued from death by force though pale and faint.
Mine as whom washed from spot of child-bed taint,
  Purification in the old law did save,
  And such, as yet once more I trust to have
  Full sight of her in heaven without restraint,
Came vested all in white, pure as her mind:
  Her face was veiled, yet to my fancied sight,
  Love, sweetness, goodness, in her person shined
So clear as in no face with more delight.
  But O as to embrace me she inclined
  I waked, she fled, and day brought back my night.

VELVET SHOES

Elinor Wylie

Let us walk in the white snow
  In a soundless space;
With footsteps quiet and slow,
  At a tranquil pace,
  Under veils of white lace.

I shall go shod in silk,
  And you in wool,
White as a white cow's milk,
  More beautiful
  Than the breast of a gull.

We shall walk through the still town
  In a windless peace;
We shall step upon white down,
  Upon silver fleece,
  Upon softer than these.

We shall walk in velvet shoes;
  Wherever we go
Silence will fall like dews
  On white silence below.
  We shall walk in the snow.

WAIT TILL THE SUN SHINES, NELLIE *

Andrew B. Sterling

On a Sunday morn sat a maid forlorn,
With her sweetheart by her side;
Thro' the window pane she looked at the rain,—
"We must stay home, Joe," she cried;
"There's a picnic, too, at the Old Point View,
It's a shame it rained today."
Then the boy drew near, kissed away each tear,
And she heard him softly say:

Chorus:
  "Wait till the sun shines, Nellie,
  When the clouds go drifting by,
  We will be happy, Nellie,
  Don't you sigh;
  Down lover's lane we'll wander,
  Sweetheart, you and I;
  Wait till the sun shines, Nellie,
  Bye and bye."

"How I long," she sighed, "for a trolley ride,
Just to show my brand-new gown."
Then she gazed on high with a gladsome cry,—
For the sun came shining down.
And she looked so sweet, on the big front seat,
As the car sped on its way,
And she whispered low, "Say you're all right, Joe,
You just won my heart today."

WHAT IS AN AMERICAN?

Michel Guillaume Jean de Crèvecœur

What then is the American, this new man? He is either an European, or the descendant of an European, hence that strange mixture of blood, which you will find in no other country. I could point out to you a family whose grandfather was an Englishman, whose wife was Dutch, whose son married a French woman, and whose present four sons now have four wives of different nations. *He* is an American, who, leaving behind him all his ancient prejudices and manners, receives new ones from the new mode of life he has embraced, the new government he obeys, and the new rank he holds. He becomes an American by being received in the broad lap of our great *Alma Mater.* Here individuals of all nations are melted into a new race of men, whose labor and posterity will one day cause great changes in the world. Americans are the western pilgrims, who are carrying along with them that great mass of arts, sciences, vigor, and industry which began long since in the east; they will finish the great circle. The Americans were once scattered all over Europe; here they are incorporated into one of the finest systems of population which has ever appeared, and which will hereafter become distinct by the power of the different climates they inhabit. The American ought therefore to love his country much better than that wherein either he or his forefathers were born. Here the rewards of his industry follow with equal steps the progress of his labor; his labor is founded on the basis of nature, *self-interest;* can it want a stronger allurement? Wives and children, who before in vain demanded of him a morsel of bread, now, fat and frolicsome, gladly help their father to clear those fields whence exuberant crops are to arise to feed and to clothe them all; without any part being claimed, either by a despotic prince, a rich abbot, or a mighty lord. Here religion demands but little of him; a small voluntary salary to the minister, and gratitude to God; can he refuse these? The American is a new man, who acts upon new principles; he must therefore entertain new ideas, and form new opinions. From involuntary idleness, servile dependence, penury, and useless labor, he has passed to toils of a very different nature, rewarded by ample subsistence.—This is an American.

(From Letters of an American Farmer, 1782)

INDEPENDENCE

Henry David Thoreau

My life more civil is and free
  Than any civil polity.

Ye princes, keep your realms
  And circumscribèd power,
Not wide as are my dreams,
  Nor rich as is this hour.

What can ye give which I have not?
What can ye take which I have got?
  Can ye defend the dangerless?
  Can ye inherit nakedness?

To all true wants Time's ear is deaf,
Penurious States lend no relief
  Out of their pelf:
But a free soul—than God—
Can help itself.

  Be sure your fate
Doth keep apart its state,—
Not linked with any band,
Even the noblest in the land,—

In tented fields with cloth of gold
  No place doth hold,
But is more chivalrous than they are,
  And sigheth for a nobler war;

  A finer strain its trumpet rings,
  A brighter gleam its armor flings.

The life that I aspire to live,
  No man proposeth me;
No trade upon the street
  Wears it emblazonry.

THE NOBLEST ROMAN

William Shakespeare

This was the noblest Roman of them all:
All the conspirators, save only he,
Did that they did in envy of great Caesar;
He only, in a general honest thought
And common good to all, made one of them.
His life was gentle, and the elements
So mix'd in him that Nature might stand up
And say to all the world "This was a man!"
(From Julius Caesar)

THE SAD TALE OF MR. MEARS

Anonymous

There was a man who had a clock,
His name was Matthew Mears;
And every day he wound that clock
For eight and twenty years.

And then one day he found that clock
An eight-day clock to be;
And a madder man than Matthew Mears
You would not wish to see.

DOMINUS ILLUMINATIO MEA

R. D. Blackmore

In the hour of death, after this life's whim,
When the heart beats low, and the eyes grow dim,
And pain has exhausted every limb—
The lover of the Lord shall trust in Him.

When the will has forgotten the lifelong aim,
And the mind can only disgrace its fame,
And a man is uncertain of his own name—
The power of the Lord shall fill this frame.

When the last sigh is heaved, and the last tear shed,
And the coffin is waiting beside the bed,
And the widow and child forsake the dead—
  The angel of the Lord shall lift this head.

For even the purest delight may pall,
And power must fail, and the pride must fall,
And the love of the dearest friends grow small—
  But the glory of the Lord is all in all.

FIRE AND ICE

Robert Frost

Some say the world will end in fire,
Some say in ice.
From what I've tasted of desire
I hold with those who favor fire.
But if it had to perish twice,
I think I know enough of hate
To say that for destruction ice
Is also great
And would suffice.

ELIZA AND HER CHILD ESCAPE FROM THE SLAVE-OWNER

Harriet Beecher Stowe

It is impossible to conceive of a human creature more wholly desolate and forlorn than Eliza, when she turned her footsteps from Uncle Tom's cabin.

Her husband's suffering and dangers, and the danger of her child, all blended in her mind with a confused and stunning sense of the risk she was running in leaving the only home she had ever known, and cutting loose from the protection of a friend whom she loved and revered. Then there was the parting from every familiar object,—the place where she had grown up, the trees under which she had played, the groves where she had walked many an evening in happier days by the side of her young husband,—everything, as it lay in the clear, frosty starlight, seemed to speak reproachfully to her, and ask her whither she could go from a home like that?

But stronger than all was maternal love, wrought into a paroxysm of frenzy by the near approach of a fearful danger. Her boy was old enough to have walked by her side, and, in an indifferent case, she would only have led him by the hand; but now the bare thought of putting him out of her arms made her shudder, and she strained him to her bosom with a convulsive grasp as she went rapidly forward.

The frosty ground creaked beneath her feet, and she trembled at the sound; every quaking leaf and fluttering shadow sent the blood backward to her heart, and quickened her footsteps. She wondered within herself at the strength that seemed to be come upon her; for she felt the weight of her boy as if it had been a feather, and every flutter of fear seemed to increase the supernatural power that bore her on, while from her pale lips burst forth, in frequent ejaculations, the prayer to a Friend above,—"Lord, help! Lord, save me!"

If it were *your* Harry, mother, or your Willie, that were going to be torn from you by a brutal trader, to-morrow morning,—if you had seen the man, and heard that the papers were signed and delivered, and you had only from twelve o'clock till morning to make good your escape,—how fast could *you* walk? How many miles could you make in those few brief hours, with the darling at your bosom,—the little sleepy head on your shoulder,—the small, soft arms trustingly holding on to your neck?

For the child slept. At first, the novelty and alarm kept him waking; but his mother so hurriedly repressed every breath or sound, and so assured him that if he were only still she would certainly save him, that he clung quietly round her neck, only asking, as he found himself sinking to sleep,—

"Mother, I don't need to keep awake, do I?"

"No, my darling; sleep, if you want to."

"But, mother, if I do go to sleep, you won't let him get me?"

"No! so may God help me!" said his mother, with a pale cheek and a brighter light in her large, dark eyes.

"You're *sure,* ain't you, mother?"

"Yes, *sure!*" said the mother, in a voice that startled herself; for it seemed to her to come from a spirit within, that was no part of her; and the boy dropped his little weary head on her shoulder and was soon asleep. How the touch of those warm arms, and gentle breathings that came in her neck, seemed to add fire and spirit to her movements! It seemed to her as if strength poured in to her in electric streams from every gentle touch and movement of the sleeping, confiding child. Sublime is the dominion of the mind over the body, that, for a time, can make flesh and nerve impregnable, and string the sinews like steel, so that the weak become mighty.

The boundaries of the farm, the grove, the wood-lot, passed by her dizzily as she walked on; and still she went, leaving one familiar object after another, slacking not, pausing not, till the reddening daylight found her many a long mile from all traces of any familiar objects upon the open highway.

She had often been with her mistress, to visit some connections in the little village of T——, not far from the Ohio River, and knew the road well. To go thither, to escape across the Ohio River, were the first hurried outlines of her plan of escape; beyond that, she could only hope in God.

When horses and vehicles began to move along the highway, with that alert perception peculiar to a state of excitement, and which seems to be a sort of inspiration, she became aware that her headlong pace and distracted air might bring on her remark and suspicion. She therefore put the boy on the ground, and, adjusting her dress and bonnet, she walked on at as rapid a pace as she thought consistent with the preservation of appearances. In her little bundle she had provided a store of cakes and apples, which she used as expedients for quickening the speed of the child, rolling the apple some yards before them, when the boy would run with all his might after it; and this ruse, often repeated, carried them over many a half-mile.

After a while, they came to a thick patch of woodland, through which murmured a clear brook. As the child complained of hunger and thirst, she climbed over the fence with him; and, sitting down behind a large rock which concealed them from the road, she gave him a breakfast out of her little package. The boy wondered and grieved that she could not eat; and when, putting his arms round her neck, he tried to wedge some of his cake into her mouth, it seemed to her that the rising in her throat would choke her.

"No, no, Harry darling! mother can't eat till you are safe! We must go on,—on,—till we come to the river!" And she hurried again into the road, and again constrained herself to walk regularly and composedly forward.

She was many miles past any neighborhood where she was personally known. If she should chance to meet any who knew her, she reflected that the well-known kindness of the family would be of itself a blind to suspicion, as making it an unlikely supposition that she could be a fugitive. As she was also so white as not to be known as of colored lineage without a critical survey, and her child was white also, it was much easier for her to pass on unsuspected.

On this presumption, she stopped at noon at a neat farmhouse to rest herself, and buy some dinner for her child and self; for, as the danger decreased with the distance, the supernatural tension of the nervous system lessened, and she found herself both weary and hungry.

The good woman, kindly and gossiping, seemed rather pleased than otherwise with having somebody come in to talk with; and accepted without examination Eliza's statement that she "was going on a piece to spend a week with her friends,"—all which she hoped in her heart might prove strictly true.

An hour before sunset, she entered the village of T——, by the Ohio River, weary and footsore, but still strong in heart. Her first glance was at the river, which lay, like Jordan, between her and the Canaan of liberty on the other side.

It was now early spring, and the river was swollen and turbulent; great cakes of floating ice were swinging heavily to and fro in the turbid waters. Owing to the peculiar form of the shore on the Kentucky side, the land bending far out into the water, the ice had been lodged and detained in great quantities, and the narrow channel which swept round the bend was full of ice, piled one cake over another, thus forming a temporary barrier to the descending ice, which lodged, and formed a great undulating raft, filling up the whole river, and extending almost to the Kentucky shore.

Eliza stood, for a moment, contemplating this unfavorable aspect of things, which she saw at once must prevent the usual ferry-boat from running, and then turned into a small public house on the bank to make a few inquiries.

The hostess, who was busy in various fizzing and stewing operations over the fire, preparatory to the evening meal, stopped, with a fork in her hand, as Eliza's sweet and plaintive voice arrested her.

"What is it?" she said.

"Isn't there any ferry or boat that takes people over to B—— now?" she said.

"No, indeed!" said the woman; "the boats has stopped running."

Eliza's look of dismay and disappointment struck the woman, and she said inquiringly,—

"Maybe you're wanting to get over?—anybody sick? Ye seem mighty anxious."

"I've got a child that's very dangerous," said Eliza. "I never heard of it till last night, and I've walked quite a piece today in hopes to get to the ferry."

"Well, now, that's onlucky," said the woman, whose motherly sympathies were much aroused; "I'm re'lly consarned for ye. Solomon!" she called, from the window, toward a small back building. A man, in leather apron and very dirty hands, appeared at the door.

"I say, Sol," said the woman, "is that ar man going to tote them bar'ls over tonight?"

"He said he should try, if't was anyway prudent," said the man.

"There's a man a piece down here, that's going over with some truck this evening, if he durs' to; he'll be in here to supper tonight, so you'd better set down and wait. That's a sweet little fellow," added the woman, offering him a cake.

But the child, wholly exhausted, cried with weariness.

"Poor fellow! he isn't used to walking, and I've hurried him on so," said Eliza.

"Well, take him into this room," said the woman, opening into a small bedroom, where stood a comfortable bed. Eliza laid the weary boy upon it, and held his hand in hers till he was fast asleep. For her there was no rest. As a fire in her bones, the thought of the pursuer urged her on; and she gazed with longing eyes on the sullen, surging waters that lay between her and liberty.

* * *

It was about three quarters of an hour after Eliza laid her child to sleep in the village tavern that the [pursuit] party came riding into the same place. Eliza was standing by the window, looking out in another direction, when Sam's quick eye caught a glimpse of her. Haley and Andy were two yards behind. At this crisis, Sam contrived to have his hat blown off, and uttered a loud and characteristic ejaculation, which startled her at once; she drew suddenly back; the whole train swept by the window, round to the front door.

A thousand lives seemed concentrated into that one moment for Eliza. Her room opened by a side door to the river. She caught her child, and sprang down the steps towards it. The trader caught a full glimpse of her, just as she was disappearing down the bank; and throwing himself from his horse, and calling loudly on Sam and Andy, he was after her like a hound after a deer. In that dizzy moment her feet to her scarce seemed to touch the ground, and a moment brought her to the water's edge. Right on behind they came; and, nerved with strength such as God gives only to the desperate, with one wild cry and flying leap, she vaulted sheer over the turbid current by the shore, on to the raft of ice beyond. It was a desperate leap,—impossible to anything but madness and despair; and Haley, Sam, and Andy instinctively cried out, and lifted up their hands, as she did it.

The huge green fragment of ice on which she alighted pitched and creaked as her weight came on it, but she stayed there not a moment. With wild cries and desperate energy she leaped to another and still another cake;—stumbling,—leaping,—slipping, —springing upwards again! Her shoes are gone,—her stockings cut from her feet,—while blood marked every step; but she saw nothing, felt nothing, till dimly, as in a dream, she saw the Ohio side, and a man helping her up the bank.

"Yer a brave gal, now, whoever ye ar!" said the man, with an oath.

Eliza recognized the voice and face of a man who owned a farm not far from her old home.

"Oh, Mr. Symmes!—save me,—do save me,—do hide me!" said Eliza.

"Why, what's this?" said the man. "Why, if't ain't Shelby's gal!"

"My child!—this boy!—he'd sold him! There is his Mas'r," said she, pointing to the Kentucky shore. "Oh, Mr. Symmes, you've got a little boy!"

"So I have," said the man, as he roughly, but kindly, drew her up the steep bank. "Besides, you're a right brave gal. I like grit, wherever I see it."

When they had gained the top of the bank, the man paused. "I'd be glad to do something for ye," said he; "but then there's nowhar I could take ye. The best I can do is to tell ye to go *thar*," said he, pointing to a large white house which stood by itself, off the main street of the village. "Go thar; they're kind folks. Thar's no kind o' danger but they'll help you,—they're up to all that sort o' thing."

"The Lord bless you!" said Eliza earnestly.

"No 'casion, no 'casion in the world," said the man. "What I've done's of no 'count."

"And oh, surely, sir, you won't tell any one!"

"Go to thunder, gal! What do you take a feller for? In course not," said the man. "Come, now, go along like a likely, sensible gal, as you are. You've arnt your liberty, and you shall have it, for all me."

The woman folded her child to her bosom, and walked firmly and swiftly away. The man stood and looked after her.

(From Uncle Tom's Cabin)

THE BELLS OF SHANDON

Francis Mahony

With deep affection,
And recollection,
I often think of
  Those Shandon bells,
Whose sounds so wild would,
In the days of childhood,
Fling around my cradle
  Their magic spells.
On this I ponder
Where'er I wander,
And thus grow fonder,
  Sweet Cork, of thee;
With thy bells of Shandon,
That sound so grand on
The pleasant waters
  Of the River Lee.

I've heard bells chiming
Full many a clime in,
Tolling sublime in
  Cathedral shrine,
While at a glib rate
Brass tongues would vibrate—
But all their music
  Spoke naught like thine;
For memory, dwelling
On each proud swelling
Of the belfry knelling
  Its bold notes free,
Made the bells of Shandon
Sound far more grand on
The pleasant waters
  Of the River Lee.

I've heard bells tolling
Old Adrian's Mole in,
Their thunder rolling
  From the Vatican,
And cymbals glorious
Swinging uproarious
In the gorgeous turrets
  Of Notre Dame;
But thy sounds were sweeter
Than the dome of Peter
Flings o'er the Tiber,
  Pealing solemnly—
O, the bells of Shandon
Sound far more grand on
The pleasant waters
  Of the River Lee.

There's a bell in Moscow,
While on tower and kiosk O!
In Saint Sophia
  The Turkman gets,
And loud in air
Calls men to prayer
From the tapering summits
  Of tall minarets.
Such empty phantom
I freely grant them;
But there's an anthem
  More dear to me,—
'Tis the bells of Shandon,
That sound so grand on
The pleasant waters
  Of the River Lee.

WATCHMAN, TELL US OF THE NIGHT

John Bowring

Watchman, tell us of the night,
  What its signs of promise are.
Traveler, o'er yon mountain's height,
  See that glory-beaming star.

Watchman, does its beauteous ray
  Aught of joy or hope foretell?
Traveler, yes; it brings the day,
  Promised day of Israel.

Watchman, tell us of the night;
  Higher yet that star ascends.
Traveler, blessedness and light,
  Peace and truth its course portends.
Watchman, will its beams alone
  Gild the spot that gave them birth?
Traveler, ages are its own;
  See, it bursts all o'er the earth.

Watchman, tell us of the night,
  For the morning seems to dawn.
Traveler, darkness takes its flight,
  Doubt and terror are withdrawn.
Watchman, let thy wanderings cease:
  Hie thee to thy quiet home.
Traveler, lo! the Prince of Peace,
  Lo! the Son of God is come!

A LIFE-LESSON

James Whitcomb Riley

There! little girl, don't cry!
They have broken your doll, I know;
  And your tea-set blue,
  And your play-house, too,
Are things of the long ago;
But childish troubles will soon pass by,—
    There! little girl, don't cry!

There! little girl, don't cry!
They have broken your slate, I know;
  And the glad, wild ways
  Of your school-girl days
Are things of the long ago;
  But life and love will soon come by;—
    There! little girl, don't cry!

There! little girl, don't cry!
They have broken your heart, I know;
  And the rainbow gleams
  Of your youthful dreams
Are things of the long ago;
  But Heaven holds all for which you sigh.—
    There! little girl, don't cry!

"BE OF GOOD CHEER; I HAVE OVERCOME THE WORLD"

Holy Bible, John 16:19–33

Now Jesus knew that they were desirous to ask him, and said unto them, Do ye inquire among yourselves of that I said, A little while, and ye shall not see me: and again, a little while, and ye shall see me? Verily, verily, I say unto you, That ye shall weep and lament, but the world shall rejoice: and ye shall be sorrowful, but your sorrow shall be turned into joy. A woman when she is in travail hath sorrow, because her hour is come: but as soon as she is delivered of the child, she remembereth no more the anguish, for joy that a man is born into the world. And ye now therefore have sorrow: but I will see you again, and your heart shall rejoice, and your joy no man taketh from you. And in that day ye shall ask me nothing. Verily, verily, I say unto you, Whatsoever ye shall ask the Father in my name, he will give it you. Hitherto have ye asked nothing in my name: ask, and ye shall receive, that your joy may be full. These things have I spoken unto you in proverbs: but the time cometh, when I shall no more speak unto you in proverbs, but I shall shew you plainly of the Father. At that day ye shall ask in my name: and I say not unto you, that I will pray the Father for you: For the Father himself loveth you, because ye have loved me, and have believed that I came out from God. I came forth from the Father, and am come into the world: again, I leave the world, and go to the Father. His disciples said unto him, Lo, now speakest thou plainly, and speakest no proverb. Now we are sure that thou knowest all things, and needest not that any man should ask thee: by this we believe that thou camest forth from God. Jesus answered them, Do ye now believe? Behold, the hour cometh, yea, is now come, that ye shall be scattered, every man to his own, and shall leave me alone: and yet I am not alone, because the Father is with me. These things I have spoken unto you, that in me ye might have peace. In the world ye shall have tribulation: but be of good cheer; I have overcome the world.

WHATEVER IS—IS BEST

Ella Wheeler Wilcox

I know, as my life grows older,
  And mine eyes have clearer sight,
That under each rank wrong somewhere
  There lies the root of Right;
That each sorrow has its purpose,
  By the sorrowing oft unguessed;
But as sure as the sun brings morning,
  Whatever is—is best.

I know that each sinful action,
  As sure as the night brings shade,
Is somewhere, sometime punished,
  Though the hour be long delayed.
I know that the soul is aided
  Sometimes by the heart's unrest,
And to grow means often to suffer—
  But whatever is—is best.

I know there are no errors,
  In the great Eternal plan,
And all things work together
  For the final good of man.
And I know when my soul speeds onward,
  In its grand Eternal quest,
I shall say as I look back earthward,
  Whatever is—is best.

BURIAL OF THE DEAD

The Book of Common Prayer

Man, that is born of a woman, hath but a short time to live, and is full of misery. He cometh up, and is cut down, like a flower; he fleeth as it were a shadow, and never continueth in one stay.

In the midst of life we are in death: of whom may we seek for succour, but of thee, O Lord, who for our sins art justly displeased?

Yet, O Lord God most holy, O Lord most mighty, O holy and most merciful Saviour, deliver us not into the bitter pains of eternal death.

Thou knowest, Lord, the secrets of our hearts; shut not thy merciful ears to our prayer; but spare us, Lord most holy, O God most mighty, O holy and merciful Saviour, thou most worthy Judge eternal, suffer us not, at our last hour, for any pains of death, to fall from thee.

A BIRTHDAY

Christina Georgina Rossetti

My heart is like a singing bird
  Whose nest is in a water'd shoot;
My heart is like an apple-tree
  Whose boughs are bent with thick-set fruit;
My heart is like a rainbow shell
  That paddles in a halcyon sea;
My heart is gladder than all these,
  Because my love is come to me.

Raise me a dais of silk and down;
  Hang it with vair and purple dyes;
Carve it in doves and pomegranates,
  And peacocks with a hundred eyes;
Work it in gold and silver grapes,
  In leaves and silver fleurs-de-lys;
Because the birthday of my life
  Is come, my love is come to me.

A PRAYER

Frank Dempster Sherman

It is my joy in life to find
At every turning of the road
The strong arm of a comrade kind
To help me onward with my load.

And since I have no gold to give,
And love alone must make amends,
My only prayer is, while I live—
God make me worthy of my friends.

THE CONSTANT LOVER

Sir John Suckling

Out upon it, I have loved
  Three whole days together!
And am like to love three more,
  If it prove fair weather.

Time shall moult away his wings
  Ere he shall discover
In the whole wide world again
  Such a constant lover.

But the spite on 't is, no praise
  Is due at all to me;
Love with me had made no stays,
  Had it any been but she.

Had it any been but she,
  And that very face,
There had been at least ere this
  A dozen dozen in her place.

O WORLD, THOU CHOOSEST NOT THE BETTER PART!

George Santayana

O World, thou choosest not the better part!
It is not wisdom to be only wise,
And on the inward vision close the eyes,
But it is wisdom to believe the heart.
Columbus found a world, and had no chart,
Save one that faith deciphered in the skies;
To trust the soul's invisible surmise

Was all his science and his only art.
Our knowledge is a torch of smoky pine
That lights the pathway but one step ahead
Across a void of mystery and dread.
Bid, then, the tender light of faith to shine
By which alone the mortal heart is led
Unto the thinking of the thought divine.

EVERYBODY WORKS BUT FATHER *

Charles W. McClintock

Every morning at six o'clock, I go straight to my work,
And button my coat round my neck, for no job would I shirk,
Winter winds blow round my head, cutting up my face,
I tell you what I'd like to have: my dear old father's place.

Chorus:

Everybody works but father, and he sits around all day;
Feet in front of the fire, passing the time away,
Mother takes in washing, so does sister Ann,
Everybody works in our house, but my old man.

Father always sleeps till noon, he tells us folks he's wise,
He said he read when quite a boy that daylight hurts the eyes,
You ask him why he never works, "I'm laying off" he'll say.
Vacation time comes round for Dad every New Year's day.

Father's quite a noble man, but lazy as a Turk,
It keeps the old man very busy steering clear of work.
A man named Work moved in to town and dad began to whine,
He said, "That Mister Work's all right, but to me he's a shine."

DIFFERENCES

Paul Laurence Dunbar

My neighbor lives on the hill,
And I in the valley dwell,
My neighbor must look down on me,

* Copyright, Edward B. Marks Music Corporation, Radio City, New York, N. Y. Used by permission.

Must I look up?—ah, well,
My neighbor lives on the hill,
And I in the valley dwell.

My neighbor reads, and prays,
And I—I laugh, God wot,
And sing like a bird when the grass is green
In my small garden plot;
But ah, he reads and prays,
And I—I laugh, God wot.

His face is a book of woe,
And mine is a song of glee;
A slave he is to the great "They say,"
But I—I am bold and free;
No wonder he smacks of woe,
And I have the tang of glee.

My neighbor thinks me a fool,
"The same to yourself," says I;
"Why take your books and take your prayers,
Give me the open sky;"
My neighbor thinks me a fool,
"The same to yourself," says I.

THE LIGHT OF OTHER DAYS

Alfred Bunn

The light of other days is faded,
And all their glories past,
For grief with heavy wing hath shaded,
The hopes too bright to last;
The world which morning's mantle clouded,
Shines forth with purer rays,
But the heart ne'er feels, in sorrow shrouded,
The light of other days.

The leaf which autumn tempests wither,
The birds which then take wing,
When winter's winds are past, come hither,
To welcome back the spring;

The very ivy on the ruin
In gloomful life displays,
But the heart alone sees no renewing
The light of other days.

I LOVE YOU TRULY

Carrie Jacobs-Bond

I love you truly, truly, dear,
Life with its sorrow, life with its tear,
Fades into dreams when I feel you are near,
For I love you truly, truly, dear.

Ah, love, 'tis something to feel your kind hand,
Ah yes, 'tis something by your side to stand;
Gone is the sorrow,
Gone doubt and fear,
For you love me truly, truly, dear.

THOMAS JEFFERSON ASSURES JOHN ADAMS OF HIS FRIENDSHIP AND RESPECT

Monticello, October 12, 1823

Dear Sir:

I do not write with the ease which your letter of September the 18th supposes. Crippled wrists and fingers make writing slow and laborious. But while writing to you, I lose the sense of these things in the recollection of ancient times, when youth and health made happiness out of everything. I forget for a while the hoary winter of age, when we can think of nothing but how to keep ourselves warm, and how to get rid of our heavy hours until the friendly hand of death shall rid us of all at once. Against this *tedium vitae,* however, I am fortunately mounted on a hobby, which, indeed, I should have better managed some thirty or forty years ago; but whose easy amble is still sufficient to give exercise and amusement to an octogenary writer. This is the establishment of a University, on a scale more comprehensive, and in a country more healthy and central than our old William and Mary, which these obstacles have long kept in a state of languor and inefficiency. But the tardiness with which such works proceed may render it doubtful whether I shall live to see it go into action.

Putting aside these things, however, for the present, I write this letter as due to a friendship coeval with our government, and now attempted to be poisoned, when too late in life to be replaced by new affections. I had for some time observed in the public papers, dark hints and mysterious innuendoes of a correspondence of yours with a friend, to whom you had opened your bosom without reserve, and which was to be made public by that friend or his representative. And now it is said to be actually published. It has not yet reached us, but extracts have been given, and such as seemed most likely to draw a curtain of separation between you and myself. Were there no other motive than that of indignation against the author of this outrage on private confidence, whose shaft seems to have been aimed at yourself more particularly, this would make it the duty of every honorable mind to disappoint that aim, by opposing to its impression a seven-fold shield of apathy and insensibility. With me, however, no such armor is needed. The circumstances of the times in which we have happened to live, and the partiality of our friends at a particular period, placed us in a state of apparent opposition, which some might suppose to be personal also; and there might be wanting those who wished to make it so, by filling our ears with malignant falsehoods, by dressing up hideous phantoms of their own creation, and presenting them to you under my name, to me under yours, and endeavoring to instil into our minds things concerning each other the most destitute of truth. And if there had been, at any time, a moment when we were off our guard, and in a temper to let the whispers of these people make us forget what we had known of each other for so many years, and years of so much trial, yet all men who have attended to the workings of the human mind, who have seen the false colors under which passion sometimes dresses the actions and motives of others, have seen also those passions subsiding with time and reflection, dissipating like mists before the rising sun, and restoring to us the sight of all things in their true shape and colors. It would be strange indeed, if, at our years, we were to go back an age to hunt up imaginary or forgotten facts, to disturb the repose of affections so sweetening to the evening of our lives. Be assured, my dear Sir, that I am incapable of receiving the slightest impression from the effort now made to plant thorns on the pillow of age, worth, and wisdom, and to sow tares between friends who have been such for near half a century. Beseeching you then, not to suffer your mind to be disquieted by this wicked attempt to poison its peace, and praying you to throw it by among the things which have never happened, I add sincere assurances of my unabated and constant attachment, friendship, and respect.

STAND UP FOR JESUS

George Duffield, Jr.

Stand up, stand up, for Jesus,
Ye soldiers of the cross!
Lift high his royal banner!
It must not suffer loss:
From victory unto victory
His army shall he lead;
Till every foe is vanquished,
And Christ is Lord indeed.

Stand up, stand up, for Jesus!
The trumpet call obey!
Forth to the mighty conflict
In this his glorious day!
Ye that are men now serve him
Against unnumbered foes!
Let courage rise with danger,
And strength to strength oppose.

Stand up, stand up, for Jesus!
Stand in his strength alone!
The arm of flesh will fail you,
Ye dare not trust your own:
Put on the Gospel armour,
And watching unto prayer,
When duty calls, or danger,
Be never wanting there!

Stand up, stand up, for Jesus,
The strife will not be long:
This day, the noise of battle;
The next, the victor's song.
To him that overcometh,
A crown of life shall be;
He with the King of glory
Shall reign eternally.

"CARE-CHARMER SLEEP, SON OF THE SABLE NIGHT"

Samuel Daniel

Care-charmer Sleep, son of the sable Night,
Brother to Death, in silent darkness born:
Relieve my anguish, and restore the light;
With dark forgetting of my care, return!
And let the day be time enough to mourn
The shipwreck of my ill-adventured youth:
Let waking eyes suffice to wail their scorn,
Without the torment of the night's untruth.
Cease, dreams, the images of day-desires,
To model forth the passions of the morrow;
Never let rising sun approve you liars,
To add more grief to aggravate my sorrow.
  Still let me sleep, embracing clouds in vain;
  And never wake to feel the day's disdain.

AMERICA FOR ME

Henry van Dyke

'Tis fine to see the Old World, and travel up and down
Among the famous palaces and cities of renown,
To admire the crumbly castles and the statues of the kings,—
But now I think I've had enough of antiquated things.

So it's home again, and home again, America for me!
My heart is turning home again, and there I long to be,
In the land of youth and freedom beyond the ocean bars,
Where the air is full of sunlight and the flag is full of stars.

Oh, London is a man's town, there's power in the air;
And Paris is a woman's town, with flowers in her hair;
And it's sweet to dream in Venice, and it's great to study Rome;
But when it comes to living, there is no place like home.

I like the German fir-woods, in green battalions drilled;
I like the garden of Versailles, with flashing fountains filled;
But oh, to take your hand, my dear, and ramble for a day
In the friendly Western woodland where Nature has her way!

I know that Europe's wonderful, yet something seems to lack;
The Past is too much with her, and the people looking back.
But the glory of the Present is to make the Future free,—
We love our land for what she is and what she is to be.

Oh, it's home again, and home again, America for me!
I want a ship that's westward bound to plow the rolling sea,
To the blessed Land of Room Enough beyond the ocean bars,
Where the air is full of sunlight and the flag is full of stars.

GO WHERE GLORY WAITS THEE

Thomas Moore

Go where glory waits thee,
But while fame elates thee,
  Oh! still remember me.
When the praise thou meetest
To thine ear is sweetest,
  Oh! then remember me.
Other arms may press thee,
Dearer friends caress thee,
All the joys that bless thee
  Sweeter far may be;
But when friends are nearest,
And when joys are dearest,
  Oh! then remember me.

When at eve thou rovest
By the star thou lovest,
  Oh! then remember me.
Think, when home returning,
Bright we've seen it burning,
  Oh! thus remember me.
Oft as summer closes,
When thine eye reposes
  On its lingering roses,
  Once so loved by thee,
Think of her who wove them,
Her who made thee love them,
  Oh! then remember me.

When, around thee dying,
Autumn leaves are lying,
  Oh! then remember me.
And, at night, when gazing,
On the gay hearth blazing,
  Oh! still remember me.
Then, should music, stealing
All the soul of feeling,
To thy heart appealing,
  Draw one tear from thee;
Then let memory bring thee
Strains I used to sing thee—
  Oh! then remember me.

BENJAMIN FRANKLIN'S METHOD OF "DOING A GREAT DEAL OF GOOD WITH A LITTLE MONEY"

Passy, France, 22 April, 1784

Dear Sir:

Your situation grieves me and I send you herewith a banknote for ten louis d'ors. I do not pretend to give such a sum; I only lend it to you. When you shall return to your country, you cannot fail of getting into some business that will in time enable you to pay all your debts. In that case, when you meet with another honest man in similar distress, you must pay by lending this sum to him, enjoining him to discharge the debt by a like operation when he shall be able and shall meet with another such opportunity. I hope it may thus go through many hands before it meets with a knave that will stop its progress. This is a trick of mine for doing a great deal of good with a little money. I am not rich enough to afford much in good works, and so am obliged to be cunning and make the most of a little. With best wishes for your future prosperity, I am, dear sir, your most obedient servant,

B. FRANKLIN (letter to Benjamin Webb)

THE MULE DEFINED BY SAMUEL JOHNSON

Without pride of ancestry or hope of posterity.

THE AGED STRANGER

Bret Harte

"I was with Grant"—the stranger said;
  Said the farmer, "Say no more,
But rest thee here at my cottage porch,
  For thy feet are weary and sore."

"I was with Grant"—the stranger said;
  Said the farmer, "Nay, no more.
I prithee sit at my frugal board,
  And eat of my humble store.

"How fares my boy,—my soldier boy,
  Of the old Ninth Army Corps?
I warrant he bore him gallantly
  In the smoke and the battle's roar!"

"I know him not," said the aged man,
  "And, as I remarked before,
I was with Grant"—"Nay, nay, I know,"
  Said the farmer, "say no more."

"He fell in battle,—I see, alas!
  Thou'dst smooth these tidings o'er.
Nay, speak the truth, whatever it be,
  Though it rend my bosom's core."

"I cannot tell," said the aged man,
  "And should have remarked before,
That I was with Grant,—in Illinois,—
  Three years before the war."

Then the farmer spake him never a word,
  But beat him with his fist full sore
That aged man, who had worked for Grant
  Three years before the war.

A NEWSPAPER HOAX THAT FOOLED THE NATION

Popular Young Couple Married This Week

The groom is a popular young bum who hasn't done a lick of work since he got shipped in the middle of his junior year at college. He manages to dress well and to keep a supply of spending money because his dad is a soft-hearted old fool who takes up his bad checks instead of letting him go to jail where he belongs.

The bride is a skinny, fast little idiot who has been kissed and handled by every boy in town since she was twelve years old. She paints like a Sioux Indian, sucks cigarettes in secret, and drinks mean corn-liquor when she is out joy-riding in her dad's car at night. She doesn't know how to cook, sew or keep house.

The groom wore a rented dinner suit over athletic underwear of imitation silk. His pants were held up by pale green suspenders. His number eight patent-leather shoes matched his state in tightness and harmonized nicely with the axle-grease polish of his hair. In addition to his jag he carried a pocket-knife, a bunch of keys, a dun for the ring and his usual look of imbecility.

The bride wore some kind of white thing that left most of her legs sticking out at one end and her bony upper end sticking out at the other. The young people will make their home with the bride's parents, which means they will sponge on the old man until he dies and then she will take in washing. The happy couple anticipate a great event in about five months.

Postscript.—This may be the last issue of *The Tribune,* but my life ambition has been to write up one wedding and tell the unvarnished truth. Now that it is done, death can have no sting.

(By Robert E. Quillen in the Fountain Inn, S. C., *Tribune*)

TEARS

Lizette Woodworth Reese

When I consider Life and its few years—
A wisp of fog betwixt us and the sun;
A call to battle, and the battle done
Ere the last echo dies within our ears;
A rose choked in the grass; an hour of fears;
The gusts that past a darkening shore do beat;
The burst of music down an unlistening street,—
I wonder at the idleness of tears.
Ye old, old dead, and ye of yesternight,
Chieftains, and bards, and keepers of the sheep,
By every cup of sorrow that you had,
Loose from me my tears, and make me see aright
How each hath back what once he stayed to weep:
Homer his sight, David his little lad!

ON THE DEATH OF JOSEPH RODMAN DRAKE

Fitz-Greene Halleck

Green be the turf above thee,
  Friend of my better days!
None knew thee but to love thee,
  Nor named thee but to praise.

Tears fell when thou wert dying,
  From eyes unused to weep,
And long, where thou art lying,
  Will tears the cold turf steep.

When hearts, whose truth was proven,
  Like thine, are laid in earth,
There should a wreath be woven
  To tell the world their worth;

And I who woke each morrow
  To clasp thy hand in mine,
Who shared thy joy and sorrow,
  Whose weal and woe were thine;

It should be mine to braid it
  Around thy faded brow,
But I've in vain essayed it,
  And feel I cannot now.

While memory bids me weep thee,
  Nor thought nor words are free,—
The grief is fixed too deeply
  That mourns a man like thee.

BLACK-EYED SUSAN

John Gay

All in the Downs the fleet was moored,
  The streamers waving in the wind,
When black-eyed Susan came aboard;

"O, where shall I my true-love find?
Tell me, ye jovial sailors, tell me true
If my sweet William sails among the crew."

William, who high upon the yard
  Rocked with the billow to and fro,
Soon as her well-known voice he heard
  He sighed, and cast his eyes below:
The cord slides swiftly through his glowing hands,
And quick as lightning on the deck he stands.

So the sweet lark, high poised in air,
  Shuts close his pinions to his breast
If chance his mate's shrill call he hear,
  And drops at once into her nest:—
The noblest captain in the British fleet
Might envy William's lips those kisses sweet.

"O Susan, Susan, lovely dear,
  My vows shall ever true remain:
Let me kiss off that falling tear;
  We only part to meet again.
Change as ye list, ye winds; my heart shall be
The faithful compass that still points to thee.

"Believe not what the landmen say
  Who tempt with doubts thy constant mind:
They'll tell thee, sailors, when away,
  In every port a mistress find:
Yes, yes, believe them when they tell thee so,
For Thou art present wheresoe'er I go.

"If to fair India's coast we sail,
  Thy eyes are seen in diamonds bright,
Thy breath is Africa's spicy gale,
  Thy skin is ivory so white.
Thus every beauteous object that I view
Wakes in my soul some charm of lovely Sue.

"Though battle call me from thy arms,
  Let not my pretty Susan mourn;
Though cannons roar, yet safe from harms

William shall to his dear return.
Love turns aside the balls that round me fly,
Lest precious tears should drop from Susan's eye."

The boatswain gave the dreadful word,
The sails their seeling bosom spread;
No longer must she stay aboard:
They kissed, she sighed, he hung his head.
Her lessening boat unwilling rows to land;
"Adieu!" she cried; and waved her lily hand.

LENORE

Edgar Allan Poe

Ah, broken is the golden bowl! the spirit flown forever!
Let the bell toll!—a saintly soul floats on the Stygian river.
And, Guy de Vere, hast *thou* no tear?—weep now or never more
See! on yon drear and rigid bier low lies thy love, Lenore!
Come! let the burial rite be read—the funeral song be sung!—
An anthem for the queenliest dead that ever died so young—
A dirge for her, the doubly dead in that she died so young.

"Wretches! ye loved her for her wealth and hated her for her pride,
And when she fell in feeble health, ye bless her—that she died!
How *shall* the ritual, then, be read?—the requiem how be sung
By you—by yours, the evil eye—by yours, the slanderous tongue
That did to death the innocence that died, and died so young?"

Peccavimus; but rave not thus! and let a Sabbath song
Go up to God so solemnly the dead may feel no wrong!
The sweet Lenore hath "gone before," with Hope, that flew beside,
Leaving thee wild for the dear child that should have been thy bride—
For her, the fair and *débonnaire,* that now so lowly lies,
The life upon her yellow hair but not within her eyes—
The life still there, upon her hair—the death upon her eyes.

"Avaunt! to-night my heart is light. No dirge will I upraise,
But waft the angel on her flight with a paean of old days!
Let *no* bell toll—lest her sweet soul, amid its hallowed mirth,

Should catch the note, as it doth float up from the damned Earth.
To friends above, from fiends below, the indignant ghost is riven—
From Hell unto a high estate far up within the Heaven—
From grief and groan to a golden throne beside the King of
Heaven."

THE LAST MESSAGE FROM THE ALAMO

Commandancy of the Alamo, Bexar, February 24, 1836.—To the people of Texas and all Americans in the world. Fellow citizens and compatriots: I am besieged by a thousand or more of the Mexicans under Santa Anna. I have sustained a continual bombardment and cannonade for twenty-four hours and have not lost a man. The enemy has demanded a surrender at discretion; otherwise the garrison are to be put to the sword if the fort is taken. I have answered the demand with a cannon shot, and our flag still waves proudly from the walls. *I shall never surrender nor retreat.* Then, I call on you in the name of liberty, of patriotism, and everything dear to the American character, to come to our aid with all dispatch. The enemy is receiving reinforcements daily and will no doubt increase to three or four thousand in four or five days. If this call is neglected, I am determined to sustain myself as long as possible and die like a soldier who never forgets what is due to his own honor and that of our country. VICTORY OR DEATH.

William Barret Travis
Lieutenant Colonel Commandant

P.S. The Lord is on our side. When the enemy appeared in sight we had not three bushels of corn. We have since found in deserted houses eighty or ninety bushels and got into the walls twenty or thirty head of beeves.

WHO HATH A BOOK

Wilbur D. Nesbit

Who hath a book
Has friends at hand,
And gold and gear
At his command;

And rich estates,
  If he but look,
Are held by him
  Who hath a book.

Who hath a book
  Has but to read
And he may be
  A king indeed;

His Kingdom is
  His inglenook;
All this is his
  Who hath a book.

OUT OF THE CRADLE ENDLESSLY ROCKING

Walt Whitman

Out of the cradle endlessly rocking,
Out of the mocking-bird's throat, the musical shuttle,
Out of the Ninth-month midnight,
Over the sterile sands, and the fields beyond, where the child, leaving his bed, wander'd alone, bare-headed, barefoot,
Down from the shower'd halo,
Up from the mystic play of shadows, twining and twisting as if they were alive,
Out from the patches of briers and blackberries,
From the memories of the bird that chanted to me,
From your memories, sad brother—from the fitful risings and fallings I heard,
From under that yellow half-moon, late-risen, and swollen as if with tears,
From those beginning notes of sickness and love, there in the transparent mist,
From the thousand responses of my heart, never to cease,
From the myriad thence-arous'd words,
From the word stronger and more delicious than any,
From such, as now they start, the scene revisiting,
As a flock, twittering, rising, or overhead passing,
Borne hither—ere all eludes me, hurriedly,
A man—yet by these tears a little boy again,

Throwing myself on the sand, confronting the waves,
I, chanter of pains and joys, uniter of here and hereafter,
Taking all hints to use them—but swiftly leaping beyond them,
A reminiscence sing.

2

Once, Paumanok,
When the snows had melted—when the lilac-scent was in the air, and the Fifth-month grass was growing,
Up this sea-shore, in some briers,
Two guests from Alabama—two together,
And their nest, and four light-green eggs, spotted with brown,
And every day the he-bird, to and fro, near at hand,
And every day the she-bird, crouch'd on her nest, silent, with bright eyes,
And every day I, a curious boy, never too close, never disturbing them,
Cautiously peering, absorbing, translating.

3

Shine! shine! shine!
Pour down your warmth, great Sun!
While we bask—we two together.

Two together!
Winds blow South, or winds blow North,
Day come white, or night come black,
Home, or rivers and mountains from home,
Singing all time, minding no time,
While we two keep together.

4

Till of a sudden,
May-be kill'd, unknown to her mate,
One forenoon the she-bird crouch'd not on the nest,
Nor return'd that afternoon, nor the next,
Nor ever appear'd again.
And thenceforward, all summer, in the sound of the sea,
And at night, under the full of the moon, in calmer weather,
Over the hoarse surging of the sea,
Or flitting from brier to brier by day,
I saw, I heard at intervals, the remaining one, the he-bird,
The solitary guest from Alabama.

5

Blow! blow! blow!
Blow up, sea-winds, along Paumanok's shore!
I wait and I wait, till you blow my mate to me.

6

Yes, when the stars glisten'd,
All night long, on the prong of a moss-scallop'd stake,
Down, almost amid the slapping waves,
Sat the lone singer, wonderful, causing tears.

He call'd on his mate;
He pour'd forth the meanings which I, of all men, know.

Yes, my brother, I know;
The rest might not—but I have treasur'd every note;
For once, and more than once, dimly, down to the beach gliding.
Silent, avoiding the moonbeams, blending myself with the shadows,
Recalling now the obscure shapes, the echoes, the sounds and sights after their sorts,
The white arms out in the breakers tirelessly tossing,
I, with bare feet, a child, the wind wafting my hair,
Listen'd long and long.

Listen'd, to keep, to sing—now translating the notes,
Following you, my brother.

7

Soothe! soothe! soothe!
Close on its wave soothes the wave behind,
And again another behind, embracing and lapping, every one close,
But my love soothes not me, not me.

Low hangs the moon—it rose late;
O it is lagging—O I think it is heavy with love, with love,

O madly the sea pushes, pushes upon the land,
With love—with love.

O night! do I not see my love fluttering out there among the breakers?
What is that little black thing I see there in the white?

Loud! loud! loud!
Loud I call to you, my love!

High and clear I shoot my voice over the waves;
Surely you must know who is here, is here;
You must know who I am, my love.

Low-hanging moon!
What is that dusky spot in your brown yellow?

O it is the shape, the shape of my mate!
O moon, do not keep her from me any longer.

Land! land! O land!
Whichever way I turn, O I think you could give me my mate back again, if you only would;
For I am almost sure I see her dimly whichever way I look.

O rising stars!
Perhaps the one I want so much will rise, will rise with some of you.

O throat! O trembling throat!
Sound clearer through the atmosphere!
Pierce the woods, the earth;
Somewhere listening to catch you, must be the one I want.

Shake out, carols!
Solitary here—the night's carols!
Carols of lonesome love! Death's carols!
Carols under that lagging, yellow, waning moon!
O, under that moon, where she droops almost down into the sea!
O reckless, despairing carols.

But soft! sink low;
Soft! let me just murmur;
And do you wait a moment, you husky-noised sea;
For somewhere I believe I heard my mate responding to me,
So faint—I must be still, be still to listen;
But not altogether still, for then she might not come immediately to me.

Hither, my love!
Here I am! Here!

With this just-sustain'd note I announce myself to you;
This gentle call is for you, my love, for you.

Do not be decoy'd elsewhere!
That is the whistle of the wind—it is not my voice;
That is the fluttering, the fluttering of the spray;
Those are the shadows of leaves.

O darkness! O in vain!
O I am very sick and sorrowful.

O brown halo in the sky, near the moon, drooping upon the sea!
O troubled reflection in the sea!
O throat! O throbbing heart!
O all—and I singing uselessly, uselessly all the night.

Yet I murmur, murmur on!
O murmurs—you yourselves make me continue to sing, I know not why.

O past! O life! O songs of joy!
In the air—in the woods—over fields;
Loved! loved! loved! loved! loved!
But my love no more, no more with me!
We two together no more.

8

The aria sinking,
All else continuing—the stars shining,
The winds blowing—the notes of the bird continuous echoing,
With angry moans the fierce old mother incessantly moaning,
On the sands of Paumanok's shore, gray and rustling;
The yellow half-moon enlarged, sagging down, drooping, the face of the sea almost touching;
The boy ecstatic—with his bare feet the waves, with his hair the atmosphere dallying,
The love in the heart long pent, now loose, now at last tumultuously bursting,
The aria's meaning, the ears, the Soul, swiftly depositing,
The strange tears down the cheeks coursing,
The colloquy there—the trio—each uttering,
The undertone—the savage old mother, incessantly crying.

To the boy's Soul's questions sullenly timing—some drown'd secret hissing,
To the outsetting bard of love.

9

Demon or bird! (said the boy's soul,)
Is it indeed toward your mate you sing? or is it mostly to me?
For I, that was a child, my tongue's use sleeping,
Now I have heard you,
Now in a moment I know what I am for—I awake,
And already a thousand singers—a thousand songs, clearer, louder and more sorrowful than yours,
A thousand warbling echoes have started to life within me, never to die.
O you singer, solitary, singing by yourself—projecting me;
O solitary me, listening—never more shall I cease perpetuating you;
Never more shall I escape, never more the reverberations,
Never more the cries of unsatisfied love be absent from me,
Never again leave me to be the peaceful child I was before what there, in the night,
By the sea, under the yellow and sagging moon,
The messenger there arous'd—the fire, the sweet hell within,
The unknown want, the destiny of me.

O give me the clew! (it lurks in the night here somewhere;)
O if I am to have so much, let me have more!
O a word! O what is my destination? (I fear it is henceforth chaos;)
O how joys, dreads, convolutions, human shapes, and all shapes, spring as from graves around me!
O phantoms! you cover all the land and all the sea!
O I cannot see in the dimness whether you smile or frown upon me;
O vapor, a look, a word! O well-beloved!
O you dear women's and men's phantoms!

A word then, (for I will conquer it,)
The word final, superior to all,
Subtle, sent up—what is it?—I listen;
Are you whispering it, and have been all the time, you seawaves?
Is that it from your liquid rims and wet sands?

10

Whereto answering, the sea,
Delaying not, hurrying not,
Whisper'd me through the night, and very plainly before daybreak,
Lisp'd to me the low and delicious word DEATH,
And again Death—ever Death, Death, Death,
Hissing melodious, neither like the bird, nor like my arous'd child's heart,
But edging near, as privately for me, rustling at my feet,
Creeping thence steadily up to my ears, and laving me softly all over,
Death, Death, Death, Death, Death.

Which I do not forget,
But fuse the song of my dusky demon and brother,
That he sang to me in the moonlight on Paumanok's gray beach,
With the thousand responsive songs, at random,
My own songs, awaked from that hour;
And with them the key, the word up from the waves,
The word of the sweetest song, and all songs,
That strong and delicious word which, creeping to my feet,
The sea whisper'd me.

SUNRISE AND SUNSET

Emily Dickinson

I'll tell you how the sun rose,—
A ribbon at a time.
The steeples swam in amethyst,
The news like squirrels ran.

The hills untied their bonnets,
The bobolinks begun.
Then I said softly to myself,
"That must have been the sun!"

But how he set, I know not.
There seemed a purple stile
Which little yellow boys and girls
Were climbing all the while

Till when they reached the other side,
A dominie in gray
Put gently up the evening bars,
And led the flock away.

THE DEATH OF STONEWALL JACKSON

Lieut.-Col. George F. R. Henderson

About noon, when Major Pendleton came into the room, he [Stonewall Jackson] asked, "Who is preaching at headquarters today?" He was told that Mr. Lacy was, and that the whole army was praying for him. "Thank God," he said; "they are very kind to me." Already his strength was fast ebbing, and although his face brightened when his baby was brought to him, his mind had begun to wander. Now he was on the battle-field, giving orders to his men; now at home in Lexington; now at prayers in the camp. Occasionally his sense came back to him, and about half-past one he was told that he had but two hours to live. Again he answered, feebly but firmly, "Very good; it is all right." These were almost his last coherent words. For some time he lay unconscious, and then suddenly he cried out: "Order A. P. Hill to prepare for action! Pass the infantry to the front! Tell Major Hawks—" then stopped, leaving the sentence unfinished. Once more he was silent; but a little while after he said very quietly and clearly, "Let us cross over the river, and rest under the shade of the trees," and the soul of the great captain passed into the peace of God.

DELIGHT IN DISORDER

Robert Herrick

A sweet disorder in the dress
Kindles in clothes a wantonness.
A lawn about the shoulders thrown
Into a fine distraction;
An erring lace, which here and there
Enthrals the crimson stomacher;
A cuff neglectful, and thereby
Ribbands to flow confusedly;

A winning wave, deserving note,
In the tempestuous petticoat;
A careless shoestring, in whose tie
I see a wild civility;—
Do more bewitch me, than when art
Is too precise in every part.

A TERRIBLE INFANT

Frederick Locker-Lampson

I recollect a nurse called Ann,
  Who carried me about the grass;
And one fine day, a fine young man
Came up and kiss'd the pretty lass;
She did not make the least objection!
  Thinks I, *Aha!*
When I can talk I'll tell mama;
And that's my earliest recollection.

GEORGE WASHINGTON

Thomas Jefferson

His mind was great and powerful, without being of the very first order; his penetration strong, though not so acute as that of a Newton, Bacon or Locke; and as far as he saw, no judgment was ever sounder. It was slow in operation, being little aided by invention or imagination, but sure in conclusion. . . . Hearing all suggestions, he selected whatever was best; and certainly no General ever planned his battles more judiciously. But if deranged during the course of the action . . . he was slow in readjustment. . . . He was incapable of fear, meeting personal dangers with the calmest unconcern.

Perhaps the strongest feature in his character was prudence, never acting until every circumstance, every consideration was maturely weighed. . . . His integrity was most pure, his justice the most inflexible I have ever known, no motives of interest or consanguinity, of friendship or hatred, being able to bias his decision. He was, indeed, in every sense of the words, a wise, a good, and a great man. His temper was naturally irritable and high toned; but reflection and resolution had obtained a firm and habitual ascendancy over it. If ever, however, it broke its bonds, he was most tremendous in his wrath.

In his expenses he was honorable, but exact; liberal in contributions to whatever promised utility; but frowning and unyielding on all visionary projects and all unworthy calls on his charity. His heart was not warm in its affections; but he exactly calculated every man's value, and gave him a solid esteem proportioned to it.

His person, you know, was fine, his stature exactly what one would wish, his deportment easy, erect and noble; the best horseman of his age, and the most graceful figure that could be seen on horseback.

Although in the circle of his friends, where he might be unreserved with safety, he took a free share in conversation, his colloquial talents were not above mediocrity, possessing neither copiousness of ideas, nor fluency of words. In public, when called on for a sudden opinion, he was unready, short and embarrassed. Yet he wrote readily, rather diffusely, in an easy and correct style. This he had acquired by conversation with the world, for his education was merely reading, writing and common arithmetic, to which he added surveying at a later day. His time was employed in action chiefly, reading little, and that only in agriculture and English history. . . . His agricultural proceedings occupied most of his leisure hours within doors.

On the whole, his character was, in its mass, perfect, in nothing bad, in few points indifferent; and it may truly be said, that never did nature and fortune combine more perfectly to make a man great, and to place him . . . in an everlasting remembrance.

(1814)

ALL QUIET ON THE POTOMAC

Ethel L. Beers

"All quiet along the Potomac to-night."
Except here and there a stray picket
Is shot as he walks on his beat to and fro,
By a rifleman hid in the thicket.

'Tis nothing, a private or two now and then
Will not count in the news of the battle;
Not an officer lost. Only one of the men
Moaning out all alone the death rattle.
"All quiet along the Potomac to-night."

"All quiet along the Potomac to-night,"
There the soldiers lie peacefully dreaming,
And their tents in the rays of the clear autumn moon
And the rays of the camp-fires are gleaming.

A tremulous sigh as the gentle night wind
Through the forest leaves slowly is creeping,
While the stars up above, with their glittering eyes
Keep guard o'er the army while sleeping.

Hark! Was it the night wind that rustles the leaves?
Was it the moonlight so wondrously flashing?
It looked like a rifle! "Ha! Mary, good-bye!"
And his life-blood is ebbing and plashing.

"All quiet along the Potomac to-night."
No sound save the sound of the river;
While soft falls the dew on the face of the dead,
The picket's off duty forever.

A CHILD'S PRAYER

(Ex ore Infantium)

Francis Thompson

Little Jesus, wast Thou shy
Once, and just so small as I?
And what did it feel like to be
Out of Heaven, and just like me?
Didst Thou sometimes think of *there,*
And ask where all the angels were?
I should think that I would cry
For my house all made of sky;
I would look about the air,

And wonder where my angels were;
And at waking 'twould distress me—
Not an angel there to dress me!

Hadst Thou ever any toys,
Like us little girls and boys?
And didst Thou play in Heaven with all
The angels, that were not too tall,
With stars for marbles? Did the things
Play *Can you see me?* through their wings?

And did Thy mother let Thee spoil
Thy robes with playing on *our* soil?
How nice to have been always new
In Heaven, because 'twas clean blue!

Didst Thou kneel at night to pray,
And didst Thou join Thy hands, this way?
And did they tire sometimes, being young,
And make the prayer seem very long?
And dost Thou like it best, that we
Should join our hands and pray to Thee?
I used to think, before I knew,
The prayer not said unless we do.
And did Thy mother at the night
Kiss Thee and fold the clothes in right?
And didst Thou feel quite good in bed,
Kissed, and sweet, and Thy prayers said?

Thou canst not have forgotten all
That it feels like to be small:
And Thou know'st I cannot pray
To Thee in my father's way—
When Thou wast so little, say,
Could'st Thou talk Thy Father's way?—

So, a little child, come down
And hear a child's tongue like Thy own;
Take me by the hand and walk,
And listen to my baby-talk.
To Thy Father show my prayer

(He will look, Thou art so fair),
And say: "O Father, I Thy Son,
Bring the prayer of a little one."

And He will smile, that children's tongue
Has not changed since Thou wast young!

WE NEVER SPEAK AS WE PASS BY

Anonymous

The spell is past, the dream is o'er,
And tho' we meet, we love no more!
One heart is crushed to droop and die,
And for relief must heav'nward fly!
The once bright smile has faded, gone;
And given way to looks forlorn!
Despite her grandeur's wicked flame,
She stoops to blush beneath her shame.

Chorus:

We never speak as we pass by,
Altho' a tear bedims her eye;
I know she thinks of her past life,
When we were loving man and wife!

In guileless youth I sought her side,
And she became my virtuous bride,
Our lot was peace, so fair, so bright.
One sunny day, no gloomy night;
No life on earth more pure than ours,
In that dear home, 'midst fields and flowers,
Until the tempter came to her,
It dazzled her, alas, she fell!

In gilded halls 'midst wealth she dwells,
How her heart aches, her sad face tells,
She fain would smile, seem bright and gay,
But Conscience steals her peace away;
And when the flatterer casts aside
My fallen dishonored bride,
I'll close her eyes, in death forgive,
And in my heart her name shall live.

IS THERE A SANTA CLAUS?

We take pleasure in answering at once and thus prominently the communication below, expressing at the same time our great gratification that its faithful author is numbered among the friends of THE SUN:

Dear Editor—I am 8 years old.

Some of my little friends say there is no Santa Claus.

Papa says, "If you see it in THE SUN it's so."

Please tell me the truth, is there a Santa Claus? Virginia O'Hanlon 115 West ninety-fifth street.

Virginia, your little friends are wrong. They have been affected by the skepticism of a skeptical age. They do not believe except they see. They think that nothing can be which is not comprehensible by their little minds. All minds, Virginia, whether they be men's or children's, are little. In this great universe of ours man is a mere insect, an ant, in his intellect, as compared with the boundless world about him, as measured by the intelligence capable of grasping the whole of truth and knowledge.

Yes, Virginia, there is a SANTA CLAUS. He exists as certainly as love and generosity and devotion exist, and you know that they abound and give to your life its highest beauty and joy. Alas! how dreary would be the world if there were no SANTA CLAUS! It would be as dreary as if there were no Virginias. There would be no child-like faith then, no poetry, no romance to make tolerable this existence. We should have no enjoyment, except in sense and sight. The eternal light with which childhood fills the world would be extinguished.

Not believe in SANTA CLAUS! You might as well not believe in fairies! You might get your papa to hire men to watch in all the chimneys on Christmas Eve to catch SANTA CLAUS, but even if they did not see SANTA CLAUS coming down, what would that prove? Nobody sees SANTA CLAUS, but that is no sign there is no SANTA CLAUS. The most real things in the world are those that neither children nor men can see. Did you ever see fairies dancing on the lawn? Of course not, but that's no proof that they are not there. Nobody can conceive or imagine all the wonders there are unseen and unseeable in the world.

You tear apart a baby's rattle and see what makes the noise inside, but there is a veil covering the unseen world which not the strongest man, nor even the united strength of all the strongest men that ever lived, could tear apart. Only faith, fancy, poetry, love, romance, can push aside that curtain and view and picture the supernal beauty and glory beyond. Is it all real? Ah, Virginia, in all this world there is nothing else real and abiding.

No SANTA CLAUS! Thank GOD! he lives, and he lives forever. A thousand years from now, Virginia, nay, ten times ten thousand years from now, he will continue to make glad the heart of childhood.

(Editorial in the New York SUN, Sept. 21, 1897, by Francis P. Church)

ETERNAL FATHER, STRONG TO SAVE

William Whiting

Eternal Father, strong to save,
Whose arm hath bound the restless wave
Who bidd'st the mighty ocean deep
Its own appointed limits keep:
  O hear us when we cry to Thee
  For those in peril on the sea.

O Christ, whose voice the waters heard,
And hushed their raging at Thy word,
Who walkedst on the foaming deep,
And calm amid the storm didst sleep:
  O hear us when we cry to Thee
  For those in peril on the sea.

O Holy Spirit, who didst brood
Upon the waters dark and rude,
And bid their angry tumult cease,
And give, for wild confusion, peace:
  O hear us when we cry to Thee
  For those in peril on the sea.

O Trinity of love and power,
Our brethren shield in danger's hour;
From rock and tempest, fire and foe,
Protect them wheresoe'er they go:
  Thus evermore shall rise to Thee
  Glad hymns of praise from land and sea.

THE DINKEY-BIRD

Eugene Field

In an ocean, 'way out yonder
  (As all sapient people know),
Is the land of Wonder-Wander,
  Whither children love to go;
It's their playing, romping, swinging,
  That give great joy to me
While the Dinkey-Bird goes singing
  In the amfalula tree!

There the gum-drops grow like cherries
  And taffy's thick as peas—
Caramels you pick like berries
  When, and where, and how you please;
Big red sugar-plums are clinging
  To the cliffs beside that sea
Where the Dinkey-Bird is singing
  In the amfalula tree.

So when children shout and scamper
  And make merry all the day,
When there's naught to put a damper
  To the ardor of their play;
When I hear their laughter ringing
  Then I'm sure as sure can be
That the Dinkey-Bird is singing
  In the amfalula tree.

For the Dinkey-Bird's bravuras
  And staccatos are so sweet—
His roulades, apoggiaturas,
  And robustos so complete,
That the youth of every nation—
  Be they near or far away—
Have especial delectation
  In that gladsome roundelay.

Their eyes grow bright and brighter
  Their lungs begin to crow,
Their hearts get light and lighter,

And their cheeks are all aglow;
For an echo cometh bringing
The news to all and me,
That the Dinkey-Bird is singing
In the amfalula tree.

I'm sure you like to go there
To see your feathered friend—
And so many goodies grow there
You would like to comprehend!
Speed, little dreams, your winging
To that land across the sea
Where the Dinkey-Bird is singing
In the amfalula tree!

THE KID IN UPPER 4

It is 3.42 a.m. on a troop train.
Men wrapped in blankets are breathing heavily.
Two in every lower berth. One in every upper.
This is no ordinary trip. It may be their last in the U.S.A. till the end of the war. Tomorrow they will be on the high seas.
One is wide awake . . . listening . . . staring into the blackness.
It is the kid in Upper 4.

* * *

Tonight, he knows, he is leaving behind a lot of little things—and big ones.
The taste of hamburgers and pop—the feel of driving a roadster over a six-lane highway . . . a dog named Shucks, or Spot, or Barnacle Bill.
The pretty girl who writes so often . . . that gray-haired man, so proud and awkward at the station . . . the mother who knit the socks he'll wear so soon.
Tonight he's thinking them over.
There's a lump in his throat. And maybe—a tear fills his eye.
It doesn't matter, Kid. Nobody will see . . . it's too dark.

* * *

A couple of thousand miles away, where he's going, they don't know him very well.

But people all over the world are waiting, praying for him to come.
And he will come, this kid in Upper 4.
With new hope, peace and freedom for a tired, bleeding world.

* * *

Next time you are on the train, *remember the kid in Upper 4.*
If you have to stand en route—*it is so he may have a seat.*
If there is no berth for you—*it is so that he may sleep.*
If you have to wait for a seat in the diner—*it is so he—and thousands like him . . . may have a meal they won't forget in the days to come.*
For to treat him as our most honored guest is the least we can do to pay a mighty debt of gratitude.

THE NEW HAVEN R.R.
(Written by Nelson C. Metcalf)

THE SHEPHERDESS

Alice Meynell

She walks—the lady of my delight—
  A shepherdess of sheep.
Her flocks are thoughts. She keeps them white;
  She guards them from the steep;
She feeds them on the fragrant height,
  And folds them in for sleep.

She roams maternal hills and bright,
  Dark valleys safe and deep.
Into that tender breast at night
  The chastest stars may peep.
She walks—the lady of my delight—
  A shepherdess of sheep.

She holds her little thoughts in sight,
  Though gay they run and leap.
She is so circumspect and right;
  She has her soul to keep.
She walks—the lady of my delight—
  A shepherdess of sheep.

"A WET SHEET AND A FLOWING SEA"

Allan Cunningham

A wet sheet and a flowing sea,
  A wind that follows fast
And fills the white and rustling sail
  And bends the gallant mast;
And bends the gallant mast, my boys,
  While like the eagle free
Away the good ship flies, and leaves
  Old England on the lee.

O for a soft and gentle wind!
  I heard a fair one cry;
But give to me the snoring breeze
  And white waves heaving high;
And white waves heaving high, my lads,
  The good ship tight and free—
The world of waters is our home,
  And merry men are we.

There's tempest in yon hornéd moon,
  And lightning in yon cloud;
But hark the music, mariners!
  The wind is piping loud;
The wind is piping loud, my boys,
  The lightning flashes free—
While the hollow oak our palace is,
  Our heritage of the sea.

THE INCHCAPE ROCK

Robert Southey

No stir in the air, no stir in the sea,
The ship was still as she could be;
Her sails from heaven received no motion,
Her keel was steady in the ocean.

Without either sign or sound of their shock,
The waves flowed over the Inchcape Rock;
So little they rose, so little they fell,
They did not move the Inchcape Bell.

The holy Abbot of Aberbrothok
Had placed that bell on the Inchcape Rock;
On a buoy in the storm it floated and swung,
And over the waves its warning rung.

When the rock was hid by the surge's well,
The mariners heard the warning Bell;
And they knew the perilous Rock,
And blessed the Abbot of Aberbrothok.

The Sun in heaven was shining gay,
All things were joyful on that day;
The sea-birds screamed as they wheeled around,
And there was joyance in their sound.

The buoy of the Inchcape Bell was seen,
A darker speck on the ocean green;
Sir Ralph, the Rover, walked his deck,
And he fixed his eye on the darker speck.

He felt the cheering power of spring,
It made him whistle, it made him sing;
His heart was mirthful to excess;
But the Rover's mirth was wickedness.

His eye was on the Inchcape float;
Quoth he: "My men, put out the boat;
And row me to the Inchcape Rock,
And I'll plague the Abbot of Aberbrothok."

The boat is lowered, the boatmen row,
And to the Inchcape Rock they go;
Sir Ralph bent over from the boat,
And cut the Bell from the Inchcape float.

Down sank the Bell with a gurgling sound;
The bubbles rose, and burst around.
Quoth Sir Ralph, "The next who comes to the Rock
Won't bless the Abbot of Aberbrothok."

Sir Ralph, the Rover, sailed away,
He scoured the seas for many a day;
And now, grown rich with plundered store,
He steers his course for Scotland's shore.

So thick a haze o'erspreads the sky
They cannot see the Sun on high;
The wind hath blown a gale all day;
At evening it hath died away.

On the deck the Rover takes his stand;
So dark it is they see no land.
Quoth Sir Ralph, "It will be lighter soon,
For there is the dawn of the rising moon."

"Canst hear," said one, "the breakers roar?
For yonder, methinks, should be the shore."
"Now where we are I cannot tell,
But I wish I could hear the Inchcape Bell."

They hear no sound; the swell is strong;
Though the wind hath fallen, they drift along,
Till the vessel strikes with a shivering shock,—
"O Christ! it is the Inchcape Rock!"

Sir Ralph, the Rover, tore his hair;
He cursed himself in his despair.
The waves rush in on every side;
The ship is sinking beneath the tide.

But, even in his dying fear,
One dreadful sound could the Rover hear,—
A sound as if, with the Inchcape Bell,
The Devil below was ringing his knell.

DREAM CHILDREN: A REVERIE

Charles Lamb

Children love to listen to stories about their elders, when *they* were children; to stretch their imagination to the conception of a traditionary great-uncle, or grandame, whom they never saw. It was in this spirit that my little ones crept about me the other evening to hear about their great-grandmother Field, who lived in a great house in Norfolk (a hundred times bigger than that in which they and papa lived) which had been the scene—so at least it was generally believed in that part of the country—of the tragic incidents which they had lately become familiar with from the ballad of the Children in the Wood. Certain it is that the whole story of the children and their cruel uncle was to be seen fairly carved out in wood upon the chimney-piece of the great hall, the whole story down to the Robin Redbreasts; till a foolish rich person pulled it down to set up a marble one of modern invention in its stead, with no story upon it. Here Alice put out one of dear mother's looks, too tender to be called unbraiding. Then I went on to say, how religious and how good their great-grandmother Field was, how beloved and respected by everybody, though she was not indeed the mistress of this great house, but had only the charge of it (and yet in some respects she might be said to be the mistress of it too) committed to her by the owner, who preferred living in a newer and more fashionable mansion which he had purchased somewhere in the adjoining county; but still she lived in it in a manner as if it had been her own, and kept up the dignity of the great house in a sort while she lived, which afterwards came to decay, and was nearly pulled down, and all its old ornaments stripped and carried away to the owner's other house, where they were set up, and looked as awkward as if some one were to carry away the old tombs they had seen lately at the Abbey, and stick them up in Lady C.'s tawdry gilt drawing-room. Here John smiled, as much as to say, "that would be foolish indeed." And then I told how, when she came to die, her funeral was attended by a concourse of all the poor, and some of the gentry too, of the neighbourhood for many miles round, to show their respect for her memory, because she had been such a good and religious woman; so good indeed that she knew all the Psaltery by heart, ay, and a great part of the Testament besides. Here little Alice spread her hands. Then I told what a tall, upright, graceful person their great-grandmother Field once was; and how in her youth she was esteemed the best dancer—here Alice's little right foot played an involuntary movement, till, upon my looking grave, it desisted—the best dancer, I was saying, in the county, till a cruel disease, called a cancer, came, and bowed her down with pain; but it could never bend her good spirits, or make them stoop, but they were still upright, because she was so good and religious. Then I told how she was used to sleep by herself in a lone chamber of the great lone house; and how she believed that an apparition of two infants was to be seen at midnight gliding up and down the great staircase near where she slept, but she said "those innocents would do her no harm"; and how frightened I used to be, though in those days I had my maid to sleep with me, because I was never half so good or religious as she—and yet I never saw the infants. Here John expanded all his eyebrows and tried to look courageous. Then I told how good she was to all her grandchildren, having us to the great house in the holydays, where I in particular used to spend many hours by myself, in gazing upon the old busts of the twelve Caesars, that had been Emperors of Rome, till the old marble heads would seem to live again, or I to be turned into marble with them; how I never could be tired with roaming about that huge mansion, with its vast empty rooms, with their worn-out hangings, fluttering tapestry, and carved oaken panels, with the gilding almost rubbed out—sometimes in the spacious old-fashioned gardens, which I had almost to myself, unless when now and then a solitary gardening man would cross me—and how the nectarines and peaches hung upon the walls, without my ever offering to pluck them, because they were forbidden fruit, unless now and then,—and because I had more pleasure in strolling about among the old melancholy-looking yew-trees, or the firs, and picking up the red berries, and the fir-apples, which were good for nothing but to look at—or in lying about upon the fresh grass with all the fine garden smells around me—or basking in the orangery, till I could almost fancy myself ripening too along with the oranges and the limes in that grateful warmth—or in watching the dace that darted to and fro in the fish-pond, at the bottom of the garden, with here and there a great sulky pike hanging midway down the water in silent state, as if it mocked at their impertinent friskings, —I had more pleasure in these busy-idle diversions than in all the sweet flavours of peaches, nectarines, oranges, and such-like common baits of children. Here John slyly deposited back upon the plate a bunch of grapes, which, not unobserved by Alice, he had meditated dividing with her, and both seemed willing to relinquish them for the present as irrelevant. Then, in somewhat a more heightened tone, I told how, though their great-grandmother Field loved all her grandchildren, yet in an especial manner she might be said to love their uncle, John L——, because he was so handsome and spirited a youth, and a king to the rest of us; and, instead of moping about in solitary corners, like some of us, he would mount the most mettlesome horse he could get, when but an imp no bigger than themselves, and make it carry him half over the county in a morning, and join the hunters when there were any out—and yet he loved the old great house and gardens too, but had too much spirit to be always pent up within their boundaries—and how their uncle grew up to man's estate as brave as he was handsome, to the admiration of everybody, but of their great-grandmother Field most especially; and how he used to carry me upon his back when I was a lame-footed boy—for he was a good bit older than me—many a mile when I could not walk for pain; —and how in after life he became lame-footed too, and I did not always (I fear) make allowances enough for him when he was impatient, and in pain, nor remember sufficiently how considerate he had been to me when I was lame-footed; and how when he died, though he had not been dead an hour, it seemed as if he had died a great while ago, such a distance there is betwixt life and death; and how I bore his death as I thought pretty well at first, but afterwards it haunted and haunted me; and though I did not cry or take it to heart as some do, and as I think he would have done if I had died, yet I missed him all day long, and knew not till then how much I had loved him. I missed his kindness, and I missed his crossness, and wished him to be alive again, to be quarrelling with him (for we quarrelled sometimes), rather than not have him again, and was as uneasy without him, as he their poor uncle must have been when the doctor took off his limb.—Here the children fell a-crying, and asked if their little mourning which they had on was not for uncle John, and they looked up, and prayed me not to go on about their uncle, but to tell them some stories about their pretty dead mother. Then I told how for seven long years, in hope sometimes, sometimes in despair, yet persisting ever, I courted the fair Alice W—n; and, as much as children could understand, I explained to them what coyness, and difficulty, and denial, meant in maidens—when suddenly, turning to Alice, the soul of the first Alice looked out at her eyes with such a reality of re-presentment, that I became in doubt which of them stood there before me, or whose that bright hair was; and while I stood gazing, both the children gradually grew fainter to my view, receding, and still receding, till nothing at last but two mournful features were seen in the uttermost distance, which, without speech, strangely impressed upon me the effects of speech: "We are not of Alice, nor of thee, nor are we children at all. The children of Alice call Bartrum father. We are nothing; less than nothing, and dreams. We are only what might have been, and must wait upon the tedious shores of Lethe millions of ages before we have existence, and a name"—and immediately awaking, I found myself quietly seated in my bachelor arm-chair, where I had fallen asleep, with the faithful Bridget unchanged by my side—but John L. (or James Elia) was gone for ever.

JEAN

Robert Burns

Of a' the airts the wind can blaw,
  I dearly like the west,
For there the bonnie lassie lives,
  The lassie I lo'e best:
There wild woods grow, and rivers row
  And monie a hill between;
But day and night my fancy's flight
  Is ever wi' my Jean.

I see her in the dewy flowers,
  I see her sweet and fair:
I hear her in the tunefu' birds,
  I hear her charm the air:
There's not a bonnie flower that springs
  By fountain, shaw, or green;
There's not a bonnie bird that sings,
  But minds me o' my Jean.

A WISH

Samuel Rogers

Mine be a cot beside the hill;
  A bee-hive's hum shall soothe my ear;
A willowy brook that turns a mill,
  With many a fall shall linger near.

The swallow, oft, beneath my thatch
  Shall twitter from her clay-built nest;
Oft shall the pilgrim lift the latch,
  And share my meal, a welcome guest.

Around my ivied porch shall spring
  Each fragrant flower that drinks the dew;
And Lucy, at her wheel, shall sing
  In russet gown and apron blue.

The village church among the trees,
  Where first our marriage vows were given,
With merry peals shall swell the breeze
  And point with taper spire to heaven.

PIED BEAUTY

Gerard Manley Hopkins

Glory be to God for dappled things—
  For skies of couple-colour as a brinded cow;
  For rose-moles all in stipple upon trout that swim;

Fresh-fire-coal chestnut-falls; finches' wings;
  Landscape plotted and pieced—fold, fallow, and plough;
    And áll trádes, their gear and tackle and trim.

All things counter, original, spare, strange;
  Whatever is fickle, freckled (who knows how?)
    With swift, slow; sweet, sour; adazzle, dim;
He fathers-forth whose beauty is past change:
  Praise him.

A HAPPY MAN

Anatole France

(Translator: D. B. Stewart)

Note: A fabled king, tormented by imaginary ills, was advised to wear the shirt of a happy man. This is the experience of the king's emissaries, sent in search of the shirt of a happy man.

Having travelled through the country for a year in vain, Quatrefeuilles and Saint-Sylvain returned to the Chateau de Fontblande, whither the King had gone to enjoy the coolness of the woods. They found him in a state of prostration which was alarming the Court.

The guests did not lodge at the Chateau de Fontblande, which was hardly more than a hunting-box. The secretary and the equerry had taken lodgings in the village, and every day they walked through the woods to visit their Sovereign. On the way they often met a little man who lived in a great hollow plane-tree in the forest. His name was Mousque, and he was far from handsome, with his pug face, prominent cheek-bones, and large nose with round nostrils. But his square teeth, which his red lips often uncovered in laughter, gave his wild face an appearance of brightness and cheeriness. How he had taken possession of the great hollow plane-tree no one knew; but he had made himself a very tidy room there, furnished with all that he required. Truth to tell, he needed little. He lived on the forest and lake, and he lived very well. The irregularity of his condition was overlooked, because he made himself useful, and knew how to please people. When the ladies at the chateau drove in the forest, he would offer them, in baskets of osier plaited by himself, sections of honey, wild strawberries, or the tart, sweet fruit of the wild cherry. He was always ready to put his shoulder to the wheel of a cart foundered in the mire, and would help to fetch in the hay if the weather was threatening. He would do more than others without getting tired. His strength and activity were extraordinary. He could break a wolf's jaw-bone with his hands, run down a hare, and climb trees like a cat. To amuse the children he made reed flutes, little windmills, and Hieron's fountains.

Quatrefeuilles and Saint-Sylvain often heard it said in the village: "Happy as Mousque." This proverb impressed their minds, and one day, passing the hollow plane-tree, they saw Mousque playing with a young puppy, and apparently as happy as the dog. It occurred to them to ask whether he was happy.

Mousque was unable to answer, not having reflected on the subject of happiness. They explained generally and very simply what it meant. After thinking it over for a moment he answered that he possessed it.

At this reply Saint-Sylvain called out impetuously:

"Mousque, we will get you everything that you can want, gold, a palace, new shoes, anything that you would like; but give us your shirt."

His kindly face expressed neither regret nor disappointment, which he was quite incapable of feeling, but a great surprise. He made a sign that he could not give what they asked of him. He had not a shirt.

(From The Shirt—)

MY MIND TO ME A KINGDOM IS

Sir Edward Dyer

My mind to me a kingdom is;
  Such present joys therein I find
That it excels all other bliss
  That earth affords or grows by kind.
Though much I want which most would have,
Yet still my mind forbids to crave.

No princely pomp, no wealthy store,
  No force to win the victory,
No wily wit to salve a sore,
  No shape to feed a loving eye;
To none of these I yield as thrall—
For why? My mind doth serve for all.

I see how plenty surfeits oft,
  And hasty climbers soon do fall;
I see that those which are aloft
  Mishap doth threaten most of all;
They get with toil, they keep with fear—
Such care my mind could never bear.

Content to live, this is my stay;
  I seek no more than may suffice;
I press to bear no haughty sway;
  Look, what I lack my mind supplies.
Lo, thus I triumph like a king,
Content with that my mind doth bring.

Some have too much, yet still do crave;
  I little have, and seek no more.
They are but poor, though much they have,
  And I am rich with little store.
They poor, I rich; they beg, I give;
They lack, I leave; they pine, I live.

I laugh not at another's loss;
  I grudge not at another's pain;
No worldly waves my mind can toss;

My state at one doth still remain.
I fear no foe, I fawn no friend;
I loathe not life, nor dread my end.

Some weigh their pleasure by their lust,
Their wisdom by their rage of will;
Their treasure is their only trust;
A cloakéd craft their store of skill.
But all the pleasure that I find
Is to maintain a quiet mind.

My wealth is health and perfect ease;
My conscience clear my chief defense;
I neither seek by bribes to please
Nor by deceit to breed offense,
Thus do I live; thus will I die;
Would all did so as well as I!

PILGRIMAGE

Sir Walter Raleigh

Give me my scallop-shell of quiet,
My staff of faith to walk upon,
My scrip of joy, immortal diet,
My bottle of salvation,
My gown of glory, hope's true gage,
And thus I'll take my pilgrimage.

THE SECOND SPRING

John Henry Newman

We have familiar experience of the order, the constancy, the perpetual renovation of the material world which surrounds us. Frail and transitory as is every part of it, restless and migratory as are its elements, never-ceasing as are its changes, still it abides. It is bound together by a law of permanence, it is set up in unity; and, though it is ever dying, it is ever coming to life again. Dissolution does but give birth to fresh modes of organization, and one death is the parent of a thousand lives. Each hour, as it comes, is but a testimony, how fleeting, yet how secure, how certain, is the great whole. It is like an image on the waters, which is ever the same, though the waters ever flow. Change upon change—yet one change cries out to another, like the alternate Seraphim, in praise and in glory of their Maker. The sun sinks to rise again; the day is swallowed up in the gloom of the night, to be born out of it, as fresh as if it had never been quenched. Spring passes into summer, and through summer and autumn into winter, only the more surely, by its own ultimate return, to triumph over that grave, towards which it resolutely hastened from its first hour. We mourn over the blossoms of May, because they are to wither; but we know, withal, that May is one day to have its revenge upon November, by the revolution of that solemn circle which never stops—which teaches us in our height of hope, ever to be sober, and in our depth of desolation, never to despair.

And forcibly as this comes home to every one of us, not less forcible is the contrast which exists between this material world, so vigorous, so reproductive, amid all its changes, and the moral world, so feeble, so downward, so resourceless, amid all its aspirations. That which ought to come to naught, endures; that which promises a future, disappoints and is no more. The same sun shines in heaven from first to last, and the blue firmament, the everlasting mountains, reflect his rays; but where is there upon earth the champion, the hero, the lawgiver, the body politic, the sovereign race, which was great three hundred years ago, and is great now? Moralists and poets, often do they descant upon this innate vitality of matter, this innate perishableness of mind. Man rises to fall: he tends to dissolution from the moment he begins to be; he lives on, indeed, in his children, he lives on in his name, he lives not on in his own person. He is, as regards the manifestations of his nature here below, as a bubble that breaks, and as water poured out upon the earth. He was young, he is old, and he is never young again. This is the lament over him, poured forth in verse and in prose, by Christians and by heathen. The greatest work of God's hand under the sun, he, in all the manifestations of his complex being, is born only to die.

His bodily frame first begins to feel the power of this constraining law, though it is the last to succumb to it. We look at the bloom of youth with interest, yet with pity; and the more graceful and sweet it is, with pity so much the more; for, whatever be its excellence and its glory, soon it begins to be deformed and dishonored by the very force of its living on. It grows into exhaustion and collapse, till at length it crumbles into that dust out of which it was originally taken.

So is it, too, with our moral being, a far higher and diviner portion of our natural constitution; it begins with life, it ends with what is worse than the mere loss of life, with a living death. How beautiful is the human heart, when it puts forth its first leaves, and opens and rejoices in its spring-tide. Fair as may be the bodily form, fairer far, in its green foliage and bright blossoms, its natural virtue. It blooms in the young, like some rich flower, so delicate, so fragrant, and so dazzling. Generosity and lightness of heart and amiableness, the confiding spirit, the gentle temper, the elastic cheerfulness, the open hand, the pure affection, the noble aspiration, the heroic resolve, the romantic pursuit, the love in which self has no part,—are not these beautiful? and are they not dressed up and set forth for admiration in their best shapes, in tales and in poems? and ah! what a prospect of good is there! who could believe that it is to fade! and yet, as night follows upon day, as decrepitude follows upon health, so surely are failure, and overthrow, and annihilation, the issue of this natural virtue, if time only be allowed to it to run its course. There are those who are cut off in the first opening of this excellence, and then, if we may trust their epitaphs, they have lived like angels; but wait a while, let them live on, let the course of life proceed, let the bright soul go through the fire and water of the world's temptations and seductions and corruptions and transformations; and alas for the insufficiency of nature! alas for its powerlessness to persevere, its waywardness in disappointing its own promise! Wait till youth has become age; and not more different is the miniature which we have of him when a boy, when every feature spoke of hope, put side by side of the large portrait painted to his honor, when he is old, when his limbs are shrunk, his eye dim, his brow furrowed, and his hair grey, than differs the moral grace of that boyhood from the forbidding and repulsive aspect of his soul, now that he has lived to the age of man. For moroseness, and misanthropy, and selfishness, is the ordinary winter of that spring.

Such is man in his own nature, and such, too, is he in his works. The noblest efforts of his genius, the conquests he has made, the doctrines he has originated, the nations he has civilized, the states he has created, they outlive himself, they outlive him by many centuries, but they tend to an end, and that end is dissolution. Powers of the world, sovereignties, dynasties, sooner or later come to nought; they have their fatal hour. The Roman conqueror shed tears over Carthage, for in the destruction of the rival city he discerned too truly an augury of the fall of Rome; and at length, with the weight and the responsibilities, the crimes and the glories, of centuries upon centuries, the Imperial City fell.

Thus man and all his works are mortal; they die, and they have no power of renovation.

THE PELICAN

Anonymous

A rare old bird is the Pelican;
His beak holds more than his belican.
He can take in his beak
Enough food for a week.
I'm darned if I know how the helican.

THE GATE OF THE YEAR

M. Louise Haskins

And I said to the man who stood at the gate of the year:
"Give me a light, that I may tread safely into the unknown!"
And he replied:
"Go out into the darkness and put your hand into the Hand of God.
That shall be to you better than light and safer than a known way."
So, I went forth, and finding the Hand of God, trod gladly into the night.
And He led me toward the hills and the breaking of day in the lone East.
So, heart, be still!
What need our little life,
Our human life, to know,
If God hath comprehension?
In all the dizzy strife
Of things both high and low
God hideth His intention.

THE NYMPH'S REPLY TO THE SHEPHERD

Sir Walter Raleigh

If all the world and love were young,
And truth in every shepherd's tongue,
These pretty pleasures might me move
To live with thee and be thy love.

But time drives flocks from field to fold,
When rivers rage, and rocks grow cold;
And Philomel becometh dumb;
The rest complain of cares to come.

The flowers do fade, and wanton fields
To wayward Winter reckoning yields;
A honey tongue, a heart of gall,
Is fancy's spring, but sorrow's fall.

Thy gowns, thy shoes, thy beds of roses,
Thy cap, thy kirtle, and thy posies,
Soon break, soon wither, soon forgotten,
In folly ripe, in reason rotten.

Thy belt of straw and ivy buds,
Thy coral clasps and amber studs,
All these in me no means can move
To come to thee and be thy love.

But could youth last, and love still breed,
Had joys no date, nor age no need,
Then these delights my mind might move
To live with thee and be thy love.

THE MAD GARDENER'S SONG

Lewis Carroll

He thought he saw a Buffalo
  Upon the chimney-piece:
He looked again, and found it was
  His Sister's Husband's Niece.
"Unless you leave this house," he said,
  "I'll send for the Police!"

He thought he saw a Rattlesnake
  That questioned him in Greek:
He looked again, and found it was
  The Middle of Next Week.
"The one thing I regret," he said,
  "Is that it cannot speak!"

He thought he saw a Banker's Clerk
  Descending from the 'bus:
He looked again, and found it was
  A Hippopotamus.
"If this should stay to dine," he said,
  "There won't be much for us!"

He thought he saw a Kangaroo
  That worked a coffee-mill:
He looked again, and found it was
  A Vegetable-Pill.
"Were I to swallow this," he said,
  "I should be very ill!"

He thought he saw a Coach-and-Four
  That stood beside his bed:
He looked again, and found it was
  A Bear without a Head.
"Poor thing," he said, "poor silly thing!
  "It's waiting to be fed!"

He thought he saw an Albatross
  That fluttered round the lamp:
He looked again, and found it was
  A Penny-Postage Stamp.
"You'd best be getting home," he said:
  "The nights are very damp!"

THE THREE JOHNS

Oliver Wendell Holmes

But remember that talking is one of the fine arts—the noblest, the most important, and the most difficult—and that its fluent harmonies may be spoiled by the intrusion of a single harsh note.

Therefore conversation which is suggestive rather than argumentative, which lets out the most of each talker's results of thought, is commonly the pleasantest and most profitable. It is not easy, at the best, for two persons talking together to make the most of each other's thoughts, there are so many of them.

[The Company looked as if they wanted an explanation.]

When John and Thomas, for instance, are talking together, it is natural enough that among the six there should be more or less confusion and misapprehension.

[Our landlady turned pale—no doubt she thought there was a screw loose in my intellect—and that involved the probable loss of a boarder. A severe-looking person, who wears a Spanish cloak and a sad cheek, fluted by the passions of the melodrama, whom I understand to be the professional ruffian of the neighboring theater, alluded, with a certain lifting of the brow, drawing down of the corners of the mouth and somewhat rasping *voce di petti,* to Falstaff's nine men in buckram. Everybody looked up. I believe the old gentleman opposite me was afraid I should seize the carving-knife; at any rate, he slid it to one side, as it were carelessly.]

I think, I said, I can make it plain to Benjamin Franklin here, that there are at least six personalities distinctly to be recognized as taking part in that dialogue between John and Thomas.

<table>
<tr><td>Three Johns</td><td>1. The real John; known only to his Maker.
2. John's ideal John; never the real one, and often very unlike him.
3. Thomas's ideal John; never the real John, nor John's John but often very unlike either.</td></tr>
<tr><td>Three Thomases</td><td>1. The real Thomas.
2. Thomas's ideal Thomas.
3. John's ideal Thomas.</td></tr>
</table>

Only one of the three Johns is taxed; only one can be weighed on a platform-balance; but the other two are just as important in the conversation. Let us suppose the real John to be old, dull, and ill-looking. But as the Higher Powers have not conferred on men the gift of seeing themselves in the true light, John very possibly conceives himself to be youthful, witty, and fascinating, and talks from the point of view of this ideal. Thomas, again believes him to be an artful rogue, we will say; therefore he *is,* so far as Thomas's attitude in the conversation is concerned, an artful rogue, though really simple and stupid. The same conditions apply to the three

Thomases. It follows that, until a man can be found who knows himself as his Maker knows him, or who sees himself as others see him, there must be at least six persons engaged in every dialogue between two. Of these, the least important, philosophically speaking, is the one that we have called the real person. No wonder two disputants often get angry, when there are six of them talking and listening all at the same time.

[A very unphilosophical application of the above remarks was made by a young fellow, answering to the name of John, who sits near me at table. A certain basket of peaches, a rare vegetable, little known to boarding houses, was on his way to me *via* this unlettered Johannes. He appropriated the three that remained in the basket, remarking that there was just one apiece for him. I convinced him that his practical inference was hasty and illogical, but in the meantime he had eaten the peaches.]

(From The Autocrat of the Breakfast-Table)

THE FATAL WEDDING

W. H. Windom

The wedding bells were ringing on a moonlight winter's night,
The church was decorated, all within was gay and bright.
A mother with her baby came and saw the lights aglow,
She thought of how these same bells chimed for her three years ago!
"I'd like to be admitted, sir," she told the sexton old,
"Just for the sake of baby, to protect him from the cold."
He told her that the wedding there was for the rich and grand,
And with the eager watching crowd outside she'd have to stand.
While the wedding bells were ringing, while the bride and groom were there,
Marching up the aisle together, as the organ pealed an air;
Telling tales of fond affection, vowing never more to part,
Just another fatal wedding; just another broken heart.

She begged the sexton once again to let her pass inside.
"For baby's sake you may step in," the gray-haired man replied.
"If any one knows reason why this couple should not wed,
Speak now, or hold your peace forever," soon the preacher said!
"I must object," the woman cried, with voice so meek and mild,
"The bridegroom is my husband, sir, and this our little child."

"What proof have you?" the preacher asked. "My infant," she replied.
She raised her babe, then knelt to pray, the little one had died.

The parents of the bride then took the outcast by the arm,
"We'll care for you through life," they said, "you've save our child from harm."
The outcast wife, the bride and parents, quickly drove away,
The husband died by his own hand, before the break of day.
No wedding feast was spread that night; two graves were made next day,
One for the little baby, and in the other the father lay.
The story has been often told by firesides warm and bright,
Of bride and groom, of outcast, and the fatal wedding night.

LET ME LIVE OUT MY YEARS

John G. Neihardt

Let me live out my years in heat of blood!
  Let me die drunken with the dreamer's wine!
Let me not see this soul-house built of mud
  Go toppling to the dust—a vacant shrine!

Let me go quickly like a candle-light
  Snuffed out just at the heyday of its glow!
Give me high-noon—and let it then be night!
  Thus would I go.

And grant me when I face this grisly Thing,
  One haughty cry to pierce the gray Perhaps!
Let me be as a tune-swept fiddle-string
  That feels the Master Melody—and snaps!

THE MISTLETOE BOUGH

Thomas Haynes Bayly

The mistletoe hung in the castle hall,
The holly branch shone on the old oak wall;

And the baron's retainers were blithe and gay,
And keeping their Christmas holiday.
The baron beheld with a father's pride
His beautiful child, young Lovell's bride;
While she with her bright eyes seemed to be
The star of the goodly company.

"I'm weary of dancing now," she cried;
"Here, tarry a moment—I'll hide, I'll hide!
And, Lovell, be sure thou'rt first to trace
The clew to my secret lurking place."
Away she ran—and her friends began
Each tower to search, and each nook to scan;
And young Lovell cried, "O where dost thou hide?
I'm lonesome without thee, my own dear bride."

They sought her that night, and they sought her next day,
And they sought her in vain while a week passed away;
In the highest, the lowest, the loneliest spot,
Young Lovell sought wildly—but found her not.
And years flew by, and their grief at last
Was told as a sorrowful tale long past;
And when Lovell appeared the children cried,
"See! the old man weeps for his fairy bride."

At length an oak chest, that had long lain hid,
Was found in the castle—they raised the lid,
And a skeleton form lay moldering there
In the bridal wreath of that lady fair!
O sad was her fate!—in sportive jest
She hid from her lord in the old oak chest.
It closed with a spring!—and, dreadful doom,
The bride lay clasped in her living tomb!

COMPENSATION

Ralph Waldo Emerson

Polarity, or action and reaction, we meet in every part of nature; in darkness and light; in heat and cold; in the ebb and flow of waters; in male and female; in the inspiration and expiration of plants and animals; in the systole and diastole of the heart; in the undulations of fluids, and of sound; in the centrifugal and centripetal gravity; in electricity, galvanism, and chemical affinity. Superinduce magnetism at one end of a needle; the opposite magnetism takes place at the other end. If the south attracts, the north repels. To empty here, you must condense there. An inevitable dualism bisects nature, so that each thing is a half, and suggests another thing to make it whole; as spirit, matter, woman, subjective, objective; in, out; upper, under; motion, rest; yea, nay.

Whilst the world is thus dual, so is every one of its parts. The entire system of things gets represented in every particle. There is somewhat that resembles the ebb and flow of the sea, day and night, man and woman, in a single needle of the pine, in a kernel of corn, in each individual of every animal tribe. The reaction so grand in the elements is repeated within these small boundaries. For example, in the animal kingdom, the physiologist has observed that no creatures are favorites, but a certain compensation balances every gift and every defect. A surplusage given to one part is paid out of a reduction from another part of the same creature. If the head and neck are enlarged, the trunk and extremities are cut short.

The theory of the mechanic forces is another example. What we gain in power is lost in time; and the converse. The periodic or compensating errors of the planets is another instance. The influences of climate and soil in political history are another. The cold climate invigorates. The barren soil does not breed fevers, crocodiles, tigers, or scorpions.

The same dualism underlies the nature and condition of man. Every excess causes a defect; every defect an excess. Every sweet hath its sour; every evil its good. Every faculty which is a receiver of pleasure has an equal penalty put on its abuse. It is to answer for its moderation with its life. For every grain of wit there is a grain of folly. For everything you have missed, you have gained something else; and for everything you gain, you lose something. If riches increase, they are increased that use them. If the gatherer gathers too much, nature takes out of the man what she puts into his chest; swells the estate, but kills the owner. Nature hates monopolies and exceptions. The waves of the sea do not more speedily seek a level from their loftiest tossing than the varieties of condition tend to equalize themselves. There is always some leveling circumstance that puts down the over-bearing, the strong, the rich, the fortunate, substantially on the same ground with all others. Is a man too strong and fierce for society, and by temper and position a bad citizen,—a morose ruffian with a dash of the pirate in him;—nature sends him a troop of pretty sons and daughters who are getting along in the dame's classes at the village school, and love and fear for them smooths his grim scowl to courtesy. Thus she contrives to intenerate the granite and felspar, takes the boar out and puts the lamb in, and keeps her balance true. . . .

This Law writes laws of the cities and nations. It will not be baulked of its end in the smallest iota. It is in vain to build or plot or combine against it. Things refuse to be mismanaged long. *Res nolunt diu male administrari.* Though no checks to a new evil appear, the checks exist and will appear. If the government is cruel, the governor's life is not safe. If you tax too high, the revenue will yield nothing. If you make the criminal code sanguinary juries will not convict. Nothing arbitrary, nothing artificial can endure. . . .

Life invests itself with inevitable conditions, which the unwise seek to dodge, which one and another brags that he does not know; brags that they do not touch him;—but the brag is on his lips, the conditions are in his soul. If he escapes them in one part, they attack him in another more vital part. If he has escaped them in form, and in the appearance, it is that he has resisted his life, and fled from himself, and the retribution is so much death. So signal is the failure of all attempts to make this separation of the good from the tax, that the experiment would not be tried,—since to try it is to be mad,—but for the circumstance, that when the disease began in the will, of rebellion and separation, the intellect is at once infected, so that the man ceases to see God whole in each object, but is able to see the sensual allurement of an object, and not see the sensual hurt; he see the mermaid's head but not the dragon's tail; and thinks he can cut off that which he would have from that which he would not have. "How secret art thou who dwellest in the highest heavens in silence, O thou only great God, sprinkling with an unwearied Providence certain penal blindnesses upon such as have unbridled desires!" * . . .

All things are double, one against another.—Tit for tat; an eye for an eye; a tooth for a tooth; blood for blood; measure for measure; love for love.—Give and it shall be given you.—He that watereth shall be watered himself.—What will you have? quoth God; pay for it and take it.—Nothing venture, nothing have.—Thou shalt be paid exactly for what thou hast done, no more, no less.—Who doth not work shall not eat.—Harm watch, harm catch.—Curses always recoil on the head of him who imprecates

* St. Augustine: Confessions, Bk. I.

them.—If you put a chain around the neck of a slave, the other end fastens itself around your own.—Bad counsel confounds the adviser.—The devil is an ass.

It is thus written, because it is thus in life. Our action is overmastered and characterized above our will by the law of nature. We aim at a petty end quite aside from the public good, but our act arranges itself by irresistible magnetism in a line with the poles of the world.

SAILING

Godfrey Marks

Y'heave ho! my lads, the wind blows free,
A pleasant gale is on our lee,
And soon across the ocean clear
Our gallant barque shall bravely steer;
But ere we part from homeland's shores to-night
A song we'll sing for home and beauty bright:
Then here's to the sailor, and here's to hearts so true,
Who will think of him upon the waters blue!

Chorus:

Sailing, sailing over the bounding main,
For many a stormy wind shall blow,
Ere Jack comes home again;
Sailing, sailing over the bounding main,
For many a stormy wind shall blow,
Ere Jack comes home again.

The sailor's life is bold and free,
His home is on the rolling sea;
And never heart more true and brave
Than he who launches on the wave.
Afar he speeds in distant climes to roam,
With jocund song he rides the sparkling foam;
Then here's to the sailor, and here's to the hearts so true,
Who will think of him upon the waters blue!

The tide is flowing with the gale,
Y'heave ho! my lads, set every sail!
The harbor bar we soon shall clear,

Farewell once more to home so dear,
For when the tempest rages loud and long,
That home shall be our guiding star among;
Then here's to the sailor, and here's to the hearts so true,
Who will think of him upon the waters blue.

JULIUS CAESAR'S PREFERENCE

William Shakespeare

Let me have men about me that are fat,
Sleek-headed men, and such as sleep o' nights:
Yond Cassius has a lean and hungry look;
He thinks too much: such men are dangerous.
(From Julius Caesar)

THE PRINTING PRESS

Robert H. Davis

I am the printing press, born of the mother earth. My heart is of steel, my limbs are of iron, and my fingers are of brass.

I sing the songs of the world, the oratorios of history, the symphonies of all time.

I am the voice of today, the herald of tomorrow. I weave into the warp of the past the woof of the future. I tell the stories of peace and war alike. I make the human heart beat with passion or tenderness. I stir the pulse of nations, and make brave men do braver deeds, and soldiers die.

I inspire the midnight toiler, weary at his doom, to lift his head again and gaze with fearlessness into the vast beyond, seeking the consolation of a hope eternal.

When I speak, a myriad people listen to my voice. The Saxon, the Latin, the Celt, the Hun, the Slav, the Hindu, all comprehend me.

I am the tireless clarion of the news. I cry your joys and sorrows every hour. I fill the dullard's mind with thoughts uplifting. I am light, knowledge, power. I epitomize the conquests of mind over matter.

I am the record of all things mankind has achieved. My offspring comes to you in the candle's glow, amid the dim lamps of poverty, the splendor of riches; at sunrise, at high noon and in the waning evening.

I am the laughter and tears of the world, and I shall never die until all things return to their immutable dust.

I am the printing press.

LOST LOVE

Alfred, Lord Tennyson

I envy not in any moods
  The captive void of noble rage,
  The linnet born within the cage,
That never knew the summer woods:

I envy not the beast that takes
  His license in the field of time,
  Unfetter'd by the sense of crime,
To whom a conscience never wakes;

Nor, what may count itself as blest,
  The heart that never plighted troth
  But stagnates in the weeds of sloth;
Nor any want-begotten rest.

I hold it true, whate'er befall;
  I feel it, when I sorrow most;
  'Tis better to have loved and lost
Than never to have loved at all.
(From In Memoriam)

GOOD AND BAD

There is so much good in the worst of us,
And so much bad in the best of us,
That it hardly becomes any of us
To talk about the rest of us.
(Attributed to Edward Wallis Hoch)

LETTER FROM GEORGE WASHINGTON WHEN HE ACCEPTED COMMAND

It has been determined in Congress, that the whole army raised for the defense of the American cause shall be put under my care, and that it is necessary for me to proceed immediately to Boston to take upon me the command of it.

I have been called upon by the unanimous voice of the Colonies to the command of the Continental Army. It is an honor I by no means aspired to. It is an honor I wished to avoid, as well from an unwillingness to quit the peaceful enjoyment of my family, as from a thorough conviction of my own incapacity and want of experience in the conduct of so momentous a concern; but the partiality of the Congress, added to some political motives, left me without a choice. May God grant, therefore, that my acceptance of it, may be attended with some good to the common cause, and without injury (from want of knowledge) to my own reputation. I can answer but for three things: a firm belief in the justice of our cause, close attention in the prosecution of it, and the strictest integrity.

(Letter to Mrs. Martha Washington, June, 1775)

HYMN TO THE NIGHT

Henry Wadsworth Longfellow

I heard the trailing garments of the Night
   Sweep through her marble halls!
I saw her sable skirts all fringed with light
   From the celestial walls!

I felt her presence, by its spell of might,
   Stoop o'er me from above;
The calm, majestic presence of the Night,
   As of the one I love.

I heard the sounds of sorrow and delight,
   The manifold, soft chimes,
That fill the haunted chambers of the Night,
   Like some old poet's rhymes.

From the cool cisterns of the midnight air
  My spirit drank repose;
The fountain of perpetual peace flows there,—
  From those deep cisterns flows.

O holy Night! from thee I learn to bear
  What man has borne before!
Thou layest thy finger on the lips of Care,
  And they complain no more.

Peace! Peace! Orestes-like I breathe this prayer!
  Descend with broad-winged flight,
The welcome, the thrice-prayed for, the most fair,
  The best-beloved Night!

PROPHETIC WORDS BY WOODROW WILSON

A steadfast concert for peace can never be maintained except by a partnership of democratic nations. No autocratic government could be trusted to keep faith within it or observe its covenants. It must be a league of honor, a partnership of opinion. Intrigue would eat its vitals away; the plottings of inner circles who could plan what they would and render account to no one would be a corruption seated at its very heart. Only free peoples can hold their purpose and their honor steady to a common end and prefer the interests of mankind to any narrow interest of their own.

(From the Address to Congress asking for Declaration of War Against Germany, April 2, 1917)

THE CRY OF A DREAMER

John Boyle O'Reilly

I am tired of planning and toiling
  In the crowded hives of men;
Heart-weary of building and spoiling,
  And spoiling and building again.
And I long for the dear old river,
  Where I dreamed my youth away;
For a dreamer lives forever,
  And a toiler dies in a day.

I am sick of the showy seeming,
  Of a life that is half a lie;
Of the faces lined with scheming
  In the throng that hurries by.
From the sleepless thoughts' endeavour,
  I would go where the children play;
For a dreamer lives forever,
  And a thinker dies in a day.

I can feel no pride, but pity
  For the burdens the rich endure;
There is nothing sweet in the city
  But the patient lives of the poor.
Oh, the little hands too skillful
  And the child mind choked with weeds!
The daughter's heart grown willful,
  And the father's heart that bleeds!

No, no! from the street's rude bustle,
  From the trophies of mart and stage,
I would fly to the woods' low rustle
  And the meadow's kindly page.
Let me dream as of old by the river,
  And be loved for the dream alway;
For a dreamer lives forever,
  And a toiler dies in a day.

ADDRESS TO THE UNCO GUID, OR THE RIGIDLY RIGHTEOUS

Robert Burns

My son, these maxims make a rule,
  And lump them aye thegither:
The RIGID RIGHTEOUS is a fool.
  The RIGID WISE anither:
The cleanest corn that e'er was dight,
  May hae some pyles o' caff in:
So ne'er a fellow-creature slight
  For random fits o' daffin.

SOLOMON.—Eccles. vii:16

O ye what are sae guid yoursel,
  Sae pious and sae holy,
Ye've naught to do but mark and tell
  Your Neebor's fauts and folly!
Whase life is like a weel-gaun mill,
  Supply'd wi' store o' water,
The heapet happer's ebbing still,
  And still the clap plays clatter.

Hear me, ye venerable Core,
  As Counsel for poor mortals,
That frequent pass douce Wisdom's door,
  For glaikit Folly's portals;
I, for their thoughtless, careless sakes,
  Would here propone defences,
Their donsie tricks, their black mistakes,
  Their failings and mischances.

Ye see your state wi' theirs compar'd
  And shudder at the niffer,
But cast a moment's fair regard,
  What maks the mighty differ;
Discount what scant occasion gave
  That purity ye pride in,
And (what's aft mair than a' the lave),
  Your better art o' hiding.

Think, when your castigated pulse
  Gies now and then a wallop,
What raging must his veins convulse
  That still eternal gallop:
Wi' wind and tide fair i' your tail,
  Right on ye scud your sea-way;
But in the teeth o' baith to sail,
  It maks an unco leeway.

See Social life and Glee sit down,
  All joyous and unthinking,
Till, quite transmugrify'd, they're grown
  Debauchery and Drinking:
O would they stay to calculate
  Th' eternal consequences;
Or your more dreaded hell to state,
  Damnation of expenses!

Ye high, exalted, virtuous Dames,
  Ty'd up in godly laces,
Before ye gie poor Frailty names,
  Suppose a change o' cases;
A dear lov'd lad, convenience snug,
  A treacherous inclination—
But, let me whisper i' your lug,
  Ye're aiblins nae temptation.

Then gently scan your brother Man,
  Still gentler sister Woman;
Tho' they may gang a kennin wrang,
  To step aside is human:
One point must still be greatly dark,
  The moving *Why* they do it;
And just as lamely can ye mark,
  How far perhaps they rue it.

Who made the heart, 'tis He alone
  Decidedly can try us,
He knows each chord its various tone,
  Each spring its various bias:
Then at the balance let's be mute,
  We never can adjust it;
What's *done* we partly may compute,
  But know not what's *resisted*.

MY CHOICE

Robert G. Ingersoll

I would rather go to the forest, far away, and build me a little cabin—build it myself—and daub it with clay, and live there with my wife and children; and have a winding path leading down to the spring where the water bubbles out, day and night, whispering a poem to the white pebbles, from the heart of the earth; a little hut with some hollyhocks at the corner, with their bannered bosoms open to the sun, and a thrush in the air like a winged joy —I would rather live there and have some lattice work across the window so that the sun-light would fall checkered on the babe in the cradle—I would rather live there, with my soul erect and free, than in a palace of gold, and wear a crown of imperial power, and feel that I was superstition's cringing slave, and dare not speak my honest thought.

TO BOSTON

John Collins Bossidy

And this is good old Boston,
The home of the bean and the cod,
Where the Lowells talk only to Cabots
And the Cabots talk only to God.
(Toast, Midwinter Dinner, Holy Cross Alumni, 1910)

TO NEW HAVEN

Frederick Scheetz Jones

Here's to the town of New Haven,
The home of the Truth and the Light,
Where God talks to Jones
In the very same tones
That he uses with Hadley and Dwight.
(Toast, dinner of the Yale Alumni Association, Waterbury, Conn., 1915)

TO NEW HAVEN AND BOSTON

Walter Foster Angell

Here's to New Haven and Boston,
And the turf that the Puritans trod,
In the rest of mankind little virtue they find,
But they feel quite chummy with God.
(Toast, Brown University)

LOVE WILL FIND OUT THE WAY

Anonymous

Over the mountains,
  And over the waves;
Under the fountains,
  And under the graves;
Under floods that are deepest,
  Which Neptune obey;
Over rocks that are steepest,
  Love will find out the way.

Where there is no place
  For the glow-worm to lie;
Where there is no space
  For receipt of a fly;
Where the midge dares not venture,
  Lest herself fast she lay;
If love come, he will enter,
  And soon find out his way.

You may esteem him
  A child for his might;
Or you may deem him
  A coward from his flight;
But if she, whom love doth honour,
  Be conceal'd from the day,
Set a thousand guards upon her,
  Love will find out the way.

Some think to lose him,
  By having him confin'd;
And some do suppose him,
  Poor thing, to be blind;
But if ne'er so close ye wall him,
  Do the best that you may,
Blind love, if ye so call him,
  Will find out his way.

You may train the eagle
  To stoop to your fist;
Or you may inveigle
  The phenix of the east;

The lioness, ye may move her
  To give o'er her prey;
But you will ne'er stop a lover;
  He will find out his way.

THE DEATH OF COWARDS

William Shakespeare

Cowards die many times before their deaths;
The valiant never taste of death but once.
Of all the wonders that I yet have heard,
It seems to me most strange that men should fear;
Seeing that death, a necessary end,
Will come when it will come.

(From Julius Caesar)

SAMUEL JOHNSON ANSWERS A CHALLENGE

(Johnson had said that some poems, which MacPherson claimed to have translated, were forgeries. MacPherson sent Johnson a challenge)

Mr. James MacPherson,—I received your foolish and impudent letter. Any violence offered me I shall do my best to repel, and what I cannot do for myself, the law shall do for me. I hope I shall never be deterred from detecting what I think a cheat, by the menaces of a ruffian.

What would you have me retract? I thought your book an imposture; I think it an imposture still. For this opinion I have given my reasons to the publick which I here dare you to refute. Your rage I defy. Your abilities, since your Homer, are not so formidable; and what I hear of your morals, inclines me to pay regard not to what you shall say, but to what you shall prove. You may print this if you will.

SAM. JOHNSON

OUT IN THE FIELDS

Anonymous

The little cares that fretted me,
I lost them yesterday
Among the fields above the sea,
Among the winds that play,
Among the lowing of the herds,
The rustling of the trees,
Among the singing of the birds,
The humming of the bees.

The foolish fears of what might pass,
I cast them all away
Among the clover-scented grass,
Among the new-mown hay,
Among the hushing of the corn,
Where drowsy poppies nod,
Where ill thoughts die and good are born—
Out in the fields of God.

ODE TO THE WEST WIND

Percy Bysshe Shelley

I

O Wild West Wind, thou breath of Autumn's being,
Thou, from whose unseen presence the leaves dead
Are driven, like ghosts from an enchanter fleeing,

Yellow, and black, and pale, and hectic red,
Pestilence-stricken multitudes: O thou,
Who chariotest to their dark wintry bed

The winged seeds, where they lie cold and low,
Each like a corpse within its grave, until
Thine azure sister of the Spring shall blow

Her clarion o'er the dreaming earth, and fill
(Driving sweet buds like flocks to feed in air)
With living hnes and odours plain and hill:

Wild Spirit, which art moving everywhere;
Destroyer and preserver; hear, oh, hear!

II

Thou on whose stream, mid the steep sky's commotion,
Loose clouds like earth's decaying leaves are shed,
Shook from the tangled boughs of Heaven and Ocean,

Angels of rain and lightning: there are spread
On the blue surface of thine aery surge,
Like the bright hair uplifted from the head

Of some fierce Maenad, even from the dim verge
Of the horizon to the zenith's height,
The locks of the approaching storm. Thou dirge

Of the dying year, to which this closing night
Will be the dome of a vast sepulchre,
Vaulted with all thy congregated might

Of vapours, from whose solid atmosphere
Black rain, and fire, and hail will burst: oh, hear!

III

Thou who didst waken from his summer dreams
The blue Mediterranean, where he lay,
Lulled by the coil of his crystalline streams,

Beside a pumice isle in Baiae's bay,
And saw in sleep old palaces and towers
Quivering within the wave's intenser day,

All overgrown with azure moss and flowers
So sweet, the sense faints picturing them! Thou
For whose path the Atlantic's level powers

Cleave themselves into chasms, while far below
The sea-blooms and the oozy woods which wear
The sapless foliage of the ocean, know

Thy voice, and suddenly grow gray with fear,
And tremble and despoil themselves: oh, hear!

IV

If I were a dead leaf thou mightest bear,
If I were a swift cloud to fly with thee;
A wave to pant beneath thy power, and share

The impulse of thy strength, only less free
Than thou, O uncontrollable! If even
I were as in my boyhood, and could be

The comrade of thy wanderings over Heaven,
As then, when to outstrip thy skiey speed
Scarce seemed a vision; I would ne'er have striven

As thus with thee in prayer in my sore need.
Oh, lift me as a wave, a leaf, a cloud!
I fall upon the thorns of life! I bleed!

A heavy weight of hours has chained and bowed
One too like thee: tameless, and swift, and proud.

V

Make me thy lyre, even as the forest is:
What if my leaves are falling like its own!
The tumult of thy mighty harmonies

Will take from both a deep autumnal tone,
Sweet though in sadness. Be thou, Spirit fierce,
My spirit! Be thou me, impetuous one!

Drive my dead thoughts over the universe
Like withered leaves to quicken a new birth!
And, by the incantation of this verse,

Scatter, as from an unextinguished hearth
Ashes and sparks, my words among mankind!
Be through my lips to unawakened earth

The trumpet of a prophecy! O Wind,
If Winter comes, can Spring be far behind?

THE DEATH OF LITTLE NELL

Charles Dickens

She was dead. No sleep so beautiful and calm, so free from trace of pain, so fair to look upon. She seemed a creature fresh from the hand of God, and waiting for the breath of life; not one who had lived, and suffered death. Her couch was dressed with here and there some winter berries and green leaves, gathered in a spot she had been used to favor. "When I die, put near me something that has loved the light, and had the sky above it always." These were her words.

She was dead. Dear, gentle, patient, noble Nell was dead. Her little bird, a poor, slight thing the pressure of a finger would have crushed, was stirring nimbly in its cage, and the strong heart of its child-mistress was mute and motionless forever! Where were the traces of her early cares, her sufferings, and fatigues? All gone. Sorrow was dead, indeed, in her; but peace and perfect happiness were born, imaged in her tranquil beauty and profound repose.

And still her former self lay there, unaltered in this change. Yes! the old fireside had smiled upon that same sweet face; it had passed, like a dream, through haunts of misery and care; at the door of the poor schoolmaster on the summer evening, before the furnace fire upon the cold wet night, at the still bedside of the dying boy, there had been the same mild and lovely look. So shall we know the angels, in their majesty, after death.

The old man held one languid arm in his, and had the small hand tight folded to his breast for warmth. It was the hand she had stretched out to him with her last smile; the hand that had led him on through all their wanderings. Ever and anon he pressed it to his lips; then hugged it to his breast again, murmuring that it was warmer now, and as he said it, he looked in agony to those who stood around, as if imploring them to help her.

She was dead, and past all help, or need of help. The ancient rooms she had seemed to fill with life, even while her own was waning fast, the garden she had tended, the eyes she had gladdened, the noiseless haunts of many a thoughtful hour, the paths she had trodden, as it were, but yesterday, could know her no more.

"It is not," said the schoolmaster, as he bent down to kiss her on the cheek, and gave his tears free vent, "It is not in *this* world that heaven's justice ends. Think what earth is, compared with the world to which her young spirit has winged its early flight, and say, if one deliberate wish, expressed in solemn tones above this bed, could call her back to life, which of us would utter it?"

She had been dead two days. They were all about her at the time, knowing that the end was drawing on. She died soon after day-break. They had read and talked to her in the earlier portion of the night; but, as the hours crept on, she sank to sleep. They could tell by what she faintly uttered in her dreams, that they were of her journeyings with the old man; they were of no painful scenes, but of the people who had helped them, and used them kindly; for she often said "God bless you!" with great fervor.

Waking, she had never wandered in her mind but once, and that was at beautiful music, which, she said, was in the air. God knows. It may have been. Opening her eyes, at last, from a very quiet sleep, she begged that they would kiss her once again. That done, she turned to the old man, with a lovely smile upon her face, such, they said, as they had never seen, and could never forget, and clung, with both her arms, about his neck. She had never murmured or complained; but, with a quiet mind, and manner quite unaltered, save that she every day became more earnest and more grateful to them, faded like the light upon the summer's evening.

(From The Old Curiosity Shop)

WHEN LOVELY WOMAN

Phoebe Cary

When lovely woman wants a favor,
And finds, too late, that man won't bend,
What earthly circumstance can save her
From disappointment in the end?

The only way to bring him over,
The last experiment to try,
Whether a husband or a lover,
If he have a feeling is—to cry.

* * *

How sad it is to think that eyes that are too old to see are yet not too old to shed tears.—François René de Chateaubriand

O LOVE, THAT WILT NOT LET ME GO

George Matheson

O Love, that wilt not let me go,
  I rest my weary soul in Thee;
I give Thee back the life I owe,
That in Thine ocean depth its flow
  May richer, fuller be.

O Light, that followest all my way,
  I yield my flickering torch to Thee;
My heart restores its borrowed ray,
That in Thy sunshine's blaze its day
  May brighter, fairer be.

O Joy, that seekest me through pain,
  I cannot close my heart to Thee;
I trace the rainbow through the rain,
And feel the promise is not vain,
  That morn shall tearless be.

O Cross, that liftest up my head,
  I dare not ask to fly from Thee;
I lay in dust life's glory dead,
And from the ground there blossoms red
  Life that shall endless be.

A FAMOUS BUT SPURIOUS DESCRIPTION OF JESUS CHRIST

There has appeared in these our days, a man of great virtue, named Jesus Christ, who is living among us, and of the Gentiles is accepted as a Prophet, but his disciples call him the "Son of God." He raiseth the dead, and cures all manner of diseases; a man of stature somewhat tall and comely, with very revered countenance, such as the beholders both love and fear; his hair the color of chestnut, full ripe, plain to his ears, whence downwards it is more orient, curling and waving about his shoulders.

In the midst of his head is a seam or partition of his hair after the manner of Nazarites, his forehead plain and very delicate; his face without a spot or wrinkle, beautiful with a most lovely red; his nose and mouth so formed that nothing can be reprehended; his beard thickish, in color like his hair, not very long but forked; his look, innocent and mature; his eyes, gray, clear and quick. In reproving he is terrible; in admonishing, courteous and fair-spoken; pleasant in conversation, mixed with gravity. It cannot be remarked that any one saw him laugh, but many have seen him weep. In proportion of body, most excellent, his hands and arms most delicate to behold. In speaking, very temperate, modest and wise. A man, for his singular beauty, surpassing the children of men.

> (This is supposed to have been a letter sent by Publius Lentulus to the Emperor Tiberius and the Roman senate. But authorities have repeatedly rejected its authenticity, some of them attributing it to an unnamed 14th century monk, possibly adapted from a letter found in one of works of a credulous and not very critical Greek historian.)

THE DEATH BED

Thomas Hood

We watch'd her breathing thro' the night,
  Her breathing soft and low,
As in her breast the wave of life
  Kept heaving to and fro.

So silently we seem'd to speak,
  So slowly moved about,
As we had lent her half our powers
  To eke her living out.

Our very hopes belied our fears,
  Our fears our hopes belied—
We thought her dying when she slept,
  And sleeping when she died.

For when the morn came dim and sad
  And chill with early showers,
Her quiet eyelids closed—she had
  Another morn than ours.

LIVE JOYFULLY

Holy Bible, Ecclesiastes 9:7–11

Go thy way, eat thy bread with joy, and drink thy wine with a merry heart; for God now accepteth thy works. Let thy garments be always white; and let thy head lack no ointment. Live joyfully with the wife whom thou lovest all the days of the life of thy vanity, which he hath given thee under the sun, all the days of thy vanity: for that is thy portion in this life, and in thy labour which thou takest under the sun. Whatsoever thy hand findeth to do, do it with thy might; for there is no work, nor device, nor knowledge, nor wisdom, in the grave, whither thou goest.

I returned, and saw under the sun, that the race is not to the swift, nor the battle to the strong, neither yet bread to the wise, nor yet riches to men of understanding, nor yet favour to men of skill; but time and chance happeneth to them all.

FLOWER IN THE CRANNIED WALL

Alfred, Lord Tennyson

Flower in the crannied wall,
I pluck you out of the crannies,
I hold you here, root and all, in my hand,
Little flower—but *if* I could understand
What you are, root and all, and all in all,
I should know what God and man is.

METHUSELAH

Anonymous

Methuselah ate what he found on his plate,
And never, as people do now,
Did he note the amount of the calory count:
He ate it because it was chow.
He wasn't disturbed as at dinner he sat,
Devouring a roast or a pie,
To think it was lacking in granular fat

Or a couple of vitamins shy.
He cheerfully chewed each species of food,
Unmindful of troubles or fears
Lest his health might be hurt
By some fancy dessert;
And he lived over nine hundred years.

LETTER FROM A YUGOSLAVIAN GUERRILLA FIGHTER TO HIS UNBORN CHILD

(Found on his body sometime in 1942)

My Child, sleeping now in the dark and gathering strength for the struggle of birth, I wish you well. At present you have no proper shape, and you do not breathe, and you are blind. Yet, when your time comes, your time and the time of your mother, whom I deeply love, there will be something in you that will give you power to fight for air and life. Such is your heritage, such is your destiny as a child born of woman—to fight for light and hold on without knowing why.

May the flame that tempers the bright steel of your youth never die, but burn always; so that when your work is done and your long day is ended, you may still be like a watchman's fire at the end of a lonely road—loved and cherished for your gracious glow by all good wayfarers who need light in their darkness and warmth for their comfort.

The spirit of wonder and adventure, the token of immortality, will be given to you as a child. May you keep it forever, with that in your heart which always seeks the gold beyond the rainbow, the pasture beyond the desert, the dawn beyond the sea, the light beyond the dark.

May you seek always and strive in good faith and high courage, in this world where men grow so tired.

Keep your capacity for faith and belief, but let your judgment watch what you believe.

Keep your power to receive everything, only learn to select what your instinct tells you is right.

Keep your love of life, but throw away your fear of death. Life must be loved or it is lost; but it should never be loved too well.

Keep your delight in friendship; only learn to know your friends.

Keep your intolerance—only save it for what your heart tells you is bad.

Keep your wonder at great and noble things like sunlight and thunder, the rain and the stars, the wind and the sea, the growth of trees and the return of harvests, and the greatness of heroes.

Keep your heart hungry for new knowledge; keep your hatred of a lie; and keep your power of indignation.

Now I know I must die, and you must be born to stand upon the rubbish heap of my errors. Forgive me for this. I am ashamed to leave you an untidy world. But so it must be.

In thought, as a last benediction, I kiss your forehead. Good night to you—and good morning and a clear dawn.

TO A SKYLARK

Percy Bysshe Shelley

Hail to thee, blithe Spirit!
Bird, thou never wert,
That from Heaven, or near it,
Pourest thy full heart
In profuse strains of unpremeditated art.

Higher still and higher
From the earth thou springest
Like a cloud of fire;
The blue deep thou wingest,
And singing still dost soar, and soaring ever singest.

In the golden lightning
Of the sunken sun,
O'er which clouds are bright'ning,
Thou dost float and run;
Like an unbodied joy whose race is just begun.

The pale purple even
Melts around thy flight;
Like a star of Heaven,
In the broad daylight
Thou art unseen, but yet I hear thy shrill delight.

Keen as are the arrows
Of that silver sphere,
Whose intense lamp narrows
In the white dawn clear
Until we hardly see—we feel that it is there.

All the earth and air
With thy voice is loud,
As, when night is bare,
From one lonely cloud
The moon rains out her beams, and Heaven is overflowed.

What thou art we know not;
What is most like thee?
From rainbow clouds there flow not
Drops so bright to see
As from thy presence showers a rain of melody.

Like a Poet hidden
In the light of thought,
Singing hymns unbidden,
Till the world is wrought
To sympathy with hopes and fears it heeded not:

Like a high-born maiden
In a palace-tower,
Soothing her love-laden
Soul in secret hour
With music sweet as love, which overflows her bower:

Like a glow-worm golden
In a dell of dew,
Scattering unbeholden
Its aërial hue
Among the flowers and grass, which screen it from the view:

Like a rose embowered
In its own green leaves,
By warm winds deflowered,
Till the scent it gives
Makes faint with too much sweet those heavy-winged
thieves:

Sound of vernal showers
On the twinkling grass,
Rain-awakened flowers,
All that ever was
Joyous, and clear, and fresh, thy music doth surpass:

Teach us, Sprite or Bird,
What sweet thoughts are thine:
I have never heard
Praise of love or wine
That panted forth a flood of rapture so divine.

Chorus Hymeneal,
Or triumphal chaunt,
Matched with thine would be all
But an empty vaunt,
A thing wherein we feel there is some hidden want.

What objects are the fountains
Of thy happy strain?
What fields, or waves, or mountains?
What shapes of sky or plain?
What love of thine own kind? what ignorance of pain?

With thy clear keen joyance
Languor cannot be:
Shadow of annoyance
Never came near thee:
Thou lovest—but ne'er knew love's sad satiety.

Waking or asleep,
Thou of death must deem
Things more true and deep
Than we mortals dream,
Or how could thy notes flow in such a crystal stream?

We look before and after,
And pine for what is not:
Our sincerest laughter
With some pain is fraught;
Our sweetest songs are those that tell of saddest thought.

Yet if we could scorn
  Hate, and pride, and fear;
If we were things born
  Not to shed a tear,
I know not how thy joy we ever should come near.

Better than all measures
  Of delightful sound,
Better than all treasures
  That in books are found,
Thy skill to poet were, thou scorner of the ground!

Teach me half the gladness
  That thy brain must know,
Such harmonious madness
  From my lips would flow
The world should listen then—as I am listening now.

A CHILD'S GRACE

Robert Herrick

Here a little child I stand
Heaving up my either hand;
Cold as paddocks though they be,
Here I lift them up to Thee,
For a benison to fall
On our meat and on us all, Amen.

HAMLET'S INSTRUCTIONS TO THE PLAYERS

William Shakespeare

Speak the speech, I pray you, as I pronounced it to you, trippingly on the tongue: but if you mouth it, as many of your players do, I had as lief the town-crier spoke my lines. Nor do not saw the air too much with your hand, thus; but use all gently: for in the very torrent, tempest, and, as I may say, the whirlwind of passion, you must acquire and beget a temperance that may give it smoothness. O, it offends me to the soul to hear a robustious periwig-pated fellow tear a passion to tatters, to very rags, to split the ears of the groundlings, who for the most part are capable of nothing but inexplicable dumb-shows and noise: I would have such a fellow whipped for o'erdoing Termagant; it out-herods Herod: pray you, avoid it.

Be not too tame neither, but let your own discretion be your tutor. Suit the action to the word, the word to the action; with this special observance, that you o'erstep not the modesty of nature: for any thing so overdone is from the purpose of playing, whose end, both at the first and now, was and is, to hold, as 'twere, the mirror up to nature; to show virtue her own feature, scorn her own image, and the very age and body of the time his form and pressure. Now this overdone, or come tardy off, though it make the unskilful laugh, cannot but make the judicious grieve; the censure of the which one must in your allowance o'erweigh a whole theatre of others. O, there be players that I have seen play, and heard others praise, and that highly, not to speak it profanely, that, neither having the accent of Christians nor the gait of Christian, pagan, nor man, have so strutted and bellowed that I have thought some of nature's journeymen had made men, and not made them well, they imitated humanity so abominably.

(From Hamlet)

THE HIGH TIDE AT GETTYSBURG

Will Henry Thompson

A cloud possessed the hollow field,
The gathering battle's smoky shield.
  Athwart the gloom the lightning flashed,
  And through the cloud some horsemen dashed,
And from the heights the thunder pealed.

Then at the brief command of Lee
Moved out that matchless infantry,
  With Pickett leading grandly down,
  To rush against the roaring crown
Of those dread heights of destiny.

Far heard above the angry guns
A cry across the tumult runs,—
  The voice that rang through Shiloh's woods
  And Chickamauga's solitudes,
The fierce South cheering on her sons!

Ah, how the withering tempest blew
Against the front of Pettigrew!
  A Khamsin wind that scorched and singed
  Like that infernal flame that fringed
The British squares at Waterloo!

A thousand fell where Kemper led;
A thousand died where Garnett bled:
  In blinding flame and strangling smoke
  The remnant through the batteries broke
And crossed the works with Armistead.

"Once more in glory's van with me!"
Virginia cried to Tennessee;
  "We two together, come what may,
  Shall stand upon these works to-day!"
(The reddest day in history.)

Brave Tennessee! In reckless way
Virginia heard her comrade say:
  "Close round this rent and riddled rag!"
  What time she set her battle-flag
Amid the guns of Doubleday.

But who shall break the guards that wait
Before the awful face of fate?
  The tattered standards of the South
  Were shriveled at the cannon's mouth.
And all her hopes were desolate.

In vain the Tennessean set
His breast against the bayonet!
  In vain Virginia charged and raged,
  A tigress in her wrath uncaged,
Till all the hill was red and wet!

Above the bayonets, mixed and crossed,
Men saw a gray, gigantic ghost
  Receding through the battle-cloud,
  And heard across the tempest loud
The death-cry of a nation lost!

The brave went down! Without disgrace
They leaped to Ruin's red embrace.
  They only heard Fame's thunders wake,
  And saw the dazzling sun-burst break
In smiles on Glory's bloody face!

They fell, who lifted up a hand
And bade the sun in heaven to stand!
  They smote and fell, who set the bars
  Against the progress of the stars,
And stayed the march of Motherland!

They stood, who saw the future come
On through the fight's delirium!
  They smote and stood, who held the hope
  Of nations on that slippery slope
Amid the cheers of Christendom.

God lives! He forged the iron will
That clutched and held that trembling hill.
  God lives and reigns! He built and lent
  The heights for Freedom's battlement
Where floats her flag in triumph still!

Fold up the banners! Smelt the guns!
Love rules. Her gentler purpose runs.
  A mighty mother turns in tears
  The pages of her battle years,
Lamenting all her fallen sons!

ON FLEAS

The vermin only tease and pinch
Their foes superior by an inch;
So, naturalists observe a flea

Has smaller fleas that on him prey,
And these have smaller still to bite 'em,
And so proceed *ad infinitum.*

Jonathan Swift

Great fleas have little fleas upon their backs to bite 'em,
And little fleas have lesser fleas, and so ad infinitum.
The great fleas themselves in turn have greater fleas to go on,
While those again have greater still, and greater still, and so on.

Augustus De Morgan

WEST POINT CADETS PRAYER

Clayton E. Whear

O God, our Father, Thou Searcher of Men's hearts, help us to draw near to Thee in sincerity and truth. May our religion be filled with gladness and may our worship of Thee be natural.

Strengthen and increase our admiration for honest dealing and clean thinking, and suffer not our hatred of hypocrisy and pretense ever to diminish. Encourage us in our endeavor to live above the common level of life. Make us to choose the harder right instead of the easier wrong, and never to be content with a half truth when the whole can be won. Endow us with courage that is born of loyalty to all that is noble and worthy, that scorns to compromise with vice and injustice and knows no fear when truth and right are in jeopardy. Guard us against flippancy and irreverence in the sacred things of life. Grant us new ties of friendship and new opportunities of service. Kindle our hearts in fellowship with those of a cheerful countenance, and soften our hearts with sympathy for those who sorrow and suffer. Help us to maintain the honor of the Corps untarnished and unsullied and to show forth in our lives the ideals of West Point in doing our duty to Thee and to our Country. All of which we ask in the name of the Great Friend and Master of man.—Amen.

THE BARGAIN

Sir Philip Sidney

My true love hath my heart, and I have his,
By just exchange one for another given:
I hold his dear. and mine he cannot miss

There never was a better bargain driven:
My true love hath my heart, and I have his.

His heart in me keeps him and me in one,
My heart in him his thoughts and senses guides:
He loves my heart, for once it was his own,
I cherish his because in me it bides:
My true love hath my heart, and I have his.

"IF THOU MUST LOVE ME, LET IT BE FOR NOUGHT"

Elizabeth Barrett Browning

If thou must love me, let it be for nought
Except for love's sake only. Do not say
"I love her for her smile—her look—her way
Of speaking gently,—for a trick of thought
That falls in well with mine, and certes brought
A sense of pleasant ease on such a day"—
For these things in themselves, Belovèd, may
Be changed, or change for thee,—and love, so wrought,
May be unwrought so. Neither love me for
Thine own dear pity's wiping my cheeks dry,—
A creature might forget to weep, who bore
Thy comfort long, and lose thy love thereby!
But love me for love's sake, that evermore
Thou mayest love on, through love's eternity.

OTHELLO'S FAREWELL

William Shakespeare

Soft you; a word or two before you go.
I have done the state some service, and they know't.
No more of that. I pray you, in your letters,
When you shall these unlucky deeds relate,
Speak of me as I am; nothing extenuate,
Nor set down aught in malice; then must you speak
Of one that loved not wisely but too well;
Of one not easily jealous, but, being wrought,

Perplex'd in the extreme; of one whose hand,
Like the base Indian, threw a pearl away
Richer than all his tribe; of one whose subdued eyes,
Albeit unused to the melting mood,
Drop tears as fast as the Arabian trees
Their medicinal gum. Set you down this;
And say besides, that in Aleppo once,
Where a malignant and a turban'd Turk
Beat a Venetian and traduced the state,
I took by the throat the circumcised dog
And smote him, thus.

[*Stabs himself*]

(From Othello)

GEORGE WASHINGTON'S ADVICE TO HIS NEPHEW

Be courteous to all, but intimate with few; and let those few be well tried before you give them your confidence. True friendship is a plant of slow growth, and must undergo and withstand the shocks of adversity before it is entitled to the appellation. Let your heart feel for the afflictions and distresses of every one, and let your hand give in proportion to your purse; remembering always the estimation of the widow's mite, that it is not every one that asketh that deserveth charity; all, however, are worthy of the inquiry, or the deserving may suffer.

Do not conceive that fine clothes make fine men, any more than fine feathers make fine birds. A plain, genteel dress is more admired, obtains more credit, than lace and embroidery, in the eyes of the judicious and sensible.

(1783)

A CRADLE HYMN

Isaac Watts

Hush! my dear, lie still and slumber,
  Holy angels guard thy bed!
Heavenly blessings without number
  Gently falling on thy head.

Sleep, my babe; thy food and raiment,
  House and home, thy friends provide;
All without thy care or payment:
  All thy wants are well supplied.

How much better thou'rt attended
  Than the Son of God could be,
When from heaven He descended
  And became a child like thee!

Soft and easy is thy cradle:
  Coarse and hard thy Saviour lay,
When His birthplace was a stable
  And His softest bed was hay.

Blessed babe! what glorious features—
  Spotless fair, divinely bright!
Must He dwell with brutal creatures?
  How could angels bear the sight?

Was there nothing but a manger
  Cursèd sinners could afford
To receive the heavenly stranger?
  Did they thus affront their Lord?

Soft, my child: I did not chide thee,
  Though my song might sound too hard;
'Tis thy mother sits beside thee,
  And her arms shall be thy guard.

Yet to read the shameful story
  How the Jews abused their King,
How they served the Lord of Glory,
  Makes me angry while I sing.

See the kinder shepherds round Him,
  Telling wonders from the sky!
Where they sought Him, there they found Him,
  With His Virgin mother by.

See the lovely babe a-dressing;
  Lovely infant, how He smiled!
When He wept, the mother's blessing
  Soothed and hush'd the holy child.

Lo, He slumbers in His manger,
  Where the hornèd oxen fed:
Peace, my darling; here's no danger,
  Here's no ox anear thy bed.

'Twas to save thee, child, from dying,
  Save my dear from burning flame,
Bitter groans and endless crying,
  That thy blest Redemeer came.

May'st thou live to know and fear Him,
  Trust and love Him all thy days;
Then go dwell for ever near Him,
  See His face, and sing His praise!

THE RAGGEDY MAN

James Whitcomb Riley

O The Raggedy Man! He works fer Pa;
An' he's the goodest man ever you saw!
He comes to our house every day,
An' waters the horses, an' feeds 'em hay;
An' he opens the shed—an' we all ist laugh
When he drives out our little old wobble-ly calf;
An' nen—ef our hired girl says he can—
He milks the cow fer 'Lizabuth Ann,—
  Ain't he a' awful good Raggedy Man?
  Raggedy! Raggedy! Raggedy Man!

W'y, The Raggedy Man—he ist so good
He splits the kindlin' an' chops the wood;
An' nen he spades in our garden, too,
An' does most things 'at *boys* can't do!—
He clumbed clean up in our big tree
An' shooked a' apple down fer me—
An' nother'n, too, fer 'Lizabuth Ann—
An' nother'n, too, fer The Raggedy Man,—
  Ain't he a' awful kind Raggedy Man!
  Raggedy! Raggedy! Raggedy Man!

An' The Raggedy Man, he knows most rhymes
An' tells 'em, ef I be good, sometimes:
Knows 'bout Giunts, an' Griffuns, an' Elves,
An' the Squidgicum-Squees 'at swallers therselves!
An', wite by the pump in our pasture-lot,
He showed me the hole 'at the Wunks is got,
'At lives 'way deep in the ground, an' can
Turn into me, er 'Lizabuth Ann,
Er Ma er Pa er The Raggedy Man!
  Ain't he a funny old Raggedy Man?
  Raggedy! Raggedy! Raggedy Man!

The Raggedy Man—one time when he
Wuz makin' a little bow-'n'-orry fer me,
Says "When *you're* big like your Pa is,
Air *you* go' to keep a fine store like his—
An' be a rich merchunt—an' wear fine clothes?—
Er what *air* you go' to be, goodness knows!"
An' nen he laughed at 'Lizabuth Ann,
An' I says "M go' to be a Raggedy Man!—
  I'm ist go' to be a nice Raggedy Man!"
  Raggedy! Raggedy! Raggedy Man!

WHEN EARTH'S LAST PICTURE IS PAINTED

Rudyard Kipling

When Earth's last picture is painted and the tubes are twisted and dried,
When the oldest colours have faded, and the youngest critic has died,
We shall rest, and, faith, we shall need it—lie down for an aeon or two,
Till the Master of All Good Workmen shall put us to work anew.

And those that were good shall be happy: they shall sit in a golden chair;
They shall splash at a ten-league canvas with brushes of comets' hair;
They shall find real saints to draw from—Magdalene, Peter, and Paul;
They shall work for an age at a sitting and never be tired at all!

And only the Master shall praise us, and only the Master shall blame;
And no one shall work for money, and no one shall work for fame,
But each for the joy of the working, and each, in his separate star,
Shall draw the Things as he sees It for the God of Things as They are!

ABRAHAM LINCOLN'S LETTER TO JOHNSTON, HIS STEP-BROTHER

Dear Johnston: Your request for eighty dollars I do not think it best to comply with now. At the various times when I have helped you a little you have said to me, "We can get along very well now"; but in a very short time I find you in the same difficulty again. Now this can only happen by some defect in your conduct. What that defect is, I think I know. You are not lazy, and still you are an idler. I doubt whether, since I saw you, you have done a good whole day's work in any one day. You do not very much dislike to work, and still you do not work much, merely because it does not seem to you that you could get much for it. This habit of uselessly wasting time is the whole difficulty; it is vastly important to you, and still more so to your children, that you should break the habit. It is more important to them, because they have longer to live, and can keep out of an idle habit before they are in it, easier than they can get out of it after they are in.

You are now in need of some money; and what I propose is, that you shall go to work, "tooth and nail," for somebody who will give you money for it. Let father and your boys take charge of your things at home, prepare for a crop, and make a crop, and you go to work for the best money wages, or in discharge of any debt you owe, that you can get; and, to secure you a fair reward for your labor, I now promise you, that for every dollar you will, between this and the first of May, get for your own labor, either in money or as your own indebtedness, I will then give you one other dollar. By this, if you hire yourself at ten dollars a month, from me you will get ten more, making twenty dollars a month for your work. In this I do not mean you shall go off to St. Louis, or the lead mines, or the gold mines in California, but I mean for you to go at it for the best wages you can get close to home in Coles County Now, if you will do this, you will soon be out of debt, and, what is better, you will have a habit that will keep you from getting in debt again. But if I should now clear you out of debt, next year you would be just as deep in as ever. You say you would almost give your place in heaven for seventy or eighty dollars. Then you value your place in heaven very cheap, for I am sure you can, with the offer I make, get the seventy or eighty dollars for four or five months' work. You say if I will furnish you the money you will deed me the land, and, if you don't pay the money back, you will deliver possession. Nonsense! If you can't live with the land, how will you then live without it? You have always been kind to me, and I do not mean to be unkind to you. On the contrary, if you will but follow my advice, you will find it worth more than eighty times eighty dollars to you.

Affectionately your brother,

A. Lincoln

ALONG THE ROAD

Robert Browning Hamilton

I walked a mile with Pleasure;
 She chattered all the way,
But left me none the wiser
 For all she had to say.

I walked a mile with Sorrow
 And ne'er a word said she;
But oh, the things I learned from her
 When Sorrow walked with me!

THE SAILOR'S CONSOLATION

Charles Dibdin

One night came on a hurricane,
 The sea was mountains rolling,
When Barney Buntline turned his quid,
 And said to Billy Bowling:
"A strong nor-wester's blowing, Bill;
 Hark! don't ye hear it roar, now?
Lord help 'em, how I pities them
 Unhappy folks on shore now!

"Foolhardy chaps who live in towns,
What danger they are all in,
And now lie quaking in their beds,
For fear the roof should fall in;
Poor creatures! how they envies us,
And wishes, I've a notion,
For our good luck, in such a storm,
To be upon the ocean!

"And as for them who're out all day
On business from their houses,
And late at night are coming home,
To cheer their babes and spouses,
While you and I, Bill, on the deck
Are comfortably lying,
My eyes! what tiles and chimney-pots
About their heads are flying!

"And very often have we heard
How men are killed and undone
By overturns of carriages,
By thieves, and fires in London;
We know what risks all landsmen run,
From noblemen to tailors;
Then, Bill, let us thank Providence
That you and I are sailors."

THE TIME TO STRIKE

William Shakespeare

There is a tide in the affairs of men
Which taken at the flood leads on to fortune;
Omitted, all the voyage of their life
Is bound in shallows and in miseries.
On such a full sea are we now afloat,
And we must take the current when it serves,
Or lose our ventures.

(From Julius Caesar)

THE JESTER'S SERMON

George Walter Thornbury

The Jester shook his hood and bells, and leap'd upon a chair,
The pages laugh'd, the women scream'd, and toss'd their scented hair;
The falcon whistled, staghounds bay'd, the lapdog bark'd without,
The scullion dropp'd the pitcher brown, the cook rail'd at the lout;
The steward, counting out his gold, let pouch and money fall,
And why? because the Jester rose to say grace in the hall!

The page play'd with the heron's plume, the steward with his chain,
The butler drumm'd upon the board, and laugh'd with might and main;
The grooms beat on their metal cans, and roar'd till they were red,
But still the Jester shut his eyes and roll'd his witty head;
And when they grew a little still, read half a yard of text,
And, waving hand, struck on the desk, then frown'd like one perplex'd.

"Dear sinners all," the Fool began, "man's life is but a jest,
A dream, a shadow, bubble, air, a vapor at the best.
In a thousand pounds of law I find not a single ounce of love;
A blind man kill'd the parson's cow in shooting at the dove;
The fool that eats till he is sick must fast till he is well;
The wooer who can flatter most will bear away the belle.

"Let no man halloo he is safe till he is through the wood;
He who will not when he may, must tarry when he should;
He who laughs at crookèd men should need walk very straight;
Oh, he who once has won a name may lie abed till eight!
Make haste to purchase house and land, be very slow to wed;
True coral needs no painter's brush, nor need be daub'd with red.

"The friar, preaching, cursed the thief (the pudding in his sleeve).
To fish for sprats with golden hooks is foolish, by your leave,—
To travel well—an ass's ears, ape's face, hog's mouth, and ostrich legs,
He does not care a pin for thieves who limps about and begs.
Be always first man at a feast and last man at a fray;
The short way round, in spite of all, is still the longest way.

When the hungry curate licks the knife, there's not much for the clerk;
When the pilot, turning pale and sick, looks up,—the storm grows dark."

Then loud they laugh'd, the fat cook's tears ran down into the pan:
The steward shook, that he was forced to drop the brimming can;
And then again the women scream'd, and every staghound bay'd,--
And why? because the motley Fool so wise a sermon made.

IN PRAISE OF LITERATURE

Marcus Tullius Cicero

(Translator: N. H. Watts)

But this gives stimulus to our youth and diversion to our old age; this adds a charm to success, and offers a haven of consolation to failure. In the home it delights, in the world it hampers not. Through the night-watches, on all our journeying, and in our hours of country ease, it is an unfailing companion.

THE WORLD

Henry Vaughan

I saw Eternity the other night,
Like a great *Ring* of pure and endless light,
All calm, as it was bright,
And round beneath it, Time, in hours, days, years,
Driven by the spheres,
Like a vast shadow moved, in which the world
And all her train were hurled.
The doting lover, in his quaintest strain,
Did there complain;
Near him his lute, his fancy, and his flights,
Wit's sour delights;
With gloves, and knots, the silly snares of pleasure,
Yet his dear treasure,
All scattered lay, while he his eyes did pour
Upon a flower.

The darksome Statesman, hung with weights and woe,
Like a thick midnight fog, moved there so slow,
He did not stay, nor go;
Condemning thoughts (like sad eclipses) scowl
Upon his soul,
And Clouds of crying witnesses without
Pursued him with one shout;
Yet digged the Mole, and, lest his ways be found,
Work'd under ground,
Where he did clutch his prey; but one did see
That policy;
Churches and altars fed him; perjuries
Were gnats and flies;
It rained about him blood and tears, but he
Drank them as free.

The fearful Miser, on a heap of rust
Sat pining all his life there; but did scarce trust
His own hands with the dust;
Yet would not place one piece above, but lives
In fear of thieves:
Thousands there were as frantic as himself,
And hugged each one his pelf;
The downright Epicure placed heaven in sense,
And scorned pretence;
While others, slipt into a wide excess,
Said little less;
The weaker sort, slight, trivial wares enslave,
Who think them brave;
And poor, despisèd Truth sat counting by
Their victory.

Yet some, who all this while did weep and sing,
And sing, and weep, soared up into the *Ring;*
But most would use no wing.
"O fools," said I, "thus to prefer dark night
Before true light!
To live in grots, and caves, and hate the day
Because it shews the way,—
The way which, from this dead and dark abode,
Leads up to God;
A way where you might tread the sun and be
More bright than he!"

But, as I did their madness so discuss,
One whispered thus,—
"This Ring the Bridegroom did for none provide,
But for his Bride."

CASEY'S REVENGE

Being a Reply to the Famous Baseball Classic, "Casey at the Bat"

James Wilson

There were saddened hearts in Mudville for a week or even more;
There were muttered oaths and curses—every fan in town was sore.
"Just think," said one, "how soft it looked with Casey at the bat!
And then to think he'd go and spring a bush-league trick like that."

All his past fame was forgotten; he was now a hopeless "shine,"
They called him "Strike-out Casey" from the mayor down the line,
And as he came to bat each day his bosom heaved a sigh,
While a look of helpless fury shone in mighty Casey's eye.

The lane is long, someone has said, that never turns again,
And Fate, though fickle, often gives another chance to men.
And Casey smiled—his rugged face no longer wore a frown;
The pitcher who had started all the trouble came to town.

All Mudville had assembled; ten thousand fans had come
To see the twirler who had put big Casey on the bum;
And when he stepped into the box the multitude went wild.
He doffed his cap in proud disdain—but Casey only smiled.

"Play ball!" the umpire's voice rang out, and then the game began;
But in that throng of thousands there was not a single fan
Who thought that Mudville had a chance; and with the setting sun
Their hopes sank low—the rival team was leading "four to one."

The last half of the ninth came round, with no change in the score;
But when the first man up hit safe the crowd began to roar.
The din increased, the echo of ten thousand shouts was heard
When the pitcher hit the second and gave "four balls" to the third.

Three men on base—nobody out—three runs to tie the game!
A triple meant the highest niche in Mudville's hall of fame;
But here the rally ended and the gloom was deep as night
When the fourth one "fouled to catcher" and the fifth "flew out to right."

A dismal groan in chorus came—a scowl was on each face—
When Casey walked up, bat in hand, and slowly took his place;
His bloodshot eyes in fury gleamed; his teeth were clinched in hate;
He gave his cap a vicious hook and pounded on the plate.

But fame is fleeting as the wind, and glory fades away;
There were no wild and woolly cheers, no glad acclaim this day.
They hissed and groaned and hooted as they clamored, "Strike him out!"
But Casey gave no outward sign that he had heard this shout.

The pitcher smiled and cut one loose; across the plate it spread;
Another hiss, another groan. "Strike one!" the umpire said.
Zip! Like a shot, the second curve broke just below his knee—
"Strike two!" the umpire roared aloud; but Casey made no plea.

No roasting for the umpire now—his was an easy lot;
But here the pitcher whirled again—was that a rifle shot!
A whack! a crack! and out through space the leather pellet flew,
A blot against the distant sky, a speck against the blue.

Above the fence in center field, in rapid whirling flight,
The sphere sailed on; the blot grew dim and then was lost to sight.
Ten thousand hats were thrown in air, ten thousand threw a fit;
But no one ever found the ball that mighty Casey hit!

Oh, somewhere in this favored land dark clouds may hide the sun,
And somewhere bands no longer play and children have no fun;
And somewhere over blighted lives there hangs a heavy pall;
But Mudville hearts are happy now—for Casey hit the ball!

* * *

As a goose is not frightened by cackling nor a sheep by bleating, so do not let the clamor of a senseless multitude alarm you.
—Epictetus

THE COMMON PEOPLE

Walt Whitman

The genius of the United States is not best or most in its executives or legislatures, nor in its ambassadors or authors or colleges or churches or parlors, nor even in its newspapers or inventors . . . but always most in the common people. Their manners, speech, dress, friendships,—the freshness and candor of their physiognomy—the picturesque looseness of their carriage . . . their deathless attachment to freedom—their aversion to anything indecorous or soft or mean—the practical acknowledgment of the citizens of one state by the citizens of all other states—the fierceness of their roused resentment—their curiosity and susceptibility to a slight—the air they have of persons who never knew how it felt to stand in the presence of superiors—the fluency of their speech—their delight in music, the sure symptom of manly tenderness and native elegance of soul . . . their good temper and openhandedness—the terrible significance of their elections—the President's taking off his hat to them and not they to him—these too are unrhymed poetry.

(From the preface to Leaves of Grass)

A MIGHTY FORTRESS IS OUR GOD

Martin Luther

(Translator: Frederic H. Hedge)

A mighty Fortress is our God,
A Bulwark never failing;
Our Helper He amid the flood
Of mortal ills prevailing;
For still our ancient foe
Doth seek to work us woe;
His craft and power are great,
And, armed with cruel hate,
On earth is not his equal.

Did we in our own strength confide,
Our striving would be losing;
Were not the right Man on our side,

The Man of God's own choosing:
Dost ask who that may be?
Christ Jesus, it is He;
Lord Sabaoth His name,
From age to age the same,
And He must win the battle.

And though this world, with devils filled,
Should threaten to undo us;
We will not fear, for God hath willed
His truth to triumph through us:
The Prince of Darkness grim,
We tremble not for him;
His rage we can endure,
For lo! his doom is sure,
One little word shall fell him.

That word above all earthly powers,
No thanks to them, abideth;
The Spirit and the gifts are ours
Through Him who with us sideth:
Let goods and kindred go,
This mortal life also;
The body they may kill:
God's truth abideth still,
His Kingdom is forever.

CLIFF KLINGENHAGEN

Edwin Arlington Robinson

Cliff Klingenhagen had me in to dine
With him one day; and after soup and meat,
And all the other things there were to eat,
Cliff took two glasses and filled one with wine
And one with wormwood. Then, without a sign
For me to choose at all, he took the draught
Of bitterness himself, and lightly quaffed
It off, and said the other one was mine.

And when I asked him what the deuce he meant
By doing that, he only looked at me
And smiled, and said it was a way of his.
And though I know the fellow, I have spent
Long time a-wondering when I shall be
As happy as Cliff Klingenhagen is.

WHERE TO BURY A DOG

Ben Hur Lampman

[The following editorial appeared originally in *The Oregonian* and was used in a book compilation of some of Mr. Lampman's work, entitled "How Could I Be Forgetting?"]

A subscriber of the Ontario *Argus* has written to the editor of that fine weekly, propounding a certain question, which, so far as we know, yet remains unanswered. The question is this—"Where shall I bury my dog?" It is asked in advance of death. THE OREGONIAN trusts the *Argus* will not be offended if this newspaper undertakes an answer, for surely such a question merits a reply, since the man who asked it, on the evidence of his letter, loves the dog. It distresses him to think of his favorite as dishonored in death, mere carrion in the winter rains. Within that sloping canine skull, he must reflect when the dog is dead, were thoughts that dignified the dog and honored the master. The hand of the master and of the friend stroked often in affection this rough, pathetic husk that was a dog.

We would say to the Ontario man that there are various places in which a dog may be buried. We are thinking now of a setter, whose coat was flame in the sunshine, and who, so far as we are aware, never entertained a mean or an unworthy thought. This setter is buried beneath a cherry tree, under four feet of garden loam, and at its proper season the cherry tree strews petals on the green lawn of his grave. Beneath a cherry tree, or an apple, or any flowering shrub of the garden, is an excellent place to bury a good dog. Beneath such trees, such shrubs, he slept in the drowsy summer, or gnawed at a flavorous bone, or lifted head to challenge some strange intruder. These are good places, in life or in death. Yet it is a small matter, and it touches sentiment more than anything else. For if the dog be well remembered, if sometimes he leaps through your dreams actual as in life, eyes kindling, questing, ask-ing, laughing, begging, it matters not at all where that dog sleeps at long and at last. On a hill where the wind is unrebuked, and the trees are roaring, or beside a stream he knew in puppyhood, or somewhere in the flatness of a pasture land, where most exhilarating cattle graze. It is all one to the dog, and all one to you, and nothing is gained, and nothing lost—if memory lives. But there is one best place to bury a dog. One place that is best of all.

If you bury him in this spot, the secret of which you must already have, he will come to you when you call—come to you over the grim, dim frontiers of death, and down the well-remembered path, and to your side again. And though you call a dozen living dogs to heel they shall not growl at him, nor resent his coming, for he is yours and he belongs there. People may scoff at you, who see no lightest blade of grass bent by his footfall, who hear no whimper pitched too fine for mere audition, people who may never really have had a dog. Smile at them then, for you shall know something that is hidden from them, and which is well worth the knowing. The one best place to bury a good dog is in the heart of his master.

OWED TO NEW YORK

Byron Rufus Newton

Vulgar of manner, overfed,
Overdressed and underbred,
Heartless, Godless, hell's delight,
Rude by day and lewd by night;
Bedwarfed the man, o'ergrown the brute,
Ruled by boss and prostitute:
Purple-robed and pauper-clad,
Raving, rotting, money-mad;
A squirming herd in Mammon's mesh,
A wilderness of human flesh;
Crazed by avarice, lust and rum,
New York, thy name's "Delirium."

* * *

I'm lonesome. They are all dying. I have hardly a warm personal enemy left.—James McNeill Whistler

MACBETH'S WORDS BEFORE MURDERING

William Shakespeare

Is this a dagger which I see before me,
The handle toward my hand? Come, let me clutch thee.
I have thee not, and yet I see thee still.
Art thou not, fatal vision, sensible
To feeling as to sight? or art thou but
A dagger of the mind, a false creation,
Proceeding from the heat-oppressed brain?
I see thee yet, in form as palpable
As this which now I draw.
Thou marshall'st me the way that I was going;
And such an instrument I was to use.
Mine eyes are made the fools o' the other senses,
Or else worth all the rest: I see thee still;
And on thy blade and dudgeon gouts of blood,
Which was not so before. There's no such thing:
It is the bloody business which informs
Thus to mine eyes. Now o'er the one half-world
Nature seems dead, and wicked dreams abuse
The curtain'd sleep; witchcraft celebrates
Pale Hecate's offerings; and wither'd murder,
Alarum'd by his sentinel, the wolf,
Whose howl's his watch, thus with his stealthy pace,
With Tarquin's ravishing strides, towards his design
Moves like a ghost. Thou sure and firm-set earth,
Hear not my steps, which way they walk, for fear
Thy very stones prate of my whereabout,
And take the present horror from the time,
Which now suits with it. Whiles I threat, he lives:
Words to the heat of deeds too cold breath gives.
[*A bell rings.*]
I go, and it is done: the bell invites me.
Hear it not, Duncan, for it is a knell
That summons thee to heaven, or to hell.

* * *

Who builds a church to God, and not to fame,
Will never mark the marble with his name.
Alexander Pope

I HEAR AMERICA SINGING

Walt Whitman

I hear America singing, the varied carols I hear;
Those of mechanics—each one singing his, as it should be, blithe and strong;
The carpenter singing his, as he measures his plank or beam,
The mason singing his, as he makes ready for work, or leaves off work;
The boatman singing what belongs to him in his boat—the deck-hand singing on the steamboat deck;
The shoemaker singing as he sits on his bench—the hatter singing as he stands;
The wood-cutter's song—the ploughboy's, on his way in the morning, or at the noon intermission, or at sundown;
The delicious singing of the mother—or of the young wife at work—or of the girl sewing or washing;
Each singing what belongs to him or her, and to none else;
The day what belongs to the day—at night, the party of young fellows, robust, friendly,
Singing, with open mouths, their strong melodious songs.

A LAST WILL

IN THE NAME OF GOD, AMEN: I, Charles Lounsbery, being of sound and disposing mind and memory, do now make and publish this, my LAST WILL AND TESTAMENT, in order, as justly as I may, to distribute my interests in the world among succeeding men.

And first, that part of my interests which is known in the law and recognized in the sheep-bound volumes as my property, being inconsiderable and of no account, I make no account of it in this my will.

My right to live, it being but a life estate, is not at my disposal, but, these excepted, all else in the world I now proceed to devise and bequeath.

ITEM—And first, I give to good fathers and mothers, but in trust for their children, nevertheless, all good little words of praise and all quaint pet names, and I charge said parents to use them justly but generously, as the needs of their children shall require.

ITEM—I leave to children exclusively, but only for the life of their childhood, all and every, the dandelions of the fields and the daisies thereof, with the right to play among them freely, according to the custom of children, warning them at the same time against thistles. And I devise to children the yellow shores of creeks and the golden sands beneath the waters thereof, with the dragonflies that skim the surface of said waters, and the odors of the willows that dip into said waters, and the white clouds that float high over the giant trees.

And I leave to children the long days to be merry in, in a thousand ways, and the Night and the Moon and the Train of the Milky Way to wonder at, but subject, nevertheless, to the right thereinafter given to lovers; and I give to each child the right to choose a star that shall be his, and I direct that the child's father shall tell him the name of it, in order that the child shall always remember the name of that star after he has learned and forgotten astronomy.

ITEM—I devise to boys jointly all the useful idle fields and commons where ball may be played, and all the snow-clad hills where one may coast, and all the streams and ponds where one may skate, to have and to hold the same for the period of their boyhood. And all meadows with the clover-blooms and the butterflies thereof; and all woods, with their appurtenances of squirrels and whirring birds and echoes and strange noises: And all distant places which may be visited, together with the adventures there found, I do give to said boys to be theirs; and I give to said boys each his own place at the fireside at night, with all the pictures that may be seen in the burning wood or coal, to enjoy it without let or hindrance, and without any encumbrance of cares.

ITEM—To lovers I devise their imaginary world, with whatever they may need, as the stars of the sky, the red, red roses by the wall, the snow of the hawthorn, the sweet strains of music, of aught else they may desire to figure to each other the lastingness and beauty of their love.

ITEM—To young men jointly, being joined in a brave, mad crowd, I devise and bequeath all boisterous, inspiring sports of rivalry. I give to them the disdain of weakness and undaunted confidence in their own strength. Though they are rude and rough, I leave to them alone the power of making lasting friendships and of possessing companions; and to them exclusively I give all merry songs and brave choruses to sing, with smooth voices to troll them forth.

ITEM—And to those who are no longer children or youths, or

lovers, or young men, I leave a memory, and I leave to them the volumes of the poems of Shakespeare and Burns, and of other poets, if there are others, to the end that they may live over again the old days freely and fully, without tithe or diminution: and to those who are no longer children or youths or lovers I leave, too, the knowledge of what a rare, rare world it is.

(Actually written by Williston Fish, but often mistakenly believed to have been found among the effects of one deceased)

CANTICLE OF THE SUN

St. Francis of Assisi

(Translator: Matthew Arnold)

O most high, almighty, good Lord God, to Thee belong praise, glory, honour, and all blessing!

Praised be my Lord God with all His creatures; and specially our brother the sun, who brings us the day, and who brings us the light; fair is he, and shining with a very great splendour: O Lord, to us he signifies Thee!

Praised be my Lord for our sister the moon, and for the stars, the which He has set clear and lovely in heaven.

Praised be my Lord for our brother the wind, and for air and cloud, calms and all weather, by the which Thou upholdest in life all creatures.

Praised be my Lord for our sister water, who is very serviceable unto us, and humble, and precious, and clean.

Praised be my Lord for our brother fire, through whom Thou givest us light in the darkness; and he is bright, and pleasant, and very mighty, and strong.

Praised be my Lord for our mother the earth, the which doth sustain us and keep us, and bringeth forth divers fruits, and flowers of many colours, and grass.

Praised be my Lord for all those who pardon one another for His love's sake, and who endure weakness and tribulation; blessed are they who peaceably shall endure, for Thou, O most Highest, shall give them a crown!

Praised be my Lord for our sister, the death of the body, from whom no man escapeth. Woe to him who dieth in mortal sin! Blessed are they who are found walking by Thy most holy will, for the second death shall have no power to do them harm.

Praise ye, and bless ye the Lord, and give thanks unto Him, and serve Him with great humility.

DOROTHY Q.

Oliver Wendell Holmes

Grandmother's mother: her age, I guess,
Thirteen summers, or something less;
Girlish bust, but womanly air,
Smooth, square forehead with uprolled hair,
Lips that lover has never kissed;
Taper fingers and slender wrist;
Hanging sleeves of stiff brocade;
So they painted the little maid.

On her hand a parrot green
Sits unmoving and broods serene.
Hold up the canvas full in view,—
Look! there's a rent the light shines through,
Dark with a century's fringe of dust,—
That was a Red-Coat's rapier-thrust!
Such is the tale the lady old,
Dorothy's daughter's daughter, told.

Who the painter was none may tell,—
One whose best was not over well;
Hard and dry, it must be confessed,
Flat as a rose that has long been pressed;
Yet in her cheek the hues are bright,
Dainty colors of red and white,
And in her slender shape are seen
Hint and promise of stately mien.

Look not on her with eyes of scorn,—
Dorothy Q. was a lady born!
Ay! since the galloping Normans came,

England's annals have known her name;
And still to the three-hilled rebel town
Dear is that ancient name's renown,
For many a civic wreath they won,
The youthful sire and the gray-haired son.

O Damsel Dorothy! Dorothy Q.!
Strange is the gift that I owe to you;
Such a gift as never a king
Save to daughter or son might bring,—
All my tenure of heart and hand,
All my title to house and land;
Mother and sister and child and wife
And joy and sorrow and death and life!

What if a hundred years ago
Those close-shut lips had answered No,
When forth the tremulous questions came
That cost the maiden her Norman name,
And under the folds that look so still
The bodice swelled with the bosom's thrill?
Should I be I, or would it be
One tenth another, to nine-tenths me?

Soft is the breath of a maiden's YES:
Not the light gossamer stirs with less;
But never a cable that holds so fast
Through all the battles of wave and blast,
And never an echo of speech or song
That lives in the babbling air so long!
There were tones in the voice that whispered then
You may hear to-day in a hundred men.

O lady and lover, how faint and far
Your images hover,—and here we are,
Solid and stirring in flesh and bone,—
Edward's and Dorothy's—all their own,—
A goodly record for Time to show
Of a syllable spoken so long ago!—
Shall I bless you, Dorothy, or forgive
For the tender whisper that bade me live?

It shall be a blessing, my little maid!
I will heal the stab of the Red-Coat's blade,
And freshen the gold of the tarnished frame,
And gild with a rhyme your household name;
So you shall smile on us brave and bright
As first you greeted the morning's light,
And live untroubled by woes and fears
Through a second youth of a hundred years.

SELF-KNOWLEDGE

Blaise Pascal

(Translator: W. F. Trotter)

It is dangerous to make man see too clearly his equality with the brutes without showing him his greatness. It is also dangerous to make him see his greatness too clearly, apart from his vileness. It is still more dangerous to leave him in ignorance of both. But it is very advantageous to show him both. Man must not think that he is on a level with the brutes or with the angels, nor must he be ignorant of both sides of his nature; but he must know both.

(From Pensées)

KING HENRY VI YEARNS FOR THE SIMPLE LIFE

William Shakespeare

O God! methinks it were a happy life,
To be no better than a homely swain;
To sit upon a hill, as I do now,
To carve out dials quaintly, point by point,
Thereby to see the minutes how they run,
How many make the hour full complete;
How many hours bring about the day;
How many days will finish up the year;
How many years a mortal man may live.
When this is known, then to divide the times:
So many hours must I tend my flock;
So many hours must I take my rest;

So many hours must I contemplate;
So many hours must I sport myself;
So many days my ewes have been with young;
So many weeks ere the poor fools will ean;
So many years ere I shall shear the fleece:
So minutes, hours, days, months, and years,
Pass'd over to the end they were created,
Would bring white hairs unto a quiet grave.
Ah, what a life were this! how sweet! how lovely!
Gives not the hawthorn-bush a sweeter shade
To shepherds looking on their silly sheep,
Than doth a rich embroider'd canopy
To kings that fear their subjects' treachery?
O, yes, it doth; a thousand-fold it doth.
And to conclude, the shepherd's homely curds,
His cold thin drink out of his leather bottle,
His wonted sleep under a fresh tree's shade,
All which secure and sweetly he enjoys,
Is far beyond a prince's delicates,
His viands sparkling in a golden cup,
His body couched in a curious bed,
When care, mistrust, and treason waits on him.

(From King Henry VI)

THE FIRST CHRISTMAS

Holy Bible, Luke 2:1–19

And it came to pass in those days, that there went out a decree from Caesar Augustus, that all the world should be taxed. (And this taxing was first made when Cyrenius was governor of Syria.) And all went to be taxed, every one into his own city. And Joseph also went up from Galilee, out of the city of Nazareth, into Judaea, unto the city of David, which is called Bethlehem; (because he was of the house and lineage of David:) To be taxed with Mary his espoused wife, being great with child. And so it was, that, while they were there, the days were accomplished that she should be delivered. And she brought forth her firstborn son, and wrapped him in swaddling clothes, and laid him in a manger; because there was no room for them in the inn. And there were in the same country shepherds abiding in the field, keeping watch over their flock by night. And, lo, the angel of the Lord came upon them, and the glory of the Lord shone round about them: and they were sore afraid. And the angel said unto them, Fear not: for, behold, I bring you good tidings of great joy, which shall be to all people. For unto you is born this day in the city of David a Saviour, which is Christ the Lord. And this shall be a sign unto you; Ye shall find the babe wrapped in swaddling clothes, lying in a manger. And suddenly there was with the angel a multitude of the heavenly host praising God, and saying, Glory to God in the highest, and on earth peace, good will toward men. And it came to pass, as the angels were gone away from them into heaven, the shepherds said one to another, Let us now go even unto Bethlehem, and see this thing which is come to pass, which the Lord hath made known unto us. And they came with haste, and found Mary, and Joseph, and the babe lying in a manger. And when they had seen it, they made known abroad the saying which was told them concerning this child. And all they that heard it wondered at those things which were told them by the shepherds. But Mary kept all these things, and pondered them in her heart.

THE LOST LEADER

Robert Browning

Just for a handful of silver he left us,
  Just for a riband to stick in his coat—
Found the one gift of which fortune bereft us,
  Lost all the others she lets us devote;
They, with the gold to give, doled him out silver,
  So much was theirs who so little allowed:
How all our copper had gone for his service!
  Rags—were they purple, his heart had been proud!
We that had loved him so, followed him, honored him,
  Lived in his mild and magnificent eye,
Learned his great language, caught his clear accents,
  Made him our pattern to live and to die!
Shakespeare was of us, Milton was for us,
  Burns, Shelley, were with us,—they watch from their graves!
He alone breaks from the van and the freemen,
  —He alone sinks to the rear and the slaves!

We shall march prospering,—not through his presence;
  Songs may inspirit us,—not from his lyre;
Deeds will be done,—while he boasts his quiescence,
  Still bidding crouch whom the rest bade aspire:
Blot out his name, then, record one lost soul more,
  One task more declined, one more footpath untrod,
One more devils'-triumph and sorrow for angels,
  One wrong more to man, one more insult to God!
Life's night begins: let him never come back to us!
  There would be doubt, hesitation and pain,
Forced praise on our part—the glimmer of twilight,
  Never glad confident morning again!
Best fight on well, for we taught him—strike gallantly,
  Menace our heart ere we master his own;
Then let him receive the new knowledge and wait us,
  Pardoned in heaven, the first by the throne!

KILLARNEY

Edward Falconer

By Killarney's lakes and fells, em'rald isles and winding bays,
Mountain paths and woodland dells, mem'ry ever fondly strays,
Bounteous nature loves all lands, beauty wanders ev'rywhere,
Footprints leaves on many strands, but her home is surely there!
Angels fold their wings and rest, in that Eden of the West,
  Beauty's home, Killarney, ever fair Killarney.

Innisfallen's ruined shrine may suggest a passing sigh;
But man's faith can ne'er decline such God's wonders floating by;
Castle Lough and Glena Bay; mountains Tore and Eagle's Nest;
Still at Mucross you must pray though the monks are now at rest.
Angels wonder not that man there would fain prolong life's span,
  Beauty's home, Killarney, ever fair Killarney.

No place else can charm the eye with such bright and varied tints,
Ev'ry rock that you pass by, verdure broiders or besprints,
Virgin there the green grass grows, ev'ry morn spring's natal day,
Bright-hued berries daff the snows, smiling winter's frown away.
Angels often pausing there, doubt if Eden were more fair,
  Beauty's home, Killarney, ever fair Killarney.

Music there for echo dwells, makes each sound a harmony;
Many-voiced the chorus swells, till it faints in ecstasy.
With the charmful tints below, seems the heav'n above to vie,
All rich colors that we know, tinge the cloud-wreaths in that sky.
Wings of angels so might shine, glancing back soft light divine,
Beauty's home, Killarney, ever fair Killarney.

A LITTLE WORK, A LITTLE PLAY

George du Maurier

A little work, a little play
To keep us going—and so, good-day!

A little warmth, a little light
Of love's bestowing—and so, good-night!

A little fun, to match the sorrow
Of each day's growing—and so, to-morrow!

A little trust that when we die
We reap our sowing! And so—good-bye!

FATHER FORGETS

William Livingston Larned

Listen, son, I am saying this to you as you lie asleep, one little paw crumpled under your cheek and the blond curls stickily wet on your damp forehead. I have stolen into your room alone. Just a few moments ago, as I sat reading my paper in the library, a hot, stifling wave of remorse swept over me. I could not resist it. Guiltily I came to your bedside.

These were the things I was thinking, son: I had been cross to you. I scolded you as you were dressing for school because you gave your face merely a dab with a towel. I took you to task for not cleaning your shoes. I called out angrily when I found you had thrown some of your things on the floor.

At breakfast, I found fault, too. You spilled things. You gulped down your food. You put your elbows on the table. You spread butter too thick on your bread. And as you started off to play and I made for my train, you turned and waved a little hand and called, "Good-by, Papa!" and I frowned and said in reply, "Hold your shoulders back!"

Then it began all over again in the late afternoon. As I came up the hill road, I spied you, down on your knees, playing marbles. There were holes in your stocking. I humiliated you before your boy friends, by making you march on ahead of me, back to the house. Stockings were expensive—and if *you* had to buy them you would be more careful. Imagine that, son, from a father! It was such a stupid, silly logic.

But do you remember, later, when I was reading in the library, how you came in softly, timidly, with a sort of hurt, hunted look in your eyes? When I glanced up, over my paper, impatient at the interruption, you hesitated at the door.

"What is it you want?" I snapped.

You said nothing, but you ran across, gathering all your childish courage, in one tempestuous plunge, and threw your arms around my neck, and kissed me, again and again, and your small arms tightened with an affection that God had set blooming in your heart and which even neglect could not wither. And then you were gone, pattering up the stairs.

Well, son, it was shortly afterwards that my paper slipped from my hands and a terrible, sickening fear came over me. Suddenly I saw myself as I really was, in all my horrid selfishness, and I felt sick at heart.

What had habit been doing to me? The habit of complaining, of finding fault, of reprimanding—all these were my rewards to you for being a boy. It was not that I did not love you; it was that I expected so terribly much of youth. I was measuring you by the yardstick of my own years.

And there is so much that is good, and fine, and true in your character. You did not *deserve* my treatment of you, son. The little heart of you was as big as the dawn itself, over wide hills. All this was shown by your spontaneous impulse to rush in and kiss me goodnight. Nothing else matters, tonight, son. I have come to your bedside in the darkness, and I have knelt here, choking with emotion and so ashamed!

It is a feeble atonement. I know you would not understand these things if I told them to you during your waking hours. Yet I must say what I am saying. I must burn sacrificial fires, alone, here in your own bedroom, and make free confession.

And I have prayed God to strengthen me in my new resolve.

Tomorrow I will be a *real* daddy! I will chum with you and suffer when you suffer and laugh when you laugh. I will bite my tongue when impatient words come. I will keep saying, as if it were a ritual: "He is nothing but a boy—a little boy!"

I am afraid I have visualized you as a man. Yet as I see you now, son, crumpled and weary in your cot, I see that you are still a baby. Yesterday you were in your mother's arms, your head on her shoulder. I have asked too much, too much!

Dear boy! Dear little son! A penitent kneels at your infant shrine, here in the moonlight. I kiss the little fingers, and the damp forehead, and the yellow curls, and, if it were not for waking you, I would snatch you up and crush you to my breast.

Tears came and heartache and remorse and, I think, a greater, deeper love, when you ran through the library door and *wanted* to kiss me!

DO THEY MISS ME AT HOME?

S. M. Grannis

Do they miss me at home? Do they miss me?
'Twould be an assurance most dear,
To know that this moment some loved one,
Were saying, "I wish he were here";
To feel that the group at the fireside
Were thinking of me as I roam,
Oh, yes, 'twould be joy beyond measure
To know that they miss'd me at home.

When twilight approaches, the season
That ever is sacred to song,
Does someone repeat my name over,
And sigh that I tarry so long?
And is there a chord in the music
That's miss'd when my voice is away,
And a chord in each heart that awaketh
Regret at my wearisome stay?
Regret at my wearisome stay?

Do they set me a chair near the table
When evening's home pleasures are nigh,

When the candles are lit in the parlor,
And the stars in the calm azure sky?
And when the "good-nights" are repeated,
And all lay them down to their sleep,
Do they think of the absent, and waft me
A whisper'd "good-night" while they weep,
A whisper'd "good-night" while they weep?

Do they miss me at home—do they miss me.
At morning, at noon, or at night?
And lingers one gloomy shade round them,
That only my presence can light?
Are joys less invitingly welcome,
And pleasures less hale than before,
Because one is missed from the circle,
Because I am with them no more,
Because I am with them no more?

SONG

Christina Georgina Rossetti

When I am dead, my dearest,
  Sing no sad songs for me;
Plant thou no roses at my head,
  Nor shady cypress tree:
Be the green grass above me
  With showers and dewdrops wet;
And if thou wilt, remember,
  And if thou wilt, forget.

I shall not see the shadows,
  I shall not feel the rain;
I shall not hear the nightingale
  Sing on, as if in pain;
And dreaming through the twilight
  That doth not rise or set,
Haply I may remember,
  And haply may forget.

LINCOLN CHALLENGES ROBERT ALLEN

New Salem, June 21, 1836

Dear Colonel: I am told that during my absence last week you passed through this place, and stated publicly that you were in possession of a fact or facts which, if known to the public, would entirely destroy the prospects of N. W. Edwards and myself at the ensuing election; but that, through favor to us, you should forbear to divulge them. No one has needed favors more than I, and, generally, few have been less unwilling to accept them; but in this case favor to me would be injustice to the public, and therefore I must beg your pardon for declining it. That I once had the confidence of the people of Sangamon, is sufficiently evident; and if I have since done anything, either by design or misadventure, which if known would subject me to a forfeiture of that confidence, he that knows of that thing, and conceals it, is a traitor to his country's interest.

I find myself wholly unable to form any conjecture of what fact or facts, real or supposed, you spoke; but my opinion of your veracity will not permit me for a moment to doubt you at least believed what you said. I am flattered with the personal regard you manifested for me; but I do hope that, on more mature reflection, you will view the public interest as a paramount consideration, and therefore determine to let the worst come. I here assure you that the candid statement of facts on your part, however low it may sink me, shall never break the tie of personal friendship between us. I wish an answer to this, and you are at liberty to publish both, if you choose.

A. Lincoln

YOU NEVER CAN TELL

Ella Wheeler Wilcox

You never can tell when you send a word
  Like an arrow shot from a bow
By an archer blind, be it cruel or kind,
  Just where it may chance to go.
It may pierce the breast of your dearest friend,
  Tipped with its poison or balm,

To a stranger's heart in life's great mart
  It may carry its pain or its calm.

You never can tell when you do an act
  Just what the result will be,
But with every deed you are sowing a seed,
  Though the harvest you may not see.
Each kindly act is an acorn dropped
  In God's productive soil;
You may not know, but the tree shall grow
  With shelter for those who toil.

You never can tell what your thoughts will do
  In bringing you hate or love,
For thoughts are things, and their airy wings
  Are swifter than carrier doves.
They follow the law of the universe—
  Each thing must create its kind,
And they speed o'er the track to bring you back
  Whatever went out from your mind.

STABAT MATER

Anonymous

(Translators: Richard Mant and Edward Caswall)

At the cross her station keeping,
Stood the mournful mother weeping,
  Where he hung, the dying Lord;
For her soul of joy bereaved,
Bowed with anguish, deeply grieved,
  Felt the sharp and piercing sword.

O how sad and sore distressed
Now was she, that mother blessed
  Of the sole-begotten One.
Deep the woe of her affliction,
When she saw the crucifixion
  Of her ever-glorious Son.

Who, on Christ's dear mother gazing,
Pierced by anguish so amazing,
  Born of woman, would not weep?
Who, on Christ's dear mother thinking,
Such a cup of sorrow drinking,
  Would not share her sorrow deep?

For his people's sins chastised,
She beheld her Son despised,
  Scourged, and crowned with thorns entwined;
Saw him then from judgment taken,
And in death by all forsaken,
  Till his spirit he resigned.

Jesus, may her deep devotion
Stir in me the same emotion,
  Fount of love, Redeemer kind;
That my heart fresh ardòur gaining,
And a purer love attaining,
  May with Thee acceptance find.

(Latin, Twelfth Century)

AN OLD STORY

Edwin Arlington Robinson

Strange that I did not know him then,
  That friend of mine!
I did not even show him then
  One friendly sign;

But cursed him for the ways he had
  To make me see
My envy of the praise he had
  For praising me.

I would have rid the earth of him
  Once in my pride. . . .
I never knew the worth of him
  Until he died.

LITTLE GIFFEN

Francis Orray Ticknor

Out of the focal and foremost fire,
  Out of the hospital walls as dire,
Smitten of grapeshot and gangrene,
Eighteenth battle and he sixteen—
Specter such as you seldom see,
Little Giffen of Tennessee.

"Take him and welcome," the surgeon said;
"Not the doctor can help the dead!"
So we took him and brought him where
The balm was sweet in our summer air;
And we laid him down on a wholesome bed;
Utter Lazarus, heel to head!

And we watched the war with abated breath
Skeleton boy against skeleton death!
Months of torture, how many such!
Weary weeks of the stick and crutch—
And still a glint in the steel-blue eye
Told of a spirit that wouldn't die,

And didn't! Nay! more! in death's despite
The crippled skeleton learned to write—
"Dear mother!" at first, of course, and then
"Dear Captain!" inquiring about the men.
Captain's answer: "Of eighty and five,
Giffen and I are left alive."

"Johnston pressed at the front," they say;—
Little Giffen was up and away!
A tear, his first, as he bade good-by,
Dimmed the glint of his steel-blue eye.
"I'll write, if spared!" There was news of fight,
But none of Giffen—he did not write!

I sometimes fancy that were I King
Of the courtly Knights of Arthur's ring,
With the voice of the minstrel in mine ear
And the tender legend that trembles here,

I'd give the best on his bended knee—
The whitest soul of my chivalry—
For Little Giffen of Tennessee.

THE SON OF GOD GOES FORTH TO WAR

Reginald Heber

The Son of God goes forth to war,
A kingly crown to gain;
His blood-red banner streams afar;
Who follows in His train?
Who best can drink his cup of woe
Triumphant over pain,
Who patient bears his cross below,—
He follows in His train.

The martyr first, whose eagle eye
Could pierce beyond the grave,
Who saw his Master in the sky,
And called on Him to save;
Like Him, with pardon on his tongue,
In midst of mortal pain,
He prayed for them that did the wrong;
Who follows in his train?

A glorious band, the chosen few
On whom the Spirit came,
Twelve valiant saints, their hope they knew,
And mocked the cross and flame;
They met the tyrant's brandished steel,
The lion's gory mane;
They bowed their necks the stroke to feel;
Who follows in their train?

A noble army, men and boys,
The matron and the maid,
Around the Saviour's throne rejoice,
In robes of light arrayed:
They climbed the steep ascent of heaven
Through peril, toil and pain.
O God, to us may grace be given
To follow in their train.

THE WALLOPING WINDOW-BLIND

Charles E. Carryl

A capital ship for an ocean trip
Was the Walloping Window-Blind!
No wind that blew dismayed her crew,
Or troubled the Captain's mind.
The man at the wheel was made to feel
Contempt for the wildest blow,
Tho' it often appeared when the gale had cleared
That he'd been in his bunk below.

Chorus:
Then blow ye winds, heigh-ho!
A-roving I will go!
I'll stay no more on this bright shore,
So let the music play,
I'm off for the morning train,
I'll cross the raging main!
I'm off to my love with a boxing glove,
Ten thousand miles away.

The bo'swain's mate was very sedate,
Yet fond of amusement too;
He played hopscotch with the starboard watch
While the Captain, he tickled the crew,
And the gunner we had was apparently mad,
For he sat on the after rail,
And fired salutes with the Captain's boots,
In the teeth of the booming gale!

The Captain sat on the Commodore's hat,
And dined in a royal way,
Off toasted pigs and pickles and figs,
And gunnery bread each day.
And the cook was Dutch, and behaved as such,
For the diet he gave the crew
Was a number of tons of hot cross buns
Served up with sugar and glue!

All nautical pride we laid aside,
And we ran the vessel ashore
On the Gullibly Isles, where the Poo-poo smiles,

And the Rubly Ubdugs roar.
And we sat on the edge of a sandy ledge
And shot at the whistling bee;
And the cinnamon bats wore wet-proof hats
As they dipped in the shiny sea.

On Rugbug bark, from morn till dark,
We dined till we all had grown
Uncommonly shrunk; when a Chinese junk
Came up from the Torribly Zone.
She was chubby and square,
But we didn't much care,
So we cheerily put to sea;
And we left all the crew of the junk to chew
On the bark of the Rugbug tree.

PROSPICE

Robert Browning

Fear death?—to feel the fog in my throat,
  The mist in my face,
When the snows begin, and the blasts denote
  I am nearing the place,
The power of the night, the press of the storm,
  The post of the foe;
Where he stands, the Arch Fear in a visible form,
  Yet the strong man must go:
For the journey is done and the summit attained,
  And the barriers fall,
Though a battle's to fight ere the guerdon be gained,
  The reward of it all.
I was ever a fighter, so—one fight more,
  The best and the last!
I would hate that death bandaged my eyes, and forbore,
  And bade me creep past.
No! let me taste the whole of it, fare like my peers
  The heroes of old,
Bear the brunt, in a minute pay glad life's arrears
  Of pain, darkness and cold.
For sudden the worst turns the best to the brave
  The black minute's at end.

And the elements' rage, the fiend-voices that rave,
  Shall dwindle, shall blend,
Shall change, shall become first a peace out of pain,
  Then a light, then thy breast,
O thou soul of my soul! I shall clasp thee again,
  And with God be the rest!

THE SECRET HORROR OF THE LAST

Samuel Johnson

There are few things, not purely evil, of which we can say, without some emotion of uneasiness, this is the last. Those who could never agree together shed tears when mutual discontent has determined them to final separation; of a place which has been frequently visited, though without pleasure, the last look is taken with heaviness of heart; and the Idler, with all his chilliness of tranquillity, is not wholly unaffected by the thought that his last essay is before him.

The secret of horror of the last is inseparable from a thinking being, whose life is limited, and to whom death is dreadful. We always make a secret comparison between a part and a whole; the termination of any period of life reminds us that life itself has likewise its termination; when we have done anything for the last time we involuntarily reflect that a part of the days allotted to us is past, and that as more is past there is less remaining.

THE COURTSHIP OF MILES STANDISH

Henry Wadsworth Longfellow

I

In the Old Colony days, in Plymouth the land of the Pilgrims,
To and fro in a room of his simple and primitive dwelling,
Clad in doublet and hose, and boots of Cordovan leather,
Strode, with a martial air, Miles Standish the Puritan Captain.
Buried in thought he seemed, with his hands behind him, and
    pausing
Ever and anon to behold his glittering weapons of warfare,
Hanging in shining array along the walls of the chamber,—

Cutlass and corselet of steel, and his trusty sword of Damascus,
Curved at the point and inscribed with its mystical Arabic
sentence,
While underneath, in a corner, were fowling-piece, musket, and
matchlock.
Short of stature he was, but strongly built and athletic,
Broad in the shoulders, deep-chested, with muscles and sinews of
iron;
Brown as a nut was his face, but his russet beard was already
Flaked with patches of snow, as hedges sometimes in November.
Near him was seated John Alden, his friend and household
companion,
Writing with diligent speed at a table of pine by the window;
Fair-haired, azure-eyed, with delicate Saxon complexion,
Having the dew of his youth, and the beauty thereof, as the
captives
Whom Saint Gregory saw, and exclaimed, "Not Angles, but
Angels."
Youngest of all was he of the men who came in the Mayflower. . . .

II

Nothing was heard in the room but the hurrying pen of the
stripling,
Or an occasional sigh from the laboring heart of the Captain,
Reading the marvellous words and achievements of Julius Caesar.
After a while he exclaimed, as he smote with his hand, palm
downwards,
Heavily on the page: "A wonderful man was this Caesar!
You are a writer, and I am a fighter, but here is a fellow
Who could both write and fight, and in both was equally skilful!"
Straightway answered and spake John Alden, the comely, the
youthful:
"Yes, he was equally skilled, as you say, with his pen and his
weapons.
Somewhere have I read, but where I forget, he could dictate
Seven letters at once, at the same time writing his memoirs.". . .

All was silent again; The Captain continued his reading.
Nothing was heard in the room but the hurrying pen of the
stripling
Writing epistles important to go next day by the Mayflower,
Filled with the name and the fame of the Puritan maiden Priscilla;
Every sentence began or closed with the name of Priscilla,

Till the treacherous pen, to which he confided the secret,
Strove to betray it by singing and shouting the name of Priscilla!
Finally closing his book, with a bang of the ponderous cover,
Sudden and loud as the sound of a soldier grounding his musket,
Thus to the young man spake Miles Standish the Captain of Plymouth:
"When you have finished your work, I have something important to tell you.
Be not however in haste; I can wait; I shall not be impatient!"
Straightway Alden replied, as he folded the last of his letters,
Pushing his papers aside, and giving respectful attention;
"Speak; for whenever you speak, I am always ready to listen,
Always ready to hear whatever pertains to Miles Standish."
Thereupon answered the Captain, embarrassed, and culling his phrases:
" 'Tis not good for a man to be alone, say the Scriptures.
This I have said before, and again and again I repeat it;
Every hour in the day, I think it, and feel it, and say it.
Since Rose Standish died, my life has been weary and dreary;
Sick at heart have I been, beyond the healing of friendship;
Oft in my lonely hours have I thought of the maiden Priscilla.
She is alone in the world; her father and mother and brother
Died in the winter together; I saw her going and coming,
Now to the grave of the dead, and now to the bed of the dying,
Patient, courageous, and strong, and said to myself, that if ever
There were angels on earth, as there are angels in heaven,
Two have I seen and known; and the angel whose name is Priscilla
Holds in my desolate life the place which the other abandoned.
Long have I cherished the thought, but never have dared to reveal it,
Being a coward in this, though valiant enough for the most part.
Go to the damsel Priscilla, the loveliest maiden of Plymouth,
Say that a blunt old Captain, a man not of words but of actions,
Offers his hand and his heart, the hand and heart of a soldier.
Not in these words, you know, but this in short is my meaning;
I am a maker of war, and not a maker of phrases.
You, who are bred as a scholar, can say it in elegant language,
Such as you read in your books of the pleadings and wooings of lovers,
Such as you think best adapted to win the heart of a maiden."

When he had spoken, John Alden, the fair-haired, taciturn stripling,

All aghast at his words, surprised, embarrassed, bewildered,
Trying to mask his dismay by treating the subject with lightness,
Trying to smile, and yet feeling his heart stand still in his bosom,
Just as a timepiece stops in a house that is stricken by lightning,
Thus made answer and spake, or rather stammered than answered:
"Such a message as that, I am sure I should mangle and mar it;
If you would have it well done,—I am only repeating your maxim,—
You must do it yourself, you must not leave it to others!"
But with the air of a man whom nothing can turn from his purpose,
Gravely shaking his head, made answer the Captain of Plymouth:
"Truly the maxim is good, and I do not mean to gainsay it;
But we must use it discreetly, and not waste powder for nothing.
Now, as I said before, I was never a maker of phrases.
I can march up to a fortress and summon the place to surrender,
But march up to a woman with such a proposal, I dare not.
I'm not afraid of bullets, nor shot from the mouth of a cannon,
But of a thundering 'No!' point-blank from the mouth of a woman,
That I confess I'm afraid of, nor am I ashamed to confess it!
So you must grant my request, for you are an elegant scholar,
Having the graces of speech, and skill in the turning of phrases."
Taking the hand of his friend, who still was reluctant and doubtful,
Holding it long in his own, and pressing it kindly, he added:
"Though I have spoken thus lightly, yet deep is the feeling that prompts me;
Surely you cannot refuse what I ask in the name of our friendship!"
Then made answer John Alden: "The name of friendship is sacred;
What you demand in that name, I have not the power to deny you!"
So the strong will prevailed, subduing and moulding the gentler,
Friendship prevailed over love, and Alden went on his errand.

III

So the strong will prevailed and Alden went on his errand,
Out of the street of the village, and into the paths of the forest,
Into the tranquil woods, where bluebirds and robins were building
Towns in the populous trees, with hanging gardens of verdure,
Peaceful, aerial cities of joy and affection and freedom.

All around him was calm, but within him commotion and conflict,
Love contending with friendship, and self with each generous
impulse.
To and fro in his breast his thoughts were heaving and dashing,
As in a foundering ship, with every roll of the vessel,
Washes the bitter sea, the merciless surge of the ocean!
"Must I relinquish it all," he cried with a wild lamentation,—
"Must I relinquish it all, the joy, the hope, the illusion?
Was it for this I have loved, and waited, and worshipped in
silence?
Was it for this I have followed the flying feet and the shadow
Over the wintry sea, to the desolate shores of New England?
Truly the heart is deceitful, and out of its depths of corruption
Rise, like an exhalation, the misty phantoms of passion;
Angels of light they seem, but are only delusions of Satan.
All is clear to me now; I feel it, I see it distinctly!
This is the hand of the Lord; it is laid upon me in anger,
For I have followed too much the heart's desires and devices,
Worshipping Astaroth blindly, and impious idols of Baal.
This is the cross I must bear; the sin and the swift retribution."

So through the Plymouth woods John Alden went on his errand;
Crossing the brook at the ford, where it brawled over pebble and
shallow,
Gathering still, as he went, the May-flowers blooming around him,
Fragrant, filling the air with a strange and wonderful sweetness,
Children lost in the woods, and covered with leaves in their
slumber.
"Puritan flowers," he said, "and the type of Puritan maidens,
Modest and simple and sweet, the very type of Priscilla!
So I will take them to her; to Priscilla the May-flower of Plymouth,
Modest and simple and sweet, as a parting gift will I take them;
Breathing their silent farewells, as they fade and wither and perish,
Soon to be thrown away as is the heart of the giver."
So through the Plymouth woods John Alden went on his errand;
Came to an open space, and saw the disk of the ocean,
Sailless, sombre and cold with the comfortless breath of the east-
wind;
Saw the new-built house, and people at work in a meadow;
Heard, as he drew near the door, the musical voice of Priscilla
Singing the hundredth Psalm, the grand old Puritan anthem,
Music that Luther sang to the sacred words of the Psalmist,
Full of the breath of the Lord, consoling and comforting many.

Then, as he opened the door, he beheld the form of the maiden
Seated beside her wheel, and the carded wool like a snow-drift
Piled at her knee, her white hands feeding the ravenous spindle,
While with her foot on the treadle she guided the wheel in its motion.
Open wide on her lap lay the well-worn psalm-book of Ainsworth,
Printed in Amsterdam, the words and the music together,
Rough-hewn, angular notes, like stones in the wall of a churchyard,
Darkened and overhung by the running vine of the verses.
Such was the book from whose pages she sang the old Puritan anthem,
She, the Puritan girl, in the solitude of the forest,
Making the humble house and the modest apparel of homespun
Beautiful with her beauty, and rich with the wealth of her being!
Over him rushed, like a wind that is keen and cold and relentless,
Thoughts of what might have been, and the weight and woe of his errand;
All the dreams that had faded, and all the hopes that had vanished,
All his life henceforth a dreary and tenantless mansion,
Haunted by vain regrets, and pallid, sorrowful faces.
Still he said to himself, and almost fiercely he said it,
"Let not him that putteth his hand to the plough look backwards;
Though the ploughshare cut through the flowers of life to its fountains,
Though it pass o'er the graves of the dead and the hearths of the living,
It is the will of the Lord; and his mercy endureth forever!"

So he entered the house: and the hum of the wheel and the singing
Suddenly ceased; for Priscilla, aroused by his step on the threshold,
Rose as he entered, and gave him her hand, in signal of welcome,
Saying, "I knew it was you, when I heard your step in the passage;
For I was thinking of you, as I sat there singing and spinning."
Awkward and dumb with delight, that a thought of him had been mingled
Thus in the sacred psalm, that came from the heart of the maiden,
Silent before her he stood, and gave her the flowers for an answer,
Finding no words for his thought. He remembered that day in the winter,

After the first great snow, when he broke a path from the village,
Reeling and plunging along through the drifts that encumbered the doorway,
Stamping the snow from his feet as he entered the house, and Priscilla
Laughed at his snowy locks, and gave him a seat by the fireside,
Grateful and pleased to know he had thought of her in the snow-storm.
Had he but spoken then! perhaps not in vain had he spoken;
Now it was all too late; the golden moment had vanished!
So he stood there abashed, and gave her the flowers for an answer.

Then they sat down and talked of the birds and the beautiful Spring-time,
Talked of their friends at home, and the Mayflower that sailed on the morrow.
"I have been thinking all day," said gently the Puritan maiden,
"Dreaming all night, and thinking all day, of the hedge-rows of England,
They are in blossom now, and the country is all like a garden;
Thinking of lanes and fields, and the song of the lark and the linnet,
Seeing the village street, and familiar faces of neighbors
Going about as of old, and stopping to gossip together,
And, at the end of the street, the village church, with the ivy
Climbing the old gray tower, and the quiet graves in the church-yard.
Kind are the people I live with, and dear to me my religion;
Still my heart is so sad, that I wish myself back in Old England.
You will say it is wrong, but I cannot help it: I almost
Wish myself back in Old England, I feel so lonely and wretched."

Thereupon answered the youth: "Indeed I do not condemn you;
Stouter hearts than a woman's have quailed in this terrible winter.
Yours is tender and trusting, and needs a stronger to lean on;
So I have come to you now, with an offer and proffer of marriage
Made by a good man and true, Miles Standish the Captain of Plymouth!"

Thus he delivered his message, the dexterous writer of letters,—
Did not embellish the theme, nor array it in beautiful phrases,
But came straight to the point, and blurted it out like a school-boy;

Even the Captain himself could hardly have said it more bluntly.
Mute with amazement and sorrow, Priscilla the Puritan maiden
Looked into Alden's face, her eyes dilated with wonder,
Feeling his words like a blow, that stunned her and rendered her speechless;
Till at length she exclaimed, interrupting the ominous silence:
"If the great Captain of Plymouth is so very eager to wed me,
Why does he not come himself, and take the trouble to woo me?
If I am not worth the wooing, I surely am not worth the winning!"
Then John Alden began explaining and smoothing the matter,
Making it worse as he went, by saying the Captain was busy,—
Had no time for such things;—such things! the words grating harshly
Fell on the ear of Priscilla; and swift as a flash she made answer:
"Has he no time for such things, as you call it, before he is married,
Would he be likely to find it, or make it, after the wedding?
That is the way with you men; you don't understand us, you cannot.
When you have made up your minds, after thinking of this one and that one,
Choosing, selecting, rejecting, comparing one with another,
Then you make known your desire, with abrupt and sudden avowal,
And are offended and hurt, and indignant perhaps, that a woman
Does not respond at once to a love that she never suspected,
Does not attain at a bound the height to which you have been climbing.
This is not right nor just; for surely a woman's affection
Is not a thing to be asked for, and had for only the asking.
When one is truly in love, one not only says it, but shows it.
Had he but waited awhile, had he only showed that he loved me,
Even this Captain of yours—who knows?—at last might have won me,
Old and rough as he is; but now it never can happen."

Still John Alden went on, unheeding the words of Priscilla,
Urging the suit of his friend, explaining, persuading, expanding;
Spoke of his courage and skill, and of all his battles in Flanders,
How with the people of God he had chosen to suffer affliction;
How, in return for his zeal, they had made him Captain of Plymouth;
He was a gentleman born, could trace his pedigree plainly
Back to Hugh Standish of Duxbury Hall, in Lancashire, England,

Who was the son of Ralph, and the grandson of Thurston de Standish;
Heir unto vast estates, of which he was basely defrauded,
Still bore the family arms, and had for his crest a cock argent,
Combed and wattled gules, and all the rest of the blazon.
He was a man of honor, of noble and generous nature;
Though he was rough, he was kindly; she knew how during the winter
He had attended the sick, with a hand as gentle as woman's;
Somewhat hasty and hot, he could not deny it, and headstrong,
Stern as a soldier might be, but hearty, and placable always,
Not to be laughed at and scorned, because he was little of stature;
For he was great of heart, magnanimous, courtly, courageous;
Any woman in Plymouth, nay, any woman in England,
Might be happy and proud to be called the wife of Miles Standish!

But as he warmed and glowed, in his simple and eloquent language,
Quite forgetful of self, and full of the praise of his rival,
Archly the maiden smiled, and, with eyes overrunning with laughter,
Said in a tremulous voice, "Why don't you speak for yourself, John?"

IV

Into the open air John Alden, perplexed and bewildered,
Rushed like a man insane, and wandered alone by the sea-side;
Paced up and down the sands, and bared his head to the east-wind,
Cooling his heated brow, and the fire and fever within him.
Slowly as out of the heavens, with apocalyptical splendors,
Sank the City of God, in the vision of John the Apostle,
So, with its cloudy walls of chrysolite, jasper, and sapphire,
Sank the broad red sun, and over its turrets uplifted
Glimmered the golden reed of the angel who measured the city.

"Welcome, O wind of the East!" he exclaimed in his wild exultation,
"Welcome, O wind of the East, from the caves of the misty Atlantic!
Blowing o'er fields of dulse, and measureless meadows of sea-grass,
Blowing o'er rocky wastes, and the grottoes and gardens of ocean!
Lay thy cold, moist hand on my burning forehead, and wrap me
Close in thy garments of mist, to allay the fever within me!"

Like an awakened conscience, the sea was moaning and tossing,
Beating remorseful and loud the mutable sands of the sea-shore.
Fierce in his soul was the struggle and tumult of passions contending;
Love triumphant and crowned, and friendship wounded and bleeding.
Passionate cries of desire, and importunate pleadings of duty!
"Is it my fault," he said, "that the maiden has chosen between us?
Is it my fault that he failed,—my fault that I am the victor?"
Then within him there thundered a voice, like the voice of the Prophet:
"It hath displeased the Lord!"—and he thought of David's transgression,
Bathsheba's beautiful face, and his friend in the front of the battle!
Shame and confusion of guilt, and abasement and self-condemnation,
Overwhelmed him at once; and he cried in the deepest contrition:
"It hath displeased the Lord! It is the temptation of Satan!"

Then, uplifting his head, he looked at the sea, and beheld there
Dimly the shadowy form of the Mayflower riding at anchor,
Rocked on the rising tide, and ready to sail on the morrow;
Heard the voices of men through the mist, the rattle of cordage
Thrown on the deck, the shouts of the mate, and the sailors' "Ay, ay, Sir!"
Clear and distinct, but not loud, in the dripping air of the twilight,
Still for a moment he stood, and listened, and stared at the vessel,
Then went hurriedly on, as one who, seeing a phantom,
Stops, then quickens his pace, and follows the beckoning shadow.
"Yes, it is plain to me now," he murmured; "the hand of the Lord is
Leading me out of the land of darkness, the bondage of error,
Through the sea, that shall lift the walls of its waters around me,
Hiding me, cutting me off, from the cruel thoughts that pursue me.
Back will I go o'er the ocean, this dreary land will abandon,
Her whom I may not love, and him whom my heart has offended.
Better to be in my grave in the green old churchyard in England,
Close by my mother's side, and among the dust of my kindred;
Better be dead and forgotten, than living in shame and dishonor!
Sacred and safe and unseen, in the dark of the narrow chamber
With me my secret shall lie, like a buried jewel that glimmers

Bright on the hand that is dust, in the chambers of silence and darkness,—
Yes, as the marriage ring of the great espousal hereafter!"

Thus, as he spake, he turned, in the strength of his strong resolution,
Leaving behind him the shore, and hurried along in the twilight,
Through the congenial gloom of the forest silent and sombre,
Till he beheld the lights in the seven houses of Plymouth,
Shining like seven stars in the dusk and mist of the evening.
Soon he entered his door, and found the redoubtable Captain
Sitting alone, and absorbed in the martial pages of Caesar,
Fighting some great campaign in Hainault or Brabant or Flanders.
"Long have you been on your errand," he said with a cheery demeanor,
Even as one who is waiting an answer, and fears not the issue.
"Not far off is the house, although the woods are between us;
But you have lingered so long, that while you were going and coming
I have fought ten battles and sacked and demolished a city.
Come, sit down, and in order relate to me all that has happened."

Then John Alden spake, and related the wondrous adventure,
From beginning to end, minutely, just as it happened:
How he had seen Priscilla, and how he had sped in his courtship,
Only smoothing a little, and softening down her refusal.
But when he came at length to the words Priscilla had spoken,
Words so tender and cruel: "Why don't you speak for yourself, John?"
Up leaped the Captain of Plymouth, and stamped on the floor, till his armor
Clanged on the wall, where it hung, with a sound of sinister omen.
All his pent-up wrath burst forth in a sudden explosion,
E'en as a hand-grenade, that scatters destruction around it.
Wildly he shouted, and loud: "John Alden! you have betrayed me!
Me, Miles Standish, your friend! have supplanted, defrauded, betrayed me!
One of my ancestors ran his sword through the heart of Wat Tyler;
Who shall prevent me from running my own through the heart of a traitor?
Yours is the greater treason, for yours is a treason to friendship!

You, who lived under my roof, whom I cherished and loved as a brother;
You, who have fed at my board, and drunk at my cup, to whose keeping
I have intrusted my honor, my thoughts the most sacred and secret,—
You too, Brutus! ah woe to the name of friendship hereafter!
Brutus was Caesar's friend, and you were mine, but henceforward
Let there be nothing between us save war, and implacable hatred!"

So spake the Captain of Plymouth, and strode about in the chamber,
Chafing and choking with rage; like cords were the veins on his temples.
But in the midst of his anger a man appeared at the doorway,
Bringing in uttermost haste a message of urgent importance,
Rumors of danger and war and hostile incursions of Indians!
Straightway the Captain paused, and, without further question or parley,
Took from the nail on the wall his sword with its scabbard of iron,
Buckled the belt round his waist, and, frowning fiercely, departed. . . .

V

There with his boat was the Master, already a little impatient
Lest he should lose the tide, or the wind might shift to the eastward,
Square-built, hearty, and strong, with an odor of ocean about him,
Speaking with this one and that, and cramming letters and parcels
Into his pockets capacious, and messages mingled together
Into his narrow brain, till at last he was wholly bewildered.
Nearer the boat stood Alden, with one foot placed on the gunwale,
One still firm on the rock, and talking at times with the sailors,
Seated erect on the thwarts, all ready and eager for starting.
He too was eager to go, and thus put an end to his anguish,
Thinking to fly from despair, that swifter than keel is or canvas,
Thinking to drown in the sea the ghost that would rise and pursue him.
But as he gazed on the crowd, he beheld the form of Priscilla
Standing dejected among them, unconscious of all that was passing.
Fixed were her eyes upon his, as if she divined his intention,
Fixed with a look so sad, so reproachful, imploring, and patient,
That with a sudden revulsion his heart recoiled from its purpose,

As from the verge of a crag, where one step more is destruction.
Strange is the heart of man, with its quick, mysterious instincts!
Strange is the life of man, and fatal or fated are moments,
Whereupon turn, as on hinges, the gates of the wall adamantine!
"Here I remain!" he exclaimed, as he looked at the heavens above him,
Thanking the Lord whose breath had scattered the mist and the madness,
Wherein, blind and lost, to death he was staggering headlong.
"Yonder snow-white cloud, that floats in the ether above me,
Seems like a hand that is pointing and beckoning over the ocean.
There is another hand, that is not so spectral and ghost-like,
Holding me, drawing me back, and clasping mine for protection.
Float, O hand of cloud, and vanish away in the ether!
Roll thyself up like a fist, to threaten and daunt me; I heed not
Either your warning or menace, or any omen of evil!
There is no land so sacred, no air so pure and so wholesome,
As is the air she breathes, and the soil that is pressed by her footsteps.
Here for her sake will I stay, and like an invisible presence
Hover around her forever, protecting, supporting her weakness;
Yes! as my foot was the first that stepped on this rock at the landing,
So, with the blessing of God, shall it be the last at the leaving!"

Meanwhile the Master alert, but with dignified air and important,
Scanning with watchful eye the tide and the wind and the weather,
Walked about on the sands, and the people crowded around him
Saying a few last words, and enforcing his careful remembrance.
Then, taking each by the hand, as if he were grasping a tiller,
Into the boat he sprang, and in haste shoved off to his vessel,
Glad in his heart to get rid of all this worry and flurry,
Glad to be gone from a land of sand and sickness and sorrow,
Short allowance of victual, and plenty of nothing but Gospel!
Lost in the sound of the oars was the last farewell of the Pilgrims.
O strong hearts and true! not one went back in the Mayflower!
No, not one looked back, who had set his hand to this ploughing! . . .

Lo! as they turned to depart, they saw the form of an Indian.
Watching them from the hill; but while they spake with each other,

Pointing with outstretched hands, and saying, "Look!" he had vanished.
So they returned to their homes; but Alden lingered a little,
Musing alone on the shore, and watching the wash of the billows
Round the base of the rock, and the sparkle and flash of the sunshine,
Like the spirit of God, moving visibly over the waters.

VI

Thus for a while he stood, and mused by the shore of the ocean,
Thinking of many things, and most of all of Priscilla;
And as if thought had the power to draw to itself, like the loadstone,
Whatsoever it touches, by subtile laws of its nature,
Lo! as he turned to depart, Priscilla was standing beside him.

"Are you so much offended, you will not speak to me?" said she.
"Am I so much to blame, that yesterday, when you were pleading
Warmly the cause of another, my heart, impulsive and wayward,
Pleaded your own, and spake out, forgetful perhaps of decorum?
Certainly you can forgive me for speaking so frankly, for saying
What I ought not to have said, yet now I can never unsay it;
For there are moments in life, when the heart is so full of emotion,
That if by chance it be shaken, or into its depths like a pebble
Drops some careless word, it overflows, and its secret,
Spilt on the ground like water, can never be gathered together.
Yesterday I was shocked, when I heard you speak of Miles Standish,
Praising his virtues, transforming his very defects into virtues,
Praising his courage and strength, and even his fighting in Flanders,
As if by fighting alone you could win the heart of a woman,
Quite overlooking yourself and the rest, in exalting your hero.
Therefore I spake as I did, by an irresistible impulse.
You will forgive me, I hope, for the sake of the friendship between us,
Which is too true and too sacred to be so easily broken!"
Thereupon answered John Alden, the scholar, the friend of Miles Standish:
"I was not angry with you, with myself alone I was angry,
Seeing how badly I managed the matter I had in my keeping."
"No!" interrupted the maiden, with answer prompt and decisive;
"No; you were angry with me, for speaking so frankly and freely.
It was wrong, I acknowledge; for it is the fate of a woman

Long to be patient and silent, to wait like a ghost that is speechless,
Till some questioning voice dissolves the spell of its silence.
Hence is the inner life of so many suffering women
Sunless and silent and deep, like subterranean rivers
Running through caverns of darkness, unheard, unseen, and unfruitful,
Chafing their channels of stone, with endless and profitless murmurs."
Thereupon answered John Alden, the young man, the lover of women:
"Heaven forbid it, Priscilla; and truly they seem to me always
More like the beautiful rivers that watered the garden of Eden,
More like the river Euphrates, through deserts of Havilah flowing,
Filling the land with delight, and memories sweet of the garden!"
"Ah, by these words, I can see," again interrupted the maiden,
"How very little you prize me, or care for what I am saying.
When from the depths of my heart, in pain and with secret misgiving,
Frankly I speak to you, asking for sympathy only and kindness,
Straightway you take up my words, that are plain and direct and in earnest,
Turn them away from their meaning, and answer with flattering phrases.
This is not right, is not just, is not true to the best that is in you;
For I know and esteem you, and feel that your nature is noble,
Lifting mine up to a higher, a more ethereal level.
Therefore I value your friendship, and feel it perhaps the more keenly
If you say aught that implies I am only as one among many,
If you make use of those common and complimentary phrases
Most men think so fine, in dealing and speaking with women,
But which women reject as insipid, if not as insulting."

Mute and amazed was Alden; and listened and looked at Priscilla,
Thinking he never had seen her more fair, more divine in her beauty.
He who but yesterday pleaded so glibly the cause of another,
Stood there embarrassed and silent, and seeking in vain for an answer.
So the maiden went on, and little divined or imagined
What was at work in his heart, that made him so awkward and speechless.

"Let us, then, be what we are, and speak what we think, and in all things
Keep ourselves loyal to truth, and the sacred professions of friendship.
It is no secret I tell you, nor am I ashamed to declare it:
I have liked to be with you, to see you, to speak with you always.
So I was hurt at your words, and a little affronted to hear you
Urge me to marry your friend, though he were the Captain Miles Standish.
For I must tell you the truth: much more to me is your friendship
Than all the love he could give, were he twice the hero you think him."
Then she extended her hand, and Alden, who eagerly grasped it,
Felt all the wounds in his heart, that were aching and bleeding so sorely,
Healed by the touch of that hand, and he said, with a voice full of feeling:
"Yes, we must ever be friends; and of all who offer you friendship
Let me be ever the first, the truest, the nearest and dearest!"

Casting a farewell look at the glimmering sail of the Mayflower,
Distant, but still in sight, and sinking below the horizon,
Homeward together they walked, with a strange, indefinite feeling,
That all the rest had departed and left them alone in the desert.
But, as they went through the fields in the blessing and smile of the sunshine,
Lighter grew their hearts, and Priscilla said very archly:
"Now that our terrible Captain has gone in pursuit of the Indians,
Where he is happier far than he would be commanding a household,
You may speak boldly, and tell me of all that happened between you,
When you returned last night, and said how ungrateful you found me."
Thereupon answered John Alden, and told her the whole of the story,—
Told her his own despair, and the direful wrath of Miles Standish.
Whereat the maiden smiled, and said between laughing and earnest,
"He is a little chimney, and heated hot in a moment!"
But as he gently rebuked her, and told her how he had suffered,—
How he had even determined to sail that day in the Mayflower,

And had remained for her sake, on hearing the dangers that
threatened,—
All her manner was changed, and she said with a faltering accent,
"Truly I thank you for this: how good you have been to me
always!"

Thus, as a pilgrim devout, who toward Jerusalem journeys,
Taking three steps in advance, and one reluctantly backward,
Urged by importunate zeal, and withheld by pangs of contrition;
Slowly but steadily onward, receding yet ever advancing,
Journeyed this Puritan youth to the Holy Land of his longings,
Urged by the fervor of love, and withheld by remorseful mis-
givings.

VII

Meanwhile the stalwart Miles Standish was marching steadily
northward,
Winding through forest and swamp, and along the trend of the
sea-shore,
All day long, with hardly a halt, the fire of his anger
Burning and crackling within, and the sulphurous odor of powder
Seeming more sweet to his nostrils than all the scents of the
forest.
Silent and moody he went, and much he revolved his discomfort;
He who was used to success, and to easy victories always,
Thus to be flouted, rejected, and laughed to scorn by a maiden,
Thus to be mocked and betrayed by the friend whom most he had
trusted!
Ah! 'twas too much to be borne, and he fretted and chafed in his
armor!

"I alone am to blame," he muttered, "for mine was the folly.
What has a rough old soldier, grown grim and gray in the harness,
Used to the camp and its way, to do with the wooing of maid-
ens?
'Twas but a dream,—let it pass,—let it vanish like so many others!
What I thought was a flower is only a weed, and is worthless;
Out of my heart will I pluck it, and throw it away, and hence-
forward
Be but a fighter of battles, a lover and wooer of dangers!"
Thus he revolved in his mind his sorry defeat and discomfort,
While he was marching by day or lying at night in the forest,
Looking up at the trees, and the constellations beyond them. . . .

VIII

Month after month passed away, and in Autumn the ships of the merchants
Came with kindred and friends, with cattle and corn for the Pilgrims.
All in the village was peace; the men were intent on their labors,
Busy with hewing and building, with garden-plot and with merestead,
Busy with breaking the glebe, and mowing the grass in the meadows,
Searching the sea for its fish, and hunting the deer in the forest.
All in the village was peace; but at times the rumor of warfare
Filled the air with alarm, and the apprehension of danger.
Bravely the stalwart Standish was scouring the land with his forces,
Waxing valiant in fight and defeating the alien armies,
Till his name had become a sound of fear to the nations.
Anger was still in his heart, but at times the remorse and contrition
Which in all noble natures succeed the passionate outbreak,
Came like a rising tide, that encounters the rush of a river,
Staying its current awhile, but making it bitter and brackish.

Meanwhile Alden at home had built him a new habitation,
Solid, substantial, of timber rough-hewn from the firs of the forest.
Wooden-barred was the door, and the roof was covered with rushes;
Latticed the windows were, and the window-panes were of paper,
Oiled to admit the light, while wind and rain were excluded.
There too he dug a well, and around it planted an orchard:
Still may be seen to this day some trace of the well and the orchard.
Close to the house was the stall, where, safe and secure from annoyance,
Raghorn, the snow-white bull, that had fallen to Alden's allotment
In the division of cattle, might ruminate in the night-time
Over the pastures he cropped, made fragrant by sweet pennyroyal.

Oft when his labor was finished, with eager feet would the dreamer
Follow the pathway that ran through the woods to the house of Priscilla,
Led by illusions romantic and subtile deceptions of fancy,
Pleasure disguised as duty, and love in the semblance of friendship.
Ever of her he thought, when he fashioned the walls of his dwelling;

Ever of her he thought, when he delved in the soil of his garden;
Ever of her he thought, when he read in his Bible on Sunday
Praise of the virtuous woman, as she is described in the Proverbs,—
How the heart of her husband doth safely trust in her always,
How all the days of her life she will do him good, and not evil,
How she seeketh the wool and the flax and worketh with gladness,
How she layeth her hand to the spindle and holdeth the distaff,
How she is not afraid of the snow for herself or her household,
Knowing her household are clothed with the scarlet cloth of her weaving!

So as she sat at her wheel one afternoon in the Autumn,
Alden, who opposite sat, and was watching her dexterous fingers,
As if the thread she was spinning were that of his life and his fortune,
After a pause in their talk, thus spake to the sound of the spindle.
"Truly, Priscilla," he said, "when I see you spinning and spinning,
Never idle a moment, but thrifty and thoughtful of others,
Suddenly you are transformed, are visibly changed in a moment;
You are no longer Priscilla, but Bertha the Beautiful Spinner."
Here the light foot on the treadle grew swifter and swifter; the spindle
Uttered an angry snarl, and the thread snapped short in her fingers;
While the impetuous speaker, not heeding the mischief, continued:
"You are the beautiful Bertha, the spinner, the queen of Helvetia;
She whose story I read at a stall in the streets of Southampton,
Who, as she rode on her palfrey, o'er valley and meadow and mountain,
Ever was spinning her thread from a distaff fixed to her saddle.
She was so thrifty and good, that her name passed into proverb.
So shall it be with your own, when the spinning-wheel shall no longer
Hum in the house of the farmer, and fill its chambers with music.
Then shall the mothers, reproving, relate how it was in their childhood,
Praising the good old times, and the days of Priscilla the spinner!"
Straight uprose from her wheel the beautiful Puritan maiden,
Pleased with the praise of her thrift from him whose praise was the sweetest,
Drew from the reel on the table a snowy skein of her spinning,
Thus making answer, meanwhile, to the flattering phrases of Alden:

"Come, you must not be idle; if I am a pattern for housewives,
Show yourself equally worthy of being the model of husbands.
Hold this skein on your hands, while I wind it, ready for knitting;
Then who knows but hereafter, when fashions have changed and the manners,
Fathers may talk to their sons of the good old times of John Alden!"
Thus, with a jest and a laugh, the skein on his hands she adjusted,
He sitting awkwardly there, with his arms extended before him,
She standing graceful, erect, and winding the thread from his fingers,
Sometimes chiding a little his clumsy manner of holding,
Sometimes touching his hands, as she disentangled expertly
Twist or knot in the yarn, unawares—for how could she help it?—
Sending electrical thrills through every nerve in his body.

Lo! in the midst of this scene, a breathless messenger entered,
Bringing in hurry and heat the terrible news from the village.
Yes; Miles Standish was dead!—an Indian had brought them the tidings,—
Slain by a poisoned arrow, shot down in the front of the battle,
Into an ambush beguiled, cut off with the whole of his forces;
All the town would be burned, and all the people be murdered!
Such were the tidings of evil that burst on the hearts of the hearers.
Silent and statue-like stood Priscilla, her face looking backward
Still at the face of the speaker, her arms uplifted in horror;
But John Alden, upstarting, as if the barb of the arrow
Piercing the heart of his friend had struck his own, and had sundered
Once and forever the bonds that held him bound as a captive,
Wild with excess of sensation, the awful delight of his freedom,
Mingled with pain and regret, unconscious of what he was doing,
Clasped, almost with a groan, the motionless form of Priscilla,
Pressing her close to his heart, as forever his own, and exclaiming:
"Those whom the Lord hath united, let no man put them asunder!" . . .

IX

This was the wedding morn of Priscilla the Puritan maiden.
Friends were assembled together; the Elder and Magistrate also
Graced the scene with their presence, and stood like the Law and the Gospel,
One with the sanction of earth and one with the blessing of heaven.

Simple and brief was the wedding, as that of Ruth and of Boaz.
Softly the youth and the maiden repeated the words of betrothal,
Taking each other for husband and wife in the Magistrate's presence,
After the Puritan way, and the laudable custom of Holland.
Fervently then, and devoutly, the excellent Elder of Plymouth
Prayed for the hearth and the home, that were founded that day in affection,
Speaking of life and of death, and imploring Divine benedictions.

Lo! when the service was ended, a form appeared on the threshold,
Clad in armor of steel, a sombre and sorrowful figure!
Why does the bridegroom start and stare at the strange apparition?
Why does the bride turn pale, and hide her face on his shoulder?
Is it a phantom of air,—a bodiless, spectral illusion?
Is it a ghost from the grave, that has come to forbid the betrothal?
Long had it stood there unseen, a guest uninvited, unwelcomed;
Over its clouded eyes there had passed at times an expression
Softening the gloom and revealing the warm heart hidden beneath them,
As when across the sky the driving rack of the rain-cloud
Grows for a moment thin, and betrays the sun by its brightness.
Once it had lifted its hand, and moved its lips, but was silent,
As if an iron will had mastered the fleeting intention.
But when were ended the troth and the prayer and the last benediction,
Into the room it strode, and the people beheld with amazement
Bodily there in his armor Miles Standish, the Captain of Plymouth!
Grasping the bridegroom's hand, he said with emotion, "Forgive me!
I have been angry and hurt,—too long have I cherished the feeling;
I have been cruel and hard, but now, thank God! it is ended.
Mine is the same hot blood that leaped in the veins of Hugh Standish,
Sensitive, swift to resent, but as swift in atoning for error.
Never so much as now was Miles Standish the friend of John Alden."
Thereupon answered the bridegroom: "Let all be forgotten between us,—
All save the dear, old friendship, and that shall grow older and dearer!"

Then the Captain advanced, and, bowing, saluted Priscilla,
Gravely, and after the manner of old-fashioned gentry in England,
Something of camp and of court, of town and of country, commingled,
Wishing her joy of her wedding, and loudly lauding her husband.
Then he said with a smile: "I should have remembered the adage,—
If you would be well served, you must serve yourself; and moreover,
No man can gather cherries in Kent at the season of Christmas!"

Great was the people's amazement, and greater yet their rejoicing,
Thus to behold once more the sunburnt face of their Captain,
Whom they had mourned as dead; and they gathered and crowded about him,
Eager to see him and hear him, forgetful of bride and of bridegroom,
Questioning, answering, laughing, and each interrupting the other,
Till the good Captain declared, being quite overpowered and bewildered,
He had rather by far break into an Indian encampment,
Than come again to a wedding to which he had not been invited.

Meanwhile the bridegroom went forth and stood with the bride at the doorway,
Breathing the perfumed air of that warm and beautiful morning.
Touched with autumnal tints, but lonely and sad in the sunshine,
Lay extended before them the land of toil and privation;
There were the graves of the dead, and the barren waste of the sea-shore,
There the familiar fields, the groves of pine, and the meadows;
But to their eyes transfigured, it seemed as the Garden of Eden,
Filled with the presence of God, whose voice was the sound of the ocean.

INDEX BY TITLES

Q

R

S

INDEX OF FAMILIAR LINES

NOTE: Many of the selections in this book contain more than one familiar line. But this index contains only one familiar line from each selection. Consequently, the choosing of lines has often been arbitrary, representing only the editor's opinion of what is most familiar.

T

INDEX BY AUTHORS

C

T